THE INFANTRY JOURNAL READER

THE
Infantry Journal
READER

SELECTED AND EDITED BY

COLONEL JOSEPH I. GREENE

DOUBLEDAY, DORAN & COMPANY, INC.

Garden City, New York

1943

PRINTED AT THE *Country Life Press,* GARDEN CITY, N. Y., U. S. A.

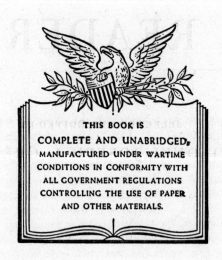

THIS BOOK IS
COMPLETE AND UNABRIDGED,
MANUFACTURED UNDER WARTIME
CONDITIONS IN CONFORMITY WITH
ALL GOVERNMENT REGULATIONS
CONTROLLING THE USE OF PAPER
AND OTHER MATERIALS.

Preface

THROUGH THE TWENTY YEARS in which the Army, as someone has said, lived on starvation rations more than a dozen professional military journals were regularly published. Seven were the unofficial magazines of branch associations, like the *Infantry Journal;* the others were official. The branch associations are simply groups of Army men, mainly officers, of the Coast Artillery, Cavalry, Infantry, Quartermaster Corps, and other arms and services. These groups were formed together, like so many lawyers or doctors, for professional discussion and the publication of journals and military books on a non-profit basis. Several of the associations are over fifty years old, and two have published a magazine for that length of time.

The Infantry Association, the largest of the groups since its branch has always been the largest, originated at Fort Leavenworth, Kansas, in 1893, but did not begin to get out the *Infantry Journal* till 1904, when Association headquarters opened in Washington. The magazine has appeared without interruption since that time, with several shifts between quarterly, bimonthly, and monthly publication. For its first thirty years the *Infantry Journal* was a serious technical and tactical magazine for Infantry readers, though from the beginning the Association welcomed members and subscribers from other Army branches. The circulation varied from the two thousand charter members (including Major Generals Arthur MacArthur and Tasker H. Bliss, First Lieutenant Hugh A. Drum, and Second Lieutenants George C. Marshall and Walter Krueger, and many others who were later of high command) to a World War I high of nearly thirteen thousand, then down to roughly a third that number again.

In 1934 the editorial handling of the magazine changed markedly with the coming of a new editor and assistant editor. Lieutenant Colonel (now Major General) E. F. Harding, the new editor, encouraged Army men to write of their profession in a more lively style, just as other editors

of the country were then seeking manuscripts which presented all kinds
of abstruse sciences in a more popular way for the general reader. He
was right in so doing. For in the four years that General Harding ran
the *Infantry Journal,* assisted editorially by Lieutenant (now Colonel)
Charles T. Lanham, the number of readers climbed right back toward
the World War I high, and articles and editorials more often became the
center of discussion and argument, some of it hot, over present and
future ways of war. Comment and quotation also increased in magazines
and papers outside of the Army, when these remembered that the nation
had an Army and that it might be used again someday in war.

The editors who have followed more recently have stuck to the same
policy. There happens to be no commercial or other military magazine in
the country devoted to broad discussion of warfare for the general reader.
It was therefore natural that a reasonably readable military journal,
which covered many sides of war not covered in general magazines,
should have a fast increase in circulation with the approach and coming of war. By the spring of 1943 there were over one hundred thousand
readers of the *Infantry Journal,* including officers and enlisted men in
every branch of the Army and many civilians. The magazine is read by
those who want to know more about war—how we can better destroy
our Axis enemies, and what a sizable part of the Army thinks concerning
methods and means of warfare.

There are two reasons for an *Infantry Journal Reader.* The first is to
help still further in some small measure to bring this country and its
Army closer together. They have been apart for a long time. There are
millions of civilians still, after eighteen months of war, who think of
the Army as a separate if vast activity which has its separate ways and
even its separate language. They do not see it as an utterly necessary
sphere of American life in which every citizen shares whether or not he
wears an Army uniform. There are, for that matter, Army men who
sometimes forget the singleness of the American nation and its Army, the
fact that the Army is of and for the nation.

A second reason for the book is to show the man of the new Army
something of the men who are his leaders. For many of those whose
ideas, gripes, researches, and stories are in this Reader are leaders in combat today. From what they wrote you cannot picture the entire history of
the Army for forty years, but you can see into many of its more articulate
minds. You can find what an Army man thinks is worth sweating out an
article about, and what other Army men think is worth reading.

There may be a third sound reason for this Reader for all that it was
not considered in making the selections. Many of the articles written in
years of peace are forceful self-criticism. They do not merely criticize;
they inveigh. They hammer at the faults of the Army itself, and often,
though mainly by implication, at the neglectful nation behind it. To

this extent this Reader is a warning against letting these conditions arise again.

Nothing in the book is put there merely because its writer held high rank or holds it now. A good many articles by officers now in high command were left out because they are no longer of interest except to the military historian. One of our highest commanders argued in 1920 that we should have fast tanks capable of making fifteen miles an hour. Fifteen miles an hour *was* fast for a tank in 1920. All such material has been omitted no matter who wrote it. It should comfort the country and its Army to know, however, that in going through the files the editor found no article by a man in high command today which evidenced a closed mind or a rigid thought. And if any reader of the sections on "The Soldier Looks Ahead" is astonished at the alertness he finds, he should remember, too, that what is in this book was written in the main by men of but one of a dozen arms and services. There were similar articles over the peacetime years in the service journals of arms and services other than the Infantry's.

Those who wrote and write for the *Infantry Journal* are largely infantrymen. But anybody who can put the common sense of war into readable prose—or even verse—is welcomed as a contributor. If a writer has something to say about war that will interest and help the soldier reader, his stuff is accepted—and paid for at a decent rate. He may belong to any army. Articles by foreign military writers have appeared regularly since the first issue of the magazine. Even articles by enemy writers from enemy publications are published now in war as in the past, if they seem to reflect the military thought of the enemy clearly. The politics of an author makes no difference. Democrat, Republican; New Deal, Old Deal; Right, Left, middle; so long as he has something to say about fighting war that makes sense, his article is printed. Nor is a military writer barred because he doesn't belong to the Infantry. There have been many articles in the *Journal* (there are a lot in this Reader) by writers from every other branch of the Army. Two of the steadiest contributors of recent years were of the Corps of Engineers and the Coast Artillery Corps. The regular, the guardsman, the reservist, all have written for the magazine. Its contributors also cover every step there is in Army promotion, from private to general. Any writer not in the Army may write for the magazine if he writes intelligently about any side of war. One civilian writer, Fletcher Pratt, has been a contributor through the better part of two decades.

Since the *Infantry Journal* is the magazine of a large association of individuals, it is privately owned (though non-profit) and not an official organ. The editor's statement in a 1937 issue covers this point:

The masthead carries an emphatic statement to the effect that the opinions expressed in our columns do not carry the stamp of official approval.

But in spite of all this, eyebrows are sometimes raised over articles that scoff at time-honored practices or criticize prevailing doctrine and methods. The eyebrow raisers seem to have an idea that such articles are subversive to discipline and damaging to the prestige of the Army. This idea has its root in the "official-publication" misconception that credits the *Infantry Journal* with an authority it does not possess.

Those who recognize the *Journal* for what it is are not disturbed by articles that inveigh against the established order. They applaud or condemn, depending on their views as to the merits of the cause and the soundness of the argument. The dissenters may write impertinently friendly letters denouncing the offending contribution or they may submit a spirited reply. But they don't suggest that the War Department exercise its power to prevent the publication of critical articles on the grounds that they undermine the foundations of the Republic. They concede to authors the right to say what they think and to the editor the privilege of publishing any literate comment on the military scene that is impersonal, restrained, and duly mindful of the proprieties.

The primary mission of the *Infantry Journal,* as we conceive it, is to encourage thought on military matters by broadcasting the most stimulating discussions of timely subjects that we can lay our hands on. It is not to prescribe how things shall be done. That is the province of regulations. The *Journal* has neither the mandate nor the desire to cultivate the fenced fields of prescribed and approved instruction. It serves best by prospecting on the frontier. It hopes to lead its followers to gold in the hills. The contributors tell where it is to be found, and more often than not it is there. But the editors do not guarantee that the alleged pay dirt won't turn out to be iron pyrites. Nor do we grieve overmuch if some of it does. For what the searcher after knowledge finds on any single intellectual expedition is of small consequence; the important thing is to get him out on the trail.

In brief, then, the *Journal* is a forum open to those who champion the things that ain't, as well as to those who champion the things that are. That the views set forth in a manuscript do not qualify as "accepted" is no barrier to publication. Original thought is here valued more highly than uncritical acceptance of military dogma rooted in the past. Since what we print goes out to subscribers without the blessing of the War Department, an article in the *Journal* can shape thought and influence action only by its inherent merit. The viewers-with-alarm need not fear that it will do more. The forward-looking would not have it do less.

Throughout the whole life of the magazine, however, it has been under a general official supervision. Up to 1920 the editors were assigned to duty in one part or another of the War Department and did their editorial work in addition to other duties. For five years during the earliest days the president of the Infantry Association was Major General John C. Bates, who held the highest place in the Army, the office corresponding to Chief of Staff, which General George C. Marshall now holds. In 1920 the office of Chief of Infantry was established and the editor of the *Journal* was naturally placed under his supervision. In 1942, when the Army was reorganized and the Chief of Infantry's office abolished, the four ground-combat journals, including that of the Infantry, came under the supervision of the Commanding General, Army Ground Forces, Lieutenant General Lesley J. McNair, with Major General Richard C. Moore of General McNair's staff in direct supervision of the editors.

The *Infantry Journal* continues in war to operate with similar editorial freedom to that of the past. There are certain natural limitations in war which do not apply in peace, and the military mission of the magazine in war is to do everything possible and appropriate in support of the war effort. But still the magazine is, as the masthead has declared for years, "not the mouthpiece of the War Department." It is the Infantry's unofficial "magazine for fighting men."

The scope of the articles the magazine has published in thirty-nine years has been broad. As a recent editor wrote:

The *Infantry Journal* scope is the Infantry scope. For a long time back good infantrymen have habitually thought in terms of the whole damned Army as the team of fighters it takes to win a war. [The scope of the magazine] covers the whole vast scope of warfare itself . . . all of war and everything connected with war, including science, world politics, and the social and even the religious aspects of life that make the fighting flier, sailor, soldier what he is.

This was a statement of editorial policy, not a description of the acceptable articles that come to the editors and get printed. But the contents of this Reader itself will best show the variety of the interests of the fighting ground soldier.

Not much of the writing you will find in this Reader is of a marked literary quality. But you will often find a directness, a force, and an effective use of the vernacular which you will not find in many professional journals. Especially during the last decade the editors have not sought for learned articles in the military jargon. They have believed that most things about war could be plainly said and that the soldier preferred them said that way. It is necessary to use military terms in military writing. But not the artificial phraseology of the kind that generally hinders the broad understanding of every profession including the military.

In a few respects this Reader is not precisely representative of the *Infantry Journal* as a whole. For one, the back files contain hundreds of articles on technical developments which are old stuff now, though they often led in the days of peace to the adoption of new weapons and new methods. For another, the Reader does not indicate the emphasis the magazine puts on books. It contains many thousand words each month on books that deal with or touch upon war. But book reviews are seldom good anthology material. The *Infantry Journal* is in a considerable degree a center for the publication and distribution of military books of all kinds

—official manuals, its own books, and those of other publishers which its editors think are a help to the fighting soldier. (Many of the selections in this Reader have also appeared in books.) One other omission is that of all long articles on specific campaigns. Some of the best things the magazine has printed are complete studies of past war which do not lend themselves to selection of separate chapters or passages.

But in brief this Reader contains what the present editors think are the most interesting things from the *Infantry Journal* for readers in general. If the job had been done for the experienced soldier alone, there would probably have been a somewhat different selection.

The book could not have been assembled in a time of heavy wartime pressure without the able help of the associate editors of the magazine: Lieutenant Colonel John R. Ulmer, Captain H. A. DeWeerd, Corporal John B. Spore, and Miss Catherine Redmond. In particular, thanks should be expressed to Mr. N. J. Anthony, assistant to the editor, whose remarkable memory of past editorial matters made a far more efficient preparation possible. Mr. Anthony, assisted by Miss Marilynn Allen, carried out the extensive secretarial work, and Captain Mark A. Rollins, assistant to the editor, helped with suggestions as to form and contents. Since the preparation of the book was a task in which the staff of the magazine shared, all royalties are to go to the *Infantry Journal* itself.

The fullest thanks are due to the scores of *Infantry Journal* contributors who wrote the words in this book, and to the past editors who judged them worth reading by men whose profession was war. Three of those editors are generals in the Army today: Major Generals Paul C. Mueller and E. F. Harding, and Brigadier General T. J. Camp. General George C. Marshall, chief of staff, was once assistant editor. Many others who were at one time on the Board of Directors of the magazine and the Executive Council of the Infantry Association, or who contributed articles to the magazine, are likewise serving in high command and staff positions. Among them are Generals Eisenhower, Fredendall, Stilwell, Krueger, Drum, and Chennault. There is a complete list of past *Infantry Journal* editors in the Appendix.

Not all able American soldiers, by any means, have written about their profession. The soldier's writing is writing done when his official tasks are over for the day or the week. The writing of articles is such hard work for many otherwise able military men that they do not attempt it. But a surprising number have done so, thus to give special aid to their Army and country beyond their regular military duties.

The free presentation of ideas is as necessary to military development as it is to the social growth of a nation and of the world. There yet appears to be no prospect of a lasting, a possibly permanent, civilization without military strength to preserve it. If we finally learn as a people to accept and cherish military strength against conquest, and to think of armed services as vital and integral agencies necessary to the common welfare, there is some hope. The thought of the nation now draws closer to the thought of its soldiers. But the soldier's duties, the soldier's work, done for all, need appreciation, understanding, and inspection by all. And one way of gaining these ends is through reading the soldier's own self-criticism and discussion of his own work. For a beginning, there is plenty of it in this *Reader*.

COLONEL JOSEPH I. GREENE
Editor, the *Infantry Journal*

Washington
March 1943

Contents

xiii

CONTENTS

PAGE

CONTENTS

III   LEADERSHIP AND DISCIPLINE

CONTENTS

PAGE

VII TODAY'S WAR

VIII THE SOLDIER LOOKS AHEAD—2

CONTENTS

IX APPENDIX

THE INFANTRY JOURNAL READER

SOLDIER[1]

The stars swing down the western steep,
And soon the east will burn with day,
And we shall struggle up from sleep
And sling our packs and march away.

In this brief hour before the dawn
Has struck our bivouac with flame
I think of men whose brows have borne
The iron wreath of deadly fame.

I see the fatal phalanx creep,
Like death, across the world and back,
With eyes that only strive to keep
Bucephalus' immortal track.

I see the legion wheel through Gaul,
The sword and flame on hearth and home,
And all the men who had to fall
That Cæsar might be first in Rome.

I see the horde of Genghis Khan
Spread outward like the dawn of day
To trample golden Khorassan
And thunder over fair Cathay.

I see the grizzled grenadier,
The dark dragoon, the gay hussar,
Whose shoulders bore for many a year
Their little emperor's blazing star.

I see these things, still am I slave
When banners flaunt and bugles blow,
Content to fill a soldier's grave
For reasons I shall never know.

C. T. LANHAM, CAPTAIN (now COLONEL), INFANTRY

[1]Reprinted by courtesy of *Harper's* and the author.

I

The Soldier Looks Ahead—1

THE FACT that a good many soldiers looked ahead during the peacetime years is perhaps evidenced by this Reader as a whole. The Army man, as a rule following at least one service journal and often two or three, knew how much discussion there was about new and improved methods and weapons of war. He might himself think that warfare should be revolutionized, or he might think the old way was the best. But there was plenty written in the 1920s and '30s that would make most Army men reach one conclusion or the other.

In fact, as this first section of the Reader appears to indicate strongly, there were many voices raised demanding change and the voices were sometimes sharp in their demands, not merely as the new World War began but for years before it.

Why there was not more action accomplished to achieve the points made individually in such magazines as the *Infantry Journal* is something that will deserve the deepest study by those who determine the future course of our armed services after this war is over. You can't go through the first section of this Reader without finding that many alert minds were represented in just one of the several service journals. But the need for modernization and change suggested and argued by these men was usually slow in coming. For example, in an *Infantry Journal* article entitled "Traditionalism and Military Defeat" (March 1941) by Lieutenant Colonel (now Colonel) Thomas R. Phillips, the author searchingly points out this lag. In speaking of motorization among other things he says:

In the use of motors for the transportation of troops, one would think that the United States, which can manufacture trucks faster than it can draft men, would have developed the tactics and equipped its Army so as to make the greatest possible use of this exceptional military asset. But not so. It was not until 1939 that a divisional organization was adopted which discarded horses and mules for hauling supplies in wagons and dragging machine-gun carts and substituted motors for them. With this reorganization it became possible to put a whole division in motors and move it rapidly. But remember, it was twenty years after 1918 when that reorganization was made.

This particular military author thought the entire trouble lay in the ingrained traditionalism of the Army as a whole, though he did not clearly distinguish between the Army as an institution and its separate members, scores of whom were thinking in such terms as those expressed in the articles in this Reader. Moreover, he forgot the fact that the people of our country had a large measure of responsibility for the state of their Army and paid little attention to it. This isn't the place to do more than say how important an exhaustive study of this old peacetime trouble is. For such a study would go far beyond the Army itself and into the relationship between the people of the United States, Congress, the War Department civilian heads, and the Army itself. All this section of the Reader does is to show how forcefully and readably individual Army men wrote about things they thought were wrong. And what they wrote was read and discussed by many thousands of others in uniform.

It was also available for editorial comment and academic study to the whole country. But only one in a thousand or so was interested.

THE AMERICAN PROFESSIONAL SOLDIER

By MAJOR JOHN H. BURNS

(1940)

Some of the most reflective thinking which our Army produced in the twenties and thirties came from the mind of Major John H. Burns. Major Burns was editor of the *Infantry Journal* for two years until his death in June 1940. He was a graduate of the Command and General Staff School and the Army War College and served much with troops as well as in staff capacities.

Major Burns believed that psychology and anthropology held some of the principal answers to the problems of war. He was a student of both. In the many articles and editorials he wrote over a period of years he continually emphasized the main thought that it is *men* who make up an army. Man, he therefore held, was a chief study for the high command. He favored a broad knowledge among Army men of our country and the types of its men in its different regions, and how they thought and worked, the better that Army leaders might know in advance of war how best to teach them to fight.

It was natural also that Major Burns's stress upon man and individual and mass psychology would lead him to reflect and write about leadership. In his *Psychology and Leadership*, which was used as a text at the Command and General Staff School for a number of years, his principal ideas are gathered. But in "The American Professional Soldier" he gave the Army his strongest statement on the future of our military men.

LET US first go back a year ago. The shadow of war lay over the world. Pacificism had failed; weakness was an invitation to partition; treaties were being cynically disregarded, and arbitration had become a mockery. The stronger, the ruthless nation had begun to dispense justice for its own benefit. Already only military power could guarantee to a nation the chance for existence and eventual survival. People of all nations were beginning to look anxiously around and to plan for their future safety; we, perhaps, not yet so much as those nations which lay close within the darkest part of the shadow. Hurriedly, nervously, they checked over their defenses—guns, tanks, planes, ships, factories, and masses of men. At that critical time in our own nation few of our citizens were noticing the men who would direct the energies of this vast nation in war—the professional soldiers. They were, for the most part, unknown and unimportant.

The intelligentsia—the jugglers of modern ideologies—looked down their noses at the Army. They forgot that the people who make a war may be silly, but that the people who wage it cannot afford to be. True, an occasional modern thinker might intellectually find a reason for an army if he could bring himself to think clearly about it. But in most of their minds there was clear animosity—an animosity based not on reason but on emotions aroused by the symbol of the one thing that human thought appears unable to solve. That one thing is war. And war, to the intellectual, was too plainly indicative of the primitive, puny state of our vaunted human intellect.

So these workers in words, ideas, and thoughts, the articulate part of the American folk, were mainly alike in their aversion—to use a mild term—to the Army. Strange, wasn't it, how this heterogeneous list of writers, speakers, idealists, scientists, religionists, philosophers, pseudo-philosophers—practically all the vocal parts of our population—had one powerful emotion in common? They disliked the professional soldier. One could also add the revolutionary communist to this group, so that often we had the spectacle of the atheist and the man of God sharing the same bed. A quaint conceit—the red nightcap of liberty on the same pillow with the churchly black one.

All of these people shuddered over the horrors of war, and rightly so. For who does not? But often the basis for their shuddering was the self-conscious feeling that they themselves were not capable of standing up in battle—unless it be waged with words. Consequently many of them acquired a sense of inferiority which grew distortedly and caused them to vent their spleen on the only symbol of war that confronted them—the professional soldier. So it was often true that back of the intellectual opposition to the military lay, not cold reason, but hot emotion.

Not that all this ever bothered the soldier. The soldier has yet to be heard of who, because of this, ever added a stroke to his golf score. But the soldier could nevertheless see the danger in certain of the modern ideologies, certain of the social processes that would not produce soldier material. He yearned for the type of man that went into the Wilderness and into the Argonne. But he had long since begun to fear that he would not get them. For to the modern educator especially—a sluggish thinker for the most part—the acquisition of ideas was paramount, the acquisition of ideals secondary, and the physical defense of either abhorrent. Thus the products of our educational timberline might perhaps be only inferior soldier material, and, by the same token, inferior human beings.

But the soldier does not make wars. He merely takes the war handed to him by the people and tries his level best to finish it in accordance with the wishes of the very people who began it. The picture of the professional soldier which for years has been so assiduously projected by the portrait of a thirsty, power-drunk individual, only too eager to engage in any war just for the fun of it, is simply silly. Indeed, many wars would have been prevented if the counsel of the professional soldier had been taken. And many future wars may likewise be prevented.

So the professional soldier gets along reasonably well and pays little attention to the attitude of any particular class. He himself knows that his government—any government, for that matter—is upheld by bayonets. He may not know how to model a statue or write a sonnet, or even turn a neat paragraph of prose, but he does know how to handle the bayonet-men. Which is important.

Little enough study is given to the professional soldier and his cohorts by the busy research worker who investigates almost everything else under the sun. The military has been called "the next to oldest profession." But fifty weighty tomes are written by sociologists and other students about "the oldest profession" to one book about the military. Yet the sociologist who neglects the significance of military force and looks on an army as a glorified police force—negligible in sociological matters—is missing a big point. He fails to observe fully modern events and fails to interpret them fully.

At almost any time in the past one could envisage wars, then in embryo, that every sensible military man would hate to see born. But those wars were born, never fear, for people make wars—not soldiers. The soldier only fights them.

The professional soldier does not start a war under any circumstances unless he is sure of the outcome. He is a practical man who regards war fundamentally as a business and not as a game. There is little romance

in it for him. And he never—no, never—gives his opponent an even break
if he can help it. The people who make the war may want to do that
and in our country generally have. It is hard going to have to wage such
a war. One hopes it will not happen again.

It could well have been asked up to about a year ago why the Army
existed when so many classes were either actively or passively hostile to
it. But in a democracy there is always a certain hardheadedness which the
illuminati often dub ignorance and which resists all attempts to inculcate
the belief that the millennium is just around the corner. Even though
democracies are usually ungrateful to their leaders, particularly the military ones, still they know in the back of their collective heads that they
need them. Furthermore, as the past year has shown, it is always astonishing in the end how little weight the writers and speakers carry when
they go against the deep swift current of public opinion.

Of all people in the modern industrial system, the professional soldier
has more insight into the minds of men than any other class. He is the
best practical psychologist extant. He does not regard men as a con-
glomeration of reflexes and conditioned responses, as the psychologists
appear to do. He knows him for what he is, an integrated personality,
with great capacity for self-sacrifice and an irritating habit of doing
thoughtless, roistering things at an inopportune time. He sees man in the
round and knows him in the raw and doesn't think he is such a bad
product after all. To the professional soldier, man is not damned by
original sin; nor is he, as our "uplifters" would have us believe, the victim
of circumstance.

Nobody in our modern civilization thinks of men as the professional
soldier does. To all others men are producers, consumers, clients, sales
prospects, cases, subscribers, parishioners, or what not. Seldom, if ever,
does any person deal with more than one facet of the perplexing phenomenon called man. But the professional soldier deals with all sides
of man. He feeds, clothes, doctors, works, amuses, shelters, disciplines;
arouses self-respect, faith, loyalty, patriotism; teaches self-reliance, courage, sex, and other subjects neglected by the schools. There is more to
the job than just teaching the art of war. The soldier therefore knows
men individually or in the mass as no other group in modern life does.
He can do more with men.

And this last by itself is something worth close study. Note, for instance,
that your industrialists cannot get a man to work overtime fifteen minutes
without giving double pay, whereas the professional soldier in peacetime
can work him twenty-four or forty-eight hours at a stretch with no more
reward offered than a good meal, a good sleep, a word of commendation.
And in war he can lead men into a sleet of deadly lead in order to gain
an objective. Men offer their lives to the professional soldier for nothing
when they won't give their employer fifteen minutes. These are the

stark facts. A strange commentary on our so-called scientific civilization.

The writer or student who dismisses all this by saying that it is only iron discipline—fear of the commander—which drives a soldier forward is only proving how little he actually knows of men and particularly of the soldier. Furthermore—and this should strike home to the gentlemen who are running our schools—the soldier calls on his men to sacrifice themselves, to offer their lives for the good of the whole, and he gets his request. On the other hand the schoolmaster could not persuade his pupils in general to sacrifice anything important for the good of anyone. Yet the schools have over ten years to produce their effect, the Army only a few short months on the average. Crude as the professional soldier may seem to most intellectuals, he still has something which puts over to those he leads a great moral lesson in a short time. He accomplishes something that almost no one else in our modern civilization can accomplish or is accomplishing.

Just what sort of fellow is the American professional soldier? He is generally the product of a middle-class home, seldom of a wealthy home. Indeed, many a laborer or mechanic or farmer now has a son wearing the shoulder straps of an officer. Men have often practically lifted themselves by their bootstraps from lowly jobs to a commission, and often these last, when placed in competition with graduates of West Point, Harvard, Columbia, Yale, or Princeton, come out on top.

The accusation is often leveled at the professional soldier that he is narrow, reactionary, with little vision and no imagination—in short, trustworthy but doltish. This will bear a little investigation. For the most part Army officers are graduates of some good college or university. But that is only the beginning of their studies. They must do much postgraduate work in the Army schools. It is not unusual for an Army officer to put in six years of study during twenty or twenty-five years of service more or less, in such schools as the Infantry School, the Artillery Schools, the Air Corps Tactical School, the Command and General Staff School, and the Army War College. You will seldom find an officer on the War Department General Staff who has not had from three to six years, or even more, of postgraduate study to fit him for his job. In civil life all of these officers would have earned through such study the magic letters Ph.D.—which would automatically entitle them to admittance into the inner circle of the intelligentsia and to respectful attention whenever they gave out an opinion.

It is doubtful if any professional group is so rigorously trained and educated as the American officer. Foreign officers, because of birth or breeding, may be selected for higher training, but the American Army tries to give it to all who can qualify, and there are a lot who do qualify. When men in other professions are beginning to relax a bit after making their niche in life, the professional soldier is still plugging at his books.

Men with gray-sprinkled hair not uncommonly work all night at their problems—a forty-eight-hour stretch is not rare. This strenuous work often goes on, not for a few months only, but over a period of years.

Narrow work, no cultural value, one might say. Again, perhaps; but not as narrow as the graduate study in medicine, psychology, engineering, or other sciences. What is there cultural about learning to snatch out a pair of tonsils, or the reactions of a rat in a maze, or the efficiency of the mercury-turbine engine? These are no more cultural than studying how to bring up Class I supplies, industrial mobilization, or the exterior ballistics of machine-gun fire, all of which are elementary subjects in the soldier's training. His proper field of study is everything that man has ever done, not only as an individual, but as a member of a nation or group of nations. From this he traces the causes of past wars and from his data he can predict why there will be future upheavals. As a consequence he is not so naïve as to accept the conclusion—so prevalent today—that our entrance into the last World War was due to the machinations of our munitions makers. Moreover, he is obliged to go back to the humanizing influence of troop duty, where he deals with men in the mass, and thus never does he get far away from the vitalizing, warming, though often crude, contact with human nature. All the theories he learned must square with this realistic environment.

True, we have a few—a very few—professional soldiers who are also professional scholars. They are great lads. They can reach down through the corridor of history and with a long arm pluck out any fact or, on the other hand, project themselves into the future and tell exactly how a gigantic regulating station should be run in the next war. They can discuss Spengler, Freud, or the Italian *condottiere*. They are clever fellows, all sib to the doctors of philosophy, but—and this is a pity—the troops are cold to them ever.

Aside from that, the professional soldier has all the weaknesses of other humans but with few of the petty virtues. He'll take a drink or several of them and on special occasions get politely tight. But he has three great virtues which are not too common: One, he is absolutely honest, and this applies not to money matters only; second, he has a clean-cut conception of what the word "duty" means, and, drolly enough in this modern age, he uses it in all seriousness; and he has faith. Faith in the country and its destiny, in democracy and its methods, in something greater outside of this puny human intellect of ours. And this last, no doubt, disqualifies him utterly from ever being a modern intellectual.

He has spent a great part of his life traveling up and down this broad continent, from Monterey to Montreal. He knows the people, has lived with them, and knows their problems. And yet he is not one of them. He is a citizen of no state but of the United States at large. He seldom, if ever, votes or becomes intellectually or emotionally entangled in political problems. He may not be a great social thinker but he knows what the common man wants because he knows the common man—is a common man. And he realizes when political or economic evils press hard on this common man and make him restive.

Furthermore, he has spent years beyond the limits of the United States. He knows the tropics, the heat, the fecund growth, the insects, the dankness, the people who live there, struggling in the grip of Nature at her cruelest. He knows the beach at Waikiki and the liquid sunshine of Hawaii, and the remnants of the giant Hawaiian chieftain class—figures such as Phidias never had to model from. The Far East is more familiar to him than New York is to the Kansan.

He admires the Chinese girls with their semi-modern garb, the throat-high military jacket and the skirt slit to the knee. Their faces of pale yellow ivory pointed to the chin, their slanting provocative dark eyes, the thin, small feet—all these he knows. And also the Chinese merchant, clothed in silks of rich hues, grave in his courtesy, calm, dignified despite his rotund shape. A gentleman in the mart of trade. But behind all this the professional soldier senses the 400,000,000 that is China, the civilization that extends back thousands of years when the western European was a half-naked, vermin-infested savage. He sees China awakening after her long sleep and just now beginning to rub her eyes. Here is vast physical power, such power as he understands well, and he hopes it never will be unleashed in his day.

And he comes home to the provincial thought of the United States wondering. What if he cannot become vitally interested in the newest social experiment, or the latest frill in psychology, philosophy, or the like? He has seen enough of the world and its people to know that neither he nor anyone else has the ability to solve all the problems that arise. Only piece by piece do we progress. No one generation can do more than make a tiny advance—just a fraction of a step. So he doesn't bother to support or oppose any scheme which, its originator thinks, solves the problem of life. After all, he is but a soldier.

Therefore, he turns to his job, which is to make this country safe from aggression so as to permit its people to develop as they must, or, as the last resort, to fight the wars of the people when—God help them—the people make such wars. If, in ordinary times, he seems importunate in his demands for weapons of war, and doubly so in times such as the present, this is not because he wants to begin a war, but because he knows this imperfect world of ours and has a very definite idea of what it means to try to fight wars without the tools it takes to win them.

It would be better for all concerned, as many non-military folk are now finding out, if thinking people knew the soldier personally—his life and his function. Merely seeing a parade or a military review is not to see the professional soldier. It would, indeed, pay any professor of history, psychology, or sociology to spend part of his sabbatical year with the Army—if only he would leave behind his preconceived notions with his books. And if such a one should make this visit, he should never tell the soldier that some new scheme is going to prevent all wars. For the soldier has heard that before, and wars are still going on and will go on when all who live today are dust. Bigger minds than any in our own crass culture have tried that and have failed miserably. Do not say to a soldier that war is silly and unscientific. He knows that perfectly well. And he knows something else often forgotten: man himself is silly and unscientific.

It is not too late now—though it is a bit late—for the intellectuals to come close to the Army. Many are already realizing that fact. Witness some of those fine minds who write for the *New Republic* and the *Nation*. At all events it is the soldier who will take the sons of the people and make soldiers of them. If he does his job well the people will win the war when next it comes. For it always does come, as the soldier knows.

OPEN MINDS FOR OPEN WAR

Editorial by
LIEUTENANT COLONEL (now MAJOR GENERAL) E. F. HARDING

(*1937*)

To think, and think in time, the muscles of the intellect must be kept supple.

INVENTIONS developed between wars have always been the bête noire of soldiers. One can almost picture the general staffs of the New Stone Age meeting in worried conference to discuss the probable effect that the introduction of bow and arrow would have in an impending clash with a neighboring tribe. Certainly the Israelites were much more concerned about the war chariots of Sisera; and the elephants of Pyrrhus gave the Romans many an anxious hour. And no wonder, for new or improved weapons have been responsible for many a great military upset.

But our predecessors had a comparatively easy time of it at that. They didn't have to contend with new weapons, new technique, and new tactics every time they went to war. Sometimes there were no notable changes for centuries. Hubert, in *Ivanhoe,* whose "grandsire drew a good bow at Hastings," was drawing the same kind of bow in King Richard's time. And the French knights who rode to their deaths at Crécy had had two centuries to devise countermeasures against that same bow used by Hubert's descendants under Edward III.

Even in relatively modern times armies seldom had to contend with more than one or two innovations at the outbreak of war. Sometimes they had none at all—witness our War of 1812. Even in 1914 there were only three weapons that had not been fully tested in a conflict between first-class powers—the machine gun, the airplane, and large-caliber mobile artillery. Moreover, these were not of transcending importance initially.

Since the World War, developments have been so extensive that nearly all of our weapons are essentially new. The modern airplane, for instance, has been so improved that it must be regarded as a new instrument whose effect cannot be predicted from the performance of its 1918 prototype. Still more unpredictable is the effect which the enormous increase in the size of air forces will have. The same goes for tanks, chemicals, and motors. Even the old familiar implements of our trade have been improved to a degree that makes unreliable all 1918 estimates of their probable influence on the issue of battle. In a word, the great armies of the world will carve the next panel to the frieze of military history with a new set of tools.

In view of the number and weight of the unknown factors that will enter into the equation of the next great war, only a crystal-gazer would venture to predict just what it will be like or just how it will be won. However, one need not be a major prophet to predict how it may be lost. Assuming that the contestants are evenly matched, our guess is that the willows will go to the army that is most thoroughly indoctrinated with the belief that it knows the answers.

Such an army will be prompt to err and slow to revise. Formerly this was not necessarily fatal. Armies so handicapped have survived initial defeat, discarded their peacetime panaceas, set their roots in reality, and emerged victorious. But that was in the days when horses and marching men set the pace. Today the army that persists in giving its dubious preconceived theories a complete battle test may never have an opportunity to try out others. We may and should entertain all reasonable theories (and perhaps a few screwy ones) as to the course future battles will take, but none must be allowed to become permanently attached to the inside of the skull.

Instead, we must prepare ourselves psychologically to make quick adjustments to actualities. We must cultivate flexibility of mind. We must be ready to relinquish our most cherished theory of what war ought to be and accept it as we find it.

And what is an airplane, by the way? It's nothing but a machine that travels in the air instead of on the ground, or on or under the water. It feeds on gasoline and is operated by human beings. It can be used to carry troops, guns, bombs, or whatever other supplies are needed. But, above all, from an airplane one can see over the hills and far away—something the infantryman most ardently desires to do.

Why can't he do it? What's so exclusive about flying?

Any soldier can administer first aid without the benefit of an M.D. after his name! No one has to join a motor outfit before driving a truck! All of us have ridden horses (and how!) whether or not we wanted to be in the Cavalry! Why, then, the monopoly on airplanes?

The horse-and-buggy days are gone. The doughboy is no longer relegated to advancing a mere twelve miles a day. Rather, he is expected to cover incredible distances—by trains, motor vehicles, and even parachutes. He can't linger by the wayside picking flowers, either. When he's gotta go, he's gotta get there in a hurry!

The burning question then is, what will he meet at the other end? Or even before he gets there, for that matter.

No one likes to be caught in his fatigue clothes or with the seat of his pants glued to a reconnaissance car! The only way to prevent that is to look ahead. And the best place to look from is in the air.

We don't need any super-duper Flying Fortresses to do that. We could dispense with the steam-heated foot warmers, the nickel-plated gadgets, and the running hot and cold water. Even the gasoline tanks could be cut in half—because we wouldn't have to fly over an ocean or cross a continent. All we want is to find out what's on the other side of the next hill.

Navigators and other high-priced help would be superfluous also. In place of a $50,000 plane and a $6,000-a-year pilot, we'd trade even for five cut-down jobs and a similar number of wild-eyed kids who would rather fly than do K.P. The woods are full of them too. The kids, that is.

As for the planes, they would not be hard to build. All we want is something that could land in a cow pasture, hide in a smokehouse, and take off from the general's pansy wagon when necessary.

Right now the aviators seem embarrassed with riches. Rumor has it they are going to get more airplanes than they know what to do with. How about giving some of them to us?

Of course we may break our fool necks trying to fly the darn things, but what of it? They're our necks. And besides, we'd rather break 'em ourselves than have the enemy do it for us!

But the brass hats and lads with embroidered wings needn't be too sure we can't make the grade. The doughboys have never fallen down yet. And if they ever do start, it won't be from airplanes!

THE NEW FACE OF WAR

By Major (now Colonel) Thomas R. Phillips

(1938)

In LONDON, Paris, Berlin, and Rome men and women live fearing to be awakened any night by the roar of exploding bombs. They are digging mole cities far beneath the surface. They are renting apartments with underground bombproofs before the buildings are even finished. They are fitting their children with gas masks. Their fears turn ever toward the skies.

Terrorism from the air stands in popular belief as the principal feature of tomorrow's war. Actually the probability of air attack on cities is steadily decreasing. It has not been effective in Spain and China. A prepared populace is immune to terror. The threat of retaliation gives pause to staffs that contemplate unlimited aerial war. Attack from the air on populous centers no longer offers hope of surprise. Five years ago it might have been tried successfully, but today antiaircraft defenses and other preparations have ended the honeymoon of aerial terrorism and war. The theory of warfare which it represents is passing into the military attic along with the French "headlong offensive" of 1914 and the "mechanized armies" of the recent past.

The Versailles Treaty army of Germany, under General von Seeckt, making a virtue of necessity, proclaimed the superiority of a small, highly trained force, largely mechanized. Von Seeckt pictured attacks with thousands of tanks breaking over the borders and disrupting all communications while a thousand airplanes paralyzed the hostile capital. The French answer to thousands of tanks and sudden attack was the Maginot Line. They established a continuous front before war could begin. But twenty years finds the cycle of military thought, after rising into the clouds with airplanes and wandering down the highways with mechanized armies, returning to the trenches and strong points of the World War.

A scornful critic of generals as a class has written that the war they prepare for is not the next war but the last. Major General J. F. C. Fuller claims it is the war *before* the last. The present model for tactics and strategy in many armies is to be found in the opening three months of the World War, when divisions, corps, and armies maneuvered into battle. In these same armies it is insisted that the continuous front was a product of the special conditions of 1914, and that these are not likely to recur. The concentration of armies some distance behind the theater of operations, their slow advance on foot toward contact, protected and screened by large units of cavalry—this is the model. To 1914 divisions a few modern weapons are added, and a little motor transport, and then battles, model 1914, are refought. Alone, in the middle of a continent, divisions, brigades, and even regiments, are maneuvered—on paper, at least—with both flanks open.

The validity of these theories is open to question. In an almost war occurring not so long ago in Europe, the two armies faced each other across their fortified border. The continuous front was formed before war started, and this may well have supplied one reason for its suppression. Had the two armies clashed, there would have been no room for maneuver. Maneuver room could only have been gained by battle. Along the Manchukuoan border Russian and Japanese forces face each other on a fortified and occupied line. The Maginot Line is paralleled by a fortified German line. Boundaries between Russia, Poland, and Finland are fortified and manned. On every boundary in the world where war might break soldiers face each other. Continuous fronts are already formed. Contact is already established. Tomorrow's war will start as the World War ended—with a continuous front—and end as the World War started—with maneuver.

Soldiers' efforts to avoid the pitfalls of the last war are represented by the Douhet theory and the dream of a mechanized, high-speed army. Both resulted from efforts to avoid stabilized fronts and wars of attrition in which even the winner loses. To Douhet the power of the defensive had become so great that fronts could not be broken. He visualized the ground armies as on the defensive along their national borders. The air armies, alone capable of passing over the trenches, were to win the war. They would attack lines of communication, manufacturing establishments, governmental headquarters, and even the civil population, and destroy the ability and will of the enemy to fight. The logic of Douhet, granted his premises, is irreproachable. But his premises were based on an exaggerated idea of the powers of air attack and an underestimate of the offensive power of ground armies and the moral resistance of civil populations.

In theory the mechanized army could prevent the formation of stabilized fronts by sudden attack at the outset. It was expected to disrupt the mobilization of the enemy and win the war by capturing key political and communications centers. But the fronts to prevent such an interruption are already in being. The hardheaded French established a checkmate. Von Seeckt's dream ship foundered on the Maginot Line.

Were the military theorists wrong when they assumed that stabilization for three years in France was a result of special conditions? No; for the formation of fronts in modern war is a product of new agencies of warfare. Stabilization on the Western Front resulted from relatively short lines, a shortage of ammunition, and an approximately equal combat power of two great armies. And now the very threat of envelopment by motorized and mechanized troops forces the continuous front. The foot soldier of 1914 could be blocked when he attempted to move at a rate of ten or twelve miles a day toward the rear of his enemy. The mechanized force of today can move two hundred miles to the flank and rear in twenty-four hours. Fronts must be extended to prevent such envelopment; barriers established in time of peace to block the sudden attack. A nation can have no flanks; an army can have no flanks. An open flank is but an invitation to a mechanized force to march around and to the rear, and render the position of the army untenable. And so lines are extended in peace to international boundaries, to the sea, to great mountain ranges—to impassable barriers. In this day of total war each nation becomes a vast fortress ringed by barriers, artificial and natural. And this protection gains time to assemble the citizen armies.

The continuous front is not a condition peculiar to a European war. A continuous, or perhaps discontinuous, front more than a thousand miles long was formed in Spain almost at once. Franco's line of communication guards, from Toledo to Don Benito, found themselves the occupants of a front. Everywhere, from the Pyrenees to the Mediterranean, isolated bodies joined to establish the continuous line. It was unforeseen but inevitable. A road or valley without its protecting barrier was a free highway for troops in motors to turn the whole battle line. The demands of the barrier took precedence over the massing of an offensive maneuvering force by either contender. They still do.

Though but a quarter as many men are fighting on each side, they are maintaining, in Spain, a continuous front more than twice as long as that of the World War in France. The war started without preparation, without thought of forming fronts. The objectives of the opposing forces were the great cities. If the continuous front was inescapable in Spain, it is inevitable in any war.

A continuous front is not, however, synonymous with stabilization. Certain military writers, reasoning from the stabilization of 1915 and 1916 on the Western Front, have assumed that stabilization is inevitable. But the front in Spain is not stabilized and never has been. The front in France was not stabilized during 1918. A stabilized front results when forces of approximately equal power face each other along a continuous front. The initial deadlock on the French front was the result of ammunition shortage. Only blasting could dislodge the burrowing soldiers, but both France and Germany had exhausted their blasting materials. Had either foreseen the unprecedented expenditure of ammunition and supplied greater stockages or possessed a higher manufacturing capacity, there would have been no stabilization. Either could thus have won the war.

Sequacious military thinkers, pointing to the period of stabilization in France, proclaim that all stabilization is the result of the power of defensive weapons and organization. The World War proves precisely the opposite. Offensives were successful when means were available and the technique of their use was understood. The defensive is never impregnable. Ample and appropriate means and suitable technique can break it. Artillery blasted through the most powerful lines in 1918. Since then the tank and airplane have been developed to aid artillery and infantry. Motors make possible the surprise concentration of the necessary mass and supply it continuously with men, ammunition, and food.

Defensive power, moreover, aids the attacker just as much as it does the defender. No army is strong enough to attack everywhere at once. The attacker must defend nine tenths of his line. Defensive organization permits him to do this with limited numbers. Thus is he able to concentrate enormous masses against a single sector and overwhelm it. The greatest art in modern war is to make the power of the defensive work for the attack. Given a definite superiority, an attacker can, by threats at many points, force the dispersion of hostile reserves while he concentrates his masses.

It is also true that combat power is more than ever dependent upon matériel. If the World War used entirely unforeseen quantities of ammunition, the requirements of tomorrow's war are equally unrealized. All weapons fire faster. To an ammunition usage of almost unimaginable vastness must be added tank and airplane replacement. The average battle life of an airplane in the World War was less than twenty hours; the average actual life at the front, about thirty days. What nation is now prepared to replace its air fleets at such a rate? The destruction of half the tanks used in a single engagement may be a commonplace. What nation can build new tanks at such a pace? It is quite possible that a future war will see stabilization again, purely for lack of factories and stockages to replace the usury of battle.

Other things being equal, the nation with the greatest stocks of war material, or, in their stead, a war industry ready to turn out ammunition, aircraft, and tanks as fast as they are used, will win. Germany's greatest strength for war does not lie in its army of a million men but in an industry rapidly expanding to equip an army suddenly increased from one hundred thousand to a full million with more than a million reserves.

Industrial mobilization is a magic word on the lips of all general staffs. But only the nation definitely preparing for offensive war at a foreseen time will develop its industry or stockages to the degree that tomorrow's war will require. The democracy with defensive strategy, unable to foresee the time of hostilities, cannot afford to stock, or be prepared to manufacture, war materials on the scale needed. If it did, its stockages and equipment might become obsolete, its plants and plans useless. Indeed, the waste of peacetime preparation now approaches the waste of war. Democratic peoples live in the present, and the facts of tomorrow are always unexpected. The nature of democratic government and the pacific inclination of democratic peoples make industrial counterpreparation for a war on tomorrow's scale a practical impossibility. The industrial requirements of modern war favor the aggressor nation.

Thus the two inescapable features on the new face of war are the continuous front and the unimaginable devouring of matériel. No longer, in the face of mechanized war, can a nation have an unfortified frontier. No longer will it suffice to have an air force in being, a tank force in being, a three-month stockage of ammunition. Behind these must be a plant in being, ready to replace unprecedented consumption. Neither plant plans nor paper plans of industrial mobilization can go into action fast enough to replace losses of matériel in the early stages of war. The nation that breaks the continuous front will be the nation that can supply ammunition and replace airplanes and tanks a month earlier than its opponent. The industrial front is as important as the fighting front. It is total war that may be expected.

Even the United States does not escape these servitudes. Our most potent allies are two great oceans. In recorded history no great nation has ever been so favored. But oceans are highways. Our frontiers are sea frontiers. Our continuous front is occupied by the Navy, backed by the air force and coast defenses. Behind those barriers we alone among the great nations may have time to organize our Army and prepare its industrial support.

Soldiers teach the practice of war by extracting little parts from the whole of war, classifying the parts as to type of operation. Then they set up situations in problems and maneuvers so that the classical solutions are applicable. Envelopment, penetration, delaying action, etc., are illustrated. The situation is made to fit the solution. Years of thus thinking about war in samples obscures the whole, and by then the pieces cannot be made to fit into a whole even if it were perfectly seen.

To gain a true picture the outset of war must be visualized. When there is tension between adjacent nations the newspapers inform us that large-scale maneuvers are taking place in the frontier areas. Both sides deny that this has any significance. But border forces are reinforced. If war then breaks, the two armies are in contact in small force, facing each other on the frontier. The opposing armies flow to the battle areas behind the border barriers. Concentration takes place on the battlefield and not in the interior.

What will the air forces, the only forces at this time capable of passing the barrier, be doing? Will they be out knocking over buildings? Hardly! They will be busy where they can serve their country most effectively.

At the outset, it seems probable, their greatest service will be to delay and disorganize the movement of enemy troops to the border. Not then are cities and industries the vital targets. Most important of all tasks will be the effort to prevent the strengthening of the continuous front. It must be kept weak to ease the problem of breaking it. Hence air forces will be used against troop movements. Every marching column will be swept with bombs and machine guns. Every railroad track will get its quota of bombs.

At the same time the air forces will have to protect their own troop movements from the hostile aviation. This may become so important that attack on hostile aviation in the air and on its airdromes will become the vital task. This decision will be difficult and one that cannot be made in advance.

In important areas activity in the air will be almost continuous. Soldiers may have to give up the immemorial march to battle, for long columns on roads are the dream targets of the aviator. Marching at night gives a partial protection. Movements by rail may be so delayed and interrupted as to be impracticable. Only the motor remains. Its roads are many, difficult to destroy, and easy to repair. A wrecked train blocks the tracks for a day. A wrecked truck is shoved into the ditch and traffic continues. These conditions will probably force the use of trucks for all troop movements to the front. And trucks will not be safe in long columns. Just as soldiers must disperse and move forward in small groups when they come into the zone of fire in battle, so in the future will they have to filter through the beaten zone of air attack by movement in single trucks. This zone is not of unlimited depth; perhaps thirty miles, perhaps fifty miles, perhaps seventy-five. But whatever its depth, within it there can be no masses, no perfect targets for the hostile aviation.

It is at the outset of a war that surprise is most easily obtained, and speed is a main element of surprise. Superior peacetime preparation is a surprise. The strength of the German armies in 1914, reinforced by their reserve corps, was a surprise to the French. The direction of the German attack was a surprise. The speed of mobilization was a surprise. The rapid reduction of Belgian fortresses, by artillery heavier than any ever used in the field before, was a surprise. The Germans were in turn surprised by the speed of Russian mobilization. New surprises are likewise being prepared for tomorrow's war. Unquestionably mobilization will take place with greater speed, and some of the former steps in the process will doubtless be eliminated.

Getting the "mostest men thar fustest" is more important at the outset of war than at any time during it. But it is a mistake to assume that surprises will repeat patterns of the past. The surprise of tomorrow may be the neutralization of air forces by ground weapons; it may even be the unexpected success of enormous masses of tanks in a break-through obtained by superior speed in the opening phases of war. No greater mistake can be made than to visualize war as if it were a fixed form.

In no field of war has uninformed imagination strayed so wildly as in the popular conception of aerial war. Soldiers and staffs who become infected with these public enthusiasms will have their surprises. Air forces are thought of as darkening the skies in numbers and performing prodigiously. The air forces of the World War are thought of as negligible in comparison with those of tomorrow's war.

Germany, England, and France each manufactured about fifty thousand airplanes during the World War. Germany surrendered eighteen thousand at the Armistice. Such numbers will probably never be produced in an equal period again. The airplanes of 1918 were small, inexpensive, and relatively simple to construct. The bombers of today cost from one hundred thousand to half a million dollars, and the cost is still mounting. Construction takes from six months to a year and a half; they cannot be replaced without long delay. Will such costly craft, fragile as a flying insect and practically irreplaceable, be used on every trifling mission? Obviously not. They will be reserved for work suitable to their cost and importance. Just as a navy is unwilling to risk its fleet without hope of compensating results, so will the air forces decline to operate their irreplaceable squadrons against trifling objectives. They will be saved until the tasks at hand are important enough to warrant the chances they may have to take.

The effectiveness of antiaircraft defense may also be a surprise. If the results obtained by German matériel in Spain can be used as a standard, it appears that localities well defended by antiaircraft artillery are immune from bombardment. Not because bombers cannot get through the antiaircraft defense, but because the losses are too great to justify the results obtained. The time is approaching when antiaircraft defense, like coast defense, will accomplish its mission of holding off the enemy by its mere presence, with never the opportunity of firing a shot. But antiaircraft matériel will always be limited in amount. There will be enough to protect certain vital localities, but it will never be available in quantities sufficient to limit air operations seriously.

The failure of air forces to perform the prodigies expected of them will be a surprise because everyone looks for some explanation, hidden as yet, to account for the small results in Spain and China. In theory, a ton of gas can kill forty-five thousand men; in the World War it took a ton to kill one man. A single rifle bullet can kill half a dozen men; in the World War twenty-eight thousand were fired for each man killed. A single bomb can destroy a bridge—in theory; perhaps two hundred will have to be dropped to accomplish the destruction, and perhaps, too, the bridge can be repaired in a day. In a year of steady bombardment the

Japanese air force, unopposed, has failed to interrupt the Canton–Hankow railway for more than a few hours at a time. In Spain two railway lines from France, supplying the Loyalist forces, have continued to operate under almost daily attacks from Franco's bombers. The single-rail line from Barcelona to Valencia continued to run for almost two years until it was cut by Franco's advance to the sea. Franco's four hundred modern bombers are not a weak force if weighed against the limited communications they have been attacking. In a major war the air forces would be larger, but so would their tasks be more numerous. Recognition of their real limitations will lead to their use in concentrations great enough, and on objectives important enough, not to dissipate their unique capabilities and unexampled power.

But though many soldiers do not exaggerate the capabilities of fighting aviation, they have unlimited faith in the powers of observation aviation. A squadron of thirteen observation planes is allotted to each division. These are each given, in maneuvers and problems, one or two missions a day. Methodically they make their scheduled flights up and down all roads in the hostile rear and photograph great areas of territory. How simple; what quantities of information they bring in! The general makes his daily flights to observe the course of the battle. Artillery fire is adjusted from the air. The whole thing is as unreal as popular belief in a five-minute destruction of Manhattan Island.

When battle is intense, pursuit aviation will operate constantly over the lines. The single observation plane fortunate enough to escape small-caliber antiaircraft cannon will be the prey of pursuit patrols. Observation, in battle, will have to be fought for. Three observation ships will need the protection of a pursuit squadron. Fishing expeditions for information will only result in the loss of plane, pilot, and observer. Specific, vital information will warrant an expenditure of the air power required to obtain it. But the G-2 practices of using observation aviation current in many armies have no basis in the reality of war. When the thirteen observation planes of each of the divisions have once been reduced to two or three before the first week of battle is over, then will they be concentrated in the larger units and sent out with proper protection on limited and specific assignments. Information worth the loss of a half-dozen airplanes and crews can only be information of the greatest importance.

The nature of tomorrow's battles depends upon the whole silhouette of tomorrow's war. The tactics of small, independent maneuvering forces have no application to the reality of the continuous front and of support by tank masses and combat aviation. Instead, tactics will be power tactics. It is not the maneuver of men that must be learned; it is the maneuver of power, of which men are but a part. What must be learned is the concentration, application, and continuity of application, of all the powers of armies. Not men alone nor aviation alone, not tanks alone nor artillery alone, but all of these, co-ordinating their action toward a uniform objective, reinforced by endless rivers of ammunition and replacements, are the tools of power tactics.

The preliminary steps of the offensive battle will be efforts to get the enemy off balance. His reserves will be dispersed in answer to feints. Secondary offensives will force him to counterattack, thus reversing the offensive-defensive balance. When the main attack takes place it will be a surprise, and initial success should follow. It may be made on a broad front to allow the massive entrance of men and material to flow through and spread out on each flank, or it may be in the form of two penetrations converging toward a point and pinching out a pocket—"pocket tactics." The break can be accomplished only with the help of all the available means of war. In 1918 it was men and artillery; now it must be men and tanks supported by artillery and combat aviation.

The first reaction of the defender will be to concentrate his air power to delay the flood pouring through the gap in his defensive dikes. Closely following will come his tanks and troops in motors to form new dams. The attacker's air force will operate with his troops to make the breakthrough. As soon as the break is made the air force will delay the movement of enemy reserves and will also protect its own troops from the defender's frantic air attacks. Will air forces be wasted at bombing cities and rail lines at a time like this? The break-through may mean total destruction for the defender and a victorious end of the war for the attacker. For both the vital need for air-force help is on the field of battle where the main decision is being resolved. Every other air-force objective is secondary.

Great battles require periods of resupply and recuperation between them. It is during these periods that air forces will be most effective in attacking the movement of ammunition toward the front and the military manufacturing establishments in the rear. Offensives may thus be delayed or disrupted. One searches in vain for justification of independent air operations against objectives not related to the objectives of the ground armies. Whatever the future may show, the gain of tomorrow's war depends upon the success of the ground armies. Air forces will make their principal contribution in support, both close and distant, of ground operations.

If the war turns into stabilization and a war of attrition, there may be some logical (but no humane) justification for the aerial attack of political and economic objectives. A people, weary and worn with years of fruitless war, may succumb to discouragement if the hostile air force constantly harasses. Who can tell? Perhaps it may be tried.

No picture of tomorrow's war is complete without the black warriors of propaganda, subversion, and sabotage in the shadows. Propaganda exalts the virtues, strength, and nobility of its sponsors. Underground organizations spread dissension and corrupt the faith of the opponent in his leadership and cause. Sabotage makes the best-laid plans go awry. In many nations in the world the black war is being fought today, the preliminary of the blood war. It is real war, a war of lies and corruption, of spies and destruction. In certain nations two- and three-year courses of subversion are given in universities. Our own nationals attend and come back to undermine our institutions. We are not prepared for war until we are prepared to fight subversion.

Among all the combat agencies of war, the Infantry remains the center of gravity of battle. Only the infantryman can *hold* ground and protect himself. But no longer can the Infantry alone *win* ground. The tragic Queen of Battles, without her servitors, is no longer queen. She remains at the center of military power but is powerless without her stanch supporters.

The silhouette of tomorrow's war shows it starting with a continuous front. The front will be broken by the application of power tactics on a new scale. All the elements of military power will be co-ordinated to help attain the objectives of the ground army. The war may be won or lost, or it may be stabilized, as a result of the battle on the industrial front. In the lines and in the factories the forces of subversion will fight. This war, pounding against the will of the soldiers and nations, may be decisive if it, too, is not prepared for and met. The sphere of war expands. A new view of the whole is needed, and a new resolution of war into its components. The classical pieces of war with which soldiers, fascinated, play and lose all sense of the world's growth and change are still, and ever will be, yesterday's and not tomorrow's war.

APPLICATION OF SCIENCE TO WAR

By Captain (now Colonel) Joseph H. Grant

(*1927*)

Although the need for new engines has led to the cultivation of some of the exact sciences—after a fashion—their study has been unsystematic. In fact, their technical contributions have been made for the most part by non-military men, and with few exceptions the Army makes no serious effort to keep in touch with scientific progress or to branch out for itself in the field of independent scientific investigation. The less exact but no less important sciences such as sociology, biology, and psychology are, with the limited exception of military medicine, totally neglected. Yet a knowledge of these latter fields of thought would have indicated to the

Western Allies in the late war just what might have been expected of Russia. In time of peace a study of psychology and the application of its principles would undoubtedly aid in abolishing many present-day evils. For example, psychology shows that the aptitudes and interests of men vary and that it is possible to devise tests which will indicate, within reasonable limits, the characteristics a man must possess for certain tasks. Although the military service recognizes the desirability of a certain amount of specialization, it sets that recognition at naught by the bland assumption that a man can be a Jack-of-all-trades and good at all. That this condition exists, the demands in the way of professional knowledge and consequent instructional ability upon the officers of the combatant arms amply demonstrate.

From these facts the need for a true science of war becomes evident. Supposedly such a science exists at present, but exactly what it is no one seems to know. Nowhere is it exactly defined. Clausewitz makes it mere knowledge, but certainly it is more than this. Because war has primarily a biological basis (it is made by human beings) and because it does represent a phase in the evolutionary progress of the race, the science of war should be as broad as life. It should take cognizance of all the other sciences, particularly those applied sciences of everyday life. In time of peace it should make use of the scientific method, substituting, wherever practicable, controlled experimental procedure for mere theory. It should also adopt the scientific attitude, resolutely putting away the tendency toward dogmatic thinking which now characterizes it. It should be scientific, as science is now understood.

The organization of science is the task for no one man or group of men, but for many men working all the time. The products of this science will make war more terrible and, paradoxically, more humane because less frequent and less lengthy.

KEEPING TWO JUMPS AHEAD

By Lieutenant (now Colonel) Joseph I. Greene

(1935)

SOME TWO OR THREE YEARS AGO Major General J. F. C. Fuller, in *Lectures on F.S.R. III,* recommended that an army have two sets of Field Service Regulations, both kept well revised at all times, one containing the latest tactical doctrine applicable to the army as it is now organized and equipped, and the other comprising the equivalent doctrine for tomorrow's army. He argued that it would be of tremendous advantage to have on hand a complete set of regulations based on the most probable and desirable changes of the near future. Then, if war came, and with it a number of the probable changes, there would be something concrete and well considered to go on.

The virtue of such a project lies in giving probabilities, and even possibilities, official recognition. We give them recognition now, it is true, but only by weighing them in our extremely sensitive scales of experimentation, which take a long time to settle and all too often have to be read over and over.

Careful experimentation is undoubtedly of utmost importance, but when war comes we are always in the middle of a number of changes. The World War, for example, found us on the point of deciding that machine guns had importance. The final jump had to be taken flat-footed and was a tremendous effort. We had to decide on a weapon and then write regulations for it, almost overnight. The small group of officers who knew anything at all about the experimental types of machine guns that had been studied for several years had to be assembled at Camp Benning and had to do their work under tremendous pressure. That work might well have been accomplished—much of it during the preceding years—while experiments were under way.

"Here is a new thing (or a new idea). It looks good. But we can't be sure that it *is* good until we've given it a lot of study. On the supposition that it will be found practicable, what use can we make of it? How would it affect our present doctrine and methods? What changes in regulations would be necessary?"

This sequence of thought today is largely individual. An occasional enthusiast for a new point of view or piece of equipment lets his mind travel ahead, but he seldom goes the whole distance. An official analysis of the new departure accompanied by a set of changes for regulations is rare indeed. In the usual case we spend several years experimenting and several more deciding upon the alterations in doctrine. It is only necessary to point to the fifteen years we have spent in approaching some definite conclusions on mechanization and motorization to prove the point.

And for the past five years we have had before us a possibility—fast becoming a probability—that upsets every doctrine we have half decided upon with regard to armored vehicles. I refer to the high-speed small-arms bullet. Five years ago, when it was first definitely known that a man had held a rifle to his shoulder and blasted a big hole through an inch and more of armor plate, then was the time to formulate tentative changes in our current tank doctrine, such as it was. An improvement that bade fair to make every known type of tank a brother to a Swiss cheese as soon as it ventured on the battlefield—and still does—deserved the immediate consideration of a group of open-minded officers who could spend their whole time on the subject; but to date nothing but hushes surround the subject. A few bold minds have asked: "What kind of tanks shall we build now?" Or, more to the point, "What kind of tanks *can* we build? Can they carry the extra armor? And if they can carry it, where shall we put it?"

The real question we face is: "If armies get the high-speed bullet before we get the tank that can stop it, then what do we do with our tanks if war pops up?" There should be some group whose business it is to reply: "Here is what you can do if *this* proves true," and, "Here is something you can go by if *that* proves true."

I suggest, therefore, that the Infantry Board be doubled in size and that the additional members be formed as a twin board whose sole duty would be to keep two jumps ahead of the game. I suggest that this parallel board be required to view every new possibility of importance as if it were already practicable and available, and evolve at least an outline of the changes in doctrine it would bring about.

Much of such work, no doubt, would never be of actual use. On the other hand, when a new development did prove out, the work of the "futurist" board would constitute a well-thought-out line of departure for the changes to be made. And in the event of war its studies would be "something to go by" until experience found a better way.

ARMY PUBLICITY
AND THE PROFESSIONAL SERVICE JOURNALS

From an article by GENERAL C. P. SUMMERALL
(then CHIEF OF STAFF)

(*1930*)

TRUTHFUL PUBLICITY is one of the most important missions of the Army in time of peace. This is also the case in time of war, with the difference that in peace great efforts are required to secure proper publicity, while in war publicity is automatic. The Army is an instrumentality of the government, as necessary in peace to prepare for defense as it is in war to execute the defense. During war the people understand perfectly well the mission of the Army; in peace its mission is obscure. Even the people who participated in war have become largely occupied with their own affairs and have little time to devote to thought on the military establishment.

The Army depends for its existence and support upon the will of the people. The extent of their interest measures the degree of support that the Army receives. It is not fair to the Executive or to Congress to expect them to act arbitrarily in providing means for the support of the Army when the people know little about the reasons for its existence. It is one of the duties of the Army to acquaint the people with its mission and its performances in time of peace.

There has been in our service an evident tendency for officers to avoid "bursting into print." As a result, our list of military writers who have achieved distinction is regrettably short. We still rely on British authors for standard works on Jackson, Lee, Sherman, Grant, and other outstanding American military leaders. Up to the close of the World War our military textbooks were largely indebted to foreign publications for their contents.

.   .   .

There is no reason for our officers to feel inferior or to imply, by their silence on military subjects, undue deference to the opinions of foreign military writers. There are many subjects of immediate importance to the Army that American officers should discuss in the pages of the professional magazines of the arms and services, which we call the service journals. The editors of these journals may be relied upon to protect authors and the War Department from untoward incidents that might arise from the publication of undesirable material.

.   .

There appears to be an idea that news consists of only such items as appear on the front pages of the metropolitan newspapers. Nothing is farther from the truth. Our service journals afford an excellent means of making military news available to the public. When an article appears in any of the service journals it comes to the attention of publishers who are constantly on the lookout for interesting material on subjects connected with national defense. Any article that has value for their purposes receives prompt attention; it may be quoted at length or may serve as the basis for articles prepared by civilian writers. In either case the author receives due recognition and the Army benefits by having its activities accurately portrayed. Many officers who are not directly connected with the Army's regularly estabished publicity agencies will find that the service journals afford the most convenient outlet for authoritative and interesting articles. They can thus pass on to the service and to the public the results of their study, their thought, and their experience.

IF THIS BE TREASON

From an article by LIEUTENANT COLONEL (later COLONEL)
ROWAN P. LEMLY

(*1934*)

IN MY JUDGMENT the Army appears more prone to orthodoxy than most professions in civil life. To put it baldly, too many officers are addicted to inertia in the origination of constructive ideas.

One can appreciate the necessity for conservatism in the adoption of new weapons and other matériel, or in the complete upheaval of doctrines on organization, or in radical changes of our views in the application of tactical principles. And no conservatively minded man can criticize the snail's pace at which (through no fault of their own) our several laboratories function in the experimentation, test, and adoption of new ideas. An economical expenditure as well as a very careful distribution of our limited military appropriations is forced upon us. As a result we seem to be striving constantly to spread our meager allotment of butter over too large a slice of bread. Requests for additional funds with which to experiment and effect radical changes are not received enthusiastically by members of the military committees in Congress. They are from Missouri and must be shown, and to this viewpoint one can attach no blame. The result is that innovations which involve expenditures other than for bare maintenance of the existing military machine go into a mill where they are ground into dust and oblivion or come to life only in the face of dire national emergencies.

But mental activity and concentration, constructive thought, exchange of ideas and argument on ways and means to improve the military, particularly in the fields of weapons, organization, and tactics, cost not one cent of appropriations. Many civil corporations hold annual competitions among their employees and give substantial prizes for the best ideas, plans, or innovations which result in material savings or increased profits to the organization. Indeed, the very fight to hold down one's job in civil life and secure advancement results in constant effort and competition among those who refuse to be drones. Yet in the military—a most interesting and absorbing profession—the tendency of some officers appears to be to do their daily jobs reasonably well but otherwise to call it a day. Serious study on ways and means to improve the machinery, concentration leading to constructive criticism, and creative thought which looks toward future and perhaps radical developments in weapons, organization, and tactics—there is not enough of this. Several years after the Armistice the first vital changes since the World War took place in our infantry defense tactics. They were born of a confidential report on certain German tactical maneuvers!

DEFENDING OUR LAST FRONTIER

By MAJOR GENERAL WILLIAM C. RIVERS

General Rivers, who retired from active service a number of years before the present war after being the Inspector General, argued continually regarding the importance of the Pacific area, especially Alaska. Everything General Rivers said in November 1935—and in a number of other articles which appeared in general magazines—has been borne out by the developments which culminated in Pearl Harbor.

UNIVERSAL USE in atlases, and in illustrating books and newspaper articles, of maps on the Mercator projection—greatly distorted and deceptive at high latitudes—has given rise to important misconceptions in the public mind. One of these is the failure to realize that the normal, straight, and short steamship lane from our West coast to Asia passes near Alaska and parallel to our Aleutian Islands. Another general misconception concerns the position of Honolulu with respect to this highway to the Orient. Study of a great circle map on the gnomonic projection, or better yet a globe, will show how far (more than two thousand miles) to the south of any part of this highway to Japan and Manila lies Honolulu. Also that Japan is more than twice as far from Honolulu as from the American Aleutians in Alaska.

Such a study will indicate the paramount strategic position of the Aleutian Islands with respect to the eastern part of the north Pacific Ocean. The question is one of defending the United States, Hawaii, and the Panama Canal by controlling the parts of the north Pacific near our shores, rather than the defense of Alaska. A hostile fleet operating from an Aleutian base would find excellent harbors. Easy mining work would make the Okhotsk and Bering seas closed areas, providing well-protected communications lines. An opposing fleet based on Honolulu would be obliged to work on longer and exterior lines—an inferior strategic position.

Our recent board of Army officers appointed to consider sites for the several air-defense bases provided by the new Wilcox Bill will doubtless suggest a location of the Army air base in Alaska with respect to possible sites for a naval base in the Aleutians region. Fairbanks and the head of Cook Inlet have been mentioned in the press as suitable for the Army air-defense base. Although dispersion in depth of air forces is now necessary, and although the speed as well as carrying capacity of the bombing plane have been doubled in the last four years, both places mentioned in Mr. Gordon's recent article in the *Journal* lie at too-great distances from any probable naval base in the Aleutians.

The Weather Bureau records, and conversations with Coast Guard officers, indicate that climatic conditions in the Aleutians are more favorable than is generally believed. The Japan current passes to the north as well as to the south of that great group. In Unalaska, for example, zero weather has never been encountered. Navigation is open all the year round in the Aleutians. Winter ice floes do not come farther south than the Pribilof Islands. Annual rainfall is from sixty to eighty inches. Many places in the United States have as much or more rain. There is some precipitation about two hundred days in the year—as in some places in the United States.

Unalaska and Bristol Bay near by—the latter closed by easy mining operations—will hold the fleets of the world. At Dutch Harbor the anchorage is some eighteen or nineteen fathoms. Wharf construction would offer no difficulties. The limited personnel for repairs to vessels would be brought from the United States, as was the case with far more numerous employees to build the canal at Panama. Fogs are frequent at times in the Aleutians. For foe and friend alike they are often a great detriment and, with the deceptive possibilities of the radio, they would be at times an advantage. The suggestion has been made—and it is here repeated—that a joint Navy-Army board should study the important questions of "defending our last frontier."

RIDE A COCKHORSE

By Major (now Brigadier General) E. D. Cooke

(*1937*)

Polo and hunting are natural pastimes for members of the horse Cavalry and horse-drawn Field Artillery units. But until the middle thirties about one half of the officers on duty with Infantry regiments and battalions were also mounted. There were, for example, five polo teams at the Infantry School, four of which were Infantry. There was also a hunt with several packs of hounds and a vociferous if small group of non-riding doughboys who kept up a running barrage on the horsy aspects of their Infantry brothers-in-arms. In "Ride a Cockhorse" General Cooke put over the points and at the same time gave *Infantry Journal* readers a good many laughs.

Bill busher was deceived early in his military career. He was led to believe that doughboys walked, artillerymen sat on caissons, and only cavalrymen rode horses.

That was all right with Bill. He got through five major engagements without needing a horse in any one of them. And he was perfectly content to continue his service as a foot soldier. But no sooner was the war over than he had to start equitating.

"The best thing for the insides of a man is the outsides of a horse," declared Bill's division commander.

So, for the sake of their insides, Bill and his contemporaries reported. each morning to a specially imported cavalry instructor. Although prisoners did not turn out until seven-thirty, the door of the riding hall opened at seven.

The condition of his insides had never bothered Bill, but after three hours of slow trotting the outside of his anatomy needed plenty of attention. If any pleasure was derived from the exercise, it existed for the instructor alone.

Swaying gently to the beauty-rest gaits of a thoroughbred mare, the cavalryman hazed his victims with caustic innuendoes. Always the riders were at fault, never the flea-bitten culls they bestrode.

"If you're going to be just a passenger, drop a nickel in his ear!" Bill was told on several occasions.

Bill's lips straightened into a hard, thin line. If ever he had any delusions about the benefits of riding, they were dispelled under that grueling. Never again would Bill associate old Dobbin with anything related to his own personal well-being.

"I'm only getting you shaken down into your saddle," the instructor said in justification of his slow-trotting methods.

"If I get shaken down any further I'll be swallowing the cinch," Bill complained.

But the pounding continued, until the general announced that he personally would conduct the class on a controlled ride. He wanted to see how they were progressing.

"Someday," he informed them, "your social status may depend upon your appearance on a horse."

Seated upon his privately owned Arabian stallion, the general presented a fine picture of an aristocratic gentleman. But Bill Busher was not so fortunate. Judging by the horseflesh beneath him, Bill ranked pretty low in the social scale at that particular moment.

The bones of his decrepit hay burner creaked in every joint as Bill pounded off across country in pursuit of social prestige and the good of his insides. The general's horse soared over a fence, light as a cloud. The instructor's mount skimmed after him like a swallow. Then came the charge of the heavy brigade.

The vanguard hit that fence with a crash that could have been heard clear down to the Rio Grande. Kindling wood flew like straws, and overgrown plow horses rolled and thrashed around in the dust. An ambulance, thoughtfully provided, picked up the casualties and rushed them to the dispensary for first aid. The remainder of the cavalcade surged through the opening made by their fallen comrades and thundered after the general.

A slide came next. A straight up-and-down slide into a gravel pit. A regular heart-stopping monster of a slide. Bill's benighted quadruped took one look over the yawning lip of that orifice and shook his head. The poor dumb beast wanted to imply that he couldn't go down that thing—not without wings. And, being no dumber than the horse, Bill agreed with him. But down below the instructor was yelling:

"Don't be a passenger! Dominate him! Come on, dominate him!"

So to show the general that he had the welfare of his insides at heart, Bill drove home the spurs with one great smack of his heels.

The horse gave a weary, resigned grunt and leaped straight out into space!

Several hours later in the hospital a doctor was fussily going over the cuts, contusions, and abrasions on Bill's body and at the same time giving him a severe lecture.

"I can't find any broken bones," he concluded, snapping on the last piece of adhesive, "but you're going to stay in bed for a while, anyhow. If you fellows must ride, why risk your necks going down slides and jumping fences when there are all the bridle paths in the world to ride on?"

Bill shrugged a painful shoulder.

"You've got me there, Doc," he admitted. "I'd like to know the answer to that one myself."

Bill was not being smart: he was honestly puzzled. He knew his experience had in no way improved the condition of his insides. As for any social aspirations—well, they lay shattered at the bottom of the gravel pit. So aside from a week in the hospital, Bill was unable to figure out just what benefits he had derived from his brief course in equitation.

A certificate announcing his proficiency in horsemanship arrived in due course, and Bill decided that was the answer. It was like any other inoculation in the Army: one took it and became immune. Bill guarded the certificate zealously, believing that with it in his possession he was finished with horses. But he was quickly disillusioned.

A new brigadier arrived on the post, and he was plenty tough. At his first review he spotted one officer having difficulty with a horse, and the brigadier immediately ordered every officer in the brigade out for equitation.

Not thinking the order would apply to anyone already proficient, Bill proceeded to headquarters and presented his certificate. The brigadier acted as though Bill had tried to hand him a rattlesnake.

"I'm the only one who gives certificates in my brigade," the brigadier fumed, pounding his desk and stomping his feet. "Unless you want a Class B, you'd better get yourself out of here and onto a horse."

Bill got himself to the stables without delay.

"I bet I don't even get up high enough on this guy's social ladder to fall off," Bill confided gloomily to his friend, John Bean.

"You needn't worry about him being social," said John. "He's out for blood."

And sure enough, the brigadier's idea of equitation proved to be a series of plain endurance tests. Eighteen to thirty miles once every week—with an extra ride thrown in whenever a new officer joined the brigade. As there frequently were not enough horses to go around, John and Bill took to riding mules.

"Not so stylish," John admitted, "but a whole lot more comfortable."

"Yes," Bill agreed, "but if equitation is the art of horsemanship, what is riding a mule?"

"It's thirty miles, no matter what you're riding. Are you still worried about your social standing?"

"Nope. Just puzzled. The brigadier hasn't said what he has us out here for."

"That's what you think," John retorted. "He has us here to do fifteen miles out and fifteen miles back, because that's the kind of a guy he is."

"But why?" Bill persisted. "What do we get out of it?"

"Maybe you'll get a diploma in mulemanship."

But the brigadier did not issue a certificate. And even if Bill had been pronounced proficient it wouldn't have done him any good because he was ordered to school at Fort Benning, and students at the Infantry School equitate, certificates or no certificates.

Bill couldn't understand why equitation was part of the curriculum in a doughboy school. He questioned a few of his classmates and their answer was a shrug. They took it for granted no military education could be complete without a horse in it, but they didn't know why.

"At least we have a doughboy instructor," Bill said as they filed into the corral for their first day's slow trotting. "He probably won't be so hard on us."

On the horse next to Bill's, "Cotton" Jones hooted derisively.

"You haven't been around one of these doughboy graduates from Fort Riley [the Cavalry School], have you?" Cotton asked. "A cavalryman teaches equitation because it's his business, but these fellows do it for pleasure. They're twice as tough."

"Do you mean that infantrymen actually go to a cavalry school just to learn horseback riding?"

"Sure! And they come back with pink coats, riding to hounds, and everything."

A puzzled furrow appeared between Bill's eyes.

"But if they like it so much, why don't they transfer to the Cavalry?"

"Then they'd be just one more man on a horse," said Cotton. "Here they are big shots. Ladies pay court to them and club together to buy them presents. They travel around to horse shows and polo games. They collect ribbons, silverware, and swell details [jobs]. They are sitting on the troops!"

Bill shook his head.

"They can have my share of it. All I want to know is, why do the rest of us have to ride?"

There was no connection between horsemanship and the rest of Bill's schoolwork. But he rode with folded arms, jumped logs, and galloped across country just the same. And on the diploma given Bill at the end of the year was a statement to the effect that Bill Busher had passed in equitation.

But that was good at the Infantry School only. It didn't buy Bill anything beyond there. Each year, it seemed, someone discovered a new way of pointing the toes or of holding the reins, and when that happened Bill had to go out and start all over again.

He rode leaning back and he rode leaning forward. He lengthened his stirrups and he shortened them again. He pointed his toes out and he pointed his heels down. But none of it seemed to get him anywhere. There just wasn't any end to a doughboy having to ride a horse.

"Don't any of these certificates mean anything?" Bill inquired of one superior.

"I'm afraid not," was the answer. "Perhaps when you get one from Leavenworth [the Command and General Staff School] it will excuse you."

"That's small comfort," said Bill, "because it doesn't look as if I'll ever get to that place."

But he did, eventually. And he was not surprised when, the very first week, all students reported for equitation.

"Look," said Captain Krims, pointing to the lists of horses, "they have a name for every one of them!"

"That's nothing." Bill spat at the tanbark. "So have I."

He was not disappointed in the horse assigned to him. The beast had a mouth of iron and a firm determination to be at the head of the column. It was no more than Bill expected.

However, the instructor was quite decent. As much as possible he avoided seeing Bill's errors and even admitted that the horse was not so good.

"We only want you to get toughened up for the terrain exercises," he said.

That certainly was reasonable enough, and Bill perked right up. At last he could see a reason for horses. And besides, if a graduate of Leavenworth didn't have to ride any more, then this was equitation to finish equitation, and Bill was all for it.

But in the second year's work there were no terrain exercises, and still they rode. Second-year students were required to be on a horse for two hours a week despite hell and high water.

"How come?" Bill wanted to know.

Again he encountered that same blank wall. It was orders, that was all.

The bottom fell out of the thermometer—for a month it was too weak even to get up to zero—and still they rode. It was not mandatory to ride outdoors. Bill could have stayed in the riding hall but, like many another, he preferred the cold to maneuvering by fours on the dot, cross, and circle.

Swathed in extra underclothes, sweaters, ear muffs, gloves, and even galoshes, Bill and his friends wandered like miserable outcasts through the brakes of the Missouri. It was equitation at its worst, but the discomforts were merely incidental to Bill's desire to learn the reason why it had to be done. The motive, however, remained obscure.

Then, long after all riding was over, Bill attended a huge Hunt Ball. And there, among the pink hunt dinner jackets of the *caballeros,* he discovered the long-sought reason for equitation.

"Look at all the whipper-uppers and tallyhoers," he said to Krims.

"Yeah," his friend replied, "and some of the whippersnappers too. Aren't they having a big time, all dressed up in boots and silks?"

But in looking closely Bill detected a note of sadness behind the gaiety, a haunted look in the eyes of those jaunty cavaliers. And suddenly Bill knew the cause of their hidden fears, and with it the reason for Army equitation.

The art of horsemanship had been kept alive by the spirit of those pink coats. The people themselves were clinging desperately to an idea, to a legend originating as far back as the ancient days of chivalry. For centuries the symbol of leadership was a man on a horse, and those people had struggled valiantly to keep it so.

They would not hear the rumbling of combat cars. Their eyes were closed to the infantry hurrying by in trucks. They still heard the creak of saddle leather above the clank of machinery. They refused to relinquish their heritage.

And to Bill the sight of them trying so hard to hold back the hands on the clock of time was all at once pathetic.

"It's not funny, after all," he said, and Krims nodded in agreement.

"No! It's not so damned funny. Let's go have a drink."

And even as they entered the taproom the orchestra started another dance. With a preliminary umpah, umpah, the trombones and clarinets sounded:

Oh, the old gray mare, she ain't what she used to be,
Ain't what she used to be . . .

TANK DIVISIONS

From an article by MAJOR (now COLONEL) C. C. BENSON

(*1931*)

This is one of the first articles to appear in America suggesting the use of tanks in such large units as divisions. We had, at that time, but a few companies of obsolete World War tanks and a few single experimental models. This writer's thought for the future was indeed clear, :or nearly everything he says turned out to be right when it came to building our armored divisions of the present.

A FEW OUTSPOKEN ENTHUSIASTS maintain that most of the fighting in future wars will be done by machines. Those who rely more upon practical experience than upon imagination can hardly accept this view without important reservations. Fighting machines are particularly sensitive to the ground; as the ground gets rougher, their efficiency falls off rapidly. In extremely difficult country they are practically useless. Infantry and cavalry take the ground as they find it, and no machine can compete with them on rugged or wooded terrain. Even in open country there are towns, patches of woods, hills, and watercourses that form reefs on which land battleships may come to grief under the anti-tank guns of the enemy. The ability of mechanized units to operate independently for brief periods should not obscure the fact that they will be organized primarily for co-operation with other arms. Both the old and the new combat elements have their parts to play. The real problem is not to carve out an exclusive role for mechanized units but to co-ordinate their uses with those of existing means.

.   .   .

In close proximity to an organized system of hostile machine guns, even infantry is pinned to the ground and deprived of that tactical mobility which is essential to offensive action. With a tactical doctrine based on aggressive offensive action, we must provide adequate means for offensive action. The armored cross-country fighting machine affords one means of disrupting the hostile machine-gun organization and assisting the whole force to overcome the power of the defensive. The purpose of mechanization is to provide ground troops with an effective offensive element.

.   .   .

There are, then, two principal combat missions that mechanized units will have to perform:

(1) To lead the assault upon well-organized positions;

(2) To maneuver rapidly and deliver sudden powerful blows against the enemy's front, flanks, and rear.

We cannot reasonably expect a single unit to execute efficiently missions so markedly different; consequently it will be necessary to consider carefully the matter of organization. The machines used for different purposes may be identical except for thickness of armor and details of armament, but the organizations will be different.

.   .   .

The organization of these units is a matter for immediate consideration, not only because of their potential value in combat, but also because their creation will affect materially the revision of present plans for mobilization and for procurement. The writer suggests that these units be organized as tank divisions.

.   .   .

Tank-versus-tank actions will develop and culminate even more rapidly than cavalry-versus-cavalry actions. Tank-division and brigade commanders can and should have highly centralized control of their units before and after an engagement; but in action they will be unable to direct in detail the fast-moving operations of their combat units. If they attempt to issue detailed orders, confusion and delay will result. Much must therefore be left to the initiative and judgment of subordinates. The adaptability of a tank division to rapid changes in the situation will depend largely upon subordinates who can assume their proper share of responsibility in action. Each unit should have an ample quota of officers, so that higher commanders will not hesitate to exploit the full powers of highly mobile combat elements.

.   .   .

It may appear premature to proceed with organization before we have had some experience in handling modern equipment. There are, however, excellent reasons for so doing. Our general mobilization plan fails in its purpose if it does not include all the units that we may expect to mobilize. To produce and maintain equipment for mechanized units will impose a heavy burden on certain of our industries. They should be fully prepared to assume that burden in wartime, but procurement plans cannot take definite shape until definite tables of organization are provided. Furthermore, the creation of mechanized units is highly desirable for training purposes. Once authorized, these units could be used in command-post exercises and in problems at the service schools. Hundreds of officers throughout the service, instead of a handful, could then apply themselves to mechanization studies. We do not hesitate to change infantry or cavalry tables of organization, nor should we hesitate to publish tables for mechanized units, even though they will be subject to change. Whether perfect or not, tables of organization [for tank divisions] should be authorized. So long as our plans are merely on paper, changes cost us nothing. The first step is to get an adequate organization established as a basis for future plans and studies.

Many years may elapse before mechanization is generally accepted in our service. The equipment is so expensive that comparatively little of it can be had in times of peace. After the first tank division is organized and equipped, its powers and limitations will have to be determined by such experience as maneuvers provide. The service schools will have to modify their teachings to accommodate the newcomers, and many a class will graduate before our future commanders are thoroughly prepared to use mechanized forces, or even to co-operate with them. In the normal course of peacetime events it will take a long time to adapt military thought to the use of fighting machines.

There are, however, certain factors that may accelerate our mechanization progress:

(1) Fighting machines appeal to the American desire for energetic action and swift decision. In other words, the weapon suits our national characteristics.

(2) Machines are now used in civil pursuits in this country far more extensively than in the Army. Americans are thoroughly accustomed to the use of mechanical devices, and we have more good mechanics than any other nation in the world. Herein lies strength if the Army is prepared to use it.

(3) Our industrial, material, scientific, and financial resources are ample to produce and maintain the necessary equipment. Increased mechanization in the Army provides an effective means of utilizing in national defense our acknowledged superiority in these matters.

(4) Mechanization is in full accord with our plan of national defense— a plan based on the maintenance of a small but highly efficient force.

(5) Armored fighting machines can be made practically immune to attacks by gas and aircraft, and can therefore be relied upon to protect ground troops from the unrestricted use of these powerful new weapons.

(6) The War Department favors a reasonable measure of mechanization in our service and is giving serious thought to the development of a definite well-considered mechanization project.

(7) Influential leaders in Congress appreciate the value of fighting machines and recognize the need for an increased number of well-equipped mechanized units. It is probable that when the time comes Congress will be prepared to grant the necessary funds.

(8) Under present conditions the necessary automotive equipment can be purchased at rock-bottom prices.

In conclusion, let us recall a paragraph from an address delivered by General Summerall on September 1, 1927:

> The temptation is ever present to view military problems in the light of past experience. It must be borne in mind that no two situations or campaigns in war are alike. Especially must it be recognized that our last experience presented a special case that cannot be repeated. Not again can we expect allies to contain the enemy for more than a year and furnish us with all essential munitions while we are organizing our armies.

THE USE OF INHERENT MOBILITY

By Major (now Major General) William C. Lee

Another student of tanks in war who early argued for the employment of large masses of mechanized units in striking depth into the enemy's territories was Major William C. Lee. (He is now a major general commanding large air-borne forces and has, more than any other man in our Army, been responsible for the rapid and thorough development of our parachute and other air-borne troops.) General Lee's ideas were expressed in the following article which appeared in January 1936.

TREMENDOUS PROGRESS in mechanical development and the almost universal mechanization of industry directs the thoughts of officers of all armies into new and fascinating paths. Everywhere mechanical development is being paralleled by studies in the tactical employment of the new weapons being developed. In our own Army progress has been retarded by a lack of matériel, but this condition is about to be relieved by the production of a new tank of much promise. We may well devote time and thought as to how we are going to use it.

From the time, soon after the war, when the British adopted the sprung track (the secret of tank speed over ten miles per hour) they have led the world in practical experimentation and in the development of new tank tactical methods. Thinking always in terms of speed and mobility, they have looked into the future and have conducted extensive experiments leading toward mechanization on a large scale.

In England, out of the many changes in organization and the great variety of thought, we see emerging a mechanized force capable of independent action and possessing a considerable radius of action and great striking power. The advocates of such a force urge that it should by no means be restricted to close operation with the less mobile foot soldier; rather it should be used either independently or in decisive attacks with other arms against the enemy's flank and rear. It is capable of frontal attacks against the main hostile position when no flanks are available, but in such case it will make a deep penetration and its objectives will be artillery in position, headquarters, communication centers, and reserves. Tank officers say that in this way they can utilize the speed of the new tank to support the infantry action more effectively.

The important element around which the British Mobile Force is built is the tank brigade, consisting of one light tank battalion and three mixed tank battalions in which we find light, medium, and "close-support" tanks. The light tanks act on security, covering, and reconnaissance missions; they screen the advance of the brigade and watch its flanks; they constitute a pivot of maneuver while the heavier elements, the medium tanks, form the maneuvering mass. When the mission of the brigade carries it far into enemy territory, beyond its normal cruising range, it is to be supported by airplanes, armored cars, and motorized protective troops of all arms.

France has contemplated the employment of the tank as an accompanying weapon for infantry, and the motorization and mechanization of cavalry.

To support the infantry, methods of tank employment in France have not changed materially since the World War. Even though a better and faster tank has been built, and great progress in anti-tank defense has been accomplished, the French tanks are still closely tied to infantry action in methodical attacks.

For protection the French lean to heavier armor and fire support from other arms rather than to great speed. They do not believe that the terrain will permit tanks to employ high speeds on the battlefield. Their new infantry tank, although faster than the old Renault, lacks the high speed of the new British and American tanks. Its somewhat improved speed, however, does give sufficient mobility to permit the new tank to operate at a somewhat greater distance from infantry than the old tank. But, contrary to the British thought, the French maintain that the tank is *not* capable of extended independent action and that it requires at all times the help of the other arms and the protection of their supporting fires.

Thus we see in Europe the armies of two powerful nations with sharply varying policies regarding mechanization: one looking ahead to warfare of the future, the other wedded to methods proven in warfare of the past. The trend of military thought of a nation is strongly influenced by its social system, its economic condition, its political relations with foreign nations, its geographic location with reference to possible enemies, and its experience in war. A brief analysis will indicate, perhaps, the reasons for the difference in French and British policies.

In Great Britain we see a small professional army which is not organized primarily for continental warfare but to imperial policing and small wars. However, owing to its obligations under various political pacts, the nation must be prepared now to support its allies on the continent. Its land forces can best do this by maintaining a modernized and well-trained army of great mobility, one capable of striking powerful and decisive blows. Quite naturally, then, the army has turned to motorization and mechanization as a means of modernization.

We realize the extraordinary value of the British experiments and they should be carefully studied. We are appreciative of the progress that they have made in the development of tank forces capable of operating as independent formations. Surely there is a great need for such forces.

The infantryman, we believe, heartily approves of the creation of mechanized forces, in his own or other arms, for he knows that the reason for such forces is to help him attain victory. But he sees the high-speed, self-contained tank formation becoming less and less a close supporting infantry weapon. He is apprehensive of the tendency to take from him the armored assistance that he so much needs for his immediate, direct, and close support. It is well to heed him, for even in England the high command still considers the infantry the backbone of modern armies.

We hear much of the new infantry in which armored machines will replace the foot soldier in the near future. We wonder. Machines will move him faster; they will move him to the battlefield and on the battlefield; but when the deadly hail of hostile bullets is met it is the foot soldier, with his weapon in his hand, crouching, crawling, from hole to hole, from cover to cover, who will clinch the victory. And it is he only who can hold conquered ground. The capabilities of the tank are great, but its limitations are actual and cannot be glossed over. Assuming that perfected armor plate will turn every bullet, that the multiplicity of maintenance, supply, and traffic problems can be solved, and that technique will eliminate mechanical limitations, the colossal problem of production precludes putting every fighting man in an armored vehicle. There is no evidence that any country today is preparing for production of tanks on such a scale.

What, then, is the true sphere of the tank? It is not to replace the infantryman but to aid him. The problem revolves around the question of how best to do this. Shall self-contained armored formations, acting as the mobile arm, support the general action—which, in fact, is a support of the infantry—by wide maneuver on the enemy's flank or rear, or shall the tank be closely tied to infantry action?

Infantry officers of the British Army cry out that close support from tanks is necessary. They say, "The power of the machine gun in the defense is too great for our unprotected bodies. Give us a tank to work closely with us." In answer to this demand the British plan to produce an infantry tank, low, heavily armored, and of necessity slower than the vehicles of the tank brigade. These tanks are to be organized on a basis of one battalion of tanks to the infantry division and allotted to army or corps. Speed is sacrificed for armor, mobility is lessened, tactical methods are back to fifteen years ago. This reversion is typical of the inconsistency surrounding the whole question.

Why sacrifice speed and mobility in the tank in order to give close support to the infantry? If we admit that armor is preferable to speed such a decision is logical, but there are other considerations. Tactical success is dependent to a great extent on strategical mobility. General Forrest's pithy comment on mobility applies to tanks as well as to men, and when strategy ends and tactics begin, it is speed and reserve engine power that give the tank the suppleness and agility to save itself at the moment it is most exposed; it is speed that makes a difficult target; and it is speed that enables the tank to close rapidly with the enemy. Until every infantryman is equipped with powerful armor-piercing weapons, we deny that a sacrifice of speed will enable the tank to support the foot soldier more effectively.

Let us turn again to France. The factors governing the tactical employment of the tank during the World War have dominated French thought ever since.

The French cannot afford to carry on extensive experiments. Moreover, their methods are dictated by their situation in Europe, which necessitates a policy of defensive frontier tactics. The French prefer proven methods, even with their new tank. One of their writers has said: "It is only from a consideration of our experience in war that we can arrive at positive and reasonable conclusions, free from foolish and unjustified hopes. There is nothing so useless as imagining combat tactics for a formation that does not exist or is not exactly defined."

The French do not become unduly excited over improvements in arms or armor. They expect an occasional upsetting of the balance between protection and offensive armament.

French doctrines are based on probable continental wars in which great masses of conscripted infantry and artillery will come to grips. Cavalry, as the mobile arm, has been reinforced by mechanization; but for general actions, tanks are employed for close infantry support on wide fronts and in density and depth. Tank units are attached to front-line infantry battalions to fight with the infantry *as infantry*. Therefore, tank action can be a surprise only to the degree that the general action is a surprise. As infantry advances in long thin lines so do the tanks advance.

The enemy will equip his front elements with long thin lines of anti-tank weapons, gun for tank, and the tank will be mastered.

With methods of this kind mobility is restricted, surprise is impossible, and protection simmers down to the questionable factor of armor.

In the American Army we have discarded the slow and obsolete war-time tanks. Our tank units are marking time while awaiting the production of our new vehicles. Soon we hope to see our tank battalions paralleling our theoretical tactical studies with practical tests and experimentation in the field with troops and machines, for it is only in this way that we can arrive at worth-while tactical conclusions.

Although, in theory, machines are designed to conform to tactical requirements, mechanical progress is at times far ahead of our tactical accomplishments. Our new tank possesses great speed and increased ability to maneuver. To limit this machine to the old tactical tank method of "accompanying tanks" is permitting tactical thought to fall far behind mechanical progress.

As in the French Army, our tanks are infantry, although our cavalry is being reinforced and strengthened by mechanization in order to provide forces for distant and independent missions. As in the past, our methods regarding tank combat methods still strongly resemble those of the French. Undoubtedly this has been because of the similarity of tank matériel. But with a new tank, positively and distinctly American, certainly we should evolve our own methods to fit its capabilities and the spirit of our tactical doctrines. In considering the knowledge obtained from a study of the experiments of the French and British, let us not ignore the capabilities of our new machine.

There has appeared in our new school texts a brief reference to "tanks in support of foot troops," and therein is the key to an effective method of employing our most recent tank. We are told that tanks, when used in the supporting role, are not attached to subordinate units of foot troops, but are kept under the control of the higher commander, to act as a unit under the tank commander. But the new texts still emphasize the employment of tanks in the accompanying mission, and this role is stressed throughout.

It is believed that, in the future, the emphasis will be put on the supporting tank method and that this idea will be developed, far beyond the short reference in our texts, with the aim of substituting it completely for the old established accompanying tank method. In this new role the tank can use its speed, its mobility, its power of maneuver. It can maneuver against the enemy's flank and rear and can penetrate his defensive positions when no flanks are available. And in doing all this *it will operate so as to closely support and work directly with the infantry.* Because the tank possesses speed is no reason to say that its speed makes it unfit to work closely with foot troops, rather is the opposite true.

Our present method of using tanks in the accompanying role necessitates the attachment of, usually, one platoon of tanks to assault infantry battalions. Our regulations state that tanks should be employed only in large numbers, on a broad front, and with a maximum of surprise.

We repeat that the attachment of tank platoons to rifle battalions on a broad, continuous front practically eliminates surprise, reduces mobility, limits the results that the new tank is capable of producing, and does *not* give the most effective close support to the foot troops. As previously pointed out in discussing French methods, it makes defense against the tank exceedingly simple.

This writer proposes that we follow the French in retaining the tank for the mission for which it was created; that is, the close support of foot troops. But there let us leave the French and borrow from the British to the extent of using the speed, the mobility, and the maneuver power of the modern tank. Let us base our solution on the principle of concentrated formations. If only one company of tanks is available to support an infantry regiment, then let us not break up that tank company for attachment to infantry battalions, dispersing the tank effort and scattering the tanks into a long thin line, or lines, whereby an opposing long thin line of anti-tank guns can meet them, gun for tank. But rather let us use the tank company as a unit, to fight and maneuver as a unit, with all the fighting power of the company concentrated within itself. Its mobility and speed will enable it to attack unexpectedly and swiftly over selected terrain, to strike from the flank, to penetrate, and, when once within the hostile lines, to move laterally over the enemy's positions opposite the front of the attacking regiment of foot troops. Such action as this can be sudden and swift and can be co-ordinated closely with the attack of the foot troops and supporting fires. But, it will be asked, what is to prevent the enemy from concentrating his anti-tank fires in order to meet the concentrated tanks? The answer is in the speed of the tank, its ability to maneuver and make rapid thrusts and move on before concentrated fires can be brought to bear on it.

The more closely the tank battalion supports the attack of the foot troops, the shorter the thrusts it makes into the hostile position, the simpler its missions, and the more often can the tanks disengage and repeat the action. The tank-battalion commander is no longer a staff officer at the command post of the infantry commander. He is now a fighting leader. Co-ordination with the foot troops and the supporting arms can be obtained by informing them promptly of the proposed tank action, including the tank missions, objectives, routes, and assembly points. The commander of the supported infantry unit can best co-ordinate this action.

We can carry the idea on to include groups of tank battalions, organized as regiments or brigades, operating as powerful mobile units, penetrating more deeply into the enemy's lines, striking his guns in position, his reserves, his command posts, and communications. We can create a mobile formation for the reserve as a powerful weapon to be used by the higher commander in pursuit, exploitation, or as a striking force to be committed for decisive action.

A company or a battalion, or even a group of battalions, of our new tanks, operating as a concentrated unit, employing surprise, swift and sudden thrusts, and rapid disengagements, will be more effective in closely supporting the foot troops than a wide dispersion of small tank units attached to battalions over a wide front.

It is not advocated that these tank units assume cavalry missions of long-range reconnaissance. We should leave that to the mechanized cavalry, which is better organized and fitted for the purpose. It is not claimed that our concentrated tank formations are capable of extended independent action. We can, however, in the supporting role, use the speed and maneuverability of the tank to strike at a decisive time, in a decisive direction.

To accept the armored fighting vehicle as a mobile weapon to be maneuvered as a concentrated force is simply to utilize its full capabilities.

The great captains have been those who used to the utmost the inherent mobility of the most effective striking force of their times and the mobility of their own brains.

Mobility! Mobile fire power! These are as necessary today and tomorrow as in the time of Genghis Khan.

ONLY SECURITY CAN GUARANTEE SPEED

By Captain (now Colonel) Joseph I. Greene

This 1937 attempt to look into the future hit the nail right on the thumb several times, especially as regards the speed at which the German armies would enter France. True, the author covers himself to some extent by saying early in his article that a highly mechanized army can only make high speed in conducting an invasion if the "invaded nation is totally unprepared." But this doesn't make up for his poor prognostication later on. "Security" is, for the benefit of the reader who may not have a clear grasp of the term, protection against sudden attack which is obtained by the commander of a force through a combined use of part of his air and ground troops out at a considerable distance from the main part of his army so that the enemy will run into it first.

THE FACTOR in mechanical warfare that is least clear in our minds and on which there is the greatest variety of muddled thought is the element of speed in fast motor or tank columns. In a previous article the writer pointed out the possibilities of using our highways to their actual capacities but confined his discussion mainly to traffic matters. There is more to the story than that, however. It is particularly necessary to consider modern security before we can draw well-founded conclusions on fast motor and mechanized movements. In this article, then, let us see what security has to do with it.

The greatest confusion regarding fast motor columns comes from the natural but mistaken conception of widespread parallel columns of great armies speeding toward each other, *and toward battle,* at forty miles an hour. We know full well by this time—or at least we should know it— that such a conception is absurd and that the flying columns of such forces would be bound to get into difficulties soon or late.

And yet this idea persists, and with some reason, since motor vehicles can travel at high speeds even in large numbers. Particularly does it persist in the newspapers, which seldom number among their writers men with a sound background of military thought.

In a recent lecture, for example, Mr. George Slocombe, well-known British correspondent and commentator on European affairs, made the statement that if Germany wars against France again, her armies will speed toward and across the border at fifty to sixty miles an hour, with vehicles moving six abreast on broad military highways. At that rate, if the layman follows Mr. Slocombe's picture to its seemingly inevitable conclusion, the German armies would reach Paris some two hours after leaving their own soil.

It is perfectly true, however, that the German Army, or any other, may move *toward* and probably *as far as* its own border with remarkable speed. But once it reaches the border there can be no continuance of such speed unless, perchance, the invaded nation is totally unprepared. Here is where security enters the picture.

Not long since, when a day's march for cavalry was twenty to thirty miles, and for infantry twelve to fifteen miles, the commander of a large force felt safe with a screen of mounted units a score or two of miles out front, and with advance and flank guards giving him a protective leeway of a few thousand yards. Moreover, the term "beyond striking distance of the enemy's main ground forces" meant, in those days, simply that his security detachments could be smaller than when he was "within striking distance" of the enemy. And so long as his cavalry kept close watch of the hostile forces, he felt secure.

Now, however, "striking distance" must be measured in terms of thirty miles an hour instead of two and one half. Where a commander once felt that an enemy twenty miles away was uncomfortably close, now a hostile force that is 20 × 30/2.5, or 240, miles away is beginning to get near enough for business. Under these circumstances a commander has but one solution—to push out his ground security many times farther than before and to use his distant air reconnaissance hundreds of miles farther than that. In fact, the Command and General Staff School now teaches that elements of distant ground security and reconnaissance may operate out to 250 miles, and distant air reconnaissance to 700 miles.

Security, moreover, is only a half measure unless it extends in all directions. Where once a commander could reasonably estimate the chief direction of his danger, today he cannot tell from what point of the compass a blow may strike. Hence he dares not leave the slightest section of his perimeter unguarded. The same Leavenworth text quoted above defines security as "the *all-around* ground and air protection of a command by the adoption of effective measures to prevent surprise, observation, and interference by the enemy."

This all-around protection at a distance is not obtained, however, by placing advance, flank, and rear guards much farther out from the main force than before, or by increasing their sizes. On the contrary, we find the following in paragraph 74 of the same text:

When our main body is beyond striking distance of the enemy's main ground forces, the necessity for advance, flank, and rear guards, and other security detachments of a size capable of effective combat, is minor as compared with a thorough distant air and ground reconnaissance which will provide adequate warning of approaching aviation, mechanized or motorized elements, and be able to delay or stop them.

And here it is that we find the essence of modern security—a distant sturdy circle of small ground combat units.

These ground units are necessary no matter how strong we may be in the air. The fact is simply that air reconnaissance at best is too uncertain. It cannot see through cloud, fog, and haze for one thing. And for another, we may not have the planes to spare to do a thorough job, especially at the beginning of a war.

The distant security units around the great perimeter of a modern force must be strong enough to prevent any undetected penetration, and powerful enough to delay and harass an approaching enemy. By resistance, road blocks, and demolitions they can reduce the speed of his approach from any direction to a crawling pace.

This job is essentially one for mechanized cavalry. (At the same time, there must be no confusion of mission between the tight ring of distant security forces and mechanized reconnaissance units that may dart out to still greater distances in order to seek definite information by contact.) Lacking mechanized cavalry in sufficient numbers, motorized infantry, assisted by artillery and demolition engineers, can do the job of distant security. This fact is recognized by the discussion of "security without cavalry" in the Command and General Staff School text previously cited. Reconnaissance detachments of the types which have appeared in Leavenworth instruction for the past two years may also be used. However composed, such units must have high speed and considerable delaying power.

Now to return for a moment to the general concept of a mechanical army speeding toward the border bent on invading a contiguous state; it is self-evident that the border itself is equivalent to a strong perimeter of distant security. Behind that border, so long as hostile defending elements of any size have not crossed it in order to establish road blocks, movement toward invasion can be conducted at maximum speeds. The only limitations are the capacities of highways and the power of motors, save, of course, the possibility of interference from the air. And of this there will be little or none, if the invaders choose a day of visibility zero to launch their thrust.

If the enemy has any defenses at all along his borders, the invading columns must, for all their initial speed, reduce their pace to a walk when they encounter them, or even come to a halt and fight. It is an absurdity, for example, to conceive of great German columns continuing on into France at high speeds.

But suppose instead that a sudden invasion strikes an ill-defended frontier. In such case it seems probable that small but tough advance combat units of the invaders' force would first push rapidly down every road, in order to advance the high-speed zone as far as possible for the larger columns following. But as the advance units go on this errand they must keep fairly abreast and make sure by rapid cross reconnaissance that the ground between roads contains no force of size. Eventually we can expect that all such advance security and reconnaissance units will find roads blocked and meet resistance strong enough to halt them. The defender, by then, will have established his own perimeter of distant security, behind which he, too, can speed forward with his forces as fast as he can muster them.

What comes after this, as far as speed of movement is concerned, depends entirely on the relative strength of invader and invaded. If the invaded nation is relatively weak we may expect determined operations by the invader to overcome the delaying forces in accordance with a plan of action involving his whole main force. These operations, when successful, will extend his area of high-speed operation and reduce that of the defender in the same degree. But in the words of the Leavenworth text, quoted before, "generally speaking, a highly mobile force will not be able to move through an area which is not controlled by friendly forces, unless the situation and the available information definitely establish the fact that hostile interference within the area is impossible."

It may be that movement for one force may be far more restricted than for the other. For example, in the event of an invasion of our own coastal frontiers, we may think of our distant security perimeter as forming a semicircle around the invader. In this situation we would have much room, and he comparatively little. We can imagine here a continuous line of mechanized or motorized units giving way where the invader presses, but placing every stumbling block in his path. And somewhere behind this line of outposts our own force would be getting ready to strike its blow. But where both main forces have some freedom of maneuver, their distant security perimeters will, of course, approach the circular in form.

In any case the first clashes will be between advanced mechanized reconnaissance elements, forming a part of the security perimeter, or pushed out still farther in advance. Thus our own main force may be called at short notice to strengthen its security perimeter. Every hour saved in making such a reinforcement may mean many square miles of maneuver area saved to our own force. Here is a time, if ever, for using the main highways to rush double staggered columns at maximum running speed to critical areas.

Let us assume now that our main force takes the offensive before the hostile commander makes a vigorous effort. If up to this time the enemy has not tried to penetrate our own distant ground security, or has not gained contact with it, our whole perimeter of security should move forward as the main force moves, perhaps leapfrogging by rapid jumps, instead of slowly advancing. Eventually some part of the security must close upon the enemy's. Indeed, these far outpost lines may touch along scores or even hundreds of miles before one main force or the other makes a sudden thrust.

When such a thrust is made, if the direction of advance is to be through a sector where the hostile security is already in contact with our own, there should be a preliminary pressure at several points in order to create deception. The security units at all these points, reinforced by detachments strong in motorized engineers, must shove forward rapidly, repairing roads, rebuilding bridges, and otherwise preparing for the main advance a few hours later. If the direction of advance is toward a part of the security perimeter where there has been no contact, feints in several directions are nevertheless desirable. Here the security preceding the main force must likewise be strong in road- and bridge-repairing units.

Thus, throughout the whole period of coming to grips, behind the shifting barrier of the security perimeter large mechanized and motorized units can move at high speed, using the highways to their full capacities. Nothing can get through that stout ground barrier to interfere with rapid movement. Hostile action, behind the barrier, can come only from the air.

Hostile action from the air may consist in attempts to block or destroy defiles and stretches of important routes, or of actual attacks upon columns by bombardment or attack aviation. Whether an enemy could keep all roads in great areas continually closed by air bombardment is open to doubt, although he may be able to interfere continuously with a few important defiles as long as the weather favors him.

Direct attacks on columns may occur as a routine harassment of traffic on main highways, or they may take the form of planned attacks upon discovered motor movements, both of which have their limitations. We are safe in assuming that the trained antiaircraft fire of a modern army—particularly that of infantry—will afford considerable protection against either.

It is also a possibility that, in order to break through our line of distant security abruptly, the enemy might concentrate his air attack directly upon the elements composing it. Here again success is doubtful. For the security units will be small, scattered, and well camouflaged. And those who fly attack planes that move between two hundred and three hundred miles an hour, and close to the ground, will have great difficulty in detecting and attacking such small deployed forces. Moreover, the effect of such attacks on the actual road blocks would be nil.

More effective, perhaps, would be the use by the enemy of the vertical envelopment, although as yet we know little about it. Whether carried out by hostile units in transport planes that land to discharge their loads, or by bodies of parachute troops, this type of operation grows closer to reality every day. And how could a hostile commander employ aerial infantry better than by using it to clear a wide breach in our distant security, thereby paving the way for the rapid and unresisted advance of his ground units? If this new method of warfare proves practicable, an operation like that just suggested could be countered only by frequent patrolling to cover the entire area inside of the distant ground security. And once a vertical envelopment is discovered, the movement of fast columns behind the distant security perimeter to deal with them would be an absolute necessity.

To sum up, then, distant security guarantees in large measure rapidity of movement in areas behind it. In turn, speed, combined with secret movement during hours and days of low air visibility—the very circumstances that also best *protect* fast columns from the hostile forces of the air—preserve for us surprise. And surprise, as always, gives the great advantage. But there can be no true speed in movements of large forces, hence no surprise, until we are thoroughly familiar with the capabilities and limitations of traffic on modern highways.

Once battle is joined by the main forces, the pace of the forefront will be greatly reduced. Yet if speed of movement is largely preserved until that time, it should give us such an advantage in the placement of forces that the conflict will never come to a World War standstill. But even if that does happen, speed of movement in rear areas will still be a vital thing. No matter what vehicular columns move, back there every resource of modern traffic knowledge and practice will still be needed.

Speed, in fact, will be vital from the first act of war to the last pursuit. We must learn how to gain it and use it, now, in time of peace. In war we must preserve it. Security alone can guarantee it.

BILL BUSHER GOES TO COLLEGE

By MAJOR (now BRIGADIER GENERAL) E. D. COOKE

Through the eyes of Bill Busher, General Cooke furnished to the readers of the *Infantry Journal* acute comment on many sides of peacetime Army life. This piece, dated 1939, is, for all its lightness, an accurate description of the reaction of an Army officer upon attending the Army's highest school.

BEING ORDERED to the War College made Bill Busher feel like a man suddenly arriving in the welcome safety of harbor waters after a long and stormy voyage at sea. From the War College on it looked like clear sailing to Bill. At least he would no longer have to dip his colors to those contemporaries who had successfully navigated their way to a military Ph.D.

Just the same, the prospect of becoming a similar Doctor of Philosophy sort of stumped Bill. He wondered if he had the necessary qualifications and made a determined effort to discover what went on down at the confluence of the Potomac and Anacostia rivers. He didn't have much luck.

"It's going to be the best year of your life," was the trite response of one officer questioned on the subject.

"You get out just what you put into it," said another.

When pressed for further details the interrogated officers became vague and their answers nebulous. So Bill decided to wait and learn for himself what it was all about when he got to Washington.

From the very beginning, starting with his first stroll down Connecticut Avenue, the habitat of our General Staff failed to make a hit with Bill Busher. He ran into less pulchritude and more personal ambition to the square inch than he'd encountered to the acre anywhere else in America. Because of this Bill feared he might be misplaced among the intelligentsia. So did his old crony from Leavenworth, John Honest.

"They must be pretty hard up when they reach down for a couple of field hands like you and me," John opined.

"They just got us here to encourage the rest," Bill retorted. "If we get by, anybody can."

Of course neither one believed what he said. Each had a sneaking idea he was pretty good. And at the first War College conference their suspicions were confirmed. From the commandant on down, every speaker assured Bill and his mates that they were superior, especially selected officers, capable of handling any situation which might arise.

Bill hoped they were right—particularly on his first committee. [Much of the work of student officers at the Army War College was done in study groups or "committees."] His name appeared as chairman, but the directive was as far over his head as the Washington Monument. Bill began to understand why no one had been able to tell him what he would be doing at the War College. He didn't even know now that he was there. And he wasn't alone in that predicament, either.

The entire committee was lost in a fog of indecision and false starts. Members spent long hours in vehement debates—which usually degenerated into windy bull fests, broken up only by spontaneous adjournments to the coffee shop. Yet as a whole there was no mental driftwood in the group, and their written report somehow lumbered forward to a ponderous conclusion.

When completed, the results had to be presented by Bill and a couple of subchairmen: the formal oration being preceded by two rehearsals. The first of these recitations disclosed all too clearly what a weird, jumbled, incoherent brain child their joint efforts had conceived. But it was too late to make more than minor changes before recording a second dry run [a marksmanship term for "practice"] the following day—which was even less encouraging than the first. And then came the final palaver, the trial for record, the high spot in a military education!

For sixty whole minutes Bill and his two sweating fellow sufferers took their turns delivering themselves of an awkward, stilted speech, from which all split infinitives, together with most of the life, had carefully been eradicated. And listening attentively was the entire faculty, not showing by so much as a single lifted eyebrow that they recognized whole passages shamelessly lifted from similar speeches of previous years. Listening, also, was a dazed student body, aghast at the spectacle presented, yet ever mindful of the time when it would be their turn to mount the speakers' platform.

Perhaps it was for that reason they were so vociferous in their congratulatory comments immediately after the lecture.

"Would you believe me," asked John Honest, "if I told you that was one of the most interesting talks I've ever heard?"

"No," said Bill, "I wouldn't believe you, but I like to hear it just the same."

In addition to the commendations, Bill's committee, being one of the first to present, escaped lightly during the period devoted to comments and questions. Even though the class had been assured from the very first day that any member could say anything he pleased—that one man's opinion was as good as another's—most of the boys were a little slow in accepting the statement. Many of them had heard it before.

But at the War College it actually was true. For the first time in his Army career Bill found himself in a place where knowledge had no rank —where opinions were judged on their merits and not according to the insignia of the opinionee!

That fact became more and more apparent as the course progressed. And, once reassured, some of the more unexpected persons developed into incorrigible sounder-offers. Bill himself lay awake many a night thinking up brilliant bits of repartee, but unfortunately they always pertained to something already past or to subjects which never came up. Several times Bill got to his feet and expounded extemporaneously. Each time he resumed his seat in utter embarrassment and self-recrimination. Again and again he swore not to repeat the performance, but he found free speech was like free drinks—hard to leave alone.

Yet it was John and not Bill who one day took the cake. The commandant in person had just pronounced a principle which, he believed, was unassailable. Whereupon John lumbered heavily to his feet.

"This may be my last official act," he announced solemnly, "but I disagree."

"Well," said Bill on the way out, "it's been nice to have known you."

"Yeah." John hunched his shoulders defensively. "Tell 'em to forward my mail to Guam."

The general, however, was as much amused as the others. And of course, except for a selected few, he had little to do with students' future stations. Most assignments, upon leaving the War College, as far as Bill could discover, were brewed up by the dark of the moon in the mystic chambers of the General Staff. The list, when completed, was then marked "Dangerous," "Secret," "Do Not Divulge," and locked behind the largest steel doors in the War Department.

None of these precautions managed to silence the chirping of the little birds. News of what was going on soon leaked out, and since Santa Claus was expected to be generous in the way of orders, the students began their Christmas snooping early. And their curiosity was as nothing compared with that of their wives.

"I wouldn't mind so much not knowing about our orders, except that I play bridge with a lady who just bursts at the seams with inside information," Mrs. Busher complained bitterly. "If she can make that

General-Staff-officer husband of hers tell her where we are going, I don't see why I can't find someone who will tell me."

Whereupon she dragged out her most expensive gowns and stalked the cocktail parties in search of officers connected with handling personnel. It was not a brass hat, however, but one of Bill's own classmates who finally disclosed where the Bill Bushers were going. This particular student had been sent for in connection with a specific job and during a conference had seen the secret list, along with Bill's name and assignment, which he promptly divulged. One by one, because of similar incidents, the rest of the class gradually ceased talking about orders—a sure sign the veil of secrecy had been pierced.

So that was that, and Bill was for leaving the cocktail parties alone. There were too many of them to begin with, and besides, the same people went to all of them.

"And what's more, they're so busy running from party to party they don't stay long enough in any one place to have a good time," Bill grumbled.

"It might be better if you didn't have quite so much of a good time yourself," Mrs. Busher admonished, "particularly when you drive through such thick traffic between parties."

"That's what makes me drink," allowed Bill. "It would anyone. Drive fast and these D.C. Potomaniacs smash your fenders racing to an intersection; slow down and they sideswipe you going past; and the minute you stop for a light everyone honks at you. By the time a fellow rubs bumpers with that company he needs stimulants."

Of course Bill was not actually driven to drink, but he didn't like having his actions questioned. He expected indulgence. As a War College student he was being pampered by everyone in the military service—including his wife. So at the first gentle touch on the matrimonial check-reins he bowed his neck and bucked. And as the course proceeded Mrs. Busher found Bill getting harder and harder to handle—not to say downright bullheaded.

He insisted, for instance, that he was still young and active enough to continue playing noonday baseball out behind the college building. Even when a Charley horse clamped down on one leg and Bill's walk began to resemble that of a dignified old rooster who had gotten one foot stuck on a piece of flypaper, he refused to give in.

He also tried to keep off sick report when he first caught the flu. He was afraid he'd miss the boat to graduation; that he had only a one-way ticket without stopover privileges, and that if he once got off the train he'd be out of luck. So instead of staying in bed at the first sign of fever, Bill struggled on down to school, trying to stave off the inevitable. Each day he got worse, until the morning arrived when he couldn't get out of bed and Mrs. Busher had to phone the outpatient service.

A doctor arrived immediately, but he was not very sympathetic.

"You fellows are all alike," he sighed resignedly, "always trying to keep up when you should go to bed."

"Will I be well enough to go to school tomorrow?" Bill asked timidly.

"And spread germs all over the rest of your class?" The medico irritably snapped his stethoscope into a satchel. "Not if I know it! You stay in bed till I say get up."

Bill's temperature went skyrocketing. He fumed and he fussed, and the more he worried about being absent, the higher his fever climbed. Finally, after not less than ten days in bed without improvement, Bill gave up. He fell back on the pillows, resigned to losing his chance at the War College. But he no sooner quit worrying than the fever departed. And to his agreeable surprise the school authorities accepted his return without comment.

Many of his friends hadn't realized Bill was sick. With everybody absorbed in committee work, only that group to which Bill was assigned noted his absence—principally because they had to do his work in addition to their own. The writing, the bulling, and the presenting were still going on. Only, as far as Bill could see, the class was becoming more and more blasé, more and more critical of the steady deluge of oratory flowing from the platform.

Fellows who at first had carried to college a sneaking suspicion that they were pretty good now were sure of it. No subject was too great for them to express an opinion on. At Leavenworth those fellows had juggled corps and armies all over the map; now they dealt with the entire universe. Indeed, not a few seemed to infer direct communication with Jupiter and Mars. Such hallucinations occasionally led the conversation so high into the stratosphere that Bill was forced to pull the rip cord on his mental parachute and get back to earth.

Bill was no military Einstein: he stuck to fundamentals. He figured out there were just two kinds of Army officers—the talkers and the listeners. And as hour followed hour in the conference hall Bill began to get all listened out. He cringed each time a speaker mounted the rostrum —and, once the harangue was over, rushed thankfully to the cool comfort of the coffee shop.

That refuge was becoming increasingly popular with the class as the course went on. It was just Bill's luck, too, that when he unexpectedly flipped five aces out of the dicebox most of his schoolmates were present. And those who weren't came running, for it is an old War College custom that the man who throws all aces in one cast must buy coffee for the house. Thereafter his name appears, framed for posterity, on the walls of the coffee shop.

"Getting your name there cost more than on the bronze tablet that will record our graduation," observed John Honest.

Bill looked around the room and grinned.

"Well, since the official plaques hang just outside the commandant's office, I bet more people will see I've been through college by looking at the list down here than at the one up there."

"That's right," John acknowledged, "and you know you've made this list, which is more than any of us know about the other."

The thought of not graduating was, of course, a standing joke. And yet the possibility was not so funny, after all. Men had been known to miss getting their names on the yearly scroll. As a matter of fact, one had been removed at the very last moment only a year previous. Therefore, it was with much relief that Bill finally saw himself listed on the plaque's facsimile, reproduced with printer's ink on a sheet of paper, and posted on the bulletin board for all to observe.

Nor was Bill alone in his elation. Not an officer in the class but experienced a thrill on seeing that simple but impressive announcement. After all, a man graduates from the Army War College but once.

"Just let me keep my health and not lose any secret documents," Bill prayed silently.

Thereafter work was merely incidental to the turning in as rapidly as possible of all confidential, restricted, and secret papers with which Bill had been burdened throughout the year. Each of those returned was as a weight removed. Bill's spirit, released of responsibilities, soared higher and higher as the time approached for his final clearance and embarkation upon the historical ride.

That tour was the grand finale, a de luxe exposition on military history. And the entire trip turned out to be just like the busses the class and instructors rode in—not only streamlined but air-conditioned as well.

For nine days Bill and his schoolfellows traveled about in solid comfort. They ate in air-cooled dining rooms, had their baggage carried in and out of hotels, were dished out ice water at every halt, and handed folding chairs to rest on during the talks. All they had to do was to sit and listen. And some of them kicked at doing that!

"Which only goes to show we're still soldiers in spite of our education," Bill remarked.

"What do you know about soldiers?" John Honest hooted. "You haven't been around any of them for the past fifteen years!"

"Maybe not," Bill conceded, "but I soon will be. I'm going where, if I want to know how many men are in my command, I won't have to look in *Reference Data* to see if it's thirty thousand or three hundred thousand. All I do is step out in front and yell, 'Count off,' and they'll count off—all thirty of them."

"Yeah," John jeered, "you will if you can squeeze that thirty-six waist into your thirty-two breeches."

"Okeh. But you're not going to feel so good when you have to wear woolen O.D. to graduate in."

"That's right," John sighed. "I wish our Army schools would either hold graduation in cool weather or else let us put on something besides winter uniforms."

"Aw, you know you can't be comfortable and military both at the same time. We'd do better to pray that for once the speechifying will be short and snappy."

As a matter of fact, it was. Not over thirty minutes elapsed between invocation and benediction. The talkers were just as uncomfortable as the listeners, and besides, some of those members of the class selected for pick-and-shovel jobs in the War Department [as members of the War Department General Staff] had to put on their working clothes that very afternoon and start digging. Their new bosses were calling for action!

Apparently members of the General Staff were not one bit impressed with the amount of arduous labor performed at the War College. They themselves had been through it. Their attitude was that the boys had taken it easy for a year, but now it was time to get down to business—and they needn't try to fool anyone about having been overworked at college, either.

Bill was not trying to fool anyone—not even himself. The school had presented him a gentleman's course, and Bill certainly hadn't done anything in any way to disturb the nomenclature of that curriculum. Nor did he have any aspirations toward doing so. Nevertheless, the mere fact of having graduated carried certain material benefits which Bill intended exploiting to the utmost.

Never again, for example, would Bill seek work for work's sake. No indeed! He intended devoting the rest of his service to the pursuit of securing positions, not to looking for jobs. He would, in fact, rely on his head for results instead of his feet. Yes sir, he was going to do a lot of sitting around, spending hours at a time, projecting deep thoughts far into the future.

And since indolence, like charity, should begin at home, his first step toward establishing the new era was to indoctrinate Mrs. Busher with the idea.

"You see, sweet," he explained carefully, "a considerable amount of time and money has been spent on my education. Naturally the Army expects intellectual results for the output. So from now on practically all my activities will be mental instead of physical."

Mrs. Busher gave several moments to considering this from all angles.

"Oh," she finally said understandingly—and then, giggling mischievously, "You're telling me!"

THE DEAD HAND

By Major John H. Burns

(1937)

Fortunate is that army whose ranks, released from the burden of dead forms, are controlled by natural, untrammelled, quickened common sense. GERMAN GENERAL STAFF ACCOUNT OF THE BOER WAR

FROM THE PAST a Dead Hand reaches out to clutch the present in an iron grip. It is all-grasping, all-powerful; it cannot be eluded. And, unless strenuously resisted, it strangles all progress. It has halted great races in the morning of a splendid culture by turning their faces from the future toward the past—that past which, contemplated too long, induces a hypnosis leading to mental stagnation. Such a fate befell China.

But the Dead Hand operates among all occidental peoples too, though not so obviously. It sews two buttons on the back of a dress coat; it notches the lapels of a coat collar; it stitches a row of buttons on the end of a coat sleeve. Once these things were useful, for the buttons on the dress coat kept the sword belt from sagging, and the lapel notches permitted the collar to be folded around the throat in severe weather. Today they are useless, yet still we follow the old patterns.

But, some may say, these are only conventions of dress. What harm is there in retaining, with slight changes, the raiment of the past to clothe our physical bodies? It may be harmless, it is true; but at the same time it is significant of something that is far deeper and nothing short of dangerous.

For the great harm comes when the Dead Hand fashions our mental rather than our physical clothing. We wear this clothing of the mind with no more idea of why it is shaped to a certain pattern than we have of why a dress suit has tails. We accept unquestioningly. Moveover, we can be as fully disturbed at any attempt to alter this mental garb as at the idea of wearing a red tie with evening clothes.

The human obstinately resists change of any sort but particularly an effort to change his mental raiment—the trousers of convention, the vest of doctrine, the coat of dogma, and the all-enveloping mantle of tradition. Man has a mind that can reason, but he uses it primarily— almost exclusively—to buttress the opinions, prejudices, and minor faiths he has unthinkingly absorbed from his environment. This he incorrectly calls *thinking*. The right name is *rationalizing*.

With regret we must acknowledge that man does not desire to think a thing out but prefers to act in accordance with a dictum or tradition. Furthermore, constant repetition of a thing, constant seeing of a thing in a certain way will ever convince him that that thing is essentially right and proper and thereafter all the logical data in the world will not persuade him otherwise. Thus his actions are impelled by dogmas instead of thoughts, and he becomes an ingenious rationalizer but a poor thinker. Not even our greatest minds are immune.

As a consequence we humans are perfect material for the deft fingers of the past to mold. For we are born into a fixed world, and the learning period of life is spent in absorbing dogmas, doctrines, opinions, and prejudices out of the past. When man *does* change it is not because logic has convinced him but because iron circumstance forces him.

Under the Dead Hand each generation hardens into the old pattern and becomes fiercely hostile to change. The great mind who tries to make obsolete governmental forms square with the realities of the present is stabbed to death on the ides of March, and the One who comes preaching a newer and better life—a New Way—is met by a snarling mob egged on by a venomous intelligentsia. He is scourged, spiked hand and foot to beams, and the Dead Hand hoists Him high against the sky on Calvary.

The Golden Age of mankind as recorded in folklore and fable appears to be that period in which every detail of daily life was regulated by taboos. It was a contented life, for every activity was fixed by tradition and custom; and although the struggle for existence was great, the struggle to think was absent. Man would far rather war against wandering head-hunters than have the horrifying experience of struggling with an original thought that stole into his head.

How many eons mankind, with all its potentialities for civilization, spent in this primitive state is not known, nor what started the change that led the nomad and the hunter to civilization. But this much is known: man is the same as of old; there has been no great degree of mental evolution; he still yearns for taboos, doctrines, dogmas—anything to escape from thinking. Yet he is now faced with the inescapable fact that the civilization he started forces him to think or die, and that the tempo of this civilization is quickening, demanding more thought, in its turn bringing more mental distress. Study might show, perhaps, that all past cultures came to their death because of the revulsion of the common man against the thinking required of him to maintain a state of civilization.

But what has all this to do with soldiering? you may ask. A great deal. For this mentally slothful, this twisty-thinking individual is man, and soldiers are men; and through this primitive type of mind the leader must work to accomplish any task. Indeed, of all military dangers the greatest is that the leader himself can only comprehend and initiate action with the same type primitive mind. Unless he watches himself carefully, and few do, he will direct events in accordance with prejudices, doctrine, dogmas, or tradition, and not in accordance with the clear facts before him. For these facts take thinking to comprehend, more thinking to synthesize into several probable courses of action, and still more careful thinking to resolve into the right course of action. With man it is always simpler, and much more consistent with the normal functioning of his inherited mental apparatus, to let a doctrine—or even a hunch—dictate his course of action. Then he uses his mind most ingeniously to prove how eminently correct the dogmatic decision is.

It would not be so serious if these doctrines were the result of real creative thinking by great minds of the past, but for the most part they are merely bald opinions strikingly, yet plausibly, expressed by some successful man of action. As Spengler, the great German historian, points out, "The man of action is often limited in his vision. He is driven without knowing the real aim. . . . Often he goes astray because he has conjured up a false picture of things around and about him." Tragically enough, the primitive mind—which is always present even under a top hat—admires exceedingly the man of action, reveres his statements, and cares not a fig for the thinkers, who are tiresome fellows all.

Hence any opinion on war by a successful soldier is received respectfully, repeated often, and by sheer repetition soon becomes a dictum or rule reaching out from the past to control present conduct—this to the exclusion of reason. Then another thing happens. Second-class minds—pedants or propagandists—select such of these remarks as bear out already fixed opinions or flatter national pride, and put them together in a plausible manner to build up a doctrine of war, a concept of national psychology, or anything that pleases their fancy. The result of all this is a mass of fixed irrational opinions in the minds of succeeding generations. Such opinions are the fingers of the Dead Hand and their strength is incalculable.

Farfetched, you think? But wait. Wellington once said that Waterloo was won on the playing fields of Eton. Field games, he meant, produced the proper soldier material. No one could claim, of course, that Wellington was a great social thinker; yet no one stopped to ask upon what playing fields Austerlitz, Marengo, Valmy, Arbela, or Cannae were won. The phrase was simply accepted as truth and more than a hundred years later is still repeated as truth. Such phrases are dangerous, but for long no one saw how dangerous and untrue this one was. This stock statement shaped the British mind until the playing of games by officers and gentlemen became a veritable fetish. It remained for the poet Kipling to point out its fallacy during the Boer War when he spoke in withering scorn of the "flanneled fool at the wicket" and the "muddied oaf at the goal" and related how the Empire had to depend, not on these products to win the war, but on "men who could shoot and ride." Of course Kipling was merely a poet, and where his opinion clashed with a dictum of the Iron Duke it was ignored. However, it does not always pay to ignore the poet; his vision is clearer, oftentimes, than that of the man of action.

The Boer War passed, and the World War came and passed, and still the Dead Hand rules; for only lately a British general officer, aged fifty-three years, was adversely reported upon because he did not take part in field games. Ponder on this situation. It is fantastic, absurd. Yet it is accepted placidly by the very people who, no doubt, smile superciliously at the Tibetan lama with his prayer wheel. But the lama has about as good grounds for believing in the efficacy of his wheel to bring salvation as the British in the efficacy of field games to produce tacticians.

When Lord Seaton, the famous Colonel Colborne of the Peninsular War and Waterloo, was asked how skill in war was obtained, he replied, "Fighting, and a damned deal of it." He never stopped to explain how a young man in his middle twenties, with no experience of high command and little of warfare, waged his first campaign in northern Italy so brilliantly that it is a military classic. Yet Lord Seaton knew Napoleon's record well, for he had been waging war against him so long that the British Empire was almost bankrupted.

The years roll on. In the middle of the nineteenth century General Sir John Fox Burgoyne railed against any education test for officers. It was "uncalled for, delusive, and mischievous. To extend these examinations to the higher grades, even to captain, would be intolerable and would destroy emulation in the real qualities of a good officer and a soldier." It would appear from the general's full statement that these good qualities were proficiency in games and sports. Wellington's remark and Lord Seaton's were here nicely blended and neatly rationalized to produce another stumbling block to progress almost fifty years later. To indicate the tremendous hold these phrase-born traditions had on the British mind it should be noted that in 1898, in the words of a distinguished British soldier, the British officer knew nothing of war, did not want to know anything, and considered himself a better soldier for his ignorance.

Wellington's fame, his methods, his casual phrases have had a greater effect on the British Army than that army has realized. One is tempted to see a connection between Wellington's almost rabid insistence that his orders be carried out punctiliously, even though in error, and the lack of initiative displayed by beach commanders during the Gallipoli landing. Did Wellington create a tradition which has been followed to this day—a tradition of waiting for orders instead of bold initiative? Compare the British at Gallipoli with the superb initiative of German officers nears Penchard in France in 1914, and one cannot help but wonder.

The British general who stated relative to trench periscopes, "It is contrary to the traditions of the British officer to seek information from a position of security by means of mechanical device," is typical of a man living and thinking under the Dead Hand. And so was the officer on the British Imperial General Staff who dismissed the first conception of a tank with the curt advice to the one presenting the idea, that he come down to earth and stop wasting his and others' time. And so was Wellington himself, for when shown the new improved cylindroconoidal bullet invented by Captain John Norton in 1823 he said that Brown Bess—the musket of Napoleonic days—was good enough. General Napier's remark when he learned of the Minié ball invented by Captain Minié of the French Army in 1853 (Captain Norton's idea taking shape again) is particularly characteristic. To have infantry able to fire a distance of one thousand yards was unthinkable. It would make infantry but "long-range assassins," to quote the words of the outraged general.

And then listen to these words delivered a few years ago in a motor civilization by a full general in the British service: "The longer we can keep horses for artillery and cavalry, the better it will be for the Army, because thereby you keep up the high standard of intelligence in the man from his association with the horse." *Reductio ad absurdum!*

Yet, you may say, new things do come and the old order finally passes. But how much the Dead Hand delays progress! Some wise man has made the point that many great inventions were so obvious that as a matter of fact they invented themselves. The soldier, however, will not even permit this process; he sets his face against it—indeed, his eyes are in the back of his head the more clearly to read the past for all that he must stumble through the present.

Exaggerated? Not at all. In an armory in the small town of Oneonta, New York, is a breech-loading rifle—one of those with which a battalion of British troops was equipped during our Revolutionary War. The rifle was invented by Major Patrick Ferguson, who also organized and trained the battalion equipped with it. In the Battle of Brandywine troops with this rifle were able to fire so rapidly that the Americans facing the battalion fled, thinking they were opposed by a large force. Here was an invention that received the service test of war and proved tactically successful. Even today the same rifle works smoothly and efficiently. Mechanically it is sound. Yet the British general in New York broke up the organization and distributed the men and rifles among other units. How many years later was it before armies were equipped with such weapons? Almost a full century! Think that over.

We have quoted the British record extensively merely because the record is handy; no nation or army is free from the domination of the Dead Hand. We might quote the experience of the Prussians going out to meet Napoleon and his new methods of war, with the withered traditions, formations, and ideas of Frederick the Great. We might tell how the Prussian machine creaked into action, how the Napoleonic avalanche swept over it, and how a torrential pursuit destroyed it.

Or we might recall how the French used the Chasseurs d'Afrique in the Franco-Prussian War. How they charged infantry in true Napoleonic style and were smashed into pulp. Yet the recent American Civil War and the still more recent Austro-Prussian War had definitely shown that the mass cavalry charge against infantry was as obsolete as the crossbow.

In both these cases revolutionary developments in the art of war occurred before the very eyes of the soldier, but tradition was stronger than facts. The old was blindly retained and disaster followed.

The same spirit lived on into the twentieth century—even into the World War. Did not Marshal Foch remark in 1909 at the Rheims aviation meet that while flying might be a good sport it had no military value? This from the keenest military mind in France!

Or take our own Army. Not so long ago, as history reckons time, our regulations prohibited all but cavalrymen from wearing mustaches. The boots and the jingling spurs were not enough to mark the man on horseback who for the span of a thousand years had dominated the battlefields of the world. Yet his day passed centuries ago with the rise of the bristling infantry pikes in the cantons of Switzerland and the twanging of the English bows at Crécy. Gunpowder, the musket, and bayonet definitely ended cavalry as the basic battle arm. All this was centuries past. Yet tradition wrapped the cavalryman in her ample, splendid cloak, and he, the *beau sabreur,* twirling his mustachios in the red afterglow of the sunset of his arm, demanded something special to distinguish him from those others—the rabble of battle. And still he dreamed of his ancient glory, and still at the dawn of the twentieth century—and I must go to England for this—he clung to the idea of riding down *unshaken* infantry—a delirious dream born of the hashish of tradition.

But the American Infantry would not be denied and eventually won the right to wear mustaches. Then, to make matters complete, they adopted a purely cavalry weapon—the saber—as a side arm. And after the World War—a strictly infantry conflict—they obtained the treasured privilege of wearing the boots and spurs of the cavalry arm. Tradition blinded everyone. The infantryman strutting proudly with his newly won spurs and the cavalry saber trailing from his hip failed to notice that the ammoniacal odors of the stable were being replaced by the stench of gasoline, denoting the rapid decomposition of the ancient horse.

As a result we have the absurd spectacle of the greatest motor nation in the world still enthralled by a tradition, still worshiping at the shrine of Eohippus. This, you may say, means little; it is only a quaint leftover from the past. But it is ominous, for it shows we are looking backward and burning punk before an ancient joss. Check the record and see where we stand in relation to other great powers in mechanization and motorization. This industrial giant of a nation, to drop into the jargon of the horse itself, is but an "also ran."

Yes, all armies are gripped by the Dead Hand and are content. Throughout the hierarchy of command they are blind to the possibilities of new things. Even that genius, Napoleon, failed to see the significance of the steamboat and the submarine, both of which were presented to him by Fulton. Yet Napoleon's archfoe was the sea power, Britain; and the steamboat, at least, was a practical invention which might have allowed him to come to grips with her. But for this once he could not see beyond the narrow rut of his times, and his star soon set. Tradition may only blind the genius, but it makes fools of common men.

Any doctrine, custom, or tradition advanced as a reason for doing a thing in war—or not doing it—indicates the presence of the Dead Hand. Suspicion should immediately arise and the matter should be examined in the cold light of logic, going back not to old quotations, old axioms, old opinions, or old doctrines, but straight to scientific fundamentals. For war is not won by traditions but by the utilization of solid facts applied logically in accordance with the psychological nature of man.

Perhaps it is this psychologically unchanging nature of man that has led to our veneration of tradition. By bloody trial and error we have learned how to control men in battle. We can advance few scientific reasons for our methods, yet actually the soldier knows more about controlling and directing men during times of stress than any scientist. This knowledge is conveyed from generation to generation by traditions and customs, the reasons for which we have not the faintest idea. Thus, while our understanding of the mechanism for controlling the conduct of man is hazy, the mechanism itself is fundamentally sound.

There is, then, some justification for this clinging to tradition where it applies to the control of men, but there is absolutely no justification for permitting the intrusion of any tradition, doctrine, or custom in the field of military thought. Furthermore, our ability to apply inherited methods would increase enormously if we turned the light of reason and science inward and traced each tradition or custom to its source to ascertain how it brings about a certain result or whether it creates any good result at all.

Then in the clear light of reason we can slough off all the outmoded crust of tradition that hampers our advance; retain the good from older days, and adapt the new, when reason proves it good. Then, and not till then, will our fighting organization fit the man, the times, and the new technology of the age of machines.

It should be remembered that we are in a great era of change. With lightning rapidity our social and industrial structure is being reshaped by the roaring machines of a mechanical age. Concomitantly the Army itself must change, for an army is but the integration of men and peace-time inventions for the purpose of war. Already the yeast is stirring the mass.

The infantry regiment is being radically changed to fit the age; the division is conforming; cavalry is taking to wheels and tractors; already the idea of great motorized and mechanized masses is being toyed with; aircraft have shouldered their way into the battle group. All is fluid—changing. Nothing is constant. Never did we need thinking officers more; never could less trust be placed in custom or tradition. We are on the threshold of a new era of war, like the one that came in after the battle of Adrianople or the one initiated by Napoleon.

But this time, under the pressure of the machine age, events will move with incredible rapidity. Instead of requiring generations or centuries to accomplish a change, it may take but a decade. The army that leisurely dabbles with the new is doomed. The military mind must be active, avid for new things, eager to try them out; searching, seeking, prying; ruthlessly scrapping the old thing or method to replace it by a better one.

But this is not all, or even the most important part. Every effort must be made to ascertain how sociological changes will affect our future soldier material. The officer who believes that American civilization as it is evolving will give him the same human material that fought at Gettysburg or in the Argonne is living in a fool's paradise. The mere existence of that belief indicates how the acceptance of the traditional concept of an American has atrophied the power of applied thinking. The philosophy of John Dewey and his disciples, for instance, is remaking our public schools and is but one of the many factors that are producing a different American. Whether this American will make a different or better soldier, no one can say, for no one is investigating the matter.

And so we have industry changing the tools of war with lightning speed and society shaping our human material—the basic weapon of war—to a different, untried pattern. Both things are occurring at the same time. It is a revolution if we could but see it.

Yes, a new technique of war is ready to break from the egg—a war of machines and of science, a war in three dimensions. No officer is so junior that he is freed from the necessity of thinking, for no custom or tradition can settle the problems which will arise. We must think out new methods, not fumble with old ones. Today, because of the flux—the fluidity—of modern life, the Dead Hand is a greater military menace than ever before in history.

THE INVISIBLE MAN

By Lieutenant (now Colonel) C. T. Lanham

(1935)

CONTENDING ARMIES wage a war of concealment. Both sides seek an ultimate invisibility. From this silent contest there emerged in the last war that strange phenomenon known as "the empty battlefield." No longer do banners and pennons signal the locations of headquarters. No longer does the sun glint from polished fieldpieces. No longer do soldiers march to battle in bright red pantaloons as did the French Infantry of 1914. Those picturesque settings for painters of battles are at an end. Today armies strive to vanish into nothingness.

Let us examine this "vanishing game" with reference to the infantryman. True, his colorful uniforms have long since gone by the board (to the infinite chagrin of his feminine admirers), but do the neutral colors—the horizon blue, the field gray, the khaki—that have been substituted carry the idea of invisibility to its logical conclusion? I think not.

The uniform of the individual soldier *still presents a single mass of color of unbroken outline*. Rarely, indeed, will the infantryman find himself in terrain whose color background blends perfectly with his uniform. When this blending does not occur the soldier presents a characteristic and unmistakable target.

We need only recall that in the realm of matériel more than mere neutral color was resorted to for purposes of concealment. The *characteristic outlines* of fieldpieces, of tanks, of battleships *were broken by a combination of colors*. The resulting bewilderment to the eye, even at short distances, was almost incredible.

Now isn't it possible for our camouflage experts to apply this same principle of the "broken outline" to the uniform? Can't the *field uniform* be fabricated from a *variety of colors* in such manner that the individual soldier will no longer present a characteristic target? I believe that experiments conducted along this line of thought will prove little less than startling and may in the end bring us perceptibly closer to our goal—*"the invisible man."*

GASES IN WARFARE

From an article by COLONEL (CONGRESSMAN)
JOHN Q. TILSON

(*1917*)

. . . WITH THE INCREASED USE of the airplane, so that bombs, instead of
being fired from mortars or howitzers, which are destructive of certain
kinds of containers and render useless certain kinds of very poisonous
gases, may be dropped from the airplane, we can do much toward making war unbearable.

You can use other and different gases from the airplane than you
can from the gun. There are now a number of chemists—I could not tell
you how many—brilliant chemists, who are working on these problems.
It is believed that with the supremacy of the air complete, the use of
bombs, including the use of gases—which was forced into the hands of
the Allies, first being used by their adversaries—may be made the turning
element in this whole contest. Think what the effect would be if used
against supply depots, if used against troops in reserve, where they are
supposed to be resting back of the lines; think what it would mean to
have these bombs constantly falling upon them, or, going even farther
back, with supremacy of the air back over German territory. Of course
I should be in favor of warning them to take away their women, children,
and old men from any part of the country that we should have to operate
over, a thing, by the way, which the enemy has not done in the case of the
Zeppelins which have gone over England. Having done that, you can
realize what kind of terror and destruction might be brought to Germany
itself by the use of all kinds of weapons used in aerial warfare, including
gas bombs of every type and kind.

THE LITERAL FOG OF WAR

By G. V.

(*1936*)

HANGING in the headquarters of the Infantry School for many years—
there it still hangs, I have no doubt—was a large composite photograph
of the infantryman in the modern sense. The details are now a little dim,

for it is some time since I have gazed upon it for inspiration. But if my memory is at all correct, a doughboy with bayonet at the ready, a tank looming over a trench, a machine gunner intent upon a remunerative target, a rifle grenadier, another soldier with hand grenade at the top of the arm-swing arc—in fact, every manifestation of modern infantry combat—are splendidly depicted. And when I spoke of inspiration just above, that is exactly what I meant.

Recently, however, that picture has come back to my mind more and more often, as the oncoming years have made me more reflective. What I have read in the papers, too, about Ethiopia and Spain has brought back that picture of the infantry spirit time after time. I felt that there was something wrong with it—something definitely missing. And at last I have decided just what it is.

It is too clear. You can see every feature of the men's determined faces. You can count the swivels on the rifle and the rounds of ammunition in the machine-gun belt. You can almost see the channeled surface of the poised grenade. But could you see these things on a modern battle-field, even if you were close to them?

I doubt it, for you would have your gas mask on. That whole symbolic picture of infantry activity, I have come to believe, should be shrouded in a heavy haze, in turn symbolic of the gas and smoke that form the fog of war in its literal modern sense.

When, indeed, are we going to stop playing ostrich? When are we going to think of battle as it will be and not as it has seldom been since 1915? When, to become more definite in my questioning, shall we cease to leave out chemicals from our training, except for one brief period of gas-mask drill per year?

To my mind here are a few of the things we well may do while there is still time:

(1) Require gas masks to be carried at all but the most elementary drills—always, in all types of combat training.

(2) Require them to be worn for a few minutes of every training period and for an hour at least once a month.

(3) Require every officer to be a proficient gas officer, not one second lieutenant per battalion.

(4) Bring persistent chemicals into every tactical problem given at the Infantry School, and in the Infantry Extension Courses.

(5) Require training not only in gas protection but in steps to be taken after troops have been heavily sprinkled by persistent chemicals. (What would *you* do if your whole company or battalion was drenched with mustard by a hostile plane? There are actually some things you can do if you think fast, which may prevent 100-per-cent casualties.)

We are by no means ignorant of gas. But gas is something very unpleasant, hence we are inclined to let it gently drift into the background and settle over a smaller and smaller part of our training schedules. We shall not be able to control its drift when war comes. All too often it will drift squarely upon us. Let us learn to look at things through the haze of gas as we shall have to see them then.

NE'ER A CLOUD
HANGS O'ER THE FIELD OF BATTLE

By Captain Mustard

(*1937*)

I can understand it and make some allowances—but not many—when regimental commanders content themselves with a farcical amount of gas-mask work in chemical training. Wearing masks is stuffy business at best and miserably uncomfortable when it is hot. And it is a fact that all regiments at least acknowledge the existence of chemicals in war by including time for gas drill on their schedules, however brief that time may be.

But the clearest evidence that we of the Infantry are failing to give their due to chemicals in war is the minor place given to them at the Infantry School. In last year's Regular Course problem after problem, in which chemicals should have been expected as an everyday part of the tactical situation, made no mention of gas or smoke. The brief course in chemical warfare, which came near the middle of the year, was as thorough as the time permitted. But once it was over many a problem followed in which chemicals played only a minor role, if any at all. And in this year's course, I understand, things are much the same.

As a matter of downright fact, most of the technique and doctrine of the attack now taught at Benning is primarily based on non-chemical warfare. It is painfully evident that gas and smoke are mainly afterthoughts. Isn't it time for somebody to remember that more than one quarter of our World War casualties were the result of German gas?

.   .   .

Smoke receives some recognition, but only a grudging one. The fact that it blows away in a twelve-mile breeze gets plenty of stress. Its use is not the commonplace tactical measure that it should be, especially in the instruction involving small units.

I make bold to say in conclusion that our largely non-chemical approach to warfare is a 1907, and not a 1937, brand of tactics. And I give it as my further opinion that, since the World War ended, any tactical problem in which gas and smoke do not spread over the ground is not worth the paper on which it is mimeographed. Worse than that, it is misleading and a highly dangerous practice.

THE CASE FOR ANTI–TANK

By Captain X

There has always been a marked tendency for the limitations of the tank to be overlooked. It is a machine of immense power which, properly controlled and directed and used in a correct tactical manner, is capable of great destruction. At the same time the tank, like every other weapon of war, no matter how powerful or how striking its power appears to the uninitiated, has limitations. Indeed, the "capabilities and limitations" of weapons is a phrase that has been in use in the Army for many, many years, for it is as dangerous to forget the limitations as to overestimate the capabilities. The Army man must see things squarely, must see all sides. Otherwise he cannot possibly estimate the general situation and decide what to do next.

By May 1938, when the following article was published, there had been a great deal written about tanks and mechanization in general, and very much about the means of combating them, the ways of attacking the serious limitations of tanks. In "The Case for Anti-Tank" the author attempted to point out the weaknesses of tanks and suggest what might be done against them. In several places he is guilty of overenthusiasm in an article which would have been stronger if it had been less argumentative. He also missed the important close-in method of combating tanks which has destroyed many of them in this present war. And he also missed half of the "tank-destroyer" application—the speedy-moving, self-propelled gun mount.

VALUABLE AS MAY BE the lessons of Cambrai, Amiens, and the other World War battles of the tank, we are inclined to build too much upon them. We have data in plenty about these battles—we know the numbers, casualties, frontages, time and depth of penetrations, and even the effect upon morale. And it is therefore natural to make these first and already olden tank engagements a chief burden of our tank discussion, and to use them as a measuring rod for future mechanical conflicts.

But when we search these limited, if solid, facts of history for an approved solution to fit some second, greater Cambrai of tomorrow, we distort our mechanized thought. In thinking too readily of tomorrow as a better yesterday we neglect, and sometimes forget entirely, factors far more vital to tomorrow's war than what happened in battle two decades ago. For it is the ground we shall have to fight upon, the tanks that we or an enemy can eventually build for traversing that ground, and the probable strength of the anti-tank defense—these are the main things we must think of, and not those first valiant, inconclusive actions of the tank.

Above all must we consider anti-tank. We must weigh tank in terms of anti-tank at every turn, remembering that anti-tank was inadequate, impromptu, and often non-existent in the few tank engagements of the World War, although isolated instances of its superiority were not lacking. We may even find, through such comparison, that advantage now lies far more with anti-tank than tank, and that the dream of iron battle that arose at Cambrai may become in the end more like an impracticable nightmare. Now more than ever is such a comparison pertinent, since it has recently been decided that we must have a special kind of tank for dealing with the enemy's anti-tank guns, before another kind, following in a second wave, can destroy the enemy's machine guns.

.   .   .

COMPARATIVE VULNERABILITY

Aside from the glib argument that the speed of a tank can take the place of resistant steel we must accept the fact that a gunproof tank cannot be built. Even tanks of 150 to 200 *tons,* carrying several inches of armor, like those seriously discussed in England and France for use in another stabilized European war, are vulnerable. "The Achilles' heel of these thick-skinned monsters," writes an anonymous author, "lies in their tracks, which cannot be completely protected." And the bigger the tank, the greater the ratio of track to its total of target surface. At least half of a 200-ton tank would be track target rather than armor target. We need not consider the possibility of still larger tanks, which are utterly impracticable short of some revolutionary development in metallurgy and mechanics. And since all tanks weighing more than ten or twelve tons are extremely limited in their strategic mobility because they have little speed and cannot cross most bridges, we shall confine this discussion mainly to the light- and medium-armored vehicles that every major nation is busy developing.

For use against these, it goes without saying, an effective anti-tank weapon can be built; in fact, it may already exist. A gun powerful enough to penetrate at most some two inches of armor or break, jam, or dismount the tank track, both at maximum range, is all that we need.

Maximum anti-tank range, of course, is determined by terrain and not by the curve of the trajectory and the propelling charge. It is limited by the distance at which a tank becomes a visible target for direct fire. On flat, treeless ground, like the wheat fields of the Middle West, a tank of any size may become a plainly visible target two or three miles away when the weather is clear. But not much of the earth's surface where wars are likely to be fought gives us this extreme. And where great level or gently rolling stretches do exist, the growth upon them, or the desert mirage, usually cuts down the distance of visibility. Thus it is safe to say, with terrain in general in mind, that a tank will seldom become an anti-tank target farther away than two thousand yards.

Actually, anti-tank range is a bracket running from a few feet to about two thousand yards. A tank may belly up over a hump of ground to find an anti-tank gun at point-blank range, as happened several times at the Benning maneuvers in 1937. Or it may, at the other extreme, come into clear view a mile or more away down a long straight stretch of road.

Thus, from the viewpoint of disabling power alone, we can say that an effective anti-tank gun must be capable of penetrating the armor or making useless the tracks of light and medium tanks at ranges from zero to two thousand yards. For this we will certainly need no Big Berthas—at least until the super-tank becomes the order of the day. The equivalent of the present 75-mm. gun should have ample power to disable any vehicle that may be used by any modern mechanized force. Indeed, a gun of this power has disabling power to spare for all our needs at present and for some time to come. Let us accept a weapon of this size as our *effective* anti-tank gun in this discussion.

How vulnerable, then, would the crew of such a gun be to the fire of attacking tanks? It would be extremely vulnerable to the close-range fire of tank machine guns at less than two hundred yards. It would be vulnerable, also, to accurate 37-mm. or larger caliber gunfire from stationary tanks at longer ranges. A shield of armor and a protective emplacement would lower its vulnerability in a considerable degree. Let us grant the shield, but for the present let us think in terms of open warfare and assume a hasty emplacement of the gun giving only the protection that the ground may accidentally afford.

In these conditions it is plain that the vulnerability of the tank is one of long range and that of the gun one of short range. Hence much depends upon which sees the other first and gets the jump in opening fire—upon comparative visibility. Since tanks may warn of their approach by sound before they are seen, let us first touch upon comparative audibility before turning to comparative visibility.

COMPARATIVE AUDIBILITY

The approach of tanks numbered in hundreds, or even in scores, is heralded by a mighty roar—a veritable Niagara of rolling sound. How far off this noise can first be detected by anti-tank gunners depends on the wind and the shape of the ground and upon how sustained the other noises of battle may be. These other sounds, however, must be highly sustained over a large area to drown out the deep tank undertone.

It is hardly necessary to point out that the crews of moving tanks cannot hear the movement of opposing truck-drawn anti-tank units. The crews of stopped tanks, lying in wait, might hear them, but they could not distinguish anti-tank trucks from any others. Thus the factor of audibility will be an advantage almost solely on the side of anti-tank.

COMPARATIVE VISIBILITY

The factor of visibility, too, will almost invariably favor anti-tank. It is difficult to imagine circumstances in which an anti-tank gun would not have the advantage here. We know to begin with that the myopia of the tank is incurable. The tank has been nearsighted from birth, and apparently there is little that can be done about it.

Seldom, if ever, will tank crews detect a gun in concealed or prepared positions until it has opened fire—and often not for some time thereafter, especially when the gun begins potting at the tank at a range of several hundred yards or more. The same thing will be true of guns firing from reconnoitered positions unless they are late in arriving. And when this is the case it will usually be better for them to go into a hasty position somewhere else. Anti-tank gun crews will often be able to go into action hastily, yet without immediate detection. Only on ground that is actually exposed is this likely to be difficult. And even there they may succeed at times, since it is hard to pick up details clearly through the eye slits of a moving tank at much beyond two hundred yards.

From the anti-tank viewpoint, visibility is a different story. The smallest tank is a big target at ranges measured in hundreds of yards. As General von Eimmannsberger says, "The tank doesn't fit into the emptiness of the modern battlefield . . . [it] has to attack across terrain in full view." Tanks, in fact, are about as capable of a stealthy approach as a herd of elephants charging through a canebrake. Whether anti-tank gun crews hear them first, or see them, they have the drop on the tanks, and a big one it is.

It is also true that the crews of attacking tanks will seldom have exact information of opposing anti-tank dispositions. The circumstances may vary all the way from an "exploratory" attack (as in a wide envelopment where the tank units know only the general direction of their enemy) to an attack against an area in which other units have already developed definite infantry resistance. In the first case, of course, the tanks are merely hunting for a prey. In the second, "definitely located infantry resistance," even in an attack against an organized defensive position, is seldom spotted point for point and machine gun for machine gun. Instead it is located "on the near slope of that hill," or "in the right edge of those woods." Rarely will a tank-unit commander know that the enemy has squads, or machine guns, or anti-tank guns at given points, as map problems get us in the habit of thinking. Nor will "definitely located" resistance necessarily *stay* definitely located—another illogical thing hard to keep away from in map problems.

Still more to the point, definitely located *infantry* resistance does not betray the location of its own anti-tank protection, for anti-tank guns lie low until their steel-clad enemies come lumbering over the landscape. And even if some super G-2 were somehow able to inform the tank crews exactly where our gun crews are crouching, there is no guarantee whatever that our anti-tankers will freeze in place. Rather will it be habitual for them to move their guns to any of the several near-by alternate positions as is necessary to meet the attack.

For similar reasons observation airplanes can be of little help to tanks in finding anti-tank movements or positions. Anti-tank units will always be well scattered. There will never be any anti-tank concentrations remotely approaching those of a mechanized force. Air photographs will tell only a readily altered story. Air spotting might keep scattered anti-tank guns in sight. This would afford some general help in planning a tank attack but would be small help to individual tank crews in finding their way across country to a given target during the attack itself. It is conceivable for a single plane to guide a single tank toward a single gun, but not for many planes to direct a regiment or two of tanks individually toward their targets.

Before a battle opens, observation aviation is almost certain to be more helpful to anti-tank than tank. When they can operate, observation units can warn anti-tank units, either directly or through a higher unit, of approaching masses of hostile tanks. Air warnings can be given in ample time, even without radio, since the plane is so much faster than the tank. Only two situations may prevent such warnings: (1) Movement of hostile mechanized forces in a manner that will keep air observers from seeing them, as on days of low air visibility, through heavy woods, or by short fast dashes from concealment to concealment, by day or night; and (2) a hostile air superiority that prohibits observation. Neither case, however, should greatly reduce the effectiveness of an otherwise thorough anti-tank defense.

No; the gun has the jump on the tank almost any way we look at it. If we think in terms of a single gun and the tank its gun crew first sees approaching, the gun will open fire before the tank, often at a range of many hundred yards. When the first shell detonates close by their tank or strikes it, the crew will know it is under fire. Chances are great that the tank crew will not locate the gun for some time afterward, assuming that the tank is not disabled at once. The sound of the gun may not be heard within the tank at all, and the position of the gun will often be difficult to determine until the tank gets closer to its target. Unfortunately the tank cannot, like the elephant, smell its enemy at great distance adown the wind.

If, however, the gun first takes the tank under fire at a short range, say two hundred to three hundred yards, a member of the tank crew may see the gun at once, particularly if the first shot is a wide miss (which will not be often at such ranges). But at any short range the gun crew will almost invariably be aware of the tank's approach from hearing it, and all set to engage it when it first looms into view.

Often a gun crew will be able to fire for some time before the crew of a hostile tank can determine the direction of fire and see just where the gun is. Maneuvers show that attacking tanks fail entirely to see many of the guns which are simulating fire against them. Simulated fire, it is true, makes no noise or smoke. But on the Infantry School maneuvers of 1937 it seemed most probable that, whether the anti-tank guns had fired blanks or not, the tank crews would not have seen many of them.

In actual combat we can expect a number of tanks to come under the fire of a number of guns at roughly the same time, and by virtue of the fact that anti-tank guns will usually open fire first, each will pick a specific target through some system of fire distribution before the tank crews can pick their own specific targets and thus distribute their own fires. When there are more guns than tanks the tanks may see some of the guns in short order, but hardly all of them. When there are more tanks than guns the same thing will often hold at first anti-tank contact, except when the guns are greatly outnumbered. Even when there are four or five tanks engaged by a single gun it may be some seconds or minutes before any tank crew spots it.

.   .   .

A single tank, or a platoon of three to five tanks under a single leader, may seek cover temporarily when they first come under anti-tank fire by moving behind defilade. This maneuver to gain breathing time, which is of course a passive measure, only succeeds when the tanks know the general direction from which the fire is coming—a fair probability, since at least the general direction of the enemy will usually be known. From defilade the tank crews can reconnoiter, either in the tanks or out of them, seeking to locate the gun or guns that picked them up, the better to resume their attack. But on the other hand, the opposing gun squads know where the tanks have gone and remain ready to lay on them when they pop in sight again. The gun crews, in this case, have temporarily accomplished their mission of defense by interrupting the attack and neutralizing the tanks for the time being. The tanks, in endeavoring to accomplish their own mission, may be able to stay behind defilade while they move for some distance to one flank or the other, but soon or late they must appear again and come under fire. They may come under the fire of the same guns, either from the same gun positions or new ones, or under the fire of other guns.

Though defilade may thus give some protection to attacking tanks, it is actually small protection except on very broken ground. How very small is only apparent if we analyze the matter. At first thought it appears that a tank protected by defilade during one half the time from the moment an anti-tank gun first sees it until it closes on the gun has achieved a 50-per-cent safety. But it is nothing of the sort.

We must not forget that an approaching tank offers a target one hundred times larger at two hundred yards than at two thousand yards. Thus the actual exposure of a tank to gunfire during the last half of its attack, assuming an even rate of speed, is many times that of the first half—by actual calculation about nine times as great. If an attacking tank comes in sight at two thousand yards and manages to reach a point two hundred yards from the gun, approximately 60 per cent of its exposure comes between four hundred and two hundred yards. Therefore, unless a tank, through some remarkable circumstance of ground, has defilade during the last part of its attack run, the degree of cover it can obtain is only a small fraction of its total exposure.

.   .   .

But what of the zigzag broken-field running that tanks may use where the ground is good? Its purpose, of course, is to disturb the aim of the anti-tank gunner, and this, in some degree, it accomplishes. But it is worth questioning whether its disadvantages do not offset its one advantage.

In the first place, a zigzagging tank is exposed to fire for a considerably longer time than a tank on a straight course. It also exposes more of its surface to fire since the side area of a tank is about twice that of the front. Furthermore, if we assume any distribution of anti-tank guns in width with overlapping sectors, which we must, a tank moving on an angular course across the line of aim of one gun may be moving on a straight, or practically straight, line toward some other gun, thus offering a point target with little angular change.

Actually the anti-tank difficulties of firing at crossing tank targets are not particularly great. The angular displacement, except when the tank is within one hundred yards or so of the gun, does not interfere seriously with accurate laying. The technique of fire at moving targets is neither complicated nor hard to apply. In anti-tank firing the difficulties due to angular movement can hardly be compared to those of machine-gun or rifle firing at airplanes in low flight—this for the simple reason that airplanes can fly from five to forty times as fast as attacking tanks will be able to move across country.

But there is still another important factor that goes far to cancel zigzagging as a disadvantage to anti-tank gunners. On the straightest of courses and the smoothest of fields the gunners within a tank are nevertheless attempting to fire from a moving, shifting, bumping, vibrating platform. Add the lurch and shift of the zigzag and it is hard to say how much of their fire will not land in the next county.

In any analysis of comparative visibility between tank and anti-tank we must also think of tank speeds. Let us briefly consider now the battle speeds of the tank as distinct from its general mobility in a more strategical sense, which we shall cover in a later part of this article. "In battle," writes General von Eimmannsberger in "Panzertaktik," "speed means life and effectiveness for the tank, while slowness means inaction and sure death." Battle speed, he believes, will vary around wide limits; therefore, "we should not tie ourselves down to any numerical figure." But that, indeed, is to evade one of the most vital and decisive of all anti-tank-tank questions. *We must know* roughly what tank speeds to expect on all kinds of ground, and fortunately this matter is open to little question. It can be settled at any time by punching a stop watch to measure a few hundred runs by tanks over a number of selected pieces of strange ground on various reservations. For the present we can estimate these speeds within a close bracket for any particular piece of road or ground and for dashes of any length across country on any particular type of ground.

It is only the part of wisdom to stop fooling ourselves and admit freely that tank cross-country speeds will run from one half to twenty miles an hour, seldom over that, with an average of little better than five. And while we are at it, we should take firm hold upon the fact that the smallest tank resembles the elephant more closely than it does the fox. And elephants are not noted for their ability to twist and turn. They are easy to hit, and a powerful gun will stop them in their charge.

The tank simply does not have, as some of us are prone to believe, the sustained cross-country speed of the antelope. Nor can it cross streams and clamber up banks with the slithering rapidity of the alligator, or wallow through marshes with the ease of the carabao. True, we find tank data in plenty on trench spanning, barrier climbing, and slope climbing. But if these data are interpreted in terms of actual ground performance, the truth is that any small, steep-banked stream is liable to stop the progress of tanks until a crossing can be found or prepared; that many a strip of muddy or marshy land is a barrier to light and heavy tanks alike, and that in sum the so-called cross-country speeds of twenty-five and thirty-five miles an hour or greater, often attributed to the tank, are only possible on the most exceptional terrain.

We must remember, too, that boulders and stumps greatly interfere with the speed of tanks and that there are hundreds of thousands of square miles of boulder-strewn and stump-covered land in our country.

We do recognize the fact that if the trees of a woods are big enough and near enough together, a tank cannot crash through them. But we usually forget, when we think about tank cross-country speeds, just how much a passable woods slows up a tank. Two miles an hour is nearer the truth than twenty, in going through a woods, whatever the size of the tank.

.   .   .

All hindrances reduce the average speed of the tank attack and give more minutes to anti-tank gunners in which to pour out their deadly fire. Indeed, a well-constructed hindrance which forces the drivers of an attacking tank to hunt for a way across it can easily double the total target exposure of the tank. And even a hindrance which forces drivers to overcome it by using the power of the tank in low speed to force a way through or over it increases the exposure considerably. No tank can be driven full speed into such obstacles without a high risk of damage to the tank or injury to the crew. At best the driver must take a minute or so of crawling speed, during which the tank is meat for an effective anti-tank gun laid to cover the obstacle.

Often, of course, a tank need not remain stationary when it encounters a hindrance. Unless restricted by the ground, the driver can cruise up and down searching for a better path. This is roughly equivalent to the zigzag in its effect on anti-tank aim, and the same factors go far to offset what the tank may gain. The period of tank target exposure is increased; the tank doubles its exposed area by presenting its side; the tank itself cannot fire with accuracy; it becomes more of a straight-on target to other anti-tank guns, and there is the additional fact that the range from gun to tank, while the tank is cruising, changes only slightly.

At this point let us recall again the comparative obscurity of the anti-tank gun as a target to the tank. Not only is it much smaller and, in most situations, stationary; it is often obscured by camouflage or natural growth, or partially defiladed by the ground or by a constructed emplacement. To apply the same term to gun as to tank, the target exposure of the gun, even on open ground, is actually but a fraction of that of the semiblind tank.

Next we must ask how smoke would affect the comparative visibility of tank and anti-tank. It seems improbable that smoke will have a great effect on mechanical war or the measures taken to oppose it. It is true that smoke can be used to support attacking tanks by covering the areas where anti-tank guns are likely to be and that with this help tanks can advance for some distance without coming under direct fire. But during this part of the tank attack their target exposure is least. Three quarters of the target exposure occurs during the last one quarter of the attack.

But of greater import is another point. When tanks have come close and the protecting smoke begins to thin out, it is a vastly different situation for tanks than foot troops. An attacking rifleman, when the smoke begins to lift, will often be so close to his enemy that he is practically on even terms with him in a short-range exchange of fire. Or he may even be close enough to hazard an immediate assault. Certainly his chance of first seeing his nearest enemy through the rising smoke, and then of taking him under fire, is practically as good as his enemy's chance. But the noise and size of a tank put it under a tremendous disadvantage in similar circumstances. And visibility from a tank is bad enough, even when there is no smoke at all. Thus opposing anti-tank gunners have every chance of placing accurate surprise fire at close range upon the tanks as their great bulks begin to loom up through the clearing smoke. It is quite true that smoke will reduce the period of exposure to anti-tank fire. But surprise fire at ranges so close that it will be hard to miss should go far to make up for it.

Certainly the value of smoke to tanks is highly debatable. On all but the flattest of terrain, tank drivers could only feel their way through smoke at very low speeds on straight courses. Smoke fired from a tank could be placed with accuracy only after the tank crew had located opposing anti-tank guns, which would usually be too late.

Now consider for a moment whether smoke does not have its anti-tank uses. Where no other means were available to reduce tank speed over good ground, smoke might be used to do it. Drivers could see nothing, nor could gunners. And anti-tank guns, as before, would get the first chance as the tanks emerged from the thick smoke at slow speeds. Again, where the ground forced an anti-tank gun crew to cover a small defile at close range, smoke would blind armored cars or tanks, while the anti-tank crew continued to pour fire into the road-wide defile at maximum rate, with crews acting unhampered by any but the wildest tank machine-gun fire. Experiment along these lines seems well worth while.

Thus, if smoke can be an asset to either, it favors anti-tank somewhat more than tank. As a hindrance to both, surely it places the tank at a much greater disadvantage.

COMPARATIVE MOBILITY

We have thus far touched only upon the battlefield mobility of the tank in our study of tank speeds and their effect on the visibility of tanks as anti-tank targets. But to gain a complete picture we must think also of the broader aspect of tank and anti-tank mobility. Most of us are inclined to think of the tank as being already upon the battlefield and charging rapidly across a thousand yards or so of ground—perhaps a mental heritage from Cambrai. Actually this is only the last mile of many, both for tanks and the guns against them, whether the situation be stabilized or open. So let us compare the general mobility of the two.

A 75-mm. truck-drawn gun weighs about a ton and a half. This is from one third to one sixth the weight of various types of light tanks. In spite of the fact that it does not run on tracks, such a gun has a mobility at least equivalent to, and often greater than, the tanks it shells are capable of disabling. Let us see why this is so.

In theory, but for the most part in theory only, a tank has greater mobility than the gun that can disable it. This gun, without a track-laying carrier of its own, can leave the roads only on ground that is hard enough for cross-country truck movement. On much terrain, and in wet weather, it must stick closely to the roads. True, if we put the gun on a track-laying carriage the whole thing may still be somewhat lighter than a tank. But by so doing we not only create a special and costly piece of armament, but also one that has the main disadvantage of the tank, which is weight. For weight cuts down the mobility of tanks far more than we ordinarily conceive. Weight confines tanks chiefly to first-class highways for moves of any length. They simply cannot cross most of the bridges of secondary roads.

In most discussions of what tanks can and cannot do it seems to be assumed that the next war will be fought in a land where all bridges—even on the veriest country lanes—will support any weight than can be moved under its own power. In our own country 90 per cent of the roads are other than primary highways. Over the bridges of these roads hundreds of thousands of trucks pass daily, carrying loads comparable to a truck-drawn or truck-carried anti-tank gun. But a six- or eight-ton tank would crash at first impact through most of these same bridges. The same thing would be true on by far the greater part of the seven million miles of motor roads which the rest of the world now boasts, except in certain European countries where bridges are purposely made strong enough to carry tanks.

This bridge-crossing limitation of tanks will often mean a big advantage for anti-tank. Where guns can be moved one hundred miles in three or four hours, tanks, halting at many a bridge until it has been strengthened, or detouring around, may well take a day to cover the same distance. Where guns are fairly certain of averaging from twenty to forty miles an hour in short or long moves by road, tanks, unless they can stick to good roads and bridges, will average only a fraction of those speeds.

When gun and tank both operate largely on roads, the gun has about the same speed and a far higher bridge-crossing ability. When the gun stays largely on roads and the tank moves across country, the gun keeps much of its speed except where the roads are very bad, but the tank's is often reduced to a few miles an hour. This means that the gun can move to meet the tank, instead of waiting for it where it may not come at all.

.   .   .

From this discussion of anti-tank and tank mobility it is apparent that the tactical method of holding some anti-tank units mobile for movement toward a threatened area has a sound basis. General Eimmannsberger, the noted European authority on mechanized warfare, insists "that any guns that are merely held back in readiness will never reach the front line in time." This might have been true at Amiens, where horse-drawn batteries, held in mobile reserve, attempted to move forward to meet the British tanks, and it is probably still sound where animal-drawn guns are concerned. But the actual performances of motorized anti-tank units at the Benning maneuvers make it hard to believe that anti-tank mobility suffers in any comparison with tank mobility. Indeed, it will often have the advantage.

.   .   .

The full effect of combat aviation upon mechanized warfare and upon anti-tank defense is yet to be realized. We can surely expect light battle planes of all kinds to affect both tank and anti-tank in some measure. It is generally thought in all armies to be a costly business to use combat planes against ground troops from low altitudes. But China and Spain seem to be proving two points in this regard: The low-flight attack is unhesitatingly used (1) when the target is important enough to warrant the risk of heavy air losses, and (2) when no great amount of antiaircraft fire is expected from ground troops. In any case it is hard to imagine the use of fighting planes to hunt out and attack specific anti-tank units, habitually scattered to front flanks and rear as they are, in attack, defense, or bivouac, or during a march. Any anti-tank unit, of course, may happen to be within the general area of an air attack like any other unit. When that happens they can only make the best of it, taking their hammering with the rest, and contributing such small-arms fire as they can to the general hail of antiaircraft reply. They will, of course, receive a stout incidental antiaircraft protection from all near-by ground units.

What the plane may eventually do in direct combat against the tank has been suggested in another article. The gun plane is not merely a distant possibility but probable and feasible as an immediate development of air warfare. When we remember that tanks stick to linear movement on roads in order to obtain high speeds and to cross streams, swamps, and rugged country, and that when they are off roads they can move only as fast as the ground allows, it seems highly probable that the gun plane will turn out to be a wicked tank foe. While armies continue to build light tanks by the thousands, can we afford to pass up a development which would convert anti-tank into an offensive element of warfare and extend its reach for hundreds of miles?

Both tanks and anti-tank units in all probability must fight their every battle in any new war through an atmosphere contaminated with gas. To consider persistent gas first, it is doubtful whether tanks will be able to pass through contaminated areas with full protection to their crews. Air-filtering devices will be necessary to keep tanks clear of non-persistent gases. This means that they must be tightly sealed with eye slits covered with thick unbreakable glass. Hence, with or without the need for wearing masks, visibility from within the tank would be hampered.

Anti-tank units subjected to gas will be hampered by masks and to some extent by protective clothing. But since anti-tank units will be motorized, the degree of interference to their activity would be far less than that imposed on foot troops. Anti-tankers should often be able to carry out their missions effectively in spite of persistent gas.

Again, it might at first thought seem as if mechanized onslaught preceded by gas planes drenching large areas in mustard is a method of modern warfare that offers success. But, in the first place, low-flying gas planes are vulnerable to antiaircraft fire from all ground troops. In the second place, we may always doubt gravely that an enemy will contaminate ground over which he will later attempt to operate. And finally, all ground troops can become accustomed to carrying on war under constant risk of exposure to chemicals in all forms, just as they once did in 1917 and 1918 (although we seem to forget that fact). We are also likely to have a more effective individual and collective anti-gas protection in the next war. In fact, our greatest danger, from the viewpoint of mechanized or any other kind of warfare, lies in our present neglect to consider chemical warfare as the probable normal state of affairs— as a common, day-by-day experience instead of a condition that may exist only from time to time, or not at all.

.   .   .

The present high degree of development of the anti-tank mine is too well known to do more than touch upon it in this article. We need to note chiefly that mines are a substantial aid to anti-tank defense which the tank so far has little to offset. A single platoon of engineers can establish an effective mine field on a half-mile front in one hour. If infantry can be trained to help in this work (and certainly infantry needs no specialist training to assist in carrying unarmed mines by hand), this time can probably be cut in half or better. The mines, moreover, can be rapidly unarmed and collected and used again and again. The fact that the modern German division, a somewhat smaller unit than ours, carries thirteen thousand such mines is a strong indication of the part they may play in modern warfare.

COMPARATIVE EFFECT UPON MORALE

There is a tendency to claim much for the moral effect of a tank attack. The roaring charge of mechanical cavalry spitting bullets by thousands is certainly more fear-inspiring than any ever made with horse and saber. And men fled before that charge until they were sure that the weapons in their hands could repel it.

Give an army an effective anti-tank weapon, powerful enough to disable any tank the enemy may use, and give it in sufficient numbers, and there will be no diminution of morale in the face of tanks. It will then be within the tank, and not outside of it, that morale is destroyed. A single battle with great tank losses will be enough. Men will realize, as they did in Spain, that a tank which cannot keep out the shells of the enemy is worse than none at all and is nothing more than a deadly trap of battle. Sabotage followed attempts in Spain to send poor tanks back over the battlefield against good anti-tank guns. It would be surprising if the same thing did not occur under similar circumstances in any army.

A tank crew is under a terrific strain when its tank comes under heavy fire. The shock of high explosives striking close to a tank may alone be enough to injure the whole crew, even without a direct hit. The rattle of small-arms fire against the armor and around the eye slits adds nothing to composure. But perhaps the greatest strain comes from being under fire from a source difficult to locate.

If a tank can reach a point from two hundred to one hundred yards from a gun, the balance of morale will swing to the tank. [Not necessarily so.] For its crew can then see what it is doing, and the anti-tank crew will come under an intense fire. On the other hand, it should be entirely possible to train anti-tank gun crews to duck into deep round fox holes, in the manner now taught at Benning, until the tanks have passed over. This measure of protection should form a firm bolster to anti-tank morale, since hostile tanks will ordinarily be content to destroy an anti-tank gun by crushing, and will hardly stop to dig individual soldiers out of their fox holes.

On the whole, the highest morale will be on the side that has the greatest confidence in its weapon. And there is no good reason why that should not be the side with an effective anti-tank defense.

.   .   .

It may be that in the end there will be found some better means of defense than the gun—the gun plane, perhaps. Or possibly some new type of ammunition may prove far more effective than high-explosive shells. The application of heat by thermite or similar shells, in order to drive tank crews into the open, is a manner of engaging tanks that demands exhaustive experiment. It is a historical fact from the World War that the heat of gasoline burning on the outer surface of a tank soon becomes more than the crew inside can endure. Reports from Spain have indicated the same thing. How much more effective, then, might be the tremendously greater heat of thermite (3,700 degrees F.) splashed upon a tank by a shell. If this proved to be practicable it could well become the prime means of anti-tank defense.

But there is only one main conclusion to be drawn at present. Anti-tank has the edge over the tank; and if we give anti-tank its full due and create that new and vital "framework" in abundant measure, we will have neutralized the greatest ground threat of modern warfare.

This does not mean that we should turn from the tank. The tank, even when anti-tank has been made truly effective, will be of great value. It will be of great use in rapid counterattacks to limited objectives and in pursuit of a beaten foe, and against horse cavalry if any foe should be so foolish as to use it in modern battle. Indeed, against any enemy whose anti-tank defense is inadequate, the tank will always be a mighty weapon.

But by all means let us concentrate on our own anti-tank defense until we know that it is unbeatable by anything that moves on wheels or crawls on tracks.

TANK TORPEDOES

By Major (now Brigadier General) E. D. Cooke

(1937)

When the greatest British fleet since Scapa Flow steamed into the Mediterranean a school of Italian sea sleds met and cut facetious capers around and about His Majesty's ships.

The possibility of a two-man powerboat being capable of sinking many million dollars' worth of battleships by means of torpedoes not only gave British naval officers a severe attack of the jitters, but introduced to the world a new weapon of offshore defense.

The exploitation of this idea should not be monopolized by the Navy. Our land battleships, or tanks, have the same relative strength as their seagoing cousins and are just as capable of being destroyed.

Heavily armored vehicles prefer open and comparatively level ground for their operations. Tanks could be met by smaller and faster vehicles, equipped with tubes and self-propelled land torpedoes. These mines on wheels could be driven by small clock engines and carry sufficient bursting charge to disable or destroy a tank.

Such projectiles could be used in stationary as well as moving defense. They could break up any tank attack over open, level ground and be particularly useful on hard-surface highways.

Imagine a hostile mechanized force in pursuit of a supply column or convoy with both clinging to a concrete highway to attain greater speed. A small vehicle darts in behind the fleeing column, aims a tube, and sends several swiftly moving torpedoes scooting to meet the pursuing armored cars. There is no doubt of the result. Just as England's navy left Mare Nostrum to Il Duce's playful sea sleds, so the hostile pursuit would abandon that particular road—or else.

THE MISUSE OF AIR POWER

By Dallas D. Irvine

(1937)

RADICAL INNOVATIONS in the art of war are almost invariably the product of desperation, for it seems that nothing else can tear the military profession from its habitual slumbering in the voluptuous embrace of ways that are old and familiar. Sometimes the desperation is more purely military, being inspired by the terrible anger of a nation against a trusted profession which has been demonstrating itself, monotonously, to be incapable of obtaining reasonable results with given resources. At other times the desperation is national, being the result of a predicament in which a nation's ordinary resources for war cannot furnish adequate insurance against early defeat. In either case extraordinary expedients are likely to be conceived and adopted. Since desperation is not very conducive to wisdom, however, a majority of these expedients are likely to be very ill advised even if some may prove to be really revolutionary.

One of the reasons why modern Germany has been fertile in military innovations has been the desperate predicament in which she is placed geographically, being virtually encircled by other great nations, a majority of which are either chronically hostile or possessed of inimical interests that make their friendship unreliable. Not all of the innovations to which Germany has had to resort in order to offset this encirclement have worked out to her credit, whether one judges on moral grounds or on the basis of effectiveness in the exercise of intelligence. The invasion of Belgium, the introduction of gas, and the resort to unrestricted submarine warfare are outstanding examples.

One German innovation in the World War was the purposeful aerial bombardment of great cities not in the zone of land operations. Such bombardment was not confined to installations of particular military importance but was directed against the civilian population in the hope of obtaining important moral effects. Important moral effects of the sort desired were certainly not obtained. But there was one important result, and that was to fix the attention of a horrified world on the potentialities in this mode of attack.

The fact that air raids were of little effect in the World War could be attributed to the relative imperfection of aircraft at the time. Since the war the capabilities of aircraft have been vastly increased in almost every respect. The tendency has been, therefore, to assume that their greatly augmented destructive power may be of important or even decisive effect in future war if used for direct attack upon enemy population and civilization. The prospect of air power being so used has naturally inspired an intense horror, and this horror has made the prospect a matter of terrible fascination, even for military men.

Hyperimaginative alarmists and air-power enthusiasts in great numbers have screamed themselves hoarse for half a generation over the danger from the air, and the skeptics and conservatives have been unable to answer them effectively because the capabilities of the latest types of aircraft have never been put to the test in a major war. Consequently civilian populations are mentally numb with dread and inclined to orient their military policies in expectation of the worst. This psychology favors emphasis on air power as a means of defense and preventive attack.

Because of the extraordinary attention which has been focused on the possibilities in the use of aircraft for waging war on civilian populations, the whole military profession in European countries has been deeply drawn into consideration of just what those possibilities are. This has involved study of the manner in which the airplane may best be used for war on civilian population, since only on the basis of such tactical study can the real potentialities be judged. But once in this favorite field of tactics the military mind is lost! It seems never to have occurred to the dervishes of air power to inquire whether attack on civilian population can really be effective in achieving the political end of war, which is the destruction of the enemy's will to resist.

It is not intended to question the power of the airplane to effect extensive material destruction, although the exact extent of this power is debatable. It may merely be pointed out that *material* destruction is effective only as it contributes to destruction of the will to resist. The military art has long since recognized that destruction of material *power* to resist, if sufficiently extensive, is certainly destructive of the will to resist. Therefore, in so far as aircraft can be used for this purpose, there can be no question of their utility as an instrument of war. There remains, however, the question of whether material destruction having no important effect upon the enemy's power to resist can have any important effect otherwise in diminishing his will to resist. It is obvious that such an effect must be expected through the creation of fright and discomfort. Wanton destruction can therefore hope to be effective only in the same way as direct attack on civilian life, namely, through breaking a people's morale.

The aeromaniacs assume that direct attack on civilian population may indeed be effective, and even decisive, in breaking a people's morale. In this assumption lies a most extraordinary fallacy. How anyone familiar with the fortitude shown by the human species among the horrors of war in the past can make this assumption is not easy to understand. The theory that the determination of a people to carry on war can be broken by mere punishment rests upon the grossest misunderstanding of the social psychology of war. Since exactly that theory is finding credence today, even in the circles of military supreme commands, it is desperately necessary to impress upon the minds of all who are thinking about future war that the determination of a people to prosecute a war is dependent not at all upon the punishment to which that people is subjected, but upon two things: (1) *its belief in the justice of its cause,* and (2) *its belief that it has a fair chance of winning or, in any case, of avoiding defeat.* For substantiation of this assertion let one study the causes of the German collapse in 1918.

If those who think and speak so much about attacks on civilian population can only be made to grasp this simple truth, the world may be saved a great deal of bootless misery. There is no more sense in the idea of such attacks than there would be in that of massacring all prisoners of war. Quite aside from the certainty of retaliation, can it be supposed that the killing of all prisoners would terrorize an enemy into submission? On the contrary, such action would reinforce the opposing people's belief in the justice of its cause to such a degree that the difficulty of subduing that people would be enormously increased. One of the main objectives in war must be the *weakening* of that belief by political strategy, and it would be madness to destroy the possibilities which lie in this direction by resort to wanton violence. The proper conduct of war demands, on the contrary, that every effort should be made to weaken the enemy's belief in the justice of his cause by magnanimously abstaining from all acts of cruelty which cannot have an important effect in weakening material power of resistance.

Let it be remembered that Germany's cause was ruined in the last war by the covetous invasion of Belgium and the resort to unrestricted submarine warfare. It was the moral indignation against such "immoral" actions which brought the lethargic Anglo-Saxon peoples wholeheartedly into the crusade against Germany. The morale factor may easily be decisive in modern war, into which many nations are all too easily drawn.

The nation that is wise will go out of its way to avoid attack on civilian population in the hope that the great force of moral opprobrium may fall upon its less astute enemy. For thus may its own will to victory be reinforced and the passive or active support of other peoples obtained.

The only proper use of violence in war is for taking away a determined people's hope of victory, and this can be accomplished only by destroying or neutralizing that people's material power for attack or resistance in whatever degree is necessary. The proper objective for interior air raids is, therefore, the mechanism of supply and communication and not the populace.

Two points may be made in conclusion. In the first place, if attack upon civilian population were effective in destroying will to resist, such attack did not have to await the advent of the airplane. It has almost always been possible, yet, as the result of painful experience, the race *had* learned, before the aeromaniacs frightened it out of its wits, that such attack was both ineffective and unwise. Hence the well-known and formerly respected rules of land warfare. In the second place, if the military profession is inclined to resort to mere punishment as a mode of prosecuting war, it will do well to refer to our existing knowledge in the field of penology, where will be found abundant proof that brutality of punishment has never been effective as a deterrent to the human will but rather a provocative stimulus.

THE GUN PLANE

By Captain X

(*1935*)

Very recently there appeared in a foreign military magazine an account of firings from an airplane with a small cannon. There has, in fact, never been any good reason to suppose that this could not be done. For years there have been planes in existence large enough to carry at least a 37-mm. weapon, or even one somewhat larger, and strong enough in construction to support the recoil of such a gun. But now that a small artillery piece has actually been carried, aimed, and discharged in the air, there is little doubt left that any nation can build artillery planes if it so desires. This being the case, I suggest that a complete investigation of the possible uses and effect on warfare of such planes is worth our immediate attention.

It requires little imagination to see that a gun plane (let us call it that for short) is, above all, the natural enemy of the tank. If an attack airplane can carry four machine guns and twenty-four hundred rounds of ammunition—in addition to two defensive guns—as modern attack planes do, it can surely carry at least one automatic 37-mm. or slightly larger piece, and fifty to seventy-five rounds of armor-piercing ammunition. With any kind of marksmanship at all, firing at tanks from a short dive, a single gun plane should be able to make several hits on one tank, or hits on several tanks, within a very few minutes' time.

The speed and mobility of the tank would be of little avail. A 20-, 40-, or 60-mile-an-hour machine whose activities are confined to a single plane—the surface of the earth—could make a poor job at best of dodging an enemy operating in the air at 150 to 250 miles an hour.

One of the most exciting minor battles of the World War proves this point if, indeed, proof is necessary. In 1918 off Vrieland, Holland, twelve German planes attacked a fleet of six British motorboats. Both planes and boats had machine guns. The best speed of the planes was less than one hundred miles an hour, and the boats could make nearly thirty-five, a ratio of speeds even lower than what we could reasonably assume for tanks and planes today. In less than twenty minutes the planes, diving time after time at the circling, scattered, zigzagging motorboats, put them all out of action, sinking three. The crews of the boats continued to fire their guns almost as long as there was a man left capable of doing so. But the exceedingly unstable conditions of firing made accuracy impossible, and the Germans lost only one plane.

What steps, then, could be taken toward defending tanks against gun-plane attacks? Armor, of course, can be made thicker. (Or can it?) But aside from this moot step, there is at least one other that could be taken to excellent advantage. The tank turret could be constructed with a cover that could be swung clear from inside the tank, and one machine gun—possibly two—could be placed on a mount that would pop the gun and gunner up to the open turret top like a jack-in-the-box in order to engage an attacking plane.

Since it is not improbable that the gun plane might carry a machine gun to deliver covering fire, the tank antiaircraft gunner might well be armored against such fire. Assuming that his head and shoulders would be above the turret top, a small plate of armor attached to the sides of the gun would protect him except from the eyes up.

The antiaircraft fire from such a gun would be aimed directly at the diving plane for some two or three seconds every time it attacked. Hits upon the propeller and engine of the plane would be well-nigh certain. Planes not attacking the tank could also be engaged, although with less effect, since leads would be necessary.

Here we shall stop visualizing the air-tank war, with the final remark that in the tank the airplane has a target undoubtedly worth its while. A tank costs as much to build as several airplanes. I leave the methods by which gun planes are to find their tank enemies, and the methods by which they are to be controlled before, during, and after their attack, to be worked out by the Futurist Board, recommended in a previous issue of the *Infantry Journal.*

How else can the gun plane be used to advantage? It should be, for one thing, a superb means against balloons. One hit, and any inflammable gas would ignite, which is not always the case with even special small-arms ammunition.

This use of the gun plane suggests its employment against such rear installations as gasometers, water tanks, ammunition dumps, and other targets that are hard to hit with bombs and receive little damage from machine-gun fire. For the one big advantage of the gun plane is that of placing accurate, if brief, fire upon targets that require more penetrating and detonating power to damage or destroy them than small-arms bullets afford.

Against other ground units than tanks the gun plane would be less effective than present types of attack planes. But against other airplanes, especially larger and less maneuverable machines than the gun plane, it might be exceedingly valuable. When we stop to think that a .50-caliber armor-piercing bullet will tear completely through the cylinder banks of an airplane engine and render it completely useless, the effect of a small gun is not difficult to imagine.

INFANTRY CATERPILLAR CLUB

By Captain (now Colonel) Wendell G. Johnson

(*1936*)

We were mildly startled when we read about a year and a half ago of the descent of battalions of fully armed parachute jumpers behind the enemy lines in Soviet maneuvers. Apparently the idea isn't as wild as it first appeared, for we now learn that the conservative French are to have two parachute companies. And, like the Russians, they are encouraging parachute jumping as a civilian sport.

Is it just a novelty, a new toy for war games, or are there suitable missions that individual and group parachute jumpers can accomplish? The World War teems with examples of intrepid individuals who carried out hazardous missions behind the enemy lines. Both the Allies and the Central Powers sent envoys by air to blow up ammunition dumps, air-dromes, and factories. These agents were set down by planes in the vicinity of their objectives and did their dirty work alone, or in collaboration with spies operating in the district. If still alive they were picked up and flown back to friendly territory several days later. This was the *modus operandi* when military aviation was passing through the diaper stage. Today such methods seem naïve when compared with Russia's trained battalions of parachute jumpers. These fighters, whose missions will be hazardous enough, are not going to float gently earthward and afford the enemy some fine target practice in the process; instead they are going to fall like hailstones. Red Army parachute jumpers are trained to drop from great heights with parachutes closed until the ground gets dangerously close. Thus they form poor targets, are not overdispersed by the wind, and can rally quickly after landing to accomplish surprise missions. It is said that the Red Army already boasts several thousand parachute jumpers.

The French plan is to have one company of parachutists in Algiers and the other in France. If the scheme proves successful there will probably be one company for every "air region" of France.

In the February issue of the French *Revue d'Infanterie* Lieutenant Colonel Desré discusses the future of these two companies. In war they will have two primary missions—covering and destruction.

A suitable covering mission might involve the seizure of an important crossroads or defile for a mechanized force making a stab at a distant objective. They might also be used to distract attention from a wide envelopment, or to cover the descent of a large force by air transport.

Among rear-area destruction tasks we have bridges, factories, dumps, nerve centers—the list is endless.

It would seem that the parachutist must be first of all a ground soldier, a doughboy. Next he should revel in demolitions and have an abiding love for TNT blocks, and lastly he needs enough flying and jumping with delayed action on the cord for it to become routine business for him. Infantryman, engineer, parachutist, he is really a hybrid trooper, but one, however, that could easily be produced from doughboy stock. With the incentive of a 50-per-cent increase for flying pay there would be no shortage of applicants for the 70th Infantry (light parachutes).

DEFENSE AGAINST AERIAL ATTACK

From article by COLONEL LOUIS JACKSON, British Army

(*1914*)

. . . OR SHOULD THERE BE an organized airplane patrol at night? Flying is more difficult at night than in the daytime, but we are told that they are practicing it in France to guard against dirigibles. Shall we lay this additional burden on our airmen? If it is asked of them they will certainly do it.

The question needs consideration and is no doubt getting it. A dockyard is a large object to hit, and twenty simultaneous fires would overtax the resources of the fire brigade. Direct protection is not possible. You can give a measure of protection to a ship by netting, but you cannot roof over a whole dockyard. The main point is that a dockyard is worth special and expensive measures of defense.

· · ·

Of the great centers of population, London is for us the prime object of consideration. Destruction and panic in the largest of provincial towns would cause trouble but need not affect our national policy. London in this respect stands alone, that it is not only the habitat of a large fraction of our whole population, but the seat of government, the center of our financial and business systems, and the nerve center of our military and naval forces. A serious blow aimed at London would be more effective against the national life than in any other capital of the world.

We are now, beyond doubt, face to face with the new era in war. If you have granted my assumptions with regard to the range of action and offensive power of the aircraft of the immediate future, those assumptions must hold good for one object as well as for another.

· · ·

If a Geneva convention were sitting now and the point were to be raised that a capital which is easily accessible to the enemy may claim exemption from attack on the ground that it is unfortified, would not the answer be, "Yes, provided that it is prepared to submit, and not offer resistance, to the enemy's armed forces"? And whether the armed force takes the form of troops ready to advance, or of the power to destroy resistance by attack from the air, the principle is the same. After all, war is a game that governments play to win, and we could hardly expect the most chivalrous enemy to refrain from striking a blow at the heart of the country, merely because we have chosen to leave it unprotected. Can any student of international law tell us definitely that such a thing as aerial attack on London is outside the rules; and, further, that there exists an authority by which the rules can be enforced?

· · ·

It seems to me that we cannot help accepting the fact that in three years or less London will be exposed to the form of attack I have indicated. What is the defense? In the first place, taking into account the size of London, it seems that no system of aerial patrol could prevent an attack by a dirigible balloon. A deliberate attempt to destroy a given building might perhaps be prevented, but if the balloon's gas were exploded and she fell in flames with all her cargo of explosives, the remedy might be as bad as the disease. Airplane attack on London is feasible but is not so formidable or so easy. Airplanes coming by day might be seen and engaged by our own patrols. As for night attack, I should think that maneuvering over London in the dark would be a dangerous task in present conditions. Perhaps some aviator will tell us if it is practicable, and if not, whether it is likely to become so. In brief, however, I do not think that any system of patrolling can entirely prevent aircraft from reaching London and doing damage when they get there. The only practical way of meeting this danger is to provide enough of our own aircraft to make it at least difficult and risky for the enemy's craft to get through and to be able to undertake a vigorous offensive. If no measures of actual defense can protect our capital with certainty from a dangerous attack, then the remedy must be found in offense. Armed airplanes are the natural balloon destroyers, and I think they should be provided in sufficient numbers to hunt their quarry out of existence.

INTERCHANGE OF PEACETIME DUTIES

From an article by MAJOR GENERAL WILLIAM C. RIVERS

(*1931*)

THE PRESENT continued isolation of the several branches of the Army, with the isolation of the several postgraduate schools, and simply theoretical study of the work of other arms, as well as only theoretical study on maps of the work of divisions and brigades, without opportunity for officers to serve with other than their own arms or to carry on their peacetime study at times in contact with a brigade or division in being, will produce just one kind of army. It must inevitably be an army that will not be at a reasonable state of efficiency in an emergency; an army with officers lacking in knowledge and experience and flexibility and mental keenness and power that could well be given them in time of peace at no appreciable additional cost to the state.

With modern methods of mobilization and transportation, war is a fast game and demands officers of high and ready mental caliber. Indeed, if the small extra cost to transfer officers to serve with other arms be a barrier to improvement, there will be many who have a keen memory of what they went through in our preparation for recent wars who will have little doubt that the saving to the budget might better be made by having fewer officers and men ordinarily—a smaller number of better-grade and better-trained officers might be, in time of need, a great national asset.

THE INFANTRY MIND

Editorial by CAPTAIN X

The accusation was so often repeated in the first months of the war that the Infantry and its leaders were accustomed to thinking in terms of millions of men with rifles on their shoulders that the *Infantry Journal* despaired editorially over the ignorance of many who were writing about the Army for the general public and who performed a disservice to the country and their Army through the use of catch phrases. As the war went on these writers and radio commentators gained a broader background and a fairer conception of military things, and their comments and opinions improved accordingly.

Those who have been in charge of the *Infantry Journal* have for a great many years believed that the infantryman, like other fighting and service specialists in the armed forces, needs to know a great deal about all phases of warfare—not simply his own. This is the reason why much that is in this Reader doesn't deal with Infantry but with Army matters in general. No part of the combat team that makes up an army can operate efficiently unless it understands the share of the other parts of the team. As a result of one irritation following another, and the impact of one especially pompous and misleading reference by a military expert to something he was pleased to call "the Infantry mind," the magazine from which this book is made carried the following editorial with that title in January 1942. It was referred to in Congress and picked up in hundreds of newspapers and widely reprinted in the Army.

SOMEBODY mentioned "the Infantry mind" to us a few days ago and since then we've been doing some thinking as to just what "the Infantry mind" is.

The Infantry mind is a mind that thinks men are the essence of fighting power—that the tougher and harder and keener and abler the soldier, the better the army. It thinks that it is men who win wars and that those who think armies can get along mainly on brains and mechanical ability are already defeated. It thinks that the iron fighting will of men in the mass is the heart of an army, whether they do their fighting in planes or in tanks, or gain their ground by the yard by the use of the ground. It thinks that "men in the mass" means every fighting man and every man who helps him fight.

The Infantry mind is a mind that wants every weapon and gadget sought for and adopted that will add strength and power and speed and sureness to the whole fighting force. It is a mind that thinks an army must have such weapons in the numbers it appears to require and a few more still. For it wants to be sure there are enough. And it wants no time to be wasted on argument about what shall be done with new weapons. It wants them to get into the hands of any partner in the fighting team in the shortest possible time so that new power can add to the strength of the team.

The Infantry mind is a mind that thinks only in terms of a strong, ready, all-out support. If it's Infantry doing the supporting, then the Infantry mind is constantly ready to add to the fight every ounce it has of drive, speed, and technical ability expressed in fire power and maneuver, to help the troops it is supporting. If it's Infantry that is getting the support, then the Infantry mind looks for this same kind of help—for co-operation without thought of collar ornaments—from every supporting man and his weapon of ground or air.

The Infantry mind doesn't care how it gets to the battle so long as it gets there in time. In time to surprise and in strength to match and outfight the enemy. It is eager to use the plane, the truck, and the jeep to cover the ground and get its men and their weapons wherever their attack can hit hardest and go farthest. It thinks that the fighter in the tank and the plane must have this same unalterable thought of striking where their powerful blows will do most good.

The Infantry mind is a crafty mind, not merely a charging, fighting, assaulting mind. For it knows that a stroke that strikes weakness is a stroke that tells heavily, and that every particle of driving power must then be applied. But if it knows that the enemy's weaknesses must be sought, it likewise knows that the enemy's strength must often be overcome first to create a weakness. And it knows that when there is a job like this it takes more than ever the fighting heart of the soldier himself, of the single man and of men in the mass—of men on the ground, in planes, and in tanks.

For the Infantry mind is a mind that thinks men are the essence of fighting, that the heart and the guts and blood of soldiers win wars, and that bombers and tanks and jeeps; howitzers, guns, and mortars; grenades and pursuit planes and rifles are tools in the hands of men, of fighting men, and can never win wars by themselves.

The Infantry mind, so the infantryman thinks, must be the same mind as the Air Forces mind, the Armored Force mind, the Quartermaster mind, the Field Artillery mind, the Ordnance mind, the Coast Artillery mind, the Finance mind, the Cavalry mind, the Chemical Warfare mind, the Signal Corps mind, the Engineer mind, the Medical Corps mind, the Morale Branch mind, and the minds of chaplains and inspectors and adjutant generals. One mind there must be—one single mind, with one single hard-driving aim—the defeat, the crushing defeat, of the enemy.

AIR FORCES

From an editorial by MAJOR (now COLONEL)
JOHN R. M. TAYLOR

I have no idea when the thought of a separate air force was first expressed. But one of the earliest suggestions in this direction was the following *Infantry Journal* editorial, here given in part, which appeared in August, 1918.

THE United States of America has embarked on the most stupendous undertaking of its existence. The efforts of the entire country, as well as those of our allies, are now being devoted to the one task of overcoming the Germans.

The fighting strength of this country now comprises the land forces and the naval forces. More than ever before in their history are these two forces working in unison. . . .

Recently . . . the Air Service has come into being and is fast assuming proportions far beyond that of a branch, or arm, of the land service. The personnel of this Air Service, owing to the nature of its work, is of a different sort from the personnel of which it is now a part. Because of the nature of its duties the personnel is much younger, and at present, at least, promotion is much more rapid. The element in which this service operates—the air—naturally places now, or will place in the not distant future, the Air Service in a category analogous to the land forces and the naval forces. It seems but reasonable, therefore, to assume that before long the Air Service will have outgrown its present bounds and will demand administrative facilities to compare with the present War Department or the Navy Department. Possibly the Air Department will be a necessity presently.

It is true that the greatest co-operation is required between air forces and land forces, but no more complete co-operation than is required between sea forces and land forces nor between sea forces and air forces. The operation between the fighting forces of the country (land, sea and air) is a governing body which is able to co-ordinate the efforts of supply, administration and control. In other words, it appears that the time is fast approaching when for proper control and unification of effort of these three forces of the United States, a great General Staff composed of individuals from all three forces and acting directly under the President or his representative—War Minister or whatever his title may be—will be a necessity, and plans should be perfected with as little delay as practicable with a view to enactment of whatever legislation may be necessary for its inauguration.

II

Better Ways of War

In a sense this second section is a continuation of the first, for it also contains articles that look ahead. But in this second group of *Infantry Journal* selections the authors are dealing more with improvement of existing methods and griping at peacetime hindrances than in more drastic suggestions. The same tone is there—the voice of the soldier who sees that his army could be better, must be better, and who fears the unnecessary losses in dead and wounded in the next war if improvements do not come before it comes.

Here, as in other sections of the Reader, there are many pieces written under pseudonyms. Naturally the editors of the magazine always knew who the authors were. There has always been, in fact, the customary rule that nothing submitted for possible publication will be considered for a moment if it is fully anonymous. But a junior officer might have something he wanted to express with some force and might be under a senior who would discourage such articles. More often the reason was diffidence —the desire not to be considered "a writer rather than a doer." This attitude, which completely overlooks the value of language as a military tool, has been a strong one in the Army. This confusion between writing as purely literature and writing as a skill every commander needs from the beginning of his career probably has its origins in many places, but chiefly in the high-school teacher of English who bases her course chiefly on the literary appeal. The historical fact of Caesar, Marshal Saxe, Napoleon, Frederick the Great, U. S. Grant, and many other soldier-writers, some of them professional writers, is overlooked, and so is the almost daily value of clear expression to every commander. And the wish to be known as a "doer" rather than a "writer" has led many soldier-authors to use pen names.

Perhaps the intense criticism and desire to see better ways of war has been, in the circumstances, strengthened by an editorial policy of this kind.

THE BATTLE–WISE FIGHTING SOLDIER

Editorial

(*1942*)

. . . TEAMWORK is of utmost importance. The welding of troops together into a co-ordinated fighting unit leads all other training. But it isn't the whole of training. The soldier as a single fighter must be thought of right on through to battle and till our war is won.

.   .   .

The battle team is the big team, and no fight can be won without it. But the whole story of Luzon, Bataan, and Corregidor doesn't lie in the battle achievements of units alone. To unit citations we must add the awards that single fighting soldiers won—the awards to men whose training and ability as individual fighters came to fulfillment where it was meant to—to men whose deeds not only reflected their guts but told of a soldier's grasp of a soldier's part in a fight.

We have read what they did, these men. We've seen their citations for awards and we've read the fine stories about them the battle correspondents have sent us. We know that they stand with the best of the fighters our Army has seen. We know them for soldiers.

And we know when we think of it thus that the trained soldier is not only a part of a team but also a fighting unit—almost a one-man fighting team—in himself.

The men who win medals stand out. But beside them are plenty of others who fight just as well but whose fighting deeds go unnoticed, perhaps, or are only less striking. Beside the men who are cited are plenty of others we know for soldiers.

.   .   .

The fighting man's confidence must rest on three things—his leader, his weapon, and himself. His leader can often do little to guide him once battle is on. His weapon cannot make him a smaller target to the aimed or unaimed fire of the enemy. Only the man by himself, through knowledge of what a trained fighter must do to live and fight, can handle himself as he must if battles are to be won.

The inspiring leader and the powerful modern weapon are not by themselves enough. It takes soldiers too. The inspiring leader who is followed by men who are sure of their weapons but who lack the habits of battle wastes their lives and weakens his army. His undertrained and overconfident troops stop bullets by dozens that should never strike a mark. A first success may be gallantly won, but there aren't enough fighting men left to go on to a second.

The battle wisdom of a soldier, his true basis for confidence can only be gained through repeated, hardening practice. Dirty, tiring, but utterly necessary, lifesaving work. The dirt of the ground is the soldier's friend in battle just as much as his weapon. The closer he can keep to the ground as he fights and advances, the more professional his fighting is and the more he will live to accomplish for his army, his country, and himself.

The leader of fighting men must never lose sight of the continual training it takes to perfect his troops as individual fighters. He receives them well trained from the training center and then it's his job to perfect them. He must constantly see, during all of his unit's training, that his troops form the fighting man's crafty habits. He must give them hours for special training in these things as they need it. He must take quick steps of criticism and even punishment to rid them of careless, overconfident, and unrealistic habits in training that would invite unnecessary death in battle. He must see that his unit grows into a fighting team made up of soldiers.

.   .   .

There is fighting to do in this war—it has only begun. And a lot of that fighting has got to be done on the ground. And if it's going to get anywhere it has got to be done by trained, hardened, battle-wise soldiers.

COUNSEL FOR THE DEFENSE

By Lieutenant Colonel (now Lieutenant General) Joseph W. Stilwell

General Joe Stilwell, who was Chief of Staff in Burma to Generalissimo Chiang Kai-shek, has always believed in plain words on war. In early 1933, when he wrote "Counsel for the Defense," he was a member of the staff of the Infantry School. He could, and doubtless still can, argue just as forcefully regarding new methods of attack as well as of defense.

To attempt a defense of anything at all debatable will probably be considered a faux pas for a man whose first case as counsel resulted in a sentence of four years in jail for his client. However, as I remember it, the defendant, far from being griped, even thanked me cordially for my perspiring, if ineffectual, oratory before a somnolent court. Anyway, there isn't anything debatable to be brought up here, and if angels fear to tread, somebody has to rush in.

In inviting a scrutiny of the generally accepted methods of conducting the defense, I want to start by recalling certain things that presumably we all agree on. First, let us examine the basic idea of defending along one long line. If we could make our single line strong enough to resist successfully everywhere, the defense would win, and everything would be very pleasant for the rear echelons. But we know that the attacker can mass enough means at any given point to break in. Besides, if we pack our strength forward in defending, we merely increase our casualties without doing compensating damage. Everybody knows this, of course. A defense along one long line is inherently weak—we cannot possibly make it strong enough to hold everywhere. Let us form two lines, then, one behind the other—or three—or four. This was the development at the outset of the World War, and it gave greatly increased resisting power to the defense.

But with such a defense, what happens? The enemy selects a point of attack, breaks down the first line, as we admit he can, and pours through the hole. The rupture causes the breakdown of the whole line for a considerable distance on either side of the penetration. The elements stationed on either side are taken in flank or rear and fall back on the second line. If the enemy is determined, the same operation is repeated on the second line, and so on. The first line broken, the only opposition now is the fire of the second, aided by a few elements in rear. But if the remnants of the first line do not stand, they will largely mask the fire of their comrades in falling back. And if these comrades insist on firing anyway, there will be a lot of hard feeling aroused. If the first-line warriors get back to the second line at all, there will be confusion and mixing of units. Also, subordinate commanders on the first line are left in doubt as to whether to go back or stay where they are. The parts of the line not ruptured cannot help the units that are broken. The artillery can only continue to shoot ahead of the so-called main line of resistance. We are opposing to the enemy's blow a series of obstacles which he can crash successively. This is about what we are in practice doing, and as usually performed, our defense is thus a rather stubborn delaying action. And it is based on the naïve hope that the direction of the enemy attack will be perpendicular to our front.

The Germans found out, beginning with the Somme battle, that this kind of defense was not so good, and they developed the idea of a defense in depth, so arranged that the attack, although it would probably meet with initial success, would gradually be disrupted and brought to a stop by increasing resistance toward the rear. This was accomplished by placing defensive elements at irregular intervals through a greatly deepened defensive zone. These elements were organized for all-around defense and were thicker and stronger around the vital points to be held. The holding of a few yards of ground was considered of no consequence, if a proper toll could be taken and the push finally brought to a standstill before the key points were captured. The difference between the two ideas is roughly indicated by comparing the gradual compression of a spring and the rupture of a series of light boards.

Well, but didn't our people learn that, and isn't it all in the Training Regulations? Yes, it's all there, mixed up with a lot of other things, to all of which we must assign their proper emphasis or else we'll go astray. Experience with several classes at the Infantry School shows that somehow this emphasis has shifted too far, and it would be well to look things over and see why.

In the first place, we have the main line of resistance. We are told that it is the front edge of the combat elements. If you will put yourself in the shoes of the emergency officer earnestly struggling in a limited time to learn a mass of things entirely strange to him, I believe you will agree that the term "main line of resistance" will mean to him the line of main resistance. He will want to make his best fight along it and he will push up to it for this purpose all his available means. Just what we don't want him to do. It is queer that we make such a point of being unmistakably clear in orders and yet retain in general use terms which can easily lead a man astray. As a matter of fact, the main line of resistance at the beginning of a fight is the line of elements first struck, but immediately afterward it is something else, and from then on it is always in a different location. At any given time it is the irregular line where the enemy is being opposed. We would be better off if we said nothing about it or else used some other term that would not confuse the boys.

In this connection are we not looking at the defense almost entirely from the viewpoint of the higher command? Of cause the corps commander and the division commander will draw a line on the map or designate two or more terrain features and say, "That is the main line of resistance." Of course. But as we go farther down and finally reach the battalion and company, conditions change. Take that line that the corps commander draws across his map with a pencil and put it under a microscope. It is no longer a continuous line of little breadth. It is now a wide series of smears and blotches irregularly disposed, with numerous intervals here and there. These smears and blotches are the dispositions of the junior commanders, and it is the resultant of them all that makes up the main line of resistance that the higher commander is thinking about. The piece of the corps commander's line that the battalion commander gets to defend is, from the viewpoint of the latter, an area. It will usually be an area for the regimental commander too. When the higher commander assigns the line he may also amplify his instructions by saying that this or that terrain feature is important or must be held. If he does not, then farther down the line someone must. It is the ground itself that determines the dispositions of the smaller units, and, based on an evaluation of the ground, the junior picks out the important features and arranges for their defense. After his dispositions are made, the so-called main line of resistance becomes apparent—it is a line tangent to the fronts of his forward combat groups. But in these small units it results from his dispositions—his dispositions do not grow from it.

There is another idea firmly implanted in our minds about the necessity of a continuous band of fire across our front. Certainly we should like to have it, and with the enormous concentrations of artillery we saw in the World War, with the adoption and issue of a suitable light machine gun, and with a big increase in our mortars, we might be able to get it, but as things stand, with one mortar per battalion, with no good substitute for a light machine gun, and with only three batteries backing up a regiment, it is simply out of the question without packing most of our weapons close to the front. And the more we close them up, the more we favor a quick rupture by the attack. Our elements up front are those most surely located by the attacker, and we must not forget that at any given point he can get superiority of fire. In the great majority of cases a little ground gained or lost is of no consequence. What we want is to disrupt and disorganize the attack, keep it constantly under pressure, and finally, by getting at it from unexpected directions, bring it to a stop. We want to gain time enough to be sure we have located the main thrust and get reserves back of that point. We should be willing to bend if we can keep from breaking. This requires that we establish points all the way back around which the attack will drape itself but beyond which it cannot pass except at a price. We want a series of snags to break the control and cohesion of the assault. Thereupon, when it halts we can counterattack. The necessity of giving the assault no rest requires that our weapons be disposed in depth and that enfilade fire of machine guns and the prepared fires of light artillery be utilized to the greatest advantage. We should be able to fire within the position as well as in front of it.

This matter of artillery fire is important. Where now do we plan our artillery fires except in advance of the position? We cannot fire within it without endangering our own people, who may be moving back anywhere in the area. To get the most of our support we should prepare for fires within our position and arrange so that our own troops will stay out of such locations. The artillery fire can then be brought down on them—the areas, not the troops—at any time, and what is now the artillery defense of the main line of resistance will be continued back through the position. If it is claimed that this is being taken care of I plead ignorance and lack of experience with units so well instructed. I have never seen it.

Again, by occupying a line we face in one direction, and although we are well disposed if the attack comes in as expected, we are greatly handicapped if it develops in another direction. The organization of switches helps us somewhat, but we are always exposed to the danger of infiltration, and any line is then subject to attack from the rear. If the attack is at an angle to our line, then surely the continuous-band-of-fire idea will not be effective, and surely, also, the effect of a rupture will be to add materially to the probability that the line will be rolled up. If we could jump around like ants on a hot rock and readjust our dispositions during the assault, it would not be so bad, but no one will question the statement that a realignment in a defensive position while under fire is a very difficult if not impossible operation. What we want is to make such dispositions that we cannot be badly hurt if the direction of attack is unexpected.

Assuming the patience of the reader up to this point, just what is it we do want? First, something simple, easy to teach a big emergency force. Second, something based on an evaluation of the ground. Third, something that will allow the maximum effective use of supporting fires. Fourth, something that will stand up if we guess wrong about the direction of attack. Fifth, something that gives definite missions to every unit down to the smallest.

We will get a simple solution as soon as we approach the problem in a reasonable way—by adjusting our means to the ground itself. Only a trial will convince you, but it appears to work at Benning. The fundamental decision is, "In my area what are the vital points that I must hold?" The answer to that question determines the dispositions. It relieves the natural anxiety of the commander to cover everything and allows him to use scanty means to the best advantage.

If enemy action dictates our dispositions we have nothing to worry about. But if we have a choice it must be based on what he may be able to do, and that depends on the ground—where and what the cover is, what the favorable approaches are, where the best fields of fire are, what is the best observation, etc. Since we do not know how his attack may develop, we plan against probabilities, but we must be prepared for all contingencies. Our defense of the main approaches may be successful, and yet a penetration may occur elsewhere. Such a contingency must not break down our whole plan. The direction of attack may be unexpected —this must not necessitate a rearrangement of our dispositions. The enemy may make considerable progress somewhere. Our supporting weapons must still be able to work on him. Our artillery particularly must be prepared to put down fire anywhere the attack is threatening.

And all concerned must know exactly what to do. Units in the front-line battalions must give up any idea of moving around. They must give one another mutual support. They must expect that the attack will get by them and they must therefore be ready to resist from flank and rear. The loss of an adjacent combat group should not break down their own resistance. There is no question of their withdrawing; they must fight in place.

.   .   .

Of course if the very idea of defense is obnoxious to all of us free and hardy Americans, what our doctrine is on the question doesn't matter much. We preach the offensive—we're going to attack and let the other fellow defend. That's what we did in the World War. But somebody did a lot of defending before we got in, and perhaps the next time it will be on us quickly and we won't have a year to get ready to attack. If we accept the idea that somebody may attack us, then we had better clarify our ideas so that we understand what we are trying to do and can give definite and simple missions to all concerned.

TRAINING FOR THE NEXT WAR

By CORPORAL (now CAPTAIN) LEON F. DENIS

(1936)

LEARNING from past experience and knowledge of the psychology of the average American from 18 to 35, I am much in disagreement with a lot of present-day "eye-wash" that is presumed to be a basis of "training" of the American soldier for the battlefield—which is, after all, the "raison d'aitre" of the entire military establishment.

Too much stress is laid upon a lot of "by-the-numbers" means of execution of much of the daily routine of the American soldier today; that in a theater of operations will serve no purpose whatever, in fact it will be more of a hindrance; in short, a lot of stuff is being taught in peace times that will have to be "unlearned" in the face of realities of battle that no amount of "book" can prepare for.

The *Tentative Infantry Drill Regulations* of a few years back that were tried out in certain sections by the Army is about the full extent of so-called close order drill; or, disciplinary drill that there will be any time for when the sad day arrives that the pressing call will be "Men, more men." Why these same new drill regulations were thrown into the discard, to eventually be forgotten by all but a few old noncoms who tried them out by unlearning "Squads East and West" is beyond me. [They were brought back. Corporal Denis is talking about the simplified close-

EDITORIAL NOTE: This is the only article that has ever escaped the ruthless blue pencil. Not even a punctuation mark has been added, changed, or deleted. It was the unanimous opinion of the editorial staff that a revision or a rewrite would destroy the vigor and earnestness of Corporal Denis' paper.

order drill, which abandoned "squads right" and other complicated parade-ground maneuvers. This drill was tried out for a year, early in the thirties, then dropped but brought back early in the emergency period which preceded the war.]

Not enough time, energy and practice is given to that important phrase of Jeb Stuart's: to "Get there fustest with the mostest men" by which I mean ordinary marching under full field equipment over all sorts of terrain and in all sorts of weather, until such time as *all* your men can cover 30 miles per day over average country without *anyone* falling out. In addition to this there is too much tendency in the "field" to take everything along from the barracks that is movable including almost the pool table from the recreation room. Nothing, other than that provided by the TBA [Tables of Basic Allowances which list official campaign equipment. Army units acquire much "company property" such as easy chairs and pool tables in time of peace], should be permitted in the field or on practice marches; and they, should be frequent—that men and equipment be always in a state of readiness of proper "shake-down." By the foregoing I also mean the abolition of a lot of junk that is brought along by officers, from special equipment for a separate mess to Morris chairs and what-not. Bedding rolls and shelter tents are all that the TBA provides; and they may as well get used to it from the very start, as well as eating out of mess kits the same food that the men of their organizations have to eat.

As to "taking the field" you would get quite an eye-opener if you stopped at most any Army post and asked the C.O. to sound "call to arms" unknown to anyone else at 2:00 A.M. some morning. The garrison would be lucky to be in ranks by 5:00 A.M. in most cases I'll venture, and even then a lot of equipment would be missing; nobody knowing why or where.

For the marching part, even Hitler with his Youth movement and Mussolini with his young Black Shirts is giving us a lead that we will have a long way to go, to catch up to in the future; when they even train school boys in the art of marching with full pack—whereas we don't even give our regular soldiers sufficient training in this self-same subject. There is a laugh somewhere; but certainly we are not the ones to be in a position to do the laughing—at least not now.

A certain amount of "display" or so-called "garrison soldiering" may be necessary I'll grant if only for the purpose of "showing off" to dignitaries; all of which can be restricted to a few units at a few posts—which units would not normally be included in the first increments ordered to the field in a major emergency. Otherwise, all this "display" and "eyewash" could as well as not be eliminated entirely. In this connection we are too much like women who are not satisfied with the way nature made them; can't stay "natural" but our vanity works as bad as theirs does with rouge, facials and permanents.

At the present time, too much effort, time and expense is devoted to "polishing" this and that, that should be used to much more advantage in tactical training. Any dumb cluck can learn to polish a pair of shoes, shine a belt or brass buttons; but, that same dumb cluck most certainly can't learn in a few weeks to take a squad and properly dispose it on the firing line and secure "fire superiority" promptly.

In this same vein, altogether too many men in the Army really think that an "outpost" or Cossack post is part of a fence; for which there is absolutely no excuse whatever. This condition prevails more in Headquarters [Headquarters companies, largely made up of clerical personnel], machine gun, and other specialized organizations; which calls for correction. The training of men of these organizations should include *all* that the rifleman in the rifle company is normally expected to know; in addition to which he is called upon to train in his "specialty" so-called, whether he be a switchboard operator or a supply office clerk should not make the slightest difference. He may, some day, find himself suddenly thrust in a rifle company for some reason or other; and if he has not learned the rudiments of a rifleman's training what good will he be to anyone or himself?

As to "fire superiority," it is freely admitted that our present system of instruction in "marksmanship" can hardly be improved upon; but, after all, do we really want so few "expert" shots as a result of so much training time; or, do we want men to know how and where their rifle shoots, in large numbers in preference? The system utilized early in the World War just prior to entering the lines for the first time early in 1918 seems to offer a solution to this problem of producing a quick, self-reliant method of instruction in shooting—not, mind you "marksmanship." The two subjects are entirely different.

Each individual sort of had to teach himself; knowing full well that results in future would either cost him his life or save it. Little personal instruction was afforded anyone—there was no time for it anyway had we wanted to. All the empty tin cans were gathered up from the company kitchens and taken to the "range," which was nothing more or less than a flat space at the foot of some hill with a little bank at the base of the hill upon which the cans were set with the bottom toward the firing line—which was 75 or 100 yards away. The firer had to adjust his elevation and windage by himself until such time as he could hit his can several times successively without changing sights. Having accomplished this, he had a "zero" for his rifle as we now call it and was practically ready for the trenches as far as his weapon was concerned. If more time was available he was allowed to train in following his can as it bounced along from shot to shot; which taught him more or less how to hit a moving target. The foregoing method of training in "shooting" (not marksmanship) most certainly told on the "shock troops" of Germany at such places as Seicheprey, Apremont and Chateau-Thierry, and elsewhere.

With "marching" and "weapons" in mind as the paramount basis of training, new men or units should spend their first six weeks under canvas (in the field) to be followed by the next two weeks in garrison then another six weeks in the field; until proficiency is attained.

As to equipment, at the present time there is too much tendency for individual commanders to dictate their own personal ideas as to how equipment should be kept and cared for; in some cases going to the extent of articles almost losing their original identity. These articles are purchased in a certain condition under certain specifications and it is quite safe to assume that it is intended that they be kept in just that condition and no other; whether they look pretty or not. As long as equipment is "clean" that is all that is required and should be asked of anyone. In this connection, I would forbid Post Exchanges from dealing in any of this "bucking material" that at the present time keeps most of the enlisted men broke. [By "bucking material" the author means fancy non-regulation uniforms, belts, shoes, and so on, which a soldier could buy to outshine other soldiers when it came to the selection of the commanding officer's orderly each day at guard mount.] The same could be applied to an overabundance of tailor shops, shoe shops and the like; all of which can be done within the organization at less cost, and, to a greater benefit to the organization fund as well as that of the poor individual soldier who does the spending. Cobbler kits are issued and if organizations maintained their own cobblers, barbers and the like, much less "collection sheet" trouble would be a result. [The "collection sheet" is the list of credits given to enlisted men during the month to be taken from their pay on payday.] As to leather, saddle soap is *issued;* it keeps leather clean and pliable hence is sufficient for all leather including shoes. If it had been intended that all this "bucking material" be essential parts of a soldier's equipment and much of his time devoted to its use; it is safe to assume the same would have been *issued* is it not? Well, then let us leave well enough alone and not be so feminine.

Not enough time and effort is devoted to "understudy"; few men and officers are taught to temporarily at least fill the shoes of someone higher up during field exercises or maneuvers; where the art of "command" may more readily be assimilated than elsewhere by juniors. This art of "command" is one of our greatest shortcomings and was in 1918 as well as previously. It is one thing that all the books in the world cannot ever hope to teach anyone, bar none; hence opportunity to exercise it frequently and "teach himself" through the medium of his own and other folks mistakes should be afforded all ranks in training.

Only recently Mussolini gave us an example of "training" that is a bit far fetched, but then again the right idea is behind it. That was when some of his Infantry was wounded and killed by their own Field Artillery in real "war condition" maneuvers. I do not advocate such measures exactly; but Infantry could be required to fire at moving targets while sandwiched in between batteries of artillery, also firing by which means each branch would come to a realization of what havoc the other can do in battle. Also this would quickly dispel that ever present "buck fever" so prevalent in the rifleman when first close to artillery fire. Closer co-operation and co-ordination between supporting weapons would naturally result from the foregoing as well and the individual soldier would quickly get an idea as to "what the score is."

The soldier, first of all must know how to march—and reach his destination without being all fagged out; ready for action; then, how to take care of himself and his equipment in the field; then, how and when to shoot and what at, also hit what he aims at. He must know something of the general scheme of events of the moment; in other words, "what the score is" to act intelligently on the firing line. Don't withhold all the information you have regarding the situation; you may get killed and someone else may have to carry on—provided they know "what the score is" to start with—see.

When your individual soldier can do these things almost instinctively without being ridden or harassed; then you have something of a soldier, not before.

BATTLE PRACTICE

By Sergeant Terry Bull

(1942)

PULL UP over there by that big tree, Gunther, and we'll park the platoon. Don't slap on your brakes like that, man! You might need 'em bad some time.

All noncoms up!

Your carrier needs another coat of mud and leaves on the front plate, Callahan. I can see the paint from here. You got to watch your camouflage when we're doing cross-country work. The brush knocks it off.

All up? You get a load of this too, Jiminez.

Today we're going to start our combat firing. The time's so short I asked the Old Man to let me skip the usual target-range "enemy on that line between those flags, look out for the surprise target" bunk, and I'm going to put you into a real war starting now.

Knudsen, your section, with a light-gun squad attached, forms a combat group up on the side of that wooded ridge, anywhere between that large white boulder and the stone fence line. You've got to be able to cover this valley from the burned barn on your right front to that wrecked tank on the hill yonder.

Remember, you've got to have all-around defense by every man, team, and squad in your section. I'll look over your position later, and any man that hasn't got a good field of fire in at least three directions I'll put out as a casualty and give him another chance after supper.

Dig in? Of course you dig in. And at the end of thirty minutes you pick out the poorest dug-in man of each squad as a casualty, and we'll arrange some special instruction for *him* too.

Now, Lenoir, take your section with the other light-gun squad up through those woods on the other ridge and dismount 'em in the pine grove on that highest knob. Then put 'em in battle formation and advance through the woods and across this valley. You can move anywhere in the area between that large spreading oak and the white boulder on your left and the stone fence line on your right. We've got to watch our safety angles, see, but that'll still give you plenty of maneuver room.

Jiminez, you follow the Second Section with your load of targets until they take cover. Then stand by until I get there.

Now this is a game and we play it like this. Knudsen has his section dug in almost anywhere in that four-hundred-yard stretch of woods—you can't tell just where—so he can cover his sector with everything he's got.

Lenoir, you and your merry men are Japs or Nazis, whichever you want to be, and you've got the job of crossing part of that sector in your zone of advance. You don't know where Knudsen is—you don't even know if the ridge is defended. So you're advancing, pretty well thinned out, in battle formation.

Knudsen, you have this blank in your gun. You're watching Lenoir come across the valley, and when his outfit gets to the point where you'd open fire, shoot the blank.

When you hear this shot, Lenoir, your outfit drops to cover—just like they would if Knudsen's section was to cut into 'em with everything they had.

Everybody got it?

No, that's all you need to know for now, Lenoir—just drop to cover and stay put.

Let's see, it's seven-thirty now—give you an hour all told—at eight-thirty the war starts. That means your men drop their shovels, Knudsen, and Lenoir's crew starts leaving the pine knob.

Jackson, since your guns are all attached, suppose you go with Lenoir as umpire. See that none of his outfit drops behind or climbs trees, peeking at Knudsen's position—till eight-thirty. I'll go with the First Section and keep *them* honest.

Move out!

Wind her up, Gunther.

II

Well, Knudsen, so your young men are all ready to massacre the murderous Japs! All right, let's take a look around.

I see that none of your light guns are placed to cover that back slope up there.

Sure, your sector is out yonder—but wouldn't you be surprised if I'd whispered to Lenoir to come bouncing in your back door? Take the bolt out of his gun—and put Corporal Borisov down for a little instruction in gun-siting—conducted by you personally.

Notice that both your mortars can cover the front beautifully but nowhere else? Put one of 'em in the middle of that little clearing twenty yards back and he can drop his puffballs anywhere. Let's have your firing pin, Simpson, and after this check for an overhead opening for your cannon.

Who'd you pick for the worst dug in? O.K., pull their bolts and give 'em hell. Then come up here where we can get a good view of Lenoir's crew.

Load? Hell no! You're not loading, are you? Well, don't until I give you the word. You see, this isn't a real war; it's just combat firing.

About eight-ten, eh? Lenoir ought to be showing up soon.

No, I didn't see him. Oh, sure, by that burned snag. And there's another! Well, would you commence firing now? Why not?

Quite a few of 'em in sight now—scouts well ahead—and they're doing pretty well, too, picking those draws and the high grass. How about it? Would you cut into 'em now? Why not?

Looks like that's the last of 'em trickling out of the woods. Yes, here comes Jiminez with the targets. Scouts at about two-fifty now. By gad, seeing those birds bobbing in and out of sight fairly gives me the creeps—reminds me of Coffin Corner when they were coming over——

BANG!

For God's sake, Knudsen! Why don't you blow your horn or hold out your hand before you blast a round off right at a man's ear?

Oh, so that's where you'd have your section open fire? O.K., call your men all up and rest easy till I get back.

Gunther! Twist her tail.

III

Nice going, Lenoir—looked pretty good from where I sat. Have your carriers come on up.

Ho, Jiminez! Over here with those targets.

Jackson, you go with Jiminez all over the section area, putting out one target for every man. Look at their positions. Any man that's in a good concealed position that he can shoot from gets a prone target. Anybody that got caught out in the open when Knudsen fired gets a kneeling target. And every man that's so far down under cover that he couldn't fire on Knudsen's outfit gets a standing target—stuck up full length.

Lenoir, have your men write their names on their targets and drive 'em in the ground right where they are now. When they get 'em drove, assemble, mount 'em up, and move up on that nose of ground on Knudsen's left to watch the show.

All right, Knudsen, Lenoir's gang is all clear and your heroes can do their worst.

Now the picture is that you men have dug in here for a defense of this ridge line. There's other combat groups within covering distance, but you can't count on 'em for sure, ever, so you're dug in all around.

You've seen the Japs or Nazis slipping down out of the woods over there. You've watched 'em close, full loaded, and with your trigger fingers twitching, but that's all. You haven't done anything about it yet because you want to knock down a dozen or so with your first blast—and Sergeant Knudsen's promised to shoot any man that squeezes one off before he blows his whistle.

Finally he gives the word "400." Notice that 400 is a bit low. Well, he was pretty cagey—let 'em keep coming until their scouts were at about two-fifty, and the bulk of 'em were caught short of the stream and clear of the woods. Then he blew his whistle; that is, he fired a blank, and you guys started blasting. Get it?

Now we're ready to go on from there.

You'll get loaded and all set to fire. Then Knudsen will really blow his whistle, and for one minute by the clock you'll cut into 'em. You corporals keep an eye on me. I'll be holding my arm up while you're firing, and when I drop it, cease fire right now.

By the way, Knudsen, return those bolts to your "casualties." I forgot that it would mess up the lieutenant's formula. Give 'em extra instruction instead.

Any questions?

Certainly you men in rear fire. You've qualified on the target range, haven't you? Well, if you can hit a ten-inch bull at two hundred yards prone, you ought to be able to miss one of your friends at fifty yards. Just be damn careful.

Targets? There's a target out there for every man in the Jap section, and they're placed so you can hit every one of 'em, if you can figure where the other fellow is apt to be. Of course you can't see but half a dozen of 'em, but I never knew a Jap or a Kraut to stay out in the open for very long, either. This is *combat firing*, sonny.

Now the idea to follow in combat firing—or battle—is this. When you fire your first shot at a man, he'll dive out of sight and you'll swear you hit him. You probably didn't. So you put another bullet where he disappeared. Then you have to figure on where another Jap would likely be, and you put your next bullet through that spot. Never fire more than one shot—burst for gunners—in the same place until you've covered 'em all. Then start over again.

That way it isn't safe for a Jap anywhere out there. What between your poor guesswork and lousy shooting, he's in great danger no matter where he goes or what he does.

One thing that don't apply to this problem—when you see one of the bastards get up and make a rush, don't be a sucker and try to catch him on the fly. You're not good enough, and he'll be down before even a good shot can draw a sight on him. Just mark where he settles, put two bullets or a burst in there, and then come back to it ever so often with one more bullet.

Any other questions?

All right, Knudsen, have 'em take posts, set sights, load, and when they're all set, toot your whistle.

Any time, Knudsen.

Tweeeeeeet!

(*The rippling, rattling, irregular crash of twelve rounds per second, punctuated by the metallic coughs of the rapidly served mortars, instantly answers the shrill bleat of the signal. Sergeant Bull, with arm upraised, is standing beside a large pine tree, in a position cannily chosen as being out of the line of fire of the wildest rifleman in rear. As the second hand of his watch jerks toward 45, the scaly bark of the tree near his hairy left ear apparently explodes, and the sergeant disappears behind a near-by boulder with the unhesitating celerity of long practice. The firing dies.*

After some moments of deafening silence have elapsed our hero cautiously comes out from behind his fortress, brushing pine needles from his "slaughter suit" and bark splinters from his lacerated cheek. His baleful glare alternates between the battle-scarred pine and the wide-eyed recruits occupying the rear area of the combat group.)

Jackson!

Take a squint along that bullet track and bring me the zombie you'll find in a rifle pit directly in line with it.

Knudsen! Send for your carriers, check to see that you're all clear, and count ammunition.

Ah, Simpson, so it was you? Well, what I'm most curious about is, were you aiming at me or the tree, or between me and the tree, or just what the hell were you aiming at? Don't bother to answer now—poor judgment, lousy shooting, jitters, or criminal intent—it'll be about the same in any case, but you can be figuring on your alibi until we see the Old Man.

Pull his bolt, Jackson.

Knudsen, mount your crew up and bring 'em down to the target area.

Crank up, Gunther, and let's go—by Lenoir's section.

Ho, Lenoir! Bring your section down to the targets. Let 'em mill around and see what happened to 'em.

IV

Tweeeeeeet!

Everybody up! Second Section, bring your own targets in with you! Start a pile here, Lenoir.

Jackson, score the targets hit and total hits. Sure you count ricochets —count everything. Anything that goes through a Bristol-board target will go through skin and make a casualty out of any man—even a Jap.

At ease! Take a look at this target. That is, or was, Popopagous. He dived behind a pine tree instead of out in the grass, and just look at him now. A hole in his pasteboard chest you can put a size-ten hand through, and the rest of him bristling with six-inch pine splinters. Remember that trees were good cover back in the days when grandpa was fighting Indians, but stay away from 'em nowadays. They draw fire and won't stop AP.

Here's Smith, G. W. He took a beautiful position with his head sticking up from behind a rock. Cowboys do it in the movies. And then somebody bounced a bullet off the lip of the rock.

This is Levine. He got himself caught right out in the open. Sixteen holes—count 'em—sixteen!

There's fifteen of you birds that are casualties—fifteen out of one section in one minute's time. No, forty-five seconds it was; Simpson cut it a little short. How many of you'd be left in an hour?

We're going to have several of these battles, and for every time you birds get hit you'll do a couple of hours of scouting, taking cover, and advancing by rushes—just as life insurance.

Forty-two hits on fifteen targets; not bad, Knudsen, considering it's the first shoot for most of your men. Not bad at all. But it's got to get a hell of a lot better before we go up against real Japs or Nazis. Most of you guys in the First Section were shooting high. Look at that limb hanging, lopped off eight feet above the ground.

You've got to learn to comb the grass roots. That's where you'll find Japs. If you're not sure of your target or range, shoot low. When you miss high, the Jap hears the pop and that's the end of your bullet's usefulness. But when you shoot low, your bullet flattens out, kicks up a cloud of gravel, bounces, screams like a wildcat, keyholes, and is apt to cripple anybody in the neighborhood beyond. Kicking up gravel isn't as foolish as it sounds. If a man gets hit by a chunk of rock he's very apt to think he's been killed, and if you just kick dust in his eyes he's going to be awful allergic to lead for a few minutes.

The score for the First Section is—here, Jackson, help me out with the decimals—

$$\text{Score} = \frac{100 \times \text{range to nearest Jap} \times \text{targets hit} \times \text{total hits}}{\text{Seconds time} \times \text{small-arms rounds fired} \times \text{targets}}$$
$$= \frac{100 \times 250 \times 15 \times 42}{45 \times 513 \times 36} = 18.9$$

That isn't bad, but it can stand improvement.

Now we'll change sides. Lenoir, you're defending and know what you're to do. Knudsen, take your men up to that pine knob and be pasting targets until the war starts.

It's nine forty-five now—at ten forty-five we go.

Bear in mind I want a score of at least twenty out of you men in the Second Section—and you birds in the First watch your cover so you don't get slaughtered like the Second did.

TRAINING AREAS

Editorial by MAJOR (now COLONEL) ROBERT C. COTTON

(1919)

No MATTER WHAT the military establishment may be, it is essential that organizations and troops must be trained in selected areas. The old garrison or post system of training should not be considered; the experiences of the war have fully proven this. The selected areas must be in the nature of training centers and technical centers. The training center should comprise camps, cantonments, firing areas, maneuver areas and school areas. The technical center should comprise technical and special postgraduate school areas. In addition, there must be combined maneuver areas which should be of sufficient size to enable large bodies of troops of different arms to operate in combined maneuvers and with service firing.

These training and technical centers are necessary to enable the troops to function properly and at the same time to enable the officers and men to maneuver and drill in an atmosphere of their arm of the service. In addition, a means is offered whereby the necessary *esprit de corps* of the arm may be developed and increased.

The location of these training and technical centers is most important. They must be located in districts which will afford open weather throughout the year, thus giving the greatest possible number of days of outdoor work. Since the day of each arm operating independently is over, and since, to operate successfully, the different arms of the service must have a knowledge of each other and must be trained in combined maneuvers, the training areas of the different arms must be situated in close proximity. In addition, to secure the best result in this connection, the officers of one arm must be trained at various times with organizations of other arms.

In order to insure proper co-ordination and results, the training centers and technical centers, as regards training, instruction, education, and tactical inspections, must be under the general supervision of the Training and Instruction Branch, General Staff.

These are the general conditions which must be met, but it is not going to be easy to work out the detailed plans, without which any general statement will not carry us very far. We shall find that it is easier to establish a training camp than it is to abolish one, for training camps at once create local interests because they bring money. There is no community in the world which is not glad to have money spent in it, and there is no really live community which will not fight to have the continuance of that spending secured.

THE BATTLE OF THE FLAGS

By Major Whitenred and Captain Blackanblue

In the days of starvation rations as to Army strength, the enemy on maneuvers was often represented by a few men with flags. Sometimes the system of flags was elaborated until it was pretty complicated, as this gripe of 1937 shows.

> *They were tattered, they were torn;*
> *From many a battle were they worn.*
> OLD BALLAD

DID YOU EVER HEAR how one tired platoon captured a fresh, full-strength, high-spirited regiment? Well, it happened one bright day in May some four years ago. The platoon was covering the right flank of a division—covering it on foot. Since daylight it had crept through brambly bushes and around swamps, working ever farther to the flank to find an enemy, if any there was. About noon, sweating and thorn-scratched, the forty men of the patrol struck a fine wide road—a road, fortunately for the footsore, which had to be investigated.

A few hundred yards down the highway, just over a rise, the point saw fifteen reconnaissance cars parked well off the road. Hurrying back to the patrol commander, the point leader reported this news.

The patrol commander was young, vigorous, intelligent—a man, moreover, full of modern, if still somewhat vague, ideas on mechanization and motors. Here, if ever, was a chance to prove out modern war.

He crawled forward over the rise and looked. Through his field glasses he could see drivers lolling sleepily in the reconnaissance cars. Some little distance from the road he spotted thirty or forty officers eating their noonday meal under two large tent flies. They looked for all the world like a bunch of umpires refreshing themselves after strenuous labors. (That's what they were, in fact.)

The patrol commander went back of the rise and gave hasty orders to his men. The patrol closed up in an irregular platoon column and followed the leader over the rise, moving slowly and cautiously.

A hundred yards from the reconnaissance cars, at the commander's signal, the platoon ran forward and captured the cars. With rifles at their breasts the drivers were compelled to drive off down the road at full speed. As the cars pulled out cries arose from the assembled group under the tent flies. The platoon leader thought he heard someone yell, "You can't do that!"

The now-motorized patrol sped down the road at forty-five miles an hour. At a crossroad that should lead approximately toward enemy headquarters the leader signaled a turn.

Ten minutes more of speeding and there appeared, under a grove of trees, the hostile command post. It must be. For there were flags everywhere—red, white, red with white centers, white with red centers—speckled reds, speckled whites, flags leaning against bushes and trees, bundles of them lying on the ground.

The leader ordered his driver to head directly in toward the command post. There he halted, and as the other cars closed up and stopped he yelled, "Grab the flags and get back in the cars!" In ten seconds the job was done.

About that time a colonel came running toward the cars. "You can't do that," he shouted. "Your men are all dead. You've come through two outpost lines."

The patrol leader didn't argue the point. His driver merely stepped on the gas, and the other fourteen conformed. They tore out of enemy territory by another road and in due course reached their own C.P., where they delivered their load to their regimental commander.

The war was definitely over, for that day at least. It couldn't go on without the flags. All afternoon and far into the night the Blue and Red commanders and their staffs wrangled with the umpires and with each other.

The troops had a good rest.

The Blue commander finally convinced the chief umpire that in this day of motors initiative was just as valuable in warfare as in any bygone day. "Moreover," he said, "a raid is a raid, and when a raid hits through to enemy headquarters it's bound to startle somebody—and turn things bottom side up. Hell, the only thing I blame my patrol leader for is not bringing the whole Red command and staff in as prisoners."

As this story (a true one) indicates, a method of combat training in which the enemy is represented by flags has been in vogue ever since things began to settle down after the World War. At first flags were used in a simple logical way. Big flags marked the assumed flanks of the enemy disposition, a representation that was reasonable enough for uncomplicated small-unit maneuvers. But gradually refinements were added until now we often find something akin to chaos. We may find red flags representing machine guns, blue flags a line of infantry, square-centered flags a 37-mm. gun; when two flags are crossed they mean one thing; when vigorously waved they mean still another, and when they droop they mean something else. The variations are endless.

The business of memorizing what each flag and its gyrations stand for is a man-sized job. In fact, the unit that boasts the best memories, or whose commander schools it the longest in the flag codes, has the best chance for recognition and commendation, regardless of its tactical skill.

In a maneuver the flags move forward and the troops fall back; the flags retire and the troops advance. This is fantastic; it is a military minuet that has no connection with war. But, nevertheless, umpires solemnly critique the situation and tell trained organizations wherein they committed grievous errors in their phantom combat with the flags. Has anyone stopped to consider that the bewildered troops who fight these Alice-in-Wonderland battles have little, if any, idea what they are all about? For example: One lone flag may be captured by an alert patrol using excellent patrol methods. But the patrol finds to its chagrin that it has actually captured a battalion. After a severe lecture from the umpire the patrol is allowed to return to its parent unit, so that tomorrow all hands can again take part in the military minuet.

What must the soldier think of all this? And how does he get any great training from it? Unless he is a memory giant he will never remember what all these fluttering flags to his front mean. He can only wait dumbly for someone to tell him what to do. For that matter, many an officer has to thumb through his mimeographed poopsheets to find out what a flag means before he can decide whether the situation calls for a hasty retreat or the dispatch of a squad to gather in a sniper.

It is no easy matter to bring a salutary reality to the maneuver field, but we can certainly avoid such absurd and unreal devices as a flag-waving enemy. In no war will soldiers peer intently for, or at, flags. Flags fluttering or flags still will not determine the movement of assaulting troops. This will be determined in large part by the fire action of hostile men—men who are concealed. Each soldier will watch for men, and lead slugs from enemy weapons will determine his actions—not flags. So, too, officers will issue orders based not on flags, but on such things as terrain, cover, areas under fire, casualties, and similar elementary realities.

The argument that we resort to flags because we do not have enough troops is fallacious. A regiment of three battalions can install one in a defensive position and attack it with the other two. This will offer at least some of the elements of a war problem. The men know they are not contending against a line of perplexing flags but against other men who may be outwitted.

If three battalions are not available, then let us use what units are available. A platoon maneuvering against a section gets real training. So far as the individual soldier is concerned, his action in a small platoon problem is identical to what it would be if he were taking part in a divisional attack.

By playing unit against unit and by using blanks umpires will be needed only to point out the areas under fire and, when necessary, to control the maneuver. In this way we approximate realities. Of course it is not a close approximation, but it is a far better method than battling a bewildering array of flags.

But what about the staffs? How can they be trained without troops, or flags to represent the troops? It is difficult enough to train any large unit without a full complement of troops, but the problem is not made simpler by converting a significant proportion of the command into Chinese bannermen and using the remainder to train staff and commanders. Need it be said that a good command-post exercise laid out on the ground will work any staff into a lather and make most commanders do a little sweating besides? Meanwhile, the troops can be engaged elsewhere learning the combat duties of small units. When a section knows how to use its weapons and advance skillfully over varied ground, or knows how to dispose itself for defense, it has the essentials of a competent combat unit. The higher commanders have only to utilize this training. Their primary part is to make reasonably correct decisions as to how, when, and where these units will be used.

For a conclusion let us move on to 1942. [This piece was written, remember, in 1937.] The scene is a company command post in battle. A sergeant has just reported to his company commander.

CAPTAIN: What did your patrol find, Sergeant?

SERGEANT: Well, not much, sir. We got near enough to that hill to our right front to see enemy soldiers all over it. Then we went farther out to the right—six hundred or eight hundred yards, I guess, sir—and couldn't find a thing.

CAPTAIN: Hell's fire, Sergeant, that sounds as if you located the flank!

SERGEANT: No sir, it wasn't no flank, sir.

CAPTAIN: Why not?

SERGEANT: Because there wasn't no flag out there, sir. We looked all over hell and couldn't see one.

The moral is: Even if we go back to using flags simply to indicate flanks, a good deal of explaining will have to be done. Soldiers know a flag when they see one, and if they see flags often enough they'll know for sure when they don't see one.

BOMBARDMENT AND PURSUIT AVIATION

By Major (now Major General) Claire L. Chennault

The general impression obtained by reading all the articles the *Infantry Journal* ever printed on air warfare is simply that the ground soldier has wanted to see as clearly as possible the place of aviation in war. He hasn't been ready to believe that war could be fought mainly by machines. But he has believed they would have a big part in the whole combat team. What follows is selected from two articles by General Chennault dated 1935 and 1936.

THE BOMBARDMENT AIRPLANE is strictly an offensive weapon, but it fights *in its own element* only on the defensive. It is not designed or intended to seek combat in the air. When forced into combat by a hostile airplane, it adopts one of the defensive formations. These formations are adopted solely for defense against an aerial attacker and are not assumed in the presence of effective antiaircraft artillery fire or for precision bombing operations. Having assumed a defensive formation, the bombardment unit depends upon mutual fire support, volume of fire, and its characteristic of speed for its defense.

A great volume of fire is available for the defense of a bombardment unit. Each airplane in the formation is capable of carrying three pairs of machine guns, a total of sixty flexible machine guns for a ten-plane squadron. However, it will seldom occur that more than twenty of these guns can be directed upon a hostile force attacking from any given direction. This limitation is due to the fact that the traverse and elevation or depression of each pair of guns are restricted by the structure of the airplane. The effectiveness of bombardment's volume of fire is further reduced by reason of the fact that flexible gunfire from an airplane is rarely effective at ranges greater than one hundred yards. The size of the individual airplanes prevents the simultaneous delivery of effective fire upon any one point by all the units of the formation.

The speed of the bombardment unit contributes to its defense by reducing the time available for combat and by making it more difficult for an attacking force to engage in concerted attacks with elements approaching simultaneously from several directions. Speed also reduces the probability of the defending force intercepting the invading bombardment unit.

It is generally accepted that bombardment will enjoy a considerable superiority of fire in any combat where hostile pursuit employs the World War method of diving to the attack with small units firing successively. Under such conditions the bombardment force should succeed in penetrating to its objective.

The greatest danger from bombardment aviation lies in the possible failure of military authorities to appreciate its power. It may prove of decisive importance in any situation where adequate measures for effectively opposing it have not been taken.

These measures must be taken in peacetime; the declaration of war is too late for their initiation. Essentially they consist of the organization of an efficient aircraft reporting service, the maintenance of an adequate number of defensive weapons of modern types, the preparation of detailed passive measures of defense, and the maintenance of an effective land-based air force capable of, and charged with the responsibility for, conducting both offensive and defensive aerial operations.

· · ·

The mission of pursuit aviation in the Army zone of action then is twofold: first, to support all classes of friendly aviation and, second, to deny freedom of action to all classes of hostile aviation. Pursuit aviation, properly equipped and employed, is capable of accomplishing this twofold mission due to the relatively limited area of operations. Employment will depend upon the circumstances of the campaign, but offensive action only will assure effective results.

Today the consensus is that pursuit has two broad functional missions: first, the denial of hostile bombardment and, second, the support of the operations of ground forces. It is also generally agreed that pursuit requires two types of airplanes for these missions.

For the denial of bombardment, an "interceptor" type is required. The interceptor should be light, have a high rate of climb, should not require a high degree of maneuverability, and should have heavy guns capable of being fired accurately at long ranges at large, non-maneuvering targets.

For the support of the operations of ground forces a fighter type with the maximum degree of maneuverability is required. The fighter need not have the maximum rate of climb but should climb as fast as observation airplanes. It does not require heavy armament, for most of its combats will be at close ranges and of the maneuvering type. Rather than heavy guns, it should have small-caliber guns capable of extremely rapid fire. The fighter should carry more fuel than the interceptor to enable it to remain in the air for longer periods.

We have endeavored to avoid the expense and inconvenience involved in the development and employment of two types of pursuit airplanes in the past by developing a compromise "interceptor-fighter" type, or all-purpose pursuit plane. Recent improvements in both bombardment- and observation-airplane designs indicate that this compromise type will be ineffective for at least one, if not both, of its two general missions. A highly specialized pursuit airplane is required for each mission. The interceptor with its high rate of climb, wide radius of turn, and limited endurance is not suitable for close combat with maneuvering observation and fighter aircraft. Relieved from the requirement of close combat and violent maneuver, the interceptor may be built lighter with improved climb and slower landing speed.

The trend of technical development indicates that the time has arrived when a distinctive, highly specialized fighter airplane must be developed for the support of the operations of our ground forces. Failure to do this will result in those forces being compelled to attempt operations without adequate aerial observation while exposed to the attack of all classes of hostile aviation.

Certainly no commander would relish such a prospect, yet the German Army at the battle of the Somme in 1916 found itself in exactly this situation. With almost an equal number of airplanes, the German air service was helpless because a majority of their planes were not of the proper type and could not carry out the missions assigned them. Later an insignificant number of single-seater pursuit fighters brought down from the Verdun front under the command of Boelcke were able to restore a satisfactory measure of freedom of action to German observation and limit the operations of all classes of British aviation.

This situation may develop in the future unless the fundamental principles governing the functional employment of fighting-type airplanes are thoroughly understood and timely measures taken to provide the proper types and trained personnel. Should we go to war today, eighteen months must elapse before we could furnish effective support for our aerial observation. Furthermore, we could not prevent hostile aviation from operating freely in the Army zone until our deficiency in fighter-type pursuit could be reinforced.

The pursuit complement of our G.H.Q. Air Force is designed primarily for the interception of hostile bombardment. It is neither large enough, nor is it properly equipped for the support of ground operations. It consists of only three groups—as compared to a conservatively estimated requirement of nine groups for the support of four armies. Its principal mission is generally stated as follows: "To provide security from hostile aerial attacks upon our air force, airdrome areas, or bases." Certainly a pursuit force of the interceptor type is required for this mission, and it is equally certain that a force assigned this mission will not be available for other missions.

MOLLYCODDLING THE ARMY

From an article by GEORGE T. FRY

(1918)

IF ALL of the misdirected energy that is being wasted on plans to rescue the morals of the young fighter and protect his chest, throat, indigestion, and home-cooking appetite from ruin were devoted to providing the essential things for a real army, the aggregation that followed Old Man Xerxes over the plains would look like the Salvation Army compared to the Army of Freedom, and the Boche would be sending out distress calls in advance.

I can say, with absolute truth, that the amount of money spent in the country for the hire of press agents alone to exploit the various schemes for raising money for military "charities" exceeds the total cost of maintaining the German General Staff.

*   *   *

That is true enough, but on the other hand, they will know what war really is. It will be no abstraction to them. They will be like dwellers on the slopes of a volcano who have lived through an eruption. They will not forget that what has been well may be again.

*   *   *

If we are not to be lapped by a tideless sea, then we must prepare against a new flood tide. Shall we do it by universal training? Shall we do it by the intense training of a selected and scientific group who prepare themselves to deal out death from more effective weapons than the world has ever seen? Shall we close our eyes and go back to the old dreams? Even if the decision cannot be made now, it should, at least, be considered now, unless peace is to find us as unprepared as the present war.

HOW TO READ THE GROUND

By Captain (now Lieutenant Colonel) James W. Bellah

(1942)

YOUR MEN are going to drive the automobile, not manufacture it. So in teaching map reading forget the classroom, field manual, and training film and get your men out on the ground. If you throw the agonic line and polyconic projection at them in the beginning you kick them off balance, frighten them, and confuse them needlessly with terminology. So don't do it. Later you can use Field Manual 21–25 (*Elementary Map and Aerial Photograph Reading*) and Training Film 5–12 (*Map Reading*), but at first use the ground.

Reconnaissance on the terrain itself and so-called "map reading" are one and the same thing. They are not closely allied—they are unified. One without the other cannot exist in the well-trained military mind. It is your job as S-2 to force this unification and to do it in the most simplified, rational way possible.

So at the start march your detachment out to the nearest available terrain (right in the area will do) and bang three major principles into their heads. And bang them in!

(1) To know where *they* are on the terrain—*always*.

(2) To know how to locate other objects on the terrain—in relation to (or in terms of) where they are.

(3) To know how to transmit that information to a third party *who isn't present*.

When you have done that you have done your job, for in spite of all the books, lectures, and films in the world that is all there is to it.

So start with it. Halt the detail.

"All right, Goldfarb, where are you?"

"Me, sir? I'm right here."

"That's fine, Goldfarb—and it's *a* solution to the problem. But it's not *the* solution because it only makes sense if I am right here with you so that I can look in your direction and actually see you standing there when you say, 'I'm right here.' If I can't see you when you say, 'I'm right here,' you might be on the road from Dakar to Timbuktu or on top of the Empire State Building for all the good it does me to hear your voice. So let's suppose for the sake of the problem that I haven't said, 'Where are you?' but that I have asked you the question in a written message from a position ten miles away from you. Obviously if you write back, 'Me, sir? I'm right here,' it won't mean a thing to me, will it?"

Let's hope that Goldfarb agrees.

"So, then, Goldfarb, in order to position yourself to me when I am ten miles away from you (or far enough not to be able to see or hear you), it becomes necessary for you to tell me where you are in relation to something else on the terrain—something that I can see or something of which I know the position.

"To do this successfully you have to give me two items of information—the *distance* you are from the object and the *direction* you are from the object. Simple?

"Now, Goldfarb, if you pick a cow for the object she may move away, so pick something a little more settled in its ways. Can you see the number of that mess building behind you?"

"Building 1106, sir."

"About how far are you from it?"

"About fifty feet, sir."

"So, then, your first item of information—*distance*—can be stated as follows: 'I am about fifty feet from Building 1106.' Now, will you agree with me that the fiery yellow disk in the sky directly behind you as you stand facing Building 1106 is the sun? Thank you. And will you agree also that it has been the consensus for a great many years that the sun rises in the east and sets in the west? Thank you again. Will you now look at your watch and tell me the time?"

"Eight-thirty, sir."

"In the morning, Goldfarb?"

"Yes sir."

"Don't smile, Goldfarb. A.M. and P.M. are most important items in a military communication—or were until recently, when the twenty-four-hour system went in.

"That being the case, Goldfarb, the sun is still in a general easterly direction from Building 1106, and as you are standing between Building 1106 and the sun you also are east of the building. So you have your second item—direction—and your position on the terrain becomes 'fifty feet east of Building 1106.' Now, if I know where Building 1106 is, I know where you are, even if I am a thousand miles away. And that, men, is the entire essence of map and terrain work. That is the basic principle—all else is merely a further refinement of *distance* and *direction*.

"So now we shall start to refine direction. As I pointed out to Goldfarb, it has been the consensus for thousands of years that the sun rises in the east and sets in the west. Or, to put it more simply, it rises in approximately the same place every morning and sets on the opposite side of the horizon from the place of rising. Any savage, any child gets that firmly established in his mind because the sun is a dramatic phenomenon that forces its attention on all human beings early in life. You men get it firmly established now because the consideration of direction begins and ends with the sun. East—or whatever other word in a primitive language was first coined to indicate that point on the horizon where the sun rises—was the first 'compass' point known to man in his attempt to describe direction to other men. West—or where the sun sets—was the second. In the beginning there was no north or south because nothing very dramatic happened in the north or in the south.

"Then one day something dramatic *did* happen. Someone floated a sliver of magnetized steel on the surface of a cup of water (later on someone else balanced a similar needle on a brass fulcrum), and both men discovered that the needle always pointed approximately halfway between sunrise and sunset—that is, in the direction you faced if you kept the rising sun on your right. Where the needle always pointed became known as north. The point on the horizon opposite north became known as south.

"After that the sun no longer had to be visible in order to help man to know his directions. He carried a compass instead."

(Produce the magnetic compass and issue one to each man.)

"Now we call this instrument the magnetic compass for the very practical reason that its needle is caused to point in a northerly direction by magnetic attraction. Something up there in the north country—some huge deposit of iron ore somewhere near the top of the world—makes that needle point to it.

"But, whatever that something is, it isn't exactly at the North Pole. Get that firmly fixed in your mind now, for it's vitally important. The needle points in a northerly direction, *but it doesn't point to the North Pole.*

"We can't help that slight imperfection of the compass any more than we can help the slight imperfection of the sun itself which, as the seasons change, rises progessively farther south of east in the wintertime and progressively farther north of east in the summertime. If you use the sun to determine your direction you allow for this difference in summer and in winter.

"So allow for it with the magnetic compass. Remember always that the north the compass needle points to is that ore deposit, not the North Pole.

"We call the ore deposit the Magnetic North.

"We call the North Pole the True North.

"Remember both terms and what they mean."

You have now laid the foundation for a demonstration of annual magnetic change later on. Don't go into that refinement now. Get on with the general principles.

Now move your class away from Building 1106 into a new area. (Change terrain frequently to keep a class alert—to keep their minds active. Using the same terrain deadens them.) Disperse them so that no man is closer than fifty feet to another man. In rotation have each man, by reading his compass and judging his distance, position himself on the terrain in relation to his closest neighbors. (Spend a lot of time on personal tutoring in this basic exercise and your time later on will not have been wasted. Don't terminate the exercise until you are sure each of your men knows the fundamental principles of *distance* and *direction*.)

Your next step is to form the class in march column, each man with his compass, and slog through the area (this can be your physical training as well, as you can walk fifty paces and dogtrot fifty paces and thus harden personnel), changing direction frequently. At intervals you halt and call on men at random to position themselves verbally in relation to any near-by object that they pick out—by *distance* and *direction*.

The final step in this preliminary work is to mount up in vehicles and run through the same exercise (not stopping) at twenty miles an hour with a sub-instructor in each vehicle checking each man. Get rid of any man who can't get the knack of it after reasonable coaching. He won't do. Vary the vehicular work by firing a continual stream of questions at different men in rotation for testing general alertness. How far are we from that bald hill? Estimate the number of men in the truck column we just passed. How far back is the nearest gas station?

You are now ready to let them handle maps. Get out of the area and seat your class on open terrain and make a map issue. Disperse the class so that no man has the distraction of a close neighbor.

"Now, men, what you have in your hands is a map. I don't care a damn if you never learn the definition of a map, but what I want you to get firmly fixed in your minds is that maps serve as form messages for the transmission of information about the terrain. They are a drawing of the terrain with a lot of prepared information printed on them."

Spend a few minutes reading everything on the border of the map and see what you can make of it. Read everything and remember when the question period comes that there are generally three kinds of questions students ask:

(1) Questions that show up their own ignorance.
(2) Questions that show up the instructor's ignorance.
(3) Questions that show off.
Skip all of them and ask only for what you want to know.

"All right, Warburton, what have you found out about the map from reading the printing on the border?"

"Well, sir, it was prepared under the direction of the Chief of Engineers, U. S. Army."

"Therefore, you are justified in trusting the information it gives you?"

"I think so, sir."

"I think so too. If it was prepared by the Latvian Army I wouldn't be so sure that I could. You, Meiklejohn—what does the border of the map tell you?"

"It was made in 1942, sir."

"Good—that means it's pretty well up to date. All right, men, two initial points to remember. Always check to see *who made the map* and *how long ago it was made*. What's troubling you, Jones?"

"Sir, there are three arrows on the lower right-hand corner of the map's border all joined at the bottom but all pointing in slightly different directions. One says 'Magnetic North' on it, and that has half an arrowhead at the top; the next one——"

"Never mind the next one, Jones. Stick to that one for a moment. Tell me what you think it is there for."

"It has something to do with that ore deposit that isn't at the North Pole. Something to do with Magnetic North—the point my compass needle points to."

"Jones, you're getting dangerously close to the Officers' Candidate School. What has that arrow got to do with Magnetic North?"

"Well, sir, obviously it doesn't point to Magnetic North as I hold the map, because my compass needle is pointing to Magnetic North all the time and my compass needle is pointing in exactly the opposite direction to the arrow on the map. But if I turn the map around I can make the arrow marked 'Magnetic North' point to exactly the same place that my compass needle points."

"Do just that, all of you. Turn your maps until the arrow marked 'Magnetic North' is parallel to your compass needle."

(Here get in a stiff plug about interference with that compass needle by local ore deposits, the tin hat, rifle, heavily shelled terrain, presence of artillery pieces, etc.)

"Now then, what you have done quite simply by turning your maps so that they lie before you in the same relationship that the actual terrain lies before you is described in the Field Manuals by the word 'orientation.' You have 'oriented' your maps. It doesn't make a particle of difference to me whether you remember that word or not, but it is important that you remember what you have done to the map because you must always do that to any map before you start to work with it. You must turn it and so place it before you that it lies as the ground itself lies before you.

"As you look at your maps now every point on them lies in exact relationship to every point you can see on the terrain before you. Three inches above the point of that arrow marked 'Magnetic North' on the map, for instance, you see a lot of little square black dots fuzzing the intersection of four roads. That's the town of East Prairie on the map, and you will see a wavy blue line. That's Gunner's Creek. Now look up at the smoke again and look to the left of it where the ridge slopes downward and you will see the sunlight glinting on water. Well, that is the actual water of Gunner's Creek.

"Now, Jones, let's take up the other two arrows that are bothering you. The second one, instead of half an arrowhead on top, has a star on top. I'll tell you in advance that the star is symbolic of the North Star. Where do you think that arrow points to?"

"To True North, sir. Right toward the North Pole."

"What could be simpler? And now the third arrow—*and one more north to remember*. The third arrow isn't really an arrow on your maps— it is a continuation of a line that goes right on across the map to the top. This line, with lines parallel to it and lines at right angles to it, cuts the entire map into three-inch squares. Where the line is extended down to the other two arrows on the border of the map it is marked 'Grid North.' This is the third north to remember. Grid North, men, is merely the top of any map when you hold the map before you in a position to read the printing on it.

"Remember Grid North.

"We have now traveled a long way in the science of practical terrain work and map reading and we have not, as yet, read a book. I will a little later give you reading assignments, but *nothing that you read will be anything more than a further explanation, a further refining of these basic principles which you have already applied*.

"Now to scales. The map you have is about two feet and a half across and two feet from top to bottom. The terrain as you look at it stretches for miles in every direction about you. The map is a small diagrammatic drawing of a portion of that terrain—and it is drawn in exact proportion to the terrain.

"This is where you are on the terrain."

(Mark each man's map; or, better still, have him mark his position and check for correctness.)

"Now the road to East Prairie is right there at the edge of this field. Our trucks are standing on it headed toward East Prairie. Mount up in the trucks now and each one of you take the reading of the speedometer of your truck before you climb aboard. I am going to move the convoy from here to the town square of East Prairie, where you will dismount again and again read your truck's speedometer—and then tell me how far it is on the terrain from here to East Prairie. This is an A-B-C exercise, but let it make an impression on your minds because it is the essence of all scalework. Mount up."

At East Prairie the speedometer readings show that the distance traveled was three miles.

"Now look at your maps and tell me in *inches* by actual measurement how long the line is that represents that straight road from where we were to where we are now. Three inches. Good. The scale of this map, then, can be stated in this way: 'One inch on this map equals one mile on the actual ground.'

"If you will look at the bottoms of your maps you will see that scale drawn there for you. You will also see it drawn in yards and in feet. You will also see a fraction which reads: Scale $\frac{1}{62,500}$. But the important thing is that you have just proved to yourselves, by actual movement on the *terrain* and *actual* measurement on the map that one inch of distance on the map represents one mile of distance on the ground."

(Later you will further refine scales for them, giving them half a dozen different maps of different scales and discussing representative fractions, but for now you will still carry on with the basic principles.)

As you move the convoy to East Prairie you will quite possibly cross a railroad track. Halt there, show them the track, and with a stick draw in the dirt beside the road the map symbols for single and double tracks. Draw them four feet long. At a bridge draw the bridge symbol. In East Prairie point out a school with its usual flag and draw the school symbol. Ditto—church. Ditto—a house. Do this for the purpose of dramatizing the logic that pertains in the entire system of map symbols. They are then ready for Field Manual 21–30 to complete their education in symbols. Later you will further refine the matter of symbols by calling to their attention the fact that practically all Japanese and German map symbols are identical to United States Army symbols, but that the meaning in many cases has shades of difference and that eventually they must acquaint themselves with those differences for purposes of working with enemy maps.

"I told you previously that maps serve as form messages for the transmission of information about the terrain—that they are a sort of drawing of the terrain with a lot of prepared information printed upon them. We will now use them as such. You have in previous map walks and rides positioned yourselves without maps by giving your distances and directions from various objects. We will now position ourselves on these maps by reference to the terrain. You are all in the town square of East Prairie. You can all find that point on your maps and put a pencil on it. Now, when you mount up, watch the roads the convoy takes, keep a running reference to them on your maps, and be ready at any moment to put a pencil on those maps at the exact position you occupy on the terrain. Mount up."

Now twist and turn the convoy completely around the area at about twenty miles an hour, changing direction frequently and checking each man's ability to have himself positioned on map and on terrain interchangeably. Sub-instructors in each truck.

Your next step in this important preliminary work is a brief runthrough on the subject of co-ordinates. Make this simple. Pin a map to a blackboard in front of the class and square it off in blue crayon first. Mark each square by letters or numerals and show how information can be transmitted by reference to arbitrarily numbered or lettered squares if two such maps are identically prepared. From that go into the Military Grid System with as little talk on the genesis of the system as possible because they don't need it. They only need to know how to *position by co-ordinate readings.*

After your talk, which again should take place on the terrain—keep out of classrooms—give them another moving-convoy exercise on positioning by co-ordinates.

By this time—by the expenditure of possibly ten to fifteen intensive hours of vital work—you have done your part of the job—done it well and done it soundly. Take your men into a theater now and run off Training Film 5–12 (*Map Reading*) for them. This is a magnificent tie-up film for them and should clarify in their minds any small questions that may be bothering them.

Follow it by supervising for another two hours a contour exercise in the field on an actual hill, with a map showing that hill in contours. Walk up and down that hill—better still, walk up and cover it and down the other side with continual reference to the map. Mark the actual hillside at the points where the map shows contour lines and thus pound that subject home, which invariably bothers most people no matter how much map and terrain work they have.

Your next tie-up is an exercise on working out differences between Magnetic and True North and Grid North—combining with that the running of Magnetic, True and Grid azimuths.

Close with your final scale talk and a demonstration of various scales. Keep this simple and as free of technicalities as you can, but drive all of your points in simple words, with simple, dramatized examples—and allow the men to do the work themselves.

You now have an intelligence detail that has the simple rudiments of terrain and map work firmly fixed in its minds by demonstration and actual doing.

We have omitted so far only one fairly important item. This war, we are coming to believe, is no longer the Spanish-American War or World War I (whatever that was), but is, instead, this war (whatever this war is)—and it is, among other things, more of an aerial-photograph war than it is a map war. Furthermore, every time you get away from the territorial limits of the United States the map supply falls off radically, the quality of maps goes rapidly downhill, and the large-scale map practically ceases to exist. When you have air, however, you can almost always get a presentable photo map and get it quickly.

So take the maps away from your detail now and substitute photo maps and polish them off by running through the whole exercise quickly once again with the photographic representation of the terrain. Teach them its limitations and its advantages, but, above all, teach them to prefer it to the drawn map—because we are only a short step from the three-dimensional photo map, and when it becomes general in its use most of our map and terrain problems in warfare are solved.

Finally, teach your men the sanctity of a map in combat. Impress it upon them that their lives and their comrades' lives may depend on one map. Keep that map from wear and tear; protect it from weather; mark it sparingly—cherish it always as a valued possession from the very start, because many a man alive today and many a man who still lives tomorrow will owe his life to the care of his map and the carefully acquired ability to read it and read his terrain.

TACTICS ISN'T COMMON SENSE

By Impertinax

(1937)

"There's nothing to tactics but using common sense."

Well, old soldiers never die, they say. And since phrases are notoriously longer-lived than their originators, presumably that one, like the babbling brook, will go on forever. Certainly, whenever and wherever tactics is mentioned someone comes out with it. You even hear it at service schools where they should know better.

Usually the someone proceeds to prove the worth of this pearl by quoting the formula of successful generalship credited to General Nathan Bedford Forrest: "Git thar fustest and with the mostest." As if this second catchword proves anything except that the general probably produced it on the spur of the moment [There is good reason to believe he never said it at all.] in order to silence some simpleton who plagued him with demands for the secret of his victories. Nevertheless, the listeners nod agreement and try to look wise and full of homely common sense.

Now, a good phrase is a dangerous thing. To cite but one example, "Rum, Romanism, and Rebellion" cost James G. Blaine the presidency. The trouble is that, true or false, people tend to believe a well-turned saying, however specious. Especially is this so if it caters to vanity or purports to be the signpost of a primrose path leading to success. And, of course, using the second aphorism to bolster the first makes an appeal to both human failings at the same time.

You say to yourself: "Hell, I'm just chock-full of good, sound, ordinary sense. I'm the possessor of normal intelligence. Why should I waste my time studying, endeavoring to evolve rules for a science that has no rules?

"Look at Forrest. He had little formal education and no military. Yet he got along. Even Jackson, Lee, Grant, and Napoleon received but a scant military education compared to mine. Obviously, the secret is common sense. Therefore, when the squeeze is put on me, I'll just dip into the old horse sense and clean up."

It sounds good, brethren. But I can't believe it. I've spent years swallowing yarns like that, but this time I pass. I won't even try to believe it.

To be sure, the illustrious gentlemen mentioned above were not educated officers after the modern fashion. But I deny that any of them, even General Forrest, lacked a higher military education. The point is, their Leavenworth and War College was that hard school whose tuition is casualty lists, lost battles, and the fate of whole peoples. True, Forrest had no military background, but he had what was infinitely better—an alert brain. He learned fast. Long before the Civil War ended he had mastered the principles of his own peculiar brand of warfare and constantly applied them.

It is ridiculous to say the solution of a tactical problem is a matter of common sense. Regard the other four of our list. "Mad Tom" Jackson rode against the foe with a Bible, Napoleon's *Maxims,* and a sack of lemons jostling each other in his saddlebags. In his fanatic heart reigned an iron god. His stern, gray eyes perceived every enemy weakness and refused any human weakness to his men. In his brilliant, dour mind revolved the plans that changed "Mad Tom" to "Stonewall." Do you name Lee the apostle of common sense? The gambles he accepted, the plans he conceived would never even have occurred to a general of common sense, but only to one of uncommon sense. Yet Lee was a fine tactician; his battles were the bulwark of one nation and almost the bane of another. Then Grant is your man! "I'll fight it out on this line if it takes all summer!" So stuffed with common sense was Grant that he was a middle-aged failure until the Civil War brought problems that demanded an unusual star. The man who dreamed of condensing Europe into an empire. The man who married a Josephine and divorced her to establish a dynasty. The general who confounded his common-sense opponents. Napoleon's intellect bore the same relation to common sense that an eagle bears to an ant: namely, they are not even the same species.

To carry this farther, *Field Service Regulations, U. S. Army, 1923,* contains military principles derived from experience just as are an actuary's tables of mortality. Both eliminate the errors of common sense. They are mathematically true over a period of time. Does your com-

mon sense tell you that "a strategically defensive mission is frequently
most effectively executed through offensive action"? Does your common
sense tell you that the safest place you can be is your home? Any insurance company can prove by figures that the contrary is true.

Let us, then, quit classing as a basic ingredient of tactical ability the
type of intelligence that tells you to come in out of the rain. Let us admit
that a high, even an unusual, order of intelligence is a requisite. At the
same time we should remember that the ability to think straight and to
the point requires exercise. Intellect grows.

We should stop doping ourselves with, "There's nothing to tactics but
using common sense." Instead, our young officers should be told:

"Tactical ability is founded upon a clear understanding of tactical
principles. It requires high intelligence and hard study to gain that understanding to the degree necessary in modern warfare. Even then, please
understand, you won't be a Napoleon. But you will be an asset to your
country."

DON'T OVERDO SOMETHING

Editorial by LIEUTENANT COLONEL (now MAJOR GENERAL) E. F. HARDING

(*1937*)

THE HIGHEST REWARDS in the military profession go to men of action.
This is as it should be, for armies are essentially instruments of emergency,
and emergencies require timely, positive action. The soldier who cannot
make decisions promptly and act upon them vigorously is not qualified
to lead troops no matter what other talents he possesses. There may be a
place for him in the military world, but it is not a place of command.

All this being universally accepted, our Army training emphasizes the
"do-something" doctrine. Since many—we nearly said most—of us are
prone to procrastination, we heartily endorse the idea. But it should be
recognized that there is some danger in it. For often the urge within and
the pressure without is to do the one thing that reason tells us is all
wrong.

Since wars began, this "do-something" obsession has driven leaders
of all grades to order attacks that had no prospect of success. Military
history teems with examples. It was the "do-something" urge that impelled McDowell to launch his abortive offensive at Bull Run against his
better judgment. It drove Burnside's Grand Divisions against the heights
of Fredericksburg in one of the most senseless frontal attacks on record.
At Gettysburg it sent Pickett against the Union center in a costly attempt

to salvage a battle already lost. The billy-goat tactics of the Western Front furnish hundreds of case histories—and not all of them are from foreign sources. Ask any American who participated in the fighting along the Vesle.

The fault is not with the slogan but with the distraught commander who interprets it to mean that he must seek a major decision forthwith. His mission is to defeat the enemy in his front. The higher commanders, the head of the state, the people at home, all expect it. The enemy's position is immensely strong, but our masters are impatient. We attack, and the history of military disaster is enriched by another bloody repulse.

We can reduce the butcher's bill of future wars by educating officers to interpret our typically American watchword intelligently. For instance, we might make it plain that its implication may sometimes be served merely by sending out a few patrols or making a personal reconnaissance. Above all, we should stress the point that "do something" doesn't necessarily mean to fight.

By way of clearing the ground for a better understanding of the "do-something" shibboleth, we might stop parroting that fallacious catch phrase, "It is better to do the wrong thing than to do nothing." The only excuse for such advice is that doing nothing is sometimes worse than almost any positive action. But, like all half-truths, this one can lead to serious error. The danger in it lies in the encouragement of hasty, ill-advised activity. Moreover, it completely overlooks the fact that the need for positive action in many situations may be fully met by *purposefully* doing nothing at the moment.

INFILTRATION

By Captain E. E. Hagler and Captain (now Colonel) A. R. Walk

(*1920*)

"Infiltration!" With what sinister, almost occult significance the word was first regarded. It was applied by the American troops in the Marne salient early in June 1918 to describe the method by which the enemy began his counterattack, working as snipers, small patrols, and finally increasingly larger bodies between our deployed units . . . particularly where they had become slightly diverged. About this time infiltration was made the subject of a general order, which indicated counterprecautions.

The French had already become practiced in this to such an extent that after July it might almost be called their normal method of advance. It is curious that of all the French units, those most adept in this style of fighting were the colonial divisions and those troops who had seen service in Africa. Our own "extended order" is a development of Indian fighting, and infiltration is nothing more than this same Indian fighting specially applied to meet such modern weapons as the machine gun, auto rifle, hand grenade, and rifle grenade. It is directly in line with the whole history of American infantry methods.

CO–ORDINATION OF THE ATTACK

By Major General J. F. C. Fuller, British Army

General Fuller is one of the foremost writers on war in the English language. His many books, all written with force and clarity, contain a greater body of sensible discussion on the hundred aspects of war than the works of any other living writer. The article appeared in the *Infantry Journal* for January 1931.

As a brigadier it occurred to me one day, after the close of the collective training season of 1930, to consider what I had found to be the weakest link in the harness of my regimental officers. I soon came to the conclusion that it was planning, and more particularly planning in the attack, which today includes so many uncertain factors—increased fire power, new arms, and imaginary ones. I feel that as regards this weakness most brigadiers will agree with me, and though I in no way pretend to be an expert of any kind, as a basis of thought and argument I have written the following brief paper. In it I do not intend to go into detail, but, instead, to elaborate a few general rules of guidance which are common to most forms of attack.

First, it must be recognized that co-operation between the arms is largely the result of co-ordination in the plan; second, that an attack is like any other physical operation. For example, take carpentry. A carpenter has an idea in his head; he has tools to work with and material to work on. In the attack there must be an idea in the mind of the commander, an idea as to what he intends to do; there are various arms—his tools—and the material is represented by the enemy and the ground. There is, however, one great difference: part of the material—the enemy—is alive and working against the plan. His plan is the unknown quantity, like immensely exaggerated stresses and strains in the carpenter's wood.

To co-ordinate simply means to work, to plan—that is, in harmony—

for no plan is purposely elaborated to create discord. If fighting were altogether like carpentry a plan could be an exact one, like a blueprint or a drawing; but this, in fact, is exactly what a plan cannot be, and because the material is alive it has to be, instead, not an inexact, but a flexible plan. That is, one which can be adjusted to circumstances—and be it remembered that common sense is nothing more than action adapted to circumstances.

The plan must also be a simple one or as simple as possible, because if simple it can be more readily adjusted. How simple it is depends almost entirely on the object of the attack. A carpenter may be called upon to make a packing case or a cabinet; the one is a much simpler piece of work than the other, yet the simplest piece of work can be done in a complicated way should the carpenter possess little understanding. Simplicity in war is one of the tests of efficiency because, as in carpentry, it saves time and material.

We thus arrive at three fundamental ideas in planning, namely:

(1) The plan must carry out the object;
(2) It must be as simple as possible;
(3) And as flexible as possible.

If soldiers will remember these three points, a foundation of rock will be laid to their planning.

What, now, is meant exactly by flexibility? Flexibility is like elastic; it is power to move where you want to without shattering your plan.

If the enemy can stop your plan working, in seven cases out of eight your command will become rigid and fixed. Conversely, to fix the enemy is the first step toward gaining flexibility. Therefore, flexibility is gained by so distributing your arms that the chances are that you will fix the enemy before he fixes you.

How is this done?

The first thing to do, which is obvious, is to find the enemy and find out all you can about him, and never rest content that you know enough of his affairs, and never suppose that you know all of them. Never paint a mental picture of what the enemy is going to do—that is, imagine something which you do not know for certain—and then act as if it were a true picture. Buying fakes in war, as in the salesroom, is not a paying proposition, and when you create your own fakes and "mug" yourself into believing that they are masterpieces, no one will sympathize with your loss.

The second thing to decide is where you intend to attack and with what force. You have got to attack to hold, and you have got to attack to hit. Should you surprise the enemy you will hold him morally in place of physically and greatly economize your force. But in such cases remember that should your surprise fail, lack of physical clinch may bring the whole of the enemy's forces on top of you; therefore, the more risky a surprise is, the stronger must be the reserves wherewith to meet the unexpected, and they must be located in such positions as will enable them at the shortest of notice to clinch.

Thirdly, you have got to protect your attacks. All attacks require a defensive, or protective, base to work from. "The whole art of war," says Napoleon, "consists in a well-reasoned and extremely circumspect defensive, followed by rapid and audacious attack." The protective troops are the bow and the offensive the arrow of the attack, for though the protective troops do not propel the offensive ones forward, they do break down the resistance to their advance, which is much the same thing in the end.

Lastly, you must be prepared to meet the unexpected; therefore, you will require reserves.

There are consequently three categories of troops in every attack:

(1) The attackers divided into those who hold and those who hit;
(2) Troops which protect the attackers;
(3) And reserves.

Your plan of attack is therefore an equation between these three forces, the object, and the enemy. Consequently it needs much working out. The usual mistake is to look upon the attackers as a close-up and the reserves as background detail. This is altogether wrong and may be compared to fishing with a rod, the top joint of which is heavier than the butt end. It almost always leads to loss of control. Napoleon once said: "I attack to be attacked." What he meant was that he threw forward a small fraction of his forces for the enemy to bite on, and when his adversary's jaws were fixed he moved up his large reserves—the capital of his tactical bank— and struck his real blow. Here is another saying of his: "Victory is to him who has the last reserve."

Now comes what would appear to be a difficult question to answer. Where is the decisive point of attack? For this point is, so to say, the pivot of the entire operation.

The decisive point is the rear of the enemy and not his front. It is always the rear, and when it is impossible to attack the enemy's rear, then the point selected must be in relationship to this true goal of the decisive attack. That the rear of an enemy's army is the point to hit at should be obvious. If I can stab a man in the back, that is the safest way to kill him. Should he see me coming, and should I be able to maneuver him into a bog, and so fix himself, I can equally well carry out this operation. This should accentuate the stupendous value of fixing an enemy in war. The vital point in an army is its rear, just as the vitals of a man are in rear of his skin. If I hit a man on the jaw it is to upset the rear of his head; if I fire a bullet at him it is to hit his vitals and not his skin—to scratch an enemy only annoys him.

Frequently an enemy has a very strong jaw and a very tough skin, and as its front more often than not protects its rear, it is impossible to strike directly at the vital point. In such cases a flank should be chosen—that is, a spot near to the rear—and when this is impossible and a frontal attack has to be made, then its object is not to destroy the enemy's front but to penetrate it so that flanks may be created and a way opened to his rear.

We thus obtain three orders of attack, which in importance are:

(1) The rear attack;
(2) The flank attack;
(3) And the frontal attack.

Whichever is decided on, then that part of the enemy's army which it is *not* intended to envelop or penetrate must be held back and pinned to its ground so that it cannot move toward the point of attack.

Now we must turn to another equation, that of our force in relationship to the nature of the ground and the enemy's force.

To take the ground first. It can either assist or resist you; also, it can assist or resist the enemy. Its assistance and resistance is threefold in nature. It can facilitate or impede.

(1) Observation;
(2) Protection;
(3) And movement.

The advantages of gaining and restricting observation are so obvious that I will examine only the last two characteristics.

Today we have two main categories of attacking troops—armored and unarmored, or petrol-driven and muscle-propelled. The first carries its own protection; the second does not. The second, however, as far as infantry are concerned, can move over more difficult ground than the first, but their average speed over normally good going is far less. Surely, then, it is obvious that:

(1) Tanks should be used over the open spaces;
(2) Infantry should be used on the broken ones;
(3) And tanks should be employed for outflanking operations.

A carpenter uses his tools according to the nature of the work and the material he is working on. He may sometimes use a chisel as a screw driver, but only if he is lacking the latter tool. Each of his tools has a purpose, so also has each weapon. By means of a combination of tools he fashions his packing case or cabinet; so also in war it is through a proper combination of weapons that battles are *economically* won. Every tool is paramount in its own proper sphere, but no single tool is paramount over all other tools—so also with weapons; there is no God Almighty in the Ordnance Department.

Use weapons according to ground and you cannot go far wrong.

To turn now to the enemy's force. You may or may not know what the enemy intends to do; nevertheless, the ground and his communications will often tell you what he is likely to do. Step into his shoes and look at the ground from his position. As you are going to attack him, he is probably on the defensive. Should he not be, then you must force him to defend himself before the decisive blow falls. The weakness in the defense is that the defender cannot be certain where the blow will fall. As long as he can move he may be able to frustrate the attack; therefore, fix him.

This now becomes your first problem. What part of your force will you require for this operation? It does not necessarily follow that you will require an equal or a superior force to the one you intend to fix. The whole art in this operation of war is to fix a large force by means of a small force. You can do one of three things:

(1) You can attack him;
(2) You can threaten to attack him;
(3) You can bluff.

Now as to your second problem, not the attack proper, but the reserves. What reserve force will you require? What are reserves for?

(1) To meet the unexpected;
(2) To support the attack or the defense;
(3) To pursue or cover a retreat.

When you have settled this point you can then turn to your decisive attack and see what you have left over for it.

It may be said, "This is a very cautious way of proceeding." My answer is that nowadays there are so many bullets flying about on a battlefield that caution has become a high virtue, as high as, if not higher than, courage itself. Few things are so expensive as a shattered attack. Large numbers in the decisive attack are not usually essential, but the following factors are:

(1) Surprise, which morally multiplies numbers;
(2) Concentration of force, which means superiority of weapon power at the point of attack;
(3) The fullest possible protective power to safeguard the attack.

Having settled all these points, we must consider two other factors without which co-ordination can remain but a theory. These are control and supply.

The brain is the chief controlling organ of the body. Note where it is placed. At the forward or top end of the body. In battle the force headquarters represents the brain, and they should be as far forward as it is safe to put them, and all the subsidiary headquarters—artillery, tank, and cavalry—should be close up to them. Remember that the force headquarters controls all the arms and services; remember also that every yard of cable which is unnecessary holds within itself a possible breakdown. Distance in war is not so much a matter of miles as of communications. What is your power to communicate? That will tell you what your radius of action is. In your plan of attack you must remember this, for loss of control means paralysis.

Lack or loss of supply may mean starvation, and in battle itself supply is largely a matter of getting ammunition up and its converse—getting the victims of the enemy's ammunition down. It is no good launching an attack which cannot be supplied; and remember also that in this day of aircraft, armored forces, and motorcars the front of an enemy does not necessarily protect its supply services. To cut these out is like removing the stomach from the body. They are the ultimate goal of the decisive attack or pursuit, for an enemy without bread and beef is soon reduced to a starving mob.

Co-ordination in the attack, which may be defined as the intimate relationship between functions, while co-operation is the intimate relationship between actions, depends on:

(1) Correct distribution;
(2) Rapid control;
(3) And adequate supply.

Distribution is arms fitted to ground in relation to the enemy and the object. Its aim is:

(1) To pin the enemy down—initial attack;
(2) To keep a reserve in hand—for unexpected attacks;
(3) And to carry out the decisive attack—final attack.

Control depends on:

(1) Full information of the enemy;
(2) Full information of our own troops;
(3) And rapid communication of orders.

Supply depends on:

(1) Adequate transportation;
(2) Good and safe roads;
(3) And traffic control.

If these four trinities are remembered, the result will go a long way toward establishing unity of action, which is the ultimate goal of co-ordination in the attack—"United we stand, divided we fall."

MACHINE GUNS

From an article by CAPTAIN (now MAJOR GENERAL) ALEXANDER M. PATCH

(1920)

IN OPPOSING our present methods of machine gunnery I am conscious of an unpopular and unsympathetic task. The kicker is rarely a welcome figure; more particularly is this the case when the burden of one's theme is a subject concerning which there exists a pronounced lack of general interest.

It is a significant fact that, of all accessible literature on military science, that pertaining to the subject of machine gunnery is the least definite and instructive. The technical aspects of the machine-gun science have been covered in clear and comprehensive form and may be found in various texts and independent articles, but treatments touching tactics and organization are, in the main, meaningless and unconvincing. Modern machine gunnery is a new science whose prominence and vital importance is a development of the late war, and obviously there is a pressing need for sound and understandable literature dealing with all of its phases. Yet this is only possible after the service has come to the point of general agreement and accordance concerning the fundamental principles of the subject.

ARMORED INFANTRY COMBAT TEAMS

From an article by COLONEL (now BRIGADIER GENERAL) T. J. CAMP

General Camp was editor of the *Infantry Journal* from 1931 to 1934. The following is from a 1942 article.

IT SEEMS more and more clear that time and space will wreck armored forces unless relatively small units are combined into balanced combat teams. Any tank commander who has to send back for help may lose out while help is coming. But if he has his whole team at hand time is in his favor.

TOWARD AN IDEAL

By INVICTUS

(*1937*)

THE FACT that the much-maligned efficiency report has remained substantially unchanged for all these years is prima-facie evidence that no better instrument has been devised. But in spite of this the hue and cry persist, and this certainly argues with equal eloquence that something is wrong. In this brief paper I intend to show what that something is and at the same time suggest a practical, workaday corrective.

First, it appears desirable to clear the ground in order that my footing may be apparent to all. To this end I make two admissions. First, I concede that there are now and that there always will be a few officers who allow their prejudices to run away with them. These will submit reports in which they deliberately underrate or overrate their subordinates. Second, I agree that there still remain a few die-hards who refuse to admit that anyone short of Bonaparte could meet the War Department definitions of "excellent" and "superior." Fortunately these two groups are so small that in a broad consideration of the subject they are virtually negligible. It is my considered belief, then, that all other officers conscientiously attempt to make the efficiency report an accurate and impartial appraisal of character.

And there is precisely where the system breaks down. The War Department evidently assumes that by the time an officer is called upon to evaluate his brothers he will be a qualified judge of character. Just how far from the truth this is is best evidenced by the riotous and ridiculous inconsistencies that mark nearly every officer's efficiency file. Of course in theory every officer is a leader, and it is the business of the leader to know men. But we are blind, indeed, if we accept this pronouncement of a theoretical idea as an axiomatic truth.

We are members of a practical profession. We do not take kindly to theory, nor do we traffic in assumptions that cannot be proved out of hand. We place our faith in schools, in training, and in salutary indoctrination. Since these things are true, it is strange, indeed, that we are willing to rely on a species of intuition in dealing with the most difficult and most important branch of military knowledge—the human psyche.

I am aware that this statement will be contradicted. It will be pointed out that from the first day of our service we begin our study of man; not out of a book, but in a laboratory of practical experience. That contention is only a half-truth. The laboratory is there, but the number of officers who *consciously* apply themselves to a study of the specimens it contains is amazingly few. We observe the men and the junior officers with whom we work in much the same manner that we observe a body of water. We see only the surface and the manifestations of the surface. We have no idea what lies beneath. It is because we base our character appraisals on these surface manifestations that the efficiency graphs do such an erratic dance.

Let me put it another way. How many of us deliberately set out to study the character of those who work under us? Do you, for instance, make it a matter of duty to discover the weak points and the strong points of your subordinates? Do you examine their daily conduct through a psychological microscope to determine their emotional range? Do you study their action and reaction under the stimulant of success and praise and under the depressant of failure and rebuke? Do you interest yourself in what they read? In what they think? In what they admire? In what they fear? In what they dislike? And in the "why" of all these things? Do you consider the amount of leisure at their disposal and find out how they utilize it? Now be honest with yourself. Do you really do these things? Do you know anyone who does? I'll leave the answers to you.

In any event, I think you will agree with me that only through such a searching and continuous study can we arrive at a true evaluation of our subordinates. The question, then, is this: Can we train those officers who are now growing up in the service and those who have already grown up to probe beneath the superficialities of character and discover the true man? I think so. Here is the method I propose.

First, let us deal with the newly commissioned officer. The responsibility for his training devolves upon the company commander under the direct supervision of the battalion commander. The regimental commander is at least morally charged with the duty of seeing that his subalterns are properly trained. Henceforth a fundamental part of that training should consist of a directed and continuous study of man and his behavior.

This is the way that study should be conducted. The new arrival must first of all be shown that the theory of leadership virtually presupposes an intimate knowledge of human nature. The fundamental necessity of this knowledge must be emphasized. The intelligent company commander will buttress his explanation by citing striking examples culled from his own experience in peace and from the experience of others in war. He must be particularly careful to underscore the point that this knowledge is not intuitive but comes only through conscious and continuous study.

Following this, the captain must explain the efficiency report. He must show the young officer that in effect it is a military character sketch of one man by another. He must stress the fact that it is the controlling factor in an officer's career and that the responsibility devolving upon the reporting officer is a grave one indeed. He must show that in order to discharge this duty equitably a profound knowledge of man is necessary.

After some such orientation as this the new lieutenant will be told that his training in this difficult subject will start immediately. The noncommissioned officers in his platoon will be the initial subjects for study. At the end of three months he will be required to submit a complete efficiency report on each of these men. He will be warned that the company commander will require him to justify (either orally or in writing) every entry he makes on these reports and that his own ratings in "judgment" and "intelligence" will be materially influenced by the soundness of his justifications. It must be made unmistakably clear that the mere process of filling out the reports is relatively unimportant, the big thing being the thoroughness and accuracy of his detailed observation during the three-month period as evidenced by the justifications he will be called upon to make in defense of his ratings.

This training procedure should be continuous throughout the ten years an officer is required to serve in the grade of lieutenant. By the end of that period he should be a capable judge of character. His powers of observation should be needle-sharp. The process of studying those under him should be a matter of second nature. In addition to these manifest advantages he will have made out hundreds of efficiency reports with the knowledge that every entry had to be justified in detail and that no glittering generalities would do. Can anyone successfully contend that ten years of such training will not produce a tremendous improvement in an officer's ability to justly evaluate his brothers-in-arms?

But this merely provides for the lieutenants. True enough, the system, if universally applied, will eventually result in an officers' corps thoroughly indoctrinated with the ideas I have tried to present. This, of course, is the goal to be sought, but in the meantime isn't there something we can do to quicken the judgment of those who already occupy the reporting grades? I believe so. I believe we need merely modify the method I have already outlined and move up a step or two in the chain of command.

This is what I suggest. Let each regimental commander assemble his battalion and company commanders and tell them that he intends to institute a training device designed to encourage a more accurate evaluation of subordinate officers. This device is in no sense to be construed as an infringement of a reporting officer's right to evaluate a subordinate according to his own judgment. It is merely intended to aid him in achieving greater accuracy. To this end battalion commanders will submit jawbone reports on their company commanders to the regimental commander, and company commanders will submit similar reports on their lieutenants to battalion commanders. These reports will be submitted about January 10 and will be held in strict confidence. As soon as they have served their purpose they will be destroyed.

In each instance the first concurring authority will require the reporting officer to justify every entry he makes on a report. Generalities will not be accepted as satisfactory explanations. When an officer is unable to give a clear-cut, logical, and factual explanation of an entry it should be pointed out to him that that entry is unfair, whether it be superior or unsatisfactory, for it shows a complete lack of detailed study and observation. This should be remedied before the official report is rendered, or the reporting officer will clearly show himself deficient in several items under which he himself must be graded. This is not a threat. It is a statement of fact. The officer who can give no adequate reason for an entry he makes on an efficiency report can scarcely be regarded as a man of sound judgment or satisfactory intelligence.

This device properly used should produce worth-while results. If, however, the overzealous convert it into a threat or seek to use it as a means whereby they, rather than the responsible officer, dictate the report, the whole purpose will be defeated. Used as a training medium and as a practical method of forcing reporting officers to study those under them as they should be studied, it will work.

I have discussed this proposition in considerable detail with one regimental commander and one battalion commander. Both have been enthusiastic over its possibilities and both have decided to put it into effect in their commands. Certainly, in justice to the individual and in justice to the service, it merits a trial. That trial will undoubtedly disclose collateral benefits that I have not touched on in this paper. Thus I commit to your hands an idea that has lived long in my mind. I trust that it will not die a-borning.

À BAS ELIGIBILITY!

By Major General Johnson Hagood

(*1937*)

THE ARMY has a predilection for tying its hands by establishing rigid rules of eligibility that eventually interfere with the most effective use of military personnel.

The procedure for regaining the freedom of action that is properly the prerogative of those responsible for the efficient administration of the Army varies. It may take the form of expanding the eligibility lists until they are meaningless. Otherwise the obstacles to placing in key positions the officers whom those in authority consider best qualified must be circumvented by a resort to technicalities. For instance, officers who for one reason or another are not eligible for detail on the General Staff are *attached* to the General Staff and serve in such capacity at almost every corps-area headquarters. They do the General Staff work, but they cannot wear the General Staff insignia or enjoy the prestige that attaches to serving on a General Staff detail. Some of them lay down their tools and go off to school to qualify for the same work they have been doing in superb fashion.

There was the case of an officer who served on the General Staff before the World War. He was re-detailed on the General Staff and served in that capacity in France during the entire period of the World War. He received the Distinguished Service Medal for his wartime General Staff work (he also received a Silver Star Citation). He was a distinguished graduate of the Infantry and Cavalry School, a graduate of the Staff College, and a prewar graduate of the Army War College. After the war, while serving as chief of staff of a corps area, he received word that he was not on the General Staff Eligible List and for that reason would be forthwith relieved from duty with the General Staff.

This blow was somewhat alleviated by the statement that he would shortly be subjected to a purifying process. He would be sent back to the Army War College to take over again the course in which he had already graduated and would by this means be made eligible to perform the duties that he had already been performing with marked distinction for a considerable period of years. And that is what was done.

The common-sense practice of utilizing capable officers in staff positions regardless of technical disqualifications for the performance of such duty brings to the fore the whole question of eligibility.

Now the purpose of an eligible list is to isolate certain supermen especially qualified for some particular class of duty. In theory all others are thereby excluded from performing that work. The inherent difficulty is that the smaller the eligible list, the greater the number of qualified men excluded therefrom. And the larger the eligible list, the less excuse there is for its existence.

I hold that the average American Army officer is qualified to perform any duty in the Army (line officers are excluded from medical work, but medical officers are not excluded from line work). When I say "qualified" I mean that they are better qualified than the average of those who have performed corresponding work in the past or will perform corresponding work in the future *in time of war*. In a great war we will have to have from three to five hundred thousand officers. Is it not ridiculous, then, to say that there is any type or class of ordinary routine peacetime duty that cannot be well performed by the average young officer of the regular forces? I say "young" because, in my opinion, age and other physical infirmities are the only limitations. It is an advantage for an officer to have had a college education, to have gone to West Point, to have been graduated from the service schools, to have exercised an independent command, to have had duty with the civilian components, to have served under the tutelage of able superiors. But Napoleon had none of these advantages, and no one of them is necessary to fit an officer for the performance of routine duty.

A man's qualification to perform staff duty is a matter of fact or a matter of opinion on the part of the man who wants to use him. It has no relation whatever to any artificial set of human standards established by law or regulation.

Up to 1920 we had no General Staff Eligible List. Prior to that date General Staff officers were selected by main strength and awkwardness. This system brought to the fore men like Colonel E. H. Crowder; Lieutenant Colonel Henry P. McCain; Majors George W. Goethals, William P. Duvall, and Montgomery M. Macomb; Captains John J. Pershing, Peyton C. March, Joseph T. Dickman, Charles H. Muir, Charles T. Menoher, William G. Haan, Dennis E. Nolan, and others of the original 1903 General Staff who today might be classed as military illiterates, since they were never educated in a General Staff school. They, like Bell, Liggett, Craig, McCoy, Malone, Moseley, Fox Conner, and others, crashed the General Staff for a period of fifteen years, but still the Army and the country managed somehow to survive. In the World War, civilians and ex-Quartermaster sergeants served creditably—even with distinction— as General Staff officers. Then with peace came the sudden realization of the importance of protecting ourselves by an eligible list.

And consider our experience in the selection of general officers. Evidently the old-fashioned method of picking out such men as Grant, Sherman, Sheridan, McClellan, Lee, Jackson, Beauregard, Johnston, Pershing, Wood, March, and Bliss was all wrong, for we now have a law providing that generals should be selected only from colonels carried on the eligible list.

It would be difficult to name the particular American officers who served with greatest distinction during the World War. But merely on an ex officio basis we may be excused for suggesting the following:

The commander of the A.E.F.	1
The army commanders	3
The corps commanders who had active service at the front	7
The commanders of the S.O.S.	2
The American representative on the Supreme War Council (Bliss)	1
The chief of staff of the Army (March)	1
The head of the War Department Supply System (Goethals)	1
The author and administrator of the Draft (Crowder)	1
The commander of the Army of Occupation (Allen)	1
The commander of the Siberian Expedition (Graves)	1
The father of preparedness (Wood)	1
Total	20

None of these except Liggett and Bliss had ever been prominently identified with the service schools. The significance of this would appear to be that intrinsic character is more important than the ever-changing military technique taught at Leavenworth. The schools are tremendously important, but there are other things that count.

Every ambitious officer in the Army wants to go to school. He will sacrifice anything for a school detail. But he does not thirst for knowledge. What he really wants is to get the schools on his record. And the sad part of it is that many of the best officers in the Army are eating their hearts out because Father Time has beaten them out in the race. While serving in the grade of captain they become forever ineligible for promotion to general. At least that is what they fear.

The present General Staff with troops is picked by corps-area commanders, by chiefs of staff, by Gs, and by others who, without access to records, paw over the voluminous eligible lists. In many cases they ask for men whom they would not recognize if they met them on the street. The original General Staff of 1903 was picked by a board of officers who knew their men. That day may come again.

It is all right to have a preferred list. It is essential to have men slated in advance for high command in war. It is of prime importance that we should develop in time of peace a system of selection that we could use in time of war. But we should not have a fast-running stream of eligibility which carries down the great mass of mediocrity and leaves behind in the eddies some of the best men in the Army.

THE LEGION OF THE LOST

By INVICTUS

(*1936*)

In the 1930s the facilities for attendance at the higher Army schools, such as the Command and General Staff School at Fort Leavenworth, Kansas, were so limited that it was not possible to send for the intensive years of instruction even all the officers of the Army of appropriate age whose records were superior. The result was that some of the finest officers in the Army who stood a little down from the top in actual record grew more and more deeply disappointed. For it was then believed, with good reason, that an officer who did not receive the higher education would be, to all intents and purposes, barred from promotion to general. Invictus, then (in 1936) a captain, made the most forceful statement of the situation to appear in print in the article below.

Invictus did, however, in the end, attend the Command and General Staff School. He is today commanding a combat regiment. And it has worked out in this war that able men are having their chances at battle leadership and high promotion with little regard to their education in the higher military schools. The period of preparation has been long enough for those who have it to show their stuff and receive assignments of increasing importance. The higher schools are daily proving the value in future wars of their command and staff training. But those with ability who miss the schools, owing to the artificial limitations discussed by Invictus, are not being overlooked by any means.

I HAVE NOT BEEN to Leavenworth and, barring an act of God, I am never going. The reason is immaterial: it may be too many "satisfactories," or too many bad breaks, or too many years. It may even be some dismal little ghost that clanks its chains whenever an adjutant general approaches my 201 file. But that is all unimportant. The only thing that counts is this: I am not going to Leavenworth and I know it.

With those words and that knowledge I automatically qualify for permanent membership in that thriving and fast-growing brotherhood—the Legion of the Lost. Frankly I would sell my membership in this order for a song, for I find my fellow legionaries a sorry lot. Their shoulders sag; their eyes are lackluster, and they continually weep in their beer. This was not always so. For more years than you need know I tramped the long infantry road with these same men. They were a different lot then. Their step was elastic, their eyes bright, their jaws firm, and they downed their beer to a rollicking soldier song. Yes, they were a different lot then, and it was an honor and a pleasure to share the dusty road with them. But now they are fit company for nothing better than the perpetual enjoyers of ill-health; they have abandoned their claim to the proud profession of the soldier.

Because I know these men and their worth, and because I am distressed at the dry rot eating out their hearts, I am going to give them hell. If they retain even a vestige of that sturdy common sense that characterized them a few years ago they will recognize the justice of my indictment on the one hand and on the other will see that their situation is not as hopeless as they believe.

Let's approach this whole Leavenworth question on a solid basis of facts. These are few and simple. The Command and General Staff School can accommodate just so many students and no more. Of that number the Infantry quota is about seventy-six. To select these there has to be some basis of comparison. At present there is only one—the efficiency report. Therefore, the efficiency report is used. These records are divided according to the age brackets; the thirty-eight officers in each bracket who have the best records go. And that is the beginning and the end of the Leavenworth selection, despite your fine rumors of influence, political and otherwise.

There are your facts, and not all the bellyaching in the world will alter them one whit. Therefore, you have only one course left open to you—accept them.

Very well, you accept them. But that doesn't help your morale at all. If anything, it steps it down another notch, for in the very acceptance you acknowledge the fact that the Leavenworth door has swung shut on you and that your career is at an end. Let's examine this career angle a bit, for therein lies the root of all this monstrous bitterness.

Now I could well start off by reminding you that our old friends, the Great Captains, worried along to their immortal niches in history without benefit of service schools. But that will not soothe you because you will immediately point out that there were no service schools in those robustious days and that if there had been this gentry would have made the very first list. Oh, would they? Are you sure of that?

I wonder if the undisciplined, hard-drinking, hell-raising Alexander would have made the grade in our democratic Army? How many superiors would the effeminate, army-hating young Frederick pull down today? Would Caesar, whose military activities did not begin until something after forty, ever see his name on a Leavenworth list? How far would the monumental intolerance and contemptuous attitude of the aristocratic Wellington advance him in this day of higher military education? And how would the one-eyed Hannibal fare, or the hump-backed Luxembourg, or the undistinguished Grant, or the illiterate Forrest? No, my fellow legionaries, I am forced to the sorry conclusion that these great and near-great soldiers and hundreds like them were not Leavenworth caliber. That is an item that merits a little thought when you can spare a moment or two from your discussions and damnations of the current selections.

But let's get back to the matter at hand. You are not going to Leavenworth; what are you going to do about it? At present you are doing a number of very silly things. First, you are bellyaching that fact night and day to anyone who will listen. You have become past masters of the alibi and apologists par excellence. Curiously enough, you appear ignorant of the fact that your unwilling audience is generally bored by your harrowing tale of injustice and usually contemptuous of the individual who displays his emotions for public inspection.

Second, you are tearing into those fortunate and decidedly worthwhile men who have made the list as if your own career depended upon the thoroughness with which you demolished both their professional and private reputations. Friendships of long standing are forgotten, and forgotten also is that ancient act of Congress which proclaims you officers and gentlemen. In passing, it might be worth while to remind you that the venomed word seldom reaches its target but always its originator.

Third, you take particular delight in exposing the absurdities, the fallacies, and the injustices inherent in the existing method of selection. Surely you must know that those grave deficiencies are thoroughly recognized by the War Department. In fact, it is likely that they can point out many flaws that have never occurred to any of us.

There can be no question that they would welcome a new and foolproof system. Yes, I know you have one, and it's a honey; it would land *you* out in Kansas at the beginning of the next school year. If, however, you put it up to a vote it would pull down only a handful of supporters—those who would directly benefit by it. The rest of the Army would howl. Actually I am willing to lay a bet that any ingenious soul who can devise a more equitable system will be rewarded with one of the much-coveted Leavenworth scholarships.

Your fourth current activity is entirely in keeping with your first three. Those of you who feel that you still have a chance, no matter how remote, are deliberately turning on the heat. You confront your immediate superior with the statement that your future lies in his hands. You must

have a superior report or you are through. Those who have grown shame-
less in their desperation put it up to their commanding officers bluntly;
the rest do it by indirection and innuendo. It is a shameful thing to see
an officer divest himself of the pride and dignity of his position and
adopt the role of mendicant. Think it over, my brothers, and try to
visualize the contempt you would hold for such a beggar-at-arms. But, in
addition to that, consider the position in which you place your commanding officer. In effect you tell him that by one word he can forever
damn you. That is a terrific load for any man to shoulder, even when he
knows that the supplicant is far from the definition of a superior officer.
And unfortunately the responsibility has been too great for many a reporting officer. At the present rate it will not be long before we have the
absurd situation of an officer corps that is solidly superior.

The fifth and final consideration applies to those of you who know full
well that Leavenworth will never be graced by your presence. You have
accepted that fact and with it you have adopted an out-and-out defeatist
attitude. "What's the use?" you say. "We're licked. We're through." And
your work reflects your words and your thought.

Now, my confreres, this fifth point is the real reason for this paper. If I
can convince you that you are not licked, that you are not through, then
this unprecedented mass hysteria will gradually subside and with it will
go the ridiculous and unsoldierly practices that I have already enumer-
ated. Of course, if you have closed your mind to the matter and take a
certain masochistic pleasure in your self-appointed martyrdom, then
neither I nor anyone else can induce a more rational state of mind. And
indeed I am not at all sure that it would be worth while if we could.
Therefore, it is only to those who have not yet reached the ultimate
hinterland of defeat that I offer the following observations.

For the past few years I have been conducting a one-man Institute of
Public Opinion. To pink-cheeked second lieutenants, to leather-necked
colonels, to sour-pussed legionaries, to graduates and non-graduates of
Benning, of Leavenworth, of the War College, I have asked this question: "If war broke tomorrow and you had any choice in the matter,
what duty would you elect?" To date there has been only one answer—
"Command duty." Even when the subject at hand was noted as a cork-
ing good staff officer and notorious as a poor troop leader, the reply was
the same—"Command duty."

This merely illustrates the well-known fact that we came in this man's
army to be leaders of men and we still cherish that idea. When the drums
start the long roll we don't want to be trapped in a swivel chair behind an
imitation-mahogany desk. Now the question is this: To whom will these
command plums fall on M day? The Leavenworth boys? Well, let's see.
Two years ago the course at that famous school was cut to one year

in order to double the number of graduates. This was not, as many of you seem to think, a benevolent gesture on the part of a paternal War Department. Armies are not run by altruistic motives. Actually the Leavenworth output was doubled because it was discovered that there were not enough graduates to man even half the *staff positions* in the major units of a wartime army.

So what? So this—you uneducated barbarians of the legion are going to roll to battle at the head of fighting commands—battalions and regiments. And that, mind you, is only a beginning as I hope to show you in a minute or two. But meanwhile where are our Command and General Staff School friends? If you call the headquarters rosters of our wartime divisions, corps, and armies, you will locate them nearly to a man. Their fighting tools will be ranged about them—maps, Humphreys scales, road rollers, colored pencils, typewriters, and that great god of modern warfare—the mimeograph. Will they be content with this role of glory? Well, would you?

Now so far you agree with me, but beyond this point you have objections. You are willing to admit that you will fall heir to a battalion or a regiment, but to a higher command—never. If you base this assumption on a month or two of war you are perfectly correct unless, of course, the existing system is changed, as it may well be in the event of a major scrap. Yes, the brigade, the divisions, and the corps will undoubtedly go at the start to the alumni of dear old A.W.C. But if the war goes on for a while, as wars usually do—what then?

You know the answer to that one too. France, Germany, England, Russia, the United States—all of them learned the answer in the Great War. They found that the hot shots in peace were too often just that—hot shots in peace. The result then and the result tomorrow will be the same: the roads to the rear will glitter with fallen stars.

And where will the *new* stars blossom? On the worthy and deserving shoulders of Leavenworth's old grads? A few will, but only a few. To discover the reason for this you need no more than a superficial knowledge of human nature. These men will be passed over because of two things—because they are too good or because they are too bad. If a commander finds his G-men batting close to 1.000 he will move heaven and hell to keep them with him. He can't advance them beyond the grade appropriate to his staff or he will lose them. Nor can he celebrate them too widely lest they be taken away by some higher commander for his own staff or to head a fighting unit. Therefore, with rare exceptions, the better the staff officer, the smaller his chance. You needn't take my word for this; verify it yourself by the people who know what happened in the last war. As for the others, the washouts, they are either herded back toward the S.O.S. or sometimes given a chance with the line. But at the best they have two strikes against them and they know it.

All of this brings us back to the question asked a moment ago—where will the new stars blossom? And the answer is pat and final. Most of them will fall to you howlers in the outer darkness who have established your claim to them *by preparation in peace and performance in battle.*

At this point my colleagues will manage a hollow laugh: this preparation in peace—where will it come from with the halls of higher learning forever closed to us? That question, actual or implied, marks the curious blind spot of the average Leavenworth shutout. Today, with service schools or without, an officer's professional knowledge is limited by only two things—his will to learn and his ability to learn. Never in the history of this country or any other country have there been such opportunities for the student of war. Military libraries abound. Invaluable books on the art of war are published at popular prices. Current thought of foreign armies is abstracted in English, indexed and cross-indexed, and published four times a year for the mentally thirsty. Month by month the service journals interpret the past, proclaim the present, and attempt to divine the future. And finally out of hallowed Leavenworth itself come the extension courses—the heart and soul of that very learning you pant for.

Now, my brothers, if your talent be so sickly that it must be spoon-fed by those highly competent practitioners at Leavenworth or die, then it is better for the Army's sake and for the country's sake that it die now. Do not delude yourself with the idea that that great school can make a Frederick out of a Daun or even a Daun out of some of us. Not all the schools in Christendom will ever make a great commander; the great commanders will make themselves with, without, and possibly in spite of schools. When Gibbon says, "The power of instruction is seldom of much efficacy except in those happy dispositions where it is almost superfluous," he speaks a fundamental truth. The Legion would do well to keep it in mind.

But peacetime preparation does not begin and end with cerebral activities. Physical and moral preparation are at least equally important.

Of the physical side I need say nothing: its necessity is self-evident, and our profession itself is admirably adapted to building and maintaining a robust health. I mention it here only to remind you that it is still a talisman of successful battle leadership and that without it you might just as well reconcile yourself to a noncombatant role.

On the other hand, moral preparation does require a few words by way of explanation. At the present writing few of you legionaries are morally equipped to wage war, no matter how great your erudition or how stout your health. The Leavenworth madness has eaten away your moral resiliency. In your overemphasized adversity you have gone down. You have lost the *will to succeed.* You have forgotten that anyone can give a dazzling performance on the crest of the wave but that only the morally great can fight their way back to that foaming crest after it has broken over them. In war only the morally strong survive. The battle-fields of the world are littered not so much with men who were defeated as with men who *admitted* they were defeated. Had our Revolution been led by a man less endowed with this moral quality than Washington we would probably be part of the British Empire today. Had little Prussia had anyone at the helm but Frederick she would have gone the way of Poland.

Today you are confronted by a situation that is fundamentally artificial. Its importance exists more in your minds than in actuality. If your moral stamina is of such a saffron hue that it cannot surmount and subdue this specter of peacetime failure, surely the most elementary common sense must tell you that you are not morally equipped to dominate and lead a fighting command.

I can offer no sovereign remedy for this moral jaundice. It is not a collective problem. It is an individual problem, and the individual must solve it himself. If he does not solve it he is no more prepared for battle command than a six-month-old child.

In summary, then, your peacetime preparation falls logically into three interlocking spheres—the educational, the physical, and the moral. Prove yourself in these and I think you need have no concern about your destiny in combat. If you succeed there, your rise to the major command roles will not be predicated upon graduation from any school—not even grammar school.

And so at long last I come to the final question: What if there be no war? For the benefit of any of our pacifist brethren who might happen on this essay I hasten to explain that this query is not a lament for war. No, whatever else the legionnaire may be, he is not a death-and-glory boy; the years have left that behind. With that momentary digression at an end, I turn to the matter of our remaining years on the assumption that peace endures.

First, then, a dip into prophecy. Regardless of the merit of the present system of selecting students for our two senior schools, the fact remains that it is enormously unpopular. Year by year the opposition grows, and that opposition does not spring exclusively from the ranks of the legion. Therefore, I foresee the day, and that not far off, when this rigid system must and will be discarded. In its place I look for some adaptation of the out-and-out competitive method used by the French in connection with their École Supérieure de Guerre. Whether this be better or worse than our existing system is relatively unimportant. The important thing is this: it will, at a single stroke, excise the cancerous growth that afflicts our officer corps today. And for that reason, if none other, it is coming and coming soon. Thus for many of you the door that now seems irrevocably closed may yet swing open.

Of course I realize that you will not accept me in the role of prophet.

But even if you did it would scarcely elicit any enthusiasm if you happen to be in your late forties or suffer from ulcers of the duodenum, fatty degeneration of the heart, or kindred ills of the flesh. So then I discard the prediction and have at the matter as it stands.

Now, my worthies, a little G-2-ing reveals three thoughts that nourish this Leavenworth lunacy. They are:

(1) No Leavenworth—no prestige.

(2) No Leavenworth—no hot detail.

(3) No Leavenworth—no War College—no stars.

Since these things disturb you I award them a few paragraphs.

I think you will agree with me that prestige is not absolute but relative. Moreover, you will admit that there are two types of prestige: the prestige that goes with a position such as the presidency of the United States or the command of a regiment, and the prestige that accrues to an individual as the result of an outstanding performance in some position. For instance, you may have established a considerable reputation as a company commander, or S-3, or rifleshot. So long as you occupy that particular role and continue to measure up to past performance, just so long will you enjoy the prestige that accrues to a highly competent company commander, S-3, rifleshot, or what have you. Remember this: prestige does not accrue to the person who is theoretically best but to the one who actually demonstrates that he is best. I rather imagine that there were a good many men much better qualified theoretically for Forrest's job than was Forrest, and yet Forrest seemed to hang onto it without any difficulty.

That's one point, and here is another. Leavenworth breezes off with the reinforced brigade, bears down hard on the division, and tapers off with the corps and Army. The War College starts off in the military stratosphere and ends there. All this is very fine and very necessary, but when these graduates return to compete with you as company and battalion commanders I fail to see wherein their knowledge of the corps and Army is going to be any great help in the jobs they are going to be called upon to do (General Staff assignments are something else again). When the Old Man looks over your outfit and your competitors' he will look for results—not diplomas. You still enjoy a fair field and no favorites.

A final word on this prestige business. How many of you know, as a matter of fact, whether your battalion or regimental commander is a graduate of either Leavenworth or the War College? My poll showed that darned few of you knew or cared. Those officers were your seniors and they enjoyed the prestige and the respect that went with their positions regardless of their school record. If they acquitted themselves well they enjoyed the second type of prestige I mentioned earlier. All of this should suggest that the Army is not pointing a finger at you and saying,

"Yah, Bill Jones didn't get to Leavenworth." No, my brothers, memory is brief and interest transient unless preceded by the little word "self."

Now for the hot-detail question. Perhaps I should preface this with the hoary observation that "one man's meat is another man's poison." Failure to make the prep school for the War College blocks you from the General Staff Eligible List and so from all the staff jobs open to those boys. I'm sorry, but I can't get around that one. If your heart yearns for a desk job in a corps-area headquarters in a big city you have my sympathy but not my understanding. With our own troop commands plus National Guard, Organized Reserve, and R.O.T.C. assignments, we have a field that no one man can master. What matter if some Guard or Reserve outfit demands a Leavenworth man? There are plenty of other outfits that don't, and it's a big country. You will find plenty of hot details in those four categories, not to mention others that occasionally pop up for the deserving, such as a tour with the faculty or tactical department at West Point, a language detail in China or Japan, an attaché job if you are well heeled, and so on. You will gather that I am not convinced that the hot detail is reserved exclusively for the Leavenworth alumnus.

This brings me to the third thorn in your flesh—no peacetime stars. Right you are, my lads; there will be no peacetime stars for us. But as a matter of interest how many stars are reserved, say for the current Leavenworth class? That class is some two hundred strong. Less than half will get to the War College. And of these about six will wear stars. Meanwhile, compute if you can the years of fantastic labor, scarred by worry, envy, and bitterness, that end in heartbreak for those who ran well but not best.

Finally, I suggest that you conduct a thoroughgoing self-examination. It is just possible, you know, that you might not be Leavenworth material. And if you discovered that fact yourself it might help you to soften your opinion of those who discovered it a long time ago. Of course there are many of you who have more than met all the requirements for this school and yet will never go. Indeed, it is said that in the Infantry alone the number of eligibles comes close to the thousand mark; this year seventy-five go. The deduction is too obvious to make.

But whether you be deserving or undeserving, you must somehow contrive to evolve a personal philosophy that will restore your sense of values and your sense of humor. We have many years left before us. There are still fine things to be done. There are still good soldiers to lead. There are still rousing songs to be sung, tall tales to be told, and good company to share. And if all these things leave you unmoved I offer you this last thought: At the end, though we boast neither the heavy-hearted honors of war nor the tinseled badges of peace, the flag will cover us as closely and taps will sound as sweet.

THE GOVERNMENT OF THE ARMY

From an editorial by CAPTAIN (now MAJOR GENERAL)
GEORGE A. LYNCH

(*1916*)

. . . EVEN the best-intentioned man may become so blinded by his own personal interests that he will in all sincerity advocate fallacious measures without a suspicion as to their fallacy. "Doctrines," wisely said Colonel Montaigne, "are the offsprings of emotions." He might have added that their professors often have no idea as to their real parentage. Certainly the emotion of self-interest has given birth to some strange doctrines of national defense in our Army. Self-interest places before the eyes a veil that makes it extremely difficult to see clearly on any military subject.

As we have already said, it will not do to brush aside this question of personal interest as a matter of inconsequential detail affecting the individual only and having no bearing on the efficiency of the Army as a whole. Without unity of purpose on the part of individuals there is no such thing as collective efficiency. Unless our military system can be so modified that individuals are constrained by interest to seek for the same ends, it is idle to talk of military efficiency. Our first and greatest problem is to devise some means of harnessing all this energy that spends itself in the advancement of purely personal interest, to the chariot of military efficiency, or at least to prevent it from clogging the wheels.

OVER, SHORT, & DAMAGED

By G. V.

In time of peace military property causes many a headache—to the careless officer. Practically all military property except "expendable" materials—things used up at a steady rate—have to be accounted for periodically. Every item with a book value is "signed for" by some officer. Thus when a commander of an infantry company, for example, is transferred to other duty, the new commander has to count the property and sign for it in order to relieve the first commander of his actual money responsibility for it. In terms of money the property in the possession of every such unit as an infantry company and artillery battery, or air squadron or cavalry troop may run into six figures and is always a matter of five figures.

The problem often came up of taking over property from a close friend. The friend who was leaving was usually anxious to get away on leave of absence before going to his new duties, and the friend who took over—if a bit weak-minded—might hurry through the count of the property and sign up and then three or four months later regret his haste when he had to dig several hundred dollars out of his pay to make up for shortages.

The following piece, dated January 1938, is one officer's solution to this situation.

IN ALL THE YEARS I have been reading the *Infantry Journal* I do not recall having seen an article or even an editorial squib dealing with the painful yet unavoidable business of taking over property. Some time ago I hit upon an idea that seems to help when turning over the keys of the royal storerooms, so I offer it for what it is worth.

Of late I have made it a custom, whenever it has fallen to my lot to count "screw drivers, rifle," and "chests, carpenter, tool, w/contents," to sit down beforehand and compose a letter to the responsible incumbent soon (and painlessly, he invariably hopes) to be relieved. The following is what I write:

MY DEAR CAPTAIN BLANKFILE:

(It is best to hold to this formal tone, even if you have known the bird you are relieving for the past twenty years.)

I once knew a supply sergeant who was considered a Napoleon of supply. His greatest feat was to convince a salvage officer that two worn-out sheets were, respectively, a somewhat bleached and shrunken "tent, wall, small," and its accompanying "fly, tent, wall, small"—worn out through the customary fair wear and tear in the military service. Unfortunately for us both, but on this occasion particularly for you, I am aware not only that this prodigy of supply has long since left the service—to turn his talents toward more remunerative rackets—but that his like does not exist within our ranks today, although your own supply sergeant is no doubt nearly as hot.

I am also aware that you are in a sweat to get your clearances and go on leave and that you feel confident that I will do my best to make the severance of your ties with Company B as painless as possible, since we have always been on the best of terms and have settled any small wrangles we may have had amicably and unofficially. But, again unfortunately, I have to inform you that since 1929 it has been my lot to keep the wolves from the respective doors of no less than seven brothers and sisters and their families, not to mention supporting my own aged parents and also those of my wife. Thus it is that I must hereby warn you that I shall count your property as it stands. I shall take all the time I need to count every item on your memorandum receipts at least twice, and anything of real value, thrice. Moreover, I shall not be able to imagine that a "screw driver, 7-inch," can magically assume the proportions of a "screw driver, 13-inch." Or that your numerous china, chipped and cracked, is safely covered by your allowance. [There was a money allowance for this, but it was minute.] Nor shall I feel called upon to spend the next three months pleading with the quartermaster to change my (your) nomenclature [of property items so that something not listed but on hand could be substituted for something similar that was missing], or in working out a system of fines through which I can make up for your china. Nor shall I feel it incumbent upon me to swipe tablespoons out of my own personal kitchen table to replace any of yours that may be bent, broken, or missing. And finally, I cannot accept, in lieu of anything you may be short, anything that you may be over—for example, "3 tent poles, odd," for a "boiler, 10-gallon, w/faucet."

In fact, much as I hate to say it, from the moment I step into your supply room tomorrow to begin my count, friendship ceases—but only, I hope, temporarily. And I shall emerge on the third, fourth, or fifth day thereafter with the most accurate over, short, and damaged list you will ever be privileged to examine.

If my count jibes to a hair with yours I shall rejoice doubly. But if it doesn't, I shall also have to rejoice in moderation, for yours will be the funds that go for the shortages and not my own.

The most courteous thing that occurs to me as I close is to hope that you may someday have the pleasure of taking over property from me in turn.

> Yours very sincerely,
>
> G. V.

AH'S HAPPY

By Captain Tracklink

(1937)

EVERYONE'S HOWLING about uniforms—how they should be cut, worn, and tinted. Everyone, that is, except yours truly. Nope, ain't nobody writ on my efficiency report: "This officer shows a marked aptitude for whistling down rainspouts, imitating Napoleon, and hooking rides on ice wagons." To date many have questioned but none have proved my sanity. Why, then, do I like my uniform? *Bueno,* I show you.

1 pr. coveralls	$ 2.50
1 pr. drawers	.50
1 pr. socks	.25
1 cap	1.25
1 pr. shoes or laced boots	4.75
1 leather jacket	8.50
Total	$17.75

That little sum will just pay for one good garrison cap and postage! Here I am all dressed up and nowhere to go, but just for the hell of it I'll go into the field. I want to sleep. O.K. *I sleep*—as is—and when the stillness of the night is shattered by the bark of a motorcycle all I have to do is yell, "Turn 'em over!" I am all dressed and ready to listen to the latest dope from the front.

If not sleeping I am eating. I reach into my pocket and pull out three sandwiches made with *buns,* not slices of bread. This type of sandwich can be stepped on, rolled on, and compressed to rice-paper thinness without losing any of its desirable characteristics. From the same or another pocket I pull a Bull Durham sack of tea, swirl it around in a can- or cupful of water. While the resultant mess may not be the nectar of the gods it is wet and hot or cold as conditions permit. Sack of tea lasts about a week.

Another thing I like about my costume—pockets, plenty of them. One for maps, pencil, message book, and notebook. Another for a change of underwear and socks. Plenty of room left for pistol and ammunition, first-aid kit, cigarettes, and odds and ends.

For a touch of swank I sport a web belt with pistol and canteen and two dabs of white paint on each shoulder. The latter to prevent Private Bogie from saying, "Git th' hell outta my tank," when verily it is *my* tank, as my insignia show.

I used to look pretty crawling across the parade ground in a two-hundred-and-forty-dollar o.d. uniform, teaching scouting and patrolling, but now! I am not pretty; I have B.O. (also T.O. and E.O.—transmission oil and engine oil); my costume is wrinkled and torn and scattered with grease, but, by golly, I am

(1) *Comfortable;*
(2) *Cool or warm,* according to the weather;
(3) *Ready* to fight, frolic, or foot-race;
(4) *Ah's happy.*

SHIRTS, WOOLEN

By Captain Tenderhide

(*1937*)

THE NOTION that a service uniform should be designed to meet the conditions of service in the field is slowly finding recognition. Eventually our Army may be ready to go to war minus constricted circulation and slow strangulation. There is one garment, however, that no one has yet seen fit to attack with the asperity it deserves—the woolen o.d. shirt.

Next, perhaps, to the shirt of hair, with which monks of olden time kept the flesh at bay and the spirit humble, no coatlike garment can be more uncomfortable. Possibly in cold weather the wool shirt causes no great discomfort except to the sizable percentage of us who find harsh wool irritating and itchy at any temperature. But when the sun beats down and the wool shirt becomes wringing and impermeable with sweat, shutting out every slightest seepage of air to the pores—then is when it inflicts an inexcusable torture upon the hides of those who must wear it. Solid areas of prickly heat break out on chest and back. Scratching and wanting to scratch use up one third of the energy that would otherwise go into training and fighting. And plain overheating from lack of air to the skin uses up at least another third.

Once it was believed that a woolen shirt kept a man from cooling off too suddenly and thus prevented pneumonia or some lesser respiratory attack. It was supposed to have some virtue, too, like the woolen belly-band, in warding off dysentery. Both are old wives' tales. Dysentery, we know well enough by now, must be swallowed to catch it. And the heat exhaustion to which the wool shirt makes a man liable in hot weather gives him a far easier entry to pneumonia than an ordinary chill. This was clearly demonstrated by experiments conducted in Panama more than ten years ago.

What do the fifty million men of the United States do when they get hot in summer? They take off their coats whenever custom permits, or leave them off entirely if custom doesn't bother them. And what do the fifty million do when they feel cool? They put their coats on again. Certainly they do not, in the midst of a heat wave, wear a thick-woven, scabrous, heat-retaining garment on the off-chance that the coming of sundown or a sudden thundershower will bring on a chill. Even an athlete waits until his exertion is over before he throws a sweater around his shoulders.

As a matter of medical fact, the risk of chill to a man not near the point of exhaustion, however hot he may be from exertion, is a small one. We seem, most of us, to suffer little damage from electric fans and air-conditioned buildings on the hottest days. And if a man has performed his exertion in light, suitable clothing—a cotton shirt—he will not be as near the point of exhaustion as if he had been ironclad in sodden, heavy wool.

In cold weather the wool shirt gives us little additional protection. In extremely cold climates perhaps it may be desirable in combination with woolen coat and overcoat. But this, too, is debatable. For in a warm building the wool shirt is almost as uncomfortable as in midsummer. And you can't take it off when you go indoors.

What we need in place of the wool shirt is a light, tough jacket of wool or leather that we can slip on and take off as we need to, like the rest of the fifty million—a garment that can be folded into a small space and carried on the belt or in the pack or musette bag. This would be ample protection against chill in summer. It could even be made of the same material as the woolen shirt, so long as wearing it was left largely voluntary and the cotton shirt became standard for summer service in garrison and in field.

WHEN WINTER COMES

By Captain Trenchcoat

(*1938*)

Now that we seem to be approaching common sense in uniforms, I hope that one of the most cumbersome and costly of our garments—the woolen overcoat—will not be spared by those who determine what we shall wear at work and play.

As a garment for fair weather in peacetime winters the overcoat has some virtue. But we are chary of taking the field in freezing weather, which makes us forget that the warmth of an Army overcoat is gained at a cost in weight that can be ruinous on campaign. Even when dry the coat weighs far more than need be. In a few hours of rain or snow its weight doubles and its warmth is reduced by half, if twenty pounds of wool and water can be said to give any warmth at all.

I once served on a post where the winter uniform regulations were rigidly enforced—in fact, well beyond the letter of the law. After a certain date in October the overcoat simply had to be worn for protection and warmth. But one winter happened to be mild and exceptionally wet. Within two days after winter had set in by order, my own overcoat dripped for an hour every time I hung it up. I soon saw that I would need two overcoats if I were to approximate a decent appearance, and so eighty dollars went into a new one. All winter I wore one while the other was being dried out at the cleaners, whose bill for the season would have gone far toward buying a third. Indeed, on the basis of my own bill and those of my company as they appeared on the collection sheet, I estimated that the post—a fairly large one—was spending around four hundred dollars a week out of its private pockets in an almost fruitless attempt to keep its overcoats free of wrinkles and water. By spring, moreover, every greatcoat in barracks and quarters looked as if it had been slept in through months of hard maneuvers.

Actually there is one way of converting an Army overcoat into a wind- and water-breaking garment of real warmth, and that is by wearing a light Alligator-type raincoat over it. But this is a poor compromise, although it does bring out the correct principles for the design of a winter coat—a warmth-giving layer on the inside and a windproof and waterproof layer on the outside, which keeps the inner layer reasonably dry.

Thus what we need is not a woolen greatcoat but a trenchcoat and preferably a coat with a detachable woolen lining. (For extreme cold a double lining or one of fleece would be needed.) I have such a coat now. It cost one fourth of what a good overcoat does, and when it is dry or wet its weight is roughly one half that of an overcoat. In either case it is far warmer. Moreover, if appearance is as vital to a working garment as it seems to be, the trenchcoat has, if anything, more style and dash to it than the other.

If we do turn sensibly from the expensive cramping tailored blouse and belt to a jacket it will be but half progress unless we get rid of that spongelike cloak of ill protection which now forms our burden when winter comes.

CHEVRONS FOR INSPIRATION

By LIEUTENANT CHEVRON

(*1938*)

THE PRESENT CHEVRON distinguishes one enlisted man from another by visually indicating his rank. This is as it should be. A corporal, for instance, wears chevrons showing that he has gained recognition for his leadership and judgment and that he ranks several million private soldiers in every army throughout the world, which is not a mean distinction. But do these chevrons also serve to inspire the recruit to put forth some honest sweat toward obtaining his own?

Today's recruit is not a soldier because he wants to be a soldier more than anything else in the world. He is a soldier because there's a war to be fought and it's his time to be a soldier. If once in a while he elects to feel miserable about it, then it's up to us to do something constructive for him.

Opportunities by the score are available in our Army for anyone tough enough to make the opportunity a reality. When I say "tough enough" I have in mind the simple story of a country boy named "Useless Sam" Grant who at one time in his life lost his commission, lost his trade, could not support his family, and took to hauling cordwood through the streets for a living.

Why don't we simply take a Napoleonic precedent for our own use and make a personal and inspirational approach to the new soldier? I propose that hereafter when the quartermaster procures and issues shirts, overcoats, blouses, dungarees, and overalls, they be manufactured with the printed outline of master sergeant's chevrons on each sleeve in the regulation position. Then, when a recruit draws his first shirt from the supply sergeant, he can see with his own eyes that the Army holds a chance for him to advance himself to the top and is challenging him to do it. He'll believe at least half of what he sees and he'll realize his future in the Army is up to him.

When he gets to be a corporal he'll sew his two stripes within the outline where they belong. If he doesn't get to be anything and goes on leave with $126 worth of base pay on his sleeves in empty outline, let him explain it. He's no baby.

Incidentally, such an indelible outline on a uniform sleeve would position the chevron uniformly throughout the Army as the regulations intended when they were written. Also, it might prevent the enemy from picking off noncoms and it would certainly stop GI shirts from being tabbed for officers. These thoughts are of the merest incidence to the idea that the mechanical advantage of an indelibly imprinted outline of master sergeant's chevrons on all sleeved garments would have considerable day-by-day inspirational value.

But whether this chevron and morale idea is worth a damn or not, let us put full faith in Johnny-come-lately. Feed him, lead him, and treat him right. Like the Rebels and Yankees who marched this way before him, he'll do his job.

ARMY CHOW

Academic minutiae are to be found in military schools also. The two articles that follow (dated 1939) were written about an argument at the Infantry School as to the proper designation for the noonday meal of the soldier.

"DINNER," NOT "LUNCH"

By Mess Officer

THAT WAS an excellent piece about better cold lunches in the *Journal* for January–February. But I disagree heartily on one point. What a soldier eats at midday—or any other time—should not be called a "lunch."

In the first place, it sounds too much as if war were thought of as a picnic and not as the serious business it is for all concerned. In the second place, the very word "lunch" carries the meaning of something light, something grabbed from a soda fountain in a hurry, something of no real substance. In other words, a bite or two to stave off hunger until the next square meal comes around.

In peacetime when a soldier sits down at mess it is not to eat a "lunch" but an honest, solid dinner. It's not a snack he expects; it's a full meal. The last one he had was six hours before, and there's been a stiff morning of drill or fatigue in between. And so at noontime the main meal of the day weighs down the table with good substantial food. It's time for "dinner," not a mere lunch, when the morning's work is done.

Even more so in war. The infantryman attacks at dawn, and by noontime, if he's not a dead or badly wounded hero, he wants as big a meal as he ever ate. No matter whether it gets up to him hot from the kitchens, which it rarely does in the midst of battle, or comes out of his haversack cold and squashed, it's a "dinner" he needs and wants, not a "lunch."

The idea of using the word "lunch" thus inappropriately arose some years ago. When you sit at a desk all morning working with your brain instead of your body, doubtless a "lunch" will do come noon. There was strong protest from some of the hardier field soldiers against replacing the word "dinner." There was even an attempt to compromise matters by calling the fresh food the soldier carries on his back a "cold meal." But the "cold lunchers" won out, and as the word has spread throughout the Infantry, cold dinners have shrunk unmistakably into cold lunches.

As long as we think in terms of lunch, that is exactly what the troops are going to get—a couple of flattened-out sandwiches and a small pickle—not enough calories to campaign on for an hour and a half at most. But begin to order cold dinners issued once again, and jolt the cooks' elbows a few times to get them back in the habit, and there won't be any more grumbling stomachs at 2:30 P.M. Call it "dinner," and give them dinner. They earn it, in peace or war.

CALL IT HASH

By HUNGRY

"MESS OFFICER" in the *Infantry Journal* for March–April slipped up on his victuals when he intimated that "cold lunches" had won out over "cold meals." And apparently he does not know that once upon a time a controversy involving those two phrases all but wrecked the tranquillity of our Infantry School.

It happened when an embryo editor, fresh from Leavenworth, encountered a "cold dinner" in his first edit. He unhesitatingly red-penciled the last word and substituted "lunch." This aroused vehement protests from the original author, who insisted that, theoretically at least, he had a perfect right to issue cold dinners any time he wanted to. But the guardian of the school's rhetoric contended that two stale crusts enfolding an oily slab of cheese, such as had frequently been issued to him in the past, scarcely constituted a lunch, let alone a whole dinner.

This discussion quickly grew into a free-for-all argument involving many sedentary citizens of Fort Benning. Sides were taken, and a good deal of verbal sniping went on up and down the noble halls of learning.

And while words became more and more heated, cold dinners and colder lunches flew back and forth like custard pies in a Hollywood comedy.

It got so bad finally that in order to preserve some semblance of academic dignity a conference became necessary to bring the two schools of thought together on a common moniker for what old-timers simply call "chow." The feud, however, had gone too far for arbitration. Squabbling became so violent, the head conferee was forced to eliminate the smaller fry and withdraw to his office—where he conducted a meeting of lesser headmen behind closed doors.

For an hour or more all waited with bated breaths. Then came the momentous decision. To all and sundry it was announced that the apples, sandwiches, or what have you issued to troops immediately after breakfast (and usually eaten or otherwise disposed of prior to 9:00 A.M.), thereafter, in the Infantry School at least, would be known as "a cold noon meal."

That took care of the paper work. But the very next day this humble writer was assigned as umpire on an outdoor exercise. At the proper time he extracted and unwrapped the waxed paper which contained, according to the day's menu, a chicken sandwich. Expectantly peering beneath the upper lid, his disillusioned gaze came to rest on the sad-looking, scrawny, and none-too-well-cooked neck of an aged chicken.

And so I for one say to hell with these academic discussions. Let us pay less attention to titles and more to actual chow. Let the food-dispensing fraternity put out a worth-while ration and we may rest assured that the name of the meal will take care of itself.

AIR SUPPORT IN TODAY'S WAR

By Colonel (now Brigadier General) Allison J. Barnett

(1942)

There is no point in beginning an article on air support with the statement that such support is of great importance to infantry and other ground troops. Actually that was axiomatical of air units by 1918, though it took a second World War to establish the fact plainly to all. But the ground leader who discounted the growing power of the air arm in past years because he didn't take the time to make a thorough and unbiased study of it, or the airman who was perhaps overenthusiastic in his claims—both have forgotten since December 7 any petty differences they may have had. And it doesn't make the slightest difference, anyway, what any of us may believe about the final place of air in relation to ground. The air is so big and so vital a part of modern warfare that the only thing we need to be sure about is having plenty of air and ground forces both, and full co-operation between them.

·   ·   ·

We know well enough how vitally necessary in today's war the closeness of teamwork is between ground and air. Here is what General Marshall said about it recently:

"The technique of 1917 is outmoded today. The specialized training for a particular type of operation gives way to the necessity for perfect teamwork in fast-moving operations over any type of terrain. A high degree of technical and tactical knowledge is necessary, from the individual soldier to the commanders of the highest units. Skilled initiative is a mandatory requirement. The complicated co-ordination of fire power, ground and air, must be managed at top speed, and for a surprising variety of weapons, with little or no opportunity to rehearse the procedure or to gain familiarity with the ground."

Our own announced doctrines also bring this out forcefully. In the first place, there has got to be a thorough familiarity on both sides. The commanders of ground forces have got to know just what the air units supporting them can do and what they can't do. Staffs have got to have air logistics and limitations at their finger tips. And in the air units likewise there must also be a full familiarity with the whole job in hand.

·   ·   ·

Now let us see how an air support command works in action. The Twentieth Army, let us say, takes the field. General Headquarters arranges for the 20th Air Support Command to be attached or assigned to its support. The observation groups of the support command are now decentralized and attached to the different corps of the Twentieth Army, with the army group held under army control. The corps commanders likewise decentralize, designating a light squadron to observe for each division and, if at all possible, for the division with which it has trained. These squadrons are not, however, attached to divisions. With the observation units thus decentralized, their employment then depends upon the G-2 and artillery requirements.

The proper use of such units needs plenty of explanation and emphasis, judging by recent maneuvers in which many ground officers demonstrated much lack of understanding of them. For one thing, observation units cannot be employed for continued surveillance of hostile ground forces in the face of enemy air opposition. Any observation plane that tries to stay in the air over enemy dispositions for more than a very short while can be counted as a plane that is lost. There is nothing whatever theoretical about this. It has been proven a fact. And it must therefore be thoroughly understood.

The observation squadrons that are to observe for infantry divisions, as stated above, are being equipped with pursuit- and liaison-type planes. The pilot-observer flying the pursuit-type ship carries out missions over hostile territory. These must be clear-cut missions that can be accomplished rapidly—missions that simply involve flying to the area from which the information is to be obtained, getting it and returning, all at full speed.

A pilot and his airplane used in this manner should, with any luck, continue to be available for mission after mission in support of his ground force. But a pilot and plane required to take part in continued surveillance will soon be lost.

The pilot of the slow and vulnerable liaison-type airplane must be given no job that will require him to cross his own front lines in the face of air opposition. The main usefulness of this plane, often referred to as "puddle jumper," is primarily in rear-area courier service.

When elements of an air support command are attached to or are assigned to the support of ground units, commanders of the supporting units, under the present system, retain command of their organizations. Under the old system attached aviation was commanded by the chiefs of aviation of armies and army corps and by air officers when observation aviation was attached to divisions. Now, however, the function of an air officer, or chief of aviation, is that of a staff officer only, and it is probable that in the future Air Corps officers will not be detailed to such staff assignments in units of the field forces below the army or armored force. In that event their role will be taken over by the commanders of supporting air units and air liaison officers.

To the ground commander with the right conception of modern warfare, air support by combat aviation means counter air action—until the air forces opposing him are neutralized. The greatest single contribution to the success of a ground operation that supporting combat aviation can possibly make lies in clearing the air of hostile airplanes. The first task must be to destroy the hostile planes and the fields they operate from. It is even better to destroy the factories where they are made, but that is a job not for air-support units, but for our air forces with their heavy long-range bombers.

It follows that we must not expect our support aviation to attack that enemy column approaching in our direction, or help us capture that resistance on Hill 608, or blow up that bridge across Big Creek, if any of these jobs are going to take away a single plane needed for the big job, the primary all-important air mission.

But when the hostile airdromes on our front have been neutralized and airplanes no longer threaten our operations, then our air-support units can begin to pound at targets not so far from our front. And their power may eventually be turned in large measure to our close support.

Once close air support is attained, perfect co-ordination becomes imperative. How we get it is of utmost importance to ground commanders.

When preliminary arrangements for an operation are made, the commander of the air support command establishes the rear echelon of his headquarters near one of his important airdromes to facilitate communication and control. He also establishes an advance control post near the command post of the unit he is supporting. At this *air-support control* all requests for air support are received and the decision made as to whether or not bomber attacks will be made in response to such requests. Thus it is an important establishment and must be manned by experienced personnel. An assistant G-3, selected for his judgment and knowledge of tactics and his ability to think clearly in battle, clothed with full authority, must be at this control at all times when air-support missions are to be dispatched. The air-support commander, or a representative he has designated, must also be at the air-support control at all times when calls for air support may come in. This control has every available means of communication, including radio to planes in the air.

To prevent casualties to our own ground troops a bomb-safety line is designated short of which no bomb from support aviation must fall. This line must be kept posted up to date, and every pilot must know its location.

The commander of the air support command knows at all times what the situation is at his bomber airdromes. There are two types of alert—air alert and ground alert. Air alert requires planes to be in the air with full bomb loads. This method, though it insures the delivery of a blow in the minimum time, is costly in gasoline and in pilot fatigue and has still other objections. A call may come when much of the gas in the planes has been used up. Or, since the type of target is not known when the bombers take off, the bombs they carry may not be of the kind most suitable for the eventual mission.

We can best see the general advantages of the other type of alert through an example. Let us assume that when a call comes in a certain per cent of all available bomber pilots are on ground alert. Their aircraft would be fully serviced and armed; all equipment would be at hand and the crews near by and ready to go. The representative of the ground commander at the air-support control receives the request for bombs on a suitable target. He consults with the air-support commander, or his representative, who advises that the mission be dispatched. The request is then approved for the ground-force commander by the G-3 representative and passed to the air-support representative, who communicates with the airdrome, giving the nature and location of the target, the approximate time of attack, and the number of bombers and type of bomb to be used.

When the mission is received at the airdrome the air-unit commander or his operations officer designates the airplanes to do the job and gives the other instructions clearly and briefly. While the pilots are getting this information, mechanics are starting the motors and other men are loading the bombs, if any change in bomb loadings is necessary.

All of this requires only a few minutes. The time required for delivering the attack will depend almost entirely upon the distance to the target and the difficulty in locating it after the bombers arrive over its vicinity. Targets in or near villages or farmhouses are easily found. But when there is no reference point clearly visible from the air it is exceedingly difficult to locate a target. In fact, the ideal method of directing support bombers to an exact spot of this kind has not yet been determined.

It is probable that bomber attacks in response to call or request will be more applicable to armored forces than to infantry. Air support in no wise takes over the role of field artillery when field artillery is available. Air support should be called upon for close support against resistances impeding the advance of assault troops only when the ground-support weapons are inadequate for the task at hand.

There is no need to emphasize the power of air support as an aid to ground forces. But in general a ground commander will get the most out of it by giving his air-support commander much latitude. It has also been demonstrated over and over in modern battle that, with such latitude, the air-support commander will discover and attack many important targets before their presence is known to the ground troops. As one ground commander of high rank put it a few weeks ago, "Give the air-support commander a job to do, and let him do it."

NLD

By Staff Sergeant (now Lieutenant Colonel) J. R. Ulmer

Every point suggested by Colonel Ulmer in this 1937 article on the disciplinary aspects of venereal disease in the Army is now in effect. The fault of the old way of handling the matter and the reasons for the new are strongly presented by this writer, who is now associate editor of the *Infantry Journal.*

Our hope of control lies in breaking the chain of infection at its weakest link— the early case. Dr. Thomas A. Parran, Surgeon General, United States Public Health Service.

MORE AND MORE do the words "venereal disease" appear in the public prints. Moreover, they are being spoken right out loud in precincts where they were hitherto taboo. Our people are belatedly acknowledging these scourges of the flesh and are co-operating with the United States Public Health Service in the fight against them. If the follow-through is strong enough, the campaign will bear fruit; optimists even hope that we may attain the excellent results gained in Sweden, where syphilis and gonorrhea are virtually unknown.

For years the Army has had to concern itself with venereal disease, and as a consequence its approach to the problem is far more realistic than that of the general public. Moreover, the Army's procedure for reducing the venereal rate has met with marked success. The results are testified to by statistics and cited by public-health officers to show what can be done. Even if we concede a liberal discount for undetected cases the figures are impressive.

But however successful the Army's method of control has been, it cannot be said to be truly scientific as long as the twin clouds of prudery and punishment hover over it. Until they are dispelled we cannot say that we are fighting disease in the most enlightened manner. Touching on this point, Dr. R. A. Vonderlehr, assistant surgeon general, United States Public Health Service, had this to say at the recent conference on venereal-disease control held at Washington.

One of the chief reasons why success has not been attained in bringing syphilis under control is because of its unfortunate association with morality. Health officers must take the lead in teaching the public to regard syphilis as a disease and not as a form of moral delinquency. *The disease, like many others, is a communicable one, and the fact should be so treated at all times.* [Dr. Vonderlehr's italics.] The fact that it is spread chiefly through sexual intercourse should be given no special prominence in the application of control measures.

The victims of these ailments are diseased—not disgraced. That is the viewpoint of modern public health. The Army might well review its methods in the light of Dr. Vonderlehr's dictum.

Let us first examine a few of our control measures to see if they square with what we know of the psychology of "single men in barracks." We shall concern ourselves only with the questions of education and administration. The cure of the infected we may safely leave to the doctors.

The regulations prescribe that, by way of education, every soldier shall receive a course in what is euphemistically called "sex morality." Generally it is given in the form of a lecture to recruits, and its character is determined by the knowledge, good humor, imagination, or garrulity of the officer who gives it. Usually it includes a description of the social diseases, a pious hope that the hearers will exercise restraint come payday, and the address of the nearest prophylaxis station. This last shows that the lecturer has his fingers crossed.

The present-day course is the lineal descendant of one given during

the World War. Then, also, no soldier escaped it; some heard it three
or four times as they were transferred about with the carefree abandon
of items in a wartime budget. Some of these much-harangued soldiers
built up an immunity to a sex-morality lecture that was truly astonishing;
they could sleep profoundly through the loudest oratory. Their 1937
counterparts are no less subject to the anesthesia of repetition.

In theory the course is sound, but in practice it fails of substantial
accomplishment. Made a bit less sketchy and perfunctory, and given by
an officer who patently believes what he is saying, the lecture can do
some good.

But let it be said here and now that the preparation of a good sex-
morality discussion, either oral or written, is a difficult task. I have never
listened to or read one that struck just the right note. The paucity of
good literature and oratory on the subject of venereal disease is not confined to the military. After years of experience in social-disease-control
work, Dr. N. A. Nelson, assistant director, Division of Communicable
Diseases, Massachusetts Department of Public Health, is rather gloomy
on the subject:

> I have yet to discover [says he] the story of syphilis (or any part of it) written
> in such a way that it could be used by the Health Department and would arouse
> the interest of the man in the street.
> If any one of us were granted an appropriation tomorrow for the employment
> of a single sane and unemotional lecturer who knew anything about syphilis,
> where would one be found? I would like to borrow a half-dozen talks . . . which
> are not dry and uninteresting tables of statistics, or emotional eruptions on sex,
> or too vivid descriptions of the anatomy involved, or the too frank discussion of
> the unpleasant signs of the disease. Who has them to lend? There is neither
> material nor anyone with both interest and ability to produce it.

About the only advice one can offer in regard to the sex talk is that
it should leave the moral side of the question strictly alone—this for the
simple reason that when you talk to a soldier about the state of his
morals you immediately get a hostile reaction. You can gain his confidence only by denuding the talks of prudery and sophistry. And let
them be given by his own officers—company commanders preferred.

As an adjunct to the World War campaign to control venereal disease,
we had the sex-morality movie. This, while a step forward, failed in some
respects to win the confidence of the troops and for curious reasons. Since
we may expect movies during the next war, a backward glance may not
be amiss.

A scenario titled *Fit to Fight* was hurriedly written by some unknown
genius, and a few soldiers and feminine war workers were pressed into
service as actors and actresses. A ukase went forth that no soldier was to
escape seeing this epic. As in the case of the lectures, many thousands

endured the film several times, and the more hardened snored gratefully through the second and subsequent performances.

Fit to Fight concerned itself with the fortunes of a quartet of likely lads who had 'listed for the wars. First they were rapidly seen out of cits into uniform (under a running barrage of critical comment from every soldier audience as to the superior style and fit of Army clothes furnished screen soldiers). Then the heroes idly stroll the city's streets.

Here they are accosted by a foursome of Jezebels whose motives are obviously immoral and pecuniary. Soldier A promptly scorns their advances. Soldier B compromises by stealing a kiss and departing. Soldiers C and D hesitate—possibly they have heard the sex-morality lecture only once. Be that as it may, they do not heed the pleadings of A, and they fade out in company with the pavement pounders. A vanishes from the picture in a close-up, wearing a look of regret and self-righteousness.

The next reel shows what happened to C and D as a result of yielding to the flesh. Indeed, we are shown with such a wealth of physiological detail and pathological exactitude that at every performance a few of the chickenhearted give up their preceding meal.

Nothing happened to D because he was sagacious enough to take out insurance at the prophylaxis station.

The showing of this shocker was usually marred by the comment of the unregenerate upon the appearance of the bogus courtesans. A few would always loudly swear that the gals were too lacking in comeliness to engage in such commerce with success. Accordingly, let that officer who spends the period of the next war in the unhappy business of procuring for a celluloid bagnio require a reasonable amount of pulchritude in his actresses, in order not to overstrain the credulity of the troops.

Dr. John H. Stokes, professor of dermatology and syphilology, University of Pennsylvania, in discussing his efforts to educate the physician along these lines, estimates the potential value of exhortative or informative talks as second to that of motion pictures. And he is not too greatly impressed by the work of motion pictures, for he says: "Of pictures, still and moving, I can only say that years of medical barnstorming and experiments performed in my own classes have convinced me that they are beguiling but comparatively ineffective."

As a possible accompaniment to the talks and pictures, it may be that we have not made the most of pamphlets. These should be in simple terms and well illustrated. A booklet will be carried away physically, for a short distance at least, and there is always the chance that it will be read. It would be helpful to leave pamphlets about in dayrooms, libraries, and other places where soldiers foregather.

So much for the educational field. On the administrative side we encounter a procedure that the experience of the public-health services of all countries has shown to be a cardinal error. Its name is *punishment.*

We say to the soldier: "If you are fool enough to get infected go on sick call at once. If you turn in early enough we can virtually guarantee a cure, and in later life you will be spared the serious consequences that follow neglect.

"Of course we will court-martial you if you haven't taken the prophylaxis, and during the period you are unfit for duty we will confiscate all but five dollars of your pay per month."

At least that's the way it sounds to a soldier.

Consequently many try to beat the game. They hide their ailments and tinker with self-treatment. The less intelligent fall for quacks or pin their faith on the fifty-cent pills and lotions advertised in the latrine of any well-conducted poolroom. Those who lack the stability of a few hash marks may even go over the hill. In their eagerness to escape punishment they disregard the serious consequences that follow neglect or improper treatment. Such men have not been touched by the educational program, nor does the threat of court-martial and loss of pay serve any other purpose than to keep their names off the venereal report—if they are clever enough or lucky enough to escape detection. And it is too much to expect that men so lacking in regard for themselves will show any for others. They become spreaders of the infection they carry—a menace to the health of the command and the community. These men must be brought under control even if this involves a complete about-face.

What shall we do about it?

As an initial step, abolish the trial by court-martial. Next, repeal the law prescribing forfeiture of pay. In brief, treat these infections as diseases and label them "line of duty."

What would happen?

The removal of the threats to purse and reputation would result in a greater number of venereals being treated—more would turn in. Thereafter the treatment rate should stabilize at a higher level, pending that happy day when the rate for the country as a whole will diminish.

This won't look so well on the monthly report, but at least it will show the true state of affairs. For all but the naïve know that the treatment curves for organizations stationed under the same conditions do not necessarily present an accurate picture of the venereal situation. Often those which indicate a relatively low disease rate actually reflect a high rate of concealment.

One gain from a more rational attitude toward the Army's social disease problem would be an improved officer morale. No longer would a dismayed company commander survey with concern for his record a mounting venereal court-martial rate which he could control only by putting his command under lock and key. Moreover, there would be less work for the courts, whose members are harried enough by their normal duties.

But these are only incidental benefits that we may reasonably expect from a policy designed to encourage men with venereal disease to turn in promptly. More important is the fact that such a policy would save from their folly and ignorance many who might otherwise suffer penalties out of all proportion to their offense. But the greatest benefit of all would result from bringing under control many sources of infection that might go undetected.

The main objective of the campaign of the Public Health Service is detection, isolation, and treatment of the infected. The Army already stands on that objective, but there is still some mopping up to do. The surest and quickest way to get it done is to abolish the penalties that operate to keep many cases under cover. Legally the failure to take the prophylaxis after exposure is a military offense, but from a medical viewpoint it is bad business to treat it as such.

WAR IS THE MAIN GAME

Anonymous

> This anonymous explosion about peacetime athletic abuses was published in November 1935. It doesn't need much explanation. The writer has been a steady contributor to the magazine for many years.

Thus we play the fools with the time, and the spirits of the wise sit in the clouds and mock us. Shakespeare

Only if the rifleman be trained to move unrestingly forward by walking, by rushing, by crouching, by crawling, by creeping, ever on and on, will the period of his travail be reduced. Major General H. Rowan-Robinson

There is a small but convinced minority within the commissioned grades of infantry today that is bitter on the subject of military athletics. I am one of them, and I believe our viewpoint is worth listening to.

It is only fair to say in the beginning that in my own case there is reason for prejudice. But the very reasons that have brought me to the point of writhing when I hear an infantry squad compared to a football squad are excellent illustrations of the very objections that I, and others who hold similarly, have to college athletics in military settings. Consequently a brief recounting of what has happened to me in twelve or fifteen years forms the first part of this considered gripe. The second part, since the editor of the *Infantry Journal* says that problems posed in these pages must be accompanied by a solution, will be, I assure you, a solution with a vengeance.

At the first post where I served as a lieutenant I roomed with the athletic officer. We were friends, and good ones (we still are).

My duties consisted of all the spare-part jobs and the command of a machine-gun company. The property on my papers totaled just short of a million dollars. I made a lot of mistakes, but I had good noncoms in most of my offices. The engineer sergeant slipped once, and I had to pay for three pairs of gloves for handling barbed wire. But my ordnance, recreational, post-library, police, post-painting, and corps-area-library assistants, and the noncommissioned staff of my company helped me through a year without other cost than a good deal of overtime work. I was also survey officer and, with the help of a kindly warrant officer at corps-area headquarters, managed to make a few others pay without paying anything myself. There were also boards and courts, which as a rule sat at night. Special duty, however, made drill a daily farce at the company, and so often was there no drill at all that I had frequent mornings in which to catch up on other things.

In that first year I learned much that is still of value, and I was not called on the carpet once for lack of attention to duty or for doing things wrong.

In the meantime, my athletic roommate, who was one of the best I have seen at his job, increased the number of athletic events at the post to an average of three a week. In fact, I watched many a boxing match and basketball game that year, when night work did not keep me home. And I accepted without a single doubt the faith that fine athletes are fine soldiers.

My roommate did little besides his athletic duties. He was assigned to a rifle company, it is true, but his company commander seldom saw him except for an hour or two in the morning. He was continually organizing teams, matches, bouts, and meets, and making trips with this team and that.

My unconsidered acceptance of all this was strained a little in the summer of my second year. I found myself in temporary charge of the baseball team for three weeks while my roommate went on leave. I knew nothing about baseball that would help a team, and to expose my ignorance for once and all I told the soldier manager, "You run the team and I'll back you up."

Three days later I found most of the team drunk at practice. Not very drunk, but drunk enough to show it. I formed them up and marched them down to my company, and all of us, drunk or sober, had three cups of coffee; then we went back to practice. There was no more trouble. And when the athletic officer came back from Kansas I was still orthodox on athletics.

My friend did not go unrewarded officially for his good work. His reports for those two years were all largely "superior," and he had several nice letters to file where they would do the most good. His many civilian contacts were also valuable, perhaps. He left that post eventually for foreign service in China.

I saw my own reports for those first two years more than ten years later. They were all "average." There were no remarks pro or con. Long before I saw them, however, I had made up my mind about athletics.

My own second station was on foreign service, too, although not in China. I had been with my new regiment only a few weeks (in a rifle company), when the regimental commander sent for me. "I'm going to turn over H Company to you," he said. "I hear you know something about machine guns, and I need your company commander up here at headquarters. You won't have another captain for two or three months. But you'll find you've got a fine company. It contains all the regimental boxing squad, many of the swimming team, and half the baseball team. I wish I could command that company myself. You know, Mr. Jones, I used to take part in athletics a good deal myself when I was younger. In fact, I used to be a regular bundle of muscle. It's my belief no soldier should be made a corporal unless he can knock down every man in his squad. Nearly every noncom you've got in H Company is a boxer."

This colonel was one of the gentlest and pleasantest in the conduct of his regiment I have ever seen, but that is what he said.

I went down to Company H feeling proud of the outfit already and glad that machine-gun officers were scarce. But what I found in the course of three months as the company commander of seventy-odd prima donnas of the squared circle, tank, mat, track, and so on, I shall not attempt to tell in the detail it deserves. The previous company commander had played first base on the ball team. Most of the company called him "Steve." There was not a single noncommissioned officer who would have known the mil formula if it had punched him a sharp left to the solar plexus. Two noncommissioned officers complained direct to the adjutant because I cut out morning work in the gymnasium. The few non-athletes in the company were doing three quarters of the fatigue and kitchen work. The stables were frowzy with filth, and over half the animals had bad feet. Beyond a little close order and gun drill and the bare knowledge of how to harness and lead—enough to get by at parades and reviews—the company knew nought of machine gunnery.

But I found one line sergeant—the first-ranking one fortunately—who was not punch drunk and had had wartime experience in a machine-gun battalion. He proved from the beginning—and to the end too—the only noncom in the company, not excepting the first sergeant, who was willing to play my kind of ball. By all the others, there was unanimous resistance.

Even so, my changes were not extreme. I simply began a schedule of four hours' machine-gun work on five mornings of the week, and for an hour or two each afternoon turned out the handful that might not be playing games by regimental or battalion order to scrub the stables and animals into some kind of shape. I showed a decent interest in the sports, too, but always as an apparently proud observer, and never to the sacrifice of military affairs or my own regular round of golf. I did not play first base, and the captains of the various teams, let alone the players, did *not* call me "Jim."

My battalion commander was a fat, fussy man who had been a certified accountant in civil life. His only passion was company fund books. He would not accept one with a single correction. He observed my handling of Company H for three or four days and then called me in to warn me that I was not only driving the company too hard but was not making neat entries in my fund book. "You are neglecting close-order drill too. At least half of your drill time should be close order, whatever your total hours scheduled may be."

So thenceforth my schedules showed two hours of close order, although I admit that I frequently stole much of that time for other drills—all of it, whenever I knew that the major was safely away from the post or auditing fund books.

One day in the middle of my first effort to teach the finer points of fire by direct laying, the major and the colonel came by. They watched awhile. Then the major said with a hearty laugh, and loudly enough for the whole company to hear, "Well, just give me enough riflemen and you can keep your damned machine guns." The colonel laughed, nodding agreement, and both walked away.

As we began to touch upon fire by indirect laying in the company training, I found that the war plans called for the actual defense of the post under certain possible conditions. So I asked what part in the defense had been assigned to Company H. The plans-and-training officer told me that the battalion had a sector to defend but that there were no company setups. On learning this I fitted into the company drill the problem of defense and eventually completed indirect data for firing on every possible approach to the post.

I took it to the battalion commander. But he was interested only in addition, not in the multiplication and division involved in the mil formula. He handed it back to me, not knowing what else to do with it. Then he spoke again about the company, warning me that I was going over the men's heads and attempting to teach them something of no practical value.

I left as soon as I could, went up to regimental headquarters, and gave my data to the plans-and-training officer. The next morning I found it on my desk with a note, "Very interesting." I still have the data and the accompanying maps. It is no longer of value since new ammunition has come in.

At the end of three months a captain came and took my boxers, swimmers, et al., out of my care. I went to another company. My report for that period says "average" in every entry, and at the bottom, "This young officer is inclined to be too hard on enlisted men."

During the remainder of that tour of foreign service, after my first-hand introduction to the ideal that "fine athletes are fine soldiers," I became much better acquainted with what athletics can accomplish. Then, and later on at other posts, I saw these things:

I have seen officer referees hissed and booed by halls full of enlisted men.

I have seen the bitterest of rivalry, and often the bitterest of feelings, as the result of the attempted wooing of soldier athletes from one organization to another.

Many times I have seen a decent standard of military efficiency sacrificed to a high standard of athletics. In one regiment, when there was only two weeks to go before range season, and preliminary training had not yet begun, I saw six out of ten drill mornings devoted to a regimental volleyball tournament. Yes, a volleyball tournament! (Nor am I a marksmanship fanatic.)

I have seen great glass cases of cups and trophies in the orderly rooms of companies whose conditions of military training—and whose interest in that training—would not for a moment stand comparison with those of a well-drilled troop of Boy Scouts.

I have seen the entire season of a regimental baseball league, with every game played at ten in the morning and everybody but one cook and one K.P. per company attending.

I have seen the entire effort of a brigade devoted for three weeks to a single athletic meet.

I have seen an officer stand to lose four thousand dollars of his pay because of his overzealous efforts (he was impelled by directives from higher authority) to make an athletic meet a financial success.

I have seen great honor rolls at the entrances of beautiful barracks bearing scores of names, not one out of ten cited for sound military accomplishments.

I have seen a field officer sitting in a grandstand, curse, groan, and well-nigh weep over the errors made by his battalion team.

I have seen a score of young officers—athletes of note at the Military Academy or other universities—spoiled, pampered, and encouraged to continue their participation in games. I have seen an excellent company commander relieved because he required such an officer to read and report briefly on three hundred pages of military history in the course of a month and because he mildly punished the same young athlete for a slight although deliberate neglect of his company duties. (I also saw the battalion commander's wife sympathize with this lieutenant, at dinner in the presence of many guests, regarding his hard existence.)

I have lent my saber to an officer who told me he had not worn one for eleven years. He had been on athletic duty of one kind or another the entire time.

But this is enough to show what I hold against military athletics. I realize that some of these abuses were exceptional. But I also realize that, in general, they do not give a false picture. The reader who doubts, I gently refer to the first sergeants of any infantry regiment. These men, better than any others, know what happens; and these men, with a few athletic exceptions, are as much against the glorification of soldier athletics as I am.

And now for a solution. I believe there is one, and a very good one. I have given this heavy gripe a personal tone so far; hence I will finish in a similar way, by telling what I would do if through some extraordinary act of God or Congress I became a regimental commander.

My whole program, in fact, would consist of one simple change. I would remove all the emphasis on college-athletic sports I possibly could. I would place that emphasis on military accomplishments. I do not mean that there would be no sports. There would, in fact, be plenty of them. But the cups and the trophies would go, not to the man who could run the fastest mile, but the man who could crawl the fastest hundred yards over rough terrain while keeping his head down; not to the winning football squad, but to the rifle and machine-gun squads with the best performance; not to the company that won the most games in the baseball league, but the company that could come in in best condition after a long day's marching, crawling, rushing, and resumption of marching.

At the same time I would not overemphasize military competition as such. I would set a standard of performance and find no fault with units that met it. This applies to marksmanship too.

And finally, these definite rulings would obtain within my regiment:

All college-type athletics would be on a purely voluntary basis, both as to units and individuals.

There would be no athletics of this kind until after the official day was over until I was satisfied with the state of training. (That would probably be a long time later.)

For six months at least there would be no regimental teams competing with teams outside the regiment, and none thereafter at any great cost of energy, time, or money.

There would be no playing officers.

No officers would coach except in an advisory capacity.

Stress, if any, would be placed on such games as volleyball, company-playground baseball, large-group relay races, and other games that turn out large numbers of players.

Above all, I would stress, in the training of the regiment, the conditioning of all men to contact with the hard ground that Mother Nature has put under their feet. A man who can creep, crawl, clamber over rocks, and force his body through undergrowth for hours on end, without excessive fatigue, is as good a man and a far better infantryman than the soldier who can run a mile in record time or pitch a shutout game. Some athletic sports harden men properly, but only a few men at a time and at much too great an effort. Infantry is not infantry, in this day, unless every fighting soldier's body is resiliently toughened to the ground he must accept full-length as his plane of combat if he is to last through a single hour.

Naturally I would try not to drive my regiment over the hill en masse by trying to toughen them up overnight. I would begin by substituting short periods of crawling exercises at half the periods for setting-up exercises, and then increase gradually. And I would have my staff submit every idea that came into their heads as to means of adding interest to this training.

Here I conclude. My mind is not closed on this subject. I am distinctly not an opponent of athletics in general. I simply believe, with a number of others, that we have sadly failed to bend them to the best military results and have often let them run away with us. But the athletic enthusiast is like any other. As Major General Sir H. Rowan-Robinson says in the same book quoted at the beginning: "Able and conscientious men, imbued with a profound conviction of the value of the branch in which they have specialized, not uncommonly, if of commanding character, succeed in persuading the authorities to allot to it a length of course, a quantity of equipment, or a number of men disproportionate to its true value. The enthusiasm is admirable, but it is advisable to guard against its evil effects." Athletic enthusiasm as we commonly see it is even worse, because it is misdirected energy that all too often shoves the military into second place, and often a poor second at that.

TEACHING HORSE SENSE BY MAIL

By Captain (now Lieutenant Colonel) E. G. Piper

About a year before the war began, when the Army started to bring into active duty large numbers of reserve officers, there was a good deal in the newspapers about "correspondence"-school officers. The term was used in a derogatory—and thoroughly ignorant—manner for the most part. The fact that tens of thousands of reserve officers had spent many hundreds of hours, which would have been hours of relaxation from their civilian jobs, in hard study of the very thorough Army Extension Courses, which the law required of them in part qualification for reserve promotion, was entirely overlooked by the self-appointed critics who cast off on them.

The Extension Courses had their shortcomings, as Captain (now Lieutenant Colonel) Piper said in 1937 in the article below. But as appropriations were in those days, there was no other earthly way of teaching the military arts to the tens of thousands of earnest members of the Officers' Reserve Corps.

GENGHIS KHAN conquered half a world in an age when fighting men knew little of the written word and nothing of typewriters, mimeograph machines, maps, calories, and similar modern military curiosa. Those robustious days are over and gone. Now even that semi-professional, the reserve officer, is required to know something of all these things and many more. Since the source of this knowledge is the Army Extension Courses, let's cast a bilious eye in that direction.

In addition to a knowledge of combat principles, the AEC offers instruction to Infantry Reserve officers on how to run a mess in four lessons and an examination, the care and operation of motor vehicles in five lessons and an examination, and the care of animals and stable management in seven lessons and an examination. This instruction is free. All the officer has to do is sign his name to a form and hop to it. Some hop reluctantly and have to be pricked upon the behind, but some also hop far and furiously, as witness:

There was once upon a time a first lieutenant of Infantry Reserve—in the course he might have been called Lieutenant A—who had completed the 60-series and was ready, so far as the Army Extension Courses were concerned, to wear eagles on his shoulders. Lieutenant A was just naturally smart and a hard worker to boot. His instructor was so proud of him that he used to point him out in meetings as a paragon. Of course some persons looked upon this lieutenant with deep suspicion, as ignoramuses are wont to look upon their betters. But then the instructor's opinion was worth something, for everyone knew that he was a gentleman, a scholar, and no fool.

Somewhat later the brilliant Lieutenant A was detailed to duty with the CCC and handed the humdrum chore of looking after two Dodge (Fargo) trucks driven by a pair of wild-haired CCC-ers. It was before the day of the governor, and the young Jehus of the reforestation army probably drove sixty miles an hour over rough roads when no one was looking. At any rate, it was not long before both trucks developed a misery in their innards and were sent to a garage for repairs.

A trusting soul, Lieutenant A did not get an estimate on the repair job. When the trucks came back from the shop he neither looked nor listened closely. He merely approved and forwarded to the quartermaster for payment an invoice in three figures, said invoice claiming that services had been rendered which one does not render on the Dodge truck on account of how Mr. Chrysler did not build them that way.

When the brass hats at District got the invoice they gnashed their teeth and tore their hair. One brass hat, the one who wrote letters on motor transportation, asked me, "Do these people think I am a damned fool?" I allowed they did and left hurriedly as he started writing on a pad either to the lieutenant or the garageman; I never knew which.

Eight months later I ran into Lieutenant A. In the course of our conversation he told me that the trucks he had caused to be repaired at great expense to the taxpayers had gone to the salvage pile shortly thereafter and that "they" were trying to make him pay the repair bill personally.

Parallels to this little incident are an everyday occurrence. I suspect, although I cannot prove this, that too many reserve officers who can move regiments here and there with the greatest of ease cannot fit shoes properly on the feet of Private Willie Jones, much less move a platoon of Willie and his playmates from here to there on a real piece of ground. As for stopping a riot engaged in by Willie and his playful pals, you guess what they would do. I have no idea.

Now this is not an attempt to pan the Army Extension Courses because they do not teach horse sense. They were not designed for that purpose. They assume that a reserve officer who enrolls already has some horse sense. A lot of them have. But it may be that too many officers who take the subcourses and pass them with nice high marks do not have much horse sense, and that no one discovers this deficiency until it is too late to do much about it. Whereupon, as the old lady said with a sigh, "There you are."

My knowledge of the 50- and 60-series of the subcourses offered by the Extension Course of the Infantry School is, to say the least, hazy. All I know is that I have seen my betters sweat over them for hours and come to no conclusion. They are, I will bet you, tough.

Nevertheless, our friend, Lieutenant A, passed them all, and yet because it was not written down in the book at that time—it has been written since—he didn't know enough to make Christians out of his truck drivers, or to get an estimate on a repair job before he authorized it, or to talk to enough mechanics and salesmen to find out how his motors were put together.

A little teaching and testing of horse sense is indicated. Horse sense and intelligence are not the same thing. Horse sense is the ability, among other things, to handle simple situations simply and directly, without recourse to approved solutions, texts, and manuals. And since horse sense implies an attitude of mind or a way of thinking rather than just the ability to think, it can be developed in the pupil by an instructor who believes in the horse-sense method himself.

The following changes in the AEC setup might have kept Lieutenant A and others of his ilk from making asses of themselves and paying repair bills from their personal funds:

(1) Make the subcourses shorter and easier, increasing the number if necessary. Reserve officers are civilians who play with military affairs as a hobby. Problems that are too difficult or go in for long-drawn-out requirements, impossible to conclude at one sitting, are not sufficiently interesting to hold the interest of the amateur. After three or four interruptions on the same problem the reserve-officer student loses interest and goes to the picture show or reads a magazine in which people shoot each other without benefit of contours and road junctions.

(2) Allow no officer to enroll for a subcourse in a series higher than that required for his certificate of capacity for the next higher grade. There was no point to Lieutenant A's taking on anything more difficult than the 30-series.

(3) Require a written examination at the completion of each subcourse which shall be taken in the presence of an examiner or instructor, preferably an officer of the Regular Army. At this examination no texts or other aids are to be used. This means that the examination must be relatively simple and not an endurance contest.

(4) Require an oral examination in addition to the written examination, all approved solutions or "answers" for both oral and written exams to be retained by the examiner and not divulged to any student, regardless of whether he passes or fails the test. This is not an insinuation that officers might cheat. But it is only natural for human beings to help their friends over the rough spots.

The oral exam is more adaptable to the teaching and testing of horse sense than any other. For instance, as one item in the oral examination following subcourse number 12 (Military Discipline, Courtesies, and Customs of the Service) this problem might be offered: "It is wartime. Your outfit has just been organized and is filled with recruits who are wild and woolly. Your noncommissioned officers are nothing but recruits themselves. A riot or free-for-all fight breaks out in one of your barracks. You and your first sergeant are the only people on hand who have enough courage to try to stop it. What do you do?"

Following the subcourse on mess management, this simple problem might be offered: "The quartermaster has made a forced issue to your mess of 120 number-10 cans of prunes at a cost of 55 cents the can. Dehydrated fruit costs 10 cents a pound. Your men do not like prunes, and you figure that at the rate you normally feed prunes for breakfast these 120 cans will last you at least four months. What do you do with the prunes?"

After subcourse number 15 (Military Sanitation and First Aid) the oral problem might be this: "You are in command of an outfit which has just been recruited and you are located near a large town. Things are not yet well organized. You and your officers are in something of a fog trying to discover what the war is all about, and your noncommissioned officers are not sure either. The chances are that unless you exercise a little foresight a number of your men will rush right out and catch themselves a venereal disease. What do you do to prevent this? Don't tell me that you would buy easy chairs and pool tables or have the chaplain make a speech. I've heard both of those before."

The oral questions are offered by an amateur and are presented only to illustrate the spirit of the horse-sense method. It seems reasonable to suppose that an officer of the common or garden variety had better learn how to quell a riot rather than how many guns to fire if a major general heaves into view, assuming that he has not time to learn both. It might also be observed that generals do not come around without being heralded from afar. Hence someone usually has time to look up the regulation that covers their proper reception. Rioters are often not so considerate.

The suggested questions have nothing to do with the theater of operations. They deal with preliminaries. But the prelims always precede the main bout and must be gotten out of the way.

As for the preparation of the exam, I am sure that a clever officer who knows his onions will be able to concoct some snappy orals which horse sense, applied to a knowledge of fundamentals, can solve without map, pencil, or paper. Or, if the clever officers can't do it, call in the grizzled first sergeants. I am a reader of the pulps and I have faith in the grizzled first sergeant. He can do anything.

WAR IN PLAIN LANGUAGE

By G. V.

One recurrent topic to be found in *Infantry Journal* articles is the military language. A few in the Army have worked and fought toward a more ready understanding of the military arts and sciences for the new soldier through a revision and reduction of military jargon. War and preparation for war, like any other major occupation, demand a special terminology. They do not, as a writer in the *Infantry Journal* said in 1935, demand "a language that too often enabled a military writer (like the Emperor of Ethiopia, who enjoys a private language of his own) to couch his thoughts in words and phrases whose true meaning is known only to himself—if even to him." But the professional soldier, like the professional educator, doctor, and lawyer, has gone right on preserving his mysteries with a protective fog of jargon until the war began to prove to him that the Army could be augmented far more rapidly and efficiently if as much plain language were used as possible. The tendency now, in the second year of the war, is away from the stilted military phraseology which, after all, as another *Journal* writer pointed out several years back, quoting Pareto, is a part of the torrent of such verbiage that has rushed tumultuously down across the ages.

"War in Plain Language," by G. V., appeared in October 1941. He presents the broad thought that the language of the Army may have contributed in large part as a barrier to the lack of military interest in the United States as a whole during the twenties and thirties.

Another viewpoint by Captain (now Colonel) Russell Skinner and two by other writers follow the first article.

EVEN NOW, a year and a half after the beginnings of our defense effort on a great scale, it is still most apparent that there is a lack of general understanding of the Army and how it operates on the part of the non-military citizens of the nation. It is true that there has been a great improvement in the accuracy and realism of articles, news stories, and books written about military matters. Some few of the "experts" are well along the road to becoming actual experts. (Only a very few were that far along when things began to hum.) And in the work of all who report to the country on its Army, the military man, when he gets a chance to look at a paper, sees far less pure nonsense than he did a year ago.

This improvement has been due to the efforts of writers and reporters to build up their backgrounds in order to write something that makes sense to citizen and soldier alike. Regardless of the criticism an article may contain, it makes the Army man who reads it feel that an honest attempt is being made to understand him and his difficulties, if only the facts are straight and the implications sound. This improvement has also been due in no small part to the effort of the Army itself to make all non-secret facts available through the Bureau of Public Relations and the public-relations officers throughout the Army. Not perfect yet, but endeavoring constantly to study and meet every problem of making information available, this greatly expanded setup should—or so we might think—leave little excuse for the writer or editor who continues to feed mistaken or twisted stories on the Army to his readers.

It is apparent at the same time that some of the best-known newsmen and article writers in America, as well as many a reporter who doesn't yet write under a by-line, have not yet acquired the requisite knowledge for the military reporting they attempt. For they cannot have done so and still write as they often do. There is some lack of attention to fact and often much distortion in what they produce. In fact, there is so much of error, especially in comment involving training and tactics, that it is worth while searching beyond the seemingly obvious reasons why this should be for some more basic reasons.

A further obvious place to put the blame is upon editors. For surely editors are even more to blame than writers if they neglect to acquire for themselves the background, the references, and, where possible, the special advisers that will help them recognize distortion, false implication, and plain error of fact. When a national magazine of tremendous circulation, whose editorial policy appears to be mainly to stir up thought, prints a succession of articles containing many misstatements, there is reason to believe that the fault may lie largely in editorial neglect.

I am not speaking here of the editor who may be operating under a directive to play up the errors and weaknesses of our immense expansion, or to slant all stories toward headlines for sales. The great bulk of American editors want to put out to their readers honest reporting and criticism of military affairs, and nothing in the policies under which they work should prevent them from doing so. And I'm not for a second implying that criticism founded on fact, and not on ignorance or distortion, shouldn't be normal today. Every man in uniform must realize that open criticism plus straight, accurate reporting on the basis of readily available facts is what by far the greater part of American editors are now trying to give their readers. But too many of them aren't succeeding. Too many of them who try hard to do so aren't succeeding.

Isn't there, then, some more underlying reason for this situation? Isn't there some basic explanation for the lack of understanding of what an army must be trained to do, and how it does it? Doesn't it lie somewhere in the field of communication between military and non-military minds? Suppose we look into this side of things for a possible clue.

It is now several months since the new *Field Service Regulations: Operations* (FM 100–5) was issued to the Army. In the three hundred pages of this volume of FSR, of course, is the "doctrine," the teachings on warfare, that govern all military training and all operations in war if we fight. It is not the final word, because methods and weapons constantly change. But at the time it came out it was the best-considered thought of the Army on American warfare. It was a general guide for training, campaign, and battle.

At the time this new FSR came off the government presses there was issued by the War Department to all interested newspapers, magazines, and individual correspondents and writers a release of several pages. This release emphasized some of the main modern doctrines covered in the new military bible, and also a number of points that might add color to any article or news story about it.

There may have been, somewhere in the United States, some able articles written about the new FSR. There may have been an attempt by some one writer to provide for the readers of his newspaper or magazine, or his radio listeners, a clear explanation or intelligent criticism on this most vital of all American military documents. But a search of a score of the country's leading newspapers and more than a score of its magazines finds no adequate treatment of this one most important source of military information and background. For the FSR tells how we are going to fight if we have to. And is there anywhere a much bigger story?

There was, it is true, one immediate story in most papers on the new FSR. Many made good use of the release on the book but treated it as just another side-light story on the Army. Some managed to botch up parts of the release into nonsense. Editorial comment? Practically none. Intelligent discussion and criticism? Practically none. Or none yet, for there may still be some on the way. Reviews by book reviewers? None.

As for the 150 or more other current manuals in the series issued by the War Department for use in training troops, some of them highly technical, there has been hardly more attention paid to any of them. The *Soldier's Handbook,* which contains the fundamentals for all men in military uniform, was perhaps the one exception, though a few others, such as the *Army Cook,* have been the basis for a few articles.

In short, this series of books—the greater part of them available to the public for purchase—the books that tell what our troops are supposed to be learning and what they will do in battle if a war is fought, are generally neglected as source material by those who are writing millions of words every day on the Army in training. As far as I have been able to ascertain, there is only one newspaper in the country that has purchased a complete set of these official books for purposes of reference. Some few newspapers and magazines have obtained the more important of the tactical texts such as *Field Service Regulations, Infantry Field Manual,* the *Soldier's Handbook,* and *Infantry Drill Regulations.*

Now almost certainly there is some reason beyond indifference or diffidence for this general lack of attention to these basic sources. For these books do contain in full detail what the Army is endeavoring to do in training and what it will be doing in war. The real reason, it is probable, lies in a remark made by a member of the staff of the leading illustrated weekly of the country. "Why are your Army books written," he asked, "in such fearful language? I thought I knew something about military things. But these manuals, especially the ones on tactical matters, stump me. Why can't the stuff be put out in plain language? If it were I should think it would be just that much easier to teach new officers and men the things they have to learn."

The series of field and technical manuals issued during the last two years and still being issued is beyond question the most complete and exhaustive set of training documents our Army has ever had. It is true that many of them have been put out under pressure of emergency. Hence there are some faults of haste to be found. But they do cover our military fields of technique, tactics, and strategy with remarkable completeness, and we have never had anything half so complete before.

But they are, with very few exceptions such as the *Soldier's Handbook* and *Arctic Manual,* written in the language of the military. They require, practically all of them, some considerable background of military education or experience, or the assistance of an instructor, if they are to be readily understood by those who read and use them. It has been said, in fact, that they come closer to being "officers' handbooks" than texts for the military beginner. Except for a few of the elementary manuals such as the *Soldier's Handbook* and *Infantry Drill Regulations,* it is probable that these books were not, in the first place, especially intended for the acquisition of military knowledge without an instructor's aid. Even the IDR, it is worth noting, has been considered sufficiently hard for un-drilled citizens of intelligence to understand, to warrant the publishing of at least one book carefully prepared for the sole purpose of explaining it in simpler language.

Since every other profession has its special language, its jargon, it is natural enough for the military profession to have one. As a matter of fact, our jargon has phrases in it that go back to the Greeks and the Romans. The military man can read Vegetius and Caesar and find an occasional turn of words still present in our manuals. And many another word or phrase has come down to us from other Great Captains and military writers of different periods. Through the centuries the soldier has thus acquired the special language in which he expresses his professional thoughts.

But I suggest that there is now the soundest of reasons for asking ourselves whether this language isn't in several ways a barrier to understanding and a hindrance to national defense. Doesn't it form the main reason why so few of the writers outside the Army who are writing constantly today about military things have undertaken to comment on the basic tasks and duties of troops as they are explained in readily available books? Isn't this also the reason why there has been so little comment on the official books themselves? And why so much that is written about the Army sounds absurd to the ear of a soldier?

But farther than these questions lie even broader ones. When unit leaders by tens of thousands and troops by hundreds of thousands must be trained in a period of emergency, wouldn't it save much training time if military books, particularly the ones that teach men how to fight, were written in the main like first-rate modern popular introductions to other sciences and arts? And wouldn't we find young men all over the country reading such books—thoroughly readable military books—long before their numbers were up? And other citizens, too, of non-military ages?

Since the emergency began many a publisher has hastened to press with what he thought was a good popular book on the Army. These have been aimed, the greater part of them, toward the new American soldier, but some toward what the citizen should know. Most of the publishers were wrong in their judgments despite the excellent sales that some of these books have had. Those who have followed the reviews of military books and the listings in the *Infantry Journal* have been able to get some idea of how much written about the Army has been indifferent or bad and how little has been good, even when they haven't had time to look into the books themselves. But suppose the Army itself had been producing books on the Army all the time, better than anything else obtainable, or at least as good as anything else?

Indeed, let's take the thing to its broadest implication. Let us suppose that instead of writing every military manual in the jargon of our Army it has been a consistent military policy for the last two decades to prepare thoroughly readable Army texts. Isn't it possible that the very availability of such books would have held the gap that grew between the nation and its military forces to a span considerably narrower? And hence far easier to leap when a new emergency came?

And to be thoroughly frank, wouldn't we in the Army read our own new books *as soon as they come out?* Instead of dreading and putting off the duty until it becomes a necessity? There is no denying that our own general attitude toward our books as reading matter shows plainly why "the language of regulations" is a byword for dry and often difficult reading.

If through the years there had been kept current even one fairly complete and readable book on the Army for general distribution to libraries, colleges, schools, and to newspapers and writers in general, members of Congress, and all others who might have read it or used it for reference, communication between the minds of citizens in general and their Army would have been far closer than it was when the present emergency arose. I am not suggesting here simply a descriptive handbook on the Army. I mean a text that would have spoken at some length of strategy and tactics. I mean a book that would have told what an American Army is for and how it must fight if it must.

Well, there is no such book even yet. And now that we're down to the desperately serious business of making an army in much less time than it takes, we need such books. We need to have every one of our military books done as well as they can possibly be done. We need this to help speed the training of our troops and the understanding of our citizens as to what our Army and the wars it may have to fight must be like.

What I am going to suggest must in no way be taken as finding fault with our military books as they stand or expressing criticism of the abilities and hard, grinding work of those who wrote them. Those who wrote them have often done so with a good deal of clarity—but in the language in which they were accustomed to think and write—the military language. There was no direct effort, except in the *Soldier's Handbook* and a very few others, to use a broader language, a language less dependent upon our habitual military phraseology, this for the sake of either the intelligent or the average-minded military beginner or non-military reader.

But let us now make a broad supposition. What if the military authorities sought the pick of the writers of the country to write its military books? What if they assigned each book, as far as this could be done, to a writer appropriate to the subject, with instructions somewhat as follows: "Here is your material. Give the subject matter interest and put the same general emphasis on different points now given them in the book you are going to rewrite. Make no attempt to write in an extensive, special military vocabulary, but use all the military terms you need to, explaining them clearly as you go. Army men who know the subjects thoroughly will be available to help you by explaining all military points you may not clearly understand and by pointing out to you where you distort the intended accurate meaning through lack of military background."

There are a good many official manuals which at first thought would hardly seem to lend themselves to this suggested treatment. For example, it might seem hard to get much life into the many separate volumes on the technique of different weapons. But here we merely have to remember some of the splendid popular books of the last few years on different sciences. And when it comes to manuals on such weapons as the rifle and pistol, there are a dozen thoroughly readable and fascinating books now in print on shooting. Army books would require a different treatment to get war into them, but they could be written just as well. And why shouldn't it be readily possible to write the same kind of books on the use of 155-mm. guns and howitzers or on any weapons of any size?

There should be no trouble either in doing a bright, lively job of writing on such technical manuals as *Aircraft Engines* (TM 1-405), the *Motor Vehicle* (TM 10-510), *Automotive Lubrication* (TM 10-540), *Meteorology* (TM 3-240), *Utilities* (TM 10-220), and *Standard Stream Crossing Equipment* (TM 5-270). For a long time now the trade magazines of the United States have known that technical articles, written informally and even lightly, are what interest many of their readers most. There is a fine example of this right in the Army today, the magazine *Army Motors,* published at the Holabird Quartermaster Depot. Its articles are practically all in a most informal style and often contain humor and current slang. But it's very probable that the voluntary reading of *Army Motors* by officers and enlisted men who have to do with military vehicles has resulted in ten times as much sound instruction as the voluntary reading of all the field and technical manuals on motor transport there are. The handling of meteorology in such a book as *Safety in Flight,* by Assen Jordanoff (Funk & Wagnalls, 1941), shows how clear this technical subject can be made through a combination of simple writing and modern diagrams and drawings. Indeed there is no technical field pertinent to military instruction in which there are not to be found examples of clear and accurate popular presentation.

There are a number of specific writers on the sciences whose aid could be sought. Weekly for years in the New York *Times*, Waldemar Kaempffert has been covering the scientific field in language the layman can enjoy and understand. In *Scientific American*, Henry Norris Russell has been writing for years on such abstruse subjects as astronomy. In *Popular Science Monthly* such writers as David M. Stearns present one technical topic after another in simplified scientific language. For the readers of *Harper's Magazine*, George Gray has long been covering new developments of science in a most readable fashion. *Mathematics for the Million*, by Lancelot Hogben (W. W. Norton & Company), an extremely able popular work, with large sales in Great Britain and the United States, is being used in both the Royal Air Force and the Royal Engineers as an instructional text. Such writers as these could make over the field and technical manuals on map reading, surveying, and the larger weapons— all books that contain such mathematics—into books that would be far easier to study and learn our technical business from. Likewise with the manuals on signal communication. They are accurate, workmanlike jobs as they stand. But bring in some of the writers on radio who contribute their popular technical articles to the radio magazines, and you would have books that would be avidly read and used.

Some of our books would fit readily into the abilities of writers in the field of sports. *Physical Training* is obvious. Suppose it were written by Grantland Rice or Gene Tunney and had the name of the author on the cover. Or suppose we gave the job of rewriting the field manual on the hand grenade to such a writer on sports as John Kieran or Moe Berg. Who could tell the new American soldier better, once he had grasped the thing himself, exactly how throwing the hand grenade differs from throwing a baseball, and how to make use of knowledge of sports in lobbing grenades into an enemy position?

Manuals on medical subjects? There have been several excellent popular books by doctors in the past ten years. Paul de Kruif's *Microbe Hunters* and other works; Logan Clendening's *The Human Body;* Karl Meninger's *The Human Mind.*

Manuals on animals, such as *Dog-Team Transportation* (FM 25-6) and *Animal Transportation* (FM 25-5)? How about Albert Payson Terhune, or Rex Beach, or Peter B. Kyne to give a hand with these?

The technical manual on tractors (TM 9-2777: *Track-Tractor, Heavy, Diesel Model* TD-18)? William Hazlitt Upson, through his Alexander Botts in the *Saturday Evening Post,* has told this country more about tractors than all the textbooks on them ever written.

But what of the most important books of all, the many tactical manuals and the *Field Service Regulations* itself? These, I suggest, could be broken down into parts to best advantage. And it might not be necessary to go far beyond the Army itself for writers to produce many of the sections, except for the fact that the names and abilities of nationally known writers would doubtless carry the work to a far wider audience of readers. Perhaps the best way here is to combine the work of national and military writers. For certainly such forcefully realistic writers on battle as Major William S. Triplet ("Terry Bull"), Lieutenant Colonel Edward S. Johnston (*Portrait of a Soldier, The Day Before Cantigny, Building an Army*), Colonel Ira C. Eaker (*Winged Warfare,* together with Major General H. H. Arnold), Lieutenant Colonel Elliot D. Cooke (*We Attack*), Lieutenant Colonel John U. Ayotte (*Infantry Combat Training, Red Meets Blue, A Mirror for Umpires, The Small Fights Count*), Lieutenant Colonel Thomas R. Phillips, author of many articles in military and other publications, Major Charles T. Lanham (*Panic, Where Angels Fear to Tread, Fifty Million Frenchmen Can Be Wrong,* and in part *Infantry in Battle*), Lieutenant Harvey S. Ford (*What the Citizen Should Know about the Army*) should not be passed over in working out such a project.

Among the well-known writers qualified to help with such a task, such men as James Boyd (*Drums, Marching On*), Harold Lamb (*Genghis Khan, March of the Barbarians*), Stephen Vincent Benét (*John Brown's Body*), Fletcher Pratt (*Ordeal by Fire, Road to Empire*), Kenneth Roberts (*Rabble in Arms, Northwest Passage*), Franz Werfel (*The Forty Days of Musa Dagh,* a classic of defensive combat), MacKinlay Kantor (*Long Remember,* one of the best books dealing with the Battle of Gettysburg) Ernest Hemingway (*For Whom the Bell Tolls*), Leonard H. Nason, writer of battle short stories, who lately discovered that war isn't nearly as funny as he once made it sound, and a number of others have shown themselves masters of combat analysis and description.

Can we grant perhaps that the FSR itself must remain outside of this scheme because of its central importance? I shall not attempt to say. There may be sound military reasons why the bible of the Army must be written in military language readily comprehensible only to the Command and General Staff School graduate or to his equivalent in military knowledge. If there are such reasons there could certainly be a parallel book interpreting for all others, military and non-military, the main doctrines which the FSR contains. It seems probable that if such a book were prepared we would find it the one of the two books covering the same subjects which would be more in use in the Army itself—the one that was actually studied and read.

There is already a sound precedent for what I am suggesting. The Army has been making movies as aids to its training ever since the first World War or before. This work has developed a number of officers and enlisted men experienced in moving-picture techniques. Nevertheless, there has been no hesitancy in the present emergency in seeking and accepting the best obtainable movie assistance. At the present moment the Army and the best minds in Hollywood are working out one good military picture after another for training, for morale, for any objective that will help the national defense, directly or indirectly.

But if we turn to the experts of Hollywood for help in producing their kind of training material, why shouldn't we with the same eagerness seek out the writers of the nation for the special aid they can give?

It will, of course, take more than writers alone. Illustrators, layout men, editors, publishers, and experts in the rising science of semantics would all be needed. For there is a long series of detailed technical steps between the completion of a writer's manuscript and the issuance of his book that is seldom realized by those who read and use it.

There are already a number of photographers of high rank both working for agencies of national defense and taking pictures of military activities for newspapers and news magazines. The experience and ability of the photographic sections of the Signal Corps and the Air Corps added to the work of such artists as Tommy McAvoy, Carl Mydans, Marian Post, Roy E. Stryker, Robert Y. Richie, and others who have been specializing in defense photography for the past two years would be most essential to proper illustration of the work. *The Army of the United States,* the one adequate official job of describing the Army done in recent years (1939) was superbly illustrated with photographs, only half of which came from Army sources. The bulk of the others (sixty-five pictures) were supplied through the courtesy of *Life* magazine, a number of them shots that had not appeared elsewhere before. And other commercial sources also made their contributions.

First-rate technical artists would also be needed. This present war has developed a number, but there are not many in the Army. We have but to glance at the maps and simplified drawings the newspapers and magazines use every day to see how much their work would contribute to ease of understanding.

The work of layout experts to design the appearance and sequence of the books would likewise be essential in producing books that would offer the greatest facility of use. Director of Typography Frank H. Mortimer and his layout section at the Government Printing Office have been doing first-rate work of this kind for several years—when they are given the time to do it in. The reason why field and technical manuals are not better jobs of printing, the reason why their illustrations are often not clear is not that the work couldn't be done far better by those who do it. It is simply because of the pressure of haste. *The Army of the United States* was an excellent job of layout and printing and so has been many another book and pamphlet done in recent years by the Government Printing Office.

Now, however, that huge agency is jammed with work. Consequently it would in all probability be necessary to farm out new Army books to commercial publishing houses, perhaps in much the same manner as now done to the two publishers who have been producing sound military books right on through the years of peace. The work might also well require the supervisory assistance of experienced publishers right in the War Department in co-operation with the agencies there now handling publications.

Editing is an extremely necessary evil—it is anyway an evil from the viewpoint of most writers—in the production of any book, whether Army manual, textbook, biography, songbook, or novel. Somebody has to see to it that the author's slips of fact are caught before printing, that his occasional errors of language are corrected, that his spelling and punctuation are reasonably sound, and, in expository writing of the kind we are considering, that he makes his meaning constantly clear. It is the editor's task thus to correct and co-ordinate. And in the project I have been suggesting it is possible that joint military and non-military editing would have to be done. The one would see to it that a writer somewhat unfamiliar with military things introduced no false military notes into his work. The other would endeavor to make certain that military ideas were expressed in reasonably simple and readable language. The main aim, of course, would be to avoid our customary military jargon, "the language of regulations," in the process.

But such is the state of our military language today that this could hardly be accomplished without much aid from experts in semantics. Semantics is the science that has, above all, for its study the improvement of accuracy of communication between mind and mind. It is the science that studies the shades and the shifts of the meanings of words. They are not dictionary makers, these people. Their aim is, through questioning and clarifying and simplifying language, to improve and perfect, as may be, the ability of one human being to understand accurately what another tells him through speech or writing or signs.

Experts trained in this science would discover and help us to solve many a puzzle of meaning in our present military language, many a block to understanding that hinders our training and our discussion of war but that we seldom realize to exist, if we notice them specifically at all. They would discover for us confusion of expression and inadequate and overlapping terminology which we do know exists but haven't yet been able to remedy in full. Semantic assistance could be so important that it is worth a separate study at length. The center of this work in the United States is the Committee on Communication at Harvard, where I. A. Richards and others are working out practical applications of what has been, up to recent years, a science more in the phases of preliminary study and development than of practical application.

Well, there is the idea. In it there is no question of disagreement with the contents of our official Army books and manuals. As the manuals were written, there was doubtless difference of opinion, and some of these differences must still exist. But that is how any doctrine is arrived at and how revisions of doctrine are made. There would be no military health in us at all if there were not constant differences of opinion, arguments, and discussions over the development of new tactics and techniques. With these things, however, the project I have suggested would have no concern. Its only aim would lie in what can be done through a rewriting of our military books by the best obtainable writers in order to make them clear and readable and readily understood by any reader, within the Army or without it, who will apply his mind to their contents. In the more fundamental books writers like those suggested should give us military texts that would explain every fascinating side of war in language so vivid and clear that the reader new to military matters might understand it the first time over. And the reader experienced in military matters would understand some things far better than he ever had before.

Let us think once more, in conclusion, of one of the gravest faults of our national life—our lack of understanding of military things, our feeling that the military is something apart, something that must be tolerated because it is necessary, but a strange and unpleasant and possibly bloody sort of business that in ordinary times carries on its existence away from the world on military reservations. Think of how far the Army and Navy, without which there can be no nation, had gone from the minds of the rest of the nation during the past twenty years. Think of the refusal of intelligent men (*otherwise* intelligent men) to include a national defense in the scheme of things they saw for the world. Think of their belief that the world could conceivably be controlled without some great and efficient military force to police it. Would this foreshortened outlook have developed if military lore had been on every library shelf, in every bookshop, and thus in many a home—homes of congressmen and carpenters, professors, businessmen, and clerks—in volumes written by writers who could reach the minds of all citizens if something like what I have suggested had been done long ago? Has there ever, indeed, been another way of making certain that our country accepted the military side of its national life as an integral, unquestioned part of that life?

Any step that can add to the rapidity with which military knowledge is absorbed and to the interest with which it is gained is an important direct measure of national defense. But above all, it will lead us in the direction of a broader familiarity on the part of our people with their armed forces, with what these forces do and how they think, and with what they need if they are to protect the nation. It will help them to

know and remember how constantly vital a part of the national existence
and the national strength these military forces are.

ANIMADVERSIONS ANENT ANFRACTUOSE
AND OBFUSCATORY LOCUTIONS

By Captain (now Colonel) Russell Skinner

(*1935*)

IN THE PAST FEW YEARS many of the Army officers who are radio fans
have listened to Andy talk with Lightnin' and have enjoyed his plentiful
use of four-dollar words to impress him. Probably none of them felt that
they had ever been guilty of such a thing or that they ever could be.
And yet as I think of certain words that officers have adopted for their
use I'm not so sure.

Note the eagerness with which the officers who went to France picked
up the juicy foreign terms they heard the French and English using.
The word "liaison" is an example. It may have been appealing for the
slight air of the bedroom that hung around it, but mostly it seems to have
been popular because of a childish liking for a high-sounding expression
among the staff.

Or consider coming to call a "headquarters" a "command post." There
was never anything to be gained by it except a feeling by its users that
they thus proved themselves military big-leaguers. It's foolish to call it a
headquarters until a battle starts and then give it another name merely
for the duration of the fight. They began calling a "lookout" an "observation post" too. Plainly, the only reason for that was to give the officer
doing it such added importance in his own eyes as was to be gained
from using an Andyish expression instead of a common one. It's to be remembered, too, that it had always to be "established"; it couldn't just be
"put out"; that was too ordinary.

Some time ago the writer of a paragraph in the *Journal* criticized the
use of the term "axis of signal communication." Rightly; it's a horrible
expression, invented undoubtedly by a signal officer who hoped to prove
by its use that he was the real McCoy among military high-brows. Not
that the Andys are confined to the Signal Corps or any other one branch.
Far from it. The cavalry, with a reputation in the past for plain speaking,
aren't content to call a thing by its name any longer. For instance, when
a tank is assigned to them it becomes a combat car. Shades of Tommy
Tompkins! [The most plain-spoken cavalryman who ever served in our
Army.] At that, the worst may not have happened yet. Who knows but

that at any moment they may start calling it a *sturm-panzerkraftwagen* in imitation of the Germans. The artillery, too, have invented their share of verbal horrors. In fact, one of them is probably the most ear-grating of any, the one they use when they say the artillery will "displace" forward—a bumptious substitute for the plain word "move."

The inventor of that Andyism, "hill mass," is unknown, but though we may not know his branch or who he is, we can be sure of this about him: he's an officer who thought if he called high ground by a more impressive-sounding name he'd prove his right to a seat up among the mighty. "Terrain corridor" is another term of recent appearance, apparently adopted only because it is high-sounding. Once it was called an avenue of approach; soon who can tell but that we may hear it spoken of as a "boulevard of accessibility." How refreshing if instead someone began calling it an alley. The "compartmenting of the terrain" is another phrase to be met with frequently nowadays. Nobody but an army intellectual or a German Ph.D. could have thought of such an awkward and would-be imposing group of words as that. [He's wrong; this one came from the French.] There's no end to them: "group" becomes "groupment"; "waste" turns into "wastage" (the addition of an unnecessary syllable is a favorite practice of the Army Andys); "alert" is used as a verb (to alert the reserves); "terrestrial" is used in place of "ground"; "infiltrate" for "seep"; "retrograde" for "backward," and so on and on and on.

It may seem at first as if, since these expressions are simply the product of childish vanity, there is no particular harm in their use. Sometimes that is so, but more often they are positively bad in that they substitute a strange word for a good old one about which there has grown up a host of associations, each of which is an aid to deep and thorough understanding of its meaning. The use of "observation post" for "lookout" illustrates this harm. Except for the expression "getaway man," there is no more satisfactory term in military use. Merely to designate a man as a lookout is partially to teach him his job. The use of "liaison" is harmful for the same reason also. If a man is told to keep in touch with the unit next him he understands completely what he is to do, as he seldom will if he is directed to "maintain liaison" with it.

A particularly regrettable substitution is that of "morale" for "spirit." "Spirit" is one of the tingly words in our language, rich with accrued meanings. When it is used the listener immediately interprets it in connection with other spirited things he has known: spirited horses, Spirit of '76, etc. How different when the word "morale" is used. It has no such associations for the English-speaking person; to him it is as flat and as lacking in vital meaning as a mathematical equation.

These are merely examples. In every issue of every service magazine there are dozens more. The authors, who in informal conversation often describe events in simple language which is yet racy and graphic, once they start getting something ready for formal presentation, get as solemn as owls; they outdo a Negro preacher in silly pomposity. It's a pity.

"AUXILIARY" AND "SECONDARY" ARMS

From an editorial by CAPTAIN (now MAJOR GENERAL) GEORGE A. LYNCH

(*1916*)

. . . IT IS UNFORTUNATE that in our Army there has been a tendency to confuse the function of the different arms with their importance and to consider the term "auxiliary" as equivalent to "secondary." This confusion has become evident in recent suggestions that the term "co-ordinate" should be substituted for "auxiliary" as being more in accord with the relative importance of the arms. The description of an arm as auxiliary has, however, nothing to do with its importance but relates exclusively to its tactical function. The term "co-ordinate" does not express any functional idea whatever, if not indeed a false one. For it does not define the direction from which the co-ordination must come. . . . But the term "co-ordinate" conveys no idea of the tactical bond that should exist between the arms. We conceive that in the realm of anatomy the right and left legs are co-ordinate, but we cannot comprehend that the same relation exists between the heart and the lungs.

MILITARY ENGLISH

By CAPTAIN X

(*1937*)

IS OUR PROFESSION so abstract that the matter of its instruction and regulations falls naturally into a ponderous and murky style? Are its outlines so blurred that its language must also be hazy? And is the composition of its written matter so secondary in importance that inaccurate terminology and ineffectual, careless, and even meaningless verbiage make no difference?

Far from being one of the duller sciences, military science is one of the most interesting and fascinating of all. Its bases, at least, are specific and lend themselves to the utmost precision of statement. There is every reason to write of military things in language so clear and words so carefully chosen as to be unmistakable in their intent. For upon the clarity of military language may depend the success of an army and the existence of a nation.

ABBR

By B.V.D.

(*1937*)

"PROPERLY FRAMING ORDERS is an important feature in the exercise of command," says the War Department.

"Its purpose is to enable the plan of the commander to be quickly understood," continues Leavenworth.

"The contents and method of issue depend upon the situation," adds Benning.

"So what?" asks the reader.

So nothing! But have you seen the new type of telegraphic field orders? The kind reading—"1st Tk Co (less 3 plats) div res Taneytown."

A snappy way of saying that the 1st Tank Company, minus three of its platoons, will go to Taneytown as part of the division reserve. That's O.K. The abbreviations are authorized by *Staff Officers' Field Manual.* But some of our enthusiasts want to do better. They have begun to improvise.

Catch this nifty that recently came into a rear echelon during maneuvers:

Fwd Ki and W Sup to RDP at W Tk N 1st Div Rd dark Nt 16 Oct.

By which was meant that someone wanted his kitchen and water supply forwarded to his ration distributing point at the water tanks north of the 1st Division Road under cover of the darkness on the night of October 16. But what kind of a way is that of saying so?

After all, if everyone has to carry around a list of abbreviations in his hip pocket we might as well resort to code. Deceiving the enemy is all right, but there is no sense in trying to confuse our own people. We have a hard enough time understanding orders that are completely written. What chance have we against an assortment of trick abbreviations?

Abbreviated orders look very well in our textbooks, but they are not the product of field conditions. They are written and rewritten by an instructor; cut, sliced, and amputated by a murder board; checked and double-checked by an editor, and after weeks of preparation appear as we see them. What will they look like when written under pressure, punctuated by high explosives, and subjected to the ultimate test of battle?

They might turn out all right if we were not such a nation of faddists.

But give us radio and we outtalk the world. Get us started on abbreviations and we will outabbreviate the abbreviators. We will adopt a secret
vocabulary that will put all previous jargons on the salvage pile.

Someone had better call a halt. Leave shorthand to the stenographers.
Let's spigoty English.

POLYSYLLABIFICATION

By TONGUE-TIED

(*1937*)

B.V.D.'s GRIPE on abbreviations is only half the story. I agree that short
cuts in language are bound to turn into a code after a certain point. But
is a code any harder to learn than its opposite—a list of terms each of
which fills a line?

Look at these:

> regimental ammunition distributing point
> regimental machine-gun company commander
> special-weapons battalion commander
> commanding officer 2nd Field Artillery Regiment
>   (tractor-drawn)
> outpost line of resistance
> mechanization and motorization
> advance guard when contact is imminent

The strange thing is that we already have abbreviations for most such
terms and titles, but we don't use them. Visit our academic halls, or
examine our regulations or the instructional matter that our schools produce, and what do you find? Abbreviations are limited to diagrams and
combat orders. You seldom hear them spoken or see them written. Great
mouth-filling terms strike your ear or your eye, every one of them halting
comprehension until the parade of their syllables has passed.

Only occasionally does an instructor become so informal as to speak
or write of an ammunition distributing point as a DP, and I have yet to
hear one call a line of departure an LD, or an outpost line of resistance
an OLR.

I am not suggesting a wholesale adoption of abbreviations such as B.V.D.
inveighs against—only the use of them where they seem reasonable. We
need them worst, perhaps, for titles, where we have the excellent precedent of G-1, S-4, etc. S-4 is actually the "regimental staff officer for
supply," but no one ever calls him that. Extending this practice a little
farther, we could call the four battalion commanders CO-1, CO-2, etc.,

and use CO-A to CO-M for the company commanders. True, all this could not go on forever, but a little more of it might help.

As for MLR, LD, and such terms, we have only to make more use of what we now have. And we could easily learn to speak of such things as AA and AT defense for "antiaircraft" and "anti-tank," thus to extend simplicity a little farther.

The only objection I can think of to my suggestion is the difficulty it might put in the way of our emergency officers. But suppose you ask a civilian friend, the next time you see him, what NRA, HOLC, or RFC stand for. He may not be able to tell you, but he knows what they mean.

MILITARIST OR PACIFIST?

By Lieutenant Colonel (now Colonel) John W. Lang

(*1931*)

Green shades off imperceptibly into blue at one side of the spectrum and yellow at the opposite. Green is neither blue nor yellow, though it is both. Blue has many symbolic connotations which vary from low in spirits to the poetical symbol of freedom. Yellow applies to richness as well as to cowardice.

So, too, have pacifism and militarism many connotations. Like propaganda, through loose usage they have become terms of reproach. Each has many shades and, combined, they produce many variations of thought.

The statesman should have a bit of both. He should be an advocate of arbitration as a means of settling international misunderstandings, yet he should be disposed to provide for the strength and safety of the country by maintaining adequate military force. He should heed the words of John Adams, who in his Fourth Annual Address to Congress on November 22, 1800, said, "We cannot, without committing a dangerous imprudence, abandon these measures of self-protection which are adapted to our situation and to which, notwithstanding our pacific policy, the violence and injustice of others may again compel us to resort." The statesman should weigh the costs of war and preparation against it in the balance against the probable costs of defeat and the loss of our hard-won liberty and prosperity, just as the businessman weighs the costs of insurance premiums against the value of his property and the risks to which it is subjected. He must remember that the friend of today may be the adversary of tomorrow.

Thus we see that the ideal statesman has in his mental make-up the thoughts and qualities which will prompt one group of extremists to call him "pacifist" and another group to hurl at his head the opprobrious name "militarist."

Thus is indicated how, in our living language, the contradictory terms "pacifism" and "militarism" are loosely used, even to the extent of being applied to the same person for an identical act. To Webster the terms are antonyms.

WITHOUT BENEFIT OF STENCILS

By MAJOR (now COLONEL) ARNOLD W. SHUTTER

(*1936*)

Oh, I wish I had had a commission
With J. Caesar's legions of old,
When the mimeograph, as we know it,
Was a story that hadn't been told.
The orders were then mostly verbal,
And they seldom took time out to write;
For the bulk of an officer's duties
Lay in teaching his men how to fight.

When they fought with the sturdy Helvetians
A man who was absent was missed,
For they hadn't put half their damned army
On the Detached Officers' List.
They carried their banners to Britain,
And the Britons had no cause to laugh.
But I'm told that it wasn't accomplished
By the use of the mimeograph.

Now I sit in a big city office
That's furnished with tables and chairs,
And the orderly falls down exhausted
When he's dragged my mail up the stairs.
He deposits his load in the corner
And then he is done with his chore,
While I have ten hours before me
Just reading the memos from Corps.

Now back in the days when J. Caesar
Marched from the Rhine to the Rhone,
They had to get out special orders
With a mallet and chisel on stone.

There were no carbon copies of that stuff
To bother the staff and the line.
And yet, so historians tell us,
His doughboys just got along fine.

The Senate once sent him a letter,
The kind many readers recall:
"Explain, by endorsement hereon, sir,
Results of campaigning in Gaul."
So he chiseled a snappy endorsement:
"I came and I saw and I won."
Put that in your pipe now and smoke it,
You pink-whiskered son of a gun!

Now if I should write such an answer
And send it, through channels, to Corps,
The chances, my son, are a hundred to one
That I'd not have to write any more;
For they'd hold a conclave on my record
And I'd be Class-B'd in a day;
And then they'd withdraw my commission
And stop all the rest of my pay.

Each day, as I sit in my office,
With my shoulders acquiring a stoop,
I wish that I had a commission
In J. Caesar's headquarters troop.
And yet I could die well contented
Should this be my true epitaph:
"Here Lies the American Soldier
Who Abolished the Mimeograph."

MUMBLERS, DRONERS, AND SINGSONG READERS

By D. S.

(1940)

IT IS IMPOSSIBLE to create a competent platform speaker by the mere
issuance of an order. Yet every time a new instructor is ordered to a
service school and he reports for duty, it is taken for granted that he is
capable of climbing to the platform and keeping wide awake a hallful
of students by the clarity, emphasis, and persuasiveness of his powers
of speech.

This official assumption that an instructor—any instructor—is equipped by Nature with a loud, clear voice and a platform presence simply stultifies a good third of every course presented at the schools of our arms and services. The mumblers, the droners, the singsong readers, and the speakers who have no ear for emphasis make the hours of their lectures and their illustrative problems into hours of stupefying misery for the classes that sit before them. Most of them make enough noise for sleep to be difficult. And if it were possible to measure the wanderings of the students' minds, the total would at least circle the earth every fifty minutes.

Few of these speakers are unaware of their inadequacy. Most of them are as uncomfortable on the rostrum as their hearers are in their seats. They try hard, too, most of them, because they are interested in their jobs and their topics and would like to put their stuff across to eager student minds so that one day it might be recalled to advantage in the midst of combat. But their handicaps are too great.

Nor can professional eagerness on the part of the students offset these handicaps. You may be avid to hear and learn, but if you can't hear you can't learn. And even if you can, the distraction of a poor delivery requires a superattentiveness that few possess to offset it.

Our service schools offer too much that is invaluable and their objectives are far too important for a large fraction of their instruction to be nullified by feebleness of platform presentation. There is, moreover, no sound reason why such unappetizing mental fare should be offered. A rearrangement of instructors' duties would easily remedy the fault and notably improve instruction.

Every school has a certain number of instructors who might have been preachers, professors, or possibly politicians, if they had not chosen to wear a uniform. These are the ones who actually like to lecture, and most of them do it well. Some of them are so good they can talk on any topic and hold full interest to the end. One such officer gave a fifty-minute lecture describing the Army Extension Courses to a body of mature students and received loud and long applause as he closed.

These—and no others—are the people to put on the platform. Let the best speakers give all the talks and handle all the illustrative problems. Reduce their preparatory research accordingly and let them spend most of their time in perfecting their presentations. Those to whom no amount of training could give a reasonable fluency—let them work up the materials and let them be present, in their capacity of experts, to help out speaker-instructors during the question periods. But for the sake of school efficiency—and, yes, for the sake of the national defense—keep them off the platform.

COMMANDING GROUND

By G. V.

(*1938*)

So much of war is fought in time of peace on maps rather than on the actual ground that there is a tendency toward the cut and dried at all military schools. One of the maps commonly used is that of the Gettysburg region. Contrary to the belief of many who have heard about this use of the Gettysburg map, there has not been—during the past twenty years at least—any relationship between the Battle of Gettysburg itself and the use of maps of the same ground for tactical instruction. The Army simply had good maps of that area. The area contained all kinds of ground, including mountains, rivers, lakes, flat terrain, rolling terrain, and sea-coasts and arms of the sea. The paper battles fought were modern battles, not Civil War battles.

THE SPLENDID MAPS on which we do most of our military studying tell us much about the ground of our paper wars. We pin these substitutes for miles of battle terrain upon a study wall or spread them on a dining-room table. Then, at will, we emulate that olden hero, General Jackson:

> *General Jackson had an army*
> *Of forty thousand men;*
> *He marched them up a hill*
> *And he marched them down again.*

Yes, we can look at the map and find a hill suitable for anything. And not one, but a dozen if we need them.

This bringing of mountains to Mohammed is all to the good, provided one thing is true—that the contours on the map give everyone the same mental picture. But this is not the case.

I do not mean simply that the average Army Extension Courses [correspondence courses for reserve officers] student, who seldom gets a chance to compare map with ground, may not do a fair job of terrain visualization. He often does. But even we, who have had ample opportunities to peer at a hill while our forefingers indicated the same bump of ground (approximately) on a map, are also liable to error when working with the map alone. This is particularly true when we have to estimate slopes and visibility of ground by eye. And of all people, those who offend worse in this respect should never do so; I mean the authors of map problems.

Let me cite one example—St. Luke's Church. Not a week ago I heard a service-school instructor say that St. Luke's Church stood on commanding ground. The Gettysburg map shows this decent place of worship to be about one mile southeast of Bonneauville at the top of a gentle slope. The ground drops precipitously away from the church at a rate of some twenty feet per five hundred yards on the steepest side. How far you can see in any direction, if at all, would be debatable, except for the initiative of a Benning instructor some years ago. He got so tired of arguing that the vista of St. Luke's Church was distinctly not "commanding" that he drove up to Pennsylvania to see for himself.

He sent back five snapshots, one taken toward each cardinal point of the compass, and one of himself standing in front of the church. On the back of that one he wrote, "Here I am standing at St. Luke's Church enjoying the magnificent view of thirty yards in every direction."

Yet I believe it was decided that there must be a good view from the steeple, anyhow. This, perhaps, was justifiable, if the church actually has a steeple and if General A happens to have a ladder with him so he can climb to the roof and watch his brave lads capture Gettysburg by wide envelopment.

And so this quiet country church continues to lend its name to terrain exaggeration in many a map problem. And many a similar misinterpretation can be found. The only way out is to give our school instructors a course in contour chasing [mapping] every two or three years. Or else take some more photographs on the ground to prove them wrong. Or else make General A's ladder standard equipment.

SHOTS, BIG AND LITTLE

By WILLIAM TELL

(1938)

WHEN Private Josiah Simpkins swaggered away from the firing line he knew what he'd made before the official caller of shots turned in the report. Josiah was no mean caller of shots himself. "Expert" was the answer.

In token of his skill with the U.S. rifle, caliber .30, M-1903, a grateful republic kicked his salary five dollars a month for a year and gave him a badge to wear. The government got back part of the sixty dollars, because Josiah invested most of his raise in the pink tax stamps that accompany Laughing Hyena bourbon—18 months in the wood, no neutral spirits added. The badge got a lot of the home folks to thinking that Josiah was now really a big shot, and a man who ran a shooting gallery called time on him after he had knocked loose four packs of cigarettes in rapid succession. In short, a good time was had by all.

Consider, now, Corporal Frank Merriwell. Frank is an earnest lad, and ambition just exudes from his pores. The while Josiah is downtown, giving the girls a treat, Frank studies Extension Courses. He wants to be a reserve officer, a second lieutenant of infantry, no less. This takes a little time; there are a half-dozen or so subcourses to work off, and they're not any too easy. Three or four months' night work—on his own time— and the trick is turned. Frank goes before a board for the final practical test.

He stumbles over a gobboon by way of making an effective entrance to the room where the board sits in judgment. It doesn't even get a smile. For the next couple of hours the board puts Frank over the jumps and quits only when they have him, as the saying goes, sweating profusely. On the way out he stumbles over the same gobboon, having made it a point to remember to avoid it.

About a month later Frank finds out what the board was up to after he made his exit. A letter, signed by a man with mighty poor handwriting, informs him that he is now a full-fledged shavetail of United States Infantry Reserve. From an insurance standpoint this job is so poor that Frank won't get anything but a horselaugh from an underwriter in the event of what some people quaintly call "a national emergency."

It would be nice if we could tell you that next payday Frank was rewarded by a raise of at least five dollars and a quarter by the same republic that pays Josiah sixty bucks a year for plunking holes in a bull's-eye. But we can't, for this is a true story. True stories generally wind up with the hero cutting a rather sorry figure.

Or maybe Frank wasn't the hero. Maybe it was Josiah. It's all so confusing.

NEW TRICKS—BY ORDER

By Temporarily Abreast

(*1937*)

This is a gripe about the lag between the up-to-date tactics and technique taught at the service schools and the official distribution of the same information to the troops of the Army in general. Hundreds of officers would learn new methods of war each year at the schools and then, on being assigned to a regiment, would often find that it would be another year or two before the same news would reach the regiments officially. This was, in general, caused by the fact that it took that long to get out a new field manual with the new stuff in it. Editorial staffs were small and many approvals had to be obtained.

THE PACKERS are in my quarters, and in a few days I shall be heading for my new regiment from this, the greatest Infantry School in the world.

Naturally enough, I am full of hot, up-to-the-minute infantry information, absorbed during the past nine months. And when I reach my new outfit I hope that I will be permitted to help bring it up to date on some of the excellent new methods the Infantry School has just taught me.

But all I have is a hope—and a mighty faint hope at that. The chances are five to one that when I join my regiment somebody will pin back my ears with the utmost ferocity the very first time I even suggest that "they don't do it that way at Benning any more."

I have seen that happen too many times, of course, to other enthusiastic juniors fresh from the Upatoi's sandy banks [a river at the Infantry School] to go sounding off like a new tactical or technical Messiah. I fully intend to be non-assertive and tactful. I shall not appear as a young know-it-all. I shall make only suggestions, not recommendations. But I am dead certain that unless I am very lucky and come under commanders anxious to put the latest ideas into effect, I might better keep my mouth shut from the beginning.

"We won't fool with new Benning stuff until it comes out in regulations." That is the common attitude. In free translation it simply means: "We won't make a single damn change until we have to"—or else, "The old way is plenty good enough." At bottom lies either laziness or mistrust —or sometimes sheer obstinacy.

It would not be hard to break this inertia down with a little help from high quarters. It is only a matter of getting the new methods early to the troops through authoritative channels. The simplest, cheapest way to accomplish this would be for the Infantry School to mark plainly all instructional matter suitable for immediate service use: TENTATIVE—*To be used for service instruction.* One copy of each document so marked should then be sent to all infantry regimental commanders through the office of the Chief of Infantry.

In this way new doctrine and new methods would reach every unit early. There would be no choice about keeping up to date. Regulations written in 1923 could no longer be the refuge of the cautious, the listless, the hardheaded, and the comatose. Development and progress would not be limited to the eager minds. It would be impossible for there to be a hiatus of three or four years between Benning and the service in general, as in the case of the simplified machine-gun indirect laying methods just now reaching the service officially, although taught at Benning since 1933. And not least, perhaps—the greater part of the 150 young officers who leave Benning every year would not go through the discouragement of having their commanders crown them for exhibiting a reasonable degree of professional enthusiasm.

It would be better still, of course, if late Benning information could be distributed direct, in sufficient copies, for every infantry officer to have one. This, however, would require more funds for reproduction and distribution than are now obtainable. But one copy per regiment, with the official O.K. of high infantry authority upon it, would do the trick. Suitable training matter appearing in the *Infantry School Mailing List* or the *Infantry Journal* might also be indicated as having official approval. Anything—any way—to jar us out of our postwar wagon-wheel ruts on to a speedier track.

ANCIENT SYMBOLS OF CAMPAIGN

By Captain Tentage

(*1938*)

I PROPOSE A RIDDLE: What is it that covers but discloses? What is it that makes a farce, time after time, of maneuvers in which air observation plays a part? What is it, indeed, that an air observer looks for, by night or by day, to determine the presence of a maneuver force? I'll give you one guess.

The answer is: tents.

You can see a nice clean light brown tent twenty miles away on a clear day. Nothing else on the ground resembles it at all—not even a haystack. At night you can see one with a gasoline lamp in it for at least fifteen miles, if not for twenty. And yet there must be some kind of shelter available for the rheumatic bones and tender skins of command and staff, which are not always perfectly inured to sun and rain. We need shelter, too, for maps and pencils of many colors, for typewriters and mimeographs, for telephones and radios, and for unit journals, message-center records, and the great white blankets of forms on which G-2, G-3, and G-4 estimate their respective situations and formulate their multifarious plans. And umpires, too, need shelter for snacks and snores between decisions.

In peace, unhappily, the Constitution prevents us from discommoding such theoretically ever-obliging gentlemen as Messrs. A. Trostle, M. Rudish, J. Spangler, McIlheny, and A. Plank. Nor are Luth. T. Seminary, St. Joseph's Academy, or even Mt. Vernon School and St. Luke's Church readily available except for the purposes of imaginary war. [The above are names of farm owners and places which appear on the series of maps covering the Gettysburg area, much used in theoretical military work at service schools.]

In lieu thereof, the quartermaster provides us with tentage, that ancient symbol of the rigors of campaign. And so long as self-advertising tentage is issued we may be certain that it will be used. But surely it would be no great expense or trouble to change the tentage specifications to something reasonably camouflaged. We might even stumble over the fact that camouflaged tentage would serve to hide motors as well as men.

WHO FIRES AMMUNITION— THE RIFLE OR THE MAN?

By S.A.R.

(1936)

SOME THIRTY-THREE YEARS AGO, when the United States Army took the bold step of adopting the Springfield rifle, many an old-timer shook his head. To their concreted minds it made no difference that the Springfield was a splendid weapon, mechanically tough, and more accurate by far than any shoulder piece the Army had ever had. Nor did any amount of conclusive proving ground and service tests bear weight.

Their first basis for viewing with alarm was simply the fact that a change was to be made. Something new was to take the place of something old. That, of course, is reason enough for distrust. But bolstering up this primary prejudice came a second hue and cry: "You'll never be able to get enough ammunition forward for those rifles. They can be fired too fast."

How familiar are those words to our ears at the present juncture! How frequently they are heard, now that we are about to follow at long last in the footsteps of the Mexican Army and adopt a self-loading rifle.

It may be granted that any Infantry School demonstration of the new weapon firing nearly a round a second is well calculated to bring up visions of difficulties in ammunition supply. But before we despair at the radicalism of adopting such a rifle I suggest that one brief comparison should be made.

In the excitement of battle a half-trained recruit, equipped with the semiautomatic rifle, could fire all the ammunition he carries in less than ten minutes. In fact, he could come near doing it in five if he were strong enough and his rifle functioned to perfection.

But—mark it well—the same recruit, with a Springfield at his shoulder, could spread the same number of wild shots over the landscape in less than twenty minutes.

Thus there is little difference if an hour or two must pass before more ammunition can be obtained. If either weapon has an advantage under the conditions assumed, it is the semiautomatic. It is so much easier to fire a self-loader than to pump a bolt handle that the fire of the self-loader is bound to be a little more accurate.

In the end it comes down to a matter of training and not of excessive mechanical perfection. The untrained soldier will waste ammunition with a muzzle loader. The trained man, with any weapon, will conserve ammunition until he really needs it. But when he does begin the rapid fire of battle, a semiautomatic, with twice the fire power of a bolt-action rifle available at one quarter the expenditure of energy, improves him tremendously as an element of combat.

BLAZE OF GLORY

By CAPTAIN BRASS

(*1936*)

His cohorts were gleaming in purple and gold.

Destruction of Sennacherib. BYRON

IN *The Army in My Time* Major General J. F. C. Fuller says, "Once, as a subaltern, I worked out how many hours in his service a soldier took in 'cleaning up.' I forget now the astronomical figure I arrived at. . . ." These words brought back to me a succession of scenes that my occasionally practical mind inevitably conjures up a dozen times a year. Of these scenes I shall recount only three.

(1) In Panama some years ago—nearly a thousand Springfield rifles borne by as many soldiers of the Coast Artillery at evening parade, every rifle polished to a mirror surface, bereft, even around the screwheads, of every least coating of gun metal, shining in the sunlight like the spears of Sennacherib's cohorts. Who paid for bluing them again I never learned.

(2) A day of ninety-seven in the shade—even the New Jersey applejack trees are drooping. Guard mount at four o'clock—the troops droop, too, even at attention. They spent last night until midnight—and more than one night before that—scraping, rubbing, scouring. Nothing that was brass beneath its sensible coating of o.d. paint now remains unpolished. What, nothing? Well, hardly anything. The general rides up to the guardhouse and after the customary honors have been rendered inspects the guard. In the rear rank his all-seeing eye finds an eyelet under a first-aid pouch—AN EYELET UNPOLISHED! The entire new guard is thrown off. "Captain New O.D. [also company commander of the unit furnishing the guard], report to your quarters in arrest. . . . Your lieutenant [new officer of the guard] also."

(3) One day in Georgia. A new lieutenant comes to me, an old lieutenant. "We have been told by our company commander that we are to contribute ten dollars each toward nickel-plating a machine-gun cart. I

can't afford it. The men are to pay two dollars apiece and the officers ten. Since my last kid came it's tougher than ever to keep out of debt. Do you think I should dare to refuse? I've only been commissioned a year. The whole job is to cost about $350. The company commander wants us to go on a note, too, to cover payment until all collections are in. I hate the whole idea, but I guess I'd better pay and forget it."

I said I'd give you only three fond memories, but here's a fourth for good measure:

(4) The Philippines. I fly in a simulated attack formation against an infantry regiment. As we hunt for the regiment I try my amateur eye at observation. I do my best to keep my mind on the appearance of the terrain below and off my queasy stomach. A glint, a flash, several glints and flashes, then many, down there on the slightly swaying ground. The pilot turns and grins back at me beneath his goggles as we rush down a steep channel of atmosphere to simulate an attack.

I have no personal antipathy to glinting brass and gleaming leather, but I am utterly certain that the whole business is wrong. The very idea it upholds is antagonistic, not only to the elemental habit of camouflage that modern warfare demands, but to the thoughts of military necessity that we endeavor to place in the minds of our citizens who bear no arms now but will, soon enough, when the need arises.

The greatest absurdity of all is the belief in the necessity for brassy splendor, however modest, to set off equipment and uniform. Does any uniform lend itself better to a soldierly appearance than our own combined with darkened insignia, a shoulder or waist belt of web, and leg and footwear of dull, rough-finished leather? I like the pretty brightness of brass—on door handles—but I am positive that shining equipment is (1) unnecessary to a fine, businesslike, military appearance; (2) contrary to the essential principles of modern warfare, and (3) slightly ridiculous when viewed with a calm mind.

DON'T TINKER WITH THE GOVERNOR

Anonymous

(1942)

ANY OF YOU DRIVERS ever see a Chinese fishing with cormorants—you know, those long-necked birds that dive into the water from the boat and snaffle the fish? Did you ever wonder what kept them from eating the fish, instead of taking them back and laying them in the fisherman's lap?

Damn clever, these Chinese! They put a governor on the bird's throat

—a ring big enough to let the small fish slip through into the belly, but small enough to keep the big fish out so they can go into the fisherman's pot. The cormorants get enough chow to keep them happy, but not enough to get a bellyache.

The governor on your truck works the same way. It gives the engine enough gas to keep it happy, but not enough to ruin it. But some zombies in this man's Army think they're pulling a fast one when they jimmy the governor. Soldier, it doesn't do you any good at all, but you probably won't believe it until we show you. O.K., Missouri, here goes:

The Army won't buy a governor that cuts the horsepower of an engine more than 5 per cent until the governor starts to cut out. Most of the governors now being bought hold the horsepower loss to 2 per cent. This means that the only thing a governor does is prevent excessive engine speed. With the exception of the 2-per-cent loss, a governor doesn't affect acceleration, pulling power, or anything else. Of course it stops your accelerating when you've hit the top governed road speed, but no one but a cowboy needs to step on 'er at that speed anyway.

Maybe you didn't know this: the rate of wear in an engine increases by the square of the engine speed. Which means that when you double the engine speed from 1,500 to 3,000 r.p.m., the rate of wear increases four times, and when you double it again to 6,000, the rate of wear jumps to sixteen times. To prevent this tremendous wear, most governors cut in at about 200 r.p.m. above the maximum horsepower speed of the engine.

And another thing: when you jimmy the governor you're not helping yourself a darned bit. The restriction is still there, and you have the same power loss. What do you gain? Nothing, soldier, nothing.

Actually the whole reason for a governor is not to limit your top *truck* speed, but to limit the top *engine* speed—and the only reason for that is to stop the engine shaking its guts out when you're in low gear. If you're ever hauling a load up a hill and find the governor cutting in and out, you can bet you're in too low a gear and overrevving the engine. So shift up a notch and see if you don't get the same results without punishing the engine.

Remember this: the governor can't control the speed of a truck when it's going downhill. It controls the throttle all right, but it can't control the engine speed because momentum has taken over and the wheels are driving the engine, instead of the engine driving the wheels. So if you're in too low a gear, the truck may have enough momentum to push the engine speed into the danger zone. This is happening plenty, either because some clucks don't know this or don't give a darn.

If any of you are interested, here's how a governor works. Most Army trucks have velocity-operated governors, which have no connection with any moving parts of the engine, need no lube and very little maintenance. These governors are operated by the velocity of the fuel mixture as it is sucked by the intake manifold vacuum through the governor housing. The throttle shaft of the governor is slightly offset from the center line of the throat and operates the throttle plate. Both of these are similar to the carburetor shaft and throttle, except that the governor throttle is set at an angle so that the flowing fuel mixture will move it. The harder you step on the gas, the faster the fuel mixture flows and the harder it hits the governor throttle, which starts swinging closed. The spring attached to the throttle shaft is adjusted so that its pull just equals the force of the fuel mixture on the throttle at the maximum engine speed desired. When you start pushing the accelerator beyond this set speed, the force of the fuel mixture overcomes the pull of the spring, and the throttle closes.

That's all there is to it, and if you want to go to heaven like a good gorilla, *leave that governor alone!*

AT LEAST A TECK

By CAPTAIN I. W. TURNER

(*1942*)

"It's LIKE I've told you previously," remarked Corporal Breen, the acting mess sergeant; "I should be at least a Teck [technical sergeant] with the ideas I've got. But my ideas are so simple nobody with complicated minds, like most brass hats, can appreciate them. There's no doubt about it that simple things is the essence of simplicity, which is what we need more than anything else."

"I could go for another bowl of that coffee," said Sergeant Jones, "and it's about time them pies were out of the oven."

"It's easy to see you think in a straight line and got the advantages of a one-rut mind that leads right in here to this mess hall whenever our ovens is ready to expel pie."

"Well, what I've got to listen to every time it's a rainy day and I come in here requires at least pie with coffee to give me strength to get out again."

"Anyway," said Corporal Breen, reaching for one of Sergeant Jones's cigarettes, "with my ideas I should be at least a Teck. And yet they pick clucks who can only whittle. I guess it just comes from being a lucky yokel from the wheat fields of Tennessee."

"You mean Nebraska."

"What I mean is that a cluck with practically nothing but whittling ability should get a break and go to a service school, which ever since I got transferred from the Ordnance to this outfit three years ago I been trying to do."

"You didn't have to transfer."

"And you bet your life if I'd-a known just because some cluck of a hillbilly from Nebraska could whittle out a wren house and put it in the Old Man's yard that the Old Man should say a week later, 'That birdhouse you put on my shagbark hickory is got wrens living in it, so you are a perfect example of the material we are looking to send to school.' "

"Hillbillies comes from Tennessee."

"Anyhow, I should of stayed in the Ordnance and developed some ideas I was working on. I can tell you I would now be at least a Teck at some very fine installation, instead of breathing this bad air from cheap government coal and worrying myself gray because the laundry is short four sheets."

"You got plenty of time now to develop ideas," said Sergeant Jones, "if you got any other ideas except smoking all my cigarettes just because I am sociable and come by for a bowl of coffee, which I will say is the best coffee of any company we got here."

"You know why? Because of a development I made to dry coffee bags so no goop is left in the seams. Which is why our coffee is not fit to put in storage batteries, and a child could drink it with no harm."

"Well, it is very good coffee, but I would wean no kids on it unless I wanted 'em to grow up and join the armored force."

"Now, *that's* where I should be because I have developed an idea on a type of grenade to stop tanks, and they would eat this idea up and make me a Teck at least."

"They got more land mines now than they know what to do with."

"But they ain't got a real good one. What I got is so good a six-year-old kid could use it. Do I want to blow a tank all to hell? No! All I want and got the idea for is to stop 'em by maybe gumming up a track or a bogie. And when they pile out to fix it I will look over my log and twist one right between their eyes, which you know I can do any day with a rifle even with a bigger head than I got right now after payday."

"Just what's this mine or grenade like a six-year-old kid could use?"

"It is very simple. What you got to do first is arm every man with two of them, and I would include platoon and company commanders. I got to admit I ain't worked all the details out. I haven't developed it very much yet because of the simple reason I don't intend to give out unless I get credit to be at least a Teck—which any one of my ideas is worth, counting the no-good ones. But in a training program for the use of my mine, every man has got to be able to handle a stalled or disabled tank, which even if I ain't got a plan for now I will work out later. What has got to be positive is that every man armed with an individual weapon should be able to use it because he will be so hopped up about my mine he will always be mumbling to himself that he's got no interest in life except to gum up tanks."

"Listen, Corp, I got lots to do besides listen to a guy whose old lady got scuffed with a taxi just before you were born and got a prenatural instinct against wheeled vehicles."

"I don't know nothing about that, but I will someday tell you about my nephew who's got a strawberry on his shoulder. But anyhow, every man by the thousands would each have two of my ideas on his person and put them in suitable places, which I will work out later, and when them armored vehicles come along they will find themselves unable to proceed when they run over one of my ideas, and they will stop. When they are stopped, if I never make no plans on what to do next, they are almost 100 per cent no good."

"That's all O.K., but I am still on pins and needles from not knowing what the idea is, and I am due for another bowl of coffee."

"It's very simple," said Corporal Breen as he filled the bowl. "My mine is five feet long and it's made of something flexible that looks like a heavy garden hose, and the ends hook together so it is a loop and slings over your shoulder like those Mexican bandits wear cartridge belts. It is a very simple tube filled up with granular TNT, and every six inches there is a detonator. So you can see if it is laid on the ground it goes off when it is run over. And if it ain't run over you pick it up. You keep it with you on all advances, and when them tanks and vehicles come your way they are sure as hell going to run into some of them, because if men is ten yards apart, and two each of my grenades are properly placed by each man, it is too bad when they lose a track or a bogie or get busted."

"That is all right. But now you got them tanks stopped, what the hell do you do next?"

"That is something I got to work out."

"Well, if you've got some other idea you can work out for that, it will be very fine."

"Yeah, but for me very fine is to be at least a Teck, which this idea by itself is worth any day."

TEAMWORK

From an editorial by
Major (later Major General) Merch B. Stewart

(*1917*)

. . . Some years ago the Infantry reached over the field of sport and plucked a word which it transplanted in its *Drill Regulations*. It was a good, old-fashioned American word which has grown in favor not only in the Infantry but in the service at large. That word is "teamwork," an excellent inspiring word, one to conjure with. It presents a vision of loyal, determined, shoulder-to-shoulder co-operation which hesitates at nothing, brushes aside obstacles, and with one steadfast, united effort smashes its way to the goal. . . .

PIDDLERS

From an editorial by
LIEUTENANT COLONEL (now MAJOR GENERAL) E. F. HARDING

(*1937*)

IN MORE THAN ONE ORGANIZATION useful work is subordinated to modern piddling that is on a par with the best developed in the good old days. Some is imposed by the caprices of immediate commanding officers; some draws its authority from post orders; some is buttressed by *Army Regulations*. Piddling manifests itself in eyewash, undue emphasis on competitive athletics, excessive supervision by command and staff, useless paper work, unnecessary reports, requirements that all officers attend all drills, multitudinous administrative checks, daily officers' calls indefinitely prolonged, and a hundred other time-consuming non-essentials that have nothing to do with training for war. If an officer is exposed to only one or two of these plagues he may escape the mental paralysis that afflicted the piddlers of the old Army, but real danger lurks in those garrisons where all or most of them are endemic.

Piddlers of other days were self-made. Today an officer on duty with troops runs the risk of acquiring the habit by order. That risk cannot be eliminated unless commanders of all grades forego those requirements that contribute nothing to combat efficiency. Should this be done— which, of course, it will not be—energetic officers will still find more than enough to keep them busy. But even if the rapid worker should be able to squeeze a little time from the crowded day, he can spend it profitably in study and reflection on things an infantryman should know. Not all of them would devote it to that purpose, but what of it? Better an afternoon of golf or even an occasional hour of bunk fatigue for the devotees of recreation and rest than that the zeal of the careerist be worn thin on the grindstone of a deadly routine.

ALL THE TEAMS MAKE ONE TEAM
Editorial
(1942)

THERE'S A LOT written and said about combat teams as we train our fighting units for this war. But it doesn't mean much unless everybody thinks and trains daily in terms of combat teams—everybody from Army commanders down to squad leaders.

"Combat team" means the same thing for every leader of fighters, no matter how many stripes or bars or stars he wears. It means a number of fighting men or outfits, with many different weapons, all doing their utmost to help each other get one job done. Yes, just one big job of fighting—the smashing of the enemy.

The sergeant and his rifle squad are a combat team in themselves. Garands, autorifles, carbines, hand grenades, and rifle grenades—these are the five first-rate, powerful weapons for killing used by the fighting team in the rifle squad.

But the squad is a part of another team, the team of the platoon. There are deadly 60-mm. mortars and light machine guns, and two more rifle squads—all fighting along with that first rifle squad to attack or defend, and to kill while doing either.

You can carry this idea right on up, and every modern fighting infantryman needs to do so. For a squad is not just part of a platoon combat team.

It's part of a company combat team—for the battle job of the 81-mm. mortars is teamwork with the squads and platoons.

It's part of a battalion combat team—for the battle job of heavy weapons is teamwork with the squads, platoons, and companies.

It's part of a regimental combat team—for the one battle job of the regimental weapons, the AT guns, the 75s, and the 105s is to work with the battalions, the companies, and the platoons—and the rifle squads with their Garands, their autorifles, their carbines, and their hand and rifle grenades.

You can take the thought of the combat team still higher—right on up to the top—and it still makes the good sense of modern war. The bomber and the fighting plane, the tank of every size, the gun of every caliber, the chemical mortar with its smoke (and its gas if it comes to that), the engineer fighter with his TNT are fighting members of the same great team as every rifle squad in a fighting force is, wherever the force may be fighting.

You don't have to start with a rifle squad to show these many teams.

You can start with the crew of a single plane, a single gun, or a single tank. And you reach the same simple fact. There are small teams and big teams and teams in between. The smallest are part of every other team all the way to the top. And all of these teams—there isn't a single tactical, technical, or "special" exception—have one sole purpose, to surprise, to outwit, to kill, to overwhelm, to stamp out the tough, able, coldhearted fighting men in the planes and tanks and ranks of our enemies.

A leader who ever forgets these things is a poor excuse for a fighting man. The leader who forgets the team, who lets his lower leaders try to win the war by themselves, should never be permitted to get to battle. He will lose fights and waste lives if he does get there.

This applies to the rifle-platoon leader who constantly keeps those deadly little mortars of his in reserve because he hasn't the energy and brains to get them in place where they'll be some good to his squads— who thinks they are only of use on ground perfect for observation and defilade.

It applies to the infantry battalion commander who doesn't find use for his big mortars every time they can possibly help his companies forward in the drive of their attack.

It fits, also, the regimental commander who wastes unrecoverable minutes by making the contact man from his supporting artillery or other supporting units wait till he can remember the Infantry has such powerful support.

And it fits, exactly as much, every man in the Army whose pride in the branch insignia he wears on his collar outweighs for a moment his pride as a member of the whole fighting team.

There has already been, in this war, one superb example of American combat teamwork—the troops on Bataan. Writing last month in the *Journal,* the inspector general who was with those troops said: "I never once heard of any friction of any kind between the different fighting teams. . . . The whole fighting force pitched in, and there weren't any hitches due to different collar ornaments. And this extended to the naval units and marines and air units, which operated as ground troops after their planes were gone. An army is supposed to work as a combat team, according to all the tactical doctrines taught in our military manuals. Well, the teamwork was there, in our force on Bataan, from beginning to end."

Bataan was a tough, desperate defense which welded every unit together. It's got to be the same in our attacks—in every one of them. In modern war you don't get places unless you hit the enemy with everything you've got from H hour on. And you can't hit them with everything all at once unless every combat team from squad to Army is clicking, and knows it can count on every other member of every team, and knows to perfection how to work in battle with every other team, as one fighting part of the big fighting team made up of the whole hitting force.

III

Leadership and Discipline

THE THOUGHTS of a soldier who rises to any rank or grade of command must be intent upon the ways in which he can improve his own ability as a leader. Therefore, Leadership, spelled with a capital, is the first of all themes for military writers. Articles on leadership written by soldiers of experience often turn out to be mere lists of qualifications desirable in a leader. Sometimes they speak of the Great Captains, all the way from Alexander to those rising from today's war, showing the super-traits they possessed, apparently under the assumption that raw young leaders, still uncertain of their fitness at heart, can build within themselves by inspiration the same traits which the great leaders had.

But leadership, military leadership, is at least 50 per cent a matter of practice, accustoming one's self to dealing with men, remembering the modes of speech and action that will win an extra degree of loyalty and hardest work beyond that inherent in command of itself. The "natural leader" is mainly so because he acts like one. He acts like a leader only because in some capacity he has already done so or has seen others performing as leaders or, to a much slighter degree, has read how others before him have led.

Thus written discussion about leadership has greatest value when there is within it something which the now-rising leader may be able to adapt for meeting his own problems. In its thirty-eight years of publication the *Infantry Journal* has carried all kinds of articles on battle leaders, some of the best of which are given in this section. Much of what is said in these articles will be of help to new leaders as long as there are troops to be led in war.

THINK IT OVER

By Lieutenant Colonel (now Colonel) L. M. Guyer

This article (July 1942) and the one following it (March 1943) have had a wider distribution than any other article the magazine ever printed. Nearly a year after it appeared requests were still coming in for permission to reprint for official use. The editorial note with which the editors preceded it in the magazine explains further about it.

To the unit commander:[1]

You are a leader of men, at war against an enemy who is cunning, determined, well supplied, and highly trained. He has been prepared for this war by concentrated, all-out training measures which have made him individually and collectively a skilled and ingenious enemy. In the words of a flight lieutenant who was recently in Malaya: "These fellows know more tricks than will ever be learned by the Germans . . . the first attack, believe me, will surprise you."

Your enemy knows his job. He knows his equipment and how to use it. He knows how to overcome obstacles by utilizing any and all immediate means at hand. He is not going to be stopped either by halfway preparations or halfway fighting. When the attack begins he's ready.

[1]Editor's Note (as it appeared in the magazine): This is the finest piece of official writing we have seen in this war. There have been forceful directives produced by every army fighting our enemies, and those the *Journal* has been able to find have appeared in its pages. But this is the best of all.

It was issued simply as "Notes on Training" by a general with a Coast Artillery command in an overseas theater. We'd like to name him. And we'd like to name every man who may have contributed to the writing. Often the written materials of training are the work of several official pens. But the sustained power of this one— its direct, vigorous assault upon faulty leadership—probably shows it to be the writing of a single man. [The name of the actual writer was learned later.]

Our first idea, when we saw that it was directed at the leaders of a Coast Artillery unit, was to edit it over and give it an Infantry slant. Then we decided it was too good to change, just as it stood. We figured that *Infantry Journal* readers wouldn't have the slightest trouble applying it, without any change, to themselves or their units wherever it happened to fit.

Directives with the strength and clarity of this one do more to reach the minds and hearts of an army than a thousand pages of the usual official material. We'd like to bet big odds that here was *one* issue from the mimeograph that every officer in the outfit read—and took to heart. Orders can be issued this way by every commander who will seek out the man in his outfit who can put them down in words that get out of the rut of official writing and reach into the minds of his men. He may not equal these "training notes," for they are superior indeed. But he can come near them.

The question is: Are *you* equally ready? Do *you* know *your* job? *Do your men know theirs?*

And do you honestly realize that readiness for battle is a matter of hard and intelligent training? Or are you waiting for the fight to begin in order to find out?

As the responsible commander of your men, do you know they are ready—or do you simply *think* they are? Or *hope* they are? Is your unit one of those in which inspections revealed there were men who had never seen a first-aid kit opened? Who did not know how to set their rifle sights? Who knew little or nothing about scouting, cover, and concealment? Whose gas masks had broken eyepieces? Whose bayonets would not fit on the studs of their rifles? Do you think the bayonet of the Japanese soldier is not going to fit when he needs it?

Are you driving hard every possible hour to train your men individually and as a unit to be more than a match for their enemy? Or are you loitering, leaving to chance your duties as a leader, your responsibility to every man in your command to teach him to outsmart and outfight any enemy, both as an individual and an artillery team?

Higher authority can and does plan the scope of training which will properly train your men and your unit for combat. But the implementing of this training is yours—you are the unit leader who has the final responsibility and the ultimate close contact with the soldier himself.

Refer to your training directive. Study it carefully; comply with it exactly. It has not been hastily written or written just to fill time, to get out another memorandum. On the contrary, it has been carefully written, every word of it. It has been the subject of much thought and planning. It is based upon the long experience of your commanding general, who is not guessing at what needs to be done to train both you and your men. He *knows*. He knows also the difficulties you are up against, the time you have available, and the urgency of the mission before you. And these, too, have been carefully considered in assigning you a training task you *must* accomplish.

The training objectives as stated in the directive are a vital goal to be attained by you in training your men as individual combat soldiers and your unit as a combined combat team. You would do well to frame these objectives and put them up where you will never lose sight of them, where you will see them daily, confronting you with a direct and honest question: "Am I accomplishing these objectives—*all* of them?"

The Coast Artillery individual and battery are no longer protected "concrete" soldiers facing a single seaward front. The initial attack may come from any direction. It may be made by air, by massed infantry advancing from the rear, by paratroops, by heavily armed infiltration units. You may well find yourself engaged in an all-out ground battle before you have ever seen a hostile naval vessel or fired a single artillery shot.

Consider the objectives stated in the training memorandum. Visualize the individual soldier standing before you. Visualize him from head to feet. Have you taught him that the inside headband of his helmet is adjustable, or does he neglect wearing it because it pinches his head? Have you taught him the location of neck arteries, or is another soldier someday to die because this man of yours didn't know how to apply a tourniquet? Have you taught him to wear his identification tags; do you inspect to see that he does? Have you taught him how to adjust, wear, and care for his gas mask? How to use his bayonet? His rifle? Have you taught him what armor-piercing small-arms ammunition is for and why it is issued? Or is your automatic rifleman going to fire at a landing boat with ball ammunition, while the armor-piercing he needs remains in his belt—or in an ammunition storage box somewhere? Have you inspected his shoes, taught him the importance of caring for his feet? Or are the soles worn half through, and would this soldier soon be without any shoes at all if he were suddenly cut off from his unit and isolated in the field? Can he scout, make his way as silently through brush as the Japanese? Could he use a compass if he had to? Can he dig a foxhole, a hasty trench? Does he know whether the barbed wire in front of him is properly or improperly strung to protect him? Can he throw a grenade? Identify gas? Carry a message and get to his destination? Have you taught him, every man, enough about the machine gun and automatic rifle so that if his own weapon were gone, or if a regular machine-gun crew became casualties, he could step in and load, sight, and fire those weapons?

Have you taught him gunnery, or merely how to operate mechanically an instrument without understanding it? Can your deflection-board operator also operate the range-percentage corrector? Could the chief of breech become gun pointer if he had to?

Have you taken advantage of the God-given intelligence of the American soldier and taught him the WHY of some of these things? Or are you still in only the who-what-where-and-when stage? Do your men generally know the principles of a defense plan? Do they know coast-artillery tactics? Basic infantry tactics? Do they know the mission of your own unit and how you propose to accomplish that mission? Have you passed on to them vital intelligence information about the enemy? How he operated in Malaya, and Singapore, and Java? How he is equipped? How he attacks? The ruses and trickery he has displayed—and will display again? Do your men know, for example, that the Japanese from boyhood practice and pride themselves on use of the bayonet?

The same type scrutiny may be made of your unit training as a whole. Have your men practiced your local defense plan, or is it just on paper or still in the talking stage? Do your men as a unit know the principles of ground combat? Have you ever actually practiced them? Do you know with certainty that you can carry on your primary artillery mission no matter what happens, or is your artillery drill a peacetime routine? Can you conduct fire if *all* communications go out? And do you know that at Hong Kong this was exactly what happened? Could you conduct fire under a simultaneous air or gas attack? Could you adjust fire based on only such spotting as you, yourself, can accomplish at the guns? Do you realize that naval targets may be fast-moving, fast-maneuvering, and smoke-screened? Have you trained your first sergeant, your next senior sergeant, *and* the next senior sergeant to fire your guns skillfully in case you and your other officers become casualties? Have they ever actually practiced doing it? Have you given your enemy credit for knowing your battery location, your methods of fire control and adjustment? Have you tried to visualize every emergency that may arise and prepare for those emergencies? Have you drilled and trained your unit in what to do when these things happen?

These are some of the objectives, and their accomplishment all has the same answer: the training you give your men *and how you conduct it.*

Consider the training memo again as to conduct of training. The manner in which good thorough training is conducted is as important as the nature of the training itself. There are vital precepts which inexperienced officers all too seldom know.

The first and foremost is "know your stuff," know your own job. Never get up before a group of men and read to them from a field manual or other text. To do so is an admission of ignorance and inability on your part. If the material to be covered is new to you, study it before you begin instruction. Ninety per cent of leadership is the confidence men have in their leader that he knows his job and knows what he's talking about.

Supervise your training. Supervision means actual physical presence and participation. It does not mean staying in the battery office or performing other duties. Neither does it mean an assembly of two or more officers standing off to one side and chatting while a noncommissioned officer conducts the training.

Keep a record of training progress. Elaborate charts and colored pins for the battery office may look well, but they are too often not an honest record of accomplishment. What the unit commander needs to know is the *exact* training status of every man—has Brown finished gas instruction? Has Smith completed bayonet instruction? If instruction has been only partial the record should so indicate. If a man has had no instruction at all the fact should stand out. Otherwise someday Brown is going to be the first gas casualty, and Smith is going to be bayoneted.

Utilize the value of training films and slides to the utmost possible extent. Remember that one picture is worth ten thousand words. But also remember that pictures and words by themselves will not suffice. All theoretical instruction must be followed by practical application. No man ever learned agility and skill in use of the bayonet just from pictures and words.

Note carefully the list of training topics attached as an enclosure to the training memorandum. These have been carefully selected. They will be given top priority. Many of them have been broken down into subtopics. One reason this was done was to indicate to you that most field manuals contain vastly more information of value than you realize. Dig into your manuals. The title that shows from a bookshelf is not even a partial indication of the many important subtopics that lie within.

Gunners' instruction pamphlets are valuable aids if you use them properly. But if used only to teach a man to parrot the printed answers to the printed questions, they are worse than valueless. For his answers will indicate a knowledge he does not possess.

Do not assume that a man is trained because he once qualified as an expert observer or once had rifle marksmanship in a replacement center. Training is an unending procedure, and plenty of "experts" have a lot left to learn.

Take advantage of spare moments. How many of you, for example, during the dark of early alert periods, have utilized this period to talk to your men, to instruct them, to teach them how they can determine direction by the North Star, or to discuss night tactics or night fire control?

The general plan in the training memorandum allows time for ample "breaks" or rest periods. Take advantage of these. Training that becomes tedious defeats its own end. Ten minutes of hard, alert, energetic work is worth two hours of dawdling and tedium. For the same reason vary the instruction given. Demand that your men pay attention during instruction and realize that it is part of your job to keep them interested.

Never bluff. You won't fool an American soldier—not for long, anyway. If you don't know the answer to a question be frank and admit so, and say you will find out the answer. Above all, be sure that you *do* find out.

Plan your training to be progressive. Select an important topic your men need to know and see it through. If your training schedule is just a printed list of assorted topics to look busy and imposing, you will be no farther along next month than you were this month.

There is still a further point to effective training, and that is the welfare and high morale of your men. You cannot expect a man to respond enthusiastically to instruction when he is uncomfortable, carelessly fed, dirty and deprived of a bath, poorly quartered even under field conditions, or dull-spirited because he has had no relaxation. Look to your men's comfort, their mess, their quarters, their recreation, their every need. Especially look to the welfare of those men in isolated stations and positions. Would *you* like to be serving up at the end of some of those long upward trails, day after day without being relieved, unbathed and without a place to bathe, night after night without a light to read by, a place to write, a comfortable place to sit?

Don't say these are war problems that can't be licked. They *can* be licked. A good unit commander who has the interests of his men at heart has the eye to see what's needed and the energy and resourcefulness to see that it's supplied.

And don't stop halfway either. "Eyewash" may be a term you last heard in peacetime, but it has a wartime value as well. It has a direct and immediate effect upon the morale and organizational pride of your men, and the impression which others get of the general condition and efficiency of your unit. A little paint on the inside of bunkhouse walls, men's names neatly lettered on signs before their tents, racks for clothes, holders for knickknacks, a neat log railing around an outdoor drinking fountain—whatever name you call them, eyewash or not, they raise men's morale. They turn a camp into a home. They change dreary surroundings into something pleasant to look at and cheerful to endure.

You have a big job to do, a hard and vital one—a life-and-death job that nobody else can do for you. It is beside the point to think in terms of victory or defeat. *If you think in terms of your men* all else will take care of itself. Think of Private Jones, a soldier in your unit. Tomorrow an attack begins. Have you seen to it that Private Jones is ready and trained to do his job? Are you willing, after it is over, to think back on the duties and responsibilities you had and to carry for the rest of your life the knowledge you failed to meet them? Are you willing, after it is over, to face the mother and father of an American soldier named Jones and answer the question they are going to demand of *you?*

"Johnny? Yes, I knew him. He was in my battery; he was one of my men. He didn't have a chance. A stud was bent—on his rifle—his own bayonet wouldn't fit—there was a machine gun near by, but Johnny didn't know how to use one. I failed him."

Think it over.

"THIS PLATOON *WILL* . . ."

By Major (now Lieutenant Colonel) James W. Bellah

(*1943*)

THE HEALTH and the resilient life of an army throbs in the hearts of its junior officers—or dies there. In them is reposed the immediate and close command of the men—they lead the attack personally. After all the plans are laid and the details are worked out, it is the lieutenant who faces the men and says, "This platoon *will* . . ." and it is the lieutenant that platoon follows while it does what it *will* do. And it is the lieutenant who leads the platoon, because the lieutenant is there and *can* lead it. No captain in the haze of combat can at all times lead or even see his entire company. No battalion commander can lead or see his entire battalion—certainly no CG can personally lead his division and control it by personal contact. But the lieutenant can, does, and will control the men through personal, visual, and, if necessary, physical contact.

No disparagement is intended to the sergeant or to the other noncommissioned officers, nor should any disparagement be assumed, for in the Army today they furnish the next crop of lieutenants—that lowest grade of the breed in whom, "Know Ye, that reposing special [mark the word] trust and confidence in the patriotism, valor, fidelity and abilities of [the lieutenant, and every other commissioned officer] I [the President of the United States] do appoint ———— He is therefore carefully [mark the word again!] and diligently to discharge the duty of the office to which he is appointed by doing and performing all manner of things thereunto belonging."

That is the ancient wording of your commission, Lieutenant—whether you have actually had that paper put into your hands with your name on it, or whether you have merely been informed upon graduation from OCS that you are a commissioned officer.

You are the lowest but, by the ever-increasing numbers of you, the most important grade of that breed which holds a direct contract and an implied gentleman's agreement with the President, the government, and, hence, the entire people of the United States—the most important, because from the great mass of you will come the high-ranking leaders of next year's and the year after that's and perhaps the year after that's armies of the United States:

A gentleman's agreement.

In a democracy no word is more abused than the word "gentleman," nor is it more maligned at times, pooh-poohed or less understood.

The word can be defined in many ways and is. Sometimes it is confused with manners. "He has the manners of a gentleman." But there is an instinctive realization that this is inadequate because we have coined the phrase, "one of God's gentlemen," to define the rough diamond of no particular manners or breeding who still has within him that inner spark of something that makes the gentleman. Sometimes arrogantly you run across the old feudal definition, "a gentleman's son." That definition will satisfy the College of Heralds but precious little else. Ladies have a habit of assuming that the word comes from the word *"gentle"* and, hence, invariably confuse the whole business with the moral issue. So, once and for all, let's settle it.

The word comes from *gens,* which is Latin for "people." And a gentleman, therefore, regardless of his manners, morals, clothing, breeding, conduct, or previous condition of servitude, is a man—not *of,* necessarily, but a man *for* the people.

How adequately that now fits the phrase, "an officer and a gentleman," and how thoroughly it explains why that expression has lasted through the military ages despite facetious attempts to tack "by act of Congress," or "temporary" onto it.

The first concern of the officer, and especially of this lieutenant, is for his "people"—his men. If he fails in that, he fails in everything and becomes nothing more than a travesty in uniform, a figure at a costume ball, a mountebank at a lodge meeting.

The lieutenant knows his men as soon as he possibly can. Their capabilities and individual limitations. Their temperaments and even the outside worries that militate against their working efficiently. He solves these outside problems for them when he can, by advice, by investigation, by solution through welfare agencies, if necessary and possible.

He is vitally concerned with the continued high morale of his men. Their sleeping arrangements under all conditions of garrison or campaign. Their food. Their health. Their recreation. Their punishment. Their rewards. Their training.

He is more concerned that they do not die in combat through their own ignorance or *his* ignorance or carelessness in failing to instruct them adequately and continually—so that he can lead them intelligently in all conditions of combat that may arise.

A dead soldier who has given his life because of the failure of his officer is a dreadful sight and a crime before God. Like all dead soldiers, he was tired before he died, hungry undoubtedly, dirty, wet, and possibly frightened to his soul. And there he lies—dead needlessly, on top of all that—never again to see his homeland. Don't be the officer who failed to instruct him properly—who failed to lead him well! Burn the midnight oil, Lieutenant, that you may not in later years look at your hands and find his blood still red upon them!

Now then, as a part of his contract with his President, his government, and through it with the entire people of the United States—and perhaps as a compensation for this deep, all-pervading obligation to his own "people," his men—the lieutenant has certain privileges.

If you will examine those privileges you will see that they are given for well-defined reasons—to free him from certain details of his own living, to isolate him to a small degree for thinking and studying, and to erect around him a modest individual niche and a low pedestal from which to exercise the dignity of his function of command.

And yet with all this the green lieutenant has been the butt of the military joke since the beginning of time, and in many cases rightfully so, but the lieutenant of today's Army of the United States is a shavetail of a different color in many respects—or should be.

Because very shortly he will enter combat—at the head of his men—and his worth will be weighed once and for all time in terms of the eternal values of life and death.

Where does this lieutenant of today come from?

In comparatively small quantities he still comes from West Point—where four arduous confining years have prepared him for his blooding. In larger quantities he comes from civilian colleges all over the country, where a less confining and less thorough four years of R.O.T.C. work have given him a barely adequate grounding in the fundamentals of his job. He comes from "tin" colleges in small numbers and even from "tin" preparatory schools (as young as eighteen in some cases), where his application to military life and study for four or five years lets him compare favorably in education and military background with the West Pointer. And he comes from OCS, where his background may be anything from comparatively long-service regular noncom to a short-service selectee. He has all variety of education from merely high school, through college to two or more degrees—and all variety of previous jobs. His age is from eighteen to thirty-five for service with combat troops, but his average age is about twenty-six.

He has, however, one thing in common when he serves with combat troops. He will lead those troops personally into action, and on his shoulders will rest the fate of the United States! And he will be successful in serving the future of the United States only in so far as he is successful in securing the present welfare, in all things, of his men—as an "officer and a man for his people."

No other job is left for him—no excuse can be offered for not doing this job. On the seventh of December, 1941, when the first Japanese bomb hit Hickam Field, the past, the present, and the future of the United States stood still, just as if a film had stopped in a projector. The worth of the past lay solely in how much it could inspire, influence, and activate men to face the daily, soul-searing grind of the present—on all fronts—that by facing it and forcing it to final hard-won victory a new future might unfold again.

And that, Lieutenant, is the story.

What you wear on your collar or your shoulder is a part of the government and the destiny of the United States. It is not yours personally for any grace that is in you—but it is the insignia of the militant people, the fighting government of your country. It implies a "special trust and confidence in the patriotism, valor, fidelity, and abilities" that are in you. The stripes of your corporals and of your sergeants, the bars of your captain, and the stars of your general are also an integral part of the militant people and the fighting government of this country—all graduated plainly in terms of responsibilities, accountabilities, and command functions of the ageless military hierarchies of all armies.

Look at that bar a moment as you peel off your sweaty shirt tonight. You're tired and maybe you can think of a hundred places you'd rather be; you have private worries—a wife, a girl, homesickness, a younger brother who needs your guiding hand, a frightened old mother. You are fed up with the stupidities you have had to contend with today. You are firmly convinced that that so-and-so, Major Dumbjohn, ought to be shot. You'll be double-tied if you'll keep on training men and then have them cadred away from you or sent to OCS. (You young fool, you'll still be training in the midst of combat, and this kind of expanding army where you lose your best men continually is the best training for combat, where all men are expendable.) And everyone else gets promoted but you.

All right—look at the bar again, gold or silver, look at it in the light of your blacked-out flashlight or your desk lamp in cantonments—there it is still, like the Hound of Heaven you can't escape! A part of the militant people—the fighting government of the United States—and it's on your shirt. So take a relaxing drink if you think you need it—but not the twenty that will put you on the road to town, staggering before your men and the taxpayers—and sit down and think of your thirty or so men. Have you given them that added something that is required of a military gentleman? Are you prepared for tomorrow, for next week, for combat? Will some of them die because you are not?

Reach, then, to your bookshelf with the young hand that is still clean of their blood and take down that field manual for a few brief moments before you sleep, because you won't be a lieutenant forever—not in this Army. Next month, next spring, you'll be a captain. By fall you'll be a major, perhaps, and before the last shot is fired you may be throwing armies around. But you won't be any of it or do any of it unless you fortify your professional knowledge and your inner spirit now and *always* against that dark night when your decisions will be right or wrong in terms of hot red blood—unless you spread your knowledge everywhere you go, so that those who are privates and corporals and sergeants under you today may be tomorrow's lieutenants.

But whether you face your job now, while there is yet time, or whether you scotch it; whether you realize the worth of this advice or dismiss it as the old malarkey, remember just one thing:

Prepared or not, worthy or not, competent or not, when the time comes—

"This platoon *will* . . ."

—and for better or for worse before the inexorable gods of battle, you'll lead it, Lieutenant!

PRACTICAL PEACETIME LEADERSHIP

By Major (now Major General) O. W. Griswold

In this article, published in 1931, General Griswold, now a corps commander, used the case method of discussing leadership. What he says is entirely sound for the new Army.

LEADERSHIP cannot be learned from a set of rules. However similar soldiers may be in the mass, individually each man has a distinct personality. In battle, in the face of danger and death, the soldier is stripped of all superficial attributes and reverts to the elemental man. The herd influence then becomes predominant. He ceases to think and then reacts, as a matter of habit, to the things learned on the training ground.

In peace such factors as education, previous occupation, race, antecedents, and home training make soldiers more individualistic. There is not present that common danger, as in war, to bring them all together. In peace, too, the application of disciplinary measures to suit the particular case may be efficacious as a deterrent. But in battle no disciplinary punishment, less than death itself, will affect any man who is crazed by fear.

The lives of Napoleon, Scipio, Hannibal, Caesar, Grant, Lee, Stonewall Jackson, and many other great soldiers abound in glorious exploits of leadership on the battlefield. Conversely, the student may also find in history many notable examples of its failure. Unfortunately, however, there are few examples in print concerning the practical application of leadership in time of peace. Therefore, and since it is in peace that we should prepare for war, this study concerns itself more with the peacetime aspect of the question.

The following true cases, illustrating some examples of peacetime leadership, are stated from an observation of some twenty-four years' service. They are stated, not in a spirit of criticism or commendation, but in an effort to illustrate what are considered to be certain fundamental principles that underlie the application of peacetime leadership.

Case I. Some years ago the graduating class at West Point was given opportunity, as a part of its instruction, to witness the usual Saturday inspection of one of the Regular Army detachments at that station. The detachment commander's attitude toward the men was one of extreme severity and faultfinding; any bunk not made up to his satisfaction was pulled roughly apart, and the blankets, sheets, and equipment were scattered upon the floor; noncommissioned officers, as well as privates, were admonished caustically and sarcastically before the assembled cadets;

meat cans, knives, forks, and spoons out of place or in poor condition were thrown across the room, and several times the detachment commander lost his temper and used profanity. He seemed to take pleasure in finding something wrong and failed to comment favorably on anything that was right.

The impression made on that graduating class was impressive and lasting. To their inexperienced eyes *this was the approved way to handle enlisted men.* Needless to say, every potential officer in that class was greatly handicapped during the formative years of his earlier service by the experience. It took years for some of them to readjust their ideas. This influence may have caused some of the storm of postwar protest against Regular Army methods.

This case illustrates many serious errors in the psychology of troop leadership. First of all, it is an almost criminal illustration of the power of example wrongfully applied. Secondly, it violates every semblance of dignity, justice, and good practice in the handling of enlisted men. Such treatment lowers their self-respect and exposes them to ridicule. It is unjust and arbitrary. It destroys loyalty and respect for the commander, the organization, and the entire service. Finally, the tyrannical imposition of authority on subordinates by virtue of military command can never be defended. It is the act of a bully, not that of a leader.

Conversely, analysis of the case by the observant officer will guide him to a fundamental truth, which is that in most situations commendation is more powerful than condemnation. Applied to the case in point, it means that the detachment commander's mental attitude was destructive rather than constructive.

In making an inspection, then, the best method is to find first something satisfactory. Having once found it, make favorable comment thereon. Then point out carefully the unsatisfactory things, emphasizing the idea, at the same time, that only these latter things are holding back the individual or the organization from being uniformly up to the approved standard. Instead of arbitrarily ordering "do this" or "do that," the initiative of the subordinate can be stimulated by such questions as "What do you think about this?" "Have you considered that?" leaving him the working out of the suggestion. The senior has a direct responsibility in checking up on results. This course will almost always bring home to the subordinate that the senior is a friend, not an enemy; that he is trying to build up, not to tear down. Its strength rests upon the fact that any human being is proud to have or to do something above the average. He receives pleasure and incentive from the fact that it is noticed and praised by superiors. It works irrespective of persons, whether they be generals, colonels, majors, junior officers, noncommissioned officers, cooks, or privates. It may be applied to any phase of everyday military life, whether it be between line and staff, at a drill, an inspection, a tour of guard, or even in the supervision of a police detail. The application of this principle detracts in no way from what military men call "force." If, after fair trial, good results are not obtained, then direct orders and direct action are necessary. If these latter measures do not accomplish the desired end, then the individual becomes a proper subject for prompt elimination from the service.

Case II. Immediately after the World War the then Commandant of Cadets at West Point was impressed with the necessity of developing the latent leadership of cadets while in the corps. To this end tactical officers were assigned orderly rooms in the cadet barracks. They were thus brought into direct contact with cadets. Disciplinary matters were handled under policies, exactly as in the service. Tactical officers were enjoined to be strict but absolutely just and were not empowered to use arbitrary measures of punishment. The tactical officer became, in truth, the "Old Man" of his cadet company. His daily administration of the business of that company served as a daily object lesson to the cadet throughout his course at the academy.

A textbook, *Military Man Power,* by Lieutenant Colonel L. C. Andrews, U.S.A., was obtained and a course of instruction was given by the Tactical Department. Initiative and responsibility were developed in members of the first (senior) class, by requiring each of them to rate every cadet in his company twice each year in certain fundamental qualities of character and appearance. These ratings were resolved by a mathematical formula and incorporated into the cadets' general standing for the year.

Beneficial results were immediate. Cadets began to see that officers were not hereditary enemies. On the other hand, officers began to take more interest in their cadets. They arranged for special coaching for those deficient in studies, and a community of interest developed which resulted in the cadets asking for and receiving advice and help on private, personal, and official matters. This was accomplished without lowering the standard of discipline in the least. It is certain that the relationship between commander and commanded is now much better understood at West Point than formerly.

This case illustrates a fundamental knowledge of human nature and the power of example rightly employed.

Case III. Some years ago a young married second lieutenant was ordered on foreign service. On account of a sick child who was unable to travel he applied for and obtained from the adjutant general one month's delay in sailing. Upon arrival at his new station he was severely reprimanded by his colonel for the delay in reporting. He was further told in no uncertain terms that his future actions would be guided strictly by "the law." The colonel emphasized the nature of that law by pounding on a copy of *Army Regulations.* The child died later from the effects of the trip.

Though the colonel later apologized, no amends that he could ever make could remove that subordinate's sense of resentment and injustice, shared in common with all junior officers of the regiment. The colonel had lost their loyalty and respect. Apparently, however, he learned nothing from the incident, for as long as he commanded the regiment his methods were those of a martinet. Officers were being put in arrest, and trials of officers and men were frequent. Outwardly the regiment had every appearance of being an excellent organization; within, loyalty, *esprit de corps,* and morale were very low.

This case illustrates lack of understanding and sympathy on the part of the superior. It exemplifies also rule by fear. While the power to punish is a necessary attribute of command, it should be resorted to only when necessary. In some cases punishment should and must be given. Too often, however, the rule by fear is applied by all ranks in our service. Enlisted men are too often tried by their company commanders because it is the easiest and quickest way to dispose of the cases. If a case contains any unjust or unfair elements, irreparable harm to morale is certain to result. Higher commanders sometimes centralize punishment by policy, so that an enlisted man is tried irrespective of the wishes of his company commander. If the superior is of the martinet type, such a policy is harmful.

In any well-disciplined organization the superior must uphold the authority of the junior. The superior, however, has an equal duty in seeing that the subordinate does not act unjustly.

Case IV. Incident to border trouble, a certain infantry regiment was ordered to Texas some fifteen years ago. Prior to a practice march, a company commander of that regiment, just assigned, gave his company specific orders against drinking water from unauthorized sources. He explained that much of the water in the country was unsafe to drink. As the company had many recruits, he made the necessity for the order clear. In the course of the long march the company halted, hot and tired, near a stream. Immediately on breaking ranks one of the outstanding sergeants in the company, a man of long service, was seen drinking from the brook. In the presence of the assembled company the captain quietly and without resentment cut away the sergeant's chevrons and assigned him to a squad as a private. Upon return of the company to the post the regimental commander confirmed in orders the reduction of the sergeant to the grade of private.

This case illustrates a fundamental principle of command—an order once given must be strictly enforced. The sergeant's usefulness as a leader was destroyed by his own action. Since he himself did not obey, how could he expect obedience from others? Had this offense been left unpunished, the discipline in that company would have been nil. The fact that the punishment immediately followed the delinquency is an important point to note. This case also illustrates a very human trait of soldiers, which is to try out a new commander.

Case V. A new tactical officer was assigned to and joined a cadet company at West Point on the day that it completed a week's practice march in inclement weather. At Saturday inspection the following day many rifles were found dirty and rusty. The tactical officer immediately ordered a special inspection in one hour's time for those cadets whose equipment was not in satisfactory condition. Some rifles were again found to be unsatisfactory. Two supplementary inspections were held during the day for those cadets who had failed to come up to the required standard of the previous inspection. The few who had unsatisfactory rifles or equipment at the fourth inspection were at once awarded five demerits and ten confinements or punishment tours. In addition thereto, they were confined to barracks until such time as their cadet captains had passed their equipment as satisfactory. On subsequent Saturday inspections appropriate punishment was invariably awarded without any second opportunity to make good. Needless to say, that particular tactical officer had no further trouble with the care of equipment.

This case is selected as illustrating two points.

First of all, class punishment should not be employed where individuals are at fault. While the entire company was generally unsatisfactory, there were individuals who did have excellent equipment at the first inspection. It would have been basically unsound to hold them further because others had failed to come up to the required standard. The course adopted put a premium on good work but was absolutely inflexible as to poor work.

Secondly, sincerity of purpose will always produce results. The easiest way to have handled this situation would have been to punish all delinquencies at the first inspection. However, this would not have changed the condition of equipment for that particular Saturday. Moreover, such a course might have been unfair to certain individuals on account of the short time available to prepare. The tactical officer wished to stress cleanliness of equipment rather than punishment. The series of inspections took all day and sacrificed the leisure of all concerned. It impressed the fact that the equipment *must* be in a satisfactory condition. It gave the necessary time and opportunity, and only those cadets who were not playing the game received punishment in the end.

The action was designed as an object lesson, that no matter how disagreeable the task, poor performance would not be tolerated. This principle is susceptible of extensive application in ordinary everyday military life. It is based on firmness rather than unnecessary harshness. Certain methods by one type of leader will not secure the same results when applied by another. The principle, therefore, is fixed, but the method of application often varies.

Case VI. A general officer was once visiting a large post. Part of the troops were out in a model camp erected to help with the instruction of students. Accompanied by the post commander, the colonel of the regiment, and other officers, the general made an inspection of the camp. The party came finally to the camp latrine, in the construction of which a certain corporal had displayed great interest, energy, and initiative. The corporal was present at the inspection, full of pride in the consciousness of work well done. The general turned to the post commander and complimented *him* highly on the installations, saying that it was the best field construction that he had ever seen. The corporal who had done the work stood by unnoticed by the general as the party passed on, but the wise post commander himself complimented the corporal as he left.

Passing later to the picket line, everything was found in excellent condition. Somewhat perfunctory comments were made by the general until he spied a man near by grooming a horse. He stopped and gave a long dissertation in the hearing of the men on the general unsatisfactory methods of grooming animals, not only in all branches of our service, but in that organization in particular, and called attention to that man as an example. The man was so humiliated by the gibes of the other men and by the fact that he had brought adverse criticism on the company that he later attempted to desert the service.

This case should hold some valuable lessons for the observant officer. First, men always respond to interest in themselves and their work. It would have cost the general nothing to have asked the corporal a few questions about himself and to add a quiet word of commendation.

Another striking point is the readiness of the post commander to give due credit to the man actually responsible. Selfishness is a rock upon which so many promising military careers are wrecked.

Humiliation of a junior can never be condoned. It is probable that the incident about grooming the horse passed from the general's mind within the following five minutes. He simply took that means to drive home a lesson. Yet he unwittingly humiliated one man who probably will never forgive or forget, and lowered the morale of an entire organization.

To summarize, two authorities analyze and evaluate alike the inherent qualities which they consider essential to leadership. Too often discussion on these points obscures the essence of what leadership should accomplish. The purpose of leadership is to secure wholehearted physical and moral co-operation. When such co-operation is spontaneous and free, and not until then, has true leadership been established.

Without attempting to state specifically all the principles of leadership, it may be said that they are the basis for all that a commander does to secure for himself the sincere, loyal, and voluntary co-operation.

In the analysis of cases lies the key to the practical application of troop psychology. Any officer of experience can state many examples, both

good and bad, from his own observation. The inexperienced officer, however, can only observe and benefit from the methods of others.

Granted that instruction in troop psychology is necessary, the next
consideration is to determine the best method of laying foundation. The
applicatory method, supplemented by study and lectures, is preferable to
all others.

LEADERSHIP

From an article by MAJOR (later COLONEL) C. A. BACH

(*1918*)

. . . THERE is another kind of fairness, that which prevents an officer
from abusing the privileges of his rank. When you exact respect from
soldiers, be sure you treat them with equal respect. Build up their manhood and self-respect. Don't try to pull it down. For an officer to be
overbearing and insulting in the treatment of enlisted men is the act of
a coward. He ties the man to a tree with the ropes of discipline and then
strikes him in the face, knowing full well that the man cannot strike
back. Consideration, courtesy, and respect from officers toward enlisted
men are not incompatible with discipline. They are parts of our discipline.

SECOND LIEUTENANTS AND MILITARY
COURTESY

By STONE BOREALIS

(*1940*)

THE ARMY has not gone to hell since I was a second lieutenant. In fact,
it is bigger and better than ever. Yet a distressing development has im-
pinged itself upon my consciousness in the last few years, some illustrative
incidents of which are worth thinking about.

Some weeks ago I was on maneuvers, and seven of us were present for
dinner one evening in a battalion officers' mess. The major, three captains, and three second lieutenants—all of us sat talking, and a casual
listener might not have noted anything unusual about our conversation.
But that conversation focused my attention sharply upon a tendency
which has become more and more pronounced in recent years.

The thing I noticed was that all three captains addressed the major
with an unforced but courteous respect and with a punctilious use of the
word "sir." But not once did any of the second lieutenants say "sir"
to anybody.

This is no isolated incident, for I have with some astonishment seen these newly commissioned officers slough over those evidences of respect on which I, as a second lieutenant, was raised.

Not so long ago I was celebrating, in the traditional manner, my fourteenth anniversary as a commissioned officer, when a shavetail of one year's service came in, clapped me on the back, and addressed me by my nickname. Turning around slowly, I looked the boy full in the eye and told him he had made a mistake in identity because I was Captain Sourpuss, and that the next time he addressed me to remember to use a one-syllable word of three letters.

He seemed much surprised, and honestly so, I think. He just had not been raised any better.

For some time past I have considered writing this article directed toward the education in military courtesy of those who need it. But somehow there was no overt act of sufficient violence to justify my doing it, though my own lieutenant has long since been instructed in the proper and habitual use of the term "sir." But just a few days ago there was an overt act which has stirred me to action.

We had an officers' call, and every officer in the regiment was there for a conference held by the CO himself. During the course of the discussion the colonel spoke to a major, who used the word "sir" in his reply. Next the CO spoke to our lieutenant colonel and regimental executive officer, and he also included "sir" in his reply—and then finally a second lieutenant held a conversation with the colonel, and at no time did he use that small word of respect. Further, his tone, while not disrespectful, was not definitely respectful either.

I don't intend to sound like a crusty old fuddy-duddy. Nevertheless, I believe something should be done about this new tendency, because it is becoming general and should be eliminated while in its embryonic stage. Not all young officers are offenders, but many are. And the fault is that of the older officers who permit this relaxing of the respect it is their duty to demand.

"MOST MILITARY SIR, SALUTATION"

Love's Labour's Lost, SHAKESPEARE.

By CAPTAIN DEFERENCE

(*1940*)

WITH ALL PROPER DEFERENCE to the officer who contributed the sincere cerebration on "Second Lieutenants and Military Courtesy," I believe that the lax behavior of subalterns which he "views with alarm" is more of a good sign than a bad one. Borealis is, of course, basically right in his beef about shavetails who don't say "sir." But taking his article as a whole, I think he does a good job of hitting the nail exactly on the thumb.

The reason that second lieutenants don't say "sir" is not that the Army is going to hell. No; not in the least. And it isn't because a more bigotty set of young squirts is now being commissioned in the grade of second lieutenant than in the days when Borealis and I first reported for duty.

I wonder if Borealis ever stopped to look objectively at a brand-new lieutenant who really went to town in the full sense of the word "deference." Speech in sentences beginning with "sir" and ending with "sir," and with that same small word exploded at every comma, is a language all its own—an un-American absurdity of address that has no place in our Army. Besides, it is next door to ridiculous to watch or to hear, and it is a mode of speech that interferes no little with clearness of communication between speaker and hearer.

To my idea, the reason modern-minded second lieutenants do not say "sir" is simply because they have seen too many young sirring machines in operation as I have just described them, and have become sensibly disgusted, reacting so strongly against overdone deference that for the time being they show too little. Most of them will eventually decide for themselves what degree of deference is fitting in a given situation.

As for calling your seniors by their first names and slapping them on the back, I began my career as an officer with a firm decision to call everybody "Tom" or "Dick" who called me "Harry." It worked all right, too, though my colonel must have been astonished the first time I pulled it and asked me one day in a friendly manner why I did it. I told him, and he saw my point and agreed with it at bottom but said that I'd find out it wouldn't work with a good many seniors. He then suggested that I base my degree of informality purely on friendship—to be sure a senior was my close friend before I slapped him on the back and called him "Tom."

"Anybody else who calls you 'Harry,'" said the colonel, "call him by his title once in a while, but don't bother to say 'sir' except officially. To all others say 'sir' every few sentences—a little practice will tell you what sounds decently respectful under different circumstances and what sounds deferentially redundant."

Then he ended the matter by telling me that, in his opinion, colonels as a class didn't have enough second-lieutenant friends and that he wanted to count me as one and that it was O.K. by him for me to call him "Tom" if I'd like to. "Only," he concluded, "it sounds a little better not to, up at headquarters, or in other official circumstances."

The dope my colonel gave me then is a sound basis for relations between junior officer and senior. It considers human relations in daily contact, which are even more important in an army than in the rest of life. So for every lieutenant whose ears Borealis may have knocked down for not saying "sir," there must be at least two that I myself have admonished firmly for saying "sir" so often and so fast that it made me both uncomfortable and unable to get the drift of what was being said.

The same colonel I have mentioned above always swore that there are only two kinds of officers in our Army—"young squirts" and "old poots." "Some," he would say, "get to be old poots before they're captains, and some, by good luck for the Army, never do. But once you're an old poot, set in your ways, lost to imagination, and damning things in general because the Army's gone to hell, you might as well quit for all the good you are." I'm sure my good friend Borealis is still far from coming within the latter class, though from the sound of his article he is a potential candidate.

SHAVETAILS AND COURTESY

By Captain Stone Cold

(1940)

Captain Stone Borealis
Author, "Second Lieutenants and Military Courtesy"

Dear Sir:

When distressing developments hit you between the eyes—I mean "impinge themselves upon your consciousness"—you sure go to town. Pardon me, sir, if I get right down to cases, sir, and formally assure you, sir, that I have the utmost respect for all old-timers, sir, particularly aged captains with fourteen years' service, sir.

When you so realistically related how you were rudely slapped on the back by a spanking new shavetail while you were celebrating, in the traditional manner, your fourteenth anniversary as a commissioned officer, I began to think you had won the well wishes of at least one subordinate. But when you gave the harrowing details of how you slowly turned, looked him full in the eye, and impressively told him to address you with a one-syllable word of three letters, you got me, sir. In fact, you got me down!

If that youngster does not entirely lack guts, he thinks of you not only as Captain Sourpuss, but more appropriately as an old so-and-so. To so treat an unsuspecting enthusiastic admirer shows an abysmal ignorance of human nature. How else would you want to be treated while celebrating in the traditional manner? After all, the difference in rank between a lieutenant and a fourteen-year captain is not such an insurmountable barrier that it can't be crossed. When I had fourteen years' service I was still a lieutenant. But let us suppose the gap is too large. There is a time and place for everything, a time to insist on the letter of the law and a time to relax from the fixities of military custom. But there is never a time to humiliate a subordinate whose intentions are good and who is merely misguided. If there was any good judgment displayed, the lieutenant showed it.

Suppose he had clicked his heels, bowed stiffly from the waist, and let go a blurb in this manner: "Captain, sir, I see that you are celebrating your fourteenth anniversary as a commissioned officer. I do not wish to appear presumptuous, sir, but if a second lieutenant may congratulate an older officer I desire to do so now. I wish you, sir, many happy returns of the day. I thank you, sir, for permitting me the privilege of addressing you."

Captain, I have been observing these lieutenants a damn sight longer than you have. In fact, I see more of them each year than you have seen in your entire service. Take my word for it, sir, do not mistake lip service for the real thing. There is nothing wrong with the younger officers. Take a close look at yourself, sir, and scramble off your high horse, pronto. You will get closer to earth, where all good doughboys belong. Besides, you will then be able to see plenty of the right kind of younger officers around you. Don't let a few isolated cases warp your viewpoint, sir.

Sympathetically yours,
CAPTAIN STONE COLD

SELF–RESPECT

From an article by VICE-ADMIRAL WILLIAM S. SIMS, U.S. Navy

(*1918*)

. . . NEVER DESTROY or decrease a man's self-respect by humiliating him before others. If his self-respect is destroyed, his usefulness will be seriously diminished. A man who is called down in the presence of others can hardly help resenting it. Frequent "sanding down" of your men is an all-too-common mistake, and a very detrimental one.

Do not let the state of your liver influence your attitude toward your men.

THE NEW LEADERSHIP

From the Annual Report of BRIGADIER GENERAL (*now* GENERAL) DOUG-
LAS MACARTHUR, *Superintendent of the U.S. Military Academy, 1920,
as reprinted in the* Infantry Journal *of June 1922.*

UNTIL THE WORLD WAR, armed conflicts between nations had been fought
by comparatively a small fraction of the populations involved. These professional armies were composed very largely of elements which frequently
required the most rigid methods of training, the severest forms of discipline, to weld them into a flexible weapon for use on the battlefield.
Officers were therefore developed to handle a more or less recalcitrant
element along definite and simple lines, and a fixed psychology resulted.
Early in the World War it was realized, to the astonishment of both sides,
that the professional armies, upon which they had relied, were unable to
bring the combat to a definite decision. It became evident . . . that
national communities had become so intimate that war was a condition
which involved the efforts of every man, woman, and child in the countries affected. War had become a phenomenon which truly involved the
nation in arms. Personnel was of necessity improvised, both at the front
and at the rear; the magnitude of the effort, both of supply and of
combat, was so great that individuals were utilized with the minimum of
training. In general result, this was largely offset by the high personal
type of those engaged. Discipline no longer required extreme methods.
Men gradually needed only to be told what to do rather than to be
forced by the fear of consequences of failure.. The great numbers involved made it impossible to apply the old, rigid methods which had
been so successful when battle lines were not so extensive. The rule of
this war can but apply to that of the future. Improvisation will be the
watchword. Such changed conditions will require a modification in type
of the officer, a type possessing all of the cardinal military virtues as of
yore, but possessing an intimate understanding of the mechanics of human feelings, a comprehensive grasp of world and national affairs, and a
liberalization of conception which amounts to a change in his psychology
of command. This standard became the basis of the construction of the
new West Point in the spirit of old West Point.

ALL GOD'S CHILLUN AIN'T GOT WINGS

BY ARCADES AMBO

Promotion in our Army has always crept in time of peace, and ways
to improve it without costing the country much took not only the time of

successive chiefs of staff but that of many a lieutenant of twelve, fifteen, or more years of service. A lot of them wrote about it for the *Infantry Journal*.

There was at least one World War general who was a lieutenant for twenty years, and probably many who approached that mark. There were many hundreds of officers who, when Congress finally did something in 1935, had been lieutenants for eighteen years.

Such lingering in the lower ranks is not merely a matter of not getting more pay faster. The thing has an unquestionable psychological effect, even upon those lieutenants who become professionally as close to the equivalent of generals as they can in a small army, through study and seeking for staff jobs where they can learn more and more about war. It keeps an officer immature in his relationships with his superiors and his mental attitudes toward them. It does this to a degree, in many men, that cannot readily be overcome when promotion comes fast in war. It is bad for any army.

"All God's Chillun Ain't Got Wings" is the most thorough discussion of a vital subject ever to appear in any service journal. It was published in 1935, and it looks sharply toward a new great war—a habit of most Regular Army men based on the inevitability of war throughout history.

BELSHAZZAR'S FEAST

THE OUTSTANDING PROBLEM in the military service is promotion. Everywhere the times are out of joint. Organized knowledge in the field of the physical sciences has so outstripped the slow advance of the social sciences that the control of society has become difficult. The same is true in the armed forces. Material preparedness has progressed at the expense of intellectual preparedness. Somehow the art of war must be brought into harmony with the science of war.

Still punch-drunk from the past great conflict, civilized society sees another war casting its ominous shadow before. The old worlds are seething with baffled purposes. Statesmen are straining to stave off temporarily what is once more being spoken of as "inevitable war." Thoughtful men in responsible positions have expressed serious doubts whether our present level of civilization can survive another great bloodletting.

We are in the midst of economic difficulties which themselves are grave enough. Even discounting the more fantastic imaginings of alarmists, the destructive powers it is possible to unleash in war have greatly increased. There is reason to fear in all soberness that their misuse may spell catastrophe.

This has happened before. Critics have demonstrated that the military systems tested in the recent great war were barren of all except deadly fruits. They have diagnosed the malady to be a constitutional deficiency of brain power. The armies of the world are therefore faced with a crucial problem and an awful responsibility. Unless we can find a way to mobilize and utilize the best brain power in armies more effectively, another general conflict will indeed be fraught with danger to civilization.

A *little* more brains will not serve. The destructiveness of war has become too dangerous and the problems of war too complicated. We must have the fullest possible service from the best brains that we can muster. Nor will it do to wait until the blast of war blows in the ears: then it will be too late.

Under modern conditions of fast transport and rapid movement an initial decision may come with headlong quickness—and it may be final. If the original Schlieffen plan had been adhered to in 1914, France might well have been smashed to a bleeding pulp within three months, as was expected. But at that time regular use of motor transport had not yet lent to armies the speed of movement away from railways which is now possible. Full use of the gasoline engine has since made it far more probable that opening engagements will be decisive. As a corollary we can no longer safely rely upon learning the way to victory after war has begun. The fate of nations has thus come to depend pre-eminently upon (1) intelligent preparation of war and (2) intellectual preparedness for the conduct of war. This means that no other military problem of today is comparable in importance with that of getting the ablest men to the top in time of peace.

The story of 1914 should haunt us. It is a story of what happens when the preparation and conduct of war are left to mediocrities. It is a story of divine obliviousness to the implications of technological progress and of ideas on war long disassociated from realities. Above all, there is the artistic tragedy of the Schlieffen plan, conceived by a first-rate intelligence and thoroughly botched by the tinkering and fiddling of mere journeymen soldiers.

The importance of methods of promotion to success in war is illustrated by another story: that of 1870. The world has long since taken the measure of the French generals who repeatedly led a veteran professional soldiery of premier quality down to ignominious defeat and futile death. Armies of lions were led by asses, while the great genius of an Ardant du Picq was allowed to fall at the head of a mere regiment. This came to pass because the French Army was saddled with a system of promotion by seniority and favoritism which almost guaranteed that exceptional ability should never attain the higher grades. The War of 1870–71 was lost to the French by the provisions governing advancement in the law of March 16, 1838!

From across the Rhine came the half-amateur army of Prussia, led by a military genius and seconded by a whole constellation of able men. Its preparation for war was far superior in organization, efficiency, plans, tactics, training of officers, and some of its weapons. Its higher commanders and staff officers were thoroughly prepared intellectually for the conduct of war. The superb troops of France were rolled back and rolled under, while the world gasped.

In seeking to account for the phenomenal victory of Prussia, soldier-men have ascribed great importance to her general staff institution and her army's possession of the philosophy of Clausewitz. They have missed the main point. France had the philosophy of Bourcet, Guibert, and Jomini to draw upon. In the *Dépôt de la Guerre* she had an institution corresponding far more closely to the Great General Staff than has been realized. In the *corps d'état-major* she had an equivalent of the *General-stab der Armee*. There was only one vital difference: the Prussian staff had a system of selection and promotion which drew out the last ounce of brain power in the Prussian Army under the inspired direction of a man who was himself, in part, only a product of the system. The brain power of the staff made itself felt in every department. *The greatness of the Prussian Army under Moltke thus rested upon its method of sifting out ability.*

The incubus which weighs upon the military systems of today is promotion by seniority. Seniority alone can never hope to get brains to the top. If by a happy chance a man of brains should climb the weary files to high command, by the time he has passed all the milestones of the years his energy and enthusiasm will almost certainly have been dissipated along the road and his creative genius long since have flowered—and gone to seed. Youth has an important place in high command. Fuller, in his *Generalship: Its Diseases and Their Cure,* presents the extreme view of this subject, the importance of which was recognized by Onosander 2,500 years ago. Today promotion is hopelessly handicapped in the race with senile decay. The ability which springs from long experience is too often counteracted by an increased ossification on mental habits. Nature may be wise and kindly to the generals in not allowing them to recognize these limitations in themselves, but that does not make it any easier on the Army. Today we have an almost ironclad guarantee that our generals will be a generation behind in their thinking. They reach their rank at a time when it is more natural to look backward than forward, where youth instinctively casts its eyes.

When he first read a volume of Jomini's works Napoleon nearly had an apoplectic stroke.

"How did Fouché ever let this book be published?" he demanded. "It will give away all my secrets."

Then upon second thought he said:

"After all, it doesn't matter. The young men who read it will never command against me—and the old ones will never read it."

Napoleon knew that the vices of seniority in the armies of his enemies were fighting on his side; that interminable imprisonment in the lower grades had dwarfed the imagination and sterilized the brains of his opponents so that he could tell just what they could and would do. The advantages of flexibility and of surprise were all on his side.

Seniority is a fetish which for purposes of promotion can show no more solid proofs of virtue than the time-honored use of spunk water and dead cats at midnight as a cure for warts.

Why does this archaic device survive in modern days? Is it because of military conservatism and inertia? Is it because army officers have as their chief concern the acquisition of "property" in higher grades by a sort of compound interest and regard their calling as a semiprivate business guild engaged in haggling with the state and within itself over the "spoils of peace" in the spirit of the old *condottieri?* Or is it because every system of selection which has yet been tried has proven vicious and raised an outcry?

Probably something of all these factors comes into play in varying degree, according to individual characteristics. Military men in their tactical studies make a great to-do about elaborate and complete "estimates of the situation," assessing pertinent facts in the light of their "mission." But in the conduct of routine affairs they make momentous decisions without taking account of these systematic safeguards, and with much the same combination of rationalized feeling and instinctive, cold self-interest as a romantic young woman casting an appraising eye over an unconscious candidate for her hand. Promotion is discussed on the basis of how to get rid of the "hump" so as to improve morale, prevent stagnation in grade, and let the lowly move toward the Promised Land. This Promised Land is more often envisaged as though it were a sort of transcendental Old Soldiers' Home for the faithful rather than a busy workshop for the turning out of a superlative instrument for the winning of victory in war.

While it seems to be true that our volunteer and conscript veterans have been willing to lay down their lives for the welfare of the country but not to give up their bonus, something better can be said for our professional soldiers. As a rule they live by a code of ethics whose roots lie deep in the soil of sacrifice for the public weal. It is necessary only to state the problem clearly to know how they will answer. They will submit readily to any method of selection that will do what it is supposed to do, that can be shown to be in the true public interest, and that does not by creating rancor and mistrust destroy the very breath of an army— its morale. Officers care as much for the future of their families as any normal human beings. Promotion by seniority does give a certain guarantee of future security as comforting to the soul as to lie in a hammock in the shade with a book and pipe and glass, listening idly to the clank of an oil well pumping one up a black fortune out of the ground. But the demands of war are harsh. The soldier is as much vowed to sacrifice and service as a member of a monastic order. His cannot be a life of ease.

Epic deeds such as he must be ready to perform are not spawned in security and comfort but in uncertainty, straining effort, and mastery of confusion in flux. Like the sharp notes of First Call on a bitter morning, the realization must come that the conditions of war have so changed that continued reliance upon promotion by seniority as the principal method of advancement is now madness. The only question is how a satisfactory method of selection can be divided. We must find an answer, for it is a decree of Nature: "Adapt or die!"

Mene, Mene, Tekel, Upharsin

The crucial problem of getting brains to the top of armies has been examined by Liddell Hart in his *Remaking of Modern Armies* (pp. 196–98), but for all his acumen he has not been able to offer any really new suggestions. All the old schemes have been tried and found wanting. No one will hold a brief for election. No competitive examinations yet devised by man can get at the qualities it is necessary to evaluate. Promotion by seniority is an evil to be escaped. Some sort of selection alone remains.

The really serious objection to this method is not to be found in the injustices that result. It is to be found in the fact that the systems of selection which have been tried cannot be relied upon to deliver the goods. If they do not, then the injustice is flagrant and serious. It has no justification in results and has a serious effect upon the morale of the army.

The Moltkean system of personal selection offers no general solution because it inexorably calls for a very great man to do the selecting. It can be applied effectively only within the limits of a small establishment such as a general staff, for it requires close and prolonged personal contact. Under other than these conditions personal selection will become pure favoritism without being effective. If this favoritism be frivolous, if the system be ill devised, rigid, and not subject to change in the light of trial and error, there is likely to be an inverse or freakish selection. Some years ago a distinguished scholar was asked why at that time so many weird theories were being put forth by German professors. He replied that the University of Berlin, once upon a time, decided to encourage originality and had taken pains to select men of greater originality to the faculty, and that the result had been that the most original professors had selected the most original pupils, until in time there had been raised a faculty of crackpots.

One of the difficulties with selection in the past has been that it has been done by boards. The esteem in which boards are held may be judged from the common definition: "Long, narrow, and wooden." The evils of a council of war are proverbial. A board is a council of peace and shares many of the disadvantages of a council of war and has in addition many peculiarities of its own. If the sad tales now going around about "Class B" boards [the boards before which officers of poor record appeared with a view to their elimination from the Army] are only 10 per cent true, the board as a means of selection stands condemned.

After the Franco-Prussian War French officers were reclassified by a board upon which sat none other than Marshals MacMahon and Canrobert. This board was thoroughly imbued with the spirit of the Second Empire and derided as "Cossacks" any officers who studied their profession. Before this board came the name of a certain Lafourge. It was recorded that this officer of his own free will and at great personal sacrifice had long occupied himself with the study of geology. "Peuh!" said one member of the board. "An officer who occupies himself with geology!" Another member of the august commission remarked dreamily, "But who rides a horse like a centaur!" Thereupon promotion was promptly accorded. Such is the way of boards. They may be as capricious as a coquette.

If boards rely upon opinions of members who have had some contact with particular officers—as fair-minded boards are prone to do—they do not really take corporate action but engage in a sort of "logrolling." The alternative is to fall back upon an officer's "record." For many reasons this is an inadequate basis for selection. One reason is decisive: An officer's record is one of accomplishment rather than of ability. What goes into that record depends largely upon chance or favor—upon the opportunities given him to demonstrate ability.

An officer brilliantly saves the day. He is suitably recognized. But what of the officer, perhaps of far greater ability, who never got to the front but loyally did his drudgery far from the sound of battle? A military attaché reports a foreign war with great insight. He must be rewarded. But does that prove him better than those stuck in some hole at home? Another officer brings a laggardly outfit to a high level of efficiency. It is proper to recognize this fact. But does it prove him any abler than that officer who has inherited a unit at an exceptional level of efficiency and maintains it there? In time of peace the opportunity to demonstrate ability depends pre-eminently upon assignment. Assignment is a matter of preferment. Who gets first crack at the service schools? Is it not in many cases those who have been "dog robbers" on Olympus? Soldiers are human beings and subject to human failings. To judge an officer wholly on his record merely removes favoritism to the level of assignment and makes selection on that basis a mockery.

It is a natural human failing to honor accomplishment without taking into account opportunity. General Pershing did a good job. That does not prove that he was a better man than others who did not have his opportunities. Lacking any other measure of ability, a conscientious board is almost certain to follow this failing blindly. Too many aides-de-camp promoted, too many promotions for actions of éclat in Algeria contributed largely to bring France to Sedan [the Sedan of 1870].

Where selection is practiced it is inequality of opportunity that rankles in the souls of the less fortunate. If reasonable equality of opportunity could be assured no true soldier would grumble over errors of judgment. He can always prove his case by trying harder. It is being doomed to helplessness that makes men bitter. Sportsmanship will concede another better man if the trial be in a free and fair competition, but no one takes his defeat with good grace if he knows that the deck was stacked.

Great ability is so rare that all defer to it and the entire army must be combed to find it. If it is to be recognized everywhere, it must be allowed to identify itself everywhere. It can be made to grow. That is another reason why we must find some means to identify it and stimulate it wherever it can be found. Napoleon knew his hegemonics when he said that each of his soldiers carried a marshal's baton in his knapsack. To stimulate the general growth of ability there must be an approximately equal opportunity to win reward. Such stimulus acts not only upon the cream of the crop but indirectly upon the whole corps of officers. The prospect of winning to the top works to endow the whole army with an almost epic spirit. This was the secret of Napoleon and of Von Moltke.

The Review of the Wooden Soldiers

I divide my officers into four classes as follows: The clever, the industrious, the lazy, and the stupid. Each officer always possesses two of these qualities. Those who are clever and industrious I appoint to the General Staff. Use can under certain circumstances be made of those who are stupid and lazy. The man who is clever and lazy qualifies for the highest leadership posts. He has the requisite nerves and the mental clarity for difficult decisions. But whoever is stupid and industrious must be got rid of, for he is too dangerous.

> General Freiherr von Hammerstein-Equord,
> Former head of German War Department,
> Chief of Army Direction.

The problem of promotion is complicated by the need for more than one type in the leadership of armies. As Machiavelli wrote: "There are three kinds of brains: the first can learn by itself; the second can appreciate what others have learned; the third can neither learn of itself nor from others."

The idea that all officers should be standardized and interchangeable parts in a military machine needs only to be looked at to be known for what it is, an imbecility and a fraud. We deny the thesis when we commission officers in different arms and services, although this is largely an artificial differentiation, and yet we fail to recognize important and natural differences. Blois during the World War was a madhouse peopled by round pegs who had been thrust into square holes and by square pegs who had been forced into round holes. Officers who would have been invaluable elsewhere were wrenched savagely out of jobs to which they were unsuited, to the injury of their reputations and without benefit to the service. It was a cruel and brutal system based upon the stupidity of this assumption that every officer should be able to fill any job in the Army. Someday, perhaps, our equally absurd and stupid subservience to the gross superstition of "appropriate command" will exact its penalty also.

The basic fallacy in all previous and existing systems of selection had been "blind" selection with no clear idea of what one must select for. Napoleon would have been no more than General Bonaparte had it not been for Carnot and Berthier. Alexander owed his army to his father, Philip of Macedon; Caesar, his to Marius, and Grant owed his army to McClellan. More than one type of officer is needed to win a war.

We may distinguish five types of necessary ability, with essential characteristics substantially as follows:

(1) The "Staff Brain-Truster" or Jomini Type:

Grasp, or power of comprehending the essential nature of problems or situations.

Originality and profusion of ideas, stemming from great imaginative powers.

Foresight, stemming from great imaginative powers and a strong sense of realities.

(2) The "Balance Wheel" or Blücher Type:

Suggestibility, or readiness to consider the ideas of others before deciding.

Sound judgment of values and of risks.

Decision: promptness in deciding and resolution in adhering to plans once made.

Coolness and steady, unshakable confidence.

(3) The "Staff Executive" or Berthier Type:

Refined technical skill in elaborating details of directives according to a system.

Unfailing precision and reliability.

Systematic providence: systematic forethought in the provision of information and dispositions necessary to a proper state of readiness for any conceivable eventuality.

(4) The "Subcommander" or Napoleonic Marshal Type:

Orientation, or a supreme sense for the necessity for a particular mission.

Intellectual discipline and fortitude in pursuit of that mission.

Leadership, or the capacity to get the utmost effort and teamwork out of men.

(5) The "Organizer of Victory" or Carnot Type:

Driving energy that overrides all obstacles and "red tape" to get maximum results at maximum speed.

Systematic capacity that can improvise order in any confusion.

"Hand over your money or I'll blow out your brains!" said the highwayman to the New Yorker. "Blow away," said the New Yorker. "You can live in New York without brains, but you can't without money." The same is true (to some extent) about brains in command of an army. You can command an army without brains, but you can't without character. In all except one type of officer character and skill are predominant. "Brains" is the necessary characteristic only of the Jomini type.

Thomas Conway and Charles Lee were both the superiors of George Washington as technically trained soldiers. Both failed utterly in the command of troops and had to be court-martialed. Washington is enrolled among the great military leaders of all times. Both character and skill are based upon ingrained habit, and the more such habit is reduced to the level of highly ingrained reflex action, the greater the ability. But habit is developed at the expense of brain power. It achieves speed and efficiency by dispensing with any necessity for constant recourse to fresh reasoning and so weakens the higher reasoning powers. It must be so. The last four types are "brainless" in their purity. They are the types of the "wooden soldiers." It is the first type alone that is endowed with the peculiar *problem-solving capacity* now peculiarly required. It is the only type that can hope to deal effectively with problems *of a new kind* not adequately provided for by stereotyped reactions. It is the only type that can hope to deal effectively with problems *whose elements are highly uncertain or largely unknown.*

The present military system has demonstrated that it can produce plenty of excellent wooden soldiers. It is sadly deficient in its production of "bright-idea" soldiers. This may be due in part to our theory that all officers should be standardized and interchangeable, and in part to the influence of the general service schools which teach how to make omelets without breaking eggs. It is necessary to put a special premium on "brains." This does not mean that a premium should not be placed on exceptional ability in other types. It would be folly to entrust the conduct of war to a mere book soldier. A combination of all abilities is necessary. We should search high and low for combinations in particular men, for it is they who are the Marlboroughs, the Napoleons, and the Von Moltkes. Failing such, we must resort to teams. For these the best of the wooden soldiers should be selected up. But only the very best, for the officers of any healthy army are on the average of high-standard wooden soldiers. They are the backbone of any army, and for precisely that reason ought not to be the head. It is the brain-trusters that are hard to find. Wherever found, "brains" should be selected up rapidly to the level where they are most needed. This will not be the highest level unless "brains" is combined with other types of ability. It will be the general staff level. In the lack of combinations, high command must go to the "Hindenburg," the "Blücher," the "Joffre," and the "Napoleonic-marshal" types of ability, with staffs of Ludendorffs, Scharnhorsts, and Jominis.

The two commander types do not need to be selected up as rapidly as brains. They are hardy plants that can thrive and grow under present system. The Hindenburg-Blücher type may reach full bloom in advanced years; the other in middle age. But "brains" must be gotten up before they settle into a rut. They must be plucked before they wither and go to seed. Here, then, one principle suggests itself. *Mere "bright-idea" soldiers should be selected up fast to the middle grades to stay there; the commander types should be selected up fast from the middle grades to the highest.* This principle would let the rare *combination types* go up fast all the way, but only such combination types.

The crux of the problem lies in equalization of opportunity to demonstrate ability. The problem of equalization is not the same for all types of ability. The commander types depend largely upon strength of character. Character can manifest itself to a high degree under almost any conditions. It already has a considerable measure of equal opportunity. If rapid advancement be left to take place in the higher grades, it becomes possible to rely more upon a sort of personal selection. There are fewer officers to consider, and they are known better by their long service. In the middle grades the opportunity to demonstrate ability is much larger, no matter what the assignment. The distribution of opportunity is somewhat more equitable. It is doubtful if any premium should be put upon these types in the lower grades. There is every reason to encourage the "wooden" types to develop into other types of ability as well.

The Berthier and Carnot types of ability can manifest themselves pretty well in executive positions and to a lesser extent in all administrative activity, at which every officer gets plenty of chance. If proper account be taken of opportunity, an officer's achievement may be a valueless clue to ability in these types. It is not enough, but it should not be difficult to arrange for a closer approach to equality of opportunity in this field by means of greater system in assignment. *The whole business of assignment should be redesigned so as to aim at giving every officer approximately equal chance to show these types of ability.* The greater possibilities which lie in the use of assignment for the systematic testing of the officer corps are not adequately exploited.

"Brains" gets little chance to demonstrate itself in ordinary military duties. The problem of equal opportunity is here a serious one. It is said that General Summerall as commander of the Hawaiian Division called upon each officer annually to report what progress he had made in his profession during the year: what he regarded as his outstanding achievement. Here is an attempt to get at the bottom of the business. It has not been unknown for officers to win recognition and preferment for achievements made on their own initiative above or outside of line of duty. Here is a field for study with a view to finding a basis for systematic selection for promotion.

There is one ideal of advancement in the world today which has never been prospected thoroughly for military use but which comes in here with peculiar relevance. It is that of the "brain trust" par excellence of civilization: the academic ideal of advancement for scholars and scientists. These form a loosely organized army fighting a leisurely and bloodless but endless battle on the frontier of knowledge. They have their hierarchy, both of grades and commands, and hence a problem of advancement. But their problem differs from that of armies in that it knows no two distinct phases of war and peace.

Armies, in the occasional intense conflicts of actual war, are forced to fall back in greater or lesser degree upon arbitrary selection. They can do so with confidence at such times because the test of actual war measures ability as nothing else can. But in time of peace measurement of military ability becomes a baffling problem. The elements of such ability are so various, so intangible, and so uncertain that, unlike the forces of mechanics, their presence can be detected with accuracy only through results. But results *in war* cannot be produced in time of peace, nor can war be simulated in even a hundredth part of its condition.

The sciences are always at war, in a sense. They can measure ability by results achieved in their war. In another sense they are always in a state of peace. Results can be achieved, but they do not have to be achieved at any particular time or place. The sciences have therefore hit upon a scheme of advancement in which prospective candidates are given the responsibility of demonstrating amply their ability by achieving results on their own initiative and at such time and in such manner as they see fit. It is somewhat as if candidates for high command were allowed to take an army and go conquer whatever smaller country might strike their fancy in order to demonstrate their ability to command in war.

The ability that it is vitally necessary to draw out of armies is not merely ability to conduct war but also ability to prepare for war. We need not only great war commanders but men who can recognize and develop such commanders and equip them with the best military machine that it is possible to build. We need not only virtuosos but composers and impresarios. The ability of the latter can be measured with certainty only through ultimate results in war, but there are also certain peacetime results capable of some evaluation. Armies might take a cue from the academic world by taking as a criterion for special advancement *distinguished or significant contributions to material or intellectual preparedness above and beyond the call of duty.*

NAPOLEONS, FRONT AND CENTER!

Let us try to sketch a system of advancement that embraces routine promotion for the main body of officers by seniority and exceptional advancement for a percentage of officers *in such a manner that there would be no retarding of promotion by seniority.* The last would be achieved by retiring field officers at the top to make room for exceptional promotions, thus stimulating the flow of the best ability toward the top while still young.

The essential element in this scheme is an adaptation of the system of cumulative "honor points" used at the Military Academy to determine military as distinct from academic standing. Honor points would be given for achievement under four heads:

(1) Exceptional knowledge of subjects, or exceptional proficiency in techniques, of patent or probable military utility, acquired other than in line of duty by notable voluntary effort;

(2) Significant contributions to material or intellectual preparedness for war made out of line of duty, or in line of duty in notable excess of reasonable expectations;

(3) Demonstration of the capacity to get results from plans, in the conduct of wartime or similar operations, in notable excess of what might reasonably be expected and as a consequence of exceptional force of character;

(4) Exceptional skill and efficiency in the performance of regular military duties (other than wartime conduct of operations) or non-military functions of related nature.

The purpose of the system of honor points is to get away from any judgment of officers by boards and to decentralize the process of judgment. Any particular award of points would be only contributory to determining an officer's standing. The more one increases the number of these infinitesimal judgments, the more one reduces the likelihood of any large error and approaches true evaluation as a limit. There would be, not a single judgment based upon a record, but a series of judgments by superiors, boards, or examiners, made as a result of direct knowledge or investigation *at the time.* The whole army would judge, not a single board.

"Skill-and-efficiency points" would be given upon approved recommendation of appropriate commanders who would be required to give consideration to written estimates by intermediate commanders. The company officers would be graded by the regimental commander with the written estimates from his field officers. Any large discrepancy between these ratings would call for inquiry before final approval.

"Contribution points" would be given by special corps-area boards upon presentation of substantial facts and competent testimonials on the value of the contributions made, either by the officer himself or by his commander, and after such investigations by the board as may seem fitting. An officer invents a gadget to improve fire power or makes a striking advance in methods of communications: let the facts be determined, the value of the device assessed, and let points be set to his credit.

"Command-ability points" would be given by citing for achievements under conditions calling for command ability, as actual or simulated warlike operations or emergencies of all sorts. Whenever a soldier distinguishes himself in a crisis of any kind—at a fire, in an earthquake, or other disaster—by his coolness and energy, it should be set down to his everlasting credit and noted in his record as an indication of his capacity to handle himself and others under stress. In this connection it might be advisable to study the use of psychological tests, such as are used in the Air Corps to test such things as reaction times and sense of balance, or as are being developed to test ability to handle an automobile in an emergency. It might be possible to develop a type of war exercise to test character and resistance to fatigue, confusion, uncertainty, surprise, and breathless speed. The fruits of science are at our service. The rewards offered are great.

"Education points" would be given by the same or a like board upon examination or application by the officer concerned, supported by the testimony of a superior officer or civilian expert. An officer who compiles a useful manual, who learns a foreign language, or translates a useful book; or one who masters a fresh field of knowledge, writes the history of some campaign, or proposes a practical application of some new knowledge to military uses, should be remembered by credits against the Judgment Day of selection. These boards might have the power to endorse applications for exceptional leaves of absence on two-thirds or three-quarters pay to study at civilian institutions, or for foreign travel with a specific purpose, and give credit for such fruits as may be garnered.

At the end of each two years exceptional promotion would be accorded to a number of officers in *each* grade below that of lieutenant colonel equal to, say, 2 per cent of the total number of officers in the Army.

.   .   .

The flexibility of this method could be insured by adjusting from time to time the premiums set upon the various types of ability.

Under this system it would be theoretically possible for a very exceptional officer to reach the grade of lieutenant colonel after some eight years of commissioned service or at about the age of thirty. In practice close competition would tend to raise this age considerably—and at the same time raise the general standard of efficiency enormously. Brigadier generals of forty years are conceivable. Most of the seniority men would retire as majors or lieutenant colonels. Colonels would be drawn overwhelmingly from "honors" men of greater youth. The newer generals would be younger men too. But since general officers would continue to serve until normal retirement age, a plentiful supply of "wise old heads" would be preserved. The long service and wide experience of the men at the top would be all to the good. Yet it would still be possible in theory and could happen in practice that we might get a commander in chief in time of war of only forty-five years of age. Since Napoleon was only twenty-seven at the beginning of his first Italian campaign, this is not exactly radical.

A further advantage of this system is that it would mark men for the particular type of work for which they were best fitted by segregating honor points under the four heads mentioned. That officer who had a preponderance of points for extraordinary knowledge and few for efficiency would be the last man to use as a chief of staff or G-4, but might be singularly useful as a G-2. The officer who has been prolific in invention or the development of methods might be the last man to trust with important operations. That is no reason to turn him adrift. Here we have a method for fitting round pegs into round holes and square pegs into square holes.

The proposal herein does not offer a full-fledged system to be set up by spontaneous creation. It offers a suggestion toward the development through evolution and adaptation of a working hypothesis capable of being tested progressively by trial and error so as to work gradually toward perfection with both feet firmly planted on the ground. It is a conception worthy of systematic study and experiment because of the number and importance of the advantages it offers. Colin in France and Spenser Wilkinson in England have illuminated for us the various factors which went into the making of the military genius of Napoleon. If the General Staff is not equipped to study how to create or how to discover and advance the best brains of the Army, some other agency should be set up to analyze the factors which go into the making of great leaders and to study our military system and its methods in detail from the broadest possible point of view. Such an agency might seek to determine whether it is necessary or desirable to join together in holy wedlock rank and appropriate command, or rank and pay.

.   .   .

The promotion problem is the fundamental problem of modern armies. Certain lines along which it might be attacked have been suggested. The General Staff is the proper agency to elaborate any·detailed plan. It has many important duties. But it has none more important than this and none that offers greater rewards in the task of perfecting the national defense.

SUCCESS IN WAR

By Major (now Lieutenant General) George S. Patton, Jr.

(*1931*)

WAR IS AN ART and as such is not susceptible of explanation by fixed formula. Yet from the earliest time there has been an unending effort to subject its complex and emotional structure to dissection, to enunciate rules for its waging, to make tangible its intangibility. As well strive to isolate the soul by the dissection of the cadaver as to seek the essence of war by the analysis of its records. Yet despite the impossibility of physically detecting the soul, its existence is proven by its tangible reflection in acts and thoughts.

Above armed hosts there hovers an impalpable something which on occasion so dominates the material as to induce victory under circumstances quite inexplicable. To understand this something we should seek it in a manner analogous to our search for the soul; and, so seeking, we shall perchance find it in the reflexes produced by the acts of the Great Captains.

But whither shall we turn for knowledge of their very selves? Not in the musty tomes of voluminous reports or censored recollections wherein they strove to immortalize their achievements. Nor yet in the countless histories where lesser wormish men have sought to snare their parted ghosts.

The great warriors were too busy and often too inapt to write contemporaneously of their exploits. What they later put on paper was colored by strivings for enhanced fame or by political conditions then confronting them. War was an ebullition of their perished past. The violent simplicity in execution which procured them success and enthralled them looked pale and uninspired on paper, so they seasoned it.

The race yearns to adore. Can it adore the simple or venerate the obvious? All mythology and folklore rise in indignant protest at the thought. The sun gave light; therefore, he was not hot gas or a flame, but a god or a chariot. The *ignis fatuus* deluded men of nights. It was a spirit; nothing so simple as decomposition could serve the need.

So with the soldier, to pander to self-love and racial urge he attributes to his acts profound thoughts which never existed. The white-hot energy of youth which saw in obstacles but inspirations and in the enemy but the gage to battle becomes to complacent and retrospective age the result of mathematical calculation and metaphysical erudition, of knowledge he never had and plans he never made.

With the efforts of the historians the case is even worse. Those who write at the time are guilty of partisanship and hero worship. While those who write later are forced to accept contemporaneous myths and to view their subject through the roseate light which distance, be it that of time or space, sheds ever to deprive us of harsh truth. In peace the scholar flourishes; in the war the soldier dies; so it comes about that we view our soldiers through the eyes of scholars and attribute to them scholarly virtues.

Seeking obvious reasons for the obscure, we analyze their conduct as told by historians and assign as reasons for their success apparent, trivial things. Disregarding wholly the personality of Frederick, we attribute his victories to a tactical expedient, the oblique order of battle. Impotent to comprehend the character of Rome's generals, a great historian coins the striking phrase: "At this time the Roman legionary shortened his sword and gained an empire." Our research is further muddled by the fabled heroism of all former fighters. Like wine, accounts of valor mellow with age, until Achilles, dead three thousand years, stands peerless.

Yet through the murk of fact and fable rises to our view this truth. The history of war is the history of warriors; few in number, mighty in influence. Alexander, not Macedonia, conquered the world. Scipio, not Rome, destroyed Carthage. Marlborough, not the Allies, defeated France. Cromwell, not the Roundheads, dethroned Charles.

Were this true only of warriors we might well exclaim: "Behold the work of the historian!" But it is equally the case in every phase of human endeavor. Music has its myriad of musicians but only its dozen masters. So with painting, sculpture, literature, medicine, or trade. "Many are called, but few are chosen."

Nor can we concur wholly with the alluring stories in the advertising sections of our magazines which point the golden path of success to all and sundry who will follow some particular phase of home education they happen to advocate. "Knowledge is power," but to a degree only. Its possession per se will raise a man to mediocrity but not to distinction. In our opinion, indeed, the instruction obtained from such courses is of less moment to future success than is the ambition which prompted the study.

In considering these matters we should remember that while there is much similarity there is also a vast difference between the successful soldier and the successful man in other professions. Success due to knowledge and personality is the measure of ability in each case, but to all save the soldier it has vital significance only to the individual and to a limited number of his associates. With the soldier success or failure means infinitely more, as it must of necessity be measured not in terms of personal honor or affluence but in the life, happiness, and honor of his men—his country. Hence the search for that elusive secret of military success, soul, genius, personality—call it what you will—is of vital interest to us all.

·　　　　　·　　　　　·

In our efforts to provide for the avoidance, in future, of the mistakes which we personally have encountered, and to ensure to ourselves or to our successors the same mathematical ease of operation of which we have read, we proceed to enunciate rules. In order to enunciate anything we must have a premise. The most obvious is the last war. Further, the impressions we gained there were the most vivid we have ever experienced; burned on the tablets of our memories by the blistering flash of exploding shell, etched on our souls by the incisive patter of machine-gun bullets, our own experiences become the foundation of our thoughts and, all unconscious of personal bias, we base our conceptions of the future on our experience of the past.

Beyond question, personal knowledge is a fine thing, but unfortunately it is too intimate. When, for example, we recall a railroad accident the picture that most vividly presents itself to us is the severed blue-gray hand of some child victim, not the misread signals which precipitated the tragedy. So with war experiences, the choking gas that strangled us sticks in our memory to the more or less complete exclusion of the important fact that it was the roads and consequent abundant mechanical transportation peculiar to western Europe which permitted the accumulation of enough gas shells to do the strangling.

Even when no personal experience exists we are bound to be influenced by the most recent experience of others. Because in the Boer War the bayonet found no employment, we all but abandoned it, only to seize it again when the Russo-Japanese conflict redemonstrated its value. Going back farther, we might point to countless other instances of similar nature, as witness the recurrent use and disuse of infantry and cavalry as the dominant arms according to the most recent "lesson" derived from the last war, based invariably on special conditions, in no way bound to recur, yet always presumed as immutable.

So much for the conservatives; now for the optimists—the "nothing-old" gentry. These are of several species, but first in order of importance come the specialists.

Due either to superabundant egotism and uncontrolled enthusiasm, or else to limited powers of observation of the activities of other arms, these people advocate in the most fluent and uncompromising manner the vast future potentialities of their own special weapons. In the next war, so they say, all the enemy will be crushed, gassed, bombed, or otherwise speedily exterminated, depending for the method of his death upon the arm to which the person declaiming belongs. Their spectacular claims attract public attention. The appeal of their statements is further strengthened because they deal invariably in mechanical devices which intrigue the simple imagination and because the novelty of their schemes and assertions has a strong news interest which ensures their notice by the press. Earlier examples of this newspaper tendency to exploit the bizarre is instanced in the opening accounts of the Civil War where "masked batteries" and "black-horse cavalry" seemed to infest the whole face of Nature.

Both the standpatters and the progressives have reason of sorts, and, as we have pointed out, we must seek to harmonize the divergent tendencies.

.   .   .

No matter what the situation as to clarity of his mental perspective, the conscientious soldier approaches the solution of his problem more or less bemuddled by phantoms of the past and deluded by unfounded or unproved hopes for the future. So handicapped, he assumes the unwonted and labored posture of a student and plans for perfection, so that when the next war comes that part of the machine for which he may be responsible shall instantly begin to function with a purr of perfect preparation.

In this scholarly avocation soldiers of all important nations use at the present time what purports to be the best mode of instruction—the applicatory method. The characteristics of some concrete problem are first studied in the abstract and then tested by applying them, with assumed forces and situations, in solving analogous problems either on the terrain or on a map representation of it. This method not only familiarizes the student with all the tools and technicalities of his trade, but also develops the aptitude for reaching decisions and the self-assurance derived from demonstrated achievement.

But as always there is a fly in the amber. High academic performance demands infinite intimate knowledge of details, and the qualities requisite to such attainments often inhabit bodies lacking in personality. Also, the striving for such knowledge often engenders the fallacious notion that capacity depends upon the power to acquire such details rather than upon the ability to apply them. Obsessed with this thought, students plunge in deeper and ever deeper, their exertions but enmeshing them the more until, like mired mastodons, they perish in a morass of knowledge where they first browsed for sustenance.

When the prying spade of the unbiased investigator has removed the muck of official reports and the mire of self-laudatory biographies from the swamp of the World War, the skeletons of many such military mammoths will be discovered. Amid their mighty remains will lurk elusive the secret of German failure. Beyond question no soldier ever sought more diligently than the Germans for prewar perfection. They built and tested and adjusted their mighty machine and became so engrossed in its visible perfection, in the accuracy of its bearings and the compression of its cylinders, that they neglected the battery. When the moment came their masterpiece proved inefficient through lack of the divine afflatus, the soul of a leader. Truly in war "Men are nothing; a man is everything."

Here we must deny that anything in our remarks is intended to imply belief in the existence of spontaneous, untutored inspiration. With the single exception of the divinely inspired Joan of Arc, no such phenomenon has ever existed, and . . . she was less of an exception than a coincidence. We require and must demand all possible thoughtful preparation and studious effort, so that in war our officers may be equal to their mighty trust—the safety of our country. Our purpose is not to discourage such preparation but simply to call attention to certain defects in its pursuit. To direct it not toward the glorification of the means—study; but to the end—victory.

In acquiring erudition we must live on, not in, our studies. We must guard against becoming so engrossed in the specific nature of the roots and bark of the trees of knowledge as to miss the meaning and grandeur of the forests they compose. Our means of studying war have increased as much as have our tools for waging it, but it is an open question whether this increase in means has not perhaps obscured or obliterated one essential detail; namely, the necessity for personal leadership.

.   .   .

War is conflict; fighting is an elemental exposition of the age-old effort to survive. It is the cold glitter of the attacker's eye, not the point of the questing bayonet, that breaks the line. It is the fierce determination of the driver to close with the enemy, not the mechanical perfection of the tank, that conquers the trench. It is the cataclysmic ecstasy of conflict in the flier, not the perfection of his machine gun, which drops the enemy in flaming ruin. Yet volumes are devoted to armament; pages to inspiration.

Since the necessary limitations of map problems inhibit the student from considering the effects of hunger, emotion, personality, fatigue, leadership, and many other imponderable yet vital factors, he first neglects and then forgets them. Obsessed with admiration for the intelligence which history has ascribed to past leaders, he forgets the inseparable connection between plans, the flower of the intellect; and execution, the fruit of the soul. Hooker's plan at Chancellorsville was masterly; its execution cost him the battle. The converse was true at Marengo. The historian, through lack of experience and consequent appreciation of the inspirational qualities of generals, fails to stress them, but he does emphasize their mental gifts, which, since he shares them, he values. The student blindly follows and, hugging the notion of mentality, pictures armies of insensate pawns moving with the precision of machines and the rapidity of light, guided in their intricate and resistless evolutions over the battlefield by the cold effulgence of his emotionless cerebrations as transmitted to them by wire and radio through the inspiring medium of code messages. He further assumes that superhuman intelligence will translate those somber sentences into words of fire which will electrify his chessmen into frenzied heroes who, heedless of danger, will dauntlessly translate the stillborn infants of his brain into deeds.

Was it so that Caesar rallied the XII Legion? Could the trackless ether have conveyed to his soldiers the inspiration that Napoleon imparted by his ubiquitous presence when before Rivoli he rode five horses to death, "to see everything himself"?

.   .   .

Shrewd critics have assigned military success to all manner of things— tactics, shape of frontiers, speed, happily placed rivers, mountains or woods, intellectual ability, or the use of artillery. All in a measure true, but none vital. The secret lies in the inspiring spirit which lifted weary, footsore men out of themselves and made them march forgetful of agony, as did Masséna's division after Rivoli and Jackson's at Winchester. No words ever imagined could have produced such prodigies of endurance as did the sight of the boy general, ill, perched on his sweating horse, or of the stern Puritan plodding ever before them on Little Sorrel. The ability to produce endurance is but an instance of that same martial soul which arouses in its followers that resistless emotion defined as *élan,* the will to victory. However defined, it is akin to that almost cataleptic burst of physical and mental exuberance shown by the athlete when he breaks a record or plunges through the tacklers, and by the author or artist in the creation of a masterpiece. The difference is that in the athlete or the artist the ebullition is autostimulated, while with an army it is the result of external impetus—leadership.

In considering war we must avoid that adoration of the material as exemplified by scientists who deny the existence of aught they cannot cut or weigh. In war tomorrow we shall be dealing with men subject to the same emotions as were the soldiers of Alexander; with men but little changed for better or for worse from the starving, shoeless Frenchmen of the Italian campaign; with men similar, save in their arms, to those whom the inspiring powers of a Greek or a Corsican changed at a breath to bands of heroes, all-enduring and all-capable.

No! History as written and read does not divulge the source of leadership. Hence its study often induces us to forget its potency. As a mirror shows us not ourselves but our reflection, so it is with the soul and with leadership; we know them but by the acts they inspire or the results they achieve. Like begets like; in the armies of the great we seek the reflection of themselves and we find Self-confidence, Enthusiasm, Abnegation of Self, Loyalty, and Courage.

.   .   .

Courage, moral and physical, is almost a synonym of all the foregoing traits. It fosters the resolution to combat and cherishes the ability to assume responsibility, be it for successes or failures. No Bayard ever showed more of it than did Lee after Gettysburg.

But as with the biblical candle, these traits are of no military value if concealed. A man of diffident manner will never inspire confidence. A cold reserve cannot beget enthusiasm, and so with the others there must be an outward and visible sign of the inward and spiritual grace.

It then appears that the leader must be an actor, and such is the fact. But with him, as with his bewigged compeer, he is unconvincing unless he lives his part.

Can men then acquire and demonstrate these characteristics? The answer is they have—they can. For "As a man thinketh, so is he." The fixed determination to acquire the warrior soul and, having acquired it, to conquer or perish with honor is the secret of success in war.

PANIC

By Mercutio

(*1936*)

THERE IS no more terrible word in the military lexicon than "panic," nor is there one so universally ignored. The reason for this strange conspiracy of silence lies in the fact that the compilers of official histories apparently confuse panic with cowardice; national pride does the rest. Therefore, the little factual evidence available on this subject is almost entirely limited to unofficial and not particularly trustworthy sources.

In our own Army I have seen or heard this subject dealt with but four times in five years; twice in lectures at the Infantry School and twice in the *Infantry School Mailing List*. Inquiry among friends in the other arms indicates that no other school or publication has even considered the matter.

Indeed, with our smug Anglo-Saxon complacency, we are inclined to think that panic is confined to other peoples. We think of the Italians at Adowa in 1896 and at Caporetto in 1917; we think of the French in 1871. Some of us may even think of the magnificently trained German XVII Corps at Gumbinnen in 1914. Of course those green-troop affairs at Bladensburg and Bull Run are well remembered. But how about our Missionary Ridge, to name but one first-class instance of panic in trained troops? And how about a little private investigation for examples of American units panicking in the World War? If we tried it sometime we might be surprised.

We delude ourselves. We are no more immune to this mass madness than any other people. No unit, no matter how thoroughly trained in peace or hardened in war, is panic-proof. Even Napoleon heard the terrible cry of *"Sauve qui peut!"* go up from his Old Guard at Waterloo. And yet in our service schools we choose to ignore this wildfire contagion.

Tomorrow we may pay heavily for our reluctance to bring it out in the open and examine its causes and its cures. Indeed, those who are best qualified to speak believe that the next great conflict will be characterized by wholesale panic on both sides . . . thanks to the terror-breeding tank and its various offspring. Certainly those leaders who have been taught to know the symptoms, the preventives, and the cures of this mass disease will be better equipped to handle it than those who think of panic only as an unmilitary and shameful word.

FEAR

From an article by WILLIAM ERNEST HOCKING,
Professor of Philosophy, Harvard University

(1918)

. . . NO ONE KNOWS IN ADVANCE how he will behave in an emergency that he has never experienced. But it may be taken for granted that everyone experiences fear. For fear is a natural reaction to an environment which is unfit for ordinary living, and the field of battle is one of the best examples of such an environment. But the knowledge that everybody feels fear is one of the most reassuring reflections when one finds himself touched by the unwelcome emotion, losing his steadiness of adjustment, his clearness of voice or vision, or his ease of breathing.

It is of value to remember that fear is a *transition state;* it prepares for action and usually vanishes when action begins. Moreover, it is a *matter of degree* and can be kept within limits by force of will. It may be true that only five out of a hundred keep cool enough to fire as they would on the range, but still ninety-five out of a hundred keep cool enough to fire in the general direction of the enemy, and nearly all keep cool enough to use a bayonet effectively. If one can make the first plunge he need have no fear of his fear after that.

Moreover, fear is no discredit. Man is more liable to fear than other animals because he is more self-conscious and more sensitive. He realizes the meaning of death as animals do not, and he hates to think of mutilation even more, usually, than of death. No one must regard himself as a coward because he is afraid; he would have more occasion to reproach himself if he were not.

For the same reason one should be very slow in judging anyone else a coward, even though he has behaved badly. Courage varies enormously with the physical condition, and the man who when weary will jump at a snap of the finger may go over the top without a tremor when he is fresh. There are, of course, obvious acts of cowardice and acts which must be sternly dealt with because of the infectious character of fear, but from the psychological standpoint nothing is more doubtful than the application of the term "coward."

FEAR: ALLY OR TRAITOR

From *Psychology For the Fighting Man*, prepared under the direction of a subcommittee of the National Research Council

(*1943*)

THE FIRST BATTLE, the first experience of having an enemy machine gun aimed at you, the first time an airplane swoops low to lay its deadly eggs in your particular patch of ground.

That is an experience anticipated by the young soldier with mingled dread and eagerness. He is eager by that time to get at the enemy. He has learned a great deal about the science of war and wants to use this knowledge to wipe out the enemy and gain victory.

But he always wonders—every man does—just how he will behave when that time comes. He doesn't feel like a hero. If he is honest—completely honest—with himself, he knows he will be scared—terrified.

The experienced soldier who has been through all this the first time and many other times has found out for certain that every man going into battle is scared. His hands tremble; his throat is dry; he must swallow constantly because his "heart is in his mouth." He does idiotic things like looking at his watch every few seconds or examining his rifle a hundred times to be sure it is loaded. The soldier green to battle may think he is the only one so disturbed, but it is true of the veteran as well. And it is true of the enemy. Germans and Japs get just as scared as Americans and Britons.

The bad moments do not come during actual combat, however, but in the time of tense waiting just before. As soon as the frightened man is able to go into action—to do something effective against the enemy, especially if it involves violent physical action—his fright is apt to be dispelled or forgotten because he is too busy fighting to remember it.

Airplane pilots who distinguished themselves in action against the Japanese said, when asked whether they were scared during those moments of acute peril, "Why, I don't know. There was too much to do. We didn't have time to think."

"Most of us were scared at first," wrote a member of a torpedoed ship; "sure we were. But when the torpedo hit us we forgot all about it. There wasn't much time and then there was too much work to do."

Encounters with the enemy are most terrifying when they are unfamiliar. As the soldier becomes used to gunfire, to explosions, to the sight and odor of death, he gradually acquires the power to meet these things more stoically. He does not actually lose his fear, but he learns to ignore it sufficiently to keep his attention mainly on the business of combat. And if he has in his trained hands a good weapon which he knows will put the enemy out of action, this gives him a feeling of confidence— a sense of power—that in large measure outweighs his fear. He knows it will soon be the other fellow's turn to be scared.

Fear, when it is experienced, is intensely uncomfortable and seems often to be incapacitating. If the period of fright is prolonged a man may feel that his nerves are "all shot" by it. For fear is disintegrating, demoralizing. It shatters morale. The soldier may be rooted to the spot, paralyzed or immobilized by fear.

Nevertheless, such awful moments before an attack, when each second seems an hour, may actually be useful to any soldier. They may really add to his efficiency.

For fear is the body's preparation for action. The heart pounds faster, pumping blood more rapidly to the arms and legs and brain, where its oxygen is needed. The lungs do their part by quickened breathing. Blood pressure goes up. Adrenalin, which is Nature's own "shot in the arm," is poured liberally into the blood stream. Sugar is released into the blood to act as fuel for the human fighting machine.

Subtle changes in body chemistry, automatically effected by powerful emotion, serve to protect the soldier in action in ways he would never think of if he had to plan them himself. His blood clots more readily. He loses temporarily the sense of fatigue, even though he may have been dog-tired.

It is sometimes difficult for a tense, frightened soldier to get started into combat—to begin the action that will relieve his fear. That part is taken care of by Army training and discipline. Months of training have taught the soldier to respond from habit to definite battle orders, even though in battle commands often cannot be given as in training. It has become second nature to him to carry out his own job as a member of the fighting team.

The parachute trooper jumping from the plane has learned to follow the man ahead. At first his "jumps" were from a mock-up only a few feet off the ground, but then he learned timing. He learned to take his cue from the man ahead. When he received his slap behind it was his turn, and out he went.

The fact that any action is so drilled in that it is mechanical helps when you are scared. No matter how distracted your mind may be by unfamiliar and terrifying sights and smells and sounds, you act from sheer force of habit. In fact, it is the habits which take care of a man, whether or not he is too frightened to think clearly, like the habit of diving for cover when bombs come down.

Then presently you are in action. You are fighting! You are at last using force against the foe! No more are you a cowering, abject soul. Fear is forgotten—provided you are well trained.

How to Fight Fear

(1) *Action dispels fear—do something.* In the time of suspense, when men are all ready for action but are waiting the signal to start, fear is at its height. If the period of waiting is to be prolonged—perhaps a delay until the weather changes—the time should be occupied with preparation for action. Fight fear with work—when expecting combat, when waiting on a raft for rescue, when waiting for enemy bombers to return.

(2) *Physical contact with friends helps.* Men should, if possible, stick within sight in time of peril but not too bunched up for bombs or shells, if possible. Just the presence of another man not far off, when no word is spoken, minimizes fear.

(3) *Roll calls help.* Men in peril should be reminded that they are not alone, that they are an integral part of a close-knit organization, that each is important to it. The artillery's "call out your numbers loud and strong" reassures each man that in the smoke of battle the others are still in their places, doing their parts. It also lets him know that the others, too, are keeping track of him. They will miss him if he is lost, will look for him. They are "all for one and one for all."

(4) *Knowledge is power over fear.* Surprise is the most important element in battle. Thus men should be kept constantly informed of the dangers they may meet, of the weapons that may be used against them,

of the tactics which the enemy uses. Every moment of leisure should be used by the men to find out what they can about what battle will be like, what the enemy is like. The known is never so fearful as the unknown.

And the knowledge that every normal man feels fear in the presence of danger, and that fear in itself is not cowardly and that most men overcome it, is often the most helpful knowledge of all.

(5) *Control of action helps.* To be afraid does not mean that a man must act afraid. Fear is contagious when it is expressed in action. If a man goes to pieces and becomes panicky he must be removed from the sight of the other men if that is at all possible. It is each man's responsibility to control the signs of his own fear if he can, so as to spare the others. And if he can manage to act as though he were calm, he may actually become more calm. At any rate, the opposite is true: giving in to fear tends to increase it.

(6) *Even statistics help.* It is reassuring to know that of all the men in an army comparatively few are killed. The chances that any one man will be among those mortally wounded in any one battle are relatively small. Unless a man is such an egoist that he believes that the enemy will single him out for special attention, he can be relieved by the thought that he has a good chance of coming through. And the longer he remains unscathed, the surer he becomes about those chances.

Prolonged Peril

Fear just before combat is not, however, the most trying fear that men in the armed forces must sometimes face. That is, after all, a thing of the moment, and men are helped to face it by the excitement of action.

There is another kind of fear that must be endured for days and weeks —perhaps months or years—if men are besieged, cut off from help, deprived of adequate defense. Then the ever-present peril from the enemy may be aggravated by the greater perils of disease, famine, exposure. And there may be little chance for action.

Men in the present war have endured primitive sorts of hardships that would seem to be beyond human endurance—in Bataan, on Corregidor, alone on a rubber life raft for five weeks in blistering sun and drenching storm, without food, without shelter, without water, without any aid but their own unquenchable spirits, their fortitude, and their faith.

This means terror mixed with despair. The misery cannot be relieved; it can only be endured. Then they must maintain sanity, courage, and life itself by their ingenuity in originating occupations for hands and minds that will relieve the tension and seem to reduce the hazards.

Men battling alone against the sea welcome a chance to learn something of navigation, to contrive means for keeping track of the directions and distances they are being carried by current and wind. They think of songs to sing and of games to play. The captain of one torpedoed boat reported:

"Our lifeboat was shelled for two hours. It had twenty-four holes in it. The crew plugged seven, but that still left seventeen. So the men in the boat held a meeting to discuss the problem of buying sheet metal to plug up the remaining holes. The meeting lasted two days and was conducted under strict parliamentary laws, according to *Robert's Rules*. The discussion was finally tabled on three counts: (1) The ship's treasurer was in another lifeboat and they couldn't reach him; (2) all their money went down with the ship anyway; (3) there weren't any stores there in the ocean. However, the debate made forty-eight hours pass quickly."

Thus a resourceful leader can exercise considerable ingenuity in keeping his men occupied. If physical activity is impossible, keeping minds occupied with talk on some subject unrelated to the immediate threat of danger relieves tension.

In such trying times and in tense moments a laugh can be a lifesaver. An Army officer relating experiences of the World War tells of a time when badly frightened, untrained soldiers of that war had taken refuge in a roadside ditch against an unforeseen horror—the fire of American guns turned on them by mistake.

Panic sent the blood pounding into my head and emptied my stomach of courage. It was bad enough to be shot at by the Boche, but there was no sense in being killed by friendly troops. My men looked wild and fingered their triggers, ready to return the fire of our other battalion. Something had to be done and done quick. And Captain Wass did it. Unintentionally, but still he did it.

"Jackson!" he yelled.

"Yes, Captain."

"Where are you?"

"Right here. Across the road."

"Stand up so I can see you."

"Captain," Jackson shouted above the crackling roar of machine-gun bullets, "if you want to see me, *you* stand up."

American humor can lick anything. Smothered chuckles ran down the line. Orders were given and listened to. Men wriggled backward out of the zone of fire. The first to reach the trees dashed down the line of the 3d Battalion, shutting off the guns.

Nor may we forget the power of religious belief as an antidote to fear. When men get into a tight spot they pray. They pray hard and from the heart, and they feel better for it. Prayer works.

FOOLHARDINESS IS NOT BRAVERY

Fear is Nature's way of meeting in an all-out way an all-out emergency. It is useful in mobilizing all the body's resources. Obviously, prolonged fear is horribly fatiguing. Long periods of anxiety are damaging in the extreme. But fear within limits increases strength and endurance.

And fear is an ally in other respects. It is of value to the Army as well as to the individual soldier, for it serves the same purposes as the red signal light on a railroad—to give warning of danger and to promote caution.

The purpose of warfare is to destroy the enemy and to gain this end with a minimum sacrifice of our own forces. The soldier who needlessly puts his own life in jeopardy is committing an act of treachery. The officer or noncom who imperils the safety of his men through his own foolhardiness or his failure to appreciate a danger is also betraying his country.

There are a few men in every army who know no fear—just a few. But these men are not normal. They would be recognized by a psychiatrist as mentally deficient. They have a callousness of mind that makes them incapable of emotion.

Such men are recognized as a danger to the Army. Wise leaders watch them zealously and are constantly on the alert to prevent them from exposing other men to peril. But in spite of—or because of—their complete lack of caution and common sense, these crazy daredevils, by taking the enemy completely by surprise, sometimes accomplish amazing things and cover themselves with glory before going to a premature death.

Their mad acts are not, however, feats of courage. They may collect a few medals, but they are not heroes.

True courage is the ability to act as you believe you should in the face of recognized danger—to act in spite of fear—to risk your life to keep the soldier's faith.

A man may succeed as a soldier without broad vision. He may be an efficient, dependable fighter with no interest in the larger objectives of the war. If he feels loyalty to his unit, that is enough. Training and experience teach him to be interested in the means of fighting without being concerned with the reasons for fighting. Such a man cannot be said, however, to be without ideals. His loyalty, his sense of responsibility are more than mere obedience and a sense of duty.

Thus the soldier who deliberately chooses to be blown up in order to wipe out an enemy tank or machine-gun nest that would otherwise cost the lives of his friends, his ideals, has, indeed, all it takes to make a soldier. The commander of a ship who coolly sends away the last lifeboat and goes down with his vessel rather than abandon it while some of his men are helplessly imprisoned in one of its compartments is afraid but governed by something more powerful than fear.

You may call this force idealism, conscience, religion, philosophy, tradition, code, or even habit, or you may be modern and call it ideology. Psychologists sometimes call it the triumph of the social over the selfish instincts. They recognize this force as the most potent weapon an army can possess.

Men fighting for their homes and armed with this spirit can stand their ground and win against tremendous opposing forces.

Courage and fear are not opposites; they may fill the same breast at the same time. But armed with courage, no soldier need worry about his own fright. The coward who must run when he is scared is the one to dread terror.

None but the brave can afford to fear.

SALUTES

By PRIVATE HEELCLICKER

(*1942*)

I JUST RECENTLY RE-ENLISTED in the Army after having been a civilian for a half-dozen years. I'm on duty in one of our large cities and when I reported to my company I made it a point to read the bulletin board thoroughly. On it I found a directive for all men to salute all of the officers of the Army, Navy, Marine Corps, and Coast Guard they met on the streets of this city. It was also suggested that the good soldier salutes the officers of the armed forces of other of the United Nations. The directive went on to mention the soldierly qualities expected to be practiced by the men of the command and mentioned among other things the "dignity of the uniform" and the "spirit of military courtesy."

All of which I agree with fully. When I did my hitch back in the quiet days of peace I always figured that saluting was as much a credit to me as to the officer. He returned it, didn't he? I must say that most of those salutes the officers returned were much better than the ones we enlisted men gave.

A few afternoons ago I met two naval officers. Did they return my salute? I'm not sure. One of them was smoking a cigarette. He didn't remove it from his mouth but did wave his hand listlessly in the direction of his cap. The other officer must have been examining the gambs of a passing blonde, for he never took his eyes from the sidewalk.

Then there is the Army officer who smiles heartily when you salute him as though to say, "Thanks for recognizing my rank, lad. You keep on saluting like that and maybe they'll make you a corporal." At the same time the salute he gives you is evidence enough that he never was a corporal.

Now I don't mean that all officers fail to return salutes at all, or return them grudgingly, or even return them in the spirit of brotherly love but without military snap. But there are enough of these types to destroy pride in military courtesy and to make us enlisted men wonder about the "dignity of the uniform."

Now I don't know what can be done, if anything. Probably most of the officers who do a poor job of saluting need a couple of hours of drill and lectures, not only to teach them how it's done but also to imbue them with the spirit of the ceremony, which, as I understand it, is the privileged exchange of courteous recognition between soldiers.

A SOLDIER THAT'S FIT FOR A SOLDIER

ANONYMOUS

(1942)

Now all you young soldiers that's sailin' the sea,
Just stop what you're doin' and listen to me,
And I'll tell you a soldier—the kind you should be—
A soldier that's fit for a soldier.

You've behaved, for most part, at the places we've been,
In a way that did proud by the outfit we're in;
You've established a standard; don't let it wear thin
And lose your good name as a soldier.

In this place where we're going, there's plenty to drink;
Just remember your stomach ain't coated with zinc;
Don't take on too much and end up in the clink
And lose half your pay as a soldier.

If you're smart you won't run with ladies too bold
(The native sex salesgirls are deadly I'm told.)
And any damned fool knows it's worse than a cold;
So it's best to go straight as a soldier.

But if you take chances—and some of you may—
Be sure to check in by the green lantern's ray.
If you don't you will rue it for many a day
And you won't be much use as a soldier.

And you're sure to see some wherever you look,
Who are out to get husbands by hook or by crook,
And they'll tie you up fast by the ring and the Book
If you don't watch your step like a soldier.

When the big push comes off, and it will pretty quick,
And you're up toward the front with the shells fallin' thick,
Here's some points to remember; I hope that they stick
For they'll help you behave like a soldier.

To kill is our business and that's what we do.
It's the main job of war for me and for you,
And the more we rub out, the sooner we're through
To return where they wait for a soldier.

You must dig a slit trench whenever you stop
For a halt of an hour where Jap bombs may drop;
And when they start dropping that's where you must flop,
If you want to fight on as a soldier.

When you get into action, don't let your hand twitch
When you see a Jap head sticking up from a ditch;
Make every round count for a son of a bitch—
Which means, get your man like a soldier.

When the little brown men come on like they tell,
Charging straight for you with a whoop and a yell,
Draw a bead on the leader and blow him to hell;
Then take on the rest like a soldier.

In hand-to-hand fighting, just keep it in mind
No matter how tough or how many you find,
An ace in this game will beat three of a kind
If the ace knows his job as a soldier.

When the captain goes down and the looie looks white
Remember it's ruin to run from a fight,
So use the ground close, keep your head and fight right,
And battle it out like a soldier.

PANIC

By Captain (now Colonel) C. T. Lanham

(*1937*)

The effect of panic on troops—even thoroughly trained and veteran troops—is feared by every commander because it has so often been disastrous to armies in past wars and in the present one. The main example in all history is the panic that followed the first action of the Battle of

France. Three years before then this study by Captain (now Colonel) Lanham ran in the pages of the *Infantry Journal*.

Colonel Lanham, who was commanding an infantry regiment at the time this Reader was issued, was for four years associate editor of the magazine and has been for a much longer time a contributor, and his varied career has included much duty in command of troops, as well as periods of editorial duty. He is imbued with the feeling that all military instruction in written, pictorial, or moving-picture form should never be presented in a professional military jargon but put over in forceful, customary language. The series of "Fighting Men" training films, the scripts for which he wrote in large part, and into which his ideas of realistic instruction have gone, are now being shown throughout the Army—pictures with such titles as *How to Get Killed—In One Easy Lesson.*

In "Panic" Colonel Lanham turns to history for striking examples of collective fear and its results, and the possible measures of prevention.

> *Fie, my Lord, fie! A soldier and afeard?*
> SHAKESPEARE.

August 15, 1866. The 34th Infantry, part of the Austrian rear guard, is falling back after the catastrophe at Königgrätz. The men are exhausted and frightened. Again and again they have been forced to form squares to withstand the harassing action of hostile cavalry. Late in the afternoon a dust cloud is seen whirling toward the regiment. The cry goes up, "The German cavalry is charging!" The order is given to form squares, but panic suddenly sweeps through the command. Formations disintegrate. Units open fire on each other. Men run in all directions. Even after it is discovered that the dust cloud was caused by the movement of a herd of frightened pigs, and not by German cavalry, order is restored only with the utmost difficulty.

1918. An American battalion holds a reserve position in a shell-torn wood. Enemy artillery has been intermittently strafing the position since dusk. The Americans in their fox holes are getting what sleep they can. At 11:00 P.M. the battalion commander, accompanied by his adjutant, starts an inspection of his lines. A runner dashes up and hands him a message. The major reads it. He calls to his adjutant, who is a short distance away, "Come on, let's beat it." The two start to the rear at a dead run. Before they have covered two hundred yards the entire battalion is in wild flight behind them. It races more than ten kilometers before it can be stopped. The message to the major had directed him to report to the regimental command post as fast as he could get there. He was complying with the order.

Summer maneuvers are in progress. A Blue infantry company is hidden in a field of tall grass. They are watching an unsuspecting Red battalion move straight toward them. When the battalion is within fifty yards the company commander gives the signal to open fire. The Blue soldiers, grinning broadly, cut loose with a volley of blanks. A strange thing happens. The battalion freezes in its tracks for an instant and then breaks. Men fling away their rifles and packs and race to the rear in insane flight. Leaders are powerless to stop them. Equipment is scattered all over the landscape. The umpires shake their heads.

These three incidents are not products of a lively imagination; they are based on hard fact. They may appear fantastic but they are nevertheless commonplace, for wherever men congregate this group madness is not far off. A word, a gesture, even a shadow, may be sufficient to transform men into stampeding cattle.

To military leaders, who must habitually deal with man in the mass, this strange psychological phenomenon is an ever-present contingency. No unit is panic-proof.

There is no miraculous formula by which panic may be averted. There is no science by which it may be predicted. A leader cannot say, "My troops are veterans; they are well equipped; they are well fed; they are fresh. There will be no panic." They may bolt before a shot has been fired. Nor can a leader say, "My men are worn out; they have not been properly fed; their equipment is inferior; the enemy outnumbers them. Panic will overtake them." They may perform prodigies of courage in the face of insuperable odds.

Is there, then, anything the leader can do that will act as a deterrent to this mass madness? Are there any provisions he can make that will tend to steady his command? From the negative viewpoint, is there anything he should avoid? And, finally, are there any particular conditions which render a unit panic-ripe? Before trying to answer these questions let us analyze a few historical instances of panic and attempt to arrive at some common denominator.

EXAMPLE I

The rhinoceros is the bravest of animals—it has no imagination. H. G. WELLS.

In spite of its victory over the Prussian I Corps near Trautenau on June 27, 1866, the Austrian X Corps was forced to begin a retirement early the next morning in order to meet a threat to its communications. The Brigade Grivicic marched as the left-flank column of the corps. Cavalry and artillery that had been ordered to report to the brigade failed to appear.

The march was difficult. It led first across the previous day's battlefield, which had not yet been cleared of the dead and wounded. The day was hot; roads were dusty, and drinking water scarce.

In the early stages of the march the brigade commander informed his subordinate leaders that it was probable the Prussians had gotten across the line of retreat. He also told them that he feared the brigade might be cut off from the corps. The general's fears and apprehensions soon spread among the troops.

At the end of a twelve-mile march the brigade ran head on into a detachment of the Prussian Second Army near Rudersdorf. A desperate frontal fight immediately developed. For three hours the Austrian brigade fought magnificently. Suddenly a few shots rang out on the right flank— the flank that was supposed to be covered by the remainder of the corps. Immediately someone cried, "We're cut off from the corps!" The cry spread like a prairie fire. In a few minutes the entire right regiment broke in panic. Men threw away their rifles and fled to the rear.

Despite the heroic efforts of its officers, the left regiment, which had not even been touched by this fire, also broke. Neither orders, pleas, nor threats could stem the tide of panic.

The remnants of the brigade continued their flight throughout the night. Morning found them some fifteen miles from the scene of the disaster. In this encounter the brigade lost 94 officers and 2,700 men, 65 per cent of its strength.

From a study of this action it appears that the two principal psychological factors which contributed to the panic of this Austrian brigade could have been avoided. It is most unlikely that tactical considerations precluded a detour around the previous day's battlefield. The sickening picture of the untended wounded and the unburied dead must have gone a long way toward counteracting the buoyant effect of the victory won the day before. The brigade commander committed his gravest error, however, when he expressed the fear that the brigade would probably be cut off from the corps. His subordinates completed the damage by discussing their commander's apprehensions before the men.

It is not difficult to imagine the reaction of the rank and file. In the first place, they probably felt that there was little use winning battles if the blunders of the high command required a retreat even after a victorious action. Rumors that the enemy had cut the line of retreat and word that the brigade commander feared he would be cut off from the corps contributed to the soldiers' loss of faith in their leaders. To the man in the ranks the depressing picture of the uncleared battlefield and the scarcity of drinking water added the finishing touches to the incompetence of the high command. The brigade was definitely panic-ripe.

It is unquestionably a testimonial to the valor of the troops that they fought at Rudersdorf so well and so long. But the tinder of panic was ready for the first igniting spark. That spark came on the dreaded flank in the form of a few inconsequential rifleshots which could not possibly have influenced the course of the action. Nevertheless, everyone immediately leaped to the conclusion that the brigade commander's fears had been realized, and panic swept the entire command.

EXAMPLE II

Dangers bring fears, and fears more dangers bring. BAXTER.

In 1896 Italy invaded Abyssinia with an army of 15,000 men, equipped and trained according to the best standards of the day. Abyssinia, a Negro state, without any army as we understand that term, opposed this formidable modern force with a savage horde of spearmen about 100,000 strong.

A poorly conducted night march prefaced the battle of Adowa. All night the Italian Army struggled through the wild mountain passes of Abyssinia. Men straggled—columns drifted apart. Dawn found the Italians divided into three groups, separated by precipitous ravines and out of effective supporting distance. Before them swarmed the savage hordes of Abyssinia. The Italian commander of the left group expressed in the presence of some of his men his apprehensions about being separated from the main army.

With a wild shout the Abyssinians advanced to the assault. The Italian artillery immediately went into action, but, owing to the badly accidented terrain, it was unable to determine the correct range. Its fire was altogether ineffective, and the hostile charge continued uninterrupted. As the tribesmen swept up the slope panic struck the left Italian group. The men flung away their rifles and raced toward the center. Officers who attempted to halt the mad flight were clubbed down or shot. The center was swept away in the insane rush. Only the right group stood fast. At nightfall it retired in relatively good order.

Of the 15,000 men in this European army, 3,500 escaped.

On the surface it appears that there is no psychological background for this disastrous panic. It seems to have been merely one more instance of that blind and unpredictable terror to which man in the mass is subject. However, if we go beyond the more obvious aspects of this appalling disaster, we begin to see the underlying cause. We find, for instance, that this Italian force was made up of small detachments detailed from various home regiments. These driblets of men were fitted together in much the same manner as the pieces of a jigsaw puzzle, and the completed unit had about the same relative degree of stability as the completed puzzle. Officers, noncommissioned officers, and soldiers were comparative strangers. The artillery had never worked with the infantry. With such a state of affairs, mutual trust, confidence, and understanding were definitely out of the question. In short, despite the equipment and the training of the individual soldier, this Italian force lacked from its inception those moral attributes which differentiate an army from a crowd.

Coupled with this we find another powerful psychological influence—the widely known cruelty of the Abyssinians, who were reported to torture their prisoners. What tales of horror circulated through the Italian ranks we can only surmise, but, knowing the mercurial Latin temperament, we can feel certain that the stories were ample, gory, and replete with anatomical detail.

Picture this force, then, on the morning of November 1, 1896. The men were exhausted from a long and poorly conducted night march. When dawn broke they found themselves confronted by the milling hordes of the dreaded Abyssinians and at the same time discovered that their own force had been split into three parts. They lacked faith in their officers and faith in themselves. When their artillery failed to stop or even punish the charging tribesmen, panic swept the infantry, and what should have been an easy victory over a savage horde of spearmen became one of the most terrible disasters ever suffered by a comparable modern force.

The startling thing is that practically every factor that contributed to this shambles could have been avoided.

Example III

Fear rushed in like an assaulting army. Bently.

On August 1, 1904, the Russian 140th Infantry Regiment and a rifle brigade were encamped near Haitshong, some miles from the front. Both units were in army reserve. Between them and the Japanese lay the main Russian armies. Local outposts provided still further security. Surprise was virtually impossible. The troops were fully rested. Both units were well trained for the Russian Army of that day and both had had combat experience.

Shortly after dusk on August 1 several Russian soldiers from the rifle brigade went into a near-by rice field to relieve themselves. One of these men, while in an awkward position, apparently saw something that frightened him. He leaped up and rushed back to camp shouting, "The Japanese are coming!" Panic was instantaneous in the rifle brigade. Men grabbed their rifles and fired in all directions. In a few minutes the entire brigade was racing to the rear in two streams, one toward the camp of the corps trains near Haitshong, the other toward the camp of the 140th Infantry Regiment.

Panic struck the corps trains even before the screaming wave of terror-stricken soldiers rolled over them. A fighting, milling mob of men and animals swept back to the north through Haitshong. Not even the personal intervention of General Kuropatkin, who happened to be in the village, could stem the tide of terror. This portion of the brigade was not rallied for days.

The part of the brigade that fled toward the camp of the 140th Infantry met with a different reception. The colonel of this regiment heard the firing and the screaming and promptly ordered his buglers to sound the call to arms. The men fell into ranks quietly and without disorder. They ignored the panic-stricken members of the brigade who were streaming past them. The sight of this regiment, calm and unperturbed, served to allay the imaginary fears of this part of the brigade, which at once became quiet and orderly.

At the beginning of this article the statement was made that "even a shadow may be sufficient to transform men into stampeding cattle." The affair at Haitshong bears out that statement. The personal panic of one soldier who had been frightened by some phantom in the dark stampeded an entire brigade, which in turn stampeded the rear echelon of an army corps. The whole story sounds like some incredible adventure of Alice in that strange land beyond the looking glass and not the sober recital of eyewitnesses duly chronicled in the annals of Russian military history.

However, as in all cases of panic, we must probe beneath the surface for the real causes. In this particular instance a comparison between the rifle brigade and the 140th Infantry proves illuminating. Outwardly both units were the same. They were well fed, well equipped, and well trained. They had both had combat experience. They were thoroughly rested. Further, and in common with the rest of the Russian Army, they were both imbued with a deep sense of pessimism as a result of repeated Japanese victories. But there the similarity stops, for we learn that in spite of its pessimism the morale of the 140th was high; the colonel, loved and respected; and the other officers, competent and co-operative. The picture of the rifle brigade is different. It appears that this unit was noted for the dissension and petty feuds among its officers; dissatisfaction was constantly in evidence. *Esprit de corps* was non-existent.

Thus while the 140th had a solidarity and high morale to counteract the disheartening defeats, the internal dissensions of the rifle brigade only plunged that unit farther into despair. The phlegmatic calm with which the 140th Infantry met this panic graphically demonstrates the stabilizing effect of the confidence that this regiment had in its leaders. It is probable that every man in this unit actually believed that the Japanese had surprised their bivouac, but despite that discouraging thought they responded as one man to the well-timed call to arms and calmly awaited their colonel's orders.

Contrast this with the instant panic that overwhelmed the rifle brigade. In that unit there was no officer who thought of the steadying effect of the call to arms. From the first cry of "The Japanese are coming!" the brigade appears to have been transformed into a wild mob in which each soldier and each officer thought only in terms of himself. When this brigade was finally rallied some days later, it was found that more than 150 men had been killed or wounded.

EXAMPLE IV

Fear is sharp-sighted, and can see under ground, and much more in the skies. CERVANTES.

On November 9, 1870, the French First Army of the Loire attacked the I Bavarian Corps at Coulmiers, where it obtained a success which might well have been decisive had it not been for the following incident:

Early on the morning of the ninth the Rayau Cavalry Division was ordered to turn the right flank of the Bavarian Corps and cut its line of retreat to Paris. This division was informed that its left flank would be protected during the turning movement by several groups of *francs-tireurs* (French irregulars).

The cavalry had scarcely gotten under way before all contact was lost with the francs-tireurs. The division moved slowly; every shot resulted in a long delay. By noon, however, it had gained a position which seriously threatened the enemy's communications.

About this time the division became involved in a fire fight for possession of a village. German artillery intervened, and the French suffered a few casualties. Suddenly a reconnaissance patrol galloped up at break-neck speed. It reported that Germans were driving in toward the left flank. This report spread like wildfire. No one thought of investigating it. Within a few minutes all nine of the cavalry regiments that composed this division had raced to the rear in panic. The flight continued until they reached the bivouac area they had left that morning.

The Bavarians retreated to Paris without difficulty.

It was subsequently learned that the "Germans" seen on the division's left flank were only the francs-tireurs who had been altogether forgotten in the excitement.

The First Army of the Loire, like all the hastily organized volunteer armies after Sedan, was poorly trained and poorly disciplined. In common with the Russians in the previous example, the French, as the result of an unending string of defeats, were sunk deep in the slough of despair. Despondency and pessimism haunted their bivouacs by night and marched with their columns by day. With such a background it is remarkable that this volunteer army achieved even a partial success at

Coulmiers, although it vastly outnumbered the Bavarian Corps. So great was this demoralization to become, that by January 1871 the sight of a few Prussian helmets was sufficient to cause whole units to flee the field.

The incident of the Rayau Cavalry Division is typical of the unit that has lost confidence in itself. When such a condition obtains, panics occur with increasing frequency. Insane rumors and wild reports honeycomb the military structure. Chronic pessimism and a sense of inferiority combine to destroy all sense of proportion. The enemy gradually comes to appear omniscient; he is seen everywhere; his strength is magnified a thousand times; his skill becomes legendary; his leaders assume the proportions of a Bonaparte; his battalions become an invincible combination of Caesar's X Legion and Napoleon's Old Guard. When the armed forces of a nation visualize their opponent as the French armies visualized Von Moltke's military machine, it is high time to conclude a peace.

EXAMPLE V

You tremble, body! You would tremble more if you knew where I am going to take you. HENRI OF NAVARRE.

In 1743 a Bavarian corps, under the command of Count von Torring, made an unsuccessful attempt to capture an Austrian fort. Following this failure the corps began a retirement toward Branau. The attack on the fort had lasted ten hours. The men, for the greater part newly raised troops, were very tired and had been without food throughout the entire day. Despite these various demoralizing factors, the corps maintained its discipline. The retirement began shortly after nightfall with all units well in hand. At first the movement was unhindered, but later the Austrians launched a vigorous pursuit.

Late that night the tired Bavarians were startled by the sound of heavy firing from the rearguard. Instantly rumors started. The report flew up and down the column that the Austrians had charged over a bridge that was supposed to have been destroyed, had broken through the rear guard, and were now driving forward to attack the main body. As this rumor spread through the command several units in the main body began to run.

Count von Torring rode up and down the column trying to reassure his troops. He told them that he had not blown up the bridge because he intended to turn about and destroy the Austrians and did not want to be thwarted in this project by an unfordable river. The men were beginning to take heart. Here and there a cheer broke out along the column. While Von Torring was still engaged in quieting his men a subordinate general galloped up and shouted that the Austrians had encircled the right flank. The result was practically instantaneous—a complete panic of the 10,000 men comprising this corps. All that Count von Torring could assemble in Branau the next morning were a few officers, a handful of cavalry, and 200 infantrymen. (Discussion follows Example VI).

EXAMPLE VI

For this, surely, is the very meaning of a panic—a fear that feeds upon itself. H. S. HOLLAND.

On October 11, 1806, the Prussian Army of Hohenlohe was assembled in and around Jena. Although their formidable French foe was still at a great distance, discouraging reports had been pouring in. Observers reported that a profound psychological depression reigned throughout the entire army.

Late that afternoon a solitary rider galloped down the road from the front. As he neared an artillery column that was drawn up alongside the road he signaled frantically with his hands and shouted, "Back! Back!" He then disappeared in the direction of Weimar at a dead gallop. Much later it was discovered that this excited officer had merely been directed to clear the road for other traffic. However, his spectacular dash from the direction of the enemy, coupled with his frantic shouts, immediately caused a wild flight of the artillery into the town of Weimar. As the artillery careened through the little town all the troops billeted there ran out of their quarters and the cry arose, "The enemy is only a half-hour from town!"

Panic rolled down the valley of the Salle like water from a broken dam. Even in Jena many miles away, the trains of the Prussian Army fled terror-stricken into the gathering night.

Order was not restored for many hours, and then not until officer patrols had definitely determined that the vicinity of Weimar was free of the enemy.

The panics at Branau and at Weimar are similar in that they both resulted from the careless and thoughtless action of an excited officer. Of course in each case the troops were panic-ripe, but at Branau the catastrophe might well have been averted but for the blundering general who shouted his bad news for the benefit of the entire command. Quick-thinking Count von Torring had just about succeeded in calming his tense troops, and it is altogether probable that there would have been no panic but for the tragic psychological error of his subordinate.

At Weimar, however, the same profound pessimism that we have noted elsewhere was universal. It appears likely that panic would have occurred sooner or later from some equally remote cause. The main point is that the immediate cause in both instances was the ill-advised action of a subordinate officer.

As battle approaches men become as tense as coiled springs. The prospect of death looms large to the soldier. Instinctively he turns to his officers for guidance and for reassurance. If at these critical times an officer betrays confusion, excitement, fear, or loss of confidence, that impression, be it real or imaginary, is instantly spread among his men with disastrous results.

Calmness, confidence, aggressiveness, determination, and a deep appreciation of the psychological reactions of the ordinary man are the characteristics of great leadership. Joffre's monumental calm at the Marne rallied his terribly defeated armies and inspired them to an almost miraculous victory. Through most of the war the German armies drew strength and courage from the unshaken and unshakable calm of their beloved Hindenburg. Of such is the stuff of leadership.

Example VII

To the youth it was an onslaught of redoubtable dragons. . . . Destruction threatened him from all points. . . . He ran like a blind man. Stephen Crane.

On June 24, 1866, the commanding general of the Italian 1st Division directed his 1st Brigade to attack the Mangalia Ridge. The 2d Brigade was ordered to move forward in support of the 1st. A platoon of artillery was directed to go into position on Mount Cricole to protect the flank of the attacking brigade.

The prescribed movements got under way. The skirmish lines of the 1st Brigade advanced against the disputed ridge. The 2d Brigade, with the division and brigade commanders at the head, moved forward in double column in support of the 1st. The 2d Brigade had made no provision for local security. Its advance was extremely slow. Every few minutes there were short, irritating halts. An air of uncertainty seemed to pervade the entire movement.

Suddenly a squadron of Austrian cavalry appeared near the crest of Mount Cricole. With a loud cheer this squadron charged. When the platoon of artillery which was moving toward Mount Cricole saw this cavalry it wheeled about and, at a dead run, raced toward the 2d Brigade. The Austrian cavalry followed the retreating artillery at a breakneck gallop. It did not draw rein when it encountered the dense columns of the 2d Brigade but, with sabers flashing, rode down the leading battalion, scattered the division and brigade staffs, and killed the division and brigade commanders.

Panic instantly swept the brigade. Five battalions flung away their packs and rifles and, in complete and utter rout, raced toward Valeggio. But now an unusual thing occurred—a startling thing in view of the panic that had seized the rest of the brigade. The battalion that had been ridden down was rallied by its officers and, facing about, attacked and destroyed the daredevil squadron.

The charge of the Austrian cavalry had nevertheless proved decisive. The 1st Brigade, finding itself unsupported, abandoned its attack on the Mangalia Ridge and withdrew on Valeggio.

The 2d Brigade was not rallied until late the next day.

This is an interesting study of psychological values. One hundred cavalrymen sow panic in practically an entire infantry brigade and, though eventually destroyed, determine the outcome of a division fight. How can it be accounted for? By two things: surprise and the inherent fear of the man on foot for the man on horseback. The moral effect of a surprise cavalry charge on the dismounted man caught in the open is terrific. Regardless of the often-proved superiority of infantry to cavalry, that moral effect still exists.

Today, owing to the tremendous fire power of automatic weapons, the horse has been ruled off the battlefield. In its place, however, a far more fearful agency has appeared—the tank. The moral effect of tanks on infantry was repeatedly demonstrated in the last war. Only those individuals who have actually been confronted by one of these modern juggernauts can fully realize the terror, the despair, the sense of impotence that they inspire.

It is generally agreed that in the next war the tank will play an important role. While we seek to enhance our knowledge of the tactics and technique of this weapon let us not lose sight of its moral implications. The unarmored infantryman who must confront this armored monster must be accorded more than a casual consideration. His is a real and a vital problem. Unless it is solved we may find our next major engagement characterized by an unending series of panics engendered by the mere appearance of the formidable and terror-breeding tank.

Example VIII

The courage of one and the same body of men is all or nothing according to circumstances. Gustave LeBon.

On November 25, 1863 ,the Confederate Army of the Tennessee occupied a position on Missionary Ridge that, to all intents and purposes, appeared impregnable. The troops of this army were not half-baked recruits but veterans with two and a half years of service behind them. Their great victory at Chickamauga was scarcely two months old. True, they were numerically inferior to the Federals who opposed them, but despite this it seemed a physical impossibility for any enemy, no matter how great his numerical superiority, to drive them from this magnificent position.

But the moral tone of this Confederate army was an altogether different matter. Shortly after their splendid victory at Chickamauga violent quarrels had broken out between Bragg, the army commander, and many of his subordinates. He had relieved Polk, one of his most popular corps commanders, and had preferred charges against him. Hindman, a division commander well beloved by his troops, had also been relieved of command, and his division had been broken up. General Longstreet, another popular corps commander, was openly resentful and, apparently, secretly disloyal. From this officer's correspondence it appears that he was actively engaged in undermining his army commander with the authorities in Richmond. As a result of these various dissensions the entire army was in a state of latent hostility toward its commander in chief.

The prelude to the battle was the marshaling of the Union forces in the great plain between the Ridge and Chattanooga. This massing of the Union troops took place in plain view of the Confederates. According to all observers, this display of the enormous Union forces massed for the attack made a tremendous impression on the defenders of the Ridge. Added to this was the fact that the Union Army was now commanded by General Grant, who had just successfully concluded the siege of Vicksburg and whose reputation was far greater than that of any other Union general. The final factor that must be considered in this battle was Bragg's serious tactical error in dividing his troops. Some were placed in trenches at the foot of the ridge, others in trenches on the military crest.

When the Union attack finally came, the Confederate trenches at the foot of the hill were quickly overrun. In complete disregard of General Grant's explicit instructions, the Union troops immediately charged up the Ridge on the heels of the withdrawing Confederates. The fire of the defenders located on the military crest was partially masked by the withdrawal of their own troops from the foot of the ridge, with the result that they were unable to bring the full volume of their fire to bear on the charging Union lines.

It was an exhausting charge for Grant's men. Terrain, absence of fatigue, trenches—in fact, every factor—favored the Confederates. And yet when a single Union flag appeared on the crest of the ridge something snapped in Bragg's army. Panic overwhelmed one Confederate division after another. What actually occurred is described by Bragg's official report written at Dalton, Georgia, on November 30, 1863.

A panic, which I had never before witnessed, seemed to have seized upon officers and men; and each seemed to be struggling for his personal safety, regardless of his duty or his character. . . .

The position was one which ought to have been held by a line of skirmishers against any assaulting column, and whenever resistance was made the enemy fled in disorder after suffering heavy losses.

Had all parts of the line been maintained with equal gallantry and persistence, no enemy could ever have dislodged us, and but one possible reason presents itself to my mind in explanation of this bad conduct in veteran troops who had never before failed in any duty assigned them, however difficult and hazardous. They had for two days confronted the enemy marshaling his immense forces in plain view and exhibiting to their sight such a superiority in numbers as may well have intimidated weak-minded and untried soldiers, but our veterans had so often encountered similar hosts when the strength of position was against us, and with perfect success, that not a doubt crossed my mind.

It is obvious that General Bragg was not altogether fair to his men in this report. As disheartening as the sight of the huge Union forces may have been to these war-weary Confederates, this was nevertheless insufficient to account for the wild panic, as Bragg himself implies. What General Bragg failed to see was the universal disloyalty, dissatisfaction, and resentment against his own regime. He had relieved one corps commander and one division commander for alleged disobedience of orders; both were exceptionally loved and respected. He had broken up one division for trivial reasons. Dissension was everywhere rampant. No one was satisfied with Bragg's leadership. This state of affairs had even undermined the buoyant effect of the great victory at Chickamauga that was only two months behind this army. By November 25 these demoralizing factors had transformed the veteran Army of the Tennessee into a potential mob. The result of the battle was not surprising.

Panic seems to split logically into two separate phases. The first consists of the gradual building up of a tense psychological state of mind. Outwardly this is characterized by excessive nervousness, a marked growth in wild and pessimistic rumors, and a heightened sensitivity to all external stimuli. More recondite symptoms include a loss of faith in leaders, a hostile and questioning attitude toward orders, a quickened imagination, and a profound pessimism.

The causes that induce this mental state in a military unit are many and varied. Of those considered in the historical illustrations cited in this paper, some were avoidable; others were not. Defeat, for instance, is one of the unavoidable fortunes of war; when two armies clash one must lose. Unfortunately defeat carries with it more than lost terrain and long casualty lists; it sows the seed of distrust in the fertile soil of the private soldier's brain; it implants the idea that the enemy may be physically superior to him and mentally superior to his leaders. With every battle lost, these doubts and questionings increase until finally they are fixed in irrevocable certainty. It is easy to lead victorious troops to fresh victories, but only great leaders can carry a defeated force through to triumph. Let us hope, then, that when we are engulfed in the next war we shall be able to give our armies a taste of victory early in the fight.

A second powerful psychological factor that attacks the morale of a command occurs when there is a mutual lack of faith and confidence. This condition is frequently found in raw, untrained troops. Unless men have lived and worked and played together—in short, been forged into one collective personality—confidence and trust, in the military sense, will be lacking. Instead of an army functioning as the expression of a single will, there will be a hundred thousand individual wills, each striving to solve its own small but all-important problem. In such cases each individual sees his own questionable reactions in his neighbor. Suspicion, fear, jealousy, and cowardice grow in these dark places of the mind. We will have troops in the next war as untrained as those in the last. Let us hope we have as much time to whip them into shape. But whatever amount of time we do have, let us expend part of it in the endeavor to foster that mutual faith and understanding which differentiates an army from a crowd.

While we consider this first—or, we might say, preparatory—phase of panic, let us not overlook the part the unthinking officer may play. One of the most definitely controllable factors is loose talk by officers in the presence of their men. In war the officer occupies a place that to his men is close to godhead. They feel that their safety and their well-being rest in his hands. His influence can be all powerful for good or for bad. If he shows confidence, cheerfulness, determination, calmness, those sterling virtues will usually be reflected in his command. If, on the other hand, he evinces nervousness, irritability, worry, fear, doubt in his superiors, uncertainty in himself, his state of mind will be quickly transmitted to his men. By controlling himself the leader will find he has solved many of the psychological problems of command.

Soldiers have been noted since antiquity for their peculiar susceptibility to rumor. In war most of the unending rumors that race through armies seem to be of a dismal nature. Owing to some pessimistic quirk in the average soldier's psychology, the darker the whispered story, the more quickly it is believed. This wild and depressing talk that runs back and forth through the ranks does no unit any good. Leaders should use every device possible to discover the vicious rumor and then lay it with the most deadly psychological weapons at their command—laughter and ridicule.

Fatigue, hunger, thirst, poorly conducted marches, countermarches, grumbling at orders, criticism of superiors are but a few of the many factors that irritate and depress a command. And irritation and depression are two of the outstanding psychological elements that make for that tense mental state which precedes panic.

So much for the first phase of this strange mass phenomenon. The second phase occurs when some sudden shock or surprise, either real or imaginary, touches off the actual panic.

In the foregoing examples we have seen some of the ridiculously trivial incidents which stampeded troops who were ready for panic—at Haitshong, one soldier frightened by a shadow; at Coulmiers, a false report; at Weimar, two words from an excited officer; at Missionary Ridge, the appearance of one Union flag on the crest; in the retreat from Königgrätz, a herd of frightened pigs. So it usually goes when troops become supercharged with nerves. The phenomenon might be likened to the electric tension in a condenser—when the tension reaches its maximum the condenser "breaks down."

Once panic has started it is almost impossible to stop it. Leaders are powerless. When the German XVII Corps broke in panic at Gumbinnen on August 20, 1914, not even the personal intervention of General von Mackensen, their respected and feared corps commander, could stem the wild rush. Indeed, history records few instances of panics that were stopped before they ran their full course.

The time to stop this group madness that feeds on fear is before it begins. The astute leader, even in the face of repeated disaster, will find ways and means of retaining the confidence and trust of his men Joffre found a way at the Marne. At Haitshong the Russian 140th Infantry stood like a rock while panic surged about it. Its commander had also found a way.

The problem is delicate and difficult. The leader's path is beset with a thousand pitfalls. There are few rules to guide him. Common sense, a sympathetic understanding of his fellow man, and a calm, cheerful, confident demeanor will prove his stanchest allies.

LEADER AND LED

By Major (now Colonel) Thomas R. Phillips

(1939)

THE COMMANDERS of large units in our Army in war will attain their high places with hardly an opportunity for observation or experience in their lofty ranks. They will have known professional soldiers and small units and will have led them in the safe exercises of peace. But leadership of citizen soldiers and large units, in the danger and urgency of battle, is a task of a different and more difficult nature. The duties and practices of the professional officer handling professional soldiers in peace not only do not prepare him for leadership in war, but in all probability burden him with a baggage of custom and theory that inhibits the development of whatever innate quality of leadership he may possess.

In our two great wars, the Civil War and the World War, the leadership of masses of civilian soldiers was a problem that baffled the majority of officers. It is to be noted that the larger part of the outstanding leaders of the Civil War—Grant, Sherman, McClellan, and Stonewall Jackson, for example—had left the Army and returned to it again from civil life. Some American officers, wrote Colonel G. F. R. Henderson of this conflict, could get as much out of volunteers as out of veteran troops. Others, who did not understand the prejudices and traits of the volunteers, never acquired their confidence and, despite their ability otherwise, failed in every operation they undertook. With Regulars these commanders would probably have been successful. With volunteers they fell from disaster to disaster. It is not sufficient to bring volunteers under military law, continues Colonel Henderson. It takes something more than the rules and regulations that govern a professional army to win and hold the confidence of citizen soldiers and make them steadfast under circumstances of danger, difficulty, and hardship.

Hancock, one of the most successful corps commanders in the Union Army, never sneered at volunteers. He made them feel by his evident respect, his warm approval of everything they did well, that he regarded them just as fully soldiers as if they belonged to his old Regular regiment. He knew with what assiduity, patience, and good feeling, what almost pathetic eagerness to learn and to imitate, the Volunteers of 1861 sought to fit themselves to take part in the great struggle. He saw that it was of extreme importance to develop self-respect and self-confidence in these regiments and to lead them to think that they could do anything and that they were the equals of anybody. But Hancock was not a mere drillmaster; he loved his men, understood them thoroughly, and was therefore fit for high command.

The return after the Civil War to a little professional army was a return to the psychology of leadership that had existed before it. In the World War the identical problem confronted us again in full force; the solution was not happy. According to a writer in the *American Legion Magazine:* "Our Regular Army disciplinary system is mainly responsible for the fact that universal military training has not become a part of the law of the United States. The discharged men carried firsthand information about army methods into thousands of homes. They told of the perpetual clicking together of heels, the incessant and wearisome saluting, of the overdone enforcement of deference toward officers of whatever grade, of the martinet's insistence upon the minutiae of useless and senseless observances, of the too-frequent lack of human touch in dealing with the bewildered men in the ranks. The system has produced many fine administrators, but the few genuine leaders developed under it have risen in spite of and not because of the training given them."

The problem will confront us anew when once again we must have a citizen army. For once again we have returned to the ancient practices of the professional army and the small unit. Army regulations on discipline remain unchanged, in all essential respects, from those of 1821, and those were copied from the regulations of the noble and peasant army of royal France of 1788. In theory man is the one unchangeable element in war. But as man's social life changes, so must the relation between leader and led be modified. Wellington remained convinced until his death that only flogging could develop a disciplined army. Rochambeau wrote in his memoirs that the whip is the sinew of all discipline. Flogging was forbidden in the United States Army in 1813, yet fifteen years later an officer was tried by court-martial for having a soldier flogged so severely that he was unable to perform duty for nine days. True, we no longer practice such methods and to that extent admit that man's attitude has changed. But other customs remain, equally ancient, equally inapplicable today, and they will undermine our effort to lead the literate, intelligent, independent, and eager young American in the next war.

War brings not only the citizen soldier with his civilian outlook, but also enormous numbers of men. The procedures of the peacetime company or the post commander supply no lessons of leadership to officers catapulted into high command. As Foch said of the leaders of the French Army of 1870, "They were superb generals in peacetime, fine soldiers, who knew everything except war." In short, they were generals completely without experience in handling men by tens of thousands.

The newly elevated generals react according to their character. This one swallows his saber, as the French put it, and spends his time making routine inspections and weighing out punishments. That one thinks his lofty place demands untouchability and withdraws into godlike seclusion. Others remain what they were—company commanders, now, of divisions. A few—a very few—discover, develop, and use the techniques of mass leadership and are rewarded with devotion that knows no bounds—that stops at no sacrifices.

It is easy to belittle the differences between the leadership procedures of the small professional army and those needed for large commands. The average officer is unaware that there are any. But it is these differences that lie between success and disaster. "In times of peoples' armies and totalitarian warfare [wrote Ludendorff] the officer will fulfill his task only if he has a clear notion of the basis upon which the unity of the people and discipline rest. In these qualities the old school of officers was lacking, for the officers lived apart from the people. That these officers were ignorant of the people's way of thinking and knew only national and monarchic principles was a consequence of the conditions of that time. That this was not enough, the result of the war showed clearly."

In France, after 1870, when the nation adopted compulsory military service, it took twenty years, says General Tanant, for the army to modify its methods of leadership to accord with the mentality of the citizen soldier. It took another fifteen years before enlightened, paternal, and affectionate leadership became general in the French Army. In our own Army we have the enormously difficult and hardly comprehended problem of making this same change within a few months after the outbreak of war. If we fail, the Army will again deserve and receive the hatred of its soldiers as they go back to their homes and will again struggle for years against an antipathy that it does not understand.

There is a technique of leadership of large commands and of civilian soldiers, and it can be acquired by all in some degree. When he reaches high command the educative process of the leader is over. The general must lead with the personality and character he is then endowed with. But then, if ever, he needs in addition a technique of leadership to guide him in his unexplored domain. If he has none he fails, and the next war's Blois will be filled with such failures. The great leaders of the past developed their methods through trial and error. Politicians of all ages have learned the technique of popular leadership by the same process. The leader in modern war will not have the time and opportunity, but the psychologists of today have clarified the problem of mass leadership for him, and the methods are no longer the secret of the occasional genius.

Of leaders and leadership there are many definitions. Perhaps the clearest is one that limits the function of leadership to the moral sphere in the exercise of command. The exercise of command involves:

Leadership: The imposition, maintenance, and direction of moral unity to our ends. This is similar to the definition given on the efficiency report.

Generalship: The tactical or strategical direction of operations.

Management: Staff functioning, administration, and supervision.

Many substitutes for leadership work well in peace. A good administrator can have a well-turned-out command without ever approaching the qualities of leadership. Fear of punishment is effective in peace; in war the guardhouse may be a reprieve from death. Supervision can be carried out in peace to the last trifling breach of uniformity; in war, the battle, when joined, must be turned over to subordinate leaders. Supervision and punishment, primarily functions of management—substitutes for leadership in peace—are not available or are only partially usable in war. The professional officer, too frequently in peace, depends upon these substitutes for leadership which in war he cannot use.

Leadership is the most important function in the exercise of command. Generalship and management, to a large degree, can be entrusted to a competent staff. But the eyes of the men are always turned upward, and no one can exercise leadership for the commander. "Technique and tactics," Foch said, "that is the business of staffs. The leader, himself, should furnish the spirit and the morale." And he adds that neither clairvoyance nor energy suffices for the leader; he must also have the power of communicating the spirit that animates him to his command. He should know his men, love them, and maintain between them and himself the mutual confidence that is more indispensable in a national army than in a professional army.

Military leaders fall into three principal classes:

(1) *The Institutional Leader,* who exercises control by virtue of his rank or position; that is, by the established prestige and legal authority attaching to his office. All Army officers are institutional leaders.

(2) *The Small-Group Leader,* who acts on individuals. He is represented in the Army by the captains, lieutenants, and noncommissioned officers.

(3) *The Mass Leader,* who impresses and dominates because of his character, his understanding, and his ability to mold and control the minds of large groups without intimate personal contact. All regimental and higher commanders should be mass leaders.

The institutional leader issues orders in accordance with his legal authority and expects them to be obeyed because of legal impulsion. His moral superiority exists in his rank and position, not in himself. Such a leader may maintain and build up a thoroughly coherent group. To do so he must be punctilious about dress, drill, formal discipline—in a word, about all the symbols of authority—and in this he will be right psychologically. Thus a man may get to a position of leadership who lacks the personal qualities either to dominate or to understand his men, yet may make a very considerable success of it, at least in peace, provided he recognizes his own limitations and suits his methods to them.

Institutional leadership is a system of leadership. It substitutes prestige of position for prestige of personality. It is implicit in a professional army. It permits frequent change of leaders without injury. There are no means in a peacetime army of selecting mass leaders, so a system of leadership must be depended on. Unfortunately the system fails to develop capable mass leaders; it apparently hinders their development. The complete flowering of the institutional leader is the antithesis of the mass leader, who is self-assertive and original and endowed with a high degree of initiative. He cannot help but be a thorn in the sides of many among the superior institutional leaders who predominate in a hierarchical organization. Institutional leadership, gone to decay, breeds that lowest form of military life—the martinet. In the growl of one colonel, "I have been taking it for thirty years, and now I am going to dish it out," is summed up all the repressions and decay of institutional leadership.

The small-group leader deals with men as individuals. He concentrates on individual psychology. Given the knowledge and desire to understand his men and take care of them, his problem in winning their confidence and devotion is simple. He is in close daily contact with them and has every opportunity to demonstrate his worthiness of their trust and his capacity to lead them. As the years go by, however, he accumulates a mind full of small-group ideas and small-group methods, which, if persisted in when he reaches high command, may be actively harmful. We have all seen senior officers who have never left behind them the interest and methods of the company commander.

Mass leadership itself is nothing new. What is really new is the psychologists' recognition of the mentality of the mass and their researches into methods through which masses of men can be influenced. In certain nations propaganda ministries sway whole peoples at will by appeal to mass psychology. All great military and political leaders have been mass leaders, able to arouse the devotion and enthusiasm of their followers. It was of such that the maxim was coined that leaders are born, not made. And like many oversimplifications, this one has in it only a portion of truth. For modern psychologists have paved the way to make this type of leadership a science. From their studies a technique of mass leadership can be developed and actually has been developed in the political field. Thus these methods of mass leadership are available to all with the intelligence to use them. With the enormous armies of today, composed largely of civilians, mass-leadership methods are essential to the conduct of war.

Institutional leadership and the institutional type of discipline have succeeded admirably in the past with professional armies. It works well with the peacetime army, because we have time to change the habit patterns of our men, to condition them to the soldierly ideals and prides of the professional. With the hastily trained national army there is not time to modify character to the pattern we desire. The ruthless attempt to do it in a short period, with too small a nucleus of professionals to give the example, arouses fear, resistance, hatred, and suspicion. All the new soldier's earnestness and anxiety to learn can be turned into cynicism and distrust if he is subjected initially to a commandership that appears to have no other object than to harass him with a thousand petty restraints. It was our uninspired institutional leadership that created the distrust of the military system in our World War Army which today still blocks civil understanding of its fine ideals and high purposes.

The mass leader must know the minds of his men. A knowledge of psychology will help him. But more than psychology is the understanding that comes from contact and sympathy with his men. The older psychologists pictured the mind as divided into conscious and instinctive parts and listed a large number of instincts. The analytical psychologists admit an instinctive basis and add the unconscious filled with fixations and complexes which they believe are the key to many of our actions. The behaviorists deny the existence of instincts and call the unconscious the "unverbalized" and make a pretty good case for their contentions. But regardless of the disagreements of psychologists concerning the origin of impulses of human behavior, all of them agree that man is characterized by certain behavior patterns. In our effort to utilize universal human tendencies it matters little whether we call these behavior patterns instincts—that is, inherited pattern reactions—or whether we consider them to be learned pattern reactions.

In his methods of influencing the led, the leader capitalizes on the human tendency to form groups. On the lower level are appetite and instinct groups. On the higher level the groups are based on interest, sentiment, and ideals. Such groupings are not necessarily physical; that is, in the form of crowds. The twelve thousand officers of the Army are an "interest-and-ideals" group. The group once formed has a definite group mentality. In *Psychology and Leadership* are listed the characteristics of the group or herd instinct as: intolerance of opinions that differ from those of the group; fearfulness of solitude; sensitiveness to the habits and customs of the group; subjection to the opinions of the herd; susceptibility to leadership; relations with his fellows dependent upon his recognition as a member of the herd, and heightened suggestibility. All of these group characteristics can and must be used by the leader.

His first problem is the development of group feeling and unity. Since man instinctively is a herd animal the development of group allegiance is simple. Let men with a common cultural background live together and work toward a common end, and they will automatically identify themselves with the group. When to this are added an identifying uniform and certain group passwords, symbols, and ideals, such as the military salute, military insignia, and military traditions, the solution is complete. "The historic fame of any military body," Hindenburg wrote, "is a bond of unity between all its members, a kind of cement which holds it together even in the worst of times." The process is hastened by drills and parades. In modern armies the primary value of drill lies in the development of group spirit. It has no other magic. The type of obedience and discipline taught by drill has small application on the battlefields of today. When men have been long in the lines and are consequently disorganized, no other method equals close-order drill in restoring group spirit. It is the visible symbol and shared actuality of the group in action with all of its members and leaders working together.

Since the soldier group is not a natural one but is formed deliberately with a definite end in view, group interests, sentiments, and ideals must be given to it. These we have in the form of all the historic virtues of the soldier: patriotism, loyalty, pride, obedience, courage, self-sacrifice, and discipline. In the professional army these ideals have continuity. They are absorbed rather than deliberately implanted, and the process is slow. In the citizen army they must be intentionally and consciously inculcated. If they are not, then in place of them must be put the iron discipline of legal authority. Discipline is defined as control gained by enforcing obedience. But how much more desirable, how much simpler, to give the soldier proper group ideals, so that authority comes from within the men themselves and they act through morale rather than discipline.

One American World War general, when still a colonel commanding a Regular Army unit, often collected his regiment to talk to his men. He would narrate from the regimental history a story of heroic action in battle. Then he would ask the question, "Who was responsible for this victory? Who actually deserves the credit?" Some assured private primed with the answer would get up and reply, "The private soldier, sir." Other questions would follow, all designed to bring out the same type of answer. It was thus that he developed the pride and sense of importance of his men, their individual responsibility for the success of the regiment in battle. This was a subject close to this commander's heart and one that he never failed to emphasize. Although his assemblies were deliberately stage-managed, there was no insincerity in them. That was his method of implanting group ideals. What his regiment did in battle later on proved how well his method worked.

This commander's method was that of suggestion. Each soldier, inside of himself, hoped to be as heroic as the examples his colonel cited, and when the test came he was. The quality in a leader that gives potency to suggestion is earnestness. Earnestness is an emotional quality that is transmitted from mind to mind. Constant affirmation and repetition of ideals will plant them forever if done with sincerity. Reason and right have little influence compared to suggestion and earnestness. The earnestness of Huey Long gained for him his position and his place in the hearts of his followers, not the logic by which he hoped to share wealth. The commander who fails to make use of suggestion and affirmation neglects one of the primary tools of leadership.

Group pride and confidence in the capacity of the group are developed through group accomplishment. But accomplishment must be reasonably gradual. The self-confidence of a green regiment can be ruined by a march beyond its capacity. "Unattainable demands prejudice the trust in the leaders and shake the spirit of the troops." (German FSR.) The leader who does not know the capacity of his group and gives his men tasks beyond their capacity destroys its morale. "No man is more valiant than Yessoutai," said Genghis Khan; "no one has rarer gifts. But as the longest marches do not tire him, as he feels neither hunger nor thirst, he believes that his officers and soldiers do not suffer such things. *That is why he is not fitted for high command.*" And of Sir John Moore's failure in the same respect, Wellington said, "He was as brave as his own sword, but he did not know what man could do or not do." French field service regulations are explicit that the capacity of green troops should be estimated prudently and that they should be supported energetically. In the World War our G.H.Q. appreciated the importance of this. In the attack of the 28th Infantry at Cantigny, the first attack of the regiment and the first wholly American attack, no chances were taken of failure. The operation was rehearsed on similar terrain in the rear. Its success was essential, not only for the morale of the regiment, but to insure confidence in the entire American Army. The same reasons kept Chaumont from sending partially trained men into battle. An early failure would have been disastrous to morale. And again at Saint-Mihiel no chances were taken of failure.

A classic example of a means used to develop group pride is the statement of a captured German colonel published in orders to the entire 1st Division in the lines.

I received orders to hold my ground at all costs [it read]. The American barrage advanced toward my position and the work of your artillery was marvelous. The barrage was so dense that it was impossible for us to move out of our dugouts. Following the barrage closely was the infantry of the 1st Division. I saw them forge ahead and I knew that all was lost. . . . Yesterday I knew that the Division was opposite me and I knew that we would have our hardest fight of the war. The 1st Division is wonderful and the German Army knows it. We did not believe that within five years the Americans would develop a division like the 1st. The work of its infantry and artillery is worthy of the best armies in the world.

The patness with which praise is distributed equally between infantry and artillery leads one to believe that the German colonel's statement had been rewritten for publication. It is unlikely that this would occur to the men. It contained the kind of praise they wanted to believe, and, coming from an enemy, it was ever so much more welcome. One can imagine the redoubled efforts they made to live up to their reputation on the other side of the line.

And just as the right orders to troops can raise their morale to the highest pitch, so can the wrong ones depress it. An example of a wrong way is the following extract from a division order. The division had been in the lines for its first month. The troops had fought bravely; they had suffered five hundred casualties and were proud of their accomplishments:

(2) The character of the service which the Division is now about to undertake demands enforcement of a stricter discipline and the maintenance of a higher standard of efficiency than any hitherto required of us.

(3) From now on the troops of this command will be held at all times to the strictest observation of that rigid discipline, in camp and upon the march, which is essential to their maximum efficiency on the day of battle.

(4) This order will be read by all organization commanders to the men of their command.

By command of ....:

Official.   *Chief of Staff.*

How would the men receive this order? Here was a scolding from the division commander. The men doubtless thought they had already done wonderfully. What did "rigid discipline" mean to them? Probably to stand at attention and salute every time they turned around. What they needed and deserved instead from their leader was praise. They had performed splendidly under new and terrible conditions. If laxity in formal discipline had resulted from a month in the lines it could be restored promptly by a little drill. This absence of understanding on the part of their general of the state of mind of his men might have wrecked the morale of the division. He had simply not found the way to their hearts.

In contrast to this can be placed General Mangin's order to the Americans of his command in July 1918:

OFFICERS, NONCOMMISSIONED OFFICERS, AND SOLDIERS OF THE III U. S. ARMY CORPS:

Shoulder to shoulder with your French comrades you have thrown yourselves into the battle of the counteroffensive which commenced July 18.

You went into it like a celebration.

Your magnificent courage overturned the surprised enemy, and your indomitable tenacity arrested the offensive of fresh divisions.

You have won the admiration of your brothers-in-arms.

American comrades, I am grateful for the blood shed on the soil of my country.

I am proud to have commanded you in such days and to have battled with you for the deliverance of the world.

MANGIN

Note, too, that this order was signed by Mangin, by the higher commander himself, not merely "by command of So-and-So," and somebody else as chief of staff, and somebody else as official, to dilute its import as a personal communication from the chief. Nor did it contain that useless and typical paragraph about reading the order to the troops.

One can search the pages of history, the general orders of Napoleon, and the orations of the ancients without finding a finer, more direct and manly message than that delivered to the 1st Division on October 29, 1918. The division had suffered more than seven thousand casualties between October 4 and October 11. The men had expected to have a month in a rest area but were ordered back into the Meuse-Argonne battle:

MEMORANDUM FOR MEMBERS OF THE 1ST DIVISION:

It will be well for us to bear in mind at all times and especially upon the eve of active operations, the following:

(1) That we are the first assault division of the AEF.

(2) That we have, on four battlefields, always taken all objectives assigned to us.

(3) That we have gone through the best German troops for a total of thirty kilometers and have never surrendered an inch of ground to the enemy.

(4) That for every prisoner, we have taken over one hundred Germans.

(5) That the above record has been due to the pride and spirit of each individual member of the Division who, each in his own place, has given to his country his entire effort of heart, mind, and body.

All men need and seek a leader. Confidence, respect, and affection are given to him instinctively. The commander who manages to arouse distrust and dislike in his group has accomplished almost a miracle of false leadership. That it is so often done indicates not that it is hard to avoid doing, but that there is a fundamental falsity in many of our conceptions of leadership. "Hero worship is the deepest root of all. No nobler feeling," Carlyle wrote, "than this admiration for one higher than himself dwells in the breast of man. It is to this hour, and at all hours, the vivifying influence in Man's life."

Here is another behavior pattern made to order for the leader. In childhood humans turn to a parent for care and solace. This desire for a superior to whom they can turn never leaves them. It expresses itself by hero worship, by constant seeking for guidance, by faith-giving to political messiahs, and, in an army, by love and devotion to the superiors who understand and fill this human need. Many a soldier has risked his life to protect a loved leader. Lee's men pleaded with him to remove himself from danger. One of Napoleon's most effective means of inspiring his men was to threaten to go into battle at their head. A flag in his hand, he charged the bridge at Arcole at the head of his grenadiers and at other times retired from dangerous places only on the demand of his soldiers. In bivouac at Austerlitz he announced: *"Soldiers,* I will hold myself far from the fire if, with your accustomed bravery, you carry disorder and confusion into the ranks of the enemy. But if the victory is uncertain for an instant, you will see your Emperor expose himself to the first blows."

The problem of the military leader is to transfer the tendency to hero worship to himself. He must supply the care and guidance to his men that every human seeks and thus make an associative shifting of allegiance from the father image to himself. The first step is unremitting care for his men. "An officer must likewise find a way to the hearts of his subordinates and gain their trust through an understanding of their feelings and thoughts and through never-ceasing care for their needs." (German FSR.)

Our own *Manual for Commanders of Large Units* emphasizes the same attitude: "His first object should be to secure the love and attachment of his men by his constant care for their well-being. The devotion that arises from this kind of attention knows no bounds and enables him to exact prodigies of valor on the day of battle."

There is no inconsistency in this and the obligation to perform the most arduous and dangerous of duties. Nor is it inconsistent with the exaction of rigid discipline, nor even with extreme severity. Love and care for the men, performance of duty, and discipline must march arm in arm.

The leader of large commands has a difficult problem in getting close to his men. He must plan deliberately and make occasions to share the dangers and privations of his lowest subordinate. This requires showmanship and is quite a different matter from the problem of the small-group leader in daily contact with his men. It also requires practice.

Not even Napoleon was born a leader. Marshal Marmont declared that the army of Italy received him without confidence and almost with derision. His early efforts at haranguing his men were laughed at. He had first to learn the chords to play upon, but he did learn. It was not long until his men wept with rage when he reproached them. And never was a general as religiously listened to. When he spoke, and this was frequently, he carried the enthusiasm of his troops to the highest pitch. The men gathered around his proclamations and orders of the day and learned them by heart. He made the emotional chords vibrate—words of action always, no vain rhetoric, no fancy speech, and, above all, no pompousness. Whenever he could he explained his intentions and maneuvers to his men. And always he declared his love for them—"My soldiers are my children."

No general in the Union Army received such unbounded devotion as McClellan. He forged the army with which Grant won the Civil War, and it remained a marvelous army as commanders followed him in rapid succession, even after defeats that would have ruined most armies. An idea of his methods can be gained from the letters of Private Henry Sproul. On June 5, 1862, after his regiment had been in action, Sproul wrote home: "General McClellan sent his thanks to us and said if we got into action again he would be with us."

He did this throughout his army. He went among the men; he strove to feed them well and organize them so that they would surely be victorious. Six weeks later, after the retreat down the peninsula, Sproul wrote home:

"I suppose people blame General McClellan, but they need not blame anyone but themselves. It was their fault for not sending him reinforcements when he called for them and needed them so badly. But no, they must leave him and his men to be slaughtered by overwhelming numbers. I see in the papers that it is the cry to recall. It would be the means of destroying the Army, for there is not a soldier here but that loves him more than his own life. There is not one but would be willing to lose his own life for him. If they do recall him I think it will raise a mutiny in the Army."

Personal appearances before troops can be done badly and react unfavorably. Invariably these failures are due to a lack of understanding the soldier. One of our major generals in France wanted his men to know who he was. His troops were marching to the front through a village in a heavy rain. He struck a pose on a balcony overlooking the route of march. No one paid any attention to him. He shouted, "I am your general! I am General So-and-So." The men could not hear him and did not know him. They only saw someone in uniform on the balcony waving his arms and saying something. Naturally they hooted and called back at him, and this was taken up along the line of march. Needless to say, they later learned who it was, and his prestige with his men was not helped.

Then there was the general who came to make an inspection of brigade. The review was called for 7:00 A.M. Some of the men left their billets, twelve miles distant, at 1:00 A.M. to get to the review on time. Seven o'clock and no general, and rain kept falling. Noon, and still no general, and the subordinate commanders held him in such terror they wouldn't let the men leave ranks to eat. At three in the afternoon an aide came down the line in a motorcycle splashing mud indiscriminately and said that the general had come and gone. Every man who was in that brigade still carries his hatred of that general and of the Army. The object of the inspection was not only to look over the troops but to give them a chance to see the commander to whom they looked for leadership. It failed in both objects. And it destroyed all confidence and affection for the general.

We may consider here, too, the dress of a commander. We are wont in peace to ascribe extreme importance to his outward appearance. But just how much does it count? General Grant had but one coat at a time, regarding it fondly as an old friend. He preferred his coats made so that he could wear them either side out, and he did wear both sides out before he ever discarded one. He was indistinguishable, except for his insignia, from a cavalry private. Mangin, who spent from daylight till noon daily in the trenches, was always immaculate. He avoided the communicating trenches in going up to the front and walked across country so that he wouldn't soil his clothes. In contrast, Pétain was plainly dressed, more often than not, in a soldier's overcoat. An encounter between the two, when both were brigade commanders at the time of the retreat from Belgium, shows all the difference between the two manners. As the two generals prepared to eat beside the road, Pétain, stumbling with fatigue, drew from a paper sack a piece of cold meat, some bread, and a piece of cheese. Mangin's orderly, on the contrary, laid linen on an improvised table and brought a hot filet of beef, fried potatoes, salad, and a bottle of wine. "How can you do all that?" demanded Pétain. "Don't you know we are at war?" "That is precisely why I need to be well nourished," responded Mangin. "I have been at war all my life and I have never felt better than at present. You have been fighting for fifteen days and you are almost dead. Follow my advice and nourish yourself decently."

But after the failure of the disastrous offensive of April 1917, the last drop of water which made the vase of discontent overflow into mutiny, it was to Pétain that France turned to restore discipline. Thanks to his patience, his intelligence, his kindness, and his profound knowledge of the human heart, he re-established order in a short time. He attacked the true cause by getting close to the men, talking to them, showing them by acts of judicious organization that they would find moral support in him. The poilu understood him at once and gave him his heart.

Napoleon also dramatized himself in his appearance before his men by wearing the clothes of a simple soldier.

Around him were arranged his staff and his marshals in gold braid and lace. When he appeared with his worn coat, the legendary little hat on his head, distinguished by a deliberate and exaggerated simplicity, he appeared to his men like one of the heroes of antiquity. It is what is inside the heart of the leader, not what clothes the outside of his body, that arouses the devotion of the led. Georges Bonnet, the present Foreign Minister of France, writing as a private in the lines in 1915 about the motives behind deeds of extraordinary heroism, stated, "This one acts because he adores his family and would be glorious for them; that one because he finds himself with comrades from the same village and will not abandon them at any cost; *a third because he has a good commander who has known how to make himself understood and loved.*"

The leader of large commands must make himself a part of his group in the minds of his men. He does this by identifying himself with their activities. The smart politico campaigning for the farm vote enters a cornhusking contest. He wears galluses and goes without a tie. He identifies himself with the farmer and thus proves his right to act as their spokesman. The military leader does the same thing on a higher plane. He must exhibit the qualities that he demands of his soldiers—courage, fortitude, loyalty, and discipline. If he shares the soldier's hardships and dangers he has gone two thirds of the way to the soldier's heart. He has also to prove his courage, and this he must do deliberately, making the opportunity or seizing it when occasion arises. The favorite picture of Grant during the Civil War was the one in which he was sitting on a log, smoking a cigar, shells bursting all around as he calmly wrote a dispatch, while two soldiers near by remarked, "Ulysses don't scare a bit." General Buck was never absent when his men were in danger or distress. He prowled the trenches day and night. With his tremendous vitality and the courage of a lion, he shared and more than shared the dangers and hardships of the men. He was as tough as they had to be, and they idolized him. But is that the place for the general in battle? Or should he be back in a dugout putting pins in maps?

Blaise de Montluc, writing in the sixteenth century, emphasized: "When the battle is hot at some place, if the leader does not go there, or at least some distinguished man, the men will . . . only complain that they are being sent to their death."

Men have not changed since. General Barbot, when he was reproached by his staff for endangering himself, replied, "I awaited this reproach. In principle you are entirely right, but one should never be absolute. In the present situation I estimated differently. The place of the division commander, whenever he is able, is, on the contrary, in the center of his poilus who are in the first line. The situation is excessively grave. It is necessary that the chiefs of the tactical units, from the smallest to the largest, do not spare themselves and give the example. And finally there is the question of morale, which at this moment has never been more important. The poilu is happy to see that there where the shells are falling *each takes his chances regardless.*"

General Barbot was placed in command of the 77th Division on September 1, 1914. In a few weeks he became the idol of his officers and men. Tall, thin, wearing the coat of a simple soldier, an Alpine beret on his head, he was to be found everywhere where his presence could exalt the will to conquer. The day he took command, on La Chipotte Ridge, charged with protecting the withdrawal of the Army of Alsace, it is said that he covered the withdrawal with his own body. At the end of October, when Arras seemed lost, he refused to abandon it, and the city was saved. He passed his days and long hours of his nights in the first lines. He talked with his men, knew how to find the words that temper the will and exalt the courage. This simplicity of attitude, Pétain said, far from diminishing his prestige, engendered a community of thought and unified in the same affection the men who pursued the same end and were exposed to the same dangers. In the eyes of his soldiers he lived for three things only: for his country, for his men, and for victory. True to his principles, General Barbot, less than a year later, in another exceedingly grave situation, fell in the first line in the midst of his troops.

Mangin, too, never spared himself. Telling of an operation, he said, "My leading battalion pushed ahead. After some hesitation I decided the pear was hard and sounded the charge. But it was too soon; the men had to be pushed; certain fractions were hesitating. My troopers, on whom I had counted to threaten the rear of the enemy, whom I thought small in number, had disappeared. It was by pushing the men ourselves, the generals fifty yards behind the line of riflemen, that we carried the first houses. Evidently it was not our proper place, but it was the place indicated by the state of our troops and the dispositions of the enemy; thus it was good. The *élan* was given by example, and they went in one rush from one end of the village to the other."

And what do the men think of this kind of general? Henri Detheil, a private in the division, wrote home after Mangin had taken command: "At last we have a leader. After having had at our head a walking ruin, we actually have one of the best generals in the French Army. Young, intrepid, a lucid mind, inspiring the men, charging at their head when necessary—always in the first line under fire at difficult times. There is a man; there is a leader, and we are all joyful to serve under him."

It is not only the men but the subordinate commanders of all grades who have to be supported by the presence of the superior. On the twenty-seventh of May, 1918, General Duchesne, in command of the French Sixth Army, had received the German attack on the Chemin des Dames. His troops disappeared like mist before him. In the days of the battle and following, no word of encouragement, no sight of the higher command came to him. On such occasions the commander looks rearward, searches for moral support there where he should find it, from his superiors, who alone can aid him morally and materially. The first higher commander to visit him was Premier Clemenceau, and it was from that General Duchesne received the encouragement he needed.

General Mordacq, Clemenceau's military adviser, remarked in telling of this incident that it is not only when everything goes well that a leader should visit his subordinates; it is especially at critical moments, and Duchesne was in such a case. Mordacq said that he remembered General Barbot at the opening of the war, always at their sides when everything was cracking; but in contrast, during the first attack, in Belgium in April 1915, neither his division nor his corps commander ever appeared as far forward as Mordacq's command post.

With some noteworthy exceptions, the American commanders in the World War did not spend much time in the lines. A single general was killed—an indication of the extent to which those high in rank were endangered. This, of course, was not from any lack of personal courage but because they did not, as a rule, have capable staffs to whom they could delegate their responsibilities. Frequently, too, it was because the higher command ordered them to remain at the end of a telephone line. In contrast, at the single battle of Antietam in September 1862, on the Union side there were six generals killed, including two corps commanders, and ten were wounded. On the Confederate side five generals were killed and six wounded, a total of twenty-seven general officers killed and wounded in one battle. But the leadership was superb. With leadership by proxy, or from a safe distance, this battle could have been a disaster for either side.

It is obvious that man is not led by reward or punishment. He cares more for the opinion of his group than for either. He will risk his life for a loved commander, for a comrade, for the respect of his organization, but not for fear of court-martial. Nevertheless, rewards and punishments are necessary adjuncts of leadership. Good leadership will make the need for punishment infrequent. An organization can be ruled by punishment in peace, but a commander who so rules is not a leader; he is a jailer. He can establish the appearance of discipline, but it is not a discipline for war, since that discipline depends upon abnegation. On the field of battle the awakening will be hard and it will be at the price of human lives. The more perfect such discipline appears, the more dangerous it is, for one is tempted to attribute to an organization that looks good, a fighting value much higher than its real worth.

Punishment should be reserved for the repression of the incorrigible, for those who shun their duty, and for those who do not wish to bend to discipline. Punishment given to many indicates a lack of moral superiority in the commander. When, in battle, any punishment less than death is a reprieve from dangerous duty, what lever of leadership remains to the commander who has depended on it?

Reward, like punishment, should be prompt. A word of praise from a respected commander is a reward. Many Americans saw the bucketfuls of medals being carried up to French organizations in the lines, to be awarded on the next day after heroic actions. But all recommendations for decorations for Americans had to be passed upon by a board at G.H.Q.—a board exceedingly slow in acting. For the Distinguished Service Cross it approved about five thousand recommendations and disapproved an equal number. But four fifths of those awarded were not approved until the war was over and so lost all value as stimulants to morale. The French were more generous, distributing between fourteen and fifteen thousand decorations among the Americans, but these were put on official ice until after the Armistice.

The leadership of peace, as we practice it, has little relation to leadership in war. Because tasks are not severe, the routine of institutional leadership and the substitute discipline of law and punishment suffice. Once again, should we go to war, we are unprepared psychologically to lead the citizen soldier. In the future greater armies than those over which our colors flew in the Meuse-Argonne will be constituted. The soldiers will come straight from civil life and to civil life they will return. It is vital that we recognize that these troops without the traditions, habit patterns, and training of Regular soldiers require leadership different from the professional. Upon our splendid institutional foundation must be built a leadership of understanding and mutual trust and mutual sacrifice. Only by knowing the nature and purpose of institutional leadership, and its limitations, by studying the methods of great leaders, by studying and applying the researches of modern psychologists, can we prevent the decay of leadership in our hands into the stupidities of the martinet, and prepare ourselves to lead the great armies of citizen soldiers of the future.

Bibliography of principal works:

Psychology and Leadership, The Command & General Staff School Press, Fort Leavenworth, 1934.

La Discipline dans les Armées Françaises, by General Tanant. The finest study of discipline and leadership found in any language.

Psychology and the Soldier, by Major F. C. Bartlett. Particularly acute; should be read by every officer.

La Guerre et Les Hommes, by General Debéney.

La Guerra Decisiva, by General Visconti-Prasca.

History of the United States Army, by Major William A. Ganoe.

Le Ministère Clemenceau, by General Mordacq.

History of the 1st Division.

Mangin, by Major Charles Bugnet.

Essai sur la Psychologie de l'Infanterie, by Lieutenant Colonel Bouchacourt.

Les Forces Morales, by Captain Reguert.

La Psychologie du Combat, by Coste.

L'Ame du Soldat, by Georges Bonnet.

The American Army in France, 1917–19, by Major General James G. Harbord.

The Science of War, by Colonel G. F. R. Henderson.

CANNED COMMANDERS

By MERCUTIO

(1935)

THE THOUGHT OCCURS with growing insistence that our magnificent school system is garroting originality. More and more the type mentality that can spot the celebrated Mr. Addison Sims of Seattle forges to the front. Slowly but surely we are creating a strange breed of military man . . . a slide-rule tactician, a mechanical brain-truster, a canned commander.

To how many others had the idea occurred that we might find our real commanders by turning the graduation lists of our service schools upside down? I can imagine few things more disconcerting to our adversaries in the next war. Today it is virtually a foregone conclusion that the first 80 or 90 per cent of any one class will turn in identical decisions in any given situation. How convenient such stereotyped mental processes will be for a first-class opponent!

But what if we delve a bit into this submerged and erratic tenth for commanders? There will we find, by eliminating the dullard and the die-hard, a small group of men who think and who think along original lines. There, too, will be found that moral courage which dares to translate thought into action regardless of "marks" in peace or pessimistic probabilities in war.

With such men at the head of our fighting forces a smug enemy can no longer expect the obvious. He will be confronted by the unexpected at every turn. Surprise, the product of originality, will no longer be paid a sorry lip service; it will again come into its own high domain.

In short, while there is still time, let us recognize Emerson's subtle distinction between "man thinking" and "thinking man." If our school system is not flexible enough for the "great" minority let us at least use it as a filter by means of which that "great" minority can be recognized.

LEADERS WIN WHERE COMMANDERS LOSE

By MAJOR (now COLONEL) RICHARD M. SANDUSKY

(1938)

For I am a man under authority, having soldiers under me: and I say to this man, Go, and he goeth; and to another, Come, and he cometh; and to my servant, Do this, and he doeth it. MATTHEW viii:9.

EVERY MAN IN AUTHORITY has his own definition of leadership and his own methods of developing it. According to Webster, it is the ability to conduct or direct. It would be possible to list perhaps a dozen qualities essential for leadership. But at best these are merely labels, inadequately suggesting the presence of an inner power, a hidden strength and fire, denoting the confidence and capacity of the man who plays the leader's role. Napoleon did not define leadership but indicated its vital importance in his statement that the moral is to the physical as three is to one.

The military student, searching the pages of history for some glimmering clue to greatness, is concerned with actions, not adjectives. History is written by historians. But first it is hammered and molded and made by leaders. If we know them, may we not, following their example, duplicate their success? Unfortunately it is not so easy as that. The world has moved too rapidly and too far; there are too many imponderables for exact and scientific comparison. Principles we may examine, yes. But it is dangerous to apply them unless we keep constantly in mind that the present is as far removed from the past as tomorrow will be from today.

The mercenary forces of Hannibal required a different leadership from the national armies of Napoleon. Proud and aristocratic knights, who furnished their own mounts and equipment and who served without pay, would have greeted with contemptuous scorn the repressive methods employed with hardheaded peasantry, or the rabble of the towns. The leadership problems of a democracy are certainly at wide variance with those of an autocracy and even with those of a liberal government in which there are rigid social and class distinctions.

Leadership, both military and political, is a jewel of countless facets reflecting the totality of human experience and relationships. It influences and is influenced by such diverse factors as science, philosophy, and religion.

It is a common belief in the military profession that the terms *command* and *leadership* are synonymous. An official order issued by constituted authority can appoint a commander. A leader, however, is an artist whose talents cannot be conferred by administrative act. Nature gives them to him in part as inherited equipment, and if she is liberal in her endowment he may become the "born leader." But in most cases he attains to leadership—or his conception of it—through study and observation and a series of experiments in the huge laboratory of human relations. A leader is a commander, but a commander is not necessarily a leader. If we could add up the characteristics of the two and subtract the difference our evaluation of leadership would be simple and definite. Unfortunately we deal with art, not science, and the intangibles of human qualities defy precise evaluation.

Besides, vitality, enthusiasm, decisiveness, sympathy, and all the rest are but instruments. The military leader is judged not by an inventory of his virtues but by the accomplishments of his men. Actions speak louder than words, and it is by this convincing language alone that the great of the world are recorded in the long sweep of history.

A leader arouses co-operative effort in the attainment of a common goal. A commander seeks a similar result by authoritative prescription. What is the difference? It is a matter of method and organization. Men work *with* the leader; they work *for* the commander. One group is a responsive and self-respecting society of co-workers, while the other is a form of contract labor. Both may produce results. But in a crisis—and war is a series of crises—the method of the inspired and magnetic leader will win where those of the dictatorial commander would fail. Commanders may survive short wars; only leaders emerge from long ones. Time and events sift them to their proper places. There is nothing new or strange in this. It is simply common sense.

Any man will work harder for himself than for anyone else, just as he will do more under praise than under censure. Recognizing these plain truths, the wise leader employs them to stimulate and energize all individuals concerned in the group effort, increasing their latent powers, quickening their interests, lifting them to levels of achievement and inspiration seemingly impossible to attain. He touches hidden sources of strength and extends the field of action both for his own keen talents and the redoubled capacity of those under his control.

Gregarious by instinct and habit, all of us like to be led—are accustomed to being led. Our civilization is built on an interdependent organization of individual and specialized abilities. These cut across all phases of contemporary life—religion, politics, education, industry, recreation. We are not happy, and indeed we can hardly exist, we moderns, unless we are together. And since we find ourselves grouped for some particular purpose, then we must have group control—that is to say, leadership— if we are to avoid the failure and futility of undirected and pointless effort.

The problem of the military leader, then, is not one of forcing an unknown or repugnant system on a hostile people, but rather one of providing them with the enlightened leadership which will fulfill their expectations and accomplish the end desired by all.

Halter or whip? This is the real meat of the leadership question. More often than not the whip wins, and it wins for two reasons: first, because it is easy, and second, because it is traditional. It usually takes less effort to *make* a man do something than to make him *want* to do it. So the whip cracks. And by virtue of fear and intimidation, authority of position, power of command, ruthless determination, vaulting ambition, grasping selfishness—by one or all of these—the ruler directs the actions and controls the lives of his subjects. It is no accident that the club and scepter are similar in appearance.

"Off with his head!" cried the Queen on the slightest provocation. It was a simple solution; it saved the labor of thought and demonstrated the efficacy of an autocratic system. But it did not contribute, Alice noted, to the happiness of Wonderland.

It is true that such policies may produce results for a time, but they do not constitute that permanent and wise investment in human reaction which we call morale. In the industrial world it is significant that there is little labor trouble in those institutions that are organized on a co-operative basis. But those that follow the coercive school of thought find themselves confronted with an armed truce engendered by suspicion and distrust. They hire the body, but not the spirit.

Human organizations are not so much the reflection of the man at the top as of the many men below him whose efforts are responsible for his position. He retains the full measure of his power only so long as he enjoys their unlimited admiration and respect. For he has given them something that they could not give themselves—namely, an assurance and pride born of past accomplishment, which no future obstacle can daunt. Leader and led have achieved oneness, and in that amalgamation they have discovered the secret of true success.

Because the soldier has as his ultimate métier war, violence, and sudden death, it was once believed that he should be steeled for his ordeal by a cultivation of the Spartan virtues and the imposition of a Draconian Code. He was formed with his fellows in masses and drilled and drilled and drilled into a robot denied the dangerous privilege of thought. By an accepted system of relentless training in peace he was so toughened in body and spirit that war represented no departure, no confusing transition, from his customary routine. He feared not the enemy less but his own officers more. The danger of death was also outweighed by the spoils of victory, and whatever degree of pride he possessed came from his own valor and exploits rather than from his ardent belief in the policies of his country and his patriotic obligations for its defense.

Today, of course, all this is far away and long ago. In our country the constitutional guarantees of freedom and equality do not make our military problems easier. People who are born, live, and die in a narrow groove of social and economic inferiority accept military service and traditional military methods with simple and uncomplaining resignation. It is just another episode in a predestined existence forever bounded by regulation and decree. But not our American. He is a sovereign, jealous of his royal prerogatives. The Declaration of Independence is his personal and daily credo. Emotional and responsive, he is likewise a bundle of inconsistencies. He can be a stubborn malcontent or a devoted disciple, faithful to the death. Who leads him to highest purpose must be an honor graduate of the School of Human Understanding.

And what is more, he changes with the times. The soldier found in our divisions of 1918 is not identical with the young man of today. This is an age of youth, defiance, self-expression, skepticism—an era of new and greater freedom. These moderns, the citizen soldiers who must meet the emergency of tomorrow, look with level eyes at life. Products of the confusing aftermath of war, they are stark realists. They demand convincing reasons, and they think through to their own conclusions.

Since the world that they have inherited is definitely sick, they are distrustful of the men and the policies responsible for its condition. They approach the possibility of war by frankly asking the stock military questions of what, when, where, how, and why. A disconcerting directness tempers their ideology. Behind the patriotic call of king and country they suspect an oil field, an investment trust, or a special interest. At what point, they ask, does notional honor leave off and economic advantage begin?

This is our youth of today, a restless and troubled group, groping in the dark for elusive objects which they believe are there yet somehow escape discovery. Political leadership in peace and military leadership in war must recognize the changed and critical qualities of this human material. It is clearly necessary for leaders to provide liberalized control techniques to meet these altered conditions.

For the modern generation has broken irrevocably with the past. They elect courses in college, attend classes on an optional basis, graduate when they master their fields, not when a time contract has expired. Resentful of restraints unless the restraining purpose is plainly justified, they are, nevertheless, a powerful reservoir of military energy capable of being used or wasted by the type of leadership which summons and directs their strength.

In time of peace our Army operates with enlisted volunteers and a small corps of professional officers so precisely trained that their duties and reactions—almost their viewpoints—become automatic. But war submerges the Regular Army in a flood of citizen officers and soldiers unaccustomed, for the most part, to the niceties and conventions of the profession. Hence the military standards and methods of peace necessarily suffer adjustment when subjected to the urgent demands of war.

Our civilian soldier is an amateur and admits it. Brought in to win a war, he is anxious to complete the job and go back home. Saluting, use of the third person in conversation, a meticulous exactness in so many details of his daily life—these things he accepts as the peculiar ritual of a new fraternity in which he has just acquired a visitor's membership. Sometimes his tongue is in his cheek. But in the main he conforms, especially when his problems and his sensibilities are properly appreciated by a wise and reasonable direction.

Too often in the Army is the recruit or the newcomer subjected to a hazing process. His initial impressions, which the proverb says are lasting, are made as difficult and embarrassing as possible. This sadistic practice is supposed to teach a man his place. Generally it convinces him that his place is not the Army, and more frequently it destroys in him the very qualities essential for his effective participation in the action of his group. This has long been true but is more applicable to the American youth of today than ever before.

Loyalty is indispensable to leadership. This keeping of the faith, this pledge of common understanding and trust, works down as well as up. In the realm of human relations *noblesse oblige* is more than a pretty phrase. The superior who demands loyalty from his subordinates, as if he were a tax collector gathering his just due, may seize the shadow, but he will never grasp the substance. He strives to harvest without planting. Things that grow cannot be produced by edict. They thrive only when richly nourished and sympathetically cultivated.

The success of the leader is dependent on the actions of his followers. Without them he is but one weak and ineffective individual, crying alone in the wilderness. If his policies quicken their desires, advance their interests, protect their rights, heighten their pride and self-respect—if they accomplish these things, he is observing the principle of halter leadership, and the result is irresistible. The perfect whole is found to be far greater than the sum of its component parts. The leader's position is safe and sure, for he is raised to his height—which is opportunity for service—and securely held there by the ardent devotion of his co-workers. There is ever a large loop of slack in the halter.

The man with the whip may make his mark too. More often than not he is the familiar, accepted figure in history. Over broken heads and hearts he has climbed to power. In his own mind his objectives justify the means employed as well as the consequences suffered by his followers. But times and people and methods have changed. The man with the whip is definitely archaic, a victim of the social sciences. Either he must modify his philosophy or else preach his doctrine in totalitarian circles where his methods find enforced acceptance.

Observe those led, and the characteristics of the leader are known. "General Lee to the rear," shouted the Confederate defenders at Spotsylvania as they caught sight of their beloved leader directing a counter-attack through the smoke of front-line battle. In this act Lee risked both his personal safety and his reputation. Not every command would tell its general to go back. Some might even volunteer to push him forward. Ordeal by fire is a dangerous test, but a sure one. The epic resistance of the South against overwhelming odds was not made by dugout commanders. Ebbing resources crumpled the armies, but their spirit was never conquered.

Sir John Monash is considered one of the most capable generals produced by the last war. From an obscure beginning he rose to the rank of lieutenant general, commanding an army corps of Australians. One secret of his success may be found in the following account which is taken from his war letters. The Anzacs apparently were having their full share of troubles after landing at Gallipoli, what with Turkish opposition and unfavorable terrain and climate. Your conventional commander, seeking a conventional solution, would have harped on missing buttons, dirty rifles, military courtesy, and violation of uniform regulations. But not Sir John. The moral factor was the important one with him. He writes to his wife:

We allow the men great freedom in dress. I started it and the others followed. You know what "shorts" are. They are khaki overalls cut down so as to finish four inches above the knee, like a Scotsman's trews. They are worn with short underpants and with boots and puttees, look really well, the leg showing from two inches below to four inches above the knee and soon getting as brown as the face and hands. I have dressed like that for some weeks with khaki shirt and no collar or tie.

Of course the men don't fight in that kit, but that is how I allow them to run about in their spare time, and they enjoy it immensely.

The gods of spit and polish would swoon at this, for it is downright heresy. The ancient citadel of soldierly qualities must indeed be crumbling when men dress for comfort instead of appearance, when a general goes without collar and tie. But somehow it seemed to work. Kindliness, thoughtful consideration, sympathetic interest and understanding—these qualities are more often associated with the corps of chaplains than the combat arms. Yet they must have a connection with successful leadership. For General Monash was being mentioned for the command of an army at the time of the Armistice, and the Australians were one of the hardest-hitting armies in the British forces, as German reports attested.

It should be understood that this is no thesis for namby-pamby, wishy-washy sentimentality. There is a time to pray and a time to curse. On occasion a hobnailed kick can advance a faltering skirmish line far better than a stirring appeal to a man's higher nature. Yet these are exceptions proving the rule. They are effective only as they are infrequently used. They are leadership's spare tire, mounted in an emergency when accepted methods have gone flat and there is no opportunity for deliberate, fundamental corrections at the source.

Little is taught of such leadership in our military instruction. We lay great stress on sound strategical and tactical objectives—a frontier, a city, a river, a ridge line. We are interested in *things*. The Army cannot attack until the railroads deliver so many trains of ammunition, so many tons of rock. But morale is assumed to flow constantly as from a spigot. Sometimes it does, and again it doesn't. When the supply of morale is depleted, the stockage of depots and refilling points becomes relatively unimportant. That army cannot win. The spiritual ammunition train is empty.

Our map problems, however, fail to emphasize this truth. No officer student at a military school, heedful of the marking committee, would attack a corps with a single division. But if his force had superb morale and if the enemy had none, any real leader would succeed either on paper or in war, because he had the high courage and the vision to estimate the spiritual as well as the material situation.

It may be difficult to evaluate intangible factors and to establish their coefficient with the physical. But is this any reason for ignoring them altogether, especially when they outweigh so definitely all other considerations? The map-problem room of today becomes the command post of tomorrow. So long as military students are trained to think in terms of numbers and size alone, we shall have an abundance of commanders but no real leaders. For they will have no course in the tactics and technique of moral forces.

Too often and too long has the human factor been allowed to shift for itself. It is in this field more than any other that, by self-inflicted wounds, we weaken our potential power and fail to produce genuine leaders. If we think of psychology at all in military human relations, it is, in most cases, a warped and outmoded psychology which does not fit at all the problems of leadership of today.

In the end, the methods of leadership are good to the exact extent that they encourage human devotion and co-operative response. Nor is there conflict between discipline and morale. Without discipline an army is a mob; without morale it is a hollow shell. Possessing both, it is invincible. Your stereotyped commander will insist on discipline though he lose morale. The true leader of enduring fame seeks rather the spirit of his men, knowing that when he has this he has all.

FIGHTERS MUST FIGHT

By Staff Sergeant (now Captain, U. S. Marine Corps)
Robert W. Gordon

(*1936*)

No one can deny that the soldier would be leaner and harder if he didn't eat so much and worked twice as hard, but that could be said for the civilian as well. Even with our periodic depressions, the United States is the most prosperous country in the world. Since we must seek voluntary recruits from among a people who are used to prosperity, we must put a little of that prosperity on the mess table, on the theory that it is better to have an overfed army than to have no army at all. The first step toward toughening up the Army is to toughen up the moral fiber of the nation as a whole.

Your future recruit is born in an expensive hospital, the bill probably being paid by taxation and charitable contributions. Immediately a bevy of nurses and female relatives start to coddle him. Perhaps his daddy has some of the old Spartan spirit left in him, but let him try to spank the toddler, and his wife divorces him for cruelty and gets the custody of the child. When the boy starts to school he has female teachers. Let one of them spank him, and she is arrested or discharged, or both. The little fellow must never know what it is to suffer pain or be disciplined.

If the family is poor, does little Johnny go out and peddle papers or sweep out the grocery store to help support it? He does not. The family goes on relief, while Johnny goes down to the Y.M.C.A. and listens to a lecture on "Safety First." He wants to live long enough to cash in on the Townsend Plan.

"Security!" "Safety First!" Fiddlesticks! Mankind has always wanted security. When he had none he fought for some. Now he wants it on a silver platter.

Of course everybody isn't like that—yet! The comedian at the local movie may get a laugh instead of the deserved boos when he places a manicured hand on hip and minces across the stage, but the kids still cheer for cowboys and Indians. You can't make sissies of us in one generation.

Let a submarine go into commission, and half the Navy volunteers for it. Let it be sunk with all on board, and the whole Navy will volunteer for duty on the next one. The Shenandoah, Akron, and Macon may crash. Can we get a new crew for the next dirigible? The only serious question is whether we can get enough clerks to handle the applications for the job.

The Army took over the air mail in the worst flying weather we have had for years. Naturally a few planes crashed. Was there a rush of Air Corps officers applying for the Finance Department? Being an Army man, you know that any rush would be the other way.

We still have plenty of young men eager for adventure, but can we promise them any of it? Instead we promise them an education of sorts, a soft job, a fine mess, and plenty of time for bunk fatigue. That being all we have to offer, we naturally get the type of recruit who wants that sort of life. If we offered only hardtack and willy, without a dash of danger for seasoning, we'd get no recruits at all.

Let the Marines go to Nicaragua to stop a revolution, and watch the fine type of men that approach the recruiting sergeant. I know, for I was a Marine recruiting sergeant for seven years. We had the best football team and the only active service to offer. Now there are no more little scraps, and the Marine Corps has decided it doesn't want a first-rate football team. Have you noticed how the leathernecks have lost their strut the last few years?

So you want lean, hard soldiers, do you? Well, the football coach wants lean, hard players. Only eleven men can play at a time, but every boy whose mama will let him, and many whose mamas won't, try out for the team. They'll put in long hours of work on the training field, take bruises and broken bones with a grin, and eat religiously at the training table, all in the faint hope that they can get into the game for a few minutes. Now let the college decide that the poor boys might get hurt. What happens to your players? Do they remain lean and hard? Don't make me laugh!

Soldiers are no different. Stick them in an office or on a bull gang, and they can see no reason for Spartan training. You've got to feed them well and give them time off or they'll desert. After all, a laborer or a clerk can make more money in normal times on the outside. Now give these same men some real soldiering and watch them snap out of it. March them twenty miles with a pack and rifle, feed them on hardtack and corned willy, and they'll like it, if you'll give them a few blanks and let them shoot up those outlined trenches on top of the ridge at the end of the twenty miles. They won't care if they have to pitch their shelter halves in a sea of soupy mud and hike back the next day in the rain, if you'll tell 'em they captured the hill or give 'em hell for not doing it. Now give them picks and shovels and try to march them two miles and listen to them grouse.

Get the idea? Good soldiers are really little boys. They like to play at soldiering, and if the bullets are real they like it even better. If you want soldiers, let them soldier. Give them a snappy uniform so they can strut before the girls when off duty. Promote the best soldier as quickly as you do the best clerk, and transfer him in rank as does the Marine Corps and Navy. Your real soldier doesn't want to settle down on one post for the rest of his life. Put a premium on soldierly virtues instead of Sunday-school goodness. If we don't, the virile Mungies will come over someday and lick our clerks and post-exchange stewards (yes, and associate editors).

Let's be realists. We'll never have a Foreign Legion until we have some Riffs and Berbers to fight; we won't have Sherman's raiders until we decide to march through Georgia again; we won't have a Roman Legion until we have a Gallic war—we won't even have another 29th Infantry until we have some more problems to demonstrate. We have plenty of husky lads right now who are eager to be lean, hard fighters, but they won't work at it until they see a fight in the offing.

Poor food does not make lean, hard fighters. It is campaigning that does that trick. Along with prosperity, Americans have achieved education and independence of thought. Your American soldier will not undergo privation and hardship merely for the sake of proving a faddist's theory. There is no necessity for a poor, scanty ration, and he knows it and will resent it by refusing to enlist or deserting. It may be that our Army is not in the fighting trim that a Spartan might desire, but the remedy lies deeper than "a simplified ration."

INITIATIVE

From an article by MAJOR (now BRIGADIER GENERAL)
RICHARD G. TINDALL

(1937)

TODAY—just as in 1914—the German Army still places the highest emphasis on initiative. However, it trains its subordinates not only to exercise initiative but under what conditions to exercise it.

We, too, recognize the importance of initiative. But mere lip service is not enough and never will be enough. The amount of initiative officers display in war will probably be in direct proportion to the effort made to inculcate it in peacetime training.

Unfortunately, with too many officers the word initiative is still synonymous with abandonment of a mission. Actually the finest examples of initiative are frequently pursuant to a mission. For instance, in a vague situation Von Gronau and his weak IV Reserve Corps, with a flank-protection mission, attacked toward Paris on September 5, 1914. The attack revealed an entire French Army moving east from Paris, and Kluck was warned before it was too late. This was initiative pursuant to the mission. German authorities consider it one of the finest decisions of the World War.

Undoubtedly there will be times when a subordinate will be justified in disregarding the orders of his superior. The difference between initiative and disobedience must be thoroughly understood. It is clearly indicated in a Command and General Staff School publication, extracts from which follow:

Only a radical change in the situation will justify an abandonment of a mission. In such circumstances the following principles will guide the commander in deciding his course of action. A mission will never be departed from in letter or spirit:

(a) So long as the officer who assigned it is present and does not himself alter it.

(b) If the officer who assigned it is not present, so long as there is time to report to him and await a reply without losing an opportunity or endangering the command.

If the above conditions do not exist, a departure from either the spirit or letter is justified if the subordinate who assumes the responsibility bases his decision on some facts which could not be known to the officer who assigned it and if he is satisfied that he is acting as his superior, were he present, would order him to act.

If a subordinate does not depart from the letter of his mission when such a departure is clearly demanded, he will be held responsible for any failure which may ensue.

It would seem to be desirable for our service schools to include among their tactical problems a certain number purposely drawn to illustrate abandonment or adherence to the mission. However, abandonment of the mission should be the exception, not the rule. *If subordinate units have to depart from their missions frequently, it merely means that higher authority is not up to its job and is assigning defective missions.* Let us trust that in war our higher commanders will not always be wrong.

Now although we wish to teach initiative, we certainly can't do much abandoning of missions in peacetime except in problems. What can we do?

One solution might be to emphasize initiative on the part of subordi-

nates in executing the orders of their superiors. This would involve not
only activity by the subordinates but considerable thought, not to mention restraint, on the part of superiors. However, it is something that
can be practiced daily, in peace as in war, in administrative as well as
in tactical matters, and in it there lurks no psychological danger.

And although it may not sound quite as high-powered as the other
kind, the initiative that is the most valuable in war and should be the
most frequent is *initiative within the framework of the mission*.

ROUGH ON THE MAJORS

Editorial by LIEUTENANT COLONEL (now MAJOR GENERAL)
E. F. HARDING

(*1935*)

IN THE July–August number of the *Infantry Journal* and the *Coast
Artillery Journal,* in two of the large-type blurbs that we smart editors
employ with malice aforethought to catch the eye and stimulate the
curiosity of the headline scanners and thus trick them into reading the
whole article, we quoted passages that referred to majors. One read:

WE CAN GET ALONG WITH MEDIOCRE COLONELS AND A FEW
DOWNRIGHT ROTTEN MAJORS, BUT GOD HELP THE ARMY THAT
DOESN'T HAVE GOOD LIEUTENANTS AND CAPTAINS.

And the other:

A CAPTAIN MIGHT POSSESS THE GENIUS OF NAPOLEON, THE
MORAL GRANDEUR OF LEE, AND THE INITIATIVE AND DRIVING
ENERGY OF THEODORE ROOSEVELT, BUT NOT EVEN THE COM-
BINATION OF ALL THESE QUALITIES WOULD SUFFICE TO PRO-
MOTE HIM OVER THE HEAD OF THE MOST MEDIOCRE MAJOR
THAT EVER PASSED THE BUCK.

Coming both in the same issue, it does seem, on first thought, that
we were taking a dirty crack at the majors, but presumably the happy-
go-lucky doughboys didn't take it much to heart, since none wrote in
about it.

Not so with the Coast Artillerymen, for our esteemed contemporary
received several vigorous protests. We quote from one of them:

May I register a complaint about the last issue of the *Journal?* I think you
used too big a type in referring to "rotten majors." It also seems to me that I've
been hearing or reading quite a number of remarks recently to the effect that inefficient field officers do exist in the Army. I think we ought to stop embarrassing
them for a while. It also probably raises too many doubts in the minds of our
junior officers and the rank and file.

The writer is a lieutenant, so his concern for the injured feelings of the allegedly maligned majors is purely impersonal. We admire his spirit. Most lieutenants take great delight in hearing the majors knocked. We have even known of some who, if driven to it, would join the anvil chorus with a right good will. It is refreshing to find one who objects to the practice, notwithstanding the fact that it is a grand old Army custom. We believe, however, that our friend makes too much out of what we prefer to regard as an amusing coincidence.

Coast Artillerymen, of course, have a peculiar psychology; otherwise they wouldn't be in the Coast Artillery. It is therefore quite possible that they are more sensitive than the typical thick-skinned doughboy whose heredity and training have equipped him to "take it." This difference may account for the fact that the Coast Artillery conjured up a derogatory implication from the blurbs while the Infantry just laughed them off.

It goes without saying that we rejoice that none of our Infantry majors took offense. A moment's reflection makes it obvious that none was intended, for there are a lot of majors now, and we think always of our growing circulation. Moreover, we can remember quite well when we were a major and we certainly thought highly of the breed in those days.

". . . AND ASSUME COMMAND THEREOF"

By Stone Borealis

(*1941*)

No two men take over a command in exactly the same way. The canned language of orders runs about like this: "Captain Dustcloud is this date transferred to Company Q and will assume command thereof."

But just how does Captain Dustcloud go about "assuming command thereof"?

First he blows into the orderly room enveloped in a haze of brusque efficiency which somehow conveys the idea he has been sent down to straighten out the outfit. You kind of get the impression he instantly sees a lot of things that need changing and that he thinks Captain Considerate, the former company commander, was perhaps a good fellow but not so hot as a commander.

After a critical look around Dustcloud sits down at his desk—and doesn't like the way the desk light is arranged. So he has that changed.

In the kitchen he tells the mess sergeant to shift the meat block. In the supply room Dustcloud asks Sergeant Noshortage how he runs his temporary receipts. This is changed, too, though it was a system that worked.

Now that he has made his presence felt Captain Dustcloud sits himself down at the desk where the light has been changed to suit him. He is satisfied—with Company Q—he has "assumed command thereof."

Yes, he has. No argument about it; everybody from the first sergeant to the KPs knows Captain Dustcloud is there—but they're not very happy about it.

Captain Considerate's method was different.

He walked into the orderly room, shook hands with the first sergeant, looked around until he saw what was obviously a new organization chart on the wall.

"Sergeant Bustle," he said, "that's a nice-looking chart. It's the kind of thing I like to have."

When he inspected the kitchen Captain Considerate found the coffee was good and he said so out loud. He saw several things he wanted to change later but said nothing about them. There was no hurry.

In the supply room Sergeant Eveready was busy checking out laundry, so Captain Considerate said, "Go ahead with your work, Sergeant. I'll be in to check property tomorrow."

After talking to the first sergeant about the current training program, Considerate assembled all the sergeants in the orderly room. His talk to them lasted about thirty seconds and was something like this:

"I have taken command of this company. It looks like a fine outfit, and I am glad to be here. I expect you to give me the same loyalty and support that I can see you have given your former company commander. For the time being I want you to go ahead just as you have been doing. Later on if there are any changes I want to make I'll let you know. That's all. . . . Thank you."

Both Captain Dustcloud and Captain Considerate have very definitely "assumed command thereof"—but if you were a soldier which one of those two company commanders would you rather have?

SLOW—MEN WORKING

Editorial by LIEUTENANT COLONEL (now MAJOR GENERAL) E. F. HARDING

(*1938*)

Would we not shatter it to bits—and then
Remold it nearer to the Heart's Desire?
OMAR KHAYYÁM.

THE TENTMAKER certainly wasn't thinking of things military when he set down the original of Fitzgerald's much-quoted quatrain, but he might have been. For armies are pyramids of little autocracies, and the head-man in an autocracy is favorably situated to remold any scheme of things. And many of us have a predilection for doing it.

We have all seen the system in operation. A newly assigned captain takes over his company and proceeds forthwith to make it over to con-form to his ideas of what a company ought to be. It may have been a good company before he got it, but it doesn't do things his way. It may still be a good company after he has finished remolding it nearer to his heart's desire, but the period of transition is hard on the troops. It isn't so easy to change fixed habits to conform to the idiosyncrasies of a new boss. And many changes, coming all at once, make for confusion and resentment. If the new boss be impatient, several good noncoms, a bit set in their ways, may lose their stripes in the process of adjustment. The company will survive and after six months or so may be as good as or possibly better than ever. But some excellent features of the preced-ing setup may be missing along with a few high privates who went over the hill.

Substitute majors, colonels, or generals for captains; battalions, regi-ments, or divisions for companies, and we get a similar picture on a larger scale. The same goes for every administrative office that depends upon the co-operation of trained personnel for smooth functioning. Stiff new brooms sweep out much that is useful along with the litter of the previous administration.

Does the foregoing imply that we advocate that a new No. 1 Man's only order for the first year of his assignment should be "Carry on"? Not at all. His first order might well be just that, if his predecessor has been doing a good job, but a few weeks of looking things over will un-cover deficiencies in any organization. Also, the able predecessor, being human, will have overemphasized some things and slighted others. Numerous opportunities for the exercise of the new CO's initiative will pop up in the normal course of events. It will not be necessary for the new skipper to remain a mere passenger for long. Our suggestion is merely that he hold to the course chartered by his predecessor until he is sure where it will take him. He may want to make the former skipper's destination a port of call on the voyage he plans to make.

Nothing we have said here applies to taking over from a certified failure. In that case, a complete overhaul is indicated and the engine may have to be torn down before it can be reconditioned to pull its load. But in these days most of the machinery of the military establishment is functioning well. The chances are that a skilled operator has been tend-ing it, and the new man should be sure that he knows what he is doing before he does much tinkering.

SMARTNESS AND DISCIPLINE

By G. V.

(1937)

Spit and polish got so all important in the twenties and thirties to some commanders that the *Infantry Journal* received dozens of articles about it, mostly against the abuses of it. In the following, G. V. tried to get down to fundamentals on it.

In the articles following this one spit and polish and the soldier's clothing similarly come in for a hammering.

IN ALL the outspoken indignation over excesses of spit and polish that has appeared in various articles and books during the past year or two, one main point has not been emphasized enough. That point, perhaps, can best be put in question form: Just what has a "neat and soldierly appearance" to do with discipline and military ability? Is smartness actually an element of success in war, or would it be possible (as a retired general officer recently suggested) to dress an efficient army in overalls? What basic part of fighting character would we lose if, tomorrow, all polishing of brass should suddenly cease by order?

In the text on training management now used at Benning and in the Army Extension Courses, we find that discipline "is indicated in the individual or unit by smartness of appearance and action; by cleanliness and neatness of dress, equipment, and quarters, and by respect for seniors and the willing execution of orders." Smartness comes first in this list and is doubly emphasized by repetition. But if we make an honest examination of history and weigh the matter squarely, we can only come to one conclusion—neatness and smartness have little to do with winning wars and are actually the most superficial indications of discipline.

Perhaps the toughest, hardest, most efficient military body that the United States has ever had in any war was the army that General William Tecumseh Sherman led from one corner of Georgia to the other, and then—an even more remarkable military feat—from Savannah to Virginia through the supposedly impassable swamps of the Carolinas. That army was also among the most slovenly in appearance that ever answered the bugle—and you cannot except its commander himself from that statement. If any member of that command polished a button or cleaned the slumgullion spots from his blouse front, his comrades looked upon him as a dude. Here and there, perhaps, an officer cut a dash with a bright sash, a gilded saber, or a new hat. But it is safe to say that if we could hold a field inspection of Sherman's army, in the light of our present ideas of discipline quoted above, we could only classify a superb body of fighting men as a rabble.

In fact, that is exactly what Bill Sherman's army looked like when it took part in a triumphant parade in Washington at the close of the war. It had forgotten how to drill, if ever it knew how. It went by in a column of flocks. Its unkempt appearance, even in comparison with other veteran units not noted for their gleaming brilliance, was so remarkable that few historical reports omit mention of it. And there had been plenty of days, too, since Appomattox for haircuts, polish, and scrubbing; but Bill Sherman's men had no use for such frippery. The only indication of their true state of discipline—the spotless bores of their rifles—remained invisible.

What, then, is the true relationship of spit and polish to discipline? It appears at first thought to be simply this: A shiny soldier has obeyed the order to shine; an unkempt soldier has not. The neat soldier is not necessarily a good one because he is neat but because he has played the game; whereas the other has failed to. But is this all?

The neatest soldiers, if we look into the matter carefully, do not put in all the time and care they do on their appearance just because it is required. Except for the occasional man of limited intellect who actually delights in the gloss of shining brass, the neatest soldiers in any unit, taking them as a group, are those who want promotion. They are first-class privates looking for more chevrons. Once they get to be noncoms, it is true, most of them will keep on shining because brass polish is a necessary evil that goes with the job. But sergeants of all grades, in general, do not wear out as many polishing rags in a given time as the upper crust of first-class privates.

Thus a smart appearance may indicate the following things: (1) a perfunctory obedience to standing orders mixed with the desire to look no worse than the next man in ranks, or to keep off extra kitchen police; (2) ambition; (3) the desire to keep a good job; (4) (rarely) a simple but honest love for shining brass, and (5) (still more rarely) a blouse-bursting pride in organization, usually pumped up through artificial (and costly) competition for the "best-company" pennon.

We would lose nothing good if we gave our troops a uniform that required only laundering or dry cleaning to make it presentable, insignia and all. And, if anything, the complete abolishment of Blitz, Brass, and Blanco would raise the discipline of troops and officers, individually and as a whole, to a considerable degree, for reasons pointed out forcibly in other recent articles in these columns.

Before concluding, perhaps it is worth while to ask what relation the frowziness of Bill Sherman's army had to its essential discipline. Would it have fought and marched any better if it had been smarter? No, it wouldn't. There were too many things to be done to waste time on close-order drill as such and on cleaning off the spots and tarnish. Time for doing such things could be taken only from time better used in rest and relaxation. And that would only have detracted from discipline.

There are sound reasons, of course, for not going the whole hog to the point of holding up slovenliness as a virtue. The fact that cleanliness and health are related is one. The fact that we are in the public eye in time of peace is another. But smartness of appearance is nevertheless an inadequate basis for judging military discipline. At Chancellorsville the XI Corps, rated as best largely on externals, broke and ran from the field, while many another less highly polished Union outfit fought like the devil's own.

Isn't it time, then, to redefine military discipline by placing its more important components ahead of smartness? In the next war there will be little enough chance for smartness, however keen we may be for it.

The foregoing article brought in a good many replies, mainly from those who disagreed with the writer and thought that spit and polish makes fighting soldiers. One correspondent pointed out a couple of historical errors. G. V. was given a chance at rebuttal as follows:

TRAMP, TRAMP, TRAMP

By G. V.

(1938)

Although six months have passed since the appearance of G. V.'s one-page article "Smartness and Discipline" (July–August 1937), the controversy he started still goes on. The latest contributions to it are a letter in retraction and rebuttal from the author and a cerebration from a true believer in the pipe-clay tradition. We print these as the closing arguments in the case.

SIR:

I seem to have stepped straight into it when I desecrated the memory of Sherman's splendid army by saying that it couldn't pass by in review. For two successive issues you have let others take it out on me, and now I ask to have my turn again.

First I admit that I was wrong about the "column of flocks" at the Grand Review. I trusted my memory and it betrayed me. What I should have written was that the Grand Review was the one Grand Exception—probably the only time that Sherman's troops ever presented anything approaching a proper parade appearance. But they did march well that day, and that despite the fact that they were treading roses underfoot. One observer said of them, "They march like the lords of the world." It was not so much their trimness as their "proud, rolling, swinging step," as Lloyd Lewis puts it in *Sherman, Fighting Prophet*. But no matter what Sherman wrote in later years in his memoirs, as the review began he was afraid they wouldn't be able to "swing into it." But they did. An army like that could do anything.

I might add that General Sherman himself was resplendent in uniform that day, too, and covered with roses. His customary uniform on campaign had included a battered cap, a wrinkled blouse, baggy trousers, low shoes, and one spur. And I still refuse to believe that he would have been any finer commander if he had worn boots of Circassian leather polished three times a day. Indeed, he would probably have been a worse general—for the boots might have taken his mind off his business because they hurt his feet.

But lest I show partiality for the North, or seem to concede that my whole theory was wrong, let me quote briefly from Henderson's *Stonewall Jackson:*

> The eye that lingers lovingly on glittering buttons and spotless belts would have turned away in disdain from Jackson's soldiers. There was nothing bright about them but their rifles. They were as badly dressed, and with as little regard for uniformity, as the defenders of Torres Vedras or the army of Italy in 1796. Like Wellington and Napoleon, the Confederate generals cared very little what their soldiers wore so long as they did their duty. Least of all can one imagine Stonewall Jackson exercising his mind as to the cut of a tunic or the polish of a buckle. The only standing order in the English army of the peninsula which referred to dress forbade the wearing of the enemy's uniform . . . fine feathers, though they may have their uses, are hardly essential to efficiency in the field. . . .

And so I say again that brass polish, cleaning fluid, and the steam of a tailor's pressing machine are unstable and entirely secondary bases for true discipline.

LANGUAGE OF THE LEADER

By Colonel E. L. Munson, Jr.

> The one recently written book on leadership for Army men when war began was *Leadership for American Army Leaders,* by Colonel Munson, most of which ran serially in the *Infantry Journal* during 1941. The author's purpose was to tell the new officers and noncommissioned officers in a brief space the principles and practices of leadership. The book has been used in many Army schools as a text.

Language, a component of manner, is another of the outward marks by which a leader can be judged. What he says and the forms of expression he uses give much information of his mental state or the attitude behind it.

The words the leader uses to his men should largely be chosen for the thought or purpose he wants to express. Particularly when he wants to put something over emphatically should his words be short, clear in their meaning, and understandable to the man he is addressing. High-flung, ten-dollar words or technical language are meaningless to the mind of a man who may never have heard the words. This does not mean, however, that a leader must speak in words of one syllable. In the Army of today he will seldom find uncultivated minds so lacking in ordinary comprehension that he will be justified in using the language he would use, in effect, to children. All he needs to do is to speak plainly and simply, and if he must use terms which he thinks the man he is talking to may not clearly understand, then he should make sure the meaning of these terms is understood, even if the terms demand a full and patiently given explanation.

An officer should never make the mistake of stooping to the vulgar or the illiterate, even if such speech is the normal talk of the particular men he is directing. But this does not mean that he must make any effort to "talk like a book," or that he should avoid good, plain, col-loquial speech. In fact, this kind of speech will usually put his meaning over much better than stiffer and more formal speech. It is astonishing how men of even considerable intelligence have difficulty in understand-ing speech not put in ordinary terms. There is, at the same time, no need to be ungrammatical or to make much use of slang except where a word of slang may convey the meaning more concisely and vividly than any other term. This is particularly true if within the leader's unit some slang term or nickname is in constant use. What particular good does it do to speak of "weapons carriers" if they are known to every man as "jeeps"? And what term puts over the idea better to troops than the word "chow"? Indeed, for some terms of slang in constant use there are no adequate substitutes.

Sentences should be short, uninvolved, and incisive. They should be positive and direct, not uncertain, inconclusive, or negative. To say, for example, "I'm sure you can do it," "You're just the man to do it," "There must be a way—I know you can find it," produces confidence, self-reliance, and determination. But such language as, "Maybe you can do it," "See if you can't do it," "I doubt if you can do it—but go ahead and try," brings doubt and wavering.

Cursing and profanity have always been common in armies. Whether this is caused by excess energy pent up by military restrictions, by the absence of the tempering influence of women, or by the mistaken idea that it is the sign of a he-man is immaterial. Ignoring purely ethical reasons, immoderate language habitually used toward subordinates almost always produces unfavorable results both in the individual and the unit.

One of George Washington's first general orders was an effort to curb loose language. Such language should certainly be kept governed, at least to the extent of not allowing it in the presence of officers. For if a leader lets his men run wild in this respect—if he permits the use of any language, however obscene—a lack of general control is apt to become taken for granted.

Yet here, too, judgment is required. A leader can overdo the thing and thus detract from his leadership if he harps continually on the subject and draws the line of niceness in language too closely. There are many situations in such an uncertain activity of man as warfare that bear strongly upon the emotions. A leader may well overlook the blowing off of steam whenever the occasion seems to warrant it. And it often may seem to in actual war. After all, a soldier is first of all things a man who fights, and if there is a traditional language of war he can be expected to use it at times. George Washington did, despite his first general order.

To curse any man himself is usually to affront him through his realization of the intent to insult. Sometimes such intent is modified or shown to be absent by manner. Then, too, there are men whose use of profanity is so habitual that it is recognized as entirely impersonal. But these are the exceptions. To permit loose language by subordinate leaders is to risk friction, resentment, quarreling—even insubordination.

Swearing at men by their superiors is bitterly resented. They are not only affronted; they are humiliated, for their self-respect has been impaired unless they retaliate. Since in the military service retaliation is impossible, they feel, and rightly so, that the superior has taken an unfair advantage of his authority. They may brood over the insult, alone or with friends. If hot-tempered, they may commit the serious offenses of disobedience or assault. At the least, the superior produces sullenness and animosity among his subordinates. And often he also produces a state of mind in which the only escape from a seemingly intolerable situation appears to be absence without leave or desertion.

The same thing applies to any immoderate language. It does not necessarily have to be actual cursing at men to arouse their antagonism and lose in great measure their esteem and admiration for their leader. An actual case in point is that of a company commander who, dissatisfied with the appearance of his company at Saturday inspection, drew them up in front of barracks and proceeded to inform them in no uncertain terms, without, however, using actual profanity, that the whole company was "lousy" in appearance. To add emphasis, this commander went on to say in his harangue, "And any man who won't properly clean up for Saturday inspection is a yellow-bellied Bolshevik."

Even though the company had often heard similar language from this particular commander, the words he used this time were taken as a direct insult by practically every man in the company, although they were not actually meant as such but were simply spoken in haste and ill temper. The result was that certain reponsible noncommissioned officers of the company were so disturbed over the state of affairs that they went to the regimental commander and reported the matter, and it naturally took all the tact in the world on the part of the regimental commander to straighten the situation out—a thing he managed to succeed in doing without particular injury to what was left of the leadership of the company commander.

This example brings out another important point about language used toward subordinates. It is not likely that there will ever be a unit in our Army or any other which will deserve a wholesale reprimand. In the company referred to above only some fifteen or sixteen men out of sixty-odd were picked up at the inspection as not having properly prepared for it. Yet the whole unit was subjected to the ranting of its commander. There were plenty of fine men in that unit, none of whom deserved criticism or blame. There is nothing better calculated to reduce the state of morale than just such wholesale criticism and wholesale punishments following it. Nothing creates resentment so readily.

Likewise, the "bawling out" of a man or men is resented as being a personal attack. It is, in fact, more often an expression of anger than a correction. The more or less impersonal point at issue is lost, and the matter becomes a mental clash between individuals.

Again, to reprimand a subordinate leader before his men lowers his prestige and correspondingly increases his resentment. It is hard to imagine any circumstances, excepting in combat when lives are at stake, when such treatment is justifiable.

Indeed, if violent language ever has any basis for use, that use should be reserved for extreme emergency—the emergency of extreme danger, of the battlefield. A tongue lashing may then have a stimulating and steadying effect which is lost if such speech is habitual.

Sarcasm or irony does not necessarily convey an insult, for the manner in which it is spoken shows the intent. Its wittiness sometimes lacks the sting of reproof, yet drives home the lesson. It is useful with some types of men, but it must be employed with care; it must not become habitual, and it must never have the apparent purpose of causing humiliation.

There are many men to whom sarcasm or irony is not readily apparent as such, and with these men it tends sooner or later to create a kind of bewildered resentment. Such a man is never quite sure what his leader means. Again, heavy sarcasm habitually used soon creates a general resentment because men feel that their leader is taking advantage of his position to be sarcastic. Even a bantering tone should not be used habitually. And when a leader makes a joke of something a subordinate does, as he occasionally may do to lighten a serious or tiring situation or otherwise cheer the spirits of his men, he should always try not to do so in a way that will hurt the feelings of the man himself.

Too much wisecracking on the part of the leader will also inevitably result in wisecrack replies from his troops. The American soldier is too used to that kind of talk to resist coming back with it if he thinks he can get away with it. He will have reason to think he can get away with it if he is habitually on the receiving end of such remarks. At the same time, any wise leader will know that in certain circumstances a certain amount of joking and wisecracking is what the situation calls for. It is good when there is discouragement in the air. A flash of humor helps at a time when exhausted troops must be called upon for another effort. It tends to give confidence in any time of stress. Indeed, it is often the American way of implying sympathy and understanding and even co-operation in the midst of difficulty.

LEADERSHIP

By a subcommittee of the National Research Council

The article that follows appeared early in 1943. It represents the combined thought of a number of the leading psychologists of the United States on military leadership prepared under the direction of a subcommittee of the National Research Council, with some assistance from Army men. It is a chapter from *Psychology for the Fighting Man,* an *Infantry Journal* book prepared under the same direction.

You can't boss a brick.

You can't even boss a dog unless the dog has been trained to obey and has formed habits of responding to commands. And before you can boss him you must know what commands he will respond to. The famous Seeing-Eye dogs can do wonderful things to aid the blind, but both dog and master must first go through a period of training.

Authority is not power. No amount of legal authority over the grizzly bears of British Columbia would enable you to get yourself obeyed by them out in the woods.

Men can be commanded only after they have acquired habits of obeying, and after their leader has learned to give them the commands that make these habits work. All successful leadership thus depends on the habits of those who are to be led.

The officer standing before his men is limited in the direct exercise of his authority by what the troops are able to get through their eyes and ears. And what the men do, in response to what they see and hear the officer do and say, is just exactly what their previous training and their previous experience with him insure that they will do.

When authority is not obeyed the fault may lie in the manner or speech of the leader, or else it may be that the men are in need of basic training.

It is often said that a good leader knows how to handle his men. Actually, however, it is not possible for any leader to *handle* men. It is himself that he handles. Then the men react to his deportment. And the way in which they react depends, in turn, upon their habits of thought and action.

DISCIPLINE

In an army much of this training on which leadership depends is established by discipline. Discipline is training in the right habits of attention and obedience. Without such habits we might have a crowd or a mob, but not an army.

It is quite possible to lead a mob, yet such leadership is uncertain, depending largely on the accidents of personal appearance and on fortunate timing. In an army, however, there have to be many leaders of many ranks, and they have to be interchangeable. If a leader is killed another must be ready to take his place and lead his men. And the men who lose a leader must be ready to follow without question the commands of a stranger.

Training in discipline is training in giving attention and obedience to authority, regardless of individual personality. That is why armies are uniformed, why the insignia of rank are standardized. Also, it is why commands and the manner of giving them are fixed by regulations. Practice in discipline makes it second nature for the soldier to give attention to the insignia of rank and grade, and obedience to commands.

LEARNING OBEDIENCE

The first requisite of command is attention.

What a soldier does not see or hear he cannot obey. Attention means stopping all activity that interferes with looking and listening.

If this attention did not become second nature through long practice, an Army leader would, in an emergency, have to compete for attention— by shouting or gesticulating. That would not do—he might not succeed.

So discipline is calculated to insure this preliminary attention by placing certain restrictions on behavior whenever an officer is present or enters the scene. If loud arguments or profanity or occupation with the soldier's own affairs were permitted to occur in the presence of an officer, then the soldier would learn to disregard the officer, and the officer would lose his ability to command attention and thus his ability to command at all.

If, on the other hand, the presence or arrival of an officer is always the signal to the soldier to come to attention, or, in combat, to pay attention, then no confusion of battle or distraction of pain or noise or close danger can cause a soldier to ignore his officer or his command.

What men do invariably and repeatedly is finally drilled into them—becomes for them second nature. They learn to perform acts or maneuvers in response to command or order because the command or order has always been accompanied by the act and the act by the command.

Mere lecturing never trains men in action. At best it makes them learn mere word sequences, except when the listeners already know enough about the required action to perform it in imagination. Learning something new, in other words, requires participation. You don't learn to swim by taking a correspondence course.

Unfortunately, bad habits, as well as good, can be learned. If, on a spoken command, men do not respond, then they are learning not to respond. Whenever they are ordered to do something they cannot do they are learning to disobey. Military manuals embody this fact in a rule: *Never give a command that you do not expect to be obeyed.*

Thus a young leader, when he finds himself so situated that his command might be disregarded, must refrain from giving it. He must try first to change the situation, to capture attention, or he must merely wait until he is reasonably certain that, when he gives his order, it will indeed be obeyed.

So attention is the first requisite of command, and practice is the second. The leader must see to it that his men get the right kind of practice. He must never give conflicting orders. He must give only directions that can be executed and then he must see to it that they are executed. Otherwise he loses his own power of command, and discipline is broken down among his men.

THE LEADER

Through training in discipline the Army prepares its men to carry out its ultimate missions under command and according to plan. Leadership would be uncertain without this discipline.

But a good leader does not depend solely on the authority that discipline gives him as an officer or noncom, for good leadership goes far beyond discipline. A good, experienced leader inspires respect, confidence, and loyalty in his subordinates, all of which enable him to get from his men performance far above what a new leader could command.

In this the leader can rely on the generous co-operation of his men, for men have a natural longing to respect and have affection for their leaders. They want to be proud of their officers and noncommissioned officers, just as they want to be proud of their unit and their branch of the service.

So soldiers look to an officer for that sort of bearing and behavior that leads to his being known as a "grand old man." They don't necessarily want him to be a model of all the virtues; they can forgive him for bursts of temper, for occasional arbitrary commands, for a rare show of weakness—even for tears over the loss of a friend. What they do demand in him is unfailing loyalty to duty and to his men—and the same sort of respect and confidence that the leader expects to receive.

When the new Army was first being formed, many of the officers had had little experience in command. They had learned the words—were capable of giving directions and instructions—but they had learned neither the action nor manner that goes with command. A young officer would utter an order, but his manner would betray his lack of confidence. This uncertainty was in effect a signal for not carrying the order out promptly and effectively as military orders must be carried out. All our lives we have depended on the manner and behavior of others, as well as on their speech, to know what was in their minds. Army discipline cannot change human nature.

What a soldier does in response to a leader's command depends not only on the words spoken by the leader but also upon the way in which they are said—it depends upon everything the soldier sees and hears.

The leader's facial expression, his movements, his posture, and the firmness or quaver in his voice all have their effects. And these effects may completely nullify the effect of the spoken command.

A leader is actually giving conflicting orders if his uncertain manner hints that he does not expect obedience or that he thinks he may not be obeyed.

Although it is possible for the new leader who has lacked experience to imitate the manner and tone of wiser leaders around him, only practice in command develops the appropriate manner and tone.

A good officer or noncom ought to have many imitators of his effective style, yet not of his irrelevant mannerisms. It is hard to keep the two distinct. Every man, unfortunately, forms and keeps many useless habits in gesturing, grimacing, and manipulating. It is not these that should be imitated, but his habits of direct address, clear speech, military manner, confident air, enthusiastic interest, friendliness mixed with reserve both in command and greeting.

Lack of a confident manner inevitably interferes with command. So also may a manner that betrays indecision, for men respond to the signs of indecision by withholding or delaying action. The rule is that a leader should make up his mind and arrive at the decision *before* he gives orders. When he confronts his men he must be ready to commit himself to this course or that. Men will accept assurance for competence, and they want competence in a leader.

A judge in a high court recently heard one of the trial lawyers say: "If the Court is in doubt . . ." The judge rapped the bench and said: "This Court may be occasionally in error, but it is never in doubt." It is the business of a judge to decide cases. No matter how evenly the issue is balanced and no matter how much trouble and time is required for him to reach a decision, the decision, once given, must appear final.

The leader of soldiers finds himself in the same position. On him depends the direction of men's actions. That direction must never be ambiguous. Always it must be clearly indicated.

What Soldiers Think of Leaders

For the first time in the history of armies, the Army of the United States has undertaken to find out what its enlisted personnel think about a large number of things important to the Army.

Some thousands of soldiers have been interviewed at length, and one of the subjects about which they were questioned is Army leadership. What the soldiers said makes it very clear that the quality of leadership in an army is the most important single determiner of morale and performance. The relationship between men and officers, commissioned and noncommissioned, determines the fighting spirit of an army quite as much as the ability of the soldiers to take training does.

In fact, it turns out that these human relations are much more important to morale than beefsteak, warm socks, ball games, and vaudeville shows, or what the men believe about war. These men mentioned seventy-seven features of Army life as definitely associated with morale, and, of the twenty most closely related to morale, sixteen have to do with man-officer relations.

What the men think of their leaders is, then, of the utmost importance to the Army and to the successful prosecution of the war.

Roughly, in the order of their association with good leadership in the minds of the enlisted men, are the following points:

(1) Ability. Competence comes first. The good officer must know his stuff, for on this depends the men's confidence in his leadership.

(2) Next to ability is interest in the welfare of the soldier. The officer who can be trusted to help the soldier in time of need, or who would be accessible for personal advice, is a good officer.

(3) "Promptness in making decisions" is next.

(4) "Good teacher or instructor" follows. The leader who has the patience and the ability to make things clear to the men under him is valued for that reason.

(5) "Judgment," "common sense," and the ability to get things done follow next in order.

(6) The good leader does not "boss you around when there is no good reason for it." Soldiers dislike an officer who throws his rank around, who tests his own authority continually. They sense that he is not sure of himself.

(7) "The man who tells you when you have done a good job" rates well as a leader. Failure in commendation is a common complaint among men in the ranks. The best incentive to good work is the prospect that it will be noticed and remembered by the leader.

(8) Physical strength and good build come next.

(9) "Good education," "sense of humor," and "guts or courage" follow in that order.

(10) Impartiality is next. Leaders who do not "save the dirty jobs for the fellows they don't like" are valued. The good leader is fair to all his command.

(11) Next in importance is industry. Leaders who "do as little work as they can get away with" are not respected by the enlisted men.

(12) When an officer "gives orders in such a way that you know clearly what to do," that, too, is a mark of merit as a leader. Soldiers also like an officer with a "clear, strong voice."

The remaining qualities which the soldiers mentioned came toward the bottom of the list. They are undoubtedly related to good leadership, but they are less important. Not "hot-tempered," do not "drive you too hard," "keep promises," "the kind of fellows you could have a good time with," "not too proud of their rank" are all characteristics which some men want in their leaders, but there is no general agreement about them. Many leaders are considered good in spite of failure on these points.

The chief things a man wants from a leader are, thus, competence and interest in his welfare.

The orders of a man who does not know his stuff cannot be depended on. They are subject to change and countermand. An incompetent leader teaches caution and hesitation in following his lead. He becomes a signal for lack of action on the part of the soldier.

Indecision in a leader has the same effect on a soldier as ignorance has. No soldier can follow a leader who is uncertain which way to turn. The essential quality of any leader is to take the lead and show the direction—quickly, clearly, emphatically, and with enthusiasm. Without these qualities a man is not even a good leader for his hunting dog.

The Role of the Soldier

Part of what makes a man a good soldier is his own adoption of the soldier's role. He comes to think and speak of himself as a soldier. He is progressing in military training when he stops thinking of himself as a plumber or a salesman who is now in the Army and begins to regard himself as an infantryman or an artilleryman or a tank man.

What a man thinks of himself affects his behavior. The rail straightener—the skilled worker who runs the machine that straightens railroad rails—

is one man when he thinks of himself with pride as a rail straightener. He becomes another when he begins, as he may, to regard himself as a mere "wage slave." The rail straightener takes pride in his work, does a good job, is happy. The "wage slave" lets crooked rails get by because he doesn't care. In the same way, the soldier who thinks proudly of himself as a soldier is doing a service to both himself and the Army.

Certain forms of punishment, public disgrace, ridicule, all disturb the role of the soldier and may lessen or destroy his usefulness to the Army and his amenability to leadership. The noncommissioned or commissioned officer who rides one of his men in such a manner as to make him doubt his own value as a soldier is shattering the man's best motive for good performance. The senior leader who reprimands a junior in the presence of his men reduces that junior's value to the Army.

Good leadership, on the other hand, causes men to build up, each for himself, a particular role—a specialty. It means a great deal to a man to take pride in being a soldier and in being a sharpshooter, an aviation mechanic, a truck driver, a cook, or a radio operator. Competent leaders criticize a poor piece of work, condemn a mistake, but take care never to make a soldier feel he is a failure in his job. When a man has accepted his leader's statement that he is "no soldier," then indeed he falls back to perfunctory work and the mere effort to keep out of trouble.

When a soldier begins to regard himself as being a part of his unit and when his job has become part of his role, then teamwork is enormously improved. The soldier who thinks of himself as only a private, temporarily on this or that assignment, is a different man from the soldier who thinks of himself as a necessary member of his outfit. Good leadership always takes advantage of this essential of teamwork and common effort.

The leader's easiest and most important contribution to the personal recognition that the soldier needs is the use of the soldier's name in addressing him. When an officer is unable to call his men by name there can be no chance that a man's good performance will be noticed and remembered. It is one of the first duties of a company officer to make clear to his men that he knows each of them.

A leader need not always speak of specific good performances. It is often enough for him to make it clear that he saw the good performance. Continuous public commendation of one man may put that man at a disadvantage with the others and have a bad effect on them. Public praise should be reserved for important and occasional performances.

COMPLAINTS

Soldiers are notorious gripers, and the griping may be useful not merely because it lets off steam but because it gives valuable information to the leader ready to profit by it. Only the smug or the incompetent leader dismisses complaints because they are common.

A collection of soldier comments on noncommissioned and commissioned leaders offers some food for reflection. Here is a selected batch of confidentially treated opinions expressed by a number of soldiers early in the war:

"This Army can't be driven; it must be led."

"Break up the old Army noncom clique and put advancement on a merit basis."

"Officers bluff too much."

"Let noncoms be chosen for what they know, not whom they know."

"Our first lieutenant is dominated by the first sergeant."

"No reward for good work; old soldiers learn never to volunteer for anything."

"They treat us like children."

"When an officer tells his men he doesn't like the Army any more than we do, he's not the one I look to."

". . . instead of changing his mind every few minutes. . . ."

". . . should take a little interest in what we eat. . . ."

". . . give us some idea of what's going on in maneuvers."

For similar reasons no single successful set of questions has ever been devised to assess leadership in an interview. The competent judge adapts his questioning to the individual candidate, knowing when to discard one answer and when to give another much weight.

This much, however, is known. Although young men can make excellent leaders, leadership develops with experience. Higher standards should, therefore, be set for older men. The man of thirty who is only just as good as the man of twenty-two is not going to improve as rapidly as his younger competitor. It has taken the older man longer to get where he is and it will take him longer to make the next advance.

There is one source of information about leadership which the Army has too often overlooked. It is possible to get the judgments of subordinates about a superior. They know whether the superior is a good leader or not, and for the most part subordinates do not grudge honest appreciation to a superior. If the leader has the loyalty of his men, they will want to express it. The use of estimates by subordinates is generally supposed not to be conducive to good discipline, but that objection lacks force when the manner of getting the estimates is the proper one.

It is known, moreover, that the men of a platoon can size each other up effectively, can pick the men who deserve advancement more consistently than the leaders can. The men know competence when they see it.

Thus it appears that the officer who fails to find out quietly the opinions of his subordinates when he is selecting a man for promotion is overlooking a valid source of information, one that is, in the long run, far more accurate than his own judgment. For this reason a good leader always has an advantage in picking potential leaders, because the good leader has the loyalty and confidence of his men. He can get their judgments of one another without jeopardizing discipline.

LEADERSHIP CAN BE LEARNED

There are no born leaders. All leadership is based on learning how to deal with men. Nearly all leaders improve after they have had experience in command. Some improve faster than others, and some continue to improve while others do not.

Consider the qualities which enlisted men believe important in leaders. The first is competence and ability. Competence is based on learning. The good leader has learned his job thoroughly. His men can trust him to know what he is doing. He knows not only what he learned in his training courses, but he has kept up to date. If he is an artilleryman he knows how the Germans use artillery and what guns they have. The rule is a simple one: *Know your stuff.*

Second to competence is the officer's interest in the soldier as a man, a demonstrated interest that gives the soldier confidence that, when he stands hardship or is in trouble, the hardship is a necessary part of the job and his troubles give his officer concern. Every man can by practice improve his skill in human understanding and increase his repertoire of actions that demonstrate interest in others. The rule here is less simple. It is: *Know your men and show it.* Know their names, their history, their weaknesses, their good points, their morale. Begin by studying their qualification cards.

Decisiveness is a skill harder to acquire. But it can with attention be cultivated. When you have a hard choice, remember you do not usually have to make a snap judgment. Careful consideration—weighing the merits of alternate courses—is not indecision. Your men will respect your judgment even more if you reserve decision until you are in possession of all the facts necessary for a wise choice. Do not set up a "council of war" to pass on things by vote; *you are the leader.* But seek advice when you need it, and do not hesitate to call on your subordinates for counsel if they are qualified to give it. *But choose your course before you give your orders.*

Probably only experience, together with genuine interest in other men, makes a good teacher. But there are many rules for good teaching that may help. One of them is: Remember that men learn to do by doing. Lectures are only the embroidery on training. It is actual performance that does the work.

Another suggestion to the leader is: Remember, when men do not understand you, *that is your fault*. You must talk their language—plain language. If you cannot express yourself clearly it may be because you do not understand the subject well yourself. Think things through carefully before you try to explain.

A leader, then, to be worthy in the eyes of his men, would do well to follow these commands:

(1) Be competent.
(2) Be loyal to your men as well as to your country and Army.
(3) Know your men, understand them, love them, be proud of them.
(4) Accept responsibility and give clear, decisive orders.
(5) Teach your men by putting them through the necessary action.
(6) Give only necessary orders, but—
(7) Get things done.
(8) Be fair.
(9) Work hard.
(10) Remember that a leader is a symbol. Men need to respect and trust you —don't let them down.

AN ALL–TIME COMMAND TEAM

By Lieutenant Colonel (now Colonel) George L. Simpson

(*1937*)

THE SOUND of the last cheer has scarcely died away before the football experts are feverishly at work compiling lists of All-Star teams. The critical equipment of many of these "experts" consists largely of enthusiasm and enjoyment of the game. A like urge impels me to hand-pick an All-Time corps command and staff. To those who object to my selections the answer is: I still like 'em.

My commanding general is Frederick the Great. Though self-assured, he was no egotist. He welcomed advice, but, unlike many another great soldier, he readily recognized the difference between good and bad counsel. Frederick never kidded himself into believing that he could conquer Russia, as did Napoleon. He was a strong disciplinarian and without Lee's weakness of excessive gentleness. In keeping the politicians lined up at home he went Hannibal one better. His strategy was of the best. He was a winner.

The berth as chief of staff goes to Generalfeldmarschall Alfred, Graf von Schlieffen. While the count's battle record is not so imposing as that of some of the others, I believe he would be able to work more harmoniously with the great Frederick than any other All-Timer.

Since Moltke the First was the best personnel procurement agent of them all, and a great soldier as well, he becomes G-1. He could be depended upon to give good advice.

His unexcelled ability for collecting enemy information and his superlative deductions make Lee my G-2. His capacity for winning the co-operation of others—especially subordinates—clinches the selection. The South will send no orchids for this choice, for to them Lee is the greatest general of all time and should have been nominated for the post of headman. But Lee's too-great intellect, his lack of ruthlessness, his inclination to listen to long-winded opinions of lesser lights with established weaknesses—these lovable shortcomings let him out.

In addition to many other qualifications a G-3 must own a disciplined, creative mind, one that can adapt itself to the ideas of others while it improves them in detail. This single capacity is rarer than skyscrapers on an Army post. But there is one man who had it. On this staff Bourcet is G-3.

Comes William Tecumseh Sherman as G-4. If you do not believe that this soldier's every movement showed his first consideration was logistics, take a trip to Georgia and speak with the old-timers.

For his statesmanlike qualities and his masterful use of the third person, Julius Caesar is awarded the position of adjutant general.

Our inspector must be a soldier who is tactful and understanding, an inspiration to those inspected rather than an arouser of red wrath in the breasts of the underlings. Meet De Guibert, inspector of the All-Star Corps.

Caulaincourt has proved that he can plead a cause. Hands down, he becomes judge advocate.

A careful, conscientious man who looked after the interests of his clients and who could, in addition, procure money, was Alcibiades, the ward of Pericles, first choice for finance officer.

For reasons that are obvious Clausewitz has been given the berth of chemical officer.

While I duck the flying missiles and avoid as best I may the wrath to come, I give you as our fightingest parson and chaplain: Mohammed.

Stonewall Jackson used artillery to better advantage than any other great military leader. He is nominated as chief of artillery.

Picking an air officer is not at all difficult. Baron von Richthofen wins the post without a struggle.

In the last war the Germans were the cleverest in the operation of railways, the canny use of mines and demolitions, and the regulation of traffic. For this and other reasons the engineer officer on this twin-six staff is Ludendorff.

There was a soldier who had good communications several centuries before the telegraph, the telephone, and the radio. His name was Scipio, called Africanus, and he is the signal officer.

Our own dapper, highly polished, and hard-boiled Winfield Scott is provost marshal. No lead-footed doughboys with unbuttoned blouses would wander about for long with old Fuss and Feathers on the job. And after the first day or so traffic would move expeditiously on white side-walled tires, come rain, come snow.

Our record for feeding our soldiers during the World War may be largely credited to Harbord. He gets the job of quartermaster.

During the World War the British excelled in their evacuation system, hospital trains, and hospitals. Whoever ran their Medical Department during the last fracas is my surgeon.

Ordnance officer is Gustavus Adolphus. It would be hard to gainsay his ability to recognize the value of new weapons at once and to change his tactics to suit them without a backward glance.

I'm attaching to my corps a cavalry division reinforced by a mechanized regiment. The commander of the cavalry is Oliver Cromwell, for he above all others was unhampered by tradition and had initiative and capability to spare. For subordinate commanders of the horsed regiments I allot Ashby, T. E. Lawrence, and Forrest; the mechanized regiment goes to Jeb Stuart.

They tell us at Leavenworth that a good tank commander has qualifications similar to those of a good leader of cavalry. To those who remember the fine job of crashing through and mopping up that was done at Cannae, my choice of the hook-nosed Hasdrubal, brother of Hannibal, as commander of the attached tank regiment will come as no surprise.

I shall announce my division commanders and then I am through. All-Timer Napoleon Bonaparte gets the 1st Division, Wellington the 2d, and Hannibal the 3d. These three fall just a little short of the qualifications I require of corps commanders. But I am the first to admit that they missed the three-star job by merely a hair.

To those who disagree I can only say: Trot out *your* corps, and name your ground. If, at the conclusion of hostilities, my politicians are not showing your politicians where to sign on the dotted line, I'll buy a round of drinks.

An All-Time Corps Command and Staff

Commanding General .... Frederick the Great
Chief of Staff .... Alfred, Graf von Schlieffen
G-1 .... Helmuth Carl Bernhard, Graf von Moltke
G-2 .... Robert Edward Lee
G-3 .... Pierre de Bourcet
G-4 .... William Tecumseh Sherman
Adjutant General .... Gaius Julius Caesar
Inspector .... Jacques Antoine Hippolyte, Comte de Guibert

Judge Advocate .... Armand Augustin Louis, Marquis de Caulaincourt
Finance Officer .... Alcibiades
Chemical Officer .... Carl von Clausewitz
Chaplain .... Mohammed
Chief of Artillery .... Thomas Jonathan Jackson
Air Officer .... Mannfred, Baron von Richthofen
Engineer .... Erich Ludendorff
Signal Officer .... Publius Cornelius Scipio Africanus Major
Provost Marshal .... Winfield Scott
Quartermaster .... James Guthrie Harbord
Surgeon .... Surgeon, British Expeditionary Forces, 1914
Ordnance Officer .... Gustavus Adolphus
CG, Attached Cavalry Division .... Oliver Cromwell
CG, 1st Division .... Napoleon Bonaparte
CG, 2d Division .... Arthur Wellesley, Duke of Wellington
CG, 3d Division .... Hannibal

WEST POINT[1]

> *O Spartan Woman, I have peered behind*
> *Your stoic pose and found the mother there*
> *At last; the proud gray eyes, the cool gray hair,*
> *The tender face a hundred years have lined*
> *With sorrow for your still, straight sons returned*
> *Upon their blameless shields; the quiet pride*
> *That they had lived by you, went forth, and died*
> *The Doric way. Gray Mother, they have earned*
> *Those shields and having justified the trust*
> *You placed in them, they come again to live*
> *And breathe as part of you. Today you give*
> *A burnished shield to me, to guard from rust . . .*
> *To hold before my heart . . . and bid me go.*
> *Stern Spartan, I salute you . . . but I know!*

LIEUTENANT (NOW COLONEL) C. T. LANHAM

[1]Courtesy of *Harper's*.

Learning War From Past Wars

THERE ARE two chief approaches to military history. You can get so lost in the details of ancient warfare—the customs, the style of buttons on the uniforms, the minute tactical details of campaigns and battles, that you lose all thought of new ways of war, or—equally dangerous—find yourself thinking, "Leading my troops, I'll remember to do it the way Marshal Saxe did it at Fontenoy." The other approach naturally is never to forget as you read of past battles to ignore every way of and aspect of the old-time fighting, and mark in your mind only the general and human lessons that still apply because wars are still fought by men.

This section of the Reader shows not only how the Infantry's magazine has generally avoided the academic approach to military history, but also contains some fine examples of the work of writers known for their writings among military men but not widely to others.

The man whose familiarity with the war is based mainly on what he has been reading in his newspaper and magazines since it began and what he has heard over the radio will have very little difficulty in applying to the present war the main military lessons in the following articles.

PROFITING BY WAR EXPERIENCES

BY MAJOR (now GENERAL) GEORGE C. MARSHALL

General George C. Marshall, Chief of Staff of the Army of the United States, was assistant editor of the *Infantry Journal* as a first lieutenant shortly before the first World War. In the World War, of course, he was in the heart of things and when it was over he saw very clearly, as the following article written in 1921 shows, that American military men must be careful to interpret their experiences of that conflict with reference to the whole broad scope of the war and not merely to their own little sectors.

ARTICLES appearing in our service magazines, discussions at the service schools or colleges, and pamphlets issued by the War Department lead to the belief that the American military student of the World War may be led astray in formulating conclusions on tactical questions and on organization, since the circumstances surrounding quoted instances of our participation in the war are not usually presented in sufficient detail to enable one to correctly judge the situation studied. Furthermore, the majority of our officers had but a brief experience in battle and were so hard-pressed before, during, and immediately after engagements that it is difficult for them to make an accurate, critical analysis of the battle tactics involved, and it is well known that a single example is apt to prove a dangerous guide for future action.

A proper study of tactical formations adopted requires a careful survey of the special conditions involved. In the occupation of the old defensive sectors where a division was required to hold a very broad front, the Americans were inclined to deride the complicated plan of defense turned over to them by the French units relieved. Long, intricate orders are bad in principle, but we must remember that where quiet sectors were occupied by a succession of divisions it was necessary to have a set plan of defense which would co-ordinate the action of the division in its particular sector with that of other divisions on the corps front. Also, that where a few troops defend a very wide stretch of terrain it is necessary to arrange in advance a series of combinations to meet possible attacks from varying directions. The French plans of defense were undoubtedly much too long, as they represented an accumulation of orders through a long period without having been carefully weeded out. But during stabilized warfare of this character a plan of defense of the same general nature as that employed in Europe is necessary, and each new division entering the sector must adjust itself accordingly.

The desirability of various formations for attack depends upon many considerations. For a long, grueling combat one formation may seem best, while for a rapid assault a different formation will probably appear advisable. In one division the maintaining of communication from front to rear and the facility of feeding the men in the front-line battalions were important considerations in determining the formation to be employed. It was found that a regiment with but one battalion in the first line could better maintain its communications and arrange for the feeding of hot meals to the companies engaged than with two battalions deployed. In this division it was felt that if communication was assured at all times and two hot meals were served to all the troops each day, a heavy assault could be maintained for a much longer period than otherwise. It is well known that some of our divisions had to be relieved because of confusion or disorganization resulting from lack of efficient communication and because of inertia or extreme fatigue due to the failure of the men to receive hot food on the battlefield.

A correct method of employing machine guns and of "accompanying guns" is a matter of constant debate. A trained machine-gun officer naturally understands better the technical employment of his weapon than does the ordinary infantry battalion commander. As a result we are prone to forget that the determining phase of a battle is usually a melee in which the infantry battalion commander alone is able to make decisions in time to take best advantage of the constantly changing situation. A divided command on the battlefield is out of the question. Control of troops closely engaged with the enemy is the most difficult feat of leadership and requires the highest state of discipline and training. It would therefore seem that the machine guns should be an integral part of the infantry battalion.

The "accompanying gun" was seldom employed in the manner intended, due to lack of such training in the infantry regimental and battalion commanders. These guns were often sacrificed by being placed among the forward waves during the first phases of a break-through, with the result that artillery officers became strongly opposed to their assignment to infantry units. There is undoubtedly an excellent place for an "accompanying gun" in a deep attack, and it usually is in some covered spot where the infantry regimental commander can quickly call it into play when the occasion arises. It is the fire of the gun and not its physical presence that is desired on the front line.

In studying examples of the orders issued for our troops in France several important points deserve consideration in determining the relative excellence of the orders issued. It is frequently the case that what appears to have been a model order was actually the reverse, and a poorly and apparently hastily prepared order will often be erroneously condemned. Many orders, models in their form, failed to reach the troops in time to affect their actions, and many apparently crude and fragmentary instructions did reach front-line commanders in time to enable the purpose of the higher command to be carried out on the battlefield. It is apparent that unless an order is issued in time for its instructions to percolate down through the organization sufficiently in advance of an engagement to enable each commander to arrange his unit accordingly, that order is a failure, however perfect it may appear on paper. Our troops suffered much from the delays involved in preparing long and complicated orders, due to the failure of the staff concerned to recognize that speed was more important than technique.

In studying orders for the movement of troops by marching, consideration of the time element involved is necessary to determine whether or not the staff, responsible for the order, prepared it in such form and issued it in such manner as to permit of the marching of the troops with a minimum of fatigue and discomfort. The same applies to instructions for sheltering troops. Inexperienced staff officers in France frequently caused heavy inroads to be made on the strength of a command just prior to its entrance into battle. At times this was unavoidable, but usually much unnecessary fatigue could have been avoided by the manner in which the orders were issued. Sometimes they were too brief and lacked too many details; again exactly the opposite was the case.

There were several distinct phases in the character of the fighting during America's participation in the war, and the methods employed should be studied with the particular phase concerned in view. Unfortunately in some ways few of our troops experienced the strain of confronting the German during the period of his great offensives. Those who fought only at Saint-Mihiel and in the Meuse-Argonne probably will never realize the vast difference between their enemy then and the German of April or May. Even those who fought in the summer of 1918 will have some difficulty in visualizing the state of mind of troops who are opposed by an enemy far superior in numbers and confident of his ability to defeat them. For this reason it is possible that officers who participated only in the last phase of the war may draw somewhat erroneous conclusions from their battle experience. Many mistakes were made in the Argonne which the German at that time was unable to charge to our account. The same mistakes, repeated four months earlier in the war, would have brought an immediate and unfortunate reaction. It is possible that methods successfully employed in the Meuse-Argonne would have invited a successful enemy counterattack in the spring of 1918. It is not intended by this discussion to belittle our efforts in the latter part of the war, for what we actually accomplished was a military miracle, but we must not forget that its conception was based on a knowledge of the approaching deterioration of the German Army, and its lessons must be studied accordingly. We remain without modern experience in the first phases of a war and must draw our conclusions from history.

WHAT ABOUT MILITARY HISTORY?

By Major John H. Burns

(1938)

The study of history of any kind is always difficult, not only because the human factor is so pronounced, but because the atmosphere of past events is not the atmosphere we breathe today. MAJOR GENERAL J. F. C. FULLER, British Army.

THERE IS only one weapon that is common to all wars. That is *man*. So far as recorded history goes we can see no change in him. It is amazing how hieroglyphic and cuneiform writings, millenniums old, echo the thoughts and feelings of today. Some of them might have been clipped from a late magazine, so modern they are. The cautious Will Durant says, "The basic masses of mankind hardly change from millennium to millennium." Perhaps man may have evolved from primeval slime, but so far as we know him as *man* he has always been the same. The cave man's infant brought up in modern surroundings would react and be exactly like his friends in the same apartment building. We like to think that we are better than the Stone Age man, but that is based on smugness, not science. We have not changed and, furthermore, cannot be changed. It is easier by far to knock an electron out of an atom than to eliminate one basic trait from man. Fundamentally his nature is fixed, fast, firm.

On the other hand, any system of society permits and even encourages the development of certain fundamental traits while, at the same time, inhibiting or suppressing others. The result is that when faced by two individuals processed by two antithetical social organizations we often think we have two different types of mankind. This is not so. We must repeat: they are the same beneath the veneer.

We can sum the matter up by saying all men are basically alike, though the processing of social institutions will make an apparent change in fundamental composition, by suppressing certain basic traits and developing others, but it never has eliminated and never will eliminate any fundamental characteristic. For instance, all men faced by death are frightened. The tendency to flee the danger is present in all, but certain individuals molded by their society will stand fast while others flee. Hence, courage is not lack of or elimination of fear but the temporary conquest of fear. Yet it must be understood that too much contact with fear-producing stimuli will sooner or later crack the veneer that society has overlaid on the natural nature of man. Eventually he will slough off this purely artificial crust and flee the danger.

But the most important point of all is that this fear-resistant attitude—called courage—is a product not of military training alone but of the entire social processing that the individual has undergone. *Other soldierly qualities evolve in the same manner.* Thus, the time necessary to make a soldier out of a civilian and the value of the soldier so produced depends almost entirely on the prior social training of the recruit. If he comes from a society that prizes the virtues of a soldier—duty, honor, self-sacrifice, and the like—a society that is willing to defend by force of arms the ideals for which it stands, then the soldier develops quickly from the civilian; in fact, he is largely made before he joins the colors.

From the foregoing it can be seen that the military historian should give careful attention to the social system which produces the armies he is studying. For, since different societies produce different soldier material, manifestly no two armies are exactly alike. Even troops from different parts of the same nation will be quite different. But the historian completely ignores this. He is content, for the most part, to count the noses in the contending armies; carefully note how the troops were placed on the battlefield, and then decide how the placing or moving of certain organizations led to victory or defeat. Yet, in all probability, the victory in a great measure may be attributed to the social processing one army received before it ever donned the uniform. Why is this so? Let us investigate a bit farther.

The history of warfare may be divided roughly into two parts. There is the narrow specialist concept of the military technician. This includes all affairs that concern handling and directing an army as an engine of force. It involves supply, administration, security, maneuver, intelligence, and the like. It deals solely with what appears to be a mechanism, but since it is composed of humans it is anything but a mechanism. The second and most important section of military history is the socioeconomic part which endeavors to integrate the development of armies and warfare with that of the state, industry, and the ideology of the people. This second part must be known in order to understand the conduct of battles and campaigns. For it is the conditioned men of a particular society, armed with the weapons of that society, that make an army determine to a great extent its method of fighting and, in the main, secure its victories.

There are many excellent histories on the technical aspect of war. The better ones deal with the particulars of war—such as *Infantry in Battle.* When an effort is made to generalize or evolve abstract and general truths, then trouble occurs, for these generalities are deduced wholly from the field of technical military history. This fault taints Von Schlieffen's *Cannae.* One cannot give a rounded picture of war, or analyze any campaign or battle, and definitely and with assurance ascribe victory to any factor without considering the whole basis of military power—technical and socioeconomic. This, however, is seldom done, and error is the consequence.

For instance, without knowing the socioeconomic factors of war no one can explain why the Army of the Potomac did not go to pieces under repeated beatings, or why it should come back to take frightful losses at Spotsylvania and Cold Harbor and still keep boring in. Nor can anyone explain why the South did not surrender when Vicksburg and Atlanta were captured. Their case was hopeless then. Yet Germany in 1918 collapsed before its borders were crossed. We must know more than the technical handling of an army if we are to apprehend these things. In short, *we must know the people if we are to understand that which grows from them and is part of them—the Army.*

Whatever helps to secure victory, be it a piece of terrain, industry, social mores, or national psychology, is military history. To concentrate on any part of this history and slur the rest will produce a distorted picture. Today military history suffers from a bad case of elephantiasis, developed because of our passionate concentration on the pure technique of handling military forces.

If we are to correct this we must learn to consider that any battle or campaign can be understood only by intimately knowing the following:

(1) What is the essential nature of man?

(2) How have the social systems of the combatants molded this particular human material for good or ill?

(3) How did the Army receive this socially prepared material and process it?

(4) And finally, how was this material led and directed in battle?

Check any military history closely. You will find that the manner in which the armies were led and directed is considered in minute detail, but not much else. Few military historians ever enter deeply into the primal, basic nature of man, and none into the effect of the social processing of this elemental man and how it produced good or poor soldier material. Thus, looking on the military problem in its broadest aspect, it can be seen that the military historian is dealing with only a fragment of it. As a consequence the larger part of military history is distorted and askew. It is thoroughly unscientific and a total failure in helping to interpret the present or to foresee the future.

The great misfortune is that there is no connecting link between the civilian social historian and the military chronicler. The soldier historian takes with little comment the soldier as produced by the age and recounts his exploits, leaving all other details to the conventional historian. The scientific military historian (if we had any) would be struck by the fact that the civilian authorities have charge of the soldier's training for some twenty years—infancy to manhood—and that this vital training period has a powerful effect on the type of soldier that will eventually enter battle. Therefore, he would study the social institutions of the times to ascertain their effect on this human material. Only by such an approach can we make military history truly scientific.

Along these lines let us investigate the subject a bit farther. Of the four essentials we might well concentrate on the military significance of social factors. The "essential nature of man" needs a complete study by itself, as does the military processing received by this socially prepared human. How humans are led in battle has been described *ad nauseam*. But the effect of social processing has been too often neglected.

How remiss the military historian has been about such matters is indicated by the following example: For centuries the Swiss infantry was the finest in Europe. Today the Swiss Guard of the Vatican is a memorial to its old-time fame. The hurricanes of heavy cavalry that one reads about became a gentle breeze before the Swiss. No knightly commander would lead his steel-sheathed men-at-arms against a bristling hedge of Swiss pikes—not more than once, anyway. It was the Swiss pikeman and not the English bowman who reduced cavalry from the basic arm of battle to a supporting one. Bowmen, unlike pikemen, were helpless in an open field against heavy cavalry. Strange how the English-speaking people pass over that point.

So the Swiss were cock of the walk for a few centuries and hired themselves out in compact companies to anyone who had the money and needed a job of fighting done. The French relied on them greatly, once they found that native infantry trained in the Swiss manner was worthless. So French kings signed and paid out good red gold for surly Swiss pikemen; the French generals shrugged their shoulders and gladly accepted the compact Swiss columns. The commentators and military thinkers of the time came forward with the plausible explanation that, after all, the stolid work of a pikeman was not suited to the native genius of the French race. And the military historian hurried on to the next chapter.

But the question naturally arises: Why were the Swiss so good? Here the glib military historian is ready with a flood of detail on tactics, drill, equipment, maneuvers, and the like. Then one wonders why other peoples did not follow the Swiss lead in equipment and tactics. But, strange to say, some people did and with no success, although the German *Landsknechte* were a fair second to the Swiss. The military explanation, therefore, despite its detail, is far wide of the mark.

The real military problem here, and one completely neglected, is, to repeat, just why were the Swiss so much better than those around them? The racial theory falls flat since the Swiss are racially very little, if any, different from their neighbors in France, Austria, Germany, or north Italy. Yet something caused these Swiss to fight better than their neighbors—no doubt of that. The military historian should have tracked that down. Naturally he evaded it, for to do this meant a serious study of the Swiss people, their life, manners, institutions, industry, customs, the molding effect this entire physical and psychic environment had on the people, and how all this made for better soldiers. There is little glitter to such work and no fighting; nevertheless, it was a military problem.

Surely a great opportunity was lost here, for the Spaniards about the same time also developed a first-class infantry soldier—though the Spanish methods of fighting differed from the Swiss. A close study of both cultures leading to a determination of the socially molding factors of each culture and then the elimination of all factors not common to both would have given a few basic social factors that enter into the pre-military molding of good foot-soldier material.

If such a study had been made the military historian would have been able to say that it was this factor, or factors, which produced a certain effect on the character of the human living in the Alps. It was this character—using the word in its broadest sense—that made the Swiss a good infantryman. Then to the soldier he could have said, "You have no such type individuals in your country. You cannot duplicate Swiss accomplishments no matter how closely you ape their drill and equipment. Therefore, you had better hire Swiss." And to the statesman he could say, "Swiss life produces Swiss soldiery. If you want such soldier material you must start at the bottom and change national institutions until they approximate the Swiss."

From this example it is plain to see that true military history does not begin with the armies, nor in the council chamber or legislative halls. It begins with the people—the culture, if you wish. And no battle, ancient or modern, can be understood without this background. No general can be properly evaluated without understanding his cultural and emotional background and that of his troop material. Battles are not fought *in vacuo* but by products of a certain system of life. The task of the military historian is to show this connection. Otherwise it is impossible to understand fully or clearly the significance of military events.

For instance, to understand Caesar without knowing Rome, its institutions, religion, law, industry, folkways, and how all these converged to produce a certain type military organization—the legion—is a sheer impossibility. The legion was excellent not simply by virtue of its mechanical organization, because that could be easily copied, and the ancient world was full of intelligent soldiers capable of doing it. It was something else, for we may be sure that the ancients saw the tactical virtues of the legion far better than we can today across the gulf of two thousand years. They could reproduce the legion pattern, but no soldier could reproduce the men that entered the legion. They were the product of Roman culture. The legion organization exploited this material to the utmost. Therein lay its strength. To explain the power of the legion as due to its flexibility, its armament, or other physical or mechanical factors is superficial and completely fallacious.

It was with this legion that Caesar fought. Caesar's wars become intelligible only when we realize that his battles were not won by adroit maneuver so much as by skillful utilization of simple humans as Rome had processed them and the legion polished them. Often, according to modern opinion, Caesar placed himself in a precarious situation; often he went against great odds; often, lacking essential troop components—as at Pharsalus—he took the offensive. Yet no matter how skillfully the enemy arranged his troops, Caesar won. We have no right to criticize him by modern standards, for Caesar was not fighting with or against modern soldiers. He was fighting with a Roman legion—the product of Roman culture.

Parenthetically we might say that to draw tactical lessons from Caesar's campaigns that can be applied to all warfare is, at the best, a dubious procedure.

So far we have only discussed the breadth of military history—how an army is but the projection of the culture of the nation. But another factor intrudes here. *What is the depth of the subject?* How far back do we go in amassing our material? How authentic is this material; what value has it in deriving principles of combat, and what effect has it had on military instruction? If we are to make a fair analysis of military history in its present form, then the "time-depth" factor needs analysis. For this purpose we cannot do better than to consult one of the greatest of modern military scholars, Marshal Foch.

Foch, in directing the École de Guerre, said he proceeded "from the facts which history delivers us. . . . Our models and the facts on which we shall base a theory we shall draw from the Revolution and the Empire." This was an arbitrary choice, neglecting later wars and thousands of years of prior warfare. Surely this is a narrow and unscientific foundation on which to base any scheme of battle instruction, but the arbitrary selection of periods is even a grosser error. If a person can select his own period of history and exclude all others he can prove almost any military absurdity sound. If military history is to form any basis of instruction, then it should be *all* military history, not a selected part.

Despite this, most military history is written about certain glamorous periods of warfare—periods when great figures were striding on the world's stage, when nations shook and melodrama and romance were abroad in the land. The soldier proves himself a romanticist, not a scientist. So each nation selects its own period, makes its own heroes, and twists the facts of history in order to indoctrinate all. This is not science; it is not art; it is nothing but claptrap—claptrap which has within it the seeds of great evil, because it is thought to be of value in preparing military minds to wage war.

That may sound like harsh criticism, but let us read what General

Hoffmann of the Imperial German Army had to say of the truthfulness of military history: "I have now for the first time during the whole war observed a 'history' from near by and know that it takes place in an entirely different manner than that which posterity learns. Since this is so, some trifles or false descriptions more or less do not matter."

Thus Hoffmann indicates that even our latest history is distorted.

And Clausewitz—what does he say about the doctrines and principles gleaned from history? Just this: "Theory must educate the future leader or rather guide him in his education, but not accompany him to the battlefield. . . . *As things are, there exist no laws at all for warfare.*" [Author's italics.] But Clausewitz was a scholar; let's see what a man of action has to say—one closer to the American scene and mind:

They [the Union generals] were always thinking what Napoleon would do. Unfortunately for their plans, the rebels would be thinking about something else. I don't underrate the value of military knowledge, but if men make war in slavish obedience to *rules* they will fail. No rules will apply to conditions of war as different as those which exist in Europe and America. Consequently, while our generals were working out problems of an ideal character . . . practical facts were neglected. To that extent I consider remembrances of old campaigns a disadvantage. . . .

That was the considered opinion of General U. S. Grant. This practical soldier stands not so far from Clausewitz, the theorist.

From all that has gone before it is not difficult to see that our present military history lacks breadth—fails to show the all-important connection between the soldier and the social state. It does not cover all the field of war but only a restricted portion arbitrarily chosen; its facts are difficult to get at, and when obtained, as Hoffmann cynically indicates, are then distorted. It can give no rules to the eager student, so Clausewitz states, and Grant goes even farther by stating that it had become an actual handicap to a large group of generals. If one tenth of that indictment is correct, then it is manifestly impossible to consider the subject in its present form as a basis for training leaders in warfare. It certainly is not a science but a sort of dogma—the foundation for a military theology, as one keen civilian historian aptly points out. And so on this matter the scientific historian lines up with the military theorist and the practical soldier.

Yet despite everything there are certain similarities between ancient and modern combat that need explaining. Our mistake lies in attributing these similarities to logical principles of war; it is simpler and sounder to attribute them to *man*—the common, unchanging instrument of war—and to recognize that these logical principles, so-called, are but simply the manifestations of humans reacting to combat. One stout fighting soldier of modern days has phrased it admirably: "In fact, there is a certain danger in the study of military history if we seek to obtain from it more than the eternal verities of leadership, morale, psychological effects, and the difficulty and confusion which battle entails. We cannot visualize war of the future merely by studying wars of the past."

On the whole, it is simpler and more practical to accept this attitude than to try to interpret war—past, present, and future—in accordance with an abstract, mechanistic pattern. Perhaps the latter can be done, but it has not been done yet—certainly not in a scientific manner—and there is more important work for the historian to do.

This work is to evolve a new kind of military history. A history that will show how men and organizations are fitted—or not fitted—for battle by their social and military training. The study must be broadened to include all war and all military history.

In a sketchy way, perhaps, we can outline this broad and unorthodox conception of the subject.

We want to know, for instance, not simply how Napoleon maneuvered his armies, but, in addition, the raw material that went into those armies. It is a strange thing that no one has yet adequately analyzed the effect the French Revolution had on French soldier material and then carried the study one step farther and shown how these qualities were superbly exploited by Napoleon.

But that is not all; we have here a curious and wondrous thing, if we could but see it. The French soldier who was unfitted to form thick columns and face the Swiss pikeman, in the sixteenth century, in the early nineteenth century formed these thick columns of attack and then proceeded to crack every line in Europe and march victoriously into every capital on the continent. Thinking of Waterloo and their thin red lines, the British may cavil at this, but a second thought will reveal that even at Waterloo a young untried French Army had the Iron Duke desperately praying for night or Blücher.

This historic change in the French people and soldiers requires careful, precise analysis, for without such an analysis our study of the armies alone is likely to lead us far astray. For example, Napoleon's first Italian campaign is studied as a military classic, but the student who comes away from his studies with a mental picture of the mechanism of the campaign and tries to apply the so-called lessons on another field is due for a rude awakening. For the campaign did not depend simply on Napoleon's brilliant schemes of maneuver, but largely on his leadership and his adroit exploitation of the French soldier, aflame with ideas released by the French Revolution. Napoleon himself thought so fine an army never had existed before, and adds significantly that the soldiers came from classes of society that had not usually furnished soldiers.

For the same reason—if for no other—one should not try to emulate General Lee in his vicious and victorious assaults at Chancellorsville against a vastly superior force, unless one has the same sort of troops that Lee had; nor should one copy Grant's hammer blows in the last days of the Civil War. To be sure, these blows won the war, but an army of softer fiber would have disintegrated under the punishment.

From all this one can see that it is all-important to know the troops that are fighting. But to know these troops we have to know thoroughly the society from which they are drawn. For the military technician that is the unexplored field of military history; therein lies the information which, with his military technique, gives him the secret of waging successful war—past, present, and future.

Let us take from this field an example or two which may illuminate our idea. The greatest of all ancient soldiers, Hannibal, despite a succession of magnificent victories, could not conquer the Roman people led— if we except Scipio and Claudius Nero—largely by inept generals. The decisive battle of Zama when analyzed reveals it was the steady quality of the Roman troops that enabled Scipio in desperation to snatch local supports from his central mass to extend his wings—an unheard-of maneuver—and so prevent the disaster of a double envelopment which faced him. Hannibal was at his old tricks. True, the Roman horse had defeated the weak Carthaginian horse, but both were far from the scene, and in any event it was the heavy foot that decided ancient battles. Scipio's desperate expedient succeeded although he was clearly outmaneuvered by Hannibal. Had the Roman common soldier wavered when he saw his supports withdrawn another Cannae would have ensued. This war was won not by generals but by the Roman people.

Coming to recent times, we find the same idea exemplified. The greatest modern soldier, Napoleon, failed to understand the Spanish people, and though he overwhelmed Spanish armies he could not conquer the country. Thus there ensued years of futile warfare. Some of the best troops in the Empire were wasted in Spain when they should have been concentrated in Poland against the Russians. The demoniac resistance of the Spanish civilians at the terrible siege of Saragossa showed the temper of the Spaniards. Napoleon had misjudged them, as he himself sadly acknowledged, and was forced to make war on two fronts—Madrid and Moscow. A fatal error.

All of which leads up to this: Say what one will, the abstract principles of tactics and strategy must be practically applied with and against humans conditioned by a certain environment. There is no pure science of war. Therefore, instead of trying to show the immutability of certain principles of tactics we should be trying to show how at any particular period the conditioned human of that period was converted to the purpose of war. And at the end, very likely, we will find that the leader of the day was no fool but used his material as best he could to solve his battle problems.

Confronted by the same problems and with all our knowledge of today, we would probably make a miserable failure with the same human material. It is knowledge of the people that is necessary and that we would lack. For example, no one in the Middle Ages could have trained and used in battle a Greek phalanx or a Roman legion, as excellent as those formations were, for the people were not Greeks and Romans but something quite, quite different. They did not come out of the same sort of social mold. Thus, the war harness had to be fitted to their mental contours and not cut on a theoretically better pattern.

General Bullard had this conception years ago. In 1906 he said, "Napoleon taught us that if we must fight with untrained men, being unable to adapt the men to the tactics, we must try to adapt the tactics to the men. . . . Without regard to prescriptions of tactical systems, try to suit your battle formations to the character of your men. . . ."

In the World War, Lawrence realized that the Arabians could not, and would not, fight according to Western standards, so he adapted his campaign methods to their make-up, not to a standard concept of war and soldiering. His results were astonishing.

Today we live in a world of national states, not amorphous empires, city-states, or feudal kingdoms. If we draw illustrations and lessons from the armies of such national states we approximate reality, but only so far as these states approximate one another in social environment. Here we must be cautious and not theorize too far. For example, the Prussians of Frederick the Great were far different from the Prussians of today. The American Civil War soldier mentally had more in common with the French revolutionary soldier or even Scipio's farmer soldier than with Frederick's Prussians. Yet Frederick's army of long-service soldiers was highly successful, and his heirs were content. Then came the French Revolution which broke down doors, shattered all precedents, and released a store of tremendous energy—psychic and physical. France was remolded, and from this France erupted the French nationalist soldier who overran Europe and swept the Frederician army into the discard.

It should be recognized that a social revolution or a long war will always produce such changes in warfare—irrespective of new weapons developed—since both shake society to its foundations and so condition the human that he is a different instrument of war—for better or for worse. The difference that develops will be great or small, depending on the change in the social structure. These matters need study.

Moreover, all this study is the soldier's job. We cannot expect civilian historians, even if they knew the military problem, to do this for us. They are not interested. It is a basic military job, and at this particular time in the history of the world, when all things are changing with great rapidity—particularly the social state—it is a vital matter.

The reason for this ceaseless change in modern life is not abstruse.

Late in the eighteenth century the Industrial Revolution struck the world first in western Europe. Tremendous changes were created. As the late Professor James Harvey Robinson says, "Material civilization has changed more since the days of Jefferson than it had between Jefferson's age and that of Tutankhamen." These great changes pressed against the social structure and steadily, sharply modified it and the individual it contained.

In the nineteenth century this tremendous revolution, deftly manipulated by the classes in power, shaped a certain type of society characterized on the political side by representative democracy and on the industrial side by a policy of *laissez faire*. The whole was enveloped in a strong spirit of nationalism. But the Industrial Revolution was a continuing process—it is still going on—and always the pressure became greater. The result was a tremendous upheaval called a World War, followed by two decades of radical social remolding which is still continuing. Democracy, formerly in the ascendancy, is now under heavy assaults; *laissez faire* in industry seems to be passing away, but nationalism is blazing up with greater heat and fury. Furthermore, several nations conceive they have a holy world mission that will be accomplished only by force of arms. They are regimenting and molding the people, beginning with the youth and reaching out hands to people in other nations who have the same political philosophy. Before the coming Armageddon we find the war being initiated on internal fronts.

Communism, Fascism, and even a type of militarism, compared to which Imperial Germany was as innocuous as a New England town meeting, are all challenging democracy. And still the Industrial Revolution goes on spawning countless machines and causing unemployment, depressions, recessions, and unbalanced budgets in a land of plenty. We are in a veritable vortex. We live in an unbalanced world characterized by rapid and sweeping changes. These changes have a marked effect on the people, and it is from these people that armies will be drawn—those we fight with and against. And why are we not studying these things? What blind, groping beings we soldiers are!

To be sure, it is beyond the province of the soldier to decide which of these political, economic, and social systems is the best. But it is strictly within his province to study them in order to ascertain what effects they are having on the people and what these changed people are worth in war. For instance, it is plain to see that a people under a dictatorship will be initially welded together and ready for war. But dictator-led people enter war on order and think about it afterward; this is ominous. Democracies enter war after considerable thinking and talking—even squabbling—but, once in, will very likely be steady and stand up under defeats. Since no one has investigated the matter from the military side, these are at best but estimates, although Marshal Foch thought a republic was the strongest in war. However, accepting them as sound for the nonce, we can say that a nation under a dictatorship had better make sure to win its war quickly, and a democracy must be certain not to be completely defeated in the early days of war. We might draw another conclusion to the effect that a dictator-led nation would be wise not to expect too much initiative or build its tactics on this quality, for initiative does not thrive under a dictatorship; democracies, on the other hand, can expect initiative but must guard against too much of it.

These are but a handful of the countless things that are awaiting study. As soldiers of democracy it is our task to investigate everything affecting the human, even going so far as to study modern trends of thought and ideals taught in schools, for these schools are producing potential soldiers. Years ago Charles M. Bakewell, professor of philosophy at Yale, analyzed this vital and neglected sociomilitary problem. The irony of it all is that we are doing nothing about it and know nothing, for example, of John Dewey's educational philosophy which is profoundly modifying the product of our schools.

Not that we advocate or even desire military training in all the schools, but we should expect an inculcation of love of country, a sense of duty, a feeling of something bigger and better than mere self, a willingness, a zeal to preserve the nation even if it means taking up arms. Are the schools doing this? Who knows? Yet without such basic feeling there is no core to the nation, and the product of the schools, no matter how brilliant intellectually, will never make soldier material. And without soldier material—not necessarily trained soldiers—there is no safety in this harsh modern world.

To many it will seem that this study is the task of the high command, but that belief is unsound. All officers should know the modern social problems and have a modern perspective. Right now it is a lack of such perspective that keeps our eyes riveted on the military training in higher schools and colleges—a training that in great part becomes obsolete as weapons, doctrines, and organizations change—and leaves us oblivious to the effect that the ordinary school subjects may have on youthful minds. Perhaps the school is training a vast mass of youngsters to receive with alacrity the Oxford Oath (an oath never under any circumstances to take up arms). We can say nothing about all this because we have never investigated it.

Moreover, there is a strictly military side to this matter that any tactician must know. For instance, one must never expect to reproduce with modern Americans Stonewall Jackson's tremendous marches, because the modern American is not a walker but a motor rider. Even if we were able to harden him to make such marches, psychologically he would resent it and fight less vigorously than Jackson's men. Nor can we expect any modern army to bore through wooded swamps as did Sherman's army in the Carolinas. Sherman led an army of frontier farmers to whom an ax was a common tool with which they were expert. Working in water up to their waists, they quickly felled trees, cut the trunks into proper lengths, and promptly rolled them into place to form corduroy roads. The speed with which these roads were constructed and the celerity with which the army moved were amazing. "When I learned that Sherman's army was marching through the Salk swamps . . . at the rate of a dozen miles a day or more . . . bringing its artillery and wagons with it, I made up my mind that there had been no such army in existence since the days of Julius Caesar." Thus spoke General Johnston, Sherman's erstwhile opponent. But the modern who tries Sherman's tricks will only come a cropper. We haven't the axmen today, and it would be a slow or impossible task to bring power tools to the center of a semiequatorial swamp.

Yes, our modern social system produces certain military defects, and yet we may have compensating military advantages if one only knew what they were and how to exploit them. That is the task of the military man studying the contemporary scene. We must know what human material our present culture produces so that we can compare it with the past and draw our lessons for future war. For armies fight in accordance with their environment and not in accordance with a set of abstract rules. As Clausewitz phrases it: "We must embrace the view that war, and the shape it is given, rises from ideas, feelings, and conditions prevailing *at the given moment. . . .*"

Despite this, nowhere have we given any great attention to the basic factor of war—*man*—yet, strangely enough, we have an intensive course of study to familiarize officers with the industrial and economic factors of war and how to utilize them. Meanwhile, the surroundings of a mechanical and urban civilization are making great changes in the modern human's reactions to certain mental stimuli and in his physical ability. But we go calmly on believing that the lessons gleaned from the actions of the agricultural soldier of the Civil War can be applied *in toto* to the urban soldier of today.

Without investigation we think we have progressed; but have we? Granted that there is more wealth, power, ease, luxury, lavishness; granted that modern man has increased in height, weight, size, and symmetry; yet the words "wealth" and "luxury" have an ominous ring, and a bigger body does not mean a greater heart or a finer brain. In fact, this physical bigness may be a sign of degeneracy as Alexis Carrel, a great scientist and a Nobel Prize winner, points out. All in all, we are faced by a gigantic problem which we solve by ignoring it.

The democracies of the world are paying little attention to the potential soldier, not so the autocracies. They are frankly training their youth and people for war. They are remodeling the very background of life itself so that it will produce soldiers—and little else. How pernicious this practice is needs no elucidation. A soldier civilization is a sterile one. We want none of it. All we wish is an environment that produces a solid core of human qualities about which we can build a soldier in time of emergency. Nothing more. We do not wish to develop a modern Sparta.

But to accomplish this vital task we must know more than the geometry of war now so assiduously studied. We must investigate, delve, study, and advise with civilian historical, economic, and educational experts. The task is only half military, and we are not doing our part. Truly, the military historian has a long and strange road to travel before he can be rated competent on his subject of prime importance.

The hour has struck for the military historian to turn his myopic eyes from the study of the geometric form of ancient wars. He must contemplate entire peoples and civilizations as a prelude to an exhaustive analysis of the peoples and cultures of today. In this must be included a study of the trends of development, particularly in the field of thought. Nothing is more explosive than an idea, and to understand a people one must understand its ideology which essentially is far more important than its armament. Our historian must recognize that the Industrial Revolution is still going on, creating rapid and revolutionary changes—changes which are of vital importance, since the war we fight will be tomorrow, not today. And nothing is surer than that tomorrow's men and materials will differ from those of today.

Furthermore, he must fully realize that his wars will be fought by humans—conditioned by the age—and not by robot soldiers. Consequently he must understand that it is exceedingly risky to generalize from old battles without knowing what sort of mental processing the old-time soldier received during his lifetime.

The historian must put aside his puttering with archaic jigsaw battle puzzles and raise his eyes to the broad horizon, the interminable ages of history, the flux of nations, the flow of life, the rise and fall of institutions, the mass molding of humans by social institutions, industry, religion, and folkways; the processing for war—all the great broad sweep of human activity. Only then will he become a real historical craftsman who will receive a respectful hearing from the masters in the craft.

In short, what military history needs is not more study of battles, but more study of the peoples who fight them.

WHY NOT SOON?

By Historicus

(1938)

It will be twenty years come November that the Heinies threw in the sponge, and yet the history of our own participation in the war, which had so much to do with the final result, is still far from being written. Not only is there no prospect in the discernible future that the official records will be generally available, but even some of the most vital experiences of the American Army live, if at all, a vicarious existence as glorified latrine rumors.

No educated soldier, certainly, will underestimate the importance of the leadership factor as applied to the command of large units, and surely a complete understanding of the relief, replacement, or retention of superior commanders is essential to a complete study of military history. So far as the World War is concerned, that material is available for every army but our own. We know the shortcomings of Von Moltke, why he was superseded by Falkenhayn, and why the latter in turn gave way to Hindenburg and Ludendorff. We know about the exit of Smith-Dorrien, and Sir John French's kick upstairs. We are tolerably informed on Haig's strong points and weak and on the characteristics of the several chiefs of staff of the BEF. We know the story of Joffre and of the bloody tragedy that was Nivelle; we know about Pétain and the ups and downs that marked Foch's fortunes. Close students are familiar with the changes in army and even corps commanders. But—where is there any reliable source for ascertaining the reasons for the changes in the American high command?

It is not a matter of morbid curiosity or of a heartless prying into some person's misfortune. The question is the vital one of learning from the past. If the AEF's personnel standard was, as many believe, one strike is out, then that policy should be examined in the light of individual instances. Was it too rigorous, so that it adversely affected morale? Or did it have the desired effect of making all ranks toe the mark? Blois needs more study than it can receive in the postprandial reminiscences of the AEF alumni, because—well, someday there will be another Blois, and officers now living should have available for their guidance the lessons to be drawn from the last set of reclassifications.

And in discussing the higher commanders we shall have to name names, just as in previous wars. McClellan was discussed up and down the country after his several removals. Committees of Congress were inquiring of Meade in the fall of 1863 why he did not pursue after Gettysburg. The successive commanders of the Army of the Cumberland were allowed no refuge in anonymity, and the Civil War was not long over before the projected relief of Thomas by Logan was argued at length. The cases of Fitz-John Porter and of G. K. Warren were fully chewed over long before the respective courts of inquiry sat. In the Spanish War the Sampson-Schley controversy was public property, and in all the instances mentioned the arguments and discussions, painful though they were to the individuals most closely concerned, have furnished useful lessons for the future, guides to how to do it and, equally important, guides to how not to do it.

But the American World War operations are still shrouded with the same anonymity which resulted in the familiar censor's slip that gave the Marines a disproportionate share of the glory. Half the country even today does not know that the 2d Division had an army brigade. And hardly anyone knows why General Summerall relieved General Cameron in the command of the V Corps, or why General Buck lost the 3d Division, or General McMahon the 5th, or the real reason why General Edwards was relieved from command of the 26th. Only recently has there been any authentic suggestion in print of how and why General Sibert was supplanted by General Bullard at the head of the 1st Division. The bare facts of supersession are not disputed; the "Order of Battle" has been available for some time.

The students of the last war—the leaders in the next—are entitled to know the circumstances, must know them as a part of their professional education. Whatever personal feeling now remains must surely have been dulled in twenty years' time, and a "blooied" general ignorant of the causes of his relief can hardly claim a vested right in the permanent suppression of those reasons. At any rate, the personal interests involved must yield to the national necessities of the situation, and no good reason is perceived why these matters must any longer be characterized by the embarrassed and furtive circumlocutions with which maiden ladies treat of the clinical pages in picture magazines.

Twenty years should be a long enough statute of limitations for a sacred cow; after that time the beast is merely sentimental bull.

MONGOL METHODS OF WAR

By Harold Lamb

Mr. Lamb's *Genghis Khan, Tamerlane, March of the Barbarians,* and other books dealing with the rise of Asian conquerors in the Middle Ages have had wide circulation among Army men as well as among the general reading public. In "Mongol Methods of War," which appeared in 1940 right after the blitzkrieg, the parallel between the early conquering armies from Asia and the drive of the Axis forces of conquest from mid-Europe is clearly drawn.

I. THE GERMAN IMITATION

IN THE LAST FEW MONTHS the nations of Norway, Holland, Belgium, and France have been stunned by the hammerblows of the Third Reich. And now, after these examples, the pattern of this new quick war is becoming clear.

But the Reich's design for war is not new. It was followed by the Mongols seven hundred years ago. Exactly seven hundred years ago this autumn the Mongol attack upon the civilized nations of the world, initiated by Genghis Khan, reached its high-water mark in the west. It penetrated the line of Poland-Vienna-the-Adriatic after conquering all that lay behind it in Europe and Asia.

This writer has before him a letter from a cardinal of the Vatican saying, "It is 1235 over again. . . . The nations will be destroyed one by one." The Mongol attack on Europe was first planned in 1235; His Eminence had made a study of the Mongols.

What was this Asiatic method of attack? How, when it was put into effect by barbarian horsemen from the isolated region of the Gobi Desert, did it succeed at every point against the greater powers of civilized peoples?

It was a method of annihilating the resistance in a nation to be conquered. A total war, terrible beyond belief to those faced by it. It was a series of operations designed to crush morale and man power. It had little to do with the conventional warfare of professional armies. In fact, it broke most of the canons of European military tradition. Call it war to the uttermost—deliberately planned destruction carried out, often, at incredible speed. In other words, the prototype of the blitzkrieg.

The deadly thing about the Mongol method was that it always accomplished its purpose. Napoleon once said, "I was not so lucky as Genghis Khan." But luck played a small part, if any, in the continuous victories of the Mongols. For thirty-nine years the Mongol attack suffered no real check. For a century the Mongol *Drang nach Osten* (and West) conquered and held in its military rule the greater part of the known world.

For a long time, because even historians were superstitious in the past, this feat was explained away as a manifestation of supernatural force. Only in these last two generations have we known enough about the Mongol method to examine it.

The Germans were the first to analyze the Mongol campaigns from a military point of view. An early account was published in 1865, followed by a study of the Mongol attack upon Poland, Silesia, Bohemia, and Moravia. While the military brains of the Hohenzollern Reich (the Bernhardi-Moltke-Schlieffen group) developed the doctrine that a nation by hardening itself to war can make its own destiny and enforce its political will on weaker neighbors, these technical studies of Mongol military achievements were in the hands of German readers.

No such study seems to have been made by British or French until several years after the 1914–18 war. The great majority of Americans knew even less about the methods of Genghis Khan. Our interest lay more in the mysteries of the archaeology and folklore of Central Asia. But these last months have shown us—in spite of our disinclination to believe it—that the military brains of the German Reich have developed a plan of attack that works along the same line as the Mongol. And it may be enlightening, now, to have a rough outline of the Mongol method before us.

There was nothing supernatural about it. Nor did it depend on pressure of superior numbers, as was believed for a time. Usually the Mongols were inferior in man power; during the first and last attack upon China they were outnumbered in startling proportion. Their rapid maneuvering simply multiplied their force in the eyes of the enemy.

Nor were their victories due to the legendary skill of Genghis Khan alone. He was a genius but also a savage who did not know the use of writing. He happened to be the one Mongol who broke, as it were, into the front page of history.

As a soldier Genghis Khan had two weaknesses: an ungovernable temper, which he held in iron restraint, and a latent savagery which drove him at times into a fury of destruction. But his dominant personality gave the barbarians of the Gobi a leader. "I shall raise this generation of those who dwell in felt tents above the other peoples of the world," he said. He instilled in them the conviction that they could accomplish the seemingly impossible.

The great field commanders—Mukhuli, who crushed North China; Batu, conqueror of Russia; Subotai, who made fools of the European generals and kings; and Bayan, who broke the power of the Sung empire in southern China—were at least the equals of Genghis Khan as strategists.

The Mongols as a whole were gifted in one way. They had the natural aptitude of horse nomads for maneuvering. Generations of hunting wild beasts over vast areas—and of tribal warfare—had accustomed them to tracking down, rounding up, and killing men and beasts without waste effort. Their natural tactics were the swift maneuvering of the steppes. And they learned many secrets of war from their enemies, the Chinese, who were masters of the art of strategy two thousand years before Von

Moltke was born. The Mongols were close students of such efficiency. In their world attack they commandeered Chinese engineers, bridgebuilders, artillerists—along with gunpowder, still unknown in Europe—and all the Chinese scientists they could prevail on to serve them.

THE PLAN OF ATTACK

The Mongol method of attack was to destroy resistance before it could be organized. There were five preparatory steps to this:

(1) Complete espionage (modern intelligence).
(2) Intimidation of the enemy.
(3) Sabotage of enemy's strength.
(4) Deception, as to the nature of the attack.
(5) Surprise, as to the time of the attack.

The Mongols never worked out their plan of operation until they had a clear picture of the enemy's territory, armament, routes of communication, and probable place of mobilization, while managing to keep their own preparations pretty well hidden. They made a practice of doing this before each campaign, without trusting—as they might have been expected to do—in the power of their own offensive. Sun-Tzu, author of the first known treatise on the art of war (490 B.C.), points out that commanders who expect to conquer must have "foreknowledge" and that this must be had from information given by spies and cannot be gained by deduction or by any past experience.

Better for the French commanders in the Franco-Prussian affair if they had obtained more of a picture of the Prussian military machine they faced and had forgotten their experience of the Napoleonic Wars. If the British Army on the Western Front from 1914–18 had not been at first under the control of elderly cavalry commanders steeped in the traditions of the Boer War, it might have been spared years of murderous blundering. And the events of May–June 1940 seem to indicate that too many commanders remembered only too well the days of 1914–18.

While the Mongol intelligence made its reports the war council planned the coming campaign to its end. The council, or *kuriltai,* was made up of the veteran commanders, and the princes of the house of Genghis Khan. They designed the coming attack—for the Mongol method of war was always to attack. They managed to avoid being put on the defensive, by expedients that will be explained.

This rehearsal of operations took time. The Mongols, like the Chinese of that day, believed that a mistake in planning would be more dangerous than an error in execution.

INTIMIDATION OF AN ENEMY

A summons to submit would be sent to the doomed nation. More of a warning than a summons. The people to be attacked would be reminded of the disasters that resulted to other people in their attempts to resist. A Mongol peace would be offered on these terms: demolition of the nation's defensive walls, payment of a yearly tax, admission of Mongol armies into the country, and a small levy of fighting men to serve with the Mongols.

Unless the terms were accepted and reigning authorities were sent to make submission in person to Mongol headquarters, the Mongols would not be responsible for consequences. "That will happen which will happen, and what it is to be we know not. Only God knows."

Even if the doomed nation submitted, the attack would be carried out deliberately, just as planned. It would be quicker and more effective, because the enemy had hoped for peace. Rarely did the invaders from the Gobi respect an agreement with an enemy. Treachery was a most useful weapon, and the methodical Mongols saw no reason not to use such a weapon in war.

Their purpose in war was not to win battles but to destroy the power of resistance of the enemy.

Moral issues have no place in the total war. A Chinese commentator wrote of such a war: "Why do scholars prate their stale formulas of 'virtue' and 'civilization,' condemning the use of military weapons? They will bring our country to impotence."

DECEPTION AS A SCREEN

The strategy of the campaign decided on, the Mongols tried to mask their purpose. The routes of attack through the doomed country would be surveyed. Grazing lands were set aside along the lines of march as far as the frontier; heavy supplies were moved ahead by slow transport to await the attacking forces.

A harmless-looking caravan escorted by riders across the frontier might have weapons and equipment concealed in its bales—the riders might be Mongol troopers, the owners of the weapons.

In fact, in moving slowly toward the frontier the Mongol *tumans*, or attack divisions, usually carried no arms. Their weapons waited for them at arsenals along the road. It was impossible to judge, from the casual movement of these bodies of horsemen, which direction their attack would take. At times a whole Mongol army would wheel through an adjacent, neutral area.

Spies sent out by the Mongols and captured within the doomed area would give, under torture, false information. The net result was that the defenders of the menaced country would be in the dark as to whether the Mongols would attack or where they would first appear. Meanwhile, across their frontier, the Mongol political agents would be sapping their powers of resistance without seeming to do so.

In their blitzkrieg against the Russian principalities, 1237–38, the Mongol armies spent two years in preparation and in working their way across mid-Asia. The attack itself destroyed most of the central Russian cities, the centers of resistance, in some three months—and in midwinter! The Russians had not believed that large armies could move in the cold and snow of those months.

THE SABOTAGE PREPARATION

The Mongols lacked the modern facilities for sabotage within an enemy area. They were not sophisticated enough to try to spread a defeatist propaganda. But they tried to create confusion or civil war, if possible.

Ingeniously, in their invasion of the great Sung empire, they broadcast the report of the double-dealing and profiteering of the Sung minister who was head of the defense measures. As it happened, these reports were fact.

They were apt to buy the allegiance of a brilliant commander on the opposing side or to win over rebels. Even a man who had fought against them to the end they would try to coax into their service.

When Subotai struck at Middle Europe, 1240–41, he chose a year when that part of Europe was divided—the German Empire being then locked in internecine war with the papal powers. And the Mongols, in preparing that blow, contrived to divide the enemies immediately in front of them. As it happened, some strong tribes of Kipchak Turks had taken refuge in Hungary to make a stand against the dreaded Mongols. By a cunningly contrived letter addressed to the Hungarian court, but written in a script that only the Turks could read, the Mongols managed to breed suspicion between the two. The result was that the Turks and Hungarians were fighting like dogs and wolves when the Mongols appeared on the scene.

As with today's German strategy, the methodical Mongols secured a decisive advantage before their first patrols crossed the frontier. Political operations had smoothed the way for the military attack.

And it came with the stunning force of surprise. Columns of war-hardened horsemen swept into the doomed area at terrific pace. They crossed wide rivers without a check, worked their way through ill-defended mountain passes, sometimes covering eighty miles in a day.

They were maneuvering according to a definite plan, often keeping to a fixed timetable, before the defenders realized the power of the attack. Such a lightning thrust got through the Chinese Maginot Line, the Great Wall, in a few hours. The Mongols had discovered that the way to penetrate such a fortification was to win over the commander of one point and to take it by surprise. They were also aware that, once penetrated, the rest of the line served no more purpose than a monument of masonry and stone.

The audacity of their attack was apt to stun defending officers. A Mongol *ming-khan,* or commander of a hundred, might appear suddenly in a district and force its surrrender because the defensive force had no means of knowing how many thousands might or might not be at the heels of the hundred.

But this was a calculated audacity. The Mongol columns were self-contained; they carried iron rations—they could supply themselves off the enemy country. It did no particular damage if their communications were cut, because they had no reserves behind them.

They had discovered, too, that safety lay in this speed of movement. By their greater mobility they could maintain the pressure of attack on the enemy. The columns, moving almost with the pace of German tanks and motorized columns of today, could scatter small defensive formations. And they could unite at equal speed against a main army. Lacking the radios of today, they kept up communication between the tumans by a combination of signals and mounted couriers. Their *yam,* or pony express, was capable of covering two hundred miles in a day.

Such maneuvering could not be attempted by new recruits. The Mongols were products of their steppes, hardened to fatigue. They were trained to a lifetime of war and aided by organization complete even to small articles of equipment.

Their nomad clans had been mobilized as a whole for war. Men from seventeen to sixty served, according to their qualifications, in the fighting ranks, in the transport, or by guarding the herds that provided most of their food. Their women, the old men, and youngsters cared for the home encampments.

Individual Mongols were equipped for speed and striking force—not for defense. Loose leather and felt capes protected them against the weather. Their helmets of light metal or lacquered leather had a leather drop to protect the neck. Few of the regiments had armor—and those only to protect the front of the body.

Their saddle kits were small and complete to ropes and a leather sack for iron rations of dried meat and milk curds. The swords were shaped like the modern cavalry saber—the lances light and serviceable.

But their effective weapon was the bow. Each rider carried two of the double-curved Turkish bows, strengthened by horn—one for handling from the saddle, the other for long-range firing on foot. Arrows were carried in two cases, one with tempered-steel points for piercing armor, the other for longer range. The rider could draw the bow from its case at his hip with his left hand and an arrow with his right and fire swiftly, without checking his horse.

The Mongol bows had power to outrange most European weapons. And their rapidity of fire took other armies by surprise. "They kill men and horses," a European spectator observed sadly, "and only when the men and horses are crippled do they advance to attack."

So careful were the Mongols to use this "fire" preparation that their divisions had machines dismounted and carried on pack animals—stone and javelin casters and flame throwers. They even used smoke screens and attacked behind burning grass. They avoided hand-to-hand fighting except as a last resource.

Since a Mongol army kept its formation for a lifetime, the various units were so trained in battle drill that their maneuvering was carried out according to a plan given in advance—without orders shouted during action. They had signals to use at need, whistling arrows and colored lanterns raised or lowered at night. "Silent and inflexible," another eye-witness relates, "and swift beyond belief, they moved as if at the command of one man."

This mechanical perfection in action came from two causes: the Mongol forces were all one arm and, like a motorized division today, they could all maintain the same pace. Also, the men in the ranks had spent a lifetime with their officers. Usually a regiment was made up of men from the same clan. (The Mongols used the decimal system of units— ten in a squad, ranging up to the tuman, the division of ten thousand.)

Like the men, the officers had in the highest degree the "intellectual discipline" demanded of soldiers by Marshal Foch. Youngsters served in the *keshik,* or elite division, which was always kept by Genghis Khan or his successors. They learned their lessons on the march or in campaign conditions.

Such officers were carefully weeded out. Physical bravery and endurance were taken for granted. They were trained to be cautious. Those who seemed to be foolhardy as well as brave were transferred to the transport service. Those showing traces of stupidity went lower down. The glory-hunting type was not wanted.

Of one officer who seemed to have every qualification, Genghis Khan said: "No man is more valiant than Yessutai; no one has rarer gifts. But as the longest marches do not tire him, as he feels neither hunger nor thirst, he believes that his officers and soldiers do not suffer from such things. That is why he is not fitted for high command. A general should think of hunger and thirst so he may understand the suffering of those under him, and he should husband the strength of his men and beasts."

MISSION OF OFFICERS

The leader of the first squad in a company took command of the company if its officer was killed. And so with a regiment. Ability was the only demarcation between troopers and officers. Officers were promoted by ability alone. Seniority, the curse of the professional army, cut no ice. At the age of twenty-five Subotai commanded a division.

The men had confidence in their officers, knowing them intimately, well aware that if an officer was not fit to lead he would not hold his rank long. This confidence was increased by enforcing a rule that will be appreciated by all servicemen. It was the first requirement of an officer *not* to risk the lives of his men. A loss of Mongol life was the unforgivable sin in the army.

Months after a battle which came near to deciding the fate of Europe, Batu Khan reproached his staff general, who happened to be Subotai, because Subotai, delayed in building a bridge over a river, had been late in supporting him. "You were the cause of my losing Bahatur [an officer] and twenty-three men," Batu complained.

Their armies were welded together by an inflexible discipline. For this the driving personality of Genghis Khan was responsible. He made death the punishment for failure of the members of a squad to carry off a wounded squad mate, and death was also the penalty for failure of a rear-rank rider to pick up an article dropped by a front-rank man. Before going into action the officers were required to inspect personally the full kit of every man under their command, to be certain that nothing was lacking.

There was even a lost-and-found department in each division, to keep track of missing equipment. This meticulous care of details gave the Mongols an advantage in equipment over the armies they faced. (The new German Army, rebuilt after Versailles by Von Seeckt, had this characteristic.) A lacquer coating of equipment protected it from dampness. A detail—yet one that made it possible for the Mongols to use their bows in the rain. The tempering of arrowheads gave them the advantage of steel over the iron used by Europeans. The extra ropes carried by the riders of the *ordus* could be attached to wagon transport and war machines to drag them up grades and over heavy going.

With such highly trained mobile columns operating under iron discipline, the Mongols were able to take risks. It was part of their strategy to take such risks at the start of a campaign in order to avoid being drawn into a major battle. Their object was to stun resistance by surprise and then to destroy the opposing man power during this second phase of a war.

They had three methods of doing this, decisive in their effect: by a paralysis of terror; by the immediate destruction of the enemy government, so the invaded region would be without control; and by out-maneuvering the armed forces, so that they could be scattered and then liquidated at leisure.

So the first aim of the invading Mongol columns was to create anarchy in front of them. It was no ordinary war but a destruction of all power to resist.

Take the campaign of 1219 that broke the resistance of the Khwarez-mian Turks. This particular Turkish empire was strong in man power and fortified cities. It had the warlike spirit of Moslems defending themselves against an attack by pagans. Its forces under arms outnumbered the Mongols three to two.

The Turkish armies were extended along the line of a wide river, the Syr, facing north. A chain of walled towns strengthened this defensive line. Behind it lay the large cities of Bokhara and Samarkand. Behind these, Turkish reserve contingents were assembling slowly. All Turkish units were facing the northwest, where the Mongol armies were emerging slowly from the mountain ranges of mid-Asia. Three Mongol columns moved into the open, storming isolated towns at either end of the Turkish line.

Once such a town was entered, the inhabitants were led out and divided into three groups—the boys and young girls sent back into Asia as slaves; the trained artisans spared to form a labor battalion to aid the Mongols in the next siege. All other living beings were tied up and killed methodically.

This slaughter stunned the inhabitants of the first defense zone. But the three armies operating along the Syr were serving to mask the fourth and strongest, under the direct command of Genghis Khan and Subotai. This fourth column slipped around the left of the Turkish defenses, crossing the Syr without being observed. And then it vanished. Genghis Khan led it straight to the south for nearly two hundred miles across the Red Sands Desert. And it emerged at headlong pace before the walls of Bokhara far in the rear of the Turkish armies.

Then began the rapid maneuver of the Mongol blitzkrieg. The garrison of Bokhara, trying to sally out, was annihilated. The surviving inhabitants were driven in a mass toward Samarkand to serve as a human shield for the main Mongol army. The regular Turkish armies were thrown into confusion by the attack from the rear and began to retreat separately. The swift-moving Mongol columns concentrated, to scatter them one at a time.

And simultaneously two picked Mongol divisions—about twenty thousand riders—were told off to isolate and destroy the government (in this case the Khwarezmian Shah, his ministers and court). This flying column located the Shah's court and attacked it suddenly. It retreated farther south *away from the remnants of the Turkish armies* toward Balkh. The two divisions picked up its trail and drove it into headlong flight. When the Shah fled from Balkh with his treasure, his immediate family, and a few nobles, his government ceased to function. Thereafter he was never allowed to gain touch with his fighting forces, and he was hunted into the waters of the Caspian where he died almost alone, haunted by fear of the inexorable horsemen who tracked him down.

Without any central authority to lead them, individual Turkish commanders made brave stands here and there. But the paralysis of growing fear numbed resistance. New recruits did not know where to assemble. Citadels remote from the area of conflict found themselves attacked before they could mobilize a defense. There was no longer a front. In five or six weeks the resistance of a powerful empire had been broken completely. Turkish remnants became isolated, uncertain what was happening ten miles away, under the pall of terror. Bands of fugitives fled like animals from the main roads where the Mongol regiments galloped.

"The living," a chronicler relates, "envied those who were already dead."

Herds of captives were driven to the task of tearing down the walls of cities. Then they were killed, their bodies left to fester in the ruins. Detachments of Mongols hid in the ruins and put to death survivors who came back to the sites of their homes. The organized life of the country was ripped open like a melon. The only law enforced was Mongol military necessity. It became a crime to resist a Mongol order.

Since the horse herds had been commandeered and the roads occupied by the invaders, the surviving Turks were without means of ordinary communication. Administration was taken over by the Mongol *darugashis* or roadmasters. Turkish routine had fallen into anarchy; it was replaced by the harsh military rule of the conquerors.

But the breakdown of resistance had been brought about in the first place by the almost incredible wheel of the column under Genghis Khan across the desert to the rear of the Turkish armies.

SURPRISE AS A WEAPON

The Mongols managed to destroy the strong Kin empire in middle China by brilliant stratagem. The Kin were a warlike nation protected by mountain ranges in the north and west and a chain of fortresses facing the Mongols in these two directions. The Mongols made no attempt at first to force these frontiers.

Instead, a small army of three divisions was sent down past Tibet, through almost impassable country, to emerge in the south, in the rear of the Kin forces. Tului, a son of Genghis Khan, asked Subotai how he was to meet the Kin armies when he approached them.

"They are town-bred people," Subotai advised him, "and they cannot endure hardships. Harry them enough, and you can defeat them in battle."

When some of the Kin forces about-faced, to meet Tului's column at their rear, the Mongol retreated before them, drawing them up into the mountain region that had already taken toll of his veteran regiments. Cold and hunger in this region nearly exhausted the heavily armed Kin forces.

And when the Mongols counterattacked in the hills they had little trouble driving the Kin covering force back to the plains. Meanwhile, Subotai with the main force of Mongols had rushed the northern frontier—getting through before the Kin garrisons could flood the lowlands along the Hwang-ho. The Kin armies were caught, disorganized by the pincer thrusts, between Tului's flying column and Subotai's main body, in the plains where the Mongols easily surrounded them.

Not until they were so caught did the Mongols engage in a major battle and annihilate the armies of defense. To gain this strategic advantage they had sacrificed the greater part of Tului's three divisions, but they had escaped serious loss to their main army.

In so doing they had obeyed to the letter the advice of Sun-Tzu: "In war the successful strategist only *seeks battle* after the victory has been won, whereas he who is destined to defeat first fights and afterwards looks for victory."

SUBOTAI TRICKS NAN-KING

The Mongols were capable of winning a campaign by deception at the end, instead of the beginning—a much more difficult feat. Subotai tried to surprise the strong walled city of Nan-king with his siege army. For six days he made attempts at different points to force a way through the defenses. When he failed he broke off the action, to avoid wasting the lives of his men. He built a blockade wall, fifty-four miles long, around the fortified area defended by the resolute Chinese. Nan-king was said to have a population of four million.

The blockade reduced the Chinese to near starvation. Epidemics broke out in the city, but it did not surrender. Then Subotai let it be known that he might be bribed. The Chinese sent out an enormous sum to him, to buy his withdrawal.

And Subotai did retire, abandoning his blockade line. Beyond the observation of the Chinese he rested his men, out of danger from the epidemic. When the Chinese were convinced that Nan-king had been spared the Mongols reappeared suddenly. Taken by surprise, the Chinese resistance collapsed.

Their will to resist had been strong enough to hold off the Mongol attack and to endure hunger. But it did not survive the letdown, when they believed the siege to be over. The Mongols gained Nan-king at the price of a small casualty list. By treachery! Certainly. That is one of the most useful weapons of the total war.

How different were the tactics of Falkenhayn and the German Crown Prince who staged the attack on Verdun in 1916, to create a mincing machine of artillery fire by which the resistance of the French would be broken. The Verdun charnel house sapped the resistance of the Germans as well as the French, and it was not broken off when it failed to accomplish the strategic aim that inspired it.

Neither Falkenhayn nor the Crown Prince could have agreed with Sun-Tzu, who said more than two thousand years ago: "You can begin a battle by *direct* methods, but indirect methods are needed to secure victory."

The commanders of the Third Reich, today, have learned this lesson.

BAYAN'S PEACE OFFENSIVE

Perhaps the most extraordinary deception worked by the Mongols was to camouflage at least one great war as a peace offensive. The staff general Bayan and Kubilai Khan worked it out together to break the resistance of the mighty Sung empire. The territory of the Sung, south of the Yang-tse, had not been invaded for centuries. Its immense population was high-spirited but accustomed only to an economy of peace.

The Mongol armies of invasion faced a potential man power thirty to forty times as great as their own. They might have been expected to experiment with a blitzkrieg. Instead—probably aware of the size and strength of the cities confronting them—they did the exact opposite.

Their strategy was to avoid rousing up such human masses against them. Bayan's armies moved south at an oxen's pace. Their expedition became a series of summer encampments. At times they displayed banners with the slogan, "It is forbidden to take human life."

Their flanking detachments distributed farming tools and seed to the peasants of the countryside. They issued food to the villages. Where Bayan came upon an epidemic he sent physicians from the Mongol divisions to check the disease.

When he was forced to give battle or to take a city by siege, he buried his enemies with honors and himself prayed publicly at the graves of the most daring of the Sung commanders. Meanwhile, the peace propaganda penetrated in advance of his armies. In regions where the Sung leaders were trying to rouse the common people to resist, Bayan would be apt to send officers to make a distribution of coins. He was gambling on the stubborn inclination of the southern Chinese toward peace. His propaganda emphasized that the Sung commanders were getting the agricultural regions into trouble, while the Mongols were aiding the economy of peace. It was a foolish business for the Sung people to leave their shops and fields to join the ranks of an army where soon or late they would be killed, in spite of the desire of the Mongols to protect their lives.

Naturally, the strategy of this bloodless war—or a war planned to be bloodless—required iron discipline in the ranks of the Mongols. The story is told of a soldier who helped himself to some onions from a field and was dismissed from the army. And it required the endless patience of a—Mongol.

But it sabotaged the military strength of the Sung. The Sung nobility, trying to promote a death-or-glory resistance, became very unpopular with the field workers. The strength of Bayan's strategy lay in the demonstrated fact that he had made resistance futile and unprofitable. After nine years the reigning city of the Sung surrendered without conflict. Bayan accomplished what had not been done in the centuries before his time, or since—the subjection of the whole of China to an invader.

This form of peace offensive, supported by propaganda, was tried rather clumsily by the Red Army in Poland during September 1939 and again in the invasion of Finland. The camouflage fell away from it in a few hours. The real purpose of the Red Army in each case was to occupy a foreign area as rapidly as possible by force. Propaganda that the Red advance was to protect inhabitants of the area against capitalistic control proved to be meaningless—a transparent screen of words flung in front of the advancing tanks.

In the same way the peace propaganda that camouflaged the German push into Norway broke down within a few hours. The Germans might explain that they had appeared to take over the Norwegian ports to safeguard them from an attack by the British, but their actions made clear at once that this was a military invasion. A Trojan horse ceases to be useful when armed men are seen climbing out of it. The Germans took the ports, but they were involved in military action with the Norwegians within twenty-four hours.

War without Battles

By the Mongol method of warfare their armies of invasion entered an enemy country with a decisive advantage already won. To put it broadly, the war was half won by the time military operations began.

With this advantage, the second phase of the war—the maneuvering of the attack columns—was certain to be successful unless something unforeseen occurred. By deception and surprise the Mongol attack columns had "got there first." They were already following a carefully prepared plan and moving at a speed the enemy could not match. They had gained, as it were, full momentum. It was their strategy not to "git thar fustest with the mostest men," but to get there first with the best men.

This momentum often proved decisive. In 1914 the momentum of the wheel of the right flank of the German armies—after deception and surprise—through the static Belgians and the scattered British and French divisions almost won Paris and the Channel ports. Which, in that case, might have meant the war.

In 1939 the momentum of the four German attack armies (each with a spearhead of motorized units) closing in on Warsaw broke through the resistance of the half-organized Polish armies immobilized by the bombardment from the air during the first three days. At least two of the four German armies were able to penetrate to Warsaw without a major battle. The resistance of the mixed Polish forces caught around Warsaw was hopeless, as we know now. It was ended by artillery fire and bombing from the air without serious loss to the German commands.

The Mongols were more successful in avoiding ranged battles. Their strategy kept enemy forces in movement, either forward or back. They knew by experience that a courageous and unbroken civilized army would almost always advance against them, and a broken army would seek safety in flight away from them. So their maneuvering during the third phase of a war—following the preparation and penetration—was intended to prevent a decisive battle. They did everything possible to keep enemy forces from gathering in strength to make a stand on favorable ground.

Napoleon, the greatest of the European opportunists, rarely accomplished or tried to accomplish this almost impossible feat. He relied upon the pressure of the "strongest battalions" to break the enemy resistance in battle, and upon victory in battle to win a war. But this procedure, from Austerlitz to Eylau and to Borodino, ended in Waterloo. His "strongest battalions" had become ineffective through wastage in lives.

We find no such glittering chain of battles in the campaigns of Genghis Khan. The Asiatic conqueror was too chary of the lives of his Mongols. By avoiding an Austerlitz he never knew a Waterloo. Subotai is said by tradition to have won thirty-two wars and sixty-five battles. If this be true, the conqueror of Europe needed an average of less than two engagements to a campaign.

Sun-Tzu, writing in the dawn of history, reminds us: "That commander is most successful who achieves victory without being drawn into battle."

A theoretical axiom? The Mongols practiced it. Their strategy avoided a massed battle in three ways: (1) By infiltration (that is, by moving past a strongly defended point like a fortress without attacking it, in order to break resistance behind it); (2) by flank attack (that is, by refusing to make a frontal advance against a stationary enemy and by forcing him to move by wheeling around him) ; (3) by counterattack.

These three movements can be carried out today only by highly trained and mobile units. Like the Mongols, the armies of the Third Reich have mastered the first and third particularly. Their tactical expedient in attack is to find weakness and slip past strong points, which are left to special units to reduce later. Their defense system is the well-known elastic type, by which a frontal position is held by small detachments, while the stronger forces are held back of the first line in readiness to counterattack.

These now-well-known tactics the Mongols employed in the larger scale of strategy. That is, in the massed movements of their divisions over the entire area of the conflict. If the infiltration attack failed to demolish the enemy resistance the Mongols would be apt to feign a general retreat, to draw the enemy out in pursuit before attacking again unexpectedly from the flanks.

Such a maneuver broke the first two Russian armies at the River Khalka in 1222. Subotai used it to demolish the main army of the European campaign of 1240. And by it he managed to avoid a pitched battle.

Battle without Loss

In March of the year 1241 the main resistance of the Europeans was gathering around the city of Buda on the wide Danube. It was gathering in the way usual to courageous but little-trained citizen soldiery. Armed men were collecting in the outlying country and marching in under their leaders to Buda, the concentration point, there to find out how they were to fight and where.

In the Buda castle their higher command—the Hungarian king, bishops, nobles, commanders of Templars—were discussing what measures they might take if the Mongols should appear on their side of the Carpathian Mountains. These Christian soldiers were accustomed to marching out against an enemy and fighting hand to hand—for the most part on foot. They felt confident enough because they knew only that the still-invisible Mongols were barbaric pagans, and an armed and armored Christian host could easily win a victory over pagans. These allies—Hungarians, Croats, Austrians, French Templars, and others— were good soldiers by the European standards of the day and determined to come to battle. They knew nothing, in reality, about the movements of the Mongols.

While the Allied Council debated the Mongols were already in full momentum, four attack columns driving through and around the Carpathians, sweeping over weak resistance and uniting against stronger forces, destroying elsewhere the Slavs, Poles, Silesians, and Transylvanian

Germans who stood against them. The Mongols were using their favorite pincers attack, overrunning the points of mobilization before closing the pincers on the main resistance at Buda. The rendezvous of their flying columns was the Danube at Buda. The date, March 17.

The first news the Allied Council had of the war was the sudden appearance of an officer of the frontier guard to report that the Mongols were through the mountain passes nearly two hundred miles away. He reached Buda March 15. The next day the Mongol advance units appeared at his heels along the river.

The Allied army, under leadership of the Hungarian king, was taken by surprise but not thrown into confusion. It did not scatter or make a hasty attack across the river. The Mongols had no means of crossing the Danube.

After two weeks or so the Allied army, now some one hundred thousand strong, crossed the river to give battle. It saw nothing of the Mongols except for patrols of horsemen that withdrew before it. As might be expected, the Hungarians and their allies followed up this retreat. For six days they marched eastward, away from the river, without being able to come up with the elusive horsemen. On the sixth night they camped in a plain hemmed in by low, vine-clad hills, with a small river—the Sayo—in front of them.

They were warned by an escaped prisoner that the Mongols were five or six miles on the other side of the river. They took the precautions of experienced soldiers. A strong advance detachment was posted at the one bridge over the Sayo—a wagon ring drawn up around the main encampment.

That night the Mongols moved to destroy this army. The advance guard at the bridge was driven back by the fire of war machines; elsewhere the Mongols built a bridge of their own. From two directions they occupied the higher ground around the Christian camp.

When the Mongols were seen at the first daylight the heavily armed Allied chivalry made a frontal charge from the camp. This charge up a slope was broken by "fire" from the Mongol bows and machines. A second charge led by the Templars still failed to come to hand-to-hand fighting.

The Mongol line in front of it withdrew; the Christian knights were enveloped in a smoke screen, decoyed off into rough ground, and cut to pieces from a distance. Not one of the Templars survived.

In the camp behind the wagon ring the main body of Christian soldiery on foot was still resolute enough. But the Mongols made no attack on their lines. Instead, they began a long-range fire of arrows and flame projectiles on the camp. This fire from above, to which the Christians could not reply effectively, broke the morale of the soldiers. They could not charge the Mongols on foot; they could not hold their position in the camp. They began to retire to the west, where the Mongols had left a wide gap in their encirclement. This was in the direction of the Danube and safety.

Still the Mongol regiments made no direct attack. For six days they followed on the flanks of that mass in retreat, killing the men who fell behind from weakness, and herding the fragments of the mass aside, to be destroyed more easily in woods and brush. Some seventy thousand of the Europeans are said to have died in this methodical operation.

Grim as was this slaughter, it was only an episode in the Mongol military conquest. Inferior in numbers to the central Europeans, Subotai had managed to destroy their mobilized armies without coming to battle at close quarters and with a wastage of lives so slight among the Mongols that his divisions were intact. Behind the strategy of the old Mongol there were two very material aids in his triumph at the Sayo—the skill of his engineers in bridgebuilding and the range of his "fire" power.

The Mongol method of attack made it impossible for the eastern Europeans, who were their equal in fighting spirit, to stand against them. Unaware of what they were facing, the Christians went into "battles" that were lost beforehand.

Zone Method of Conquest

In their general attack on civilization the Mongols limited each advance according to a fixed plan. It can be called the zone, or the avalanche, method.

Once the military blitzkrieg was over and the walls of fortified cities demolished, the Mongols proceeded swiftly to the dismemberment of a conquered nation before it could recover from the paralysis of the attack. The reigning monarch was hunted to death or exile, the travel routes taken over by a roadmaster. The horse herds were rounded up with cattle for the army. The surviving man power was divided. Trained workers were formed into labor battalions, fed by the Mongols. The strongest-appearing men were drafted into the reserve contingents of the invader's army. Noted scholars and scientists were sent east to Karakorum, the Mongol capital in the Gobi regions.

From a census taken by methodical Chinese secretaries, a tax record could be prepared. Field workers were left to harvest the next crop.

So when the armies of attack moved on to the next zone they took with them a large part of the man power of the first zone, which was now without leaders to organize a revolt. This commandeered man power would be used against the next zone. And only a minimum of guard posts would be needed to keep the first devastated zone under control.

If they anticipated an attack from an outlying power the whole frontier of the farthest zone would be ravaged and burned, to destroy the supplies that could maintain an army.

By limiting the area of each advance the Mongols dealt as far as possible with one nation at a time. But their zones were designed more for geographical reasons than any other. Each one stemmed out from the Gobi region. In their invasion of the west from 1235 to 1242 the Mongol ordus advanced as far as the Volga before concentrating against the vast steppe-and-forest area of Russia. Their second zone extended nearly to Kiev and the Baltic shore. Their third swept through the barrier of the Carpathians as far as the Danube.

By this limitation the Mongols avoided overreaching themselves. By isolating each zone in their peculiar fashion from the outer areas of the world they escaped being put on the defensive by an enemy attack. They took time to consolidate before each advance.

Not since the long-forgotten days of the Assyrians had the civilized world *in toto* faced such a total attack upon its powers of resistance. So there existed in the Mongol era no military machine that could check their advance, and the more peaceful powers of the outer civilization proved to be incapable of joining together for a combined resistance.

In their methodical advance the Mongols contented themselves with appropriating the wealth and labors of the vanquished peoples. Whether from superstition or because they found the priesthoods useful as intermediaries with the subject races, the horsemen from the Gobi never interfered with religion.

They established, in their passing, the deathly nomad peace in the conquered areas. (In their home life the Mongols proved to be kindly and good-natured men who wore no weapons and indulged in no quarreling. This brief sketch of their military strategy does not deal with the Mongols as a people.)

To a certain extent the strategy of the Third Reich now follows the zone method of the Mongols. The captured resources of Czechoslovakia—especially the munitions—were employed in the surprise attacks on Poland, the Low Countries, and France. Contingents of Slovaks, and apparently some Czechs, were ordered to advance into the second zone of Poland behind the motorized thrusts of the Reich's divisions. Such detachments were seen passing through the Tatra Mountains with German artillery moving behind them and German aviation overhead.

In their occupation of Poland the agents of the new imperialism of the Reich severed the nerve centers of the stunned nation.

They seized control of the food of the area, reducing the population to dependence on the new military authorities for the means of life itself. And they dealt with—by exile or execution—the natural leaders of the population who might head a revolt. Curiously enough, in their section of the invaded area, the Soviet agents were doing the same thing. The excuse made by the Reich was that, while the bulk of the common people were offering no resistance, the *intelligentsia* were causing trouble. The propaganda of the Red occupation was that only the *capitalistic land-owners* were being molested.

It came to the same thing. The best brains and keenest spirits among the Poles were at once canceled.

Even a brief study of the Mongol invasion brings home to us several lessons, forgotten in the West during the long era of industrialization and prevailing peace.

First, that Europeans have no monopoly of military genius. Asia can produce strategists of the highest caliber.

Second, that Asia has, in the past, understood the operation of the "new" total war that destroys resistance.

Third, that Asiatics can match the fighting power of Europeans, *if given an equality in weapon power*. In the desultory combats along the Amur frontier the Japanese have proved themselves more than a match for the Soviet forces in the air and in tactics on land.

Also, that the volunteer armies of a high-spirited citizenry with little training may go down to sudden defeat before the attack of a highly trained military machine.

There is no defense against the lightning attack on land *except an equally efficient military organization*. The increased power of the air force to cripple resistance on land has added to the danger of the blitzkrieg. Because it adds to the speed of the attack—as the Germans have proved once and for all. The fast-moving tank has also added to the speed of the attack, so long as the tank can be followed up by motorized infantry units. So these two modern inventions have made even more dangerous the strategy of the Mongol horsemen.

How close a study, if any, German military brains have made of the Mongol campaigns I do not know. There have been at least five studies of the Mongol attack upon Europe published in German, as against one in French and none in the English language.

WAR MAXIMS OF GENERAL LOUTAO

(About 1150 B.C.)

From an article translated from a German version by
LIEUTENANT (NOW LIEUTENANT GENERAL)
WALTER KRUEGER

(*1915*)

A GOOD GENERAL should never say that he will do a certain thing, come what may, for his course of action should be determined solely by the situation.

If your army is approximately equal in numbers to that of the enemy, nine of the ten advantages of the terrain should be on your side. Employ all your mental resources, all your physical efforts, all your diligence in obtaining them.

Do not go to sleep after an initial success and do not allow your troops an untimely period of rest. Do not dream of reaping the fruits of victory until the defeat of the enemy is complete.

TWO VIEWS OF WAR

By Brigadier General John McAuley Palmer

(1942)

THE ASPECTS OF WAR involving weapons and ways of moving troops have changed at each stage of human development. There is a vast difference between war as it was waged by Alexander the Great and as it is now fought by Rommel and Yamashita. But in one way war is the same now as it was when an unknown conqueror built the first pyramid as a monument to his name and its prowess. It is not a separate, isolated form of human activity. It is, instead, as the German soldier-philosopher Clausewitz said a century ago, a special, violent form of political action.

We customarily think that no two things can be more unlike than peaceful international relations and warlike international relations. And so we may be startled when we first grasp the thought that these are simply two phases of the same thing—human politics.

This was brought home to us last December. For years it had been the avowed purpose of Japan to dominate China and southeast Asia and control the western Pacific. When normal political action in Washington failed to gain our acquiescence Japan's next argument was delivered at Pearl Harbor. Her purpose was still political and precisely what it was before her treacherous surprise attack. The only difference was that she was now using dive bombers instead of diplomats.

Even before Clausewitz, George Washington understood that war is simply a phase of politics. Thus when his countrymen called him to establish a new political system he realized clearly that any complete system must include the machinery for dealing with that special violent phase of international politics known as war. This is the principal thought in his political writings from the close of the Revolution to the end of his life. In the light of his knowledge of war and its great significance in international affairs, his Farewell Address may be summarized as follows:

Rely on just dealing with other nations. Seek your legitimate political ends through peaceful negotiation and understanding. But lest some aggressor impose the other form of political action known as war upon you, maintain yourselves in a "respectably defensive posture."

If you do this other nations will not be tempted to depart from the normal and peaceful methods of political action in their dealings with you.

The non-aggressive military organization proposed by Washington to prevent normal political action from degenerating into the violent form known as war would have tended to conserve peace. But his countrymen ignored his advice for a century and a half. If he had been able to implement the new American republic with effective military institutions suited to a self-governing free people, Japan would never have dared to take a change of venue from the Court of Reason to the Court of Brute Force.

But if war is a phase of human politics it is plain that there can be a war-provocative as well as a peace-conservative type of military organization. While Washington was still a child and Japan a hermit kingdom Frederick the Great of Prussia was perfecting this other politico-military form. Frederick understood the close relation between peaceful and warlike politics as well as Washington, but he applied it in an entirely different way which we can summarize as follows:

When peaceful negotiation fails to solve a political question, the controversy assumes another form of political intercourse known as war.

Now, when a controversy assumes this second form, it is decided not by the best cause but by the most force. Therefore, if I have enough force I can always compel submission to my political will without reference to the merits of my cause.

Furthermore, if I am known to be invincible in this second form and always eager to embrace it I can enforce my will beyond my just rights even while political action is still in its normal peaceful form, because I can always threaten a resort to the second form if I am not humored.

My policy should therefore be to prepare for sudden victorious attack. With this assured, I will be able to make my neighbors pay me a sort of commutation of victory even in time of peace.

Therefore, I propose to maintain a striking force always ready for offensive military action, and I propose to employ it whenever a favorable and profitable opportunity offers.

Washington called his military organization a "respectably defensive posture." The organization Frederick bequeathed to Prussia was a truculently offensive posture. The one is highly conservative of peace; the other is highly provocative of war. Washington proposed to eliminate war as an irrational political process. Frederick proposed to cultivate war as a positive means of political advantage. Washington proposed to arm as a gentleman would arm to defend himself from highwaymen. Frederick proposed to profit by making himself an accomplished and invincible bandit. Washington's aim was essentially moral and social. Frederick's aim was essentially unsocial and criminal. Both of these constructive statesmen designed military institutions suited to their points of view. Washington's countrymen rejected his. Frederick transmitted his to his successors.

Indeed, the Prussian military system was never a *defensive* organization. It was deliberately designed as a conquest machine from the beginning. Frederick employed it to aggrandize Prussia within Germany. World mastery was not a feasible enterprise in his day, but the impulse toward future world conquest was inherent in his politico-military machine. Bismarck employed the conquest machine, as further perfected by Moltke the Elder, to crush the growing democratic movement in Germany and then to unite Germany under the domination of militarist Prussia. After Bismarck's victories over Austria and France the conquest machine was no longer needed to defend Germany or to conserve legitimate German interests. If retained, the German General Staff must seek grist for it outside of Germany, and so, step by step as opportunity broadened, it would follow the pathway toward world conquest. But for the tardy and unexpected awakening of America, the decisive victory might have been won in 1918. Since World War I, the German General Staff, as conserved in the Reichswehr, has never relinquished that purpose as an ultimate objective. But opportunity came earlier than was expected. While Hitler was re-equipping the old conquest machine for modern blitzkrieg he found that the English-speaking democracies (to whom the strategic ramparts of civilization were entrusted) were heavily doped in appeasement and pacifism. Therein lies the fundamental cause of the present world cyclone. There was a *high barometer* of overmilitarization in the region of autocracy and a *low barometer* of undermilitarization in the region of democracy. Hence the inevitable storm. Hitler and his fellow gangsters found their impelling opportunity in the stupidity of the English-speaking peoples.

When Washington became President there were two main objectives in the program of his administration. He sought to establish a sound financial system and a sound military system. With the aid of Alexander Hamilton, his Secretary of the Treasury, he attained the first of these objectives before the end of his first administration. But it was not until after Hitler conquered France, more than a century and a half later, that Congress adopted the first principle of the Washingtonian military policy—compulsory military training in time of peace.

It is a high tribute to Hamilton's financial genius that his successors have, so far, been able to devise enough taxes and borrow enough money to pay for the wastes of public wealth that have flowed through that wide gap in our national structure. For unreadiness for war has been the principal cause of all of our great national debts. If our fathers had accepted *all* of Washington's political system instead of but half of it, there probably could have been no World War I, no postwar depression, and no World War II.

And, if the modern democratic state in general had included the peace-conservative military institutions that Washington proposed for it, it is likely that Japan would now be the liberal constitutional monarchy that the wisest of her elder statesmen sought to make her; Benito Mussolini would be a respectable newspaper editor in a liberal and peace-loving Italy, and that temperamental architect's assistant, Adolf Hitler, would be enjoying his Wagner in harmless doses with his evening beer and pretzels instead of attempting to conduct a world-wide Götterdämmerung of his own.

SMOKE AT GETTYSBURG

By CAPTAIN (now LIEUTENANT COLONEL) VICTOR A. COULTER

(1937)

ON ONE POINT, at least, all those who took part in and those who have written about the third day's fighting at Gettysburg are agreed. July 3, 1863, was a gaspingly hot day, with the morning sky overcast and hardly a breath of air stirring anywhere. Private Griffin of Archer's (Fry's) Brigade wrote that he "heard the shot of a single cannon and noted . . . a puff of white smoke as it rolled along the valley," indicating that whatever breeze there may have been blew parallel to the battle lines.

Shortly before three o'clock in the afternoon the counterbattery fire of the Federal artillery was interrupted to conserve ammunition, to reorganize for the impending Confederate assault, and because General Warren, chief engineer on Meade's staff, "from the Round Tops, perceived that it was inexpedient to fill the valley with a screen of smoke."

The event that followed is familiar to every school child. Unprotected by cover and unsupported by their own artillery during the advance, eighteen thousand Confederate troops moved out of the woods on Seminary Ridge to advance across the valley and assault the center of the Federal position on the ridge opposite. The history books were to call it Pickett's Charge.

The history books were to record how the Federal artillery inflicted heavy casualties almost from the time the Confederate lines emerged from the woods on Seminary Ridge; how, under this fire, the movements of the several brigades engaged in the assault were unco-ordinated; how the fences on both sides of the Emmitsburg Road had to be torn down, and how the Confederates suffered heavy losses as men crowded to pass through the fence gaps. Finally, when the left of the assaulting force became "exposed to the enfilading fire of the guns on the western slope of Cemetery Hill, that exposure sealed their fate."

So overwhelming was the fire superiority of the defenders that perhaps not more than six thousand of the eighteen thousand men who started from Seminary Ridge ever reached the Federal lines less than a mile away.

The historians are agreed that Pickett's Charge, on that sultry July afternoon, was as futile as it was gallant. Longstreet, we are told, objected to the movement before it commenced as being impossible of success.

Yet General Warren, from the Round Tops, perceived that it was inexpedient to fill the valley with a screen of smoke.

A study of what Lee might have done at Gettysburg with modern smoke shell is interesting. The late Colonel Lull, in a keen analysis of what the war of the future may be like, concludes that "to find our closest parallel we must look, not to the World War, but rather to the War between the American States. . . ."

Pickett's Charge, with little or no natural cover, is a suitable engagement on which to superimpose a modern smoke screen. It is possible that a little smoke, judiciously laid down on Cemetery Ridge on the afternoon of July 3, 1863, might have changed all subsequent history.

The total length of the Federal line from Round Top around to below Culp's Hill was not more than seven thousand yards. A chemical company is able to screen a front of sixteen hundred yards. Accordingly, one battalion might have carried out any smoke operation needed by the Confederate Army on that day.

To the objection that the weapons and mass movements employed in 1863 make unreasonable any comparison with present conditions, the reply may be made that the need for screening depends entirely upon the distance troops must travel under direct fire. Under modern conditions the critical period of an infantry advance begins about eight hundred yards from the objective. Musket fire at Gettysburg was not effective at that range, but direct fire from the Federal artillery tore gaping holes in the assaulting lines at about that distance.

Since all the fire at Gettysburg was delivered following direct laying of the pieces, the experiments of the last ten years on the effect of covering riflemen with a smoke blanket apply properly. All these experiments have shown that when riflemen are covered by smoke the percentage of hits they secure on silhouette targets is decreased 93 per cent. Let us place two platoons about eight hundred yards apart to the west and south of the Peach Orchard to cover the Federal position from Round Top to sixteen hundred yards north of General Warren's vantage spot. It will be remembered that the breeze, if any, was a light southerly one, blowing parallel to the lines and favorable to the use of smoke. Let us place four platoons about six hundred yards apart directly behind the assaulting force to cover the remainder of the Federal line to its extreme north. The two platoons remaining let us dispose of between the town of Gettysburg and Rock Creek, with the dual mission of keeping Federal reserves between Cemetery Hill and Culp's Hill enveloped in smoke and of throwing additional smoke on Cemetery Ridge if necessary.

And now, assuming that we have our battalion of 4.2 mortars in action, let us return to the battle. The entire Federal line is covered with a blanket of smoke as Pickett's Charge commences. The planned alignment of Confederate units is maintained across the fields; the fences along the Emmitsburg Road are torn down; Pickett's and Pettigrew's divisions are marched across this road, and the supporting troops are maneuvered into position while the smoke still covers both the Federal infantry and artillery.

At this point the fire from the mortars is raised from the Federal infantry lines to Federal artillery, several hundred yards to the rear, until such time as the assaulting force shall have gained its first objective. Then smoke firing is lifted entirely except on the northern half of Cemetery Ridge.

In the actual engagement fire from the Federal lines had reduced the effectiveness of Pickett's, Pettigrew's, and Trimble's divisions at least 50 per cent by the time those divisions had crossed the Emmitsburg Road. Reducing that loss by 93 per cent, that figure to which we promised to return, we find the assaulting force 96 per cent effective and its leading elements within one hundred yards of the famous stone wall and the Federal infantry when the smoke fire is lifted.

Whether Lee could have won the engagement from this point is a matter for the infantry to decide. But with the support of three smoke companies he might have had at least an even break.

A ROMAN FSR

By Colonel (now Brigadier General) Oliver Lyman Spaulding

(1937)

When the *Infantry Journal* invited "twenty Jominis" to submit the titles of ten books that every infantry officer should own it uncovered a wide divergence of opinion. During the Middle Ages there would not have been such lack of agreement. Then, one book would have sufficed and the experts would have been unanimous. All would have named *The Epitome of the Military Art,* by Flavius Vegetius Renatus.

Vegetius was the first author of a work comparable to a modern Field Service Regulations. He did the job so well and covered his subject so thoroughly that for a thousand years and more his text was the military bible of every literate soldier of western Europe.

He dedicated his book to the reigning emperor, and intimates that it was written by royal command; the monarch's name is not mentioned, but critics generally believe him to have been Valentinian II, Emperor of the West, A.D. 375–392. Nothing is known of the writer, but he appears to have been a man of rank and consequence. Probably he was a theoretical student of the art of war rather than a practical soldier, for nowhere does he hint at personal experience. He claims no originality but insists that his work is a compilation, based upon authorities whom he names— Cato, Celsus, Frontinus, Paternus, and the Emperors Augustus, Trajan, and Hadrian. Little remains of their writings. Even the army regulations of the three emperors have been lost.

Only in a limited sense can we speak of Vegetius' work as Field Service Regulations, for it contains not only precepts, but also numerous historical and controversial passages, explaining how the ancients did things. The writer is distinctly a conservative; he defends the Roman system against the intrusion of foreign doctrines and inveighs against the indifference and neglect of a degenerate age.

Vegetius pays tribute to the discipline and training that made Rome the mistress of the world. He writes:

Victory is gained, not by weight of numbers and untrained courage, but by skill and discipline. We have seen the Romans conquer the world by no other means than skill in arms and the rigid discipline and thorough training of their troops. How otherwise could a handful of Romans overcome the multitudes of the Gauls? How else could the short-statured Roman face the giant German? The Spaniards are superior to us not only in numbers but in physique, the Africans in subtlety and in wealth, the Greeks in the arts and sciences. Against all this the Romans could oppose extreme care in the selection of recruits, diligent instruction in the use of arms, inculcation of discipline by daily habit, forethought in devising means to meet any emergency that might arise in action, and stern punishment for neglect of duty. For a thoroughly trained man will be bold and confident in action; one has no hesitation in undertaking work with which one is perfectly familiar. A small trained force is the best guarantee of success; a raw undisciplined host is foredoomed to destruction.

Vegetius divides his treatise into five books. The first of these treats of recruitment and elementary instruction.

For soldiers Vegetius prefers men from temperate climates, countrymen rather than city dwellers, and the hardier craftsmen such as carpenters or blacksmiths rather than confectioners or weavers. He attaches little importance to stature but insists upon health, strength, and agility. The new recruit served a probationary period until his aptitude had been tested.

The physical-training course included marching, running, leaping, and swimming. The recruit was expected to march twenty miles a day under a load of sixty pounds, which was still not as heavy as the full legionary equipment. Cavalry recruits, fully accoutered, were trained to mount a wooden horse by vaulting from either side. This was an important and practical exercise, for stirrups had yet to be invented.

Great pains were taken with instruction in the use of arms. Those issued to recruits were not service weapons, but dummies, and were made heavier than the regulation patterns, for the same reason that a baseball player swings two bats before he steps up to the plate. The swordsmen were taught to thrust rather than cut, for the same reasons explained in our modern cavalry *Drill Regulations*—the thrust is much more likely to inflict a dangerous wound, and in delivering it one's own body is not exposed. Posts, set up on the drill ground, served as targets for sword and javelin practice, in which both accuracy and power were demanded. Similar instruction was given in the use of the bow and the sling. Qualified men, selected as instructors in these exercises, drew additional pay, as do our marksmen and gunners today. These came to constitute a separate grade in the military hierarchy. For several centuries they held the title *campi doctor,* which means field master or master at arms. There may well be a connection between this title and *maestro de campo* used for a regimental commander in sixteenth-century Spain.

When individual instruction had progressed up to a certain point, the elements of collective instruction were taken up, especially marching. A fully instructed recruit was expected to be ready to join in the practice marches of his cohort, which were made every ten days. These marches, which averaged twenty miles a day, were made with full field kit, over varied ground, and invariably included incidental exercises in minor tactics.

The recruit was also expected to know how to dig, for Vegetius held to the old Roman plan of entrenching every camp. The camp was generally rectangular, but the trace of the wall was determined by the terrain. The capacity of the Roman for spadework is indicated by the dimensions of the fortification. A wall three feet high, with a ditch nine feet wide and seven feet deep, is spoken of as a light entrenchment. For really serious entrenching Vegetius prescribes a ditch twelve feet wide by nine deep and a wall four feet high, revetted with hurdles and crowned with a palisade. The wall was not intended to serve as a breastwork but as the *terreplein,* upon which the defenders stood. The work was carefully organized. The cavalry formed an outpost, backed up by half the infantry, while the other half of the infantry dug. Reliefs were by small units under their own officers. Upon relief the officers in immediate command measured the work completed to fix responsibility.

Book I ends with this pithy remark:

Military instruction should always be given to selected young men, for the state will find it less expensive to train its own citizens in arms than to purchase foreign assistance.

Not a bad motto for our Reserve Officers' Training Corps.

Book II deals with organization and interior economy. It describes the two great classes of Roman troops—the legions, or regulars, and the auxiliaries, or provincial contingents. Vegetius points out how much help the auxiliaries can be to the legions but at the same time recognizes a human trait which is not unfamiliar to us. When one class of troops has stricter discipline and heavier duty than another, recruits avoid the first and seek the second. He laments the decay of the legionary forces as a result of the failure to make service in them attractive. He remarks that good troops cost no more than bad and appeals to the emperor to put an end to abuses and restore the ancient Roman discipline.

Vegetius attributes much of the superiority of the legion to its well-rounded completeness, which he credits to divine inspiration. This unit was, in all truth, beautifully proportioned. It was small enough to be cohesive and to foster a healthy organization spirit and yet large enough and strong enough to undertake a major mission. At this time the first of its ten cohorts was approximately a thousand men strong while the others were only half that strength. With its light infantry and cavalry the legion of this period totaled somewhere between six and seven thousand men.

The old command system was still in existence. The military tribunes corresponded roughly to our field officers and the centurions to our company officers. There were also numerous grades of minor officers that might be compared to our noncoms. However, there was one important difference in the command setup: the institution foreshadowed in Caesar's armies had now become fully established—each legion had a single permanent commander, the legionary prefect. The *legati,* used by Caesar for such commands, had been moved up a grade and now commanded independent detached forces, or groups of legions. There was also the prefect of the camp who was responsible for establishing and fortifying the camp, for supply, for hospital service, and for transportation.

The legion had its own force of artificers of every trade—workers in wood and metal, masons, painters, and unskilled laborers. They manned mobile repair shops for arms and equipment. There was also a corps of sappers and miners. All these special troops came under the command of a staff officer called the prefect of artificers. The legionary trains carried not only regular supplies but also artillery—portable catapults and *ballistae*—heavy for the legion and light for the cohorts, just as we now provide light machine guns for our infantry battalions and heavier accompanying weapons for the regiment.

In this second book Vegetius also gives a brief sketch of the paper work of the legion—pay accounts, duty rosters, records of furloughs, deposits of pay, maintenance and administration of a legionary relief fund. He describes the system of promotion of centurions—seniority in the legion at large, not in each cohort separately. Additional instructions follow on collective training; all subjects mentioned for recruits are continued in the troop units—newly incorporated recruits attending two drills a day, old soldiers one.

We meet the real Field Service Regulations in Book III. It begins by discussing the desirable strength of an army. By reference to the examples of Xerxes, Darius, and Mithridates, Vegetius emphasizes the point that quantity should not be sought at the expense of quality. He strongly favors a small trained force over a larger one loosely organized and ill disciplined. The latter, he states, consumes supplies out of all proportion to the service it can render. Today, after a century's reign of the "nation in arms" theory, our military thought on this point seems to be leading back to Vegetius.

Sanitary regulations also receive attention. Rules are laid down for the selection of a healthy camp site. In hot weather marches should begin early so that they may be terminated before the hottest part of the day. Important, too, is an ample and pure water supply, prompt medical attention and proper diet for the sick, and the frequent moving of camps.

The discussion of supply emphasizes the importance of careful preliminary estimates, proper apportionment of requisitions to the provinces that are to fill them, and logical organization of depots. The subsistence stores named are beef on the hoof, grain, wine, vinegar, and salt. Other supplies such as fuel, forage, arms, and ammunition are also mentioned.

Vegetius speaks of discipline and discusses the effect of training methods upon it. Since idle men become discontented he believes that troops should be kept fully occupied with drills, physical training, and maneuvers. He observes that labor may be demanded freely, so long as it is evident that it has a definite military purpose. His idea of discipline is summed up in this statement:

He is the better leader whose command is well behaved through hard work and the habit of order, rather than he who must force his men to duty through fear of punishment.

This sagacious Roman also had something to say on marks of identification and methods of visual and sound signaling, and much on marching and the service of security and information. He stresses the importance of constant reconnaissance and prescribes that reconnaissance reports should be accompanied by sketches. Other points deemed important are the procurement and handling of guides; the formation of march columns, with advance and flank guards and appropriate disposition of trains; careful calculation of space and time, and close supervision of march discipline by officers. A special section is devoted to river crossings —the reconnaissance of fords and the technique of using them, the construction of pontoon bridges, and the establishment of bridgeheads. All of this has a distinctly modern flavor.

For planning a campaign and selecting ground for battle, Vegetius gives a form for making an estimate of the situation. It is similar to the one we use in our military schools today. It includes a study of the mission and of the strength and composition of the opposing forces. It lays special stress upon an estimate of the character of the enemy's leader. The estimate also takes into account the supply situation in both armies. Finally it prescribes a study of the terrain with a view to exploiting its favorable features and minimizing its disadvantages.

The manual goes into detail on the order of battle of large units. The infantry is habitually placed in the center, well organized in depth; heavy cavalry covers its flanks, and the light cavalry operates independently farther out. The importance of reserves is particularly emphasized. In his discussion of victory Vegetius refers again to the time-honored maxim which warns against driving a beaten enemy to desperation, and he quotes Virgil's line, that the only hope of the vanquished is in despair. Discussing defeat, he makes a perfectly sound analysis of the process of breaking off an engagement, forming a march column for retreat, and organizing a rear guard.

The work is generously provided with military maxims. Among them are:

Who wishes peace, let him prepare for war.

Who hopes for victory, let him be diligent in military training.

No one dares to provoke a power which is known to be superior in war.

A general must not attempt to change his plan after the battle has begun; confusion always results, offering opportunity to the enemy.

If a spy is suspected, order every man to his tent and the spy will be detected. (Napoleon used this device on the island of Löbau in the Wagram campaign.)

Seek advice from many, but keep your decision to yourself. (One thinks at once of Stonewall Jackson, who carried this virtue almost to a vice.)

Book IV treats of fortresses. The various offensive and defensive devices mentioned by earlier writers are discussed again, but little is added that is new. Among the engineering expedients is one which has only recently disappeared from military textbooks—determining the height of a wall by measuring the length of its shadow and comparing it with the shadow of a pole of known height.

Vegetius gives much space to the problems of supply of fortified places, especially the supply of water, salt meats, fruits, vegetables, grain, wine, salt, and vinegar; also poultry, for hospital diet. He insists upon the rigid rationing of all stores, both for the military garrison and for the civil inhabitants. Among ordnance stores he mentions sulphur, oil, and other incendiary materials; iron and coal; selected wood for manufacture of spears and arrows; smooth, round stones, sorted in sizes for use as projectiles for slings and for artillery; sinews and hair for the driving ropes of artillery weapons.

In closing he again emphasizes the importance of a good service of security and information. He favors the use of watchdogs and retells the tale of the geese that saved Rome from capture by the Gauls.

The subject of Book V is naval warfare. It is known that Vegetius is more at home ashore than afloat, and he admits as much. Still, he touches on the subject, since most of the sea fighting was done by soldiers.

In marked contrast to most military writings, this one never fell into obscurity. This is perhaps because it is the only comprehensive ancient treatise on the art of war that was written in Latin. Others there were, but they came later, when Latin had ceased to be the official language of the eastern empire. These were written in Greek and therefore not as widely known in western Europe. Vegetius' famous work was always widely read; it was copied over and over in manuscripts and translated into all modern languages as soon as these languages had reached a stage of development making translation worth while. The leading soldiers of the Middle Ages carried him in their saddle pockets. The earliest printers seized upon him as one of their first texts; half a dozen printed editions appeared before the end of the fifteenth century.

The innovations in warfare incident to the use of gunpowder outmoded some, but not all, of Vegetius' text. Distinguished soldiers of the modern era have studied it with profit. Indeed, many passages from this military classic seem destined to transcend both time and invention in their application.

JUNGLE WARFARE

By Colonel Cary I. Crockett

(1934)

The fighting our Army did in the early days of the century in the Philippines had many things in common with the South Pacific fighting in this war. The terrain was much the same—damp, thick jungle infested with poisonous plants, animals, and insects, including the malaria mosquito. Much of the Philippine jungle was also mountainous, and the only routes were deep-worn trails or new ones cut through the jungle by the troops themselves.

Some of the military feats of those days involved the greatest endurance and fighting skill on the part of our troops. They have never fought under tougher conditions.

The fighting, of course, was against the Insurrectos. Gradually the pacification was completed, and then our government, with the help of the Army, entered upon the phase of helping the distant Pacific peoples toward a greater degree of civilization.

The one Army man who has written extensively of the early fighting in the Philippines is Ingram Cary. This is the pen name of Colonel Cary I. Crockett, U. S. Army, retired, an alert and able infantry officer who has written not only of historical matters but of modern methods of warfare. His article on the Russian paratroops (1937) was the first one on this subject printed in the *Infantry Journal*.

. . . Gathering darkness found the column of bedraggled and weary men trailing laboriously across a valley where underfoot there was black mud, waist deep in places, and overhead the matted foliage of a forest so dense that the gloom in it was that of night. The rain continued to fall in torrents, but Cochrane pushed on, as a halt for the night in that morass was out of the question. In the middle of the valley a sluggish stream with steep and miry banks presented a formidable obstacle. The men floundered through it in mud and water reaching to their shoulders, one helping another across the stream and up the bank on the other side. Fortunately rising ground was soon encountered, and the company went into camp after a march of fourteen hours from San Ramon.

A body of white troops in a similar situation no doubt would have spent a miserable night lying shelterless in drenched clothing on the soaked ground. It was not so with Cochrane's seasoned campaigners. Within half an hour a circle of rainproof leaf huts floored with boughs had sprung up; the undergrowth had been cleared away for a field both of view and of fire, and the men were wringing out their blankets and outer garments before huge fires built against the open sides of the huts. The only things needed to make them perfectly comfortable were a bowl of smoking-hot rice and a few cigarettes apiece, but as these luxuries were not forthcoming, they philosophically made the best of it and chattered away happily over the scanty meal prepared by the cooks. Meanwhile the covering groups had been relieved and a "running guard" detailed, four double sentry posts being established near the edge of the clearing.

When supper was over the men finished drying their clothing and dressed, scraped the mud from their shoes, wiped off their arms and equipment, and, packing themselves together by squads with loaded rifles at hand, proceeded to take a well-earned rest. Cochrane had a separate hut, built in the center of the circle, and the men vied with each other in making him as comfortable as possible under the circumstances. He noticed a peculiar phenomenon on this night, which was that all the objects in the vicinity of the camp were phosphorescent, the strange brilliancy extending halfway up the tree trunks and giving the forest a weird and unearthly aspect.

The march to the westward was resumed early the next morning. The trail led over another mountain range and then down into a maze of ridges. It was impossible to determine the general slope of the land as the streams seemed to flow in every direction. Heretofore the trail had shown no indication of recent use, but numerous freshly made footprints were now observed. It was evident that the Pulajans on the San Ramon coast did not use the old trail the column had followed but had another and more direct route leading straight through the jungle.

Cochrane joined the advance guard on this morning, and the march was continued with redoubled caution. Several *camote* patches were passed during the morning, and before noon the column arrived at a burned hut where the trail forked, one leading to the southwest and the other toward the north. Cochrane took the latter because it showed more use and halted at noon only long enough for the men to roast some camotes. During the afternoon several other cultivated fields and burned houses were passed. Toward evening the column descended into a wide valley, covered with cogon grass over ten feet in height, and the trail, after branching several times, finally terminated in a series of runways tunneled under the long grass in half a dozen directions.

Cochrane halted the column and, taking a squad from the advance guard, went forward to reconnoiter. He followed a well-used runway leading in the original direction, and it was often necessary to crawl on hands and knees through the mud to avoid the saw-edge growth overhead. As it was quite dark under the closely matted grass he had to call his keenest faculties of observation into play to avoid getting bewildered in the network of runways, each of which seemed exactly like the other.

Advancing with extreme caution, he had progressed but a short distance when he emerged into a trail—almost a road—hard-packed by the pressure of hundreds of bare feet. It was not an ordinary trail worn smooth by traffic; it was more like a track left by a regiment of foot troops, only there were no shoe prints. There were many signs to indicate that the body of men by whom it had been made had passed within a few hours, traveling in an easterly direction.

The track came from the northwest. Cochrane moved along it in that direction to the first bend and, as he turned this, came face to face with three Pulajans. They had baskets strapped on their backs, but each was in full uniform and armed with two *bolos* and a dagger. Cochrane spoke to them quietly, telling them to drop the weapons they had drawn and promising to spare their lives if they would surrender. The man in front, a big muscular native, edged forward, making a motion at first as though he intended to hand over his arms. When he got within reach, however, instead of surrendering he made a terrific cut at Cochrane's neck while at the same time one of his companions tried to stab the officer in the side and the third man rushed in with an uplifted bolo in each hand. Cochrane saved himself by a quick leap to one side, and Sergeant Alalay, who appeared on the scene just at the opportune moment, let drive with his pump gun, first at the leader and then at the second man, the heavy charges of buckshot killing them both instantly. Cochrane then dropped the remaining Pulajan with his revolver, and the incident was closed.

The first sergeant brought the company up on the double time when he heard the firing. The Macabebes manifested great joy when it was found that the baskets taken from the dead men contained rice and carabao meat in sufficient quantity to provide a full meal for all. A package of cigarettes found on the big native was handed to Cochrane, who presented it to Sergeant Alalay with expressions of thanks for his timely action. When the arms and papers had been removed the corpses were thrown into the long grass and the column was re-formed. It was now nearly dark, and the usual rain was falling, so the selection of a camp site was of paramount importance.

Sergeants Bustos and Alalay estimated the strength of the force from which the three Pulajans evidently had straggled at between five hundred and eight hundred men. Cochrane was resolved to pursue the Pulajans regardless of their strength. Realizing, however, that his men were tired and hungry, he followed the trail to the eastward only to the first stream, up the bed of which he led the company until a place was found, isolated from the beaten paths, where wood for fuel and leaves for shelter could be obtained. The company then went into camp, the usual arrangements for comfort and security being made under the direction of the first sergeant, with whose measures the captain did not often find it necessary to interfere.

As soon as Cochrane's hut was finished he entered it and gave himself up to meditation. Ever since the discovery of the trail made by the Pula-jans he had been fighting off a peculiar impulse to march back to San Ramon at once by the route over which he had come. He could not understand this feeling. It was not one of fear—of this he was sure—for although the band that had passed outnumbered his own company many times over, he had often accepted similar risks voluntarily. The idea of returning empty-handed when the opportunity was present to engage under favorable circumstances an important force and also to capture food supplies and take prisoners from whom information could be gained was simply ridiculous! No. He could be on the march by daybreak and he would continue the pursuit until he struck them.

Thus he estimated the situation and made his decision, but for some reason he did not enjoy the serenity of mind which usually came after the completion of such an act. He paid little attention to the supper brought by the orderly, but when he saw Alalay's grinning face poked around the corner he did not fail to light the cigarette placed carefully on the leaf which served as a platter. After supper he inspected the ar-rangements for the night. When he returned to the hut the obsession came again. Something seemed to be pulling him by the shoulder and saying, "Go back, go back." He was not superstitious in the least and he had no faith in omens and presentiments, yet the absurd impulse persisted in returning again and again.

He was aroused from the deep reverie into which he had fallen by the sergeant of the guard, who reported that one of the sentinels had seen something white moving about near the edge of the clearing and wished to know if he should fire should it appear again. Going with the sergeant to the post, he found the corporal and several other members of the guard standing beside the sentinel. The object had reappeared and could be seen indistinctly, standing motionless a few yards beyond the circle of light cast by the fires. Cochrane directed two men to follow him and walked out to it. It was a little white dog. When he called to it in English it flew at him and leaped into his arms, barking, whimpering, licking at his hands and face, and showing unbounded delight in every way that a dog can. He carried it to the fire to examine it and was greatly astonished to find that it was a white man's dog—a fox terrier.

The mystery of its appearance was not explained when one of the Macabebes, who while recovering from wounds had spent several weeks at a station on the south coast, declared that this dog belonged to a lieutenant of Scouts named Harris, on duty then at the same station, and further that the dog's name was "Espote." Cochrane called to him, "Here Spot," and the little fellow responded by barking joyfully.

"He is Harris' dog, all right. The question is, how did he get out here in this wilderness? It is too mysterious and I give it up." So saying to himself, Cochrane took the dog in his arms and lay down, Spot pressing against him as though he could not get close enough. But he could not sleep; again and again came the impulse to return to San Ramon. He fought it off and at last dozed a little, only to awaken with the feeling that someone was tugging at his shoulder and saying, "Go back, go back." This broke down his opposition. Arousing the first sergeant, he gave the curt order to prepare the company to march within ten minutes. The noncommissioned officer looked at him in amazement, but a sharp repetition of the order brought him to his senses, and within less than the specified time the column was in readiness to move out.

It would have been difficult to find a more severe test of the discipline in the organization than the order to march, coming as it did on such a night when the men had just settled down to sleep in comfort after a hard day's journey. The Macabebes knew, however, that while the captain never spared them when effort was necessary, on the other hand he sedulously protected them from all unnecessary hardship and exertion. They resigned themselves, therefore, to a night of discomfort and fatigue and thought no more of it. Probably no other body of troops on the island could have been induced to make such a journey under similar circumstances, and, as Cochrane thought bitterly, no sane commander would ever have tried to make men do such a thing. He stopped on the trail only long enough for the men to eat what food was left and to take a few hours of rest when they became too exhausted to proceed. Late on the following night, the third after the departure from San Ramon, they staggered into the fort and threw themselves down, too utterly worn out to care for food, drink, or anything but rest.

Hazzard had no news to impart, as everything had been absolutely tranquil at the fort and in the vicinity. He expressed astonishment at the quick return but, as the captain vouchsafed no explanation, refrained from further comment upon the subject. Cochrane lay down, feeling, as he told himself, like "fifty-seven varieties of a damn fool," and this time he had no trouble in falling asleep. He was awakened by the crash of a heavy volley of musketry, followed by the ringing notes of "call to arms," and tumbled off his bunk to see what looked like a multitude of flaming meteors cleaving the air toward the fort. At the same time bullets were zipping through the nipa roof and the Pulajan war cry of *tad-tad, tad-tad* (chop, chop to pieces), was going up on all sides. The fort had been assaulted in force by the Pulajans.

Knowing that the weak point of the fort lay in the inflammable nipa thatch, the Pulajan chief had provided the first line of attackers, consisting of some fifty or sixty men, with torches fastened to long poles, his plan evidently being to set the roof on fire and thus force the defenders to evacuate the work in disorder, in which case they would become easy victims to his hordes of bolomen. The plan was well conceived, and it would have succeeded had not the white man who planned the fort taken cognizance of such a contingency and provided a countermeasure. The leading wave dashed in immediately after the opening volley and, leaning the torches against the roof, swarmed up the stockade to engage the defenders with the weapons which they carried unsheathed and swung to their wrists by thongs. It had rained during the night and the roof was damp, but, the thatching underneath being dry as tinder, it soon took fire in a dozen places and flared up, illuminating the surroundings until the scene was as clear as under the light of day.

Thinking that the defenders were doomed, the hordes of Pulajans in waiting on the edge of the jungle, as though by a prearranged signal, now charged across the open, their hideous apelike faces, red uniforms, and the long white capes flapping from their shoulders giving them the appearances of devils. Bare-armed and bare-legged, each man grasping two heavy bolos and whirling first one weapon and then the other in a double moulinet so rapidly executed that he seemed to be carrying two revolving disks of scintillating steel, the mass of fanatics struck the stockade and surged around it as breakers dash against a lighthouse built on a rock in the sea.

Meanwhile, their riflemen kept up a heavy fire at the fort, regardless of whether they struck friend or foe. There were some who in an excess of frenzy threw down their rifles and, drawing their bolos, charged blindly at the fort, cutting to the right and left and in sheer madness hewing down their own people who got in the way. The defenders, however, were in good courage. Within a few seconds after the alarm was given each soldier was at his post, and although the first wave of the fanatics succeeded in firing the roof, not one of them reached the inside of the stockade alive. Cochrane heard one Macabebe say to another as they watched a fanatic scale the fifteen-foot stockade as easily as a monkey runs up a coconut tree, "You hold him, when he gets up, and I'll stab him," and watched them do this, both laughing heartily when the corpse flopped to the ground.

The captain made a hasty tour of the fort, finding every man at his post and the pump guns doing excellent work with their flanking fire. Then he and the orderly on duty placed some open ammunition cases within easy reach of the men, after which he sent the orderly to hoist the flag and himself sprang into the bastion nearest the jungle in order to size up the situation. The volume of fire from the jungle rather astonished him, as he had not thought the Pulajans were so well provided with rifles and ammunition. From where he stood he could look along two faces of the fort, and to his eyes the sheets of flames spurting from the double tier of loopholes formed a beautiful sight. The Macabebes were yelling, cursing, singing, and daring the Pulajans to come on as they fired.

All this time he had an idea in the back of his head that something needed his attention, and when the roof flared up and the Pulajan main body charged the fort, he realized what it was. To seize a bolo and cut the *bejucos* holding the thatching in place required but a few seconds. He did this just as the heaviest rush of fanatics struck the stockade on three sides, and the flaming roof, bursting into greater blaze as it fell, dropped squarely into the thick of them, deluging them with fire. The Pulajans were prepared to meet bullets, bayonets, or bolos, but the charms they wore sewed in their uniforms or bound upon their foreheads had no provision against being roasted alive, so those who were able to move fell back, screaming with pain and rage.

The soldiers were using ammunition loaded with black powder, and a dense pall of smoke settled over the fort as soon as the flames died down in front of the stockade. There was a lull in the fighting then, and Cochrane thought the Pulajans had fled, but he was mistaken, for they charged again, this time against the face of the stockade to seaward. Then they charged on all sides and repeated this again and again, the soldiers peering through the smoke to hack at them or to shoot them down as they continued to come on as though bent upon their own destruction. At last the dawn came, suddenly, as it does in the tropics, and there in the open a few yards from the stockade stood a mere hand-ful of Pulajans chanting their prayers in preparation for a last charge. As Hazzard expressed it, killing them had ceased to become a pleasure, but a final volley brought an end to the desperate attempt, and then "cease firing" was sounded. The fight was over.

Presently the dancing notes of reveille rang out, and the sun popped up over the rim of the Pacific, its golden rays bestowing new beauty upon the flag floating above, before descending to dissipate the mists of night from a scene too ghastly to seem real. Of the six or seven hundred fanatics who had attacked the fort, nearly a hundred lay dead or mortally wounded on the field, while bloody paths leading from the clearing showed where many others had dragged themselves off to die like wild beasts—which indeed they were—in the recesses of the forest. The re-mainder of the band, including the less seriously wounded, were dispersed in every direction.

The casualties of the defenders were: one soldier killed, one mortally wounded, and eight others with wounds more or less slight, none of which appeared to be dangerous. One man had two fingers shot away and seemed to look upon the matter as a joke, judging by the grin on his face when he displayed the bloody stumps to the officers.

After the wounded Macabebes had been attended to the gate was thrown open and a party went out under Hazzard to search for any rem-nant of the band that might have reassembled. Another party under the first sergeant combed the jungle near by for survivors in hiding. Mean-while, Cochrane supervised the work of collecting the dead. The bodies were aligned in a row near the stockade, with the arms and papers taken from each placed opposite the head.

One body, that of a little boy not over nine years old, attracted his attention. As he leaned over to examine it the child opened his eyes and, with the rapidity of a vicious snake, thrust at the captain's side with a long dagger. The blow very nearly found its mark. Rendered peevish by the close shave, Cochrane knocked the child senseless with the butt of a gun and directed the corporal of the guard to carry him inside the fort. After this incident the Macabebes took no chances in handling the bodies. Without instructions they slipped their long needlelike poniards into the breast of each Pulajan before they started to move the body.

Never in the history of the island had a greater killing of Pulajans been made. The dead in the immediate vicinity of the fort numbered eighty-one; eleven other bodies were dragged in from the jungle, and various bodies found subsequently at a distance from the fort were left where they lay.

After breakfast a long trench was dug in the soft sand of the plaza opposite the pyramid of skulls, and in this the bodies of the dead were placed, two deep, and buried. The officers agreed that some sort of marker should be placed over the grave to commemorate the hecatomb which had taken place.

The mortally injured Macabebe died before evening. He had been wounded in the stomach by some curious projectile that made three perforations. Cochrane sat by his side and held his hand as he passed out. Just before he died he indicated that he had something to say. The captain bent over to listen and was barely able to catch the faint whisper, "I don't mind dying, my Captain, but I do hate to think of that six months' pay due me that I'll never be able to spend."

These were the poor fellow's last words. He and his comrade were buried at sunset. The company was paraded for the funeral and presented arms as the bodies, sewn in blankets, were borne past and placed on the edge of the double grave. The flag was then draped over the bodies, and Cochrane made a short address, saying that these men had met their death while fighting for a flag that meant justice and right and liberty for the people of the Philippine Islands; that they had died as he or any other soldier would wish to meet his end, while fighting in a good cause; and he would see to it personally that the story of their brave death be published at Macabebe. The first sergeant then spoke for a few minutes in a similar vein, and when the company had again presented arms the bodies were lowered into the grave. A firing squad then fired three volleys, and taps, beautifully played by the musician of the guard, concluded the ceremony. Two substantial wooden crosses were placed at the head of the grave, and it was carefully enclosed with blocks of red-and-white coral.

After the men had been dismissed Hazzard called Cochrane aside and with some pride displayed a piece of board on which were inscribed the following words:

Feb. 28, 1904
Here lie the bones of 100 Pulajan
murderers, who on this day were
punished for their crimes and buried
by Company A, 1st Battalion, P.C.
The wages of sin *is* death.

Cochrane was pleased with the epitaph and thought the scriptural admonition at the end of it especially impressive, but he took exception to the statement relative to the number of dead, because there were only ninety-two bodies in the trench. Hazzard mumbled something about poetic license, but the captain was inexorable, declaring that he did not wish the company to take credit for anything that it had not accomplished and that the number would have to be changed. The matter was settled only by Hazzard's agreeing to drag in eight more bodies from the jungle and inter them with the others.

TALK OF THE TROOPS

By Lieutenant Colonel (now Colonel) Elbridge Colby

Colonel Colby, a contributor to the *Infantry Journal* for many years, and one of the few Army writers who have consistently written articles for the more serious general magazines, has, among other interests, the study of military lore. His article of early 1942 is based on research done in writing his book, *Army Talk*.

Like any other, our military profession has a speech of its own. This speech differs, however, from that of most other professions because it includes much that is informal, common in the speech of soldiers when they are not talking shop. Indeed, these words are used so generally in personal conversation that it is sometimes hardly intelligible to the average citizen.

There is good reason for this, in spite of the fact that armies draw their personnel from the average of the people. Back in the days of professional armies the common talk of the soldier was bound to be different from that of ordinary folk. For long-term professionals of various nationalities lived a life apart and, limiting their conversations to the narrow military field, developed a familiar jargon of their own. Language is a picture of life; when the soldier's life was widely different from that of the people it was natural that his language should have been different too.

I stood once on a railway platform in Shanhaikwan amid a mixed crowd. My Chinese speech was almost unintelligible to the natives who surrounded me, but soldiers from the Mukden troops of Chang Hsueh-liang caught my meaning. The ticket taker asked how it was that local citizens whose dialect I was speaking could not understand me and soldiers from a different province did. I replied, "That is simple. All soldiers speak the same language."

Although originating half a world apart, our armies were descendants of the same ancient forms and not very dissimilar in type and in equipment.

Military language makes for precise speech. It has taken words with broad meanings and specialized and narrowed them in spite of the generalities of their original sense. This is the reason the civilian has to learn, almost by rote, when he enters the garrison gates, the names of units of the Army. A "squad" is a group of men, and so is a "company." But one is a small unit and the other much larger, although there is nothing inherent in the words themselves that distinguishes size. The distinction is traditional only; it is based only on the ways the words happened to be used and to continue to be used. A "corps" (in one sense) and a "division" and a "section" are all bodies or parts of bodies of troops of various sizes, and only a soldier can tell you offhand the approximate strength of each, in spite of the fact that in all armies to all soldiers the strength of each is approximately the same. Even a study of the early meanings of the words does not tell us. A "battalion" is a number of men drawn up for battle, and a "regiment" is a number of men regimented for the same purpose, and the meanings are obviously traditional. Size is not in the words.

This does not mean that military language stays unchanged in all of its words and phrases. Since it is a medium of communication in a field of activity its words do sometimes change in meaning. But the change from the original meaning is usually in the direction of greater precision. Take the words "cannon" and "gun," and it will be seen that they were long used almost interchangeably for large weapons. But with the rifling of a twist in the bore the word "gun" came to be applied exclusively to the rifled weapon, and the word "cannon" was reserved for the old-fashioned smoothbore weapons, like those of Civil War days that now stand on courthouse lawns.

Take "squadron" for another example. Originally in Italian, French, and Spanish, whence it came, it meant a small force drawn up in "square" formation. Then the implication of the "square" disappeared, and the meaning began to become generalized according to the laws of normal language. Finally the military specializing tendency became effective, as we can see from the later history of the word. In 1617 it was still used to refer to foot soldiers; by 1656 it was "most commonly appropriated to horsemen," and in Joel Barlow's *Columbiad* in 1809 we find "battalioned infantry and squadroned horse." It has been exclusively a cavalryman's word for over a hundred years, until—imitating the French during the World War—we began to apply it to aviators to indicate a definite-sized unit, somewhere between a small "flight" and a large "wing."

The word "company" has been said to have originated likewise in a broad sense, to describe any body of soldiers who lived together and together (*con*) ate their bread (*pain*). Every unit under a captain was a company, whether in the Infantry, Cavalry, or Artillery. But "company" was slowly limited in its meaning. Macaulay differentiated by using "troop" to describe horsemen of the Great Rebellion. Yet it was not until 1883 that "company" disappeared from the American Cavalry and "troop" became official in the Army. In the same year the companies of artillery were first officially named "batteries," although companies of Coast Artillery were called "companies" until 1924.

Official orders can thus actually create a language. Words which appear in regulations and on documentary forms move from the black-and-white of printer's ink to the easy syllables of speech. People have often wondered why the enlisted soldier should be called a "private" when his life is anything but private in the ordinary sense of the word. He eats at a table with many others; he sleeps in a large room with numerous beds; he even bathes practically in public. The technical Army meaning of "private" is a formalization of a certain civilian usage, a usage reflected even today in talk of the private lives of public men. Cox and Stubbs in England spoke of the "private" members of Parliament as opposed to those who held government office. Blackstone spoke of "private persons" making arrests, rather than officers of the Crown. As early as 1579—not to mention Shakespeare—we find "private soldier." The idea was, of course, the same as in politics—to indicate that the man did not hold office, was not an officer. In America in 1763, Jeffrey Amherst spoke of "private men" and other military documents of the same period simply of "privates." Indeed, the first Army Act of the United States, approved September 29, 1789, specified sixty "privates" for each company. The word in America thereafter was official, and therefore universal in the Army, as a noun standing by itself and no longer needed to be employed as an adjective with the word "soldiers."

These special words are official. The soldier is not always official. He uses these words, of course, also in common speech. He also uses other official words somewhat in a slang sense, to spice his speech. At formal parade or at guard mount the adjutant shouts, "Sound off!" and the band plays while all stand motionless and listen. And so in barracks, when a soldier is talking too much and his companions are standing around and just listening, he is said to be just "sounding off." When the commanding officer or the officer of the day approaches the guardhouse the sentry on duty there has to "turn out the guard" as a compliment to the officer, who sometimes inspects the guard. But of course if he does not he salutes as acknowledgment of the compliment, and the guard does not have to turn out, and then the sentry shouts, "Never mind the guard!" So, under almost any circumstances, when someone starts to have something done, he is likely to say, "Never mind the guard!" in a slang sense. At guard mount the order is given, "Officers and noncommissioned officers, front and center!" and these march forward to stand by the adjutant, who gives them their instructions. And so again, under almost any circumstances, "front and center" is freely used as an informal way of calling to a friend the equivalent of "Come here!" The topkick often yells it out of the orderly-room door: "Jones, front and center!"

Such tendencies as these, formal and informal, are probably natural in any organization that lives, as the Army does, a life apart from the rest of the people, with different interests, with shifting and only occasional contacts. There is a wide gulf, in language as well as in social activity, between town and garrison in ordinary times. Townsfolk live their lives out with few major changes of residence; soldiers come to the near-by Army post, stay awhile, and then move elsewhere. The uniqueness of Army speech is of course to be expected in purely professional forces, and particularly in peacetime.

The strange thing is that this speech has persisted through so many modern decades of mass armies, armies drawn from the people. It might be thought that large influxes of citizen-soldiers in great emergency years would have placed their own stamp upon the language of the Army. But the fact is that they have not. The citizen-soldier may bring civilian slang into the ranks with him, but he takes it out with him when he goes and does not leave it behind.

There are but few civilian-slang phrases which have come into common soldier talk to stay. One of these is "jawbone"—the word a soldier always uses in speaking of buying things on credit. It was known in what is now the state of Washington in territorial days and among cattlemen of the Northwest in the 1880s. Soldiers picked it up in frontier days and have made it distinctively their own while it has practically dropped out of civilian life. "Bunk" is very old and very common; it is a workingman's word to describe a not-too-comfortable sleeping place. As far back as the French and Indian War it was so used in the forces in America; in the Army it has almost completely forced out "bed" in the soldier's talk, even when he does have a bed instead of a cot for sleeping. It is official in "bunk tag" and fixed in "bunk fatigue" (daytime sleeping) and in "bunk flying" (aviation talk in barracks instead of outside).

"Buddy" has become universal in speaking of a soldier; the AEF of 1918 and the American Legion saw to that. At first it was used to refer to a companion. "Comrade" was too sentimental for the fighting men. Then "buddy" was used so freely among the highways of France that it came to apply to all American soldiers. ("What outfit, buddy?") It was new to the service in the World War. Kenneth Roberts says that it dates back to the Revolution, but he cites General Francis Marion as using it to speak of his half brother, and it has long been a family nickname. Its special sense of modern times probably comes from the coal mines of West Virginia, where men working up the same heading spoke of one another as "buddies." It received special impetus in France because the soldiers resented the "Sammy" which journalists tried to foist on them and disliked the "Yanks" which the British called them. And so "buddies" they became, to themselves and afterward to everyone else.

These words are exceptional in that they came into the Army from the outside. For the most part, soldier words arise within the service. Once adopted, they remain. New men pick up the talk of the troops in trying to act like old soldiers, and the old soldiers teach them what they know. The Army clings, even officially, to its own small ways in small things. It continues to write "inclosure" instead of "enclosure" and to use the "will" for the mandatory third person: "The regiment will form on the main parade ground." The recruit tries to make himself at home and to act as if he liked it and knew all about it. As a recruit of very short service, the actor Jimmy Stewart immediately adopted the lingo of the troops and said he liked it. Drafted men of less than two months' service have been heard glibly using "canteen check" and "topkick" and "jawbone"—because that is part of the language of their new lives, part of what they have in common with the many men from many places with whom they now live.

Sometimes the new speech habits of months become firmly enough fixed so that they take into civil life, when they leave, some of the most pat expressions they learned in the ranks. "Buddy" is an example. More interesting still is "dead soldier"—for many decades the Army name for an empty bottle. This phrase left the service at the conclusion of the World War. Discharged men found prohibition over the land. They went to bootleggers and bought—and sometimes drank—by the bottle, so "dead soldier" ran over the country for a decade. Then the Prohibition Amendment was repealed; a man could buy a drink by the glass again, and "dead soldier" disappeared generally from civilian speech. But it is still common in the Army, for the Army clings to its old ways and old phrases.

A great part of Army slang is uncomplimentary. Back during the Civil War, in 1862, when troops along the Mississippi were first issued small shelter tents, they called them "pup tents" and "doghouses." They spoke of their hardtack as "dog biscuits." Before the Battle of Fredericksburg infantrymen fastened to their uniforms little slips of paper or cloth on which their names were written. When this spontaneous method of identification was replaced by the issue of formally prescribed tags of metal to be worn about the neck, the soldier called them "dog tags" and still does. He is even likely to refer to himself as a "dog face," although he might resent your calling him that. This habit of uncomplimentary self-epithet is typical of the true soldier, who likes—although only half in jest—to speak slightingly of his station in life. In fact, probably the most popular poem in the service is Kipling's "It's Tommy this, an' Tommy that." The attitude is well illustrated by the song of Irving Berlin popularized by Fred Astaire. It is of course of a sister service, of the Navy rather than of the Army, but it is typical of the enlisted man in both. He was induced to "join the Navy to see the world" and was disappointed because all that he saw was the sea. And yet in going on to say that the Atlantic wasn't romantic and the Pacific wasn't what it was cracked up to be, he was still slyly boasting in the song that he had seen the Atlantic and the Pacific and the Black Sea too. Disappointed he might pretend to be, but he did not fail to impress his hearer that he had "been around" just the same.

Yet it is not only of himself that the soldier speaks in slang in an uncomplimentary way. He calls the eagles which his colonel wears as insignia "buzzards," and the honorable discharge he receives at the end of his enlistment a "buzzard" because of the American eagle displayed across its top. The company mechanic is a "wood butcher" and the company mess sergeant a "belly robber." Of course the soldier's meal is a "mess"—and that is official. Indeed a chief of staff of the Army has said, fortunately of meals long since eaten, "What the government bought was better than the housewife could get, but what the fellow in the kitchen did to it was something awful." And so the service has its "mess officer," mess stool, mess hall, but by some twist the man who takes care of the tables and tableware is a "dining-room orderly."

There is very little difference between officer slang and enlisted men's slang, except that perhaps the enlisted man uses more of it. One of these differences has to do with the personal orderly who voluntarily and for extra pay and after hours cleans the officer's leather and sometimes cleans his quarters. Only very rarely and very formally is he called an "orderly" by either. To the officer he is a "striker" and to the enlisted man he is a "dog robber"—and no offense is meant by the term either. Then there is also the slang term for a recruit. Although to officers and story writers he may be dubbed a "rookie"—as he was by Kipling in *Many Inventions* —he is not called that by enlisted men. They usually call him a "John," and this comes from a curious adaptation. Sample forms for enlistment papers used to be furnished, all filled out as a model in the name of John Doe. Recruiting sergeants began calling new men a "John" and then it spread. And even after he learned to march and shoot like a soldier and ceased to be a recruit he might keep a trace of this original name and call himself "Johnny Buck" or "Johnny Doughboy," or plain "John Soldier."

"Old Man" is used by both officers and enlisted men, by officers to refer to the colonel of the regiment, just as in civil life the head of the firm is often so called. Enlisted men use it almost exclusively for the company commander, however young he may be. That is, they use it if they like him, and unless they have fastened upon some particular trait or oddity of behavior and given him some other name like "Sad Sam," or "Felix the Cat," or "Groucho Marx," or "Turkey Neck."

It might perhaps be imagined that graduates of West Point would bring into the service with them year after year some of the distinctive Military Academy slang. But they actually bring in very little, and what little they bring seems soon to disappear. Among the very young lieutenants phrases from the Academy may persist for a time but not for long. Thus for a time the "goat" is the junior officer of the regiment, as he was at West Point the lowest-ranking member of a class, and an "engineer" is an excellent student, because the top students could and usually did enter the Corps of Engineers. But such terms, though of long standing at the Academy, do not become general of use. Officers on a post together soon get to care little exactly who is the "goat" of the regiment—except at the Presidio of San Francisco, where he is the only officer privileged to cut across the lawns and the "engineers" are far off on other duty.

There are also true Army words that are of the nature of pure slang, as spontaneous and descriptive as the "high hat" and "stuffed shirt" of civil life. Their meanings arise from concrete facts and actual circumstances. Their significance can be known only to those who live the Army life. They are so apt that, once learned, they are used forever. Such are "bobtail" and "pull your belt." "Bobtail" originated from a detail of administration. In the old days, when a soldier was discharged ahead of his time so as not to be entitled to a full honorable discharge, the same blank form was used as for others. But there was a space at the bottom of the paper on which might ordinarily be written the words, "Service honest and faithful." For a discharge other than honorable a pair of shears cut that comment off the bottom of the paper and made it a "bobtail." This slang epithet from some unknown soldier was so appropriate that it was universally adopted. It is still used, although the blank form has changed and the procedure too.

The phrase "pull your belt" grew out of a veteran custom of the "Old Army." When a soldier goes on guard duty his belt is a visible sign and symbol of his assignment. He wears it to mess; he wears it when resting at the guardhouse between tours of walking sentry posts; he wears it, of course, when he is actually on post as a sentinel. In the "Old Army" it used to be a tradition, if a sentry were found asleep on post, for the officer of the day to remove the sentry's hat, rifle, or belt surreptitiously as visible evidence of the soldier's somnolence. Even today, if a man on guard is delinquent in any way and has to be relieved from guard duty, his belt comes off. So to "pull your belt" is to relieve a man from guard duty for some misdeed and send him back to his company for punishment.

Some of our slang and some of our official terms are borrowed from the outside or borrowed from other armies. But the Army makes them its own, as we have seen of "jawbone" and "buddy" in the United States. New contacts mean new names. "Padre" entered the service as a kindly nickname for the chaplain when the troops were in Cuba, the Philippines, and along the Mexican border—just as it entered the British Army when Wellington was in Spain. In Spanish a *cantina* was a small store; it was adopted as "canteen" into the British Army and taken over by us from the British, although both armies already used another "canteen" to describe the soldier's portable water bottle. In 1892 the name of the soldier's store was officially changed to "post exchange," but to many it still remains "the canteen," although the abbreviation "PX" has been gaining ground and many supplant it.

When American troops were active in the Philippines on campaign against the Insurrectos we picked up the word "bolo" and gave it a special meaning. A bolo is a slightly curved heavy knife about two feet long, a common tool among the natives who also used it as a fighting weapon. When an American soldier proved to be a poor marksman with the rifle he was dubbed a "boloman" or simply a "bolo"—implying, of course, that he could never learn to shoot and had better be armed only with a knife. The word spread and stuck; indeed, one company in the Army annually presents a "bolo" to the man who makes the lowest score on the rifle range. He is the "company bolo."

In more formal matters than mere slang, however, we have altered military words originally adopted from the British, sometimes made up new ones of our own, or dropped the British ones altogether as we dropped, soon after the war, the British aviation "ace" and the equally British "brigade major." We took the bugle call "tap-to," or "tattoo," from them but during the Civil War devised a "taps" of our own for the soldier's final music at night. We took the "khaki" which the British had adopted from the Persian to designate the color of a uniform and applied it specially and solely to cotton uniforms, never using it as the British do to apply also to wool.

As regards most military words, of course, the American form comes from the British, for we got our language from them, not only the "company," "battalion," "regiment," and the word "army" that originated on the continent in military forms of organization, but even such broader and more informal words as "aide" and "general officer" and "private."

Yet we very often seem to have maintained a distinctive difference in pronunciation. It can be seen, for example, in "reveille," which is French, of course, in origin, but actually came to us from England. We call it "*rev'*-uh-lee" and the English "re-*vell'*-ee" or "re-*val'*-lee." The difference is plain in the fact that Irving Berlin rhymes it with "heavily" while Kipling's line accents it on the middle syllable: "It started at revelly and it lasted until dawn." We shorten the *a* in "khaki" while the English keep it long. Then there is "lieutenant" which the British pronounce "*leftenant,*" and there is justification for their so doing because the French earlier had it "*luftenand,*" and the British took it over early. In 1793 Walker hoped the British would change their pronunciation to "*lew-tenant,*" but in unchanging England they have not. In America we have.

This "lieutenant," moreover, reaches so far into nooks and crannies of language and organization that we cannot leave it here. It originated as a military title with a meaning more true to its form that it has now. It was accepted bodily into English from the French. It was meant, of course, to describe one "holding the place" of another. In the standing armies of seventeenth-century France and England there were numerous absentee colonels, men of noble rank who spent most of their time at court while another officer actually attended to the affairs of the regiment. It was thus that James Wolfe for years commanded a Highland regiment in Scotland while its colonel, Lord John Sackville, stayed in London. The title "lieutenant-colonel" was devised to fit such a circumstance. It became official. In America we have never had absentee colonels, and they have largely disappeared from other armies too. But the title remains. It has come in military regulations to make "lieutenant" mean simply "assistant," much as a lieutenant colonel is usually the first assistant to the colonel. When company officers were assigned under a captain they were also called "lieutenants" in the sense of "assistants." The idea that such a person "holds the place" of another has completely disappeared. Today lieutenant colonels are assigned to command battalions on their own responsibility and lieutenant generals to command field armies. It is now by custom and regulation merely a designation of rank.

To return at the end to more informal phrases and more oral language, we remark that the principal characteristic of familiar soldier speech is a tendency to shorten, to abbreviate, and to call things by their initials. The habit was in the Army long before the alphabetical riot of the New Deal. We have seen evidence of it already in the growing strength of "PX" for "post exchange" to replace "canteen." The habit had its greatest stimulus from official regulations. The common "AWOL" is officially prescribed as the abbreviation for "absent without leave." Also official are the abbreviations "o.d." for "olive drab" and "CO" for "commanding officer." Quartermaster lists spoke of a common yellow soap as "g.i." for "government issue." From these it was a short jump and slip of the tongue to speaking of the commanding officer as the "CO" or "KO" and of any standard article as "GI"—even of official dances as "GI dances" and of the girls who come as "GI girls." The habit spread to other things; the "OD" is the "officer of the day," and a "DD" is a dishonorable discharge. "IDR" is always used to describe infantry drill regulations, and "SCD" to describe a Surgeon's Certificate of Disability.

The tendency is, of course, toward a shortening and a clipping, not only into initials, but also into single words. The Field Artillery is "the Field," and the Coast Artillery is "the Coast." This is a tendency common in all spoken language. We see it in civilian circles in "aren't" and "he'll" and "can't." It appears in connection with a host of other Army terms. "Army Headquarters" gets cut to "Army" and, in France during the World War, the title "Army Corps" was cut to "Corps" even in official documents and letterheads. All of these things go on because the military language is principally a spoken rather than a written language. Most instruction is given orally rather than from books. Men living closely together do not commonly communicate in writing but in speech. And all speech tends to clip, to shorten, to abbreviate, especially, as H. L. Mencken has pointed out, American speech, so also American Army speech.

New abbreviations appear from time to time on official lists, but the soldier will keep on abbreviating of his own volition without the necessity of encouragement or suggestion from above. He will keep on inventing names for persons and for things. When they are apt and become popular, they stay as part of the talk of the troops, and sometimes for centuries. A regiment once stampeded by beasts in the Philippines is still called "The Carabaos." A regiment whose colonel once carried an umbrella while in uniform is still remembered as "The Umbrellas." A regiment that spent much of its time in Manila while fighting was going on in the brush has long been named "The Coffee Coolers." A division that tramped steadily about France without getting into much action is still called "The Sight-seeing Sixth." Perhaps the incident of the golf-course girls in Memphis will result in the permanence of "The Yoo Hoo Battalion." We cannot predict the permanence of any current word because popularity alone will decide.

Sometimes there is competition between names. One of our most recent words, from the Popeye comic strip, is "jeep," which is used for what is officially known as "truck, ¼-ton, 4 × 4." Suddenly put into service and without the benefit of an official nickname like that the "tanks" had in England, it has been widely and variously labeled. It has been called "midget," "kiddie car," "blitzbuggy," "bantam," and even "jalopy" as well as "jeep." But "jeep" seems to be gaining and gives the best promise of permanence. "Jeep" has also been used for light armored cars, for larger command cars, and even for larger trucks. At Fort Dix the word is generally employed to refer to recruits, to new soldiers, and "jeep barracks" is heard, as well as "jeep hats" and "jeep clothes" for any ill-fitting articles such as new men have not yet been able to discard or replace. The word "jeep" is thus in a turmoil. Time, however, and the settling influence of the service at large for uniformity will answer the question. If the meaning does not become settled and single, specific and fixed, the Army will drop it. The Army abhors ambiguity. That is the way of the Army.

SINGLEHANDED

By Lieutenant Colonel Dan D. Howe

The individual battle conduct of "Sergeant" Sam Woodfill is looked upon by professional military men, particularly those of the Infantry, as representing the ideal of the trained, skillful, and efficient ground fighter. Sergeant Woodfill was a Regular Army enlisted man of long experience when the first World War began. In France he was promoted to lieutenant, and for the day's work described by Colonel Howe he received the Congressional Medal of Honor and was later selected to represent the Infantry at the ceremonies of the burial of the Unknown Soldier at Arlington Cemetery at Washington, D.C., at which time General Pershing spoke of him as the finest kind of American soldier.

Woodfill was retired as a master sergeant, later as a captain, and was commissioned as a major early in the present war.

Colonel Howe was close at hand on Sam Woodfill's Big Day. In 1940 he sought out Woodfill at his home in Tennessee and went over with him minutely concerning what happened on the day he won the Congressional Medal. Colonel Howe was retired a few years before the present war and came back to active duty after the war started.

Fog and smoke helped M Company get going in the orthodox deployed formation. But as it reached a line just north of the road running east from Cunel, the Germans opened with rifle and machine-gun fire. It wasn't long before the company was pinned to the ground.

M Company's commander was in a shell hole himself and looked carefully over the edge of it to size things up. As he did so he began to do some figuring. He figured first that those troops—those Germans out there to the front—probably knew what they were doing. They had had four years, some of them, to learn how. They not only held the ground across which his company must advance—if it were to get anywhere—covered with the crossing fires of their heavy machine guns. They also had snipers protecting the crews of those guns and covering any dead ground which the fire of the machine guns didn't happen to cover.

You can't march troops across open ground toward such defenses and expect them to get there. The human body is too big a target, and there are too many bullets to find it. There were twenty or more M Company dead in getting just this far forward. No, the company commander figured, men can't advance against that kind of fire, across that kind of ground in a deployed upright formation, no matter how wide the intervals. They can't even advance by rushes. There is only one way to do it: You've got to get forward as far as you can without being seen. And when you are seen you've got to shoot first and you've got to shoot straight.

It's no different from the Philippines back in 1901, he thought.

But then he thought again how green his whole company was compared to the enemy's veterans. Many of his recent replacements knew little more than how to set their sights, if that much. In fact, he had figured this whole thing out before. And he'd known for a long time just what he was going to do if ever he found his company in the fix it was in now. His headquarters group had been carrying a star-gauge rifle for him, a new one, to use at just such a time. He had it in his hand, and it felt good.

He managed to signal "Down" to his forward platoon and then crawled out over the edge of his shell hole and worked his way forward. First getting a bandoleer of ammunition from his nearest soldier, he headed generally toward a hump in the ground about a hundred yards ahead, from which he thought he might get better observation. As he went several of his runners crawled in the same direction some distance behind him.

As he had thought, he could see much better into enemy ground from the hump. He watched closely for a few minutes and then he picked up signs of a machine gun firing in the edge of the woods over there about three hundred yards northeast of Cunel. He couldn't see any enemy soldiers, but he could hear an occasional machine-gun burst and see the puffs of smoke. So he began to crawl on farther, watching constantly in that direction.

But he had crawled only a few more yards when a blast of fire directly from his left gashed the ground beside him. Automatically he shifted toward that direction. He could see, more prominent than anything else, the church tower on the east edge of Cunel, the nearest French town. And, yes, he could see smoke curling out of a crack in the tower. He aimed straight at the small square window in the tower and fired about five shots. Then he waited a few seconds. No more fire came from the tower of the church, so now he shifted his direction back toward his original objective. Slowly and carefully, making the most of every bump and depression, he crawled along for another hundred yards or so.

Then another burst of fire, this time from his right, kicked up the dirt close enough to splatter him. He twisted to the right, clinging close to the ground, and took a quick look out from under the front of his helmet. In the edge of another patch of woods off in the new direction he thought he could see a dark square, and near it some smoke. He remembered that German blankets were black. It must be a blanket hung from the lower branches of a tree to cover the flashes of a machine gun. The blanket seemed to be hung with its lower edge two or three feet off the ground. He figured that the barrel of the gun ought to be two or three inches below the edge of the blanket. He shifted a little to a better firing position—all of this thinking and shifting took only a second or two— and then fired a full clip right on through the lower edge of the blanket. There was no return fire from behind the blanket.

Now he turned again toward the Bois de la Pultière where he had first seen activity. He was only a couple of hundred yards from there now. But he still couldn't see anything except an occasional puff of smoke after a machine-gun burst.

He couldn't, he figured, get much closer the way he was going without the enemy's spotting him. But there was a road ditch close by, and this ought to help him gain a good deal more ground before the Germans saw him.

By using the ditch he got within thirty or forty yards of the German gun position. He still couldn't see much. The field gray of the German uniform blended almost perfectly with the foliage. But once in a while he could see movement, and always the puff of smoke.

It was only a minute, however, when a face appeared among the leaves in the edge of the woods—the face, perhaps, of the leader of the German gun squad or that of the gunner himself, and for some reason there was excitement written upon it. The American company commander was already hugging the ground, holding his rifle ready to bring it to the aim. But before he fired he pulled his automatic out of its holster and laid it on the ground in easy reach. He was so close to the enemy this time he might need his maximum fire power.

Now inch by inch he moved his rifle up to the position of aim and then squeezed his trigger and fired right under the edge of the German soldier's clearly outlined helmet. He reloaded with the least possible movement of hand and wrist as the face dropped out of sight. Another appeared at once in its place. He fired again, and the second face was gone like the first. Four times he fired, and four times a face disappeared.

Then no other soldiers of the enemy, so it seemed, had enough curiosity left to venture a look from the woods out into the open ground.

But now a slight movement in the underbrush caught the eye of the American. He thought he could see a man crawling away from the position toward the rear. First the man's body, then his helmeted head, which looked like that of a big turtle as the man crawled. With the last shot in his clip the American dropped this soldier, also, to the ground. At once another gray figure jumped from concealment and headed into the shrubbery for the rear. But the American still had his automatic and shifted to it in an instant. Three or four shots he fired at top rapid-fire speed, and this last German figure staggered and fell into the bushes.

There was no more movement in the woods, no noise, no slightest sign of life. The American officer moved forward slowly and carefully, gaining finally the edge of the woods. There were six dead Germans there in the underbrush. Four lay near the gunner's position of the camouflaged machine gun back of the blanket hung from a tree. A little to one side were the two men who had tried to get away. All six had been killed without ever seeing their enemy and probably without ever knowing the exact direction of his fire.

A trail ran back into the woods from the gun position. The American crept along it with the utmost caution. A few yards farther on he found a German officer twisted in a heap by the side of the trail. He looked as if he might have been hit by an artillery shell or perhaps a machine-gun burst while running rapidly. His head rested awkwardly on his knee as if he had been taking a great stride when something felled him. All this the American took in at a glance as he moved to step past the figure. Then he caught the open eye of the German. It wasn't a dead eye. It wasn't glazed but glittered like the eye of a living man.

It was alive, all right. The German jumped up and at him with full force, grabbing his rifle with one hand and wrapping the other arm around his neck. The German had nearly wrested his rifle away when the American thought of the automatic in his belt. He suddenly released his hold on the rifle, snatched out his pistol, and fired against the side of the German. That was all there was to that.

No other enemy appeared, and it was again quiet in the woods. The company commander suddenly thought of his company. It was over an hour since he had left them. He ought to be getting contact with them again. He went back cautiously to the edge of the woods.

From there he could see what appeared to be advanced elements working along the outskirts of Cunel, not far away. He could see a few others to the east of the town approaching the woods. Not far out from the edge of the underbrush were two of his own men. He signaled to them that he was going back into the woods and that he wanted them to signal the company to keep on advancing.

He could now hear scattered firing at different places in the woods not far ahead. He decided to find out what it was and made his way toward the nearest sounds of firing. His route took him along a slope of the rising ground just inside the edge of the woods. He hadn't gone far when a rifle bullet scattered dirt on his feet.

He scrambled for cover beyond the great roots of a large elm tree and then tried to see who was shooting at him. The dying echoes of the shot seemed to come from a point not far up the slope of the hill. The angle of fire had seemed to be downward from some height. The German might be up a tree.

While he was thinking this over the company commander saw one of his sergeants crawling through the bushes to a spot behind a big tree about forty yards to his left. Then he heard the crack of a rifle from the branches above. The shot, fired straight downward, actually grazed the sergeant's nose and ripped up the ground between his feet and he jumped high off the ground in his surprise. The sergeant threw up his automatic and fired up into the tree above him. For a second or two there was no sound but the echo of the pistol shot. Then a German sniper crashed down through the branches and hit the ground at the feet of the sergeant, now doubly astonished.

While this was happening some of the forward elements of the company had crossed the road and were entering the woods at different points. German machine guns now opened a steady fire which seemed to be raking the high ground not far to the north. The trees, for the most part, were dense and tangled, but the company commander could see that strips cleared of timber and underbrush ran in angular directions toward the higher ground. These were surely fields of fire prepared for machine guns—good places to keep out of. So he decided he had better do some further reconnoitering before the bulk of his company tried to gain that higher ground.

Accordingly he moved on into the woods toward the sound of the nearest enemy machine guns. In a short time he had crept very close to the noise. Ahead of him was a treetop brought down not many hours before by artillery fire. He crawled into the tangled mass of branches and worked his way through to the other side. There he found himself looking squarely into a German machine-gun nest not forty yards away. The crew was partly under cover in the gun emplacement and near-by trenches.

The company commander aimed at the crouching gunner and fired. Another German gunner sprang to the gun. But he didn't get off a single shot. There appeared to be three more Germans left, and all three of them were now trying to turn the gun to fire at him. But the German heavy gun of those days had a traverse of only some thirty degrees, and shifting took time. It took too much time. The American fired three more shots, and then the crew of a second gun lay quietly dead in the midst of the Bois de la Pultière.

The company commander circled around this area and moved off again toward the north. It struck him as he did so that if the whole woods had to be cleaned out he had better find out how big the woods were. But already he thought he could see the far edge through the trees. As he continued on he could hear rifle fire first from one direction and then from another. And then a machine gun opened up somewhere in the woods.

He could probably get a better idea of things if now he went up to higher ground. He shifted his direction to the east toward the northern slope of Hill 300. At the first rise he stopped to observe.

Just at this moment he heard the bushes rustling near him. But before he could jump to cover, three German soldiers, ammunition carriers for a machine-gun crew, came into plain sight and close at hand. The encounter was so sudden neither American nor Germans did anything for a second. Then the company commander instinctively half raised his rifle, exclaiming something (he doesn't remember today what it was he said). The Germans dropped their ammunition, raised their hands up high, and shouted out together, *"Kameraden!"* and kept on shouting it.

The next thought that struck the American was that if he could get these soldiers to talk he might find out something about the rest of the woods and the immediate situation. He forgot for a minute that he couldn't speak any German himself—and then he tried sign language. Holding his rifle at the ready with one hand, he made a rotary motion with the other. Next he looked toward the north and waved his hand in that direction and then back and forth. What he wanted to know was whether there were any other Germans near by.

But by this time the three ammunition carriers simply seemed to be getting more and more scared. So in a last attempt to make himself understood the American lowered his gun to the ground, made a sign more or less indicating disgust, and wound up his gestures by a wave toward the rear. This the Germans had no difficulty in understanding. All three of them took off their steel helmets, dropped them on the ground, and began moving slowly over the hill toward the American lines. With their helmets off he could see that the Germans were not the seasoned veterans his outfit had been fighting during the days just passed. They were only kids with fuzz on their faces. He figured they would keep on moving toward the rear, all right, and that the advanced elements of his company, not far away, would take care of them.

But he still didn't know what was to be found farther to the north. He moved on down the slope but had only gone a few paces when he heard a machine gun again.

This time it took him the better part of half an hour to creep close enough to hear the click of the German bolt between the bursts. By this time he had reached the cover of a log and figured that the gun and its crew must not be far beyond the other side of it. He peeped cautiously over the log, and there they were—a machine gunner and a crew of four—not more than a grenade's throw from where he lay himself.

It didn't take him long to figure, this time, that he had some more fast work to do. A fight of any length this far from his own troops would bring German reinforcements running. Taking only time for this thought, he aimed and fired at the gunner. And four more times he aimed and fired.

There is no reason why an expert rifleman with a star-gauge rifle should ever miss a man at fifty yards. He didn't miss. Five shots of rapid fire, and this third German machine-gun crew joined its comrades from the first two crews.

A quick look around the immediate area and the American company commander detected no further signs of enemy movement. He now thought the best thing to do was to gain the northern edge of the woods, take a good look, and then go back to his company. So he moved carefully on until he could see open sky.

Near to the edge of the woods he found some old German trenches and decided they needed investigating. He was about to gain the nearest trench when violent firing broke out from somewhere else, apparently aimed in his direction. It seemed to be coming from the edge of the timber a few hundred yards away. The shifting of the bursts and the whistling of the bullets indicated that his particular corner of the forest was being searched by machine-gun fire. Each burst seemed closer. The nearest cover was the old German trench, if he could make it.

He jumped for it so fast he dropped his rifle. He landed in the trench on his left knee and arm but with his automatic in his right hand. He had drawn it instinctively as he dived for the trench. It was a good instinct to obey, for he landed almost on top of a German soldier on watch in the old trench. The German grabbed him, and they wrestled for the gun. But the American managed to get his pistol hand free and fire point-blank. The German backed away and fell.

The company commander had hardly caught his breath when he heard a click right behind him. He spun around, and there was another German. This new enemy had just come around a corner of the trench and by now had partly raised his rifle. He brought up his pistol and attempted to fire. It jammed, so he threw it straight at the German's face. But he had forgotten that the pistol was tied to him by a lanyard, and it flew backward and almost struck his own face instead.

But the German soldier was in a jam too, trying frantically to work the bolt of his rifle home. From the corner of his eye the American saw an engineer's pick lying in the bottom of the trench. One jump and it was in his hands. Without loss of motion he swung it from the ground with all his strength. The pick landed squarely just under the edge of the German's helmet. Soldier and rifle crashed to the ground.

The American, still clutching the pick, turned as he heard another noise again in his rear. The man he had shot at first in the trench was now on his feet, Luger in hand, and about to fire. The American swung the pick again in a swift high arc that came down on top of the German's helmet. The point went readily through the helmet and skull alike.

By this time the company commander felt that although a pick might do as an emergency weapon, he needed his rifle. He crawled slowly out of the trench to find it. It felt good in his hands again. Machine-gun fire was still whipping into the woods uncomfortably close to him. He wormed his way rapidly northeast. Maybe he could spot the machine guns from there. He couldn't see them, but there were other targets in view. A German soldier came out of the woods. The company commander followed this moving target with careful aim and at the soldier's first slight pause pressed the trigger. The German fell.

This time the crack of his rifle was heard and recognized by one of his own runners who had crept into a covered position near by. Both now took up a systematic fire at every enemy that came into view. The smoke and noise from other firing made the two snipers fairly safe from discovery as they alternately blazed away, but only at targets they could see.

This picking off of Germans continued until their bandoleer of ammunition was exhausted. By this time several large groups of enemy troops were in sight some distance off. It looked as if the Germans were getting ready to counterattack.

Once more the company commander began to think seriously about his company. He had better go back and see that it was reorganized on its objective back there in the woods. He should also find the battalion commander without delay and tell him of the situation. So he signaled his runner and moved back under cover of the woods and found it.

For this day's work Lieutenant Sam Woodfill was ordered to appear at General Headquarters to receive the Congressional Medal of Honor. When in 1920 Sam Woodfill was made the Infantry pallbearer for the Unknown Soldier, General Pershing said, "Here is America's greatest Doughboy!"

ALL-OUT MAP ERROR

By MAJOR (now LIEUTENANT COLONEL) THOMAS E. STONE

(1942)

As long as there is ground warfare—or, for that matter, air warfare —direction and orientation will be among its most important elements. Whether they fly, march, or move in trucks or tanks, armed forces need constantly to know exactly where they are and where they are going, particularly in cross-country ground movements and, of course, in all air movements. Accordingly the military topographical map which shows the forms of the ground, the streams, and the wooded areas, as well as the roads and towns and cities, is a most important item of military equipment for all armies.

Accurate maps and map reading are vital not only for high commanders but for the commanders of small ground units. How much can hang on the careful use of a map is brought out very clearly in Major Stone's article which follows. Major Stone is a reserve officer of Infantry now on active duty in his second World War.

Military maps, it should be said, are usually squared off in co-ordinates —lines running vertically and horizontally on the map, one thousand yards apart on some maps, more on others. These are numbered, and to give the location of any point on the map reference is made to the co-ordinate square in which it lies by giving first the vertical co-ordinate, which bounds the square of ground on the left, and then the horizontal co-ordinate, which lies beneath the square, with interpolation both ways within the square to indicate the exact spot. In rolling country, moreover, the contours which indicate the form of the ground are often deceptive because there are so many small hills and ridges of much the same shape. There is one practical way, however, of finding out whether your outfit is on the right hill, as Major Stone shows.

On October 6, 1918, the front of the 307th Infantry, 77th Division, lay along Hill 198 as shown on the map. To the north and west, surrounded by the Germans, lay the so-called Lost Battalion. On the right was the 306th Infantry, which the night before had relieved the 305th.

Since October 3 the 307th had attacked daily in an effort to reach the beleaguered group to the north. Most of these attacks, made in conjunction with the 308th Infantry on the left, had been directed along both sides of the ravine west of Hill 198.

In the forenoon a message from the brigade commander arrived at the headquarters of the 307th Infantry. This stated that the division commander had criticized the 307th Infantry severely for failure to keep up with the 306th Infantry on its right. The 306th, said the message, was on the ridge of the Bois d'Apremont; hence its line was farther advanced than that of the 307th Infantry. The 307th was ordered to attack that afternoon so as to straighten the line.

Colonel Eugene H. Houghton, a grain dealer who had seen four years' service with the Canadian Expeditionary Force and now commanded the 307th, asked and received permission to speak directly to the division commander. To him the colonel protested that the 306th Infantry had made a mistake in reporting its position; that it was not on the ridge in the Bois d'Apremont but on the ridge in the Bois de la Naza in extension of the line of the 307th Infantry. Furthermore, said the colonel, a lone attack by the 307th Infantry would be absolutely unsound, for it would get fire in enfilade from the Bois d'Apremont against which no countermeasures could be taken. Moreover, as the 307th advanced, its flanks would be exposed.

The division commander replied that the position of the 306th Infantry had been verified by its brigade commander and that the 307th would have to make the attack that afternoon. Colonel Houghton retorted, "Well, if the 306th Infantry is in the Bois d'Apremont, I wish you'd tell 'em to stop throwing minnie-werfers on my regiment." But the division commander was adamant—the lone attack would have to be made.

Leaving the telephone, Houghton instructed his intelligence officer to go into the area of the 306th and there on the ground to prove to the satisfaction of the regimental and leading battalion commanders that their reported map locations were in error.

Accompanied by two orderlies, the intelligence officer went first to the headquarters of the 306th. There he found that both he and the colonel of the 306th agreed on the map location of the regimental command post at 74.0–48.0. But as to the front line they could not reach agreement. The colonel insisted that it was on the ridge in the Bois d'Apremont—of this he was certain.

Leaving the headquarters of the 306th Infantry, the 307th intelligence officer started forward, instructing his men to count their paces. Following a trail (the route indicated on the map), they reached the command post of the leading battalion. Its commander at once agreed as to the map location of regimental headquarters, but with equal certainty he placed his own headquarters and his front line in the Bois d'Apremont. To support his own opinion he called in all four company commanders. Each of them agreed with the battalion commander. Aside from the intelligence officer of the 307th there was only one officer present who disagreed—the battalion intelligence officer.

Since opinion could not be reconciled on the basis of identification of the earth forms with the contour lines, a simple test was suggested: that two officers be sent to pace the distance from regimental to battalion headquarters. The battalion commander concurred and dispatched two lieutenants to make the count. Meanwhile, an estimate was made of the number of paces required to cover the distance between the two locations. Assuming that, owing to the terrain, the length of the steps would average twenty-four inches, it was estimated that if battalion headquarters were in the Bois d'Apremont, the number of paces would come to roughly 2,700. If in the Bois de la Naza, the number would be only 1,400.

The lieutenants returned. Each had twice paced the distance, once going back to regimental headquarters and once on the return. All four counts were substantially the same—between 1,300 and 1,400 paces. Approximately the same number of steps had been counted by the intelligence officer of the 307th and by each of the two orderlies on their trip in.

The difference between 1,400 and 2,700 paces could be explained only by inaccuracy of map location. The 306th Infantry battalion commander thereupon wrote a message to his colonel, reporting the test and correcting the reported location of his front. This message was delivered by the intelligence officer of the 307th Infantry to the colonel of the 306th, who immediately relayed the correction by telephone to 153d Brigade headquarters, whence it was reported at once to the division commander.

The order for the lone attack of the 307th Infantry that afternoon was canceled.

In the course of a concerted division attack which began the next morning, October 7, the 307th Infantry reached and outposted the so-called Lost Battalion.

COMMENT AND CONCLUSIONS

Excerpts from *From Upton to the Meuse with the 307th Infantry,* by Captain W. Kerr Rainsford, published in 1920:

. . . and the two battalions were deployed in double line for a concerted assault behind half an hour's artillery preparation. This artillery preparation had frankly become a thing to dread. There was no direct observation of their fire, due to the blind character of the country—nor was there any direct communication from the infantry units to the batteries. But what was also probably a fruitful cause of trouble was an almost criminal inexactness on the part of very many infantry officers in map reading.

The terrain was undoubtedly difficult for the attainment of this exactness and certainty, but that alone would not sufficiently account for the mistakes made.

It [map reading] was the one salient point on which the training of infantry officers was found to be deficient.

TACTICS AND TRAINING

From an editorial by LIEUTENANT (now MAJOR GENERAL) GEORGE A. LYNCH

(1915)

IT IS A FREQUENT OCCURRENCE in our service that when the advisability of adopting a certain tactical procedure is presented the argument is made that "you can't do that with untrained troops, and untrained men are what we must reckon with in time of war." The effect of the acceptance of this view is to interpose an insuperable obstacle between us and any goal of efficiency we may set for our efforts.

.   .   .

The error in this point of view lies in the assumption that we have waged all our past wars with untrained troops. We have attempted to fight some battles with them, it is true, but we have never won a victory or attained a material result from their employment.

MR. JUSTICE HOLMES: Soldier-Philosopher

By GEORGE R. FARNUM

(*1941*)

Most men who know battle know the cynic force with which the thoughts of common sense will assail them in times of stress; but they know that in their greatest moments faith has trampled those thoughts underfoot. HOLMES.

You see the soldier in him in his sense of the greatness of action, even more perhaps in the sense of great thought as itself great action. HAROLD J. LASKI.

WAR is a powerful forger of character, and never more so than when the ordeal comes in early youth. The experience of the late Justice Holmes in the struggle over secession shaped his thoughts, molded his sentiments, and affected his outlook upon life to a far greater degree, I think, than is generally suspected. This man, who lived so long and with such creative intensity, undoubtedly owed much of his stoical attitude and critical and realistic spirit to the purging and disillusionizing of influence of soldiering, as well, paradoxically enough, as no small part of his idealism.

He was graduated, just as the Civil War was beginning, from Harvard, whose sacrifice of young-manhood he modestly summed up years later as consisting in having "sent a few gentlemen into the field, who died there becomingly." Upon quitting the campus his thoughts turned toward the bivouac. He enlisted in the 20th Massachusetts Volunteers, a regiment which, as he said, "never talked much about itself but that stood in the first half-dozen of all the regiments of the North for the number of killed and wounded in its ranks," and whose exploits have been commemorated by a lion wrought by Saint-Gaudens and installed in the Boston Public Library.

For four years he was to endure the stalking terror which haunted fields and woods, to inure himself to the discomforts of camp, the fatigues of march, and the pitiless shambles of battle, and to steel himself to the vision of sudden death and the anguish of the broken bodies and shattered minds of many who lived on. In those fateful years he himself was to be thrice struck down—at Balls Bluff, at Antietam, and at Fredericksburg—but was to survive to tell the tale and interpret the moral in word and action.

In the ordeal his mind was matured and his heart "touched with fire." He underwent a purification of thought and a toughening of character, the effect of which he was never to lose in the long years in which he was destined to play a great and distinguished role in the pursuits of peace. This son of the New England poet and Harvard medical professor freed himself, as one commentator put it, "from the group loyalties and prejudices and passions which are a heritage of those reared in the security of the genteel tradition." He learned the unforgettable lesson "that life is a profound and passionate thing" and that, "after all, the place for a man who is complete in all his powers is in the fight."

The fratricidal madness and the brutalities of the war left no perceptible scars on his character, exerted no deteriorating influence on his work or thought. A romantic instinct, a mystic insight, and a philosophical bent—and a good deal of the poet in his nature too—enabled him to soar above the sordid, to elude most of the evil passions that war engenders, and to shake from his spirit the dirt and dust of battle. He possessed the philosopher's stone, whether he consciously used it or not, that transmitted all the dross of daily life in the Army into pure gold of the spirit. He saw the fundamental good in human motives when others could discern only the surface evil in human actions. When others perceived nothing but the ferocity of unchained primitive instincts, compromising the arduous work of civilization, to him the struggle was "a price for the breeding of a race fit for leadership and command." While he conceded that "war, when you are at it, is horrible and dull," he was convinced that "when time has passed . . . you see that its message was divine," adding, "I hope it may be long before we are called again to sit at that master's feet. But some teacher of the kind we all need."

Years after the war, at a gathering of old comrades-in-arms, he gave utterance to the spiritual moral in words winged with beauty and steeped in idealism. He said: "While we are permitted to scorn nothing but indifference and do not pretend to undervalue the worldly rewards of ambition, we have seen with our own eyes, beyond and above the gold fields, the snowy heights of honor, and it is for us to bear the report to those who come after us. But, above all, we have learned that whether a man accepts from Fortune her spade, and will look downward and dig, or from Aspiration her ax and cord, and will scale the ice, the one and only success which it is his to command is to bring to his work a mighty heart."

In the elemental emotions and basic revelations of war he discerned something of the outcropping of the essentials of character—something of the stark, strong bedrock of human stuff, what he would call "the hard steel underneath." "The greatest qualities, after all," he asserted, "are those of a man, not those of a gentleman." He perceived, "In the great democracy of self-devotion, private and general stand side by side." He was persuaded that "if the armies of our war did anything worth remembering the credit belongs not mainly to the individual who did it, but to average human nature."

He saw that war afforded scope for that "high and dangerous action" which he declared "teaches us to believe as right beyond dispute things for which our doubting minds are slow to find words of proof." He found "the faith . . . true and adorable which leads a soldier to throw away his life in obedience to a blindly accepted duty, in a cause which he little understands, in a plan of campaign of which he has no notion, under tactics of which he does not see the use."

Advising a young friend, when an old man, and weaving the thoughts of sixty years before into his text, he wrote: "The test of an ideal, or rather of an idealist, is the power to hold to it and get one's inward inspiration from it under difficulties. When one is comfortable and well off it is easy to talk high talk. I remember just before the Battle of Antietam thinking and perhaps saying to a brother officer that it would be easy after a comfortable breakfast to come down the steps of one's house, pulling on one's gloves and smoking a cigar, to get on a horse and charge a battery up Beacon Street, while the ladies wave handkerchiefs from a balcony. But the reality was to pass a night on the ground in the rain with your bowels out of order and then after no particular breakfast to wade a stream and attack the enemy. That is life."

The passing years never erased from memory those dramatic scenes of which he was a witness. Submerged under the preoccupations of an unusually busy life, they came streaming back from time to time, recalled by what he styled the "accidents" of daily life. "You see," he once said, "a battery of guns go by at a trot, and for a moment you are back at White Oak Swamp, or Antietam, or on the Jerusalem Road." Again he observed, "You hear a few shots fired in the distance, and for an instant your heart stops as you say to yourself, 'The skirmishers are at it,' and listen for the long roll of fire from the main line." And yet again, "You meet an old comrade after many years of absence; he recalls the moment when you were nearly surrounded by the enemy, and again there comes up to you that swift and cunning thinking on which once hung life or freedom." The mansions of his subconscious life were densely peopled with the dim ghosts of a past that symbolized the romance and adventure of devotion to duty and the moral beauty of sacrifice to a great cause.

In moments of reverie there came back before him the images of his companions-in-arms and the thought of those whose high hopes and great promise destiny had marked for a soldier's end. In the Van Dyke canvases of some of those who fell in the civil wars in England he saw, as he said, "the type of those who stand before my memory. Young and gracious figures, somewhat remote and proud, but with a melancholy and sweet kindness. There is upon their faces the shadow of approaching fate and the glory of generous acceptance of it. I may say of them, as I once heard it said of two Frenchmen, relics of the *ancien régime,* 'They were very gentle. They cared nothing for their lives.' High breeding, romantic chivalry—we who have seen these men can never believe that the power of money or the enervation of pleasure has put an end to them," and he moralized, "We know that life may still be lifted into poetry and lit with spiritual charm."

Although he spoke at times with that marked sentiment of which the foregoing passage is an illustration, I believe—although I hesitate to assert it confidently—that no deep perception of the great pain and pathos of life or strong compassion for the lot of the average man ever took any powerful hold on his mind. His speculative preoccupations were with race and type more than with individuals. As a realist he accepted what appeared to him to be the tendency of the cosmos to ignore the individual in its reckonings, and the preponderant role and inevitability of force in organizing life, and he shaped his philosophy accordingly. That is why he could write, "We march up a conscript with bayonets behind to die for a cause he does not believe in," and then add, "And I feel no scruples about it." That also explains in a measure, I think, his further assertion that "our morality seems to me only a check on the ultimate domination of force, just as our politeness is a check on the impulse of every pig to put his feet into the trough. When the Germans in the late war disregarded what we call the rules of the game, I don't see there was anything to be said except: 'We don't like it and shall kill you if we can.'" Unlike the Emperor Julian, who, being forced by circumstances to assume reluctantly the role of soldier, petulantly exclaimed, "Oh, Plato! what an occupation for a philosopher." Holmes in the Rosika Schwimmer case, avowing some skepticism toward certain pacifistic hopes, declared, "Nor do I think that a philosophical view of the world would regard war as absurd."

He never lost sight of the necessity of preserving the virility of the race and saving humanity from the abyss of intellectual lethargy and moral torpor. The processes of evolution exact a high price from life in one form or another. It is a paradox of existence that man pays for many of his blessings in the coin of suffering as he stumbles along the road which destiny has marked and toward a goal that he but dimly visualizes. If the clearheaded and skeptical thinker justified to a degree the recurrence of war as an "interstitial detriment" that must be tolerated in the present stage of civilization, the idealist in him certainly dreamed of a day—distant as it may be—when humanity will have attained an existence freed from its vices and tragedies.

There will be those who will recoil before an attitude toward life that seems, in a measure at least, not only to condone the evils of war but to find some philosophical necessity in their existence. With this feeling I am not here concerned. My purpose has not been to discuss an institution, bad as it may be, but to depict a man; a man who was largely the product of the American Civil War and who carried through life the stigmata of his experiences—experiences which were evinced in his moods, recurrent in phrase and metaphor, and reflected in his political opinions and social judgments. A warrior in some form of action he always remained, from the time when, as a youth in 1861, he was called to active duty by the brisk summons of reveille, until, as a man far beyond the average of years, he laid down his arms forever to the haunting melancholy of taps. It is fitting that he sleeps in the Arlington National Cemetery amid so many other fighting heroes of the country's past—he who believed from beginning to end, as he put it, "that man has in him that unmistakable somewhat which makes capable all miracles, able to lift himself by the might of his own soul, unaided, able to face annihilation for a blind belief."

TALES OF THE OLD ARMY

By Lieutenant Colonel (now Major General) E. F. Harding

(1936)

Somebody should write them up—the tales of the Old Army—before the tongues of those who tell them so well have ceased to wag. For want of a better amanuensis we shall try our hand at one or two for a starter. We do this in the hope that some of our master raconteurs will submit their classics in writing for publication in this column. If they do, the filling of these off-the-record pages will cease to be one of the editor's chief minor worries. As an incentive to the mercenary, we offer payment for the stories accepted. The rate will vary inversely with the amount of editing required.

The Old Army has a changing connotation. To many it once meant the Army of pre-Spanish War days. Today it refers to the Army prior to the World War. But go back as far as you like. The statute of limitations doesn't apply.

Our sample narrative follows:

QUALIFIED

Upon graduation from the Military Academy in 1883 Lieutenant John Heard, Cavalry, was assigned to a Western station. It was an active sector, for the government was determined to break up the practice of grazing privately owned sheep on the public domain. Then, as now, the dirty work was the unalienable prerogative of the second lieutenants. Shortly after reporting young Heard was sent forth to clear a certain government reservation of sheep and sheep owners.

Lieutenant Heard took his job seriously and did it thoroughly. Needless to say, he was not popular with the citizenry. There were mutterings and even threats of violence. One man in particular talked openly of putting the young shavetail on the mid-Victorian equivalent of the spot. This hothead had a double grievance, for Lieutenant Heard had not only run his sheep off the range but had cut him out with his best girl.

Perhaps the lieutenant should have taken precautions, but the record doesn't show that he did. True, he kept up his revolver practice, but that was just a hobby. He was remarkably good at it, too, which may have had something to do with the fact that his would-be assassin appeared to be in no hurry about making good his threat.

There came a day, however, when the young guardian of the public domain had to leave town for some purpose or other. He was unarmed, a circumstance of which the hostile G-2 service was undoubtedly aware. At any rate, Private Enemy No. 1 followed Lieutenant Heard aboard the train and opened fire.

Fortunately a gun-toting citizen was present whose frontier ethics revolted at the thought of an unarmed man being shot down in cold blood. The business was none of his, but he believed in fair play. So before taking cover he passed his six-shooter to the lieutenant. While this transaction was taking place the rancher scored two misses. When it was complete the lieutenant fired once.

At the trial Lieutenant Heard pleaded self-defense and was promptly acquitted. Meanwhile, the friends of the slain rancher had collected outside the courtroom, and there was talk of lynching. The sheriff was disturbed. He had no wish to see an innocent man strung up, but at the same time he was reluctant to shoot down his constituents in defense of an outlander. He solved the problem by giving Lieutenant Heard his revolver and notifying the embryo mob that he had done so. Evidently the lieutenant's recent one-shot demonstration had made a lasting impression; he was permitted to pass unmolested.

Obviously it was not in the interest of the public peace to leave Lieutenant Heard in the midst of hostile two-gun men who were looking for revenge. Accordingly he was transferred to another regiment at a distant station.

In due course he reported to the adjutant of his new outfit. The adjutant, who knew nothing of this second lieutenant's adventure among the sheep ranchers, took stock of his slight build and rather diffident mien and cleared his throat. Here was a youngster to be instructed in the regimental traditions, characteristics, and customs.

"Mr. Heard," he intoned impressively, "you are fortunate in being assigned to a regiment like this. You will find us a hard-riding, hard-fighting outfit. A high sense of duty is traditional with us. I must confess, however, that most of our officers drink, swear, and gamble. Do you by any chance indulge in these vices?"

"In mod-mod-mod-eration," replied Lieutenant Heard, who stuttered slightly at all times and a good deal when excited.

"I am afraid that few of our best officers could say the same," said the adjutant almost mournfully. "Most of them drink too much. They pride themselves on it. But mind you," he continued sternly, "they are real soldiers—true cavalrymen, bred in the best traditions of the service and the regiment."

"Y-yes sir," acquiesced the lieutenant.

"Another unusual characteristic of our officers," continued the adjutant, "is that most of us have been tried by court-martial. Strange as it may seem to you, a young officer just joining, we take pride in this too. We look upon it as just another indication that we are a hard, tough cavalry outfit. We even concede a certain deference to those who have been tried for the more serious offenses. You, of course, have not had this experience."

"Y-yes sir," replied Lieutenant Heard, "I ha-have."

The adjutant raised his eyebrows. "You have? And might I ask for what?"

"For m-m-m-murder," stammered the lieutenant.

THE ARMY'S TASK

From an editorial by MAJOR (later MAJOR GENERAL) MERCH B. STEWART

(*1917*)

. . . WITH OPPORTUNITY comes a serious responsibility. The people of this country are thoroughly, though tardily awakened. As far as lies within their power, they are preparing for war in its grimmest sense. In doing so they cherish no illusions. They are staring facts in the face in a most matter-of-fact manner. They are preparing to pour out their money, their material, and their manhood in defense of the principles which they believe to be right and true. The people of the country can do no more. Upon the Army rests the responsibility for converting these resources into fighting efficiency.

It is a monumental task, this building up from the very beginning, a task that might well strain a well-organized and perfected machinery. It is a task before which our meager and imperfectly prepared personnel might well quail, one which can be met successfully only by unswerving determination, unswerving effort, and unswerving enthusiasm, a task that will call for courage of the highest kind to withstand the handicaps imposed by our circumstances, and initiative of the boldest kind to hurdle the obstacles which will inevitably present themselves. It is a task for which our past experience will furnish little precedent, one in which it would be well to rid ourselves of precedent and build anew on the foundation of practical results. It is a task in which form and method should not be permitted to weigh themselves in the balance with practical results, one in which the red tape of custom, convention, and precedent should find no place.

In short, it is a task for shirt sleeves, sweat, and short cuts.

INDIAN FIGHTING

An editorial

(1943)

THE CRAFTIEST ENEMIES our Army ever fought were the native Americans themselves. The name of "Indian," to military students, is synonymous with stealth and combat skill, with scouting, with battle deceit, with a creeping, silent approach to a sudden assault. These tactics killed many a soldier of the United States forces—won many a battle over them. They caused our troops to think of the Indians as extremely able, deadly fighters, as warriors whose skill at war could be overcome only by a greater skill. They forced our Army to gain that greater skill before it could win against its early enemies in the woods and on the plains.

The most effective way of fighting has always been the way that was fitted to the terrain and that held the maximum of surprise and combat craftiness. The method of fighting that was best for open ground was never the best for the woods and jungles. The open plain and the desert have required a different way from the mountains and from the rolling ground, part field, part woods, part villages. All ground and all battle require craftiness, even in the use of the vast fighting power of machines in modern war—both the silent craftiness and the noisy yet skillful fighter's onslaught that were once typical of the Indian warrior.

Ruse, camouflage, silent movement, keenness, and minuteness of observation for signs to be seen, heard, and smelled—these are the methods of the jungle fighter. And they will continue to be, perhaps, until tanks crash down forests and bomb sights are equipped with X rays.

What the forest Indian knew of the woods and how to fight in the woods was what he learned from childhood on. He had a lifetime of training in it. For he lived in the woods and knew them so completely he could read the cause of every change in them he saw. But the Indian fighter could also learn the language of the woods, and with his broader knowledge of warfare and often his better weapons he was able in the end to win his wars against his native foes.

The Jap of the South Sea Islands is not a native jungle fighter. He has had to learn the ways of the jungle and how to fight within them. He has been at it in a thorough manner and now has more experience of jungle combat than the soldier of any other army. Our own fighting men have found by now how well he knows the jungle and the ways of combat that fit the jungle.

We recognized the special difficulties this kind of warfare would involve. We studied its problems and worked them out on similar terrain. But the necessity for rapid action made us hasten our training, and some of the main jungle lessons had to be learned at a considerable cost in jungle battle itself.

These lessons, as one high commander has said, are essentially lessons of Indian fighting. They are lessons of patience and stealth, of silent approach and sudden assault, and at the same time of watching for movement and guarding against ambush.

The skill our fighters attained in past wars is being reached by our new Army. Every special point about the fighting our forces have to do in every different theater, every correct method, every error, every success, every failure, is being sent back without loss of time to the centers where training methods are developed, the faster to incorporate the latest lessons of warfare into the general training.

But many of them, especially those of the jungle islands, are lessons we already had most of the answers to from past wars, above all, those we fought and eventually won in the early days against Indian foes.

"Indian fighter" has sometimes been used in recent prewar years as a term of ridicule. It was applied to the soldier who swore by the rifle and could see no great advantage in the tank or the plane. It seemed apt enough as a name for the reactionary in military thought.

But like most such carelessly chosen catchwords, "Indian fighter" still meant a number of things in war that are likely to continue to apply for a long time to come. Certainly we can use, out there on the jungle-covered islands and on the other fronts, every skill those old tough fighters against the Indians knew.

V

Generals

THE ACTUAL CAREERS of commanders have often formed the topic for *Infantry Journal* articles, although professional discussion does not lean as heavily upon such material as might be supposed. There have been some good American biographies of military figures by military writers, but for the most part the lives of generals have been written by biographers who have had the time to devote to research and who have produced such works as *R. E. Lee* (Dr. Douglas S. Freeman), *Sherman: Fighting Prophet* (Lloyd Lewis), and *Andrew Jackson* (Marquis James). The briefer biographical studies in the service journals have come from both military and non-military writers.

SWORD OF THE BORDER

By FLETCHER PRATT

(*1937*)

FATE tried to conceal him under one of the most common of names; Time, by pitching him into the most unmilitary period in the history of our peaceful republic; his parents, by bringing him up as a Quaker; the commanding general of the United States Army, by reporting him as the most stupid and insubordinate officer under his command; and the government, by giving him neither men nor horses nor guns. Yet he saved our Northern frontier twice; he won one of the most desperate battles in American history, and with raw militia at his back he broke the veterans who had stood unwavering before Napoleon. Not Sheridan or Longstreet or Mad Anthony Wayne more furiously rode the whirlwind.

Gentlemen, I give you General Jacob Brown, the best battle captain in the history of the nation.

A pleasant-faced man with rather sharp features and curling hair looks at us out of his portraits; there is a keen eye, an erect carriage, and a skeptical line to the mouth. He was born into a family Quaker for many generations, in Bucks County, Pennsylvania, a month after Lexington, son of a prosperous farmer who fished in the troubled waters of commercial speculation in the years following the Revolution and lost all his money. His education, says a man who knew him young, "was accurate and useful so far as it went, without aspiring to elegant literature or mere speculative science." He supplemented it by reading everything he could lay his hands on, and when the family fortunes shipwrecked at the time of his eighteenth birthday young Jacob Brown easily fulfilled the requirements for becoming a country schoolteacher, a trade which he followed for three years.

At that period the Ordinance of 1787 had recently gone through, and the West was opening to ambition. Brown went to Cincinnati and had enough mathematical equipment to get a post as a surveyor. It is interesting to note that he followed Washington in this profession and that biographies of such otherwise diverse captains as Frederick the Great, Napoleon, and Julius Caesar speak of the "surveyor's eye"—the sense of distance and direction possessed by these men. Perhaps there is here some clue to the secret of leadership in battle.

Yet Jacob Brown was still far from battles and the thought of battles when he came East again after two years of failure to make his fortune in Ohio and secured the position of head of the New York Friends' School. The life does not seem to have afforded enough scope for his intellectual activity, which was considerable; he left the post to take one as Alexander Hamilton's secretary. The table conversation at that house must frequently have turned on the Revolution and its military history; at all events we are told that it was at this period that Brown began to read Quintus Curtius and the strange military-philosophical works of the Maréchal de Saxe. His commercial fortunes also improved about this time, and in 1799 he bought "several thousand acres" of land near Watertown, New York, and formed there a small settlement which he called Brownville.

As the squire of the district and county court judge, he was elected colonel of the local militia in 1809, apparently less because he was thought able to command a regiment in war than because his big estate and comfortable house made a good spot to hold the quarterly drinking bouts which passed under the name of "militia exercises." He was politically active at the period, holding several pocket boroughs in the northern part of the state, and his appointment as brigadier general in the state service by Governor Tompkins in 1811 was in the nature of a reward for services rendered at the polls and not because he had shown military ability, for which, indeed, there had been no opportunity.

The appointment made him ex officio military commander of the northern district of the state, and when news of the declaration of war was followed by that of a proposed British descent on Ogdensburg it was Brown's duty to keep them off. His men (militia) and munitions were all at Sackett's Harbor, some distance away, with the roads so deep in October mire as to be positively impassable. The British had naval command of the lake and a fleet cruising on it, but Brown boldly loaded his force into bateaux and pulled along the shore. He remarked that he could always make land when topsails came over the horizon, and if the British stopped to attack his little force he would deal them such a buffet as would make them forget Ogdensburg. The topsails did not come until he made Ogdensburg. There Brown received the landing party with an amateurish but energetic fire, and after a few languid efforts the British went away.

That closed Brown's service till the following spring, when a rather peculiar strategic situation brought him out again. The American naval and military base on Ontario was Sackett's Harbor at the eastern end, faced across the lake by the British base of Kingston. Winter building had given the United States command of the water, but instead of striking at the enemy base, Chauncey, commanding the fleet, and Dearborn, the Army, decided to trot off to the western end of their little inland sea for an attack on the Niagara frontier and Toronto, then called York. Lieutenant Colonel Backus of the "Albany draggons" was in charge of a small detachment and a hospital at Sackett's. He should have been in general charge, but Brown was a landed proprietor of considerable substance and Dearborn, a toady if there ever was one, asked the latter to take charge of the post if any emergency arose.

Fortunate blunder! For the British learned of the American preoccupation at the wrong end of the line, and Sir George Prevost, governor of Lower Canada, came down on Sackett's Harbor with all the force he could muster. He had a fleet, not large by any absolute standard, but of overwhelming power in relation to the defense; for a landing party he had some six hundred lobster-back regulars and three hundred marines and sailors. The British sails were visible in the offing on the evening of May 27, but the airs fell light and baffling, and they could not close. All that night and the succeeding day messengers were out rousing the countryside. When the morning of the twenty-ninth came up, sunshiny and hot, Brown was at Sackett's and in command. He had four hundred regulars, invalids, of whom half were sufficiently convalescent to fight; a regiment of Albany cavalry, two hundred and fifty strong, who fell in line dismounted, and five hundred militia, whose experience was limited to the quarterly keg tapping afore-mentioned.

The only place where a landing could be made was on a spit west of the town, whence a broad beach led some distance toward the line of barracks that formed the outer boundary. Along these buildings Brown deployed the regulars under Backus, with a couple of guns. He posted the militia at the landing point behind a gravel bank. Guilford was the obvious model, where that other fighting Quaker, Nathanael Greene, had placed his militia in the front line, sure they would run, hopeful they would not do so till they had delivered a couple of telling volleys.

Colonel Baynes of the British 100th Regiment led the landing party and advance; his report speaks of a "heavy and galling fire, which made it impossible for us to wait for the artillery to be landed and come up" so that he had to charge out of hand and with infantry only against the gravel bank. In fact, the "heavy and galling fire" was a single ragged volley; as soon as the militiamen found their guns empty they became obsessed with the fear the British would be among them before they could reload, and vanished into the woods on their left.

The attackers cheered and came on; the fleet warped in and began to cannonade the flank of the little line of regulars. The naval lieutenant in charge of the building yard, foreseeing that they could not hold out long, set fire to everything, so that Backus' tiny group fought with the town and dockyard blazing in their rear and double their strength of enemies closing on their front. They fought well, but the British got a lodgment at one of the barracks and prepared to sweep out the line; Backus was mortally wounded, Brown nowhere to be seen.

As a matter of fact, he was off in the woods addressing most un-Quakerly expressions to the fugitive militia. Just what expressions they were, just what he did besides yell at them, we do not know. Psychological compulsion, leadership—call it anything you like; at all events, just as Sir George Prevost reached out to grasp his victory the militia suddenly came storming out of the forest into his flank with fixed bayonets and Brown at their head. They did not fire a shot, simply growled and flung themselves through a scattering volley onto the British regulars from whom they had run not half an hour before. Colonel Baynes ordered a precipitate retreat, covered by the ships. He had lost 259 men, nearly a third of the force, and Prevost, when criticized for not countermanding the retirement order, pointed out with some energy that he was in an excellent position to lose the whole force if he stayed.

The armies were diminutive but the results prodigious; certainly the victor saved Sackett's Harbor and probably the whole Northern frontier. And in the existing state of affairs it is difficult to see how the United States could have recovered from the loss of their one good base on the lakes. For Sackett's Harbor was the point through which went all the supplies for Oliver Perry, who had not yet fought the Battle of Lake Erie, and for Harrison, who had not yet driven the British from Detroit. Secretary of War Armstrong, greatly impressed by Brown's rare talent for making militia fight, rewarded him with a snap promotion to brigadier general of the United States Army and the command of one of the four brigades being organized for the "conquest of Canada" that fall.

The officer in general charge and ranking leader of the army of invasion was General James Wilkinson, traitor, spy, liar, and hopeless incompetent, completely antithetic to the militia general of the North. He had not been in camp with him a month before he was demanding Brown's removal because the latter refused to serve under a personal friend of the commander's, General Boyd, and because he was as ignorant as insubordinate. "He knows not enough of military duty to post the guards in a camp," wrote Wilkinson, "and he compelled his batteries to form in a hollow for the advantage of elevating the pieces to fire at the opposing heights."

That last item is too odd to be imaginary; one can only wonder what in the world Brown was thinking of—but the point is that Wilkinson's criticism can be admitted as perfectly just without denying Brown's usefulness as an officer. Winfield Scott, certainly with no animus against the fighting Quaker, said much the same thing in more friendly fashion— "Not a technical soldier; that is, he knew little of organization, tactics, police, etc."—but thought him of great value, for he was "full of zeal and vigor."

And he had something else as well. In those lugubrious fall months while the high generals wrangled over this plan and that, their men dying like flies under pouring rains and "lake fever" (whatever that was), Brown's brigade had fewer men on sick report than any other and was the only one that kept its strength. Why? We have one flash of insight into his methods. Alone among the brigade commanders he made his men build proper huts with fireplaces, drainage, and clean latrines. They worshiped him. Wilkinson complained he was coddling the privates for political purposes. Wilkinson would.

In November the expedition finally got untracked and wandered vaguely down the St. Lawrence, with its commanding general spending his days in bed aboard a bateau, weeping that he had a flux when called on to make decisions and sustaining himself with rum. The British fired at them from the bluffs. At first the opposition was not serious, but it showed an annoying tendency to coalesce. On the seventh Macomb, with the small reserve, was landed on the north bank to drive them off. He could not handle the situation he found, so on the next morning Brown's brigade also was put ashore and by night had bruised a path through the gathering clouds of Canadian militia.

Wilkinson next turned his attention to Captain Mulcaster of the British Navy, who was following the expedition up with some eight hundred men. Since it seemed that some reputation might be gained by driving him off, Wilkinson put another brigade and a half ashore under his favorite, Boyd, to turn back against Mulcaster, while Brown was instructed to keep straight on away from the battle. On the eleventh came the clash at Chrystler's Farm—it represents, perhaps, the lowest point the American Regular Army ever reached. In a blinding sleet storm Boyd fed his triply superior force into the fight in small parties, saw them riddled one by one, and himself led the disgraceful rout that ensued. Mulcaster might have cleaned up the whole force but for the brilliant covering charge of Walbach's small cavalry regiment and the skill and steadiness with which Brown, who had marched without orders toward the guns, covered the retreat.

The expedition, however, was ended, and that winter there was a housecleaning among the higher officers. Wilkinson, Boyd, Wade Hampton, Dearborn, all the old period pieces from the Revolution, were shoved into retirement, and to their horror Jacob Brown was appointed major general of the United States and commander at Sackett's Harbor.

Secretary Armstrong appears to have had a clear sense of Brown's limitations as well as his merits, for he gave him for brigadiers two of the strictest professional soldiers in the service—Ripley and Winfield Scott. It was a happy combination.

The campaign of 1814 started badly when Brown permitted the timorous Commodore Chauncey, with whom he had been instructed to confer, to convince him that nothing could be accomplished against Kingston. Accordingly he moved his troops to the Niagara frontier. A talk with Scott and Armstrong showed him the strategic error of trying to lop off a branch when he could strike for the trunk of the tree. "I am the most unhappy man in the world," he wrote, and hurried back to have the matter out with the naval commander.

But the latter was one of those officers whom nothing can persuade to fight unless odds-on. He flatly refused to give naval support for a move on Kingston or any other point until midsummer had brought his new battleship from the building ways. So Brown had to return to Niagara and make the best of things there. Meanwhile, Scott, left in charge of the little army, had drilled the troops well. But the strategic situation his commander found at the Niagara was bad.

The Americans held only the ashes of burned Buffalo at the Lake Erie inlet of the Niagara. Facing that place, on the Canadian side, was a strong but half-complete work, Fort Erie, in British hands; at the Ontario outlet of the river were similarly paired fortifications, Niagara on the American side, George on the Canadian, both excellently planned, well provided with guns, and both in British hands. This gave the British three corners of a quadrangle, split down the center by the river, which was passable only at the fortified points. Their commander, General Riall, had something over 4,000 men, all regulars and veterans. His mobile force, however, numbered not more than 2,800 men; the others were parceled out in garrison.

Brown's men, though nominally regulars, were actually the greenest of recruits, with no drill but what Scott had given them during the three spring months. This force comprised three brigades:

SCOTT'S

Organization	Commander	Recruited in	Number
9th Inf.	Maj. Leavenworth	Massachusetts	642
11th Inf.	Maj. McNeil	Vermont	577
22d Inf.	Maj. Brady	Pennsylvania	287
25th Inf.	Maj. Jesup	Connecticut	619
Staff			4
			2,129

RIPLEY'S

Organization	Commander	Recruited in	Number
21st Inf.	Maj. Miller	Massachusetts	917
23d Inf.	Maj. McFarland	New York	496
Staff			2
			1,415

Artillery...Maj. Hindman..................................... 327

PORTER'S

Pennsylvania militia 600

4,471

The size of the 21st Regiment is accounted for by the fact that it included some detachments from the 19th. The total number of effectives was certainly not over 3,500, and probably much less, when the campaign began in July.

The war in Europe was drawing to a close, and heavy reinforcements were already on the sea for Riall; his plan was simply to wait until he got them and then crush the Americans. On our side Chauncey's new warship was nearly completed. It would give him command of the water, and he had promised Brown a naval blockade and bombardment of Fort George for the early part of the month if the Army was at hand to co-operate. Brown therefore planned a quick stroke at Fort Erie, a sweep down the Canadian side of the river, and a siege of Fort George to chime with the arrival of the fleet. Fort Niagara would fall of its own weight once its companion piece was gone.

The move began on the first day of the month, Scott landing below Fort Erie, Ripley crossed above. The two pinched out the area between them, taking 170 prisoners and sustaining no casualties. Riall, who had not thought the Americans so bold, was taken by surprise. He gathered up what troops he had, not over 1,500 men, and came forward to hold the line of the Chippewa River, which flows into the Niagara some sixteen miles below Fort Erie.

Brown threw forward Porter's militia and a handful of Indian allies as scouts, with the design of feeling along the Chippewa for a spot where a crossing might be forced. They encountered Riall's skirmishers, Indians and Canadian militia in about the same number, and there was a little desultory firing. Scott was back at a smaller stream, Street's Creek, holding a parade. He had with him the three small guns of Towson's battery. Ripley was in camp behind Scott, and Brown up on reconnaissance. The date was July 4.

Riall's experience of this war had been that Americans always ran when vigorously attacked by British regulars. He ployed his 1,500 into column, whipped them across the Chippewa hard by its mouth, and punched through the scattered scouts of Porter's brigade with a cloud of militia and Indians round his front. Porter's men went back in disorder. Brown, galloping past Scott to bring up Ripley, shouted, "You are going to have a battle!"

Scott remarked that he did not think there were three hundred British within miles, but scarcely had he got his men across Street's Creek and into a crescent formation when Riall topped the last rise and came down toward him with two twenty-four-pounders and a big howitzer banging away. The Englishman got the surprise of his life. Not only did these Americans fail to run; they received him with volleys hotter than he gave. His column hesitated, came to a halt, and hung fixed in the semicircle of fire. Towson's little battery dueled fiercely with the British guns, mastered them, blew up an ammunition wagon in the English rear, and turned in on their column of assault just as Scott, catching a hint of wavering in the line opposed to him, rode out in front with his sword swinging for a countercharge.

Brown came rushing across the creek with Ripley's men to put in on the American left for a sweep, but before they reached position it was all over; Riall had lost 515 men, a third of his force, and was behind the Chippewa, trying to rally what he had left. The American casualties, including Porter's, were only 297.

Brown followed his opponent in crisply, touched the shore of Lake Ontario, and there received the dismaying news that Chauncey's new two-decker was not ready and would not be before September. The Navy could give him no help of any kind. Meanwhile, the British had been heavily reinforced by a corps of Peninsular veterans under Major General Gordon Drummond, an officer who had made a considerable reputation in Spain.

The precise extent of the British additions and their plan of campaign was unknown to Brown. He fell back to the Chippewa River, Scott's brigade holding there for observation with the rest behind. On July 25 Drummond and Riall were ready; the former came forward and established himself in a strong position along Lundy's Lane, at right angles to the flow of the Niagara, with 1,200 men and six pieces of artillery. Three miles behind him was Drummond in person with the reserve of his forces, another 1,200 men and two guns. Up near Fort George were 1,700 more men under a British Colonel Scott, all ready to cross to Fort Niagara. Their plan was simple and should have been effective: Riall to hold hard in his prepared position, Scott to cross and turn the Americans out of their position at the river mouth or trap them in Fort Erie, Drummond to throw his reserve in with whichever force met the most opposition.

Winfield Scott and his brigade were 1,400 strong with those same three little guns of Towson's; Ripley was behind near Fort Erie with 1,200 men, and Porter near the same spot with about 600 militia, maybe less. The American position was truly desperate; they had not enough men and artillery to put up a defense, and there were no good defensive positions; heavily outnumbered at every point, they had no place to which they could retire nearer than Albany.

The best device Brown could think of was to keep the British so occupied that they could not finish their turning maneuver. As soon as he had plumbed the situation he ordered Scott to hit Riall with all his strength. At the same time he ordered Ripley's brigade forward and followed with Porter. He was staking everything on one blow.

Scott formed the 9th on his left wing, with Towson's three guns next, facing Riall's battery; then the 11th, the 22d and the 25th, the latter's right against the river. The setting sun threw long shadows across the field as they took their positions in the hollow below Lundy's Lane. There was a brief cannonade; Riall, a trifle disturbed by the unshaken bearing of those regiments he had so good cause to remember, had just ordered a retreat when Drummond in person arrived with his division, giving the British a two-to-one superiority in numbers.

Scott came right on. In the center the fighting was fierce, but the three regiments could accomplish nothing against slope, numbers, and cannon; but on the right Scott himself burst through the British line at the head of Jesup's men, hurled back their flank, wounded Riall and captured him, and completely broke up one of the British regiments before artillery from the flank and Drummond's heavier weight drove him out again.

Towson's guns had now been silenced, but Scott ordered another charge and then another; three charges we count on the right and center before nine o'clock. Scott himself took a wound that finished him for the rest of the war; Majors McNeil and Brady were down; the 9th, 11th, and 22d had lost nearly all their officers and organization, but Major Leavenworth formed what was left of them into one single mass and was planning a last-ditch defense in the hollow against the now-advancing British when Brown came up on the run with Ripley and Porter. He seized the situation at a glance; nothing would go right until he got rid of that British battery which was tearing his center to pieces. Meanwhile, Drummond had called in the British Colonel Scott and there were now over 3,000 men along Lundy's Lane, less than 2,000 below it.

"Can you take those guns?" Brown asked Major Miller.

"I'll try, sir," said Miller in the words that have become a regimental motto, and went up the hill into the dark with the 21st. Brown gave him all the help possible, himself leading the 23d as an advance echelon on Miller's right, Porter and the militia going forward on the left in loose skirmishing formation around a big stone church. Under cover of their advance Miller went right into the muzzles of the guns and bayoneted the cannoneers at their pieces. Then with militia on one side and the 23d on the other, he formed a new line, not twenty paces from the British, while "the space between was all one sheet of flame." The raw Americans stood it better than the Peninsulars; Drummond's men gave up and went tumbling down the reverse slope.

It was ten o'clock, but the stubborn fight went on. The British regulars were not used to being treated in so cavalier a fashion. Drummond got them in order and came back with a furious charge—"You could see the figures on their buttons in the light of the guns"—was beaten, came again, again was beaten, but returned still a third time. Brown was wounded now, too, and in a faint; so was Leavenworth. There was hardly an officer left in the American Army, which was all one mixed line, militia and regulars together.

As the last English wave rolled back, Drummond's confused ranks began firing into one another and collapsed. The battle was won, and the whole British Army was taken had there been a regiment of cavalry or the tiniest reserve. But there was not, and Ripley, left in command, counted his own desperate state and ordered a retreat to Fort Erie.

The wagoners sent back for the captured British cannon found that a British wagon corps had had the same idea and earlier, and when Brown recovered consciousness and heard of it he called Ripley a coward and sent for General Gaines to take command till he should be on his feet again.

The charge was not just, as Ripley had proved before and would again, but this was a tiny wrangle; the important thing was that Drummond's hopeful movement was stopped as though he had been poleaxed. He had lost 878 men in the battle (Brown lost 853) and, insisting to his dying day that he had fought not less than 5,000 Americans, won commendation from the Cabinet for his "gallant stand against superior forces." "I never saw such determined charges," said the man who had faced Junot and Murat.

He was immediately and heavily reinforced; strategically his turning maneuver was as good as ever, but Lundy's Lane had embedded itself in his mind. He did not dare try anything till he had gotten rid of the little American force. Therefore, he came down to lay siege to Fort Erie, where Gaines could muster but 2,125 men, including some militia that came up. On August 15 the English tried a midnight surprise; it ended in a frightful disaster (Ripley seems to have predicted it to the day and almost the minute) with 900 British casualties against only 84 American. A boat landing off Buffalo ran into a company of squirrel-killing Kentucky riflemen who emptied two of the boats so rapidly that the rest pulled away in a hurry.

At the beginning of September the swing was toward the American side, the more so since Brown was recovered. He held a council of war, wishful to attack the British lines. The regular officers, particularly Ripley, objected that the lines were well planned, adequately supplied with artillery, and defended by some of the best troops in the British Army, including the Scots Highlanders. Assault was madness. Brown began to fidget, finally snapped that the council was closed, and sent off for some more militia. He got about a thousand, which gave him a total of 3,000 against Drummond's 4,500. This seemed to the fighting Quaker about the proper proportions for battle.

Colonel Wood of the Engineers, under cover of the racket made by the siege artillery, cut a path through the brush to a point within 150 yards of the battery on the extreme British right. On the morning of September 17 Brown took this path with his militia and the little remnant of the 23d, which was to serve as stiffening and example for the rest. Major Miller had orders to throw a column at the British center as soon as the militia began to shoot.

The attack went off like clockwork. The Scots stood their ground, but the untrained, rowdy militia—the same men who failed every other general of the war—followed Brown in on them and in a wave of fury took losses that would have staggered most regulars (over a third!), killed the Scots where they stood, captured the battery, and spiked its guns. Miller's column punched through the second battery and spiked that too; there was a little fighting around the third, but Brown pulled out before getting too deeply involved.

That finished Major General Gordon Drummond. He was a good officer and a bold man, but the sortie had cost him 700 more casualties, bringing his battle losses to more than 3,000 for the campaign. And there seemed no limit to his opponent's stomach for combat, nor to his ability to inflict further damage. Then, too, the British artillery was spoiled or spiked. Nor had Brown neglected to burn their barracks during the sortie, and the autumn rains had set in; his own men were housed in comfortable huts. Finally, it is probable that Drummond knew Brown was being reinforced at no distant date, for it was difficult to keep any big news quiet along the border. By sum total the British position had become untenable; a week after Brown's sortie Drummond beat a retreat to his fortresses.

The following week General Izard came tramping into Buffalo with 7,000 regulars, including a strong brigade of that cavalry for the lack of which on the night of Lundy's Lane Brown had wept. It is a matter of speculation as to what might have happened after another spring, of course, but in view of what Brown accomplished with inferior forces, no cavalry, and little artillery, the likelihood is that with superiority in all three arms he would have made things extremely warm for his opponents.

He was prevented by the end of the war, which also ended active service for him, though he remained in the Army, becoming its head in 1821. In 1828, still chief, he died of the aftereffects of his Lundy's Lane wound, leaving behind a record of service second to none, but a reputation overshadowed by that of the more colorful and politically minded Andrew Jackson. Yet it is not mere wonder hunting to say that Brown did more than Jackson, for New Orleans was fought after the war was over, while Sackett's Harbor and Lundy's Lane were won at its height. The loss of either might well have entailed the fall of the whole Northwest and certainly would have afforded a solid basis for the claim to a foothold south of the lakes that the British put forward with such persistence at the conference in Ghent.

When it comes to analyzing the reasons for Brown's achievement, as startling as it was brilliant, one is a little at a loss. It is the easy and the common habit among military writers to attribute everything to Scott and to set Brown down as a sterling fighter with but a single military idea— that of getting in contact with the enemy and hitting him as hard as possible. But this picture will not quite do; Brown won at Sackett's Harbor before he had Scott and in the Fort Erie sortie after Scott was gone.

Chippewa was largely Scott's victory; the discipline he put into the raw recruits did much to win Lundy's Lane, but it is surely taking nothing from the credit due him and his men to say that they behaved on both fields as they never did before and never did again. And nobody but Brown ever thought of leading militia in a charge against veteran Scots or would have gotten away with it had they done so.

There was, in short, some ineluctable secret of leadership, something in Brown's presence and manner that made green country boys fight like the devil, and it would be worth a good deal to know that secret. But it would be silly to account for Brown's success on this basis alone. Scott complained of the general's ignorance of tactics, yet Brown's major tactics were, on the whole, better than Scott's. At Chippewa, Scott's plan of a crescent resting on the river with the right wing supported by artillery was good, yet Brown had a better one—to hold hard in the center, bring Ripley in on the left, and knock Riall's whole column into the Niagara. At Lundy's Lane, Scott conceived the classical plan of breaking down a flank, the flank where the enemy thought himself strongest, but it was Brown who saw that the big British battery in the center would queer any flanking sweep while it stood and that its fall would entail the wreck of the whole line—and he saw it in an instant, in the darkness of the night, in the midst of battle. Again at Sackett's Harbor it would have been both easier and more normal for Brown to bring his rallied militia in on the line where the regulars were holding, but no, he had to lead those troops, already once broken, in a cold-metal charge against Prevost's sensitive wing. The essence of Brown's concept may be expressed by saying that while Scott played, and played well, to beat the enemy Brown meant nothing less than his destruction at every stroke.

This suggests, then, that major tactics are something innate and not to be learned; all these ideas came out of Brown's own head, without benefit of military education. One would expect the same native genius to make him a good strategist also; but, oddly enough, this turns out to be his weak point.

Then there is another suggestion in Brown's career, perhaps even more important. The fact that the general's political influence in his home district was an influence of affection makes it clear that he treated the tenants of his estate much as he later treated the soldiers who fought so well for him; that is, with an attention to their physical well-being even rarer then than it is now. It was not only Scott's drill that made the men of Lundy's Lane follow their Quaker up the hill; it was those comfortable huts and the fight the general had made to provide good food and good clothes.

Yet neither these nor any other details can be tortured into a Jacob Brown formula. His secret was the secret of all great leaders, and what man can discover that?

ACADEMIC SOLDIER: GAMELIN

By Captain H. A. DeWeerd

Captain DeWeerd, now associate editor of the *Infantry Journal,* has for many years in the academic field (until coming into the Army he was professor of history at Denison University and a member of the military section of the Institute for Advance Study at Princeton) sought for the proper recognition of the military side of history within the study of history as a whole. He has written many biographical articles on well-known military figures, among them the one on Gamelin which follows (in 1941). He was, for several years, editor of the quarterly, *Military Affairs,* and is the author of *Great Soldiers of Two World Wars* (W. W. Norton and Co.), in which the following article was included.

FATE played one of its tragic tricks on France in 1935 when into the office of vice-president of the Supreme War Council at No. 4 Boulevard des Invalides, just vacated by General Maxime Weygand, walked a short, grayish officer: Maurice Gustave Gamelin. Weygand's retirement from the control of the French Army at the age of sixty-eight was a military event of more than average importance. Famed as the military brain and alter ego of Marshal Foch (who left the advice: "Call Weygand if trouble comes"), Weygand was long regarded as the symbol of France's military supremacy. It was known that the retiring commander in chief was not enthusiastic about his successor and would have preferred General Alphonse Georges, but that was often true of commanding officers and their successors. Time had not yet healed the wounds of the bitter wartime quarrels between French generals. Weygand was a Foch man, Gamelin a Joffre man. Joffre's treatment of Foch just before his own retirement in 1916 (Foch was placed on the inactive list on the grounds of ill-health) had never been forgiven. Even after both marshals were dead their widows passed each other on the street without speaking. Weygand may have preferred Georges (who had worked with both Pétain and Foch) not because he loved Pétain more but Joffre less.

On his record Gamelin seemed to possess all the formal qualifications for his important office. From a professional standpoint he appeared to be the most accomplished officer in France—or in Europe, for that matter. Had he assumed command of the French military establishment at a less critical time, he doubtless would have carried his brightly burnished professional reputation with him to the security of the grave. Instead, it was his destiny to face one of the few great revolutionary changes in military methods and concepts with the weapons and concepts of an earlier and happier day. As a result the story of his leadership in 1939–40 is one of disaster for the country he loved.

Gamelin came from a military family. His father, Zephirin Auguste Gamelin, served in the wars of the Second Empire, was wounded at Solferino, and ultimately rose to the rank of comptroller general of the French Army. Maurice was born within the shadow of the War Ministry at No. 262 Boulevard St. Germain in Paris in 1872. His education was given a strong Catholic bent in College Stanislas, where he fell under the influence of Henri Cardinal Baudillart. He demonstrated a taste for philosophy and a talent for memory work which enabled him to graduate first in his class of 449 from St. Cyr in 1893. For three years he served in the 3d Regiment of the *Trailleurs Algériens* and put in an additional three years in the cartographical section of the Army Geographic Service.

Here he developed a fondness for painting and an interest in the topographical features of the French frontiers. As captain of a company of *chasseurs à pied* he was detailed to the École de Guerre, where Foch was making a name for himself as the foremost lecturer on French military problems. Gamelin's record at St. Cyr and his promising showing at the École de Guerre brought him to the attention of Joffre, whose star was rising in the French military firmament. In 1906 Joffre, commanding the 6th Division in Paris, made Gamelin his orderly officer. He stayed with Joffre when Joffre rose to the vice-presidency of the Supreme War Council in 1911. He was thus prepared to play a conspicuous role in the events of 1914.

Employing the tenacious memory he had developed at College Stanislas by memorizing ten lines of prose each night before retiring, Gamelin made himself master of the military literature on Napoleon. It was widely believed that he could repeat verbatim every order the Emperor ever issued. Such erudition was uncommon even in an army which made a fetish of the study of Napoleon. Two years' service with the line from 1912 to 1914 made him available for staff duty when the crisis came. In 1914 Gamelin was a trim, sleek, taciturn, quick-witted major of forty-two who had given considerable study to the problem of countering a German attack from the direction of Belgium. Joffre loved to have sharp-witted young men around him, possibly as a foil for his own ponderous mental processes. He brought Gamelin ("one of my red corpuscles") back to his staff in August 1914.

The events of August and early September gave Gamelin a chance to utilize his early study on a German attack from the direction of Belgium. Plan XVII, the French program which called for a concentric advance by the French First and Fifth armies in a brutal and relentless manner (*l'offensive brutale et à l'outrance*), broke down with heavy losses in the face of machine guns and artillery. With the apparently irresistible force of an avalanche the gigantic armies of Kluck (First) and Bulow (Second) rolled through Belgium into northern France. Berthelot was Joffre's chief of staff, but it was Gamelin who on August 25 wrote the famous Instruction No. 2 which admitted that the French plan of offensive war had failed and which announced the general plan of building up a sufficient force on the French left wing to menace the German right when the time arrived for the counterattack. For more than a week the victorious German armies rolled on, driving before them what appeared to be "the beaten French armies." By September 4 it was apparent not only to Gallièni, military governor of Paris, but also to Gamelin that Kluck's force would not envelop Paris and that the time had come to throw Maunoury's French Sixth Army, which was concentrating at Meaux, against Kluck's flank. Though historians have found it difficult to determine just who was responsible for the famous Marne maneuver,

Joffre's *Memoirs* make it clear that Gamelin understood the situation fully and explained it to a group of officers in his presence at the operations room of General Headquarters on September 4. He urged that the the counterattack be delivered the next day. Illustrating his points on a huge operations map, Gamelin raised his voice (a thing uncommon with him) and firmly declared: "Now it is the time to bottle them up!" Joffre pleaded for greater delay so that the Germans might be more definitely drawn into the trap. But when reports from French army commanders and the BEF gave some hope for an early offensive action, Joffre asked Gamelin to prepare the decisive Instruction No. 6. It called for a general attack by all armies on September 6.

The complicated story of how the German armies blundered into the Marne defeat out of the feeble hands of Moltke into the irresponsible hands of a Lieutenant Colonel von Hentsch who presided over the destiny of the German Empire from the sixth to the ninth of September has often been told. When the haggard German troops recoiled on September 9 from the menace of the advancing British Expeditionary Force and French Fifth Army, the "miracle" of the Marne raised Joffre to the stature of a hero, and long after Joffre had fallen from power it shaped the career of Gamelin.

Gamelin's first rewards were the rank of lieutenant colonel and the post of Chief of the Bureau of Operations. After the failure of the French offensives in the spring and summer of 1915 Gamelin urged Joffre to create a large mass of reserves to exploit future anticipated successes. The long-hoped-for and repeatedly announced "break-through" of the German line never materialized. But there was a mass of forty or more French divisions available when the German attack came at Verdun. The existence of this reserve made the successful but costly defense of Verdun possible, and it enabled Joffre to think in broad terms when the British needed help on the Somme. But the "blood bath" of Verdun and the Allied failure at the Somme brought Joffre into eclipse. He was replaced by the eloquent, mercurial, thrusting Nivelle. As a consequence Gamelin's position on the staff became insecure and he took command of a brigade. He distinguished himself in the stubborn fighting of the Somme, rising to the rank of brigadier general in December 1916. From 1917 to 1918 he commanded the 9th Division.

In the critical days of 1918 Gamelin made the reputation of a tough, imperturbable, tenacious, fighting commander. The 9th Division was thrown into the breach when the German offensive threatened to drive a wedge between the British and French forces on March 23. For three days his division held up the advance of six German divisions. In the confused fighting he commanded a makeshift force of French and British infantry divisions and seven squadrons of cavalry. He impressed the troops as being a cautious, economical commander who attained his objectives with minimum losses by a meticulous regard for terrain, artillery preparation, and human factors. His philosophical calm inspired confidence. "There is nothing to be gained by getting angry with things," he used to say; "it is a matter of indifference to them." He seemed to agree with Haldane that "things military must be learned not from the generals but from the philosophers." By the time the war ended he also made a distinguished record as a fighting commander. He had also taken a vital part in the staff operations early in the war. At no stage in his well-rounded career had he committed an obvious error in judgment. He was destined for rapid postwar promotion.

II

When the German armies collapsed in November 1918, the prestige of the German military system collapsed with it. Brazil, which had previously sought the services of German military missions, now asked for French officers. In 1919 Gamelin was selected to head a French military mission there and stayed in South America from 1919 until 1925. This gave him a background of foreign travel and the international outlook essential for a superior officer. In September of 1925 he was detailed to the French command in Syria, where he faced the problem of quelling a revolt of the Druses. One of his first tasks was to relieve a French outpost besieged at Soueida. His manner was so deliberate and his preparations so thorough that one correspondent wrote in a sarcastic vein: "General Gamelin now has more troops than the entire population of Druses, men, women, and children—when he gets re-enforcements he may *perhaps* attack." Six months of campaigning and bombardment of Damascus which killed fourteen hundred civilians brought peace to Syria.

Gamelin came back to France in 1928 as a corps commander. He was appointed deputy chief of staff and in 1931 he became chief of staff. His succession to Weygand as vice-president of the Supreme War Council and commander in chief designate in case of war was almost automatic in 1935. He was then regarded as the most scholarly, accomplished, and competent professional soldier on the active list. His mastery of all the topographical features of the French frontiers and its road systems was absolute. His acquaintance with the senior officers of the army was such that he could name and recognize every officer with the rank of colonel or above. His colorless personality and complete indifference to politics made him a popular choice to succeed Weygand.

Simultaneously with Gamelin's assumption of supreme command the German rearmament program began; Italy was already embarked upon a program of imperialist expansion. The situation was one of increasing hazard for France. Gamelin had to deal with rapidly changing ministries, general strikes, Left Front folly, and a foreign policy as tortuous as it was pusillanimous. In the comparative madhouse of flux the army was the one solid national element in French society. It alone could have brought national security back to its rightful place as the first objective of the government. But the voices of the soldiers had to be more resolute, their vision clear. If professional advice was repeatedly offered, with clear warnings given as to the danger facing the state, and were repeatedly ignored—there was always the honorable course of resignation.

It cannot be said that Gamelin was unaware of the growing dangers of the military situation. German and Italian military preparations were of such vast and open character that they could be and were described with fair accuracy by the European and American press correspondents. One did not need the services of a military attaché. Even so bookish a college professor as the American ambassador to Berlin could gauge the potential menace of Nazi war preparations. Pikestaff-plain, too, were the implications of doctrinal changes in the application of industry and mechanics to war. Field trials in the Spanish Civil War were not for the Fascists alone. As a student Gamelin should have been among the first to see the menace inherent in the fanatical and demonic character of the Nazi system of thought.

Gamelin did, of course, take steps to meet the dangers of a collision with the rearmed Reich. But the steps taken were dictated by the military experience of 1918. He approved the completion of the Maginot Line and unsuccessfully urged its extension to the sea. When this advice was refused he did not resign despite the fact that a defensive war was his main military concept. He attempted to offset the French numerical inferiority vis-à-vis Germany by extending the period of military service from one year to two. In simple terms this meant that he still looked at military problems as something to be solved by numbers. He did not see new doctrines, individualistic training concepts, the application of machinery to war, new co-ordination of air and ground forces as means of gaining equality or even qualitative superiority over an enemy of potentially greater numbers.

Lest the obvious snap-judgment observation be raised that these are the counsels of perfection easy to make in the clear light of afterknowledge, I can say only that my library is full of foreign and American military journals which printed millions of words on just these subjects— *at that time.* There is little or no evidence to show that Gamelin took seriously the significant postwar German military literature such as General Gröner's *Der Feldheer Wider Willen* and other treatises on German strategy. Nor did he give more than passing attention to the prophetic book of Colonel Charles de Gaulle, *Vers l'Armée de Métier,* which advanced the claim of mechanized forces, or Paul Reynaud's *Le Problème Militaire Français.* So great was his faith in the "incomparable" infantry of France (armed with almost the identical weapons of 1918) that

Gamelin allowed his country to repeat Ludendorff's error of making trucks to carry the troops rather than masses of tanks and planes to give them a chance for survival after they arrived where he wanted them to fight. Even if he could be excused for overlooking the havoc which enemy aviation could wreak on columns of entrucked infantry after Guadalajara, he still had eight months to think it over after the Polish campaign.

The existence of the Maginot Line gave Gamelin's military thinking the appearance of soundness. He strongly supported the concept of a defensive war and took comfort in General Chauvineau's dictum: "The attack must have three times as many infantry effectives, six times as much artillery, and twelve times as much ammunition if it hopes to dominate the defense." He did not believe that the German Army had developed new and effective means of breaking through the fortifications in the west. The war which he foresaw promised to be a long-drawn-out struggle of attrition in which the French armies and fortified positions would contain the German armies until the British blockade accomplished its mission of strangulation and exhaustion.

The military reorganization of 1938 in France pointed toward a preparation for this kind of conflict. A single Committee of National Defense was set up covering land, sea, and air forces and representing the economic and financial elements of the nation. As chief of staff to Daladier, who attempted to achieve this co-ordination, Gamelin was in a position to influence the whole range of French preparation for war. His crystal-clear academic discussions with the members of the Committee of National Defense, his orderly reports and minutes enabled him to dominate the organization. He towered over the less well-informed members of the committee like a well-prepared professor over a class of sophomores. Gamelin's chief opposition in the committee came from Admiral Jean Darlan, whose halting, fragmentary salt-water language was an excellent cover for his growing political ambitions.

Gamelin's relations with Georges, who was to serve as commander of the armies in France in event of war, soon became complicated by the top-heavy military organization set up. Gamelin was to be generalissimo of the Allied forces in France and responsible for land and air operations in all theaters. Prewar calculations envisaged him as a sort of super-Foch with Georges commanding the armies on the German frontier as Pétain had done under Foch in 1918. But because no war developed immediately on the Italian, African, or Syrian fronts and Poland collapsed, both Gamelin and Georges became in effect commanders in France. The separation of the French General Staff into three divisions located at Meaux, La Ferté-sous-Jouarre, and Vincennes did not help matters any. Rivalry between the two men was bound to develop under these circumstances.

If French military preparations for war were open to question in the

realm of intellect and doctrine, there is less room for question over the
state of material preparation. In the matter of light artillery the French
Army was supreme in the period from 1914–18. But in 1939 the French
field artillery, even when modernized, was out of date. The artillery-
ammunition situation was even more critical. Shells were scarce, and prolonged controversy over the type of fuse desired held up the production of
everything heavier than 75-mm. shell. Similar professional squabbles over
the type of fuse for anti-aircraft shell limited the effectiveness of this arm.
It might be well to add, for whatever warning value it may have, that
this intensely interesting professional debate over fuses was, in fact, about
to be settled at the time of the armistice with Germany in June 1940!
The experiences in Spain had shown that the French 37-mm. anti-tank
gun did not possess the penetration required. But the 47-mm. gun which
was to replace it had virtually no stock of ammunition. French efforts to
devise a perfect land mine for anti-tank protection failed. The improvisations resorted to proved to be just what improvisations always prove to be
in modern warfare—totally ineffective.

The French tanks were excellent, but there was no effective organization on larger than a divisional basis and no clear-cut doctrine on their
employment as such. Trucks were available to haul infantry, but they
were not available to transport tanks. The individual fighting capacity of
the French tank was higher than that of the average German tank of its
own weight. But maintenance service, especially refueling, had not been
worked out on the scale of continuous service which the situation soon
demanded. There was certainly nothing like the preparation which
enabled the German panzer divisions to keep rolling day after day from
Sedan to Dunkirk. It has been reported that one excellent French tank
unit in the scrambled fighting on the Somme was reduced to the "Injun-
fighting" tactics of covered-wagon days and forced to form an immobile
hollow circle for want of fuel in the logistic breakdown that followed the
unexpected character of the war. French military aviation, which was the
most formidable in Europe in 1935, was allowed to fall to a poor fourth
in 1939, well below that of Germany, Italy, and Britain.

I think it was the late Webb Miller who made the satirical observation:
"The French Army is perfectly prepared in 1939—for the war of 1914,"
and it became thoroughly familiar to the cliché-conscious make-up editors
before the outbreak of war. But the military "experts" continued to rate
the French Army as the "finest in Europe" right up to the crash. The
newspapermen were not experts—but they knew better!

III

When Germany occupied the Rhineland in 1936, Gamelin is said to
have offered to drive them out if Prime Minister Sarraut would consent

to general mobilization. He was not prepared to act against the thirty thousand German troops in the area without placing the whole French military machine on a war basis. He was also unwilling to risk the occupation of the Saar as a countermeasure. If the second Great War did not begin then, it began, according to Liddell Hart, when Italy and Germany gave active assistance to General Franco in July 1936. The formation of the Rome-Berlin Axis on November 1, 1936, ended forever the possibility of dealing with the Reich alone. From this time on Gamelin had to count on a war of two fronts.

Gamelin strongly supported the maintenance of France's alliances even when these were being undermined by diplomatic events over which he had no control. He preferred to fight at the time of Munich rather than see the bastion of Czechoslovakia and her thirty divisions surrendered. He is said to have urged that the maximum concessions given to Hitler safeguard the main line of Czech fortifications, her strategic railways and armament factories. But the appeasers had their way. Nine months after Munich, Gamelin came to the conclusion that this surrender had tipped the balance against France, since by this time the Siegfried Line had progressed to a point where it made the prospect of military pressure on the Reich unpromising. He regarded the loss of the Czech war material and armament plants as more serious than the loss of her thirty divisions. Until August 23, 1939, there was still room for hope that the vast forces of Russia might be turned against the Axis. But the German-Russian non-aggression pact swept that prospect aside. With its signature the calculations based upon a two-front war against Germany vanished. Poland could no longer be saved.

Like Joffre in 1914, Gamelin gave the impression of utter confidence and serenity in the crisis of 1939. To a public alarmed at the prospect of seeing the French Army bleed itself white on the Siegfried position he gave assurance that he did not intend to begin the war with a Verdun battle. This gave the impression that he had another less costly and more promising alternative in mind. Isolated from the impending harsh realities of war in his headquarters in Paris and later in the keep of Vincennes, surrounded by his personal staff of fifteen officers adept at flattery and skilled in the ritual of idol worship, he presided over the mobilization of the French Army like an "imperturbable military Buddha."

Under the hot sun of a late summer the mobilization of the French Army was completed without molestation from the enemy. The new British Expeditionary Force took up its position in France in the period of false calm, and the two armies marked time while Poland was struck down in a three weeks' campaign by the amazingly effective co-ordinate action of the *Luftwaffe* and the German armored forces. The press of the Allied countries treated the uninterrupted mobilization of Franco-British forces in France as if it in itself assured ultimate victory.

Since it was impossible to go to the aid of Poland many voices were raised in France, urging that action should be taken to define Italy's position and, if hostile, to strike her down while the Germans were still occupied in the east. Gamelin did not favor opening new fronts. He was content to perch *au balcon* at the head of the Alpine passes and await developments. When Weygand advocated the opening of a front in the Balkans he opposed this on the grounds that German numerical superiority and interior lines would render this dangerous. He wanted to confine operations to western Europe, which would force the Germans to attack the Allied fortified lines in the west.

Because of the German air supremacy Gamelin vetoed the British proposal to bomb German synthetic gasoline plants for fear of reprisals. Thus the air stalemate developed along with the "sitzkrieg" on the ground. The full force of the German air power remained a secret until the attack of May 10, a circumstance that worked in favor of the enemy. Boredom as thick as night fell upon the front. It was not dispelled by Gamelin's supercautious advance into the no man's land between the Maginot and Siegfried lines toward Saarbrücken. One supremely apt picture of the situation in the west reached the press and picture magazines of the world. It showed a French poilu slumped in a chair in the midst of a wood behind the front lines, his automatic rifle on the ground in front of him, on his face the unforgettable impression of utter boredom and purposelessness. "Experts" were careful to point out that the apparent shiftless appearance of the French troops, their dog-eared, untidy uniforms and amateurish looking camps, their carelessly constructed barricades over which ancient Hotchkiss machine guns pointed with faint menace at the empty skies, were all marks of a veteran, competent, cagey, battle-worthy army.

Gamelin was apparently not disturbed or impressed by the rapid collapse of Poland. The social and military weaknesses of the Polish state, in his opinion, made it impossible to draw useful military lessons from her defeat. A single small pamphlet on German tactics in the Polish campaign was circulated in the French Army, but it was not backed by action on the part of the high command. The Norwegian disaster, however, focused criticism on Gamelin since he obviously misjudged the speed and weight of the German stroke in that theater. Daladier, his chief supporter, was replaced by Reynaud as Prime Minister, and Reynaud was not so easily impressed with Gamelin's facile academic explanations of Allied strategy. In fact, Reynaud became so suspicious of Gamelin's leadership early in May that he was preparing to replace him by either Giraud, Weygand, or Huntziger when the German blow fell in the west. There was no time after Norway to apply the lessons of the campaign or to restudy the Polish disaster from the standpoint of new tactics. The German assault in the west had to be faced with the concepts and weapons of 1918.

IV

Gamelin had long considered the possibility of a German attack on Belgium and Holland. Since the repudiation of the French alliance by Belgium in 1936 no liaison existed between the two staffs. In January 1940 Gamelin warned Belgium that if France was not permitted to send troops into the country for its protection before the Germans struck, the French relief forces could not be expected to advance much beyond their own frontiers. He anticipated that Belgian resistance would hold up the German advance for at least five days and that disorganization of the German forces after pushing through the Ardennes and Belgian fortified positions would leave them in a condition favorable for the counterattack of thirty Allied divisions earmarked for the movement. When the crisis came, however, he did not adhere to this sound program.

Possibly because he knew that Reynaud had criticized him for want of energy and daring, Gamelin met the German assault in the west with more than his customary swiftness and energy. His order of the day unwittingly provided the most damaging material for a future criticism of his own policies by asserting that "the blow which we have been expecting since September has at last fallen." This informed the world that his sole aim during all the months of military reverses had been to force the Germans to attack in the west. On the morning of May 10 Gamelin felt that he was on the eve of a complete vindication of his military program. With the swift, impetuous stroke of a chess player who abandons his carefully prepared game when the opponent makes a long-expected move, Gamelin sent an Allied force of thirty divisions racing northward into Belgium and Holland. They advanced far beyond the confines of the plan announced in January 1940. At the end of the second day motorized forces of General Giraud reached Breda.

Perhaps Gamelin expected to use the northmost Allied armies as a hammer with which to strike the German armies after they pushed through the Ardennes into Belgium. The Allied divisions, moving with great swiftness and precision northward, were curiously free from air attacks, which in itself should have aroused the suspicion of Gamelin. It might have told him that the Germans were eager to have him do just what he was attempting. The long Allied columns were ignored by the Luftwaffe, which concentrated its attack on rear areas, airfields, and communications. The confusion existing in Belgium and Holland and the penetration of the Belgian and Dutch lines on the second day of assault should have made it clear to Gamelin that the five-day estimate of the German push through the Ardennes was no longer valid. Either Gamelin was not fully informed of the situation in the north or he was seized with one of his fits of academic indecision. He did not take the heroic step necessary to save the northern force from what was an obvious trap. A terrible face-destroying decision to withdraw the whole northern force, at the end of the first or second day of action, alone could have prevented the disaster of Flanders.

It took Gamelin five days (the time he calculated the Belgian lines would be able to hold the Germans) to grasp the full significance of the developments in the north. By that time the Germans had pushed the Belgian forces back from the Albert Canal line, and Holland had succumbed to a bewildering attack of four dimensions. Swarms of Stukas and highly trained small combat squads cut Corap's ill-fated Ninth Army at Sedan to shreds. The mighty armored forces of ten panzer divisions were ready to pour through the gap. Why reserves were not available to support this poorly trained and indifferently commanded force at the hinge of the Maginot Line has never been revealed. The Germans had always shown a marked tendency to strike at points where Allied armies joined or other natural lines of cleavage. Corap has been cleared of the early charges of gross neglect in failing to destroy the Meuse bridges, but the impression of slackness in the Ninth Army remains. It served no purpose to replace Corap on May 15 with General Giraud, since the confusion of the Ninth Army was so great that Giraud was never able to collect its staff and wandered into the enemy lines.

It was at this tragic hour that the division of the French General Staff into three parts proved fatal. Its ponderous machinery could not keep pace with the lightning character of developments. Gamelin was not in touch with the armies in the north. He was not correctly informed of the situation at Sedan. In a subdued but confident mood he appeared before the Committee of National Defense on the afternoon of May 15 and assured them that the situation was not beyond repair. But when he reached the castle of Vincennes and conferred with his staff the full force of the impending tragedy broke over him. His quick academic mind told him that all was lost. Like a nervous chess player who sees a sudden checkmate looming where he thought to win a coup himself, Gamelin figuratively swept the pieces off the board in an impatient gesture of surrender. He called Daladier on the phone and admitted that the situation was indescribably grave.

Reynaud, who had been deceived by the confident atmosphere of the French command, was thunderstruck. At first he refused to speak to Gamelin and tried to secure cabinet approval of his dismissal in favor of Weygand. This was not obtained until May 19, and in the meantime Pétain, the aged hero of Verdun, was brought to Paris as Vice-Premier to bolster French morale.

Two decisive acts remained to Gamelin before he was thrust from power. After spending a hectic day in uncertainty (and without consulting Reynaud) he issued his famous order of May 17 which carried the stirring "conquer-or-die" words of the Marne order of 1914. But the magic did not work this time. There was not the slightest change in the Allied strategic position to warrant it, and in view of the colossal concentration of German armored and infantry strength rolling toward the sea in the Somme area there was not the remotest hope of its fulfillment. The message was utterly meaningless. Even if all the French troops in that area obeyed the order literally and died fighting with their puny weapons against the terrifying team of the dive bomber and the tank, the situation would not have been materially altered. Morale sagged immediately and irretrievably. France was lost.

The final act of Gamelin in the fearful drama of Flanders also bore the faint remembrance of happier days at the Marne in 1914. Five hours before he was replaced on May 19 he ordered General Billotte, commanding the Allied forces in Flanders, to launch a counterattack against the Somme gap. Before this could be undertaken Weygand assumed supreme command. His first question to Gamelin was: "Where are the French and British forces in the north?" So great was the confusion and breakdown of French intelligence that Gamelin could not give Weygand any clear picture of the situation in Flanders. The order for the counterattack was postponed, and Weygand was forced to undertake personal air reconnaissance in order to judge the situation.

It becomes clear that Gamelin's eleventh-hour order for a counterattack by the northern armies was a leap in the dark. It would be unfair to suggest, as some have done, that he made this move in order to forestall his dismissal, since it would be difficult for Reynaud to remove him while the only possible measure for the relief of the entrapped northern forces was under way. Nor does it seem fair to compare Gamelin's dismissal on May 19 with a hypothetical removal of Joffre after the Battle of Charleroi in 1914 and say: "In this case there would have been no victory at the Marne." Joffre at least knew where his own forces were. He developed a plan possible of achievement. Gamelin was acting in the absence of information.

v

One is forced to admire Gamelin's composure in this moment of personal and national disaster. There were no heroics or melodrama. The mask of academic serenity was never lifted to reveal the extent to which he considered himself personally responsible for the fall of France. On May 23 he was found trimming the roses in the back yard of his apartment at No. 55 Avenue Foch in Paris. He assured his friends that he could and would defend his military policy and program. When the final collapse came he submitted to arrest and imprisonment at Riom with dignity and silence. Hard at work on the preparation of his memoirs, he has been an example and inspiration to other less confident prisoners. He looks upon his final vindication and exoneration as certain.

It is obviously too early to pass anything like final judgment on Gamelin. Some of the French archives were destroyed in the evacuation of Paris. Full documentary evidence may never be available. The findings of the Riom court should be discounted when they appear because of the political implications involved. The whole matter of Gamelin's responsibility for the French military position on May 19 is bound up with the supreme question of the Weygand-Pétain decision on June 16 that the whole war was lost and that Britain could not possibly prevail against Germany and Italy. Thus the full truth about the first stages of the war in the west may be hidden for years. But because of the immense warning value they contain, certain conclusions can and must be drawn.

Along with many others Gamelin completely misjudged the character of the social and military revolution which was taking place in the Reich during the years of his power. He compromised with the politicians instead of forcing them to provide for the security of the state. He was blind to the tactical innovations which the Germans had prepared in peace and had practiced in Poland and Norway. He staked his whole concept of a defensive war of attrition on the Maginot Line despite the ancient maxim that everything immobile can be destroyed in war. He put the discredited idea of the thin strong line to its final test despite the World War teachings as to the strength of positions in depth. He abandoned his safe and cautious program of a limited advance in Belgium in favor of a bold stroke as far north as Holland. He took no warning from the notable immunity which the Allied relief columns enjoyed from German air attack. He did not interpret the events of the first two days' fighting in Holland and Belgium as invalidating previous concepts as to time and disposition of forces. He spent five vital days in arriving at a correct estimate of the German plan of attack. It was then too late to withdraw the northern forces. By the time he turned over control to Weygand he had lost touch with the French armies in the field and had no clear grasp of the situation.

The question may well be raised: "How could a professional soldier of Gamelin's attainments perform with such incredible maladroitness in a crisis which he admitted he foresaw since the start of hostilities?" A complete answer (if it were possible) would be of immense importance to professional soldiers everywhere. A partial answer might be that Gamelin was an academic soldier. Viscount Gort said flatly: "He was not a fighter." In the isolation of high office Gamelin retired more and more into the ivory tower of philosophical reflections on past military events and paid insufficient attention to the practical aspects of war. Combat officers visiting his headquarters at Vincennes found no opportunity in the erudite discussions of philosophy and art to comment on their front-line experience. According to André Géraud, Gamelin's ideas "came ready-made—he ceased to examine whether they were still valid. He felt that he had foreseen everything, calculated everything, arranged everything, and that he had nothing more to do." When the crisis of May smashed his little academic world to bits he was incapable of elasticity of mind or resolute action. "He was a cold light."

Lord Tweedsmuir, writing about another soldier, summed up with amazing exactness the tragedy of Gamelin. He said:

He was first and foremost a highly competent professional soldier. Now, a soldier's professionalism differs from that of other crafts. He acquires a body of knowledge which may be varied and enlarged by new conditions, such as new weapons and new modes of transport, but which in essence is a closed technique. . . . A powerful mind might work brilliantly inside its limits with little impulse to alter fundamentals. Change and expansion were consequently in the nature of a revolution and were brought about either by a great genius, or slowly and grudgingly by some cataclysmic pressure. Hence the more competent and better trained the soldier was, the more averse he would be to alter his traditional creed until its failure had been proven with utter finality.

Because of the utter finality with which the career of Gamelin set the seal of failure on his methods and concepts, it may well mark the end of one military epoch and the beginning of another. Certainly any soldier after Gamelin who permits himself to enjoy the luxury of complacency and the comforts to be found in the maintenance of old concepts, who does not subject himself and his thinking to repeated and vigorous examination, whose mind is closed to the almost limitless application of science to the "new face of war," courts similar disaster for himself and for his country.

VI

Other Armies

MILITARY JOURNALS the world over reproduce each other's articles. For every nation with an army of any size has its service journals. These, like any other group of professional magazines, differ greatly in their alertness and thought. Some run strongly to justification of the past; some dig into all sides of war and seek from within their armies the men who think most proficiently.

In view of the fact that there has been for many years an official magazine in the United States, a large part of which has been devoted to translations and abstracts from foreign-language military journals (the monthly *Military Review,* formerly the *Command and General Staff School Quarterly*), the *Infantry Journal* has never had the policy of trying to cover the same ground as fully. But it has often printed articles from foreign military magazines and by foreign military writers. It has indeed printed a number of articles by men now high in command in the armies of Nazi Germany, and it has reviewed others at length. A few of the most important of these are included in this section along with other kinds of articles that come from or touch upon or deal with foreign armies and their methods of making war.

The *Infantry Journal* missed a few of the prophets of war, such as General de Gaulle, though this author's book received such scant circulation originally that it is not surprising no copy reached the *Journal* editors. Then, too, the editorial staff has not at all times had members capable of combing the military literature of several nations. But most of the well-known foreign writers, such as Guderian of Germany, Von Eimannsberger of Austria, Fuller and Hart of Britain, have appeared in the *Infantry Journal,* and usually their writings have aroused much individual interest.

GERMAN METHODS

An editorial by MAJOR (later COLONEL) JOHN R. M. TAYLOR

(*1917*)

WE ARE PUBLISHING a certain amount of information concerning German methods of warfare, as it is important to know what methods the man you are in training to conquer is using to conquer you. This war we are in is not war in general, but war against Germany, and will be fought out this year or next spring with United States troops on French soil.

So it is different from the Red and Blue forces which so many of us have maneuvered on the Leavenworth sheets without having to consider the extreme improbability that Red and Blue forces should be there.

We now have a definite problem in front of us. It is hoped that the glimpse this German information gives of how the other man is playing his cards will help us to take the trick.

ARMORED FORCES

By MAJOR GENERAL (now COLONEL GENERAL)
HEINZ GUDERIAN, German Army

(*1937*)

The pages of the *Infantry Journal* for the past twenty years have contained articles about tanks and their uses in warfare. One of the early studies ("Tank Discussion," 1920) was by Captain (now General) Dwight D. Eisenhower in which he argued for a more concentrated use of tank power. There were many other American officers, most of them now in high command, who also wrote on one aspect or another of mechanized warfare. The magazine also carried the thoughts of leading foreign writers. "Armored Forces," by General Guderian, who has been one of Hitler's principal commanders in the field, was one of the most complete studies of the tank that appeared in the *Journal's* pages during the two decades between the wars.

A MILITARY CONFLICT of the future is inconceivable without the participation of air and armored forces. As early as 1919 General Buat of the French Army expressed his reaction to the experiences of the World War in the following words:

Of the two elements of tactics, only fire power profited by the invention of the machine. In fact, mechanical aid proved so helpful to fire power that mobility in combat ceased almost completely. The horse was virtually eliminated. Fighting was carried on from trenches. The soldier could move only when all firearms of the opponent were silenced. However, with the appearance of the motor on the battlefield, mobility has regained its full importance. The infantry company of the line henceforth will be a tank company, though this does not mean that the foot soldier will disappear altogether. The automatic weapon designed for killing human beings will give way to the automatic weapon intended for the destruction of armored vehicles.

The tremendous strides made since the World War in the technical development of the air service and the mechanized arm have greatly added to their importance. Their effect on theories and plans, on strategy and tactics is increasingly felt. Therefore, it is the natural desire of the older arms to become better acquainted with their younger relatives.

In this article we shall illustrate the organization and tactics employed by today's amored forces and examine their influence upon the other arms when co-operating with them.

We may base our study on the fact that the mechanized arm is divided into two main groups, reconnaissance forces and combat forces.

MECHANIZED RECONNAISSANCE FORCES

Reconnaissance calls for highly mobile, flexible, and easily handled units that possess a wide radius of action and good means of communication. Reconnaissance forces must observe and report to a maximum, without being observed themselves. Therefore, the smaller the reconnaissance element and the more readily it lends itself to concealment, the easier the accomplishment of its mission will be. It must possess enough fighting power to be capable of defeating any similar opponent. Certain reconnaissance missions call for additional fighting power; in such cases the reconnaissance elements must be suitably reinforced.

The heavy armored scout car constitutes the principal means of modern ground reconnaissance. For this purpose most armies employ a wheeled vehicle, designed primarily for travel on roads but which, when equipped with three or more axles and a multi-wheel drive, is also capable of cross-country movement. Recent years have witnessed considerable progress in the construction of cross-country vehicles, and further advances in this field are being made constantly. These vehicles possess a maximum speed of 40 to 60 mph and a radius of action between 120 and 200 miles. They are armed with machine guns and 20-mm. to 37-mm. guns firing armor-piercing ammunition. The armament of these vehicles is limited to a certain weight because of the speed required, but it offers protection against small-arms ammunition.

Depending upon the mission, the organization of the armored-car troop varies in number and types of vehicles employed. In some instances the armored-car troop must be reinforced by engineers, motorized infantry, and heavy arms. The armored-car troop is capable of maintaining permanent contact with the enemy, even at night, and reporting its observations by radio.

The reconnaissance squadron is generally composed of two or three armored-car troops of nine to twelve armored scout cars each. As a rule its mission will be to reconnoiter the main roads and, on the basis of the results thus gained, to enlarge upon the reconnaissance net in the vital directions. When in close contact with the enemy the latter type of work may be executed best by light armored scout cars and motorcycle elements.

Reconnaissance is of value to the command only if the results are reported in time. Therefore, the problem of equipping the reconnaissance unit with adequate communication requires careful study. Of primary consideration, in this respect, are the radio and the radiotelephone. The number and radius of the communication means control the tactical employment of the reconnaissance squadron. To avoid interception and interference with radio communication, the trend is to limit its use as much as possible. Until contact with the enemy is established, reliance is placed upon other means of communication, such as the telephone, motorized messengers, and aviation.

The mechanized reconnaissance squadron is the communication center of its respective armored-car troops. It devolves upon the squadron commander to furnish timely reliefs for the troops on reconnaissance; moreover, he must have in reserve a sufficient number of armored cars to enable him to execute reconnaissance missions that may require several days and, if necessary, to make a sudden shift of the direction of his effort without depending upon outside support.

To some extent missions involving minor combat and protection of the communication centers of the mechanized ground reconnaissance elements require reinforcements of infantry carried on motorcycles or cross-country trucks, light guns or mortars, pioneers and anti-tank guns. In sudden clashes the armor and armament of the armored-car troop and reconnaissance squadron will usually permit offensive tactics. A mechanized unit on reconnaissance should not provoke combat that might divert it from its reconnaissance mission, but it may properly take advantage of a favorable opportunity to inflict damage upon the enemy. Moreover, the general rule that a reconnaissance unit avoids combat need not interfere with the occasional assignment of combat missions to it when there is a shortage of other forces. Such assignment may become necessary, for instance, in situations involving pursuit, cover of a withdrawal, screening, and protection of flank and rear.

Mechanized reconnaissance units may execute both strategic and tactical reconnaissance. In the case of strategic reconnaissance they function as army troops or as independent units operating between armies and groups of armies. They perform tactical reconnaissance for armored forces and other highly mobile bodies of troops, such as motorized infantry divisions. Strategic ground reconnaissance supplements air reconnaissance or may even replace it, especially at night, in fog, and in wooded and mountainous country. In turn, strategic ground reconnaissance, particularly that executed by mechanized elements, must be supported by air reconnaissance whose elements are much speedier and have a larger radius of action. The command and reconnaissance elements of both these arms must be carefully trained in this co-operative work.

Tactical reconnaissance for infantry divisions and army corps takes place within a narrow zone of limited depth; moreover, both flanks usually are joined by other forces. This type of reconnaissance is most suitably assigned to horse cavalry, but the combination of horse and motor in a reconnaissance unit does not seem advisable.

The mechanized reconnaissance forces are the first units to contact the enemy. Upon the outbreak of hostilities the mechanized elements are given their first as well as their greatest opportunity for speedy gains, for no one can say how the situation may develop after the initial encounters. It is vital, therefore, that the individual components of the reconnaissance units be thoroughly trained in co-operating with each other; that the leader and his command work together as a team, and that the crews of the scout cars be well acquainted with their means of communication and support weapons. For this reason the organization of the reconnaissance units in peace must be identical with the war organization.

Armored Combat Forces

The bulk of the armored forces is most usefully organized into large combat units, as is done in Great Britain and Russia. On the other hand, France continues to adhere to an organization which provides for the employment of one or more battalions within the infantry division or army corps.

The mission of the armored combat forces is the delivery of surprise attacks with concentrated strength, with the view to gaining the decision at the point determined by the command. The armored combat forces combine fire power with mobility and armor protection that is proof, at least, against small arms. They are, therefore, exclusively an offensive arm whose advantage over other ground forces consists in capacity to fight while in motion.

Compared with tanks of the types used in the World War, the modern tank is principally noted for its considerable increase in speed, which makes it impossible for the older arms to follow a tank attack closely for an extended period of time. Armament, fire effect, aiming devices, means of observation and communication have all undergone great improvement, but at the same time the defense against armored forces has also been considerably strengthened. The principal foes of the tank are the hostile tank and anti-tank gun; these compel the tank to take all possible advantage of its own speed. Other dangers are obstructions of all kinds, especially mines.

We shall briefly describe the most important types of tanks now in use.

(a) *The light tank* is armed with one cannon, 20-mm. to 50-mm. in caliber, and several machine guns. Automatic rifles, pistols, and hand grenades serve the crew in close combat. Some tanks carry smoke-screen equipment. The armor throughout is proof against steel-core projectiles; the vital parts of the superstructure and the turret are often constructed of still heavier armor. The light tank averages about 12 mph on the march and 7 to 10 mph in combat. Its maximum weight is about 18 tons. This tank is designed for combat in the forward zone of the infantry, where it attacks hostile tanks with its cannon and animate targets with its machine guns.

(b) *A lighter tank* armed exclusively with machine guns and weighing between four and seven tons, is largely used for missions involving close reconnaissance, close security, and transmission of orders. In addition this lighter tank is useful in combat against animate targets. Presenting a small target and possessing great speed and mobility, it is also one of the most dangerous foes of the anti-tank gun. Its low construction cost permits manufacture on a large scale.

(c) *The medium tank* carries guns, 75-mm. to 100-mm. in caliber. Its speed and armor are comparable to that of the light tank. It supports the light tank, especially in attacking distant objectives, immobile targets, localities, field fortifications, woods, and anti-tank guns.

(d) *The heavy tank* is armed with several machine guns, light cannon, and guns larger than 100-mm. in caliber. As a rule this type of tank is heavily armored (in France up to 50-mm. steel plates) and is designed for attack on field or permanent fortifications. Weighing up to 90 tons, it sometimes requires specially constructed carriers for railway transportation.

Medium and heavy tanks with armament larger than 100-mm. guns usually carry smoke projectiles for blinding hostile observation posts, artillery, and, above all, anti-tank guns.

Tank units designed for mobile warfare include a combination of light, medium, and heavy tanks. The ratio of light to medium tanks depends upon the kind of combat for which the particular unit is intended. The heavy tanks constitute separate units designed for attack on fortified positions. Hence the distinction drawn in some countries between battalions of light, medium, heavy, and mixed tanks. Two or more battalions form a tank regiment, several regiments a tank brigade.

While the tank unit in action is directed by radio, small elements (such as companies and platoons) may be guided by visual signals. Up to the time the radio goes into operation, orders and messages may be transmitted by telephone, motorized messengers, and aviation.

The staffs frequently have at their disposal radio-equipped command tanks and a platoon each of lighter tanks for messenger service. The command of tank units from an airplane—an idea repeatedly advanced in some countries—presupposes that control of the air over the zone of attack is established in advance. Also, it requires faultless radio communication and a special type of airplane. To date, this problem remains unsolved.

Let us assume that the command tanks, from the brigade commander down to the platoon commanders, are equipped with both transmitting and receiving sets while the other tanks contain only receiving sets. Let us assume further an average speed of 12 mph on the march and 10 mph in action and endeavor to draw a picture of the attack of a tank brigade.

We know that a tank attack ordinarily produces decisive results only when the requisite mass effect is obtained by a concentration of force. Consequently the tank brigade should be the smallest combat unit to be entrusted with an independent mission (cf. the Russian maneuvers of 1935, where one thousand tanks were massed for an attack in four waves).

As previously stated, mechanized forces fight while in motion, their attack being a combination of fire, movement, and armor protection. But the fact that they fight while moving does not mean that it is the primary object of the tank to run down an opponent steam-roller fashion. It is the actual fire effect—the destruction of the enemy by fire—which is the important thing; the crushing effect is merely incidental, of secondary consideration, and is chiefly used for the destruction of matériel.

The fire effect of the tank depends upon:

(a) *The quality of the arms and ammunition used.* In firing from a moving tank a rapid rate of fire and the use of tracer ammunition are desirable.

(b) *The perfection of the aiming devices.* Good telescopic and open sights as well as an easily manipulated elevating and traversing gear are essential.

(c) *The construction of the running gear of the tank,* especially of the springs. Good springs absorb shocks and minimize vibration.

(d) *The terrain.* Uneven ground results in unsteadiness and causes difficulty in keeping the sights on the target. Steep slopes may produce large dead angles, both horizontal and vertical. Ground covered with high grain, brush, woods, settlements, and so on, tends to interfere with the recognition of targets and reduces the fire effect.

(e) *The state of training of the tank crews.* Constant practice in the use of the aiming devices; thorough knowledge of the weapon as well as experience in serving it in dusk or poor light or while the tank is being shaken about; fixed attention upon the enemy and alertness in firing—all these qualities are vital for the tank gunner. The driver must know how to co-operate with the gunner by driving smoothly while the guns are in action.

When the vehicle is in motion machine-gun fire is effective up to five hundred yards and cannon fire up to about one thousand yards. The French training regulations state that "the tanks can use their armament at short range with precision and rapidity." The British training regulations have this to say: "One must clearly bear in mind, however, that the mission of the tanks consists not merely in gaining a certain objective but in locating and eliminating all resistance from machine-gun and small-arms fire . . ." to which I may add "and from tank cannon fire."

Of course when stationary the tank can fire effectively on more distant targets. When the situation and a due regard for the cohesion of the tank unit permits, fire from the stationary tank is preferable to fire from the moving tank. Yet this opportunity will rarely present itself in an attack by large units. Hence fire from the vehicle in motion constitutes the essence of tank gunnery training.

Possessing both strategic and tactical mobility, mechanized forces may be more speedily concentrated and employed than any other ground force. This inherent characteristic of the mechanized arm permits surprise, and the preparations for the attack must aim to get it. This calls for the utmost abbreviation of preparatory measures. The concentration must take every advantage of speed and darkness. Also necessary are careful traffic regulation, timely storage of most urgently needed supplies, and precise and comprehensive orders. In 1918, at Amiens, the British successfully concentrated their tank forces within two nights. During the night of August 6–7 the tanks occupied the concentration zones located two to three miles behind the front, from whence they proceeded the following night to the line of departure about one thousand yards behind the front line of the infantry. In the future the speed of the modern tank will generally render it unnecessary to occupy a special line of departure but will permit the mechanized forces to launch an attack from a concentration zone out of range of the hostile artillery, unless terrain obstructions and other circumstances demand the employment of a different method. The concentration zones must provide concealment and contain a good road net, for in these areas the tank forces make their final preparations for the attack, refuel, feed the troops, and replace crews wearied by long marches. Necessary reconnaissance and liaison with the other arms must be established.

The reconnaissance should take up no more time than that of the other arms. Expert map reading, correct evaluation of aerial photographs, and, in certain instances, a personal air reconnaissance of the zone of attack by the tank commanders must furnish the basis for the attack orders. Careful determination of the various approaches in friendly territory, especially for night movements, will add greatly to a smooth traffic flow. Guided by an ample number of road signs and traffic guards, the tanks may reach the concentration zones quietly and without the use of lights.

From the concentration the tanks develop for the attack. By development is meant an advance equal in width and depth to the combat formation that the tanks will assume. The individual units should remain in column to take advantage of roads, negotiate narrow defiles, and pass through the front line without interfering with the other arms already deployed there. Greatest care must be taken to avoid disturbances to the communication service.

A favorable time for the attack is at dusk or, better yet, at dawn, when fog, smoke, and poor light reduce the field of vision of the defending side to a few hundred yards, thus minimizing the effect of the hostile defensive weapons. Camouflage, artillery fire, smoke screens, air activity and attacks simulated along other parts of the front, all tend to divert the attention of the opponent from the actual zone of attack. A simultaneous advance made on a wide front will help disperse the hostile fire effect.

Immediately before entering actual combat the tanks change from the development to the combat formation. Until the tanks open fire, all maneuvers that take place within sight of the enemy must be at great speed, and advantage must be taken of all cover offered by the ground. A terrain which slopes toward the enemy will help to increase the speed of the attack and consequently favor surprise effect. Topography to a large extent determines the direction of the tank attack; it is more important to assign the tank units favorable ground than to co-ordinate their attack with that of other arms on unfavorable ground. Thus, driving home a powerful and uniform attack on a wide front and in great depth, the mechanized forces may take the enemy by surprise and penetrate his front. Each component of the tank brigade must endeavor to gain its objective as rapidly as the hostile resistance permits. Provided all weapons are held in readiness to open fire without delay and the crews are well trained and constantly on the alert, the fire action may be executed with great force and at most effective ranges. For it is the actual fire effect which, in the end, determines the moral effect of the tank attack.

From the foregoing we may draw certain conclusions regarding the conduct of the combat. Firing requires that speed be reduced to between 7 to 12 mph, depending upon terrain and vehicle types. This speed range will permit an accurate aim. The tactics must be simple and permit of an effective use of the weapons, without causing mutual interference between the tanks.

The platoon of three heavy or medium tanks or of five to seven light tanks comprises the lowest tactical unit. The platoons cross the terrain in line or wedge formation, with about fifty yards' interval between tanks. Preparatory to the attack, the companies form in waves. The companies of light tanks, which constitute the first wave, often are directly supported by a number of medium tanks armed with cannon; Great Britain, in particular, favors this practice. Similarly disposed are the battalions, which form in several lines. The brigade may form its regiments either in waves or in line. In the former case the regiments generally will form their battalions in line; in the latter they will form in column or echelon. All commanders must post themselves far in front, where they may constantly supervise the advance of their units and bring their personal influence to bear.

Each wave and, within it, each unit must receive a clearly defined combat mission. For instance, if the mission be to penetrate the hostile front, the orders would read: "First wave will penetrate to and eliminate the hostile command posts and reserves. Second wave will silence the hostile artillery. Third wave will attack the hostile infantry and contain it until the friendly infantry has moved up. Upon accomplishment of its mission, third wave will follow the commander of the tank forces and remain at his disposal."

The zone of attack covered by a tank brigade of four battalions measures one to two and a half miles in width and two to three miles in depth. The width corresponds to about that of an infantry division; however, the tank brigade brings a larger number of light and heavy firearms into action in the forward zone of combat.

At the end of the tank attack the various units are reorganized for further employment. At this point it may be necessary to bring up ammunition, supplies, and reinforcements and replace worn elements by fresh ones.

The most dangerous foes of the tank and anti-tank weapon are hostile armored forces. Therefore, they must be attacked first. Hostile tanks may be initially engaged by fire delivered from a stationary front of tanks and anti-tank guns, but if this be not feasible, or if it becomes necessary to interrupt the fire, the tanks must change to combat in motion. Since fire will determine the outcome of such an action it is important to maintain order among the various tank units and adhere to a prescribed rate of speed so that the fire may be effective. Intelligent utilization of the ground will help to reduce losses, and in certain cases it may be of advantage to use smoke screens. But fire control and a high standard of gunnery training are the factors that will contribute most toward victory. And, once launched, an attack on hostile armored forces must be carried through to annihilation; other missions must wait until that one is accomplished.

INFANTRY

In the matter of co-operation between mechanized forces and other arms there exist two directly opposing views. The advocates of one contend that the infantry is the principal arm and that all others merely exist to serve it. They believe that the tank must move no faster than the foot soldier. In a sense it should constitute a moving shield for the infantryman who is unable to attack in the face of hostile machine-gun fire without this protection. The inherent speed of the tank is not to be exploited. For the sake of the infantry the adherents of this conception are willing to accept the considerable tank losses which these tactics make inevitable. They take little account of the strategic potentialities of a speedy armored force. The protagonists of the other school look far into the future. They are not much inclined to co-operation with other arms. They prefer to combine the armored forces in purely mechanized units and use them primarily against the enemy's flanks and rear or on large-scale raids that reach far into hostile territory. By taking the defense by surprise they would overcome road obstructions, difficulties of the terrain, and fortifications. They expect this method of employing the mechanized arm to decide the war.

In point of fact various unresolved technical difficulties handicap this adventurous conception to such an extent that, for the time being, it is better to compromise between these two schools of thought. Therefore, we seek a solution that will permit the mechanized force to support the other arms and at the same time take full advantage of its strategic and tactical potentialities. Above all, we must be careful not to hamper the development of the mechanized arm by adopting a rigid and inflexible organization or by saddling it with obsolete tactical conceptions.

Co-operation is necessary, for, like any other arm, the tank is incapable of solving all combat problems by itself. This necessity for co-operation imposes certain obligations both upon the armored forces and the other arms. These obligations are especially binding upon the arms which are suited for habitual co-operation with tanks. On this point the German training regulations state:

The commander must synchronize tank operations and their support by the other arms. Within the tank zone of attack the action of the other arms depends upon that of the tanks.

The British regulations say, in substance:

The conception that armored cars must always operate in close liaison with cavalry or infantry is obsolete; armored cars are weapons of opportunity. They can exploit their inherent strength best at the time and place and with the combat methods that best suit their characteristics.

The British point out that the direction of an attack is selected with regard to its tactical results, regardless of whether or not it runs parallel to that of the infantry. The German regulations say much the same thing in a different way:

The ground is of decisive importance [for the direction of the attack]. Close contact with the infantry will deprive the tanks of their advantage in speed and possibly sacrifice them to the hostile defense.

Of late there has been a return to the conceptions that prevailed during and shortly after the World War. In Great Britain the maneuvers of 1935 were marked by close teamwork between tanks and infantry. The tank brigade was divided and a tank battalion attached to each infantry division, despite the fact that the British tank is not ideal for joint action with infantry. The British vehicles, on the whole, are too speedy and too large, and their armor is too weak for this purpose. Tank units larger than the battalion were not used. Because of this division of strength the effect of the tank was negligible. Nor did the motorized infantry brigade play a decisive part in these maneuvers, for it operated in close contact with the foot troops.

The British explain this return to World War tactics by claiming that the introduction of a heavily armored, low-speed accompanying tank would materially reduce the disadvantages cited and permit close co-operation with the infantry. However, in order to be proof against the minimum caliber (25-mm.) anti-tank gun, armor must exceed a thickness of 30 mm. The weight of such armor would require a much bigger power plant, hence a much larger tank. And the cost of producing such tanks in large numbers would be tremendous. Yet only a large number could effectively support infantry.

But even disregarding the cost, there are important strategic and tactical objections to the organization of separate low-speed tank units for the infantry. The tank units that are designed for strategic purposes may also be used tactically, either as entire units or divided. On the other hand, it would be impracticable to combine the division tank battalions for strategic employment. Aside from the fact that their equipment is not suitable for missions of this kind, the combined force would lack the requisite headquarters and could not produce them at will. The greater the speed of an arm on the march and in combat, the more important that it and its commanders be trained in units that are organized in peace the same as they would be in war. In this respect we have a valuable lesson in the misfortunes suffered by the German cavalry in 1914 as a result of untrained staffs, poor communications, inadequate equipment, and faulty march technique on the part of large units: all of this can be attributed to its prewar organization. With the exception of the Guard Cavalry Division, the cavalry was parceled out to the infantry divisions by brigades—a peacetime practice that had an unfavorable influence on the early operations of the large cavalry units. This error should not be repeated with our armored forces. Slow infantry tanks, even though their armor be reinforced, will be unable to execute their mission in infantry combat if speedier hostile tanks are encountered. The slow tanks have no chance against a similarly armed opponent of greater speed. In this connection Major General J. F. C. Fuller says:

. . . infantry cannot under their own fire attack infantry equipped with magazine rifles and machine guns. . . . They can do so only when supported by a dense shell barrage or when led forward by tanks, in which case they are but a drag on the free movement of these machines. To give them special tanks for this purpose is merely to restrict the value of these weapons. . . . (*The Army in My Time*)

In an article published in the *Army, Navy & Air Force Gazette* of September 26, 1935, General Fuller says:

Even if the frontal attack is persisted in, and even if infantry are to continue to assault—seeing that most enemies we shall meet in the next war will possess three to four times the number of machine guns they did in 1918; will have an artillery designed and trained in anti-tank tactics, and will be equipped with fast-moving tanks (the most effective of anti-tank weapons)—is it sane to suppose that in this war a slow machine will be superior, even as a protective weapon to infantry, to a fast machine? It will have more machine guns to destroy and more anti-tank projectiles fired at it, and if attacked by fast-moving tanks it will be bunkered.

Although certain British views lean toward independent employment of tank forces, the French continue to demand closest co-operation between infantry and tanks. The latest edition of *Réglément d'Infanterie, Deuxième Partie (Combat), 1935*, cites tank figures that are based upon the technical development of the tank as of the final phase of the World War. For instance, light tanks are given a maximum speed of 7 km.p.h., a combat speed of 2 km.p.h., and an average speed on tracks of 3.5 km.p.h. In other words, the regulations treating of co-operation between infantry and tanks refer to an old equipment whose speed in combat is no greater than that of the infantry.

The French call for close teamwork between the two arms and make it a rule to subordinate the tank units to the infantry. Infantry and tanks both are assigned the same objectives. The tanks are to withdraw rather than to advance independently beyond the objectives of the infantry. As a rule, the attack of an infantry company is to be supported by a platoon of tanks, that of a battalion by a company of tanks.

The principles governing the employment of the modern French tanks have not yet been released. According to a number of statements published in the French press, the modern French tank is more heavily armored, carries more powerful guns, and is a good deal faster than its World War forerunner. Discussions of the new Tank D in current publications indicate that, despite these technical improvements, the French continue to rely mainly on close co-operation between tanks, infantry, and artillery. This conception, however, is not without opponents, even in France. For instance, Colonel de Gaulle, in his book *Vers l'Armée de Métier*, has this to say:

The tanks, usually divided into three waves, form for attack a favorable distance to the rear. The first wave is made up of light tanks whose mission it is to establish contact with the enemy. The second or combat wave is composed of the mediums and heavies. . . . Finally comes the reserve wave which is designed to relieve the forward waves or to exploit their gains. . . . Leaving the line of departure at a high rate of speed, the light tanks make the initial attack. Then, organized in large groups, the combat wave enters the battle. . . . The direction of attack will usually be oblique to the hostile front, so that resistance may be taken in flank. The advance must not be unduly delayed by the time-killing task of clearing the zone of attack. . . . In other words, the forward waves must merely clear a passage for themselves and then push on to their objectives as rapidly as possible. As soon as the tank attack shows results the infantry, too, will gain ground. The infantry may advance either by cross-country vehicles or on foot. Its mission is to occupy the ground that the tanks have seized. In many cases it may be necessary for the infantry to wipe out the final vestiges of resistance; to do this it will have to put its accompanying guns into action.

Modern tank forces must not be developed merely with the object of using them in direct support of the slow, laborious attack of the infantry. On the contrary, there must be tests to see whether it is possible to utilize the characteristics of the tank more fully, so that its effect may be more beneficial to operations as a whole. Several countries, for instance, are conducting experiments to discover ways and means of increasing the infantry's battlefield mobility, thus enabling it to keep up with a faster tank attack. There are several methods of accomplishing this. One is to issue the soldier a lighter-weight uniform and to remove his pack. Another is to motorize those rifle units designed for permanent co-operation with tanks. This method has already materialized in France in the form of the *dragons portées*. The *dragons portées* are largely equipped with Citroën-Kegresse cars—half-track vehicles of considerable cross-country ability. A number of these are now protected by light armor, proof against small arms.

Co-operation between tanks and infantry may be carried out in a number of ways:

(1) The tanks attack in advance of the infantry. The infantry follows, taking advantage of the neutralizing effect of the tank attack upon the hostile infantry and machine guns. The infantry supports the tanks by assaulting positions known

or suspected of harboring hostile anti-tank guns. This situation will occur if the attacking force has to cross large exposed areas in gaining its objective.

(2) The tanks attack simultaneously with the infantry. In this case the infantry supports the attack in the same manner as above. This method is suitable if the enemy is close and the terrain favorable for the attack.

(3) The infantry attacks in advance of the tanks. In this case the infantry must be initially supported by other arms, especially by artillery and combat engineers. This method should be used if obstacles, such as rivers or blocked roads, prevent the immediate employment of tanks and if bridgeheads or passages must first be established.

(4) The tanks, jumping off from a different zone, attack obliquely to the direction of attack of the infantry. This method is contingent upon a suitable terrain.

In crossing the hostile zone of combat the tanks must clear a path for the infantry by destroying recognized targets—primarily anti-tank guns, heavy arms, and machine guns—and neutralizing suspected localities. Merely to push through the hostile combat zone with the idea of shattering the enemy's morale is not enough; the tanks must break the enemy's strength by the full use of their weapons and open a gap in the hostile defense system.

Rarely, if ever, will the tank attack completely wipe out the resistance of the hostile infantry. Individual machine guns will remain undiscovered or come to life again. Tanks can materially facilitate infantry action and, in many cases, will be indispensable in preparing the infantry attack, but they cannot take over the infantry's role in combat. The infantry's job lies in an immediate exploitation of the tank attack by a rapid advance. Nor does the foot soldier pause until the ground seized by the tanks is definitely cleared of the enemy.

While advancing with tanks the infantry must maintain formations that permit it to move rapidly and must display signs that will enable the tanks to identify it as friendly infantry, especially in twilight and fog.

ARTILLERY

Armored forces have also created new tasks for the artillery. In the World War, for example, it was practicable and advisable to cover a tank attack by an artillery barrage, but today the high rate of speed of a tank attack prohibits this method of support.

When tank units attack as part of an army, the division artillery assists mainly by firing a preparation; in this it must put forth its utmost effort. The shorter the artillery preparation, the more effective. If enough artillery is not available in the zone of attack, and if the concentration of adequate artillery and ammunition is so conspicuous and involves so much time as to render a surprise effect doubtful, it is advisable to dispense entirely with the preparation. In event of this the artillery will be charged with guarding the tanks and firing on any targets that might endanger their attack.

As a rule the artillery must shift its fire out of the zone of attack simultaneously with the opening of the tank assault. It may then box off the flanks of the zone of attack, shell suspected anti-tank positions, or engage localities unsuitable for tank attack, such as woods and steep slopes. These tasks may be carried out partly with high-explosive shell and partly with smoke projectiles. While this requires great attention and expert fire control, it is facilitated by modern means of communication, especially radio.

This type of support does not reach very deep into the hostile zone of action. Furthermore, it is impossible for the artillery observation posts to keep up with the rapid development of the tank attack. And, finally, an aggressive artillery would not be content to see itself limited to such a small battle role. Actually it is the aim of the artillery of all armies to participate in the tank attack and, with this end in view, to motorize its components. Motorized artillery may be either motor-drawn or self-propelled. Drawn artillery has been the rule so far. Its advantage lies in the divisibility of gun and tractor; the tractor can be easily exchanged and does not have to be taken into the firing position. The question of weight is of little consequence in motor-drawn artillery.

The self-propelled mount is something new; it possesses the advantage of constant readiness for fire, combined with constant readiness to move. It gives a great radius to the individual gun and to the entire battery. It also has a certain degree of armor protection. Self-propelled artillery seems to be a desirable companion of tank units. Great Britain has employed several types of this artillery for some time, and both the United States and the U.S.S.R. are experimenting with it.

As to the tactics employed by this artillery, Colonel de Gaulle says:

The rapid development of combat will not permit artillery to carry out missions in the manner customarily established for the opening of an attack. It cannot be assigned definite zones of fire as in position warfare; nor can its firing data be prepared with mathematical accuracy. On the contrary, as soon as the hostile position is taken, the artillery fire must keep up with the rapid development of events. In other words, the artillery must tread closely upon the heels of the attacking elements not only with its guns and combat trains but with its observation and communications sections as well. Thus, the artillery itself becomes a *masse mouvante* whose components, on their own initiative, select the most favorable positions in accordance with the needs of the situation and deliver their fire from all angles on the most fleeting of targets. When it is equipped with anti-tank weapons and machine guns the artillery can protect itself. It compensates for lack of established position, inability to deliver indirect fire, and the loss of uniform fire control by its mobility, direct observation, and inherent independence.

In this description Colonel de Gaulle gives his idea of an ideal artillery. He calls upon it to discard habits acquired in a long war of position, with its reliable firing bases, its careful, studied survey methods, and its abundance of time, in order to be capable of speedily following the tank attack.

CHEMICALS

Smoke screens are becoming more and more important as an adjunct to the tank attack. Three main forms of employment can be recognized: (1) smoke projectiles fired by artillery in position during the preparation and at the beginning of the tank attack; (2) smoke projectiles fired by self-propelled artillery accompanying the tank attack, and (3) smoke produced by the tanks themselves.

There is nothing new about the first method. It is used to blind enemy observation. So, too, screens are laid down between the advancing tanks and localities suspected of harboring enemy troops or anti-tank guns. This enables the tanks to approach the enemy unobserved or outflank and invest him without drawing fire. Smoke may also be used for purposes of deception.

When smoke is fired by self-propelled artillery accompanying the tanks, the fire is executed by platoons or batteries. These guns travel immediately in rear of the forward tank waves and seek to blind any anti-tank guns that put in their appearance. Smoke projectiles are fired by trench mortars or by guns of 105-mm. caliber or larger. In England light, medium, and "close-support" tanks are combined into companies with the object of assuring teamwork between tanks and accompanying artillery.

Originally great results were expected from the method of tanks concealing themselves by self-produced smoke. It was soon found, however, that, owing to the conspicuousness of its source, the smoke tends to reveal the position or course of the tanks. The tanks travel either within the smoke or—still worse—are clearly outlined by the screen they have just laid. Therefore, it is only under the most favorable weather conditions that this method can be used in the attack. On the other hand, it may serve to facilitate a withdrawal.

Tank crews are relatively immune to gas. This applies particularly to corrosive gases used in the contamination of an area. Protection is furnished either by the gas mask or by the overpressure maintained in the interior of the tank. Some countries are trying to make tanks that are inherently gasproof; others are experimenting with filters to purify the incoming air. The U.S.S.R. mentions tanks equipped with a gas-blower apparatus.

ENGINEERS

The tanks have given the combat engineer some knotty problems to solve, especially in getting them over streams, marshes, and soft ground, and in removing obstacles, particularly mines. Minor tasks of this nature may be carried out by the regimental pioneer sections, but major obstacles will usually require entire units of specially trained and specially equipped combat engineers.

Several countries, notably Great Britain and the U.S.S.R., have produced amphibious tanks that have proved highly satisfactory for crossing unfordable streams. It is to be assumed that these will be used for reconnaissance and for the establishment of bridgeheads.

Bridging material must possess a high carrying capacity because of the tremendous weights it is to support. On the other hand, bridges designed only for the accommodation of tanks do not require full decks.

Engineer units must be specially trained to recognize obstacles and schooled in ways and means of removing them. Particular emphasis should be placed on the removal of mine barriers.

Where engineers work in co-operation with tanks their jobs will ordinarily have to be accomplished in great haste and in sight of the enemy. If they are to reach their place of activity and be effective they must be protected by tanks. Some countries, especially Great Britain, have introduced bridge-carrier tanks and mine-sweeper tanks and placed them at the disposal of engineer units designed for co-operation with tanks.

Combat engineers will find another field of activity in operations against hostile field fortifications. A tank attack on field fortifications can be successful only if the size and strength of the obstacles do not exceed the capacity of the tanks. Whatever the obstacle, both the heavy and medium tanks are capable machines. For instance, the French heavy tank can negotiate a thirteen-foot trench, a slope of forty-five degrees, a vertical wall of six feet, a stream seven feet wide, and trees up to three feet in diameter. If the tanks are unable to negotiate the obstacles the engineers must go into action. Frequently they will be employed in advance as a precautionary measure. During the World War special anchors were constructed for the removal of wire entanglements, and fascines were carried along to be used in crossing trenches. There will be frequent calls for demolitions and excavations for the purpose of overcoming obstacles or enabling stalled vehicles to move on.

All of these tasks require training which in many respects goes far beyond the former sphere of action of the engineer soldier. Therefore, co-operation between tanks and engineers will be most successful if the latter are familiar with the characteristics of the tank and possess the requisite equipment. Irrespective of this requirement, however, the entire corps of engineers must train for co-operation with tanks in offensive as well as in defensive action.

SIGNAL CORPS

The width and depth of tank units and their motorized support weapons on the march and in combat, the dust clouds raised by them, smoke, fog, and rough or covered ground prohibit the use of visual signals in controlling units larger than a company. The swift maneuvers over wide areas which the tanks must execute even in combat make it impracticable to employ the field telephone except in quiet periods and during approach marchs behind the front. Therefore, we find that all command tanks carry radio transmitters, and even the light tanks carry radio receivers.

Signal troops designated for co-operation with tanks will therefore consist primarily of radio elements. Their task is to maintain communication from the commander of the tank unit down to the regiments and independent detachments, with adjoining troops, with the air service, and, in certain cases, with the next higher commander in the rear. Abbreviated codes and special signals must be used in order to assure the speedy delivery of messages and orders. To this end signal detachments permanently assigned to tank units must receive special equipment and training.

Maneuver being rapid and it being necessary for the commander of a tank unit to be at the head of his command, only armored signal vehicles that possess a high mobility and full cross-country ability can meet his demands.

AIR CORPS

Information is valueless unless it be delivered to the commander in time for him to act on it. This means that reconnaissance elements must be speedier than the troops following them and must possess highly effective means of communication. These two basic requirements throw into sharp relief the difficulties that beset tactical and combat reconnaissance for speedy tank forces.

Aerial reconnaissance promises the best results. As early as the World War, the British High Command permanently assigned aviation to the Royal Tank Corps with good results. Air reconnaissance personally conducted by the commander of the tank forces before going into action may be of material advantage.

The reconnaissance aviator receives his instructions before taking off; supplementary orders or changes may be transmitted by radio or pickup. He reports either upon arrival at his landing field or by radio or dropped messages. Of course it must not be forgotten that the aviator cannot maintain continuous contact with the enemy and that his ability to observe still depends on weather conditions.

To allow for the high rate of speed of the tank unit, instructions must be issued carefully before the movements begin. The reconnaissance air forces must be acquainted with the plan of attack and, if possible, with the general course to be followed by the tank unit. Above all, they must be able to distinguish between friendly and hostile tanks. Even with this information the aviator may encounter difficulty in locating the tanks and establishing communication. He communicates by radio, by dropped messages, or by landing in the zone of action. Training should be conducted in all three methods.

Air reconnaissance must be supplemented by a fast, strong ground reconnaissance force which relays its messages either by radio or motor vehicle. At present the demand for speed is best met by wheeled vehicles, although their cross-country performance is inferior to that of track-laying types. Of course wheeled vehicles are more sensitive to obstacles.

Combat aviation can lend considerable support to a tank attack. As early as August 8, 1918, British airplanes effectively supported the advance of tanks by bombing and machine-gunning German batteries, reserves, and troop columns. Today, owing to the great improvements in anti-tank defense and to the mobility of the enemy's motorized and armored reserves, the employment of air forces against ground targets becomes increasingly important. By attacking such targets as mentioned and lines of communication, known locations of troops and headquarters, air forces will render it practicable for the ground attack to penetrate speedily the hostile zone of defense. Particular pains must be taken, however, to synchronize the actions of the two arms both in time and space.

The U.S.S.R. is working toward a still closer teamwork between air and ground forces, specifically the landing of infantry contingents by parachute. Landed in proper time, parachute troops may seize vital points in rear of the hostile front and then establish points of support and supply bases to assist the break-through by the tanks. Parachute troops working in co-operation with tanks may seriously damage and interfere with the hostile services of supply.

ANTIAIRCRAFT

Since tanks will quickly attract the attention of hostile aviation, an antiaircraft defense must be provided. Tanks can contribute substantially to this defense by an intelligent use of their own weapons and by skillful camouflage. Though the danger is not to be minimized, only direct or very close hits will destroy the modern tank, and this is not an easy thing to do when the tank is in motion. On the other hand, an air attack that

catches the tanks at rest with their crews dismounted or—worse yet—
while fueling strikes them where they are most vulnerable.

Since most of the support weapons of tanks are not armor-protected,
separate antiaircraft weapons must be furnished them. This applies also
to all combat trains.

SUPPLY

The supply problem is the ball and chain of the tank commander.
The more far-reaching the plan of tank employment, the more vital and
the more difficult this problem becomes. Tank units cannot fight indefinitely without drawing ammunition, rations, and fuel; nor can they
stay in action without medical service, repair shops, and replacements.
It is of paramount importance that fuel and ammunition be supplied
in proper time.

When operating as part of an army tanks are supplied by the army;
when operating independently they require a separate service of supply
and a mobile base of operations. And in this connection it should be
remembered that tank units will operate independently as soon as the
desired penetration is accomplished, and particularly during an envelopment or investment of the hostile front.

Since a large part of the supply vehicles are unarmored, they require
covering elements as soon as they enter the zone of hostile fire. Furthermore, since supply trains offer a prime target for the enemy's armored
attack, the attached covering elements must have a liberal allotment
of anti-tank weapons. On occasion it may even be necessary to withdraw
armored cars or tanks from the front and assign them a protective role
with the trains.

CONCLUSIONS

Since the mechanized arm, its supplementary weapons, and its various
counteragents are still in a state of development, no final answers can
be given to the problem of co-operation between armored forces and
other arms. And yet there *are* certain conclusions which may be drawn
from the evolution of the mechanized arm to date.

First, there are a number of fundamental elements which determine
the construction, organization, training, and employment of armored
forces. These are:

(1) The matériel on hand and its past performances.
(2) The domestic facilities for the manufacture of mechanized weapons.
(3) The maintenance and supply facilities, particularly with regard to fuel.
(4) The effect of the weapons fired from and against tanks, as determined by
experience gathered on proving grounds.

(5) The organization of the command, as determined by maneuver experience.

(6) The order of battle.

(7) The nature of prospective theaters of operations.

(8) The armament of prospective opponents.

Although the various nations follow different routes in their development of the mechanized arm, they all move in a more or less common direction. This general trend can be summarized somewhat like this:

(1) The importance of aviation is incontrovertibly established and is admitted even by those who refuse, in general, to accept the doctrines of the Italian General Douhet. The air forces require the support of a partner on the ground who is in a position to supplement and exploit the results gained by aerial reconnaissance and combat. This partner must be speedy, aggressive, and strong.

(2) The older arms lack the penetrative power, mobility, and speed to carry the attack so rapidly and deeply into the hostile front that the enemy will not have time to take countermeasures. On the one hand, the defensive power of modern firearms and, on the other, the speed with which motorized reserves may be shifted to critical points prevent the older arms from decisively exploiting gains. If the defense has motorized reserves at its disposal the attack must also have motorized forces, and vice versa.

(3) The older arms cannot repulse the attack of strong armored forces. Even a large number of anti-tank guns cannot strengthen the defense enough to frustrate surprise attacks by large bodies of tanks. An attack of this kind must be met by tanks.

(4) On the other hand, the increasing effectiveness of the anti-tank defense calls for the utmost concentration of force on the part of the mechanized arm if decisive results are to be obtained. In order to be decisive, a tank attack must be launched on a wide front; this is to prevent the enemy from striking the spearhead of the attack in flank. The attacking forces must be organized in considerable depth in order to secure their flanks, effect a deep penetration, and roll up the flanks thus created. To be decisive, an attack must cover much wider zones than can be occupied by a brigade. In 1917, at Cambrai, three brigades, each three battalions strong, fought in a zone six miles wide without any organization in depth. In 1918, at Soissons, sixteen battalions attacked in two waves— twelve battalions in the first, four in the second—on a twelve-mile front. In 1918, at Amiens, fourteen British and French battalions (two battalions and several cavalry corps were combined in the second wave) attacked in a zone about eleven miles wide. The widths of the zones of attack employed in major operations during the last year of the World War must now be regarded as minimum in view of the defensive powers of modern armor-piercing weapons and armored forces. In the future many times the number of tanks that fought in 1918 will take part in battle.

(5) The tank attack must be carried out with the utmost speed in order to take advantage of the surprise effect. It must drive deep into the hostile front, prevent the reserves from going into action, and convert tactical gains into strategic ones. In other words, speed is the main requirement of armored forces.

As the great Frederick said, "The faster the attack, the fewer men it costs. By making your battle short you will deprive it of the time to rob you of many men. The soldier who is led in this manner will gain confidence in you and expose himself gladly to all dangers." The swift execution of the tank attack being of decisive importance, the auxiliary weapons of tank units must be as fast as the tanks themselves. Auxiliary weapons designed for co-operation with tanks should be combined with them into permanent units comprising all modern arms. This should not be construed as meaning that the whole army must be motorized. Nevertheless, it must be emphasized that armored forces without speedy auxiliary weapons are incomplete and will not be able to realize their maximum potentialities.

(6) Even in earliest times armies included slow infantry and more mobile units, such as chariots, elephants, and horsemen. The numerical relationship between the two arms varied according to the ideas of the commander, the ability of the arms, the technique of the weapons, and the object of the war. In periods of indecisive position warfare the armies had to be content with a few mobile units. As a rule such times indicate a decadence in the art of war. Nobody desires them, but since nobody can predict them, they cannot be provided for. Great generals have always aimed at decisive warfare, which is another way of saying mobile warfare. To that end they have seen to it that the strength of their fast troops compared favorably with that of their slower ones. Alexander, at the outset of the war against Persia, commanded 32,000 foot soldiers and 10,000 horsemen. Hannibal, at Cannae, had 40,000 dismounted and 10,000 mounted troops; Frederick the Great, at Rossbach, went into action with 27 infantry battalions and 45 cavalry squadrons. These few figures indicate that the great leaders maintained mobile elements comprising one fourth to one sixth of their entire strength. Similarly, modern mobile units can be of decisive value only if their strength is in due proportion to that of the whole army.

As early as his campaign in Spain, Hannibal entrusted his gifted brother Hasdrubal with the training and command of the mass of his cavalry. At Rossbach, Frederick placed 38 of his 45 cavalry squadrons under the brilliant General von Seydlitz. As a rule, improvisations of mobile units and their commands have proved of little value. Therefore, in the future mobile forces should have a uniform command even in time of peace and should be formed in large units. The leaders of those forces will do well to recall the trenchant expression of Frederick the Great: "Be active and indefatigable; cast off all indolence of body and mind."

It was my intention not to stray beyond the limits of the technical possibilities of today. Yet I could not deny myself the right to study new methods of employment for new weapons. There will always be men eager to voice misgivings, but only he who dares to reach into the unknown will be successful. The man who has been active will be more leniently judged by the future.

"Until then, we, whose fate is spun without our being conscious of it, are left to our own determination and courage and are consigned to the voice of our inspiration."

KAMPFWAGENKRIEG: A Review

Reviewed by MAJOR (now COLONEL) HARVEY H. SMITH

(*1938*)

Kampfwagenkrieg (Mechanized Warfare), by General Ludwig Ritter von Eimannsberger, Austrian Army, Retired. Munich: J. F. Lehmanns Verlag, 1938. 236 pages; 10 charts, and 3 maps. $3.00.

The first edition of this book, published in 1934, aroused no little interest and comment. That the French read, ponder, and respect the author's opinions is indicated by Lieutenant Colonel L. G. Rosseau's translation of the 1934 edition, published in France in 1936. Furthermore, a 64-page review and discussion appeared in *La Revue d'Infanterie* for December 1935.

At the outset General von Eimannsberger frankly admits his total lack of experience with tanks. But this handicap, if it be such, enables him to approach the subject with the open mind of a scientist. He searches for facts in thoroughgoing and methodical fashion and arrives at sincere, straightforward conclusions.

The rapid development of armament and corresponding changes in organization since 1934—not to mention combat experiences in Ethiopia, Spain, and the Far East—call for a revision of ideas concerning the employment of tanks and mechanized units. General von Eimannsberger does not hesitate to revise and correct whenever necessary. But he feels that the bulk of his earlier conclusions and predictions are substantiated by present-day developments.

"Mechanized" warfare as defined and discussed by the author is synonymous with tank warfare. His theories concerning future tank warfare are based upon a study of World War tank-combat experiences. The battles in Flanders (August to November 1917) are cited as the last major offensive which depended upon a ponderous artillery preparation. The well-known result was a long and bitter no-decision contest which finally petered out in blood and mud. Prior to the Flanders offensive tanks had been used by the British and by the French, but only in small groups and not en masse.

After Flanders came Cambrai (November 1917), the first offensive marked by the large-scale use of tanks and the absence of artillery preparation. The Germans were not entirely without warning of the attack or of the presence of tanks but were surprised by the use of the tank en masse. Hence the British Tank Corps accomplished its mission within a few hours—in striking contrast to Flanders—but the planned exploitation by tanks and cavalry failed because the employment of small tank units in narrow zones was ineffective. So, says Von Eimannsberger, Cambrai showed the British how to penetrate a position, but it did not show them how to transform this success into victory.

The French tank attack at Soissons (July 18, 1918) was planned in general like that at Cambrai—there was to be no artillery preparation, and the tanks were to follow behind a rolling barrage. After initial success the attack halted to await the forward displacement of artillery. As at Cambrai, the resumption of the attack was marked by reduced tank effectiveness because they generally encountered disaster when they ran ahead of the infantry and poked their noses into hostile artillery areas without the support of friendly weapons. Soissons showed the French that the German front could be penetrated quickly by tanks en masse but failed to show them how to exploit success.

The British attack at Amiens (August 8, 1918) was, in the main, another repetition of Cambrai—a surprise break-through without artillery preparation, the tanks advancing in mass with their infantry behind a rolling barrage. The result was almost identical—a lull in the attack after the initial success, then a continuation with insufficient forces.

From Amiens until the Armistice there were many repetitions of the same picture—the attack with tanks employed in mass, an initial success, then several days of fighting with decreasing numbers, and finally their withdrawal behind the lines for overhaul.

Thus, the author states, the experience of war ceased, and the technique of the tank attack stopped right in the middle of its development. He summarizes the tank-employment lessons of the World War as follows: Tanks, to be sure of success, must be employed in large numbers on a broad front with the defensive artillery neutralized by smoke, fog, or other suitable countermeasures.

Questions concerning technical development of offensive and defensive matériel, organization, attack methods, and exploitation can be answered finally only by the next war. But now is the time to study these problems because a nation's existence may depend upon their solution. This is a big assignment, but the author does not shrink from the task, and he submits his conclusions as *a* solution—not *the* solution.

General von Eimannsberger disagrees with the French doctrine of tank employment as laid down in the 1937 edition of *L'Emploi Tactique des Grandes Unités,* which prescribes that tanks are to be tactically employed in two groups: (1) accompanying tanks, operating subordinate to, and in close co-operation with, the assaulting foot troops; (2) general maneuver tanks, operating under orders of higher commanders and on missions relating to the unit as a whole. This latter group is the first wave in the tank attack and bears the brunt of the fight. It should be remembered that today's anti-tank defense is organized against attacking tanks, just as machine guns were organized against attacking foot troops during the World War. Accordingly the French believe that tanks can be employed only when protected by powerful artillery. As a result, the author states, the same restrictions are imposed that handicapped World War tank attacks; namely, intermittent attacks on intermediate objectives with pauses for reorganization and forward displacement of artillery and ammunition. After considering time and space factors Eimannsberger concludes that in a French attack the tank battle is in movement for five minutes and in place for sixty minutes. All of which brings up the important questions as to where the tank masses are to go and what they are to do during these pauses in the attack. And what will the enemy be doing in the meantime?

The general believes that hostile fire and the absence of cover will make it impracticable for tank masses to remain quietly in hiding for this period. Moreover, these pauses will give the enemy more time to bring up reserves and readjust his defenses. He contends that enemy reserves can be moved up faster than the attack can advance by this methodical method, thus precluding the possibility of a break-through.

As for tank employment in Spain and China, the author says that nothing new has been tried, and the experiences thus far have been simply repetitions of lessons already learned during the World War.

Von Eimannsberger also has some definite ideas on anti-tank defense. In this and in the earlier edition he states that there is but one practical defense against tanks; namely, to move the defense as far forward as possible and give the foot soldier a counterweapon. Then, and then only, can it be demanded of the rifleman that he remain under cover until his armor-piercing infantry weapons have put the tanks out of action. Thus the fate of the infantry soldier will depend upon his own skill. This infantry anti-tank gun must be a part of the infantry as is the machine gun—even more so, for in an emergency the machine gun can be replaced by a certain number of riflemen. Obviously this is not true of the anti-tank gun. He proposes to give each rifle battalion an AT company of six guns and to create a divisional AT battalion of eighteen guns—a total of seventy-two AT guns per division. In addition, the regiment should have a cannon company of at least six infantry cannon. Anti-tank defense, of course, should be considered in distributing divisional artillery. On this point the French probably will differ. A study of their World War tank losses discloses that 80 per cent were caused by direct fire from light artillery. No wonder that the French have a profound respect for the efficiency of this type of weapon and emphasize its importance.

Since there is no historical example of a defensive position organized against mechanized attack, the author again turns to World War methods and selects a defense against an attack based upon artillery. This he modifies so as to create a defense against an infantry-artillery-tank attack. The result is an interior division defending an area 6,600 yards wide and 6,600 yards in depth, with three regiments abreast. Each regimental sector is organized into three echelons. Thus he conforms to the doctrine of dispersion to avoid undue losses from artillery fire. The first echelon in each regimental sector consists of the front-line battalion, defending on a frontage of 2,200 yards with two companies abreast and one in reserve. The depth of this echelon is 1,650 yards, and it has the usual mission assigned to front-line units. The presence of the battalion AT weapons gives considerable anti-tank protection. The rear limit of the second echelon, which consists of the "readiness battalion" with one company from the divisional AT battalion attached, is about two miles behind the front line. The basic mission of this echelon is anti-tank defense. The third echelon comprises the area in rear of the second echelon, extending to the rear limit of the position. Within this area is found the division artillery and the reserve battalion.

The author realizes that he may be criticized for placing the tank defense wholly within the infantry position and for using artillery as an incidental reinforcement of the tank defense. But he feels that this procedure is essential, since it is necessary to disable the tanks before they have overrun and destroyed the front-line troops. Moreover, it would be undesirable to place the tank defense within the artillery area.

In rear of such a defensive system the army commander should have a reserve of one or more motorized divisions. These are considered indispensable to check tank attacks. Furthermore, in the mechanized battle only tanks or armored units have offensive capacity; therefore, a tank division should be in reserve for counterattack missions.

Thus we see that the author has given his assaulting tank or mechanized divisions a hard nut to crack. He does not set up a favorable situation such as the envelopment of an exposed flank or the pursuit of a defeated enemy. He may be criticized as being too pessimistic as to the effectiveness of anti-tank weapons and for placing his estimate of the numbers needed too high. Nevertheless, if tanks appear upon the battlefield in the masses contemplated, any front-line battalion commander and his men may be glad to welcome these weapons.

To illustrate his conception of a modern tank battle General Eimannsberger concludes his study with a map problem entitled "A Battle before Amiens on August 8, 194–."

The armament of the opposing armies is assumed to be that which would be available today after protracted fighting. Each army is provided with a number of normal infantry divisions and in addition has a number of motorized and mechanized divisions for whose conception the author takes responsibility.

The proposed mechanized or tank division is a self-sustained—although unproven—organization for independent strategical employment. It is composed of two tank regiments having 250 tanks each, a three-battalion *panzerschützen* or armored-rifle regiment, an artillery regiment, a reconnaissance battalion, an air squadron, and service troops. It is intended for use solely in the attack or for counterattack against similar units. In addition, there are independent tank brigades, having the historic organization and mission, which are to be attached to infantry divisions as required.

The principal missions of the motorized division are: in the defense, to stop the hostile tanks; in the offense, to occupy the ground gained by tanks.

The defense is organized along two positions about ten miles in depth. The attack consists of three phases: a penetration of the first position, four to five miles deep; a penetration of the second position; the advance of tank units through the gap thus made and their independent operations. The width of the penetration is to be about twelve and a half miles.

The requirement in tanks is computed to be about 2,500 (five tank divisions), comprising 1,000 light tanks and 1,500 medium tanks. The infantry divisional artillery is reinforced by additional batteries—principally medium and heavy—to three times ordinary strength.

With respect to air operations, the author believes that there is one irrefutable principle—the complete surprise of the enemy by the tank assault is more important than all air attacks during the previous night. During the attack, in addition to the usual air missions, some airplanes should be used to nose-dive and fire upon AT guns as these guns open fire. He realizes that opinion among fliers is divided on this point. Some contend that the modern airplane is far too fast for such missions. He substantiates his opinion by recalling that British aviators performed such missions successfully in the last war.

The tank division attacks in three echelons. The first echelon, consisting of a tank regiment (one light and two medium battalions) and one panzerschützen battalion, attacks at H-hour into the *artillery* area of the hostile position. This echelon is assisted by attack aviation.

The second echelon, consisting of a tank regiment and two panzerschützen battalions, follows the first after a seven-minute interval and attacks as far as the forward edge of the artillery area.

The third echelon, consisting of a light-tank battalion, accompanies the assaulting foot troops and remains with them until the entire hostile position is occupied.

All artillery opens fire at H-hour on every known hostile artillery and AT gun position. Observation points are blinded by smoke. The tank regiments attack with their two medium battalions abreast in the assault, each having at least two companies in the first wave. Behind them, arranged in depth, is the light battalion, followed by the panzerschützen units. Each tank battalion has available twelve tank-support guns which, advancing by bounds, furnish the battalion with artillery direct-fire support.

The author herein approaches the French plan more closely than he did in his 1934 edition, but he still intends to grab the hostile position in one bite while the French plan to take it in two or three. His assaulting tank units apparently will depend for protection chiefly upon attack aviation, organic tank-support guns, and the panzerschützen battalions until the infantry foot troops arrive to take over the conquered terrain. It will take the infantry about three hours to arrive at the rear limit of the first position, according to the author's calculation.

A successful break-through of the first position still does not make a gap in the defensive system, because ten miles farther to the rear is a second position prepared in the assumed defense. General Eimannsberger believes that separate tank units must be used for this attack, because the tank divisions engaged in the initial assault will probably suffer severe losses which is certainly no preparation for a battle with counterattacking tank forces. Besides, if the hole should close after the tanks have passed through—then what?

The attack on the second position must be supported by aircraft instead of artillery. The author calculates that 650 attack ships and 502 bombers are required for the attack on the second position.

The basis of the entire operation is founded upon the theory that an initial surprise can be preserved only by continual attack on important areas.

Skeptics may question whether such masses of fighting machines will be available—apparently they are not now. But doubt may vanish when it is recalled that, at the time of the Armistice, France and England claimed a production rate that would have put 20,000 tanks in the field by the spring of 1919.

Perhaps the Allied commanders visualized such a mechanized attack for 1919. Certainly their orders for delivery of armored combat vehicles in such numbers show that they thought the solution to the "attack problem" lay in that direction.

Naturally this leads to the conclusion that only nations or groups of nations with very highly developed industry are in a position to make war with any prospect of success. This was true even during the World War. The fate of czarist Russia is a striking example.

General von Eimannsberger, in his profound study, has tackled a complicated and controversial problem. He has attempted to devise an attack method that will not fold up and retire to its corner after one staggering blow. His attack is to follow up its initial advantage with speedy blows to ensure a knockout before the adversary has revived. As for his solution, you may ask, "How can it be true?" The answer up until now is, "How can it be otherwise?"

AUDI ALTERAM PARTEM

By Mercutio

(1936)

DESPITE the most vigorous denials, the thought persists that the brilliant campaigns of the Great Captains were brought about by adherence to some secret and potent formula. Let any embattled general rise above mediocrity, and at once the military witch finders gather their paraphernalia and set about smelling out his secret. Military men discover the secret of successful combat as regularly as the duffer discovers the secret of good golf. In each instance the result is the same. Nevertheless, the student soldier and the student golfer continue in their efforts to conform to the great masters.

Now it seems to me that success in any line of endeavor is not purely a *positive* matter. A man gets to the top not merely by doing but by *a nicely balanced combination of doing and not doing*. Indeed, it might be argued with considerable force that success in war, for instance, depends more on *not doing* certain things that are incorrect than on *doing* certain others that are correct. In any event it appears that one-sided leaders will result from a system that stresses the *positive* at the expense of the *negative*.

It will be contended, of course, that our schools are not guilty of this indictment, that they point out the "don'ts" as well as the "dos." There is no question of this so far as the marked problem is concerned. But military history is another matter. As it comes to us today, it is no more than the distilled essence of victory. We are stuffed with Caesar, Hannibal, Frederick, Napoleon, et al., to a point little short of nausea. They did this; they did that, and victory crowned their arms. The defeated army and its commanders seldom receive more than a half-contemptuous glance to determine dispositions. The thousand and one factors so meticulously dissected on the victorious side are almost universally ignored on the other. We seek our formulas for success exclusively in success, overlooking the rich fields of experience the great failures have left us.

For instance, Frederick's principal adversary was a third-rater. Therefore, we concentrate on Frederick and dismiss his enemy, General Daun, with the word "cunctatory." Actually "cunctator" Daun has as much to teach us in a left-handed way as Frederick has in a right. We cannot escape the fact that there are two sides to every battle and that if one wins the other loses. Similarly, we cannot avoid the conclusion that the victor is seldom exclusively responsible for the success of his arms; the defeated contributed, at least, an equal part.

Therefore, I suggest that we couple our study of the great conquerors with an equal study of the great failures to the end that we recognize not only those roads that lead to victory but those other deceptive highways that plunge down to ruin.

GUERRILLA WARFARE

By Bert (Yank) Levy

One of the most remarkable developments of the present war is Britain's Home Guard. The threat of enemy invasion after Dunkirk caused the Home Guard to be developed on a big scale and led to the interest in Great Britain in all possibly useful forms of guerrilla warfare. There resulted a number of handbooks and manuals of instruction, one of the most realistic and popular of which was "Yank" Levy's *Guerrilla Warfare,* which appeared in 1940 and which has had a wide distribution in the United States through the *Infantry Journal* publication in the magazine and in book form.

The author, a Canadian with much battle experience in the first World War and in Spain, covers every practical method of scouting, patrolling, ambush, assault, and destruction which irregular troops might use in conjunction with professional forces. In the following chapter the author describes some of these methods.

Ambushing is not the only method of destroying the enemy's cars, lorries, or tanks. The guerrilla is also adept in the practice of "invisible destruction." This means that you destroy the enemy's transport, stores, and so on, without letting him know about it until the time comes when he needs to use it. If you make a noise, or if you burn or blow up something, he may be able to catch you; also, he has earlier warning of his loss and therefore more time in which to replace it.

Of course some forms of destruction cannot be done invisibly and silently. You cannot destroy an ammunition dump quietly. But it is better, for instance, to let petrol leak away than to burn it. If you have to blow up objects, use delayed-action bombs so that you have time to make a getaway.

For destructive raids, usually you should not have less than three men in your party. Sometimes two is better, and there are some jobs best done by one man. To do them you may need disguises of various kinds—

not false whiskers and sunglasses, but civilian clothing, perhaps, or an enemy uniform, or women's clothes—only pick someone who can wear them naturally—or maybe a postman's uniform.

Let us say we are out to destroy a canal barge or barges. I would never try to burn it and let the enemy know for miles around that guerrillas are active. I would sink it quietly. The additional advantage of this would be that the sunken hulk might hold up traffic on the canal.

For this purpose, if it is a wooden barge, you can use a bailing hook, such as is used by dockers to handle cargo. With this you will pull out the calking between the planks. It may take you anywhere between twenty minutes and two hours to pull out sufficient to sink the barge. You might also drill holes in the barge. Circumstances and your equipment will dictate which is preferable.

In the case of a steel barge you need a spanner to take out the draining plug at the bottom of the barge. These methods, of course, can also be used with boats. If you can't use silent methods blow a vessel up with a long-delayed-action bomb.

When destroying vehicles keep an eye open always for petrol-tank lorries—to cripple or destroy them is doubly advantageous: the enemy loses the use of the vehicle and also of the petrol.

If I succeeded in entering an enemy lorry park—almost certainly by night, of course—and had plenty of time, I would quietly remove one spark plug in each engine, then insert a quarter-inch or half-inch nut or bolt and replace the plug. When they step on her to start her off the next morning, the nut or bolt will smash up the motor. Or you can damage the distributor with a screw driver.

A good trick, but a bit more elaborate, is borrowed from gangsters, who have often used it successfully to remove competitors or anti-racketeering politicians. For this you need a stick of dynamite with a detonating cap at one end to which a wire is attached. You then attach the free end of the wire to a spark plug or switch contact and have another wire grounded to the framework of the car. When the enemy steps on his starter or turns a switch he blows his car up and himself too.

One of the oldest sabotage tricks is to put some sand or emery dust into the bearings of a vehicle. This can also be done to railroad trains and engines.

Whenever you can drain off or destroy petrol, do so. Petrol is the life-blood of the modern army. Three or four lumps or spoonfuls of sugar put into the petrol tank, or a small bottle of linseed oil emptied into it, will immobilize any car after it has traveled three or four miles. Shredded cotton or waste, confetti, wool, or sand in a petrol tank will probably block the feed line or filter. Some modern German tanks have a filter good enough to prevent this blocking, but their lorries do not.

Petrol draining out of a car's tank makes a splashing or trickling noise.

So if there happens to be any sand or sawdust—or perhaps a sack—around, put it underneath to deaden the sound. You can puncture petrol tanks with an awl or drill.

Tire slashing can be done by night or day, and the guerrilla should find lots of opportunities for this, even when other jobs which take longer are impossible. Don't unscrew the air valve from the tire if there are people near, because the escaping air makes a protracted hissing noise. One good nine-inch slash with a strong, sharp knife along the wall of the tire casing will let the air out in one short gasp and will not attract so much attention.

Among the enemy's most formidable weapons are tanks. Every tank the guerrilla can destroy, or even put out of action for a time, is a minor victory for our cause. As we have seen, tanks can be ambushed by day. And the guerrilla can also go out after them at night, when they are laid up.

For tanks do have to lie up at nights. If you had ever tried riding in the hot, airless, constricted interior of a tank you would realize that tank crews must have their rest. By nighttime they are exhausted, probably suffering from headaches, perhaps "tank-sick." They are all in.

Then is the time for you to sneak in—if the tanks are not heavily guarded by infantry—and either steal the tanks or blow them up, or throw grenades into the opened turrets.

You should be able to snaffle their sentries quietly, then go down to the laager and kill their drivers and destroy the tanks. Molotov cocktails and AW bombs hurled at the bogie-wheels will set the rubber on fire.

Supposing an enemy airplane has made a forced landing not far from your guerrilla band. Here is a heaven-sent opportunity. If it is a fighter it will have only one pilot. If a bomber, only a few men. And one or more will have to go out to make contact with his forces to get help. At most you will have only three or four men to overcome.

Or sometimes it may be possible to sneak into an airdrome by night. At any rate, it is well worth while knowing how to immobilize an airplane. When working quietly the best plan is to attack the elevator, which is lightly made and therefore easily damaged. And it is the one control surface which renders it impossible for the plane to take the air. If you can use a little noise plant a Mills bomb in among the instruments, tie a fishline to the pin, and walk away. When you come to the end of the line jerk the pin out.

If you have to set fire to a plane—and don't forget that this will bring the enemy down on you in a pretty short time—remember that there is bound to be petrol somewhere near the engine. Light some oil-soaked rags there. If you find a petrol tank puncture it with any sharp object and let some of the petrol run out onto the ground. Then throw a lighted match into it and make the quickest getaway you can, before the bombs and ammunition start popping. If you have a bomb, of course that will do the trick more quickly.

If you want to destroy an ammunition dump or perhaps a big store of other war material, you must use a time bomb. The same applies to a petrol dump, if you have not the time to open up the tanks with a hand drill to let the petrol flow out.

It takes a long time to tear up railroad tracks, and the probabilities are that there will be guards posted along the line to prevent this. They can be blown up but can usually be repaired in three or four hours. Still, this delay counts when the enemy is working to a time schedule. It is better to blow up a railway bridge, however, if you can, as this takes much longer to repair.

Furthermore, you can blow up trains, which will also have the effect of blocking the track and wrenching rails out of place. This is an easier job, from the point of view of your getaway, because you can lay the detonators on the track, so that the train blows itself up. A slab of gun-cotton laid on a railway metal and properly detonated will blow a piece of the rail right out.

A land mine is good for blowing up trains because it does not function until you want it to, if you have your wires leading from it to a position where you are protected but can view the track. Then you can blow up whatever part of the train you choose, always remembering, if it is a passenger train, that generals usually ride in the last coach, or the last but one.

Rails unbolted and displaced will tip a train off the lines. Try this at an embankment, on a curve.

If all this is too difficult you can still delay a train if a couple of you slither down to the track with a few gallons of good grease—say axle grease, but even smooth tar will serve—and smear the rails, always choosing a section of track which is level or upgrade. Then the pistons will be driving the engine wheels fast, and they cannot grip the rails, and the train will be going no place fast! No engine carries enough sand to cover a long stretch of track.

Whenever there are bridges or culverts which cross rivers or streams you have an excellent opportunity of doing some long-distance exploding. The water, of course, must have a fairly good current. Find some good cover about one hundred yards from the bridge. Float a piece of wood downstream from there, timing the period it takes to reach the bridge. Then make a tiny raft and float that down, timing it too. Then you can make another raft on which you will place some sticks of dynamite or gelignite, together with a few pounds of blasting or lifting powder, with a time fuse coiled inside a can. As you have timed the current—the length of time it takes to float your raft down to the bridge—you can cut your fuse to match so that, when the raft passes under the bridge, up she goes. This is only effective when the bridge undersurface is near the water.

There are also various types of buildings which you will want to destroy, either by fire or explosives. If they contain stores, then by fire. If they contain troops, then by explosives. For this purpose you will have to learn something about explosives, how to use them, and how to improvise bombs, hand grenades, and so on. This, I am afraid, I cannot tell you about here. But the "Explosives" article in the *Encyclopædia Britannica* will give you everything. A good deal of instruction has been given to Home Guards in this subject—although not by any means to enough of them—so that in each guerrilla band there should be at least one person who can instruct the others in these matters. You can, for instance, make a fairly good bomb out of an empty tin can if only you have the explosives and know how.

No one should run away with the idea that, in performing the above destruction jobs, all we have to do is stroll quietly down to the car park, ammunition dump, or whatever it may be. We have to approach these places with infinite caution, and often we shall have to dispose of a sentry or two before we can go about our job.

Therefore, we must know how to rid ourselves of a sentry's presence silently and expeditiously. Sometimes we shall not want to kill the sentry, for then someone may find his body and give the alarm. It will not do us any harm if we now seek instruction, right in our home town, from wrestlers, jujitsu experts, and even doctors and bonesetters, who can show us the nerve centers of the body, the vulnerable places, and how to control a man or put him out swiftly.

A hammer blow between a man's shoulder blades will paralyze him. If you want to take a sentry and walk him off you must keep your left hand, with a handkerchief balled up in it, over his mouth, so that he makes no outcry. The palm or base of your hand should be pushing up under his chin, while you pinch his nose with thumb and forefinger, pulling it down. You, of course, are standing behind him. And with your other hand you are pressing your knife against his body.

Always try to take a sentry from the rear. But if you must take him from the front, never hold your gun up against his tummy and tell him to put his hands up. Odds are he knows the trick to pull and will get your gun before you can pull the trigger. If you do have to take him from the front, place the sole of your left foot—if you are right-handed; if not, reverse these instructions—on the arch of his right foot, pulling your revolver hand—or knife hand, or the hand holding whatever weapon you have chosen—as far back as possible. Then with your left hand you tear open his tunic or greatcoat, leaving the bottom button still fastened. Then grab him by the shoulder and swing him around quickly. You may slap his ears with the revolver barrel to intimidate him. Then pull his straps, tunic, greatcoat, and braces down over his shoulders to his elbows. This will lock his arms. Unless you need to march him away, you should also drop his trousers to lock his feet. Then search him from head to foot—he may have a knife too.

Never tell him to put his hands up. His hands may show up on a moon-lit night and attract attention; also, this elongates his shadow. Besides, German sentries often carry egg bombs, and he may have one in his hand. If you make him put his hands up you are helping him to chuck it at you. Or if he has his back to you he can throw it some distance away to attract attention. He won't drop it if his hands are down, for that would hurt him as much as you, and he probably doesn't care for the death-with-honor business.

Take away a sentry's pens and pencils. He may have a tear-gas gun, which looks exactly like a propelling pencil.

Practically any military or scouting manual will give you various other methods of taking sentries, so I shall not dwell on this.

But usually you will not be able to take sentries. You will just have to dispatch them as quietly as possible. For this purpose you may not be able to carry visible weapons if you are passing through, or very close to, the enemy's lines. However, there are invisible weapons which are very efficient.

Here are some of them: ladies' hatpins, five or six inches long. Or a wrist knife, strapped to your wrist with the hilt downward. A knife worn round the neck on a thong or cord. A small revolver held up your sleeve by rubber bands or in a shoulder holster. A stiletto with a nine-inch blade, no wider than three quarters of an inch at its broadest, and double-edged for its full length. Be sure it has a hilt guard on the haft. This instrument you should grasp solidly, placing the ball of the thumb along the flat of the blade. You use it with a twist of the wrist, stabbing upward and in-ward, under the lower rib toward the heart, or aiming at the spinal cord to sever it.

Other useful weapons are hammers—either to smash a man's skull or hit him between the shoulder blades to stun him; cheesecutters—the wires with wooden handles you see in the grocery stores—which are handy for strangling people; fishlines, for strangling, too, but also useful to tie a man's hands or ankles; a handkerchief with a fistful of sand in it, and so on.

If you are going to use a knife on a man, taking him from the rear, you should keep the outside of your foot against his heel, then drag him down onto your left knee while pushing a knife between his lower ribs, or in some other vulnerable spot. Your left hand is over his mouth to prevent an outcry. Note first what vulnerable points are protected by equipment.

If ever you take a sentry or any other enemy prisoner, with one of you covering him with a rifle, never forget the golden rule that, to search him or for any other reason, you should never pass between him and the man who is covering him. The other golden rule is: Have him turn his back to you at the earliest possible moment. When he can't watch you he can't think up tricks to take you off your guard.

Sometimes, also, you will blindfold a prisoner—not only if you do not want him to see where you are taking him, but also because a blindfolded prisoner is not so likely to cry out. Gags are never as good in real life as in the movies; they work loose, and a man can usually emit some sort of yell through them.

The various methods of dealing with sentries, of course, are also useful when capturing or destroying strayed enemy soldiers or small enemy patrols. These methods are so well known—particularly when used in connection with a rifle—that I can refer you to a dozen or more well-written handbooks, from any one of which you can learn all that I could teach. For while these things are part of guerrilla warfare, they are also part of regular warfare.

Sometimes, when trying to get through enemy lines, you can have a companion whose job it is to distract the sentry's attention. He can quite simply toss a stone at him and make off noisily in the brush. Or you can rattle some tin cans tied to a rope several yards away. If in or near a town or village, a fake fight between two apparently drunken men may do the trick. Sometimes, then, you can whiz by the sentry or sentries in a small light car, toss your hand grenades into the factory, car park, or other objective, drive on for a bit, immobilize your car, and take to the woods.

Good practice for taking sentries is the stalking game. One of you sits blindfolded while the others, in turn, try to walk right up to him and touch his shoulder without his hearing their approach. As soon as he hears you he claps his hands and you are technically dead, and the next fellow tries.

SIX MONTHS WITH THE JAP INFANTRY

By Lieutenant (now Colonel) Harold Doud

Colonel Doud was on duty with a Jap infantry regiment in 1934–35. In 1937 he wrote of his experiences for the *Infantry Journal*. This article and others on the Jap Army have also appeared in *How the Jap Army Fights*.

As the finishing touch to my two-and-a-half-year language detail in Japan I was to do a tour of duty with troops. To all intents and purposes I was to be a company officer of the Imperial Japanese Army. For six months [the winter of 1934–35] I was to serve with the 2d Company, 7th Infantry Regiment, at Kanazawa. I looked forward to it.

My orders were followed by letters from the regimental adjutant and my future company commander. Both expressed the hope that my stay with them would be profitable.

In the meantime I had written to a missionary acquaintance at Kanazawa asking his aid in finding suitable quarters. He replied that there was only one house in Kanazawa suitable for one of my station. It was rather expensive, he said; the rent was eighty yen (about twenty-five dollars) a month. However, its seventeen rooms would be just about right for one of my rank. We were rather staggered at the thought of seventeen rooms, but since the letter implied that nothing less would do, we accepted it. Accordingly we packed our furniture and a few days later entrained for Kanazawa.

Although it was nearly midnight when we arrived, a reception committee met us at the station. The delegation included the regimental adjutant, the color lieutenant, the captain and senior warrant officer from the 2d Company, and a detail of soldiers to handle our baggage. After the baggage had been equitably divided we marched in a body to the local inn, where we were to put up until our furniture arrived. All hands accompanied us to our rooms, and the officers and warrant officer remained for a chat and the inevitable cup of tea.

A few days of sight-seeing and I was ready to report for duty. Buckling on my saber and giving a final pat to my uniform, I started for the barracks. The regiment was housed within the walls of an old feudal castle beautifully situated on a small hill in the center of the town. A soldier met me at the front gate and conducted me to the 2d Company's barracks. At the door he handed me a new pair of slippers, neatly stenciled with my name in Japanese characters. Following his example, I took off my shoes, put on the slippers, and pattered after him to the orderly room.

There the captain introduced me to the officers and a few of the non-commissioned officers. He then announced that I was to be presented to the company. We put on our shoes and stepped out to the company parade. There I found the company drawn up in a hollow square, three sides of which were made up by the three platoons and the fourth side by the company staff and an empty table.

I was invited to climb up on the table. As soon as I had taken this elevated post the captain introduced me to the company. The company was then brought to attention; the senior warrant officer turned out a salute, and the ceremony was over.

Next we went to regimental headquarters, dropped our shoes, and went in. The adjutant escorted us to the colonel's office. Upon entering the captain and I bowed to the colors and then to the colonel. The colonel spoke a few words of welcome, saying, among other things, that if it ever seemed to me that he was not treating me with the consideration due a guest, it was merely because he wished me to feel at home. He assured me that I would be treated like any other officer of the regiment.

I thanked the colonel for this sentiment, put on my shoes, and went with the captain to make the rounds of the principal staff officers and the battalion commanders. At each place we took off our shoes before entering. Before the morning was over I was thankful I had not worn boots.

At eleven I was presented to the regiment. This time there were two tables. The colonel mounted one and I the other. The adjutant presented the regiment and the colonel introduced me, making a polite reference to the friendly relations then existing between our two countries. The adjutant brought the regiment to attention and the colonel and I faced each other and saluted. That ended that ceremony.

It was now time for lunch. In a Japanese regiment all officers lunch at the officers' mess. There my worst ordeal was the speech each new officer must make. When all were in their places I made my shoeless entrance. Having obtained the colonel's permission to speak, I delivered my prepared oration. That over, I laid aside cap, gloves, and saber and took my place at the colonel's left.

Lunch, served in an individual tray, consisted of five dishes. There was the usual enormous bowl of rice which is the main dish at every Japanese meal. A one-eyed fish head stared fixedly at me from the bottom of a bowl of bodyless soup. Another small dish contained pickled daikon, a Japanese turnip which tastes like a radish, and another a handful of sugared beans. At my first luncheon the *pièce de résistance* was an individual octopus for each officer. Boiled, but with legs and eyes still intact, it rested upon its back and glared at me. I couldn't quite stare it down.

The instant I took my seat all hands fell to with a will, not to mention speed. I took up my chopsticks and followed suit. In the Japanese fashion I smoothed the way for my rice with gulps of soup. This I supplemented with an occasional bite of daikon and sugared beans. I made a few tentative picks at my octopus, but every time I did those baleful eyes discouraged me.

I had just made a good start on the meal when I felt, or rather sensed, a silence. I glanced up to find that all hands had finished and were apparently waiting for me. I hastily laid down my chopsticks. Immediately an officer arose and launched into a talk on a technical military subject. I soon learned that this was standard procedure. Of the hour reserved for lunch only a few minutes were devoted to eating, the rest of the time to military education. The colonel left immediately after the lecture, and the officers began drifting back to their duties.

At this time the regiment was having its "dog days' training." Although it was intensely hot, training was purposely intensified in order to accustom the men to great exertion in extreme heat. During the hottest part of the day a strenuous and lengthy bayonet practice was held. The officers were not exempt; from eleven to twelve they fenced with the Japanese two-handed sword.

Since each Japanese officer owns a fencing outfit, I equipped myself and joined in the daily workout. When my opponents got over their initial politeness I began to get some bad beatings. After a few days of taking stiff raps on the bare elbow I grew wary—I began to pick field officers for opponents, avoiding the young and agile lieutenants and captains.

During this period much of our time was taken up with the ceremonies incident to the semiannual transfer of officers. In our division both the division and brigade commanders were transferred, and in our regiment we drew new commanders for the 1st and 2d battalions and for a number of the companies. The Japanese custom of the service requires farewell and welcoming formations for all outgoing and incoming officers. Hence the novelty of the hollow square, the tables, and the speechmaking soon wore off.

After the welcoming formation for the new division commander I was called aside to meet him personally. Following the usual amenities he expressed an interest in a trip I had recently taken to Formosa while he was governor general there. Since I had never met this officer I was surprised and showed it. He smiled and said that his knowledge came from my dossier made up by the military police.

I was now getting used to garrison life and looked forward to our first holiday scheduled for August 21. This was the anniversary of the storming of Banryu Hill during the siege of Port Arthur; here the regiment had distinguished itself by an assault against withering fire with the bayonet.

When the looked-for day finally arrived I soon discovered that our conception of a holiday as a day of rest was not shared by the Japanese Army. The festivities started with a 3:00 A.M. reveille. After breakfast the men filed into the orderly room, a section at a time, and bowed low before the pictures of their comrades who had been killed in action.

Following this ceremony, the 2d Company marched to a shrine of the regiment's war dead on Mukoyama (Yonder Mountain). Here, after fitting obeisance, a bayonet tournament was held in commemoration of the bayonet assault that had carried Banryu Hill. The tournament ended shortly after daylight. Another bow to the shrine and back we marched to barracks. There the supply sergeant produced sake and a species of dried flounder, which we downed with a will. Then after a few minutes' rest the regular day's work began. The other companies celebrated the holiday in similar fashion. And so I learned that if you start your holiday observance early enough it will not interfere with the drill schedule. To the Jap soldier a holiday is a day for additional sacrifice and effort in the service of his emperor.

Several days after this celebration I got my first taste of Japanese field service. It was our battalion's turn to go to Camp Johana for a few days' combat firing. This camp lay about twenty-five miles inland beyond a range of mountains. We started out at nine o'clock at night in a driving rain and marched through a steady downpour until seven the next morning, when we reached Johana.

The camp boasted several old barrack buildings which had been prepared against our coming by an advance detail. One building was allotted to each company and one reserved for the battalion officers. The soldiers slept side by side on a long wooden platform which ran the length of the barracks. The officers' accommodations were a bit more elaborate. The major, adjutant, surgeon, three company commanders, and I occupied separate rooms furnished with an iron cot, a table, and a chair. The lieutenants bunked together in one large room and the warrant officers in another.

After breakfast the senior officers and I went to bed. As I dozed off I heard the lieutenants supervising the work of cleaning equipment in preparation for an inspection at noon by their company commanders.

On these trips away from the garrison the officers ate the same food the men did. Instead of rice we had *mugimeshi,* a mixture of rice and barley, supplemented by a vegetable stew of lotus roots. This was topped off by two or three slices of daikon for dessert. Breakfast differed somewhat from this typical noonday and evening meal in that a thick, sweetish bean soup replaced the vegetable stew.

At Johana we put in two days of firing platoon combat problems and then at 4:00 A.M. on the third day began the twenty-five-mile hike back to Kanazawa. The march was completed in a burning heat at two in the afternoon.

The 1st Company did not fall out when the battalion was dismissed. Instead its company commander double-timed it around the area of barracks two or three times. This seemed so unusual to me that I asked, "Why?" The company commander smiled. "I'm just proving to my men that they still have lots of 'go' and are not nearly as tired as they may think they are," he said.

We now fell to for a week's arduous work in preparation for the regiment's organization day. Each company was scheduled to put on a stunt or act of some sort, and most of our time was devoted to this.

The ceremonies began at 7:30 A.M. with a Shinto service at the regimental shrine. At nine-thirty came a regimental review. After the review the 2d Company put on the sham battle it had been rehearsing all week. Following this, all hands returned to barracks, which had been thrown open to the public for the day.

At noon the officers gave a banquet for the principal citizens of the town. The officers' wives, children, and servants had also been invited, but these were entertained separately, because in proper Japanese society mixed parties are taboo.

After dinner we listened to speeches and watched the soldier entertainments. Our sham-battle stunt was matched by hula dances in one company, and by amateur acts in others. One company constructed a huge sphinx in front of their barracks by piling up cots and covering them with canvas. Another set up a large globe, representing the world. Atop this a life-sized, straw-filled Japanese soldier waved his rifle and a Rising Sun flag. This figure bore the date 1937 (prophetic, in view of the China incident). The day ended with a sake party at the officers' club.

The next few weeks were largely devoted to training for the division autumn maneuvers. During this time we made another trip to Johana for a two-sided maneuver against the 35th Infantry Regiment from Toyama. We also put on several two- or three-day maneuvers, using Kanazawa as a base.

The twelve-day autumn maneuvers were divided into three four-day periods devoted respectively to regimental, brigade, and divisional exercises. These exercises were chiefly remarkable for the long distances marched and the long periods without rest or sleep. One day we marched thirty-seven miles. Twice the troops went three days and two nights without sleep, except what could be snatched during ten-minute halts and brief lulls in the situation. Sometimes the men slept while walking. Our junior lieutenant caused much amusement by marching squarely into a lumber pile on the side of the road while sound asleep.

The last four-day period was the most strenuous. *We started out at five in the morning and marched almost continuously until ten the next morning. In that time we covered fifty-six miles.* At ten o'clock the umpires stopped the war long enough to untangle the situation which had gotten out of hand. Our regiment found itself halted in front of a Buddhist temple. We all piled into the temple compound, and those of us who could keep our eyes open long enough ate a couple of our *nigurimeshi* (a mess of rice rolled into balls for ease in carrying and sometimes containing a salted plum in the center).

This blessed halt was all too short. It seemed we had just closed our eyes when orders came to fall back a mile or so and go into a defensive position. Fortunately for the tired soldiers, the line of defense ran through unharvested rice paddies, so they were forbidden to dig trenches. While the company organized its position I crawled into the bushes for a short snooze and didn't come out until awakened by the smell of cooking rice.

At nightfall everybody was occupied with outpost duty and patrols. The Japanese go in for patrolling in a big way. In bivouac virtually everybody who is not actually on post as a sentry is out on a patrol of some kind. I remarked on this to Captain Teshima, and he replied that the idea was to keep everybody busy.

"But why not let some of them sleep?" I asked.

"Oh no!" he said. "That is not necessary. They already know how to sleep. They need training in how to stay awake."

The next morning at dawn the enemy attacked our position. Just as the two opposing forces confronted each other with fixed bayonets the bugles blew recall and the battle was over. The troops assembled under their NCOs and started out on the five-, six-, and seven-mile marches to their billets, where they were to rest until the following morning. The officers gathered for a critique at the primary school in a neighboring village. When this was over we boarded the local trolley and headed for the billeting area.

Japanese troops always billet on the civilian population whenever this is possible. The Japanese citizen does not look on this the way an American does. In Japan practically every family has or has had a son with the colors and therefore has a direct interest in the army. The policy of recruiting soldiers in the locality where they are to serve further adds to this interest. The people regard it as a privilege to have soldiers quartered in their homes, and they do their utmost to entertain them and make them comfortable.

The officers were quartered with the more substantial citizens. Captain Teshima and I were always billeted together. Our hosts felt it their bounden duty to entertain us with food and sake until late at night, not realizing that perhaps we had not slept for two nights in a row. In other respects, also, their attention was sometimes slightly embarrassing. On one occasion, while boiling at my ease in the family bath, the door opened and in walked my hostess to inquire if she could be of any assistance. I quickly assured her that I had everything needed.

One of the families with whom I was quartered boasted a foreign-style bed. This they had prepared for my special use. I found it too short for me and hard as a rock, but they were so proud of it that I could hardly admit that I would rather sleep on the mats.

Our last problem was a twenty-four-hour division staff exercise. This time we marched only sixteen or seventeen miles, and but for the heavy rain which began to fall during the forenoon, we would have had an easy time of it. The next morning, after the usual dawn assault, the buglers sounded recall for the last time, and a few hours later we were entraining for the trip back to Kanazawa. To me Kanazawa meant sleep, breakfast, French-fried potatoes, apple pie, and coffee.

One of my minor trials had been the matter of food. In barracks and at Johana I had learned to like the soldiers' regular garrison ration, but the field ration was another matter as far as I was concerned. There are no field kitchens in the Japanese Army. Therefore, when in the field the

Japanese soldier lives on his emergency ration of canned beef and hard-tack, plus an occasional meal of rice and barley. The rice and barley are cooked individually when time and opportunity permit. The beef is eaten uncooked just as it comes from the can.

In billets, however, we were feasted and toasted until all hours of the night. I found that special pains were taken to cater to the queer tastes of the "foreign barbarian." The billeting detail always spread the word ahead that the foreign officer was very fond of *sukiyaki,* a succulent compound of beef or chicken and several vegetables. As a consequence Captain Teshima and I had at least one meal of sukiyaki wherever we billeted. Before the maneuvers were over he said he hoped he would never see sukiyaki again as long as he lived.

A month after we returned to Kanazawa the second-year men completed their conscription period and were discharged. This was November 30. The night before the company threw a sake party for the retiring soldiers. All the company officers attended, and the captain and I both made speeches. The soldiers appeared to enjoy my description of life in the American Army, but I think they enjoyed my funny Japanese even more.

Early in the morning of the thirtieth the area of barracks was packed with relatives and friends of the soldiers who were to be discharged. Shortly after eight a formal farewell ceremony was held on each company parade. The captain congratulated the men upon the completion of their service and thanked them for their efforts in helping the company to maintain its high standards. In conclusion he urged them to remember the lessons they had learned while with the colors. A spokesman for the retiring soldiers then stepped forward and thanked the captain and the company officers and NCOs for their guidance during the past two years and wished them a successful future. An exchange of salutes between the two groups terminated the ceremony.

The next day, December 1, was the annual promotion day. When a man is promoted custom prescribes that he make the round of his superiors and friends to report his promotion. I was unaware of this custom until I found the newly promoted men waiting to report to me. Their report, identical in form, ran like this: "Sir, Sergeant Tanaka respectfully reports that by the grace of the lieutenant's honorable shadow he has this date become a sergeant in the Imperial Army. He also begs the lieutenant's continued favor."

I congratulated each man and hoped he would soon have another promotion to report.

The next few weeks were devoted largely to fatigue, such as cleaning and repairing clothing and equipment for the new men coming in in January. The men were given a six-day holiday over the New Year, but I received seven days in order to permit me to be absent on Christmas Day.

Immediately after the holidays the officers resumed fencing. Every morning we assembled in the fencing hall at six o'clock. After donning fencing equipment and removing our socks we lined up in bare feet, paired off, and fell to for an hour of strenuous slashing and whacking. The hall was unheated and the windows were wide open. This meant that we had the choice of fencing energetically or freezing.

After this workout we repaired to the officers' club for a breakfast of rice, sweet bean soup, and a raw egg. One feature of these breakfasts was a peculiar, but not unpleasant, wine made from the powdered flesh of *mamushi*, a poisonous Japanese snake. I was told that this snake wine was especially efficacious in renewing manly vigor after great physical exertion.

On January 20 eight hundred new conscripts were inducted into the regiment. They began arriving early in the morning, accompanied by all their friends and relatives. The processing clicked with machinelike precision; by noon the recruits had drawn their uniforms and were being initiated in the mysteries of making up an army bunk. To a number it was a real mystery; many of these men had never seen a bed on legs before.

The noon meal that day was attended by all the officers and the nearest male relative of each new man. The captain explained the routine of a soldier's life and told the relatives not to worry about their sons and nephews, for they would be well taken care of and well fed.

A few days later the new conscripts were issued rifles. Giving a rifle to a Japanese soldier is a ceremony of deep significance. The entire company was formed on the parade facing a long rack of rifles. Captain Teshima explained the honor and responsibility of being entrusted with a rifle. The samurai regarded his sword as his soul, he said, and the soldier must regard his rifle in the same light. Each new soldier then stepped forward as his name was called, bowed deeply to the rifle in the captain's hands, took the rifle, raised it in obeisance to his forehead, stepped back, made an awkward present arms, and resumed his place in ranks.

Shortly after this the regimental commander, who knew that I was interested in the pre-conscriptional system of training, invited me to accompany him on two inspection trips. One trip carried me to the Middle School of Komatsu and the other to the Young Men's Training Association at Tsurugi.

We were met on the station platform at Komatsu by all of the principal town and school authorities. Upon leaving the station we found all the school children of the city lined up on both sides of the street. Each child carried a Japanese flag in one hand and an American flag in the other. As soon as he saw the flags the colonel pushed me ahead of him, saying that it was my party. As I passed each group the children made a deep bow at a word of command from their teacher. This was my cue to salute —which I did for two solid blocks!

Upon arrival at the school we were conducted to a small, concrete, tomblike structure inside of which were locked the pictures of the Emperor and the Empress. All bowed to the pictures, which were not visible. We spent the rest of the day observing the military training and other school activities. On our way back to the railway station in the afternoon we again found the children and their flags on hand. Once more I walked between the lines, saluting at their bows and saying *domo arigato* (thank you) to their *banzais*.

My last few days in Kanazawa were occupied with packing, farewell calls, and parties. There was a sake party at the company, where I made my farewell speech, and another at the officers' mess, where I featured in like manner. At a final geisha party the officers of the regiment presented me with a fine large equestrian figure of Masashige, a famous Japanese warrior, engraved with my name in Japanese characters.

On the day of departure, although it was five o'clock in the morning when we arrived at the railway station, my striker, the NCOs of the 2d Company, and all the officers of the regiment with many of their wives were already there waiting to see us off. As the train pulled out I returned the last salute.

THE TACTICAL PROBLEM—AND A NEW SOLUTION

By Captain B. H. Liddell Hart, British Army

A great deal was written at the time of the blitzkrieg about Captain Hart's influence on British military thinking, with particular reference to his "defensive" preachings; most of this criticism was greatly oversimplified. It will probably take a full-length book of objective and thorough criticism to establish Captain Hart's proper place in the world military scene of the two decades between the great wars. The *Infantry Journal*, like most military magazines published in English, has published a number of articles from Captain Hart's able pen. The following appeared in 1937.

It is setting expectations high to count on any program of rearmament and mechanization to bridge the gulf that now separates armies from their desire—for successful attack. My own view is that these potential developments in offensive power are far exceeded by the actual growth, largely unrecognized, of defensive power, and that the progress of mechanization hitherto has already reinforced the capacity for resistance more than it has any good prospect of strengthening the capacity for attack. Not only fire, but the means of obstruction and demolition, may now be moved more swiftly to any threatened spot to thwart a hostile concentration of force.

The question which armies must face is whether they have any chance of overcoming resistance on present lines, even when developed. An alternative way of approaching the problem is to seek a tactical solution, not merely a material one. If we are doubtful of overcoming the defense by an increase of offensive strength, as we have cause to be, is there any prospect in a different solution by an improvement of *art?* So heavy are the present odds against effective action on land, however, that something more than the art of the individual general is needed. Even if an army could breed Napoleons, which no army can be expected to do under its peacetime professional conditions, they would make no headway without an antidote to the paralyzing machine gun. Armies need to develop their tools to suit this new type of art.

Four years ago the British War Office appointed a committee, composed of the younger generals, to investigate the lessons of the war and to see whether they were adequately applied in the training of the British Army. The experience then sifted and collated should have shaken our satisfaction with customary methods. It is common knowledge that this re-examination of war experience led to the conclusion that surprise was of paramount importance, both in attack and in defense, and that the greatest lesson of the last war was that no attack on an enemy in action was likely to succeed unless his resistance was already paralyzed by surprise in some form. It is known, too, that this committee expressed the emphatic opinion that our methods, both during and since the war, were too stereotyped; also, that the vital importance of surprise and of the indirect approach ought to receive greater attention in the training of the army.

There has been some evidence of efforts to apply this admonition, but they have not gone wide enough. Exercises have too often become a competition in obviousness. Instead of developing ingenuity, the main effort has too often been toward simplifying the enemy's problem in defending himself. This tendency was the sequel, paradoxically, to the fresh concentration of attention on training the army for European warfare—the very type of warfare in which investigation had shown the paramount importance of surprise. Under the influence of this "European" keynote methods became more stereotyped rather than more subtle. Instead of going forward to the trial of new ideas, they went back to the repetition of old practices. If this is the best we can hope for, there should be no hesitation in bowing to the present paramountcy of the defensive and resigning ourselves to the conclusion that it would be better to relegate the army to a merely protective role—as the lesser evil than its futile sacrifice.

There were, however, some features in the work of the troops, as contrasted with the ruling ideas, which held out some promise of greater effect. One was the increased skill and subtlety which many of the troops showed in concealing themselves from air observation. Another was the cultivation of night sense and increased use of attacks in the dark—by some commanders at least.

These developments point a path by which further progress is possible. By the skillful use of *obscurity* in its various forms, the attack might recover some of its lost power. Whereas today a mass attack merely spells massacre, a "masked attack," under cover of darkness or fog, natural or artificial, has potentialities that have scarcely been tapped. Obscurity is a strong antidote to the defensive machine gun and may prove a better protection than armor. Its risks are mainly those of confusion; they are certainly less than those of annihilation by machine guns with a clear field of fire, and they can be greatly reduced by training. The superiority of well-trained troops over normal troops is much more pronounced in the dark than in daylight.

The use of obscurity, however, requires judicious adaptation to the type of troops and a recognition of its limits. Darkness is a better cloak than artificial fog to attacking infantry because, if skilled, they can see through it; when moving in fog the man on foot has difficulty in keeping his direction, while he becomes a target the moment he emerges. Thus artificial fog would seem to have greater promise as a cloak for armored fighting vehicles equipped with direction finders. But night, despite its advantages for infantry who are trained in night fighting, has the disadvantage of limiting the effective depth of their attack. They may storm a position under cover of it, but if they press on, the risks of confusion are likely to increase disproportionately to the distance traveled. For control can hardly be kept once advancing troops are engaged in actual night combat. The actual assault may go well; the difficulty comes in re-forming and pushing on afterward. Perhaps the problem of exploiting a night attack and extending its reach may eventually be solved by some form of floodlighting the battlefield when the enemy's position has been stormed.

In places that afford plentiful cover—woods, villages, and rough ground—infantry may be able to overcome hostile machine guns and make headway by the use of what one may call the "stalking attack." It is a method which puts a premium on individual skill, and it offers considerable scope for development. But enthusiasm for it should not blind us to its limitations. It is a method which fits only special conditions; it is bound to be slow if it is to be efficiently executed, and it cannot be counted on to produce large-scale results. It is of its nature a preparatory or supplementary part of the attack rather than a separate form of attack.

We are thus left with the "masked attack" or the "armored attack" as the two main forms of the offensive that seem to have any promise of breaking into an enemy's position and ejecting him. But there are more ways of overcoming the enemy's army than by storming its positions, just as there are more ways of winning wars than by winning battles. It is for the art of war to find them, and the need is the greater now that the strength of the defensive has made the storming of position such a dubious proposition. The enemy may be forestalled on positions; he may be levered out of them by maneuver; he may be left in them while his general situation is weakened by developing pressure elsewhere, in directions that his position does not cover. As a sequel or otherwise, he may be caught in motion without having time to take up a defensive disposition.

There may be more scope for such alternative forms of action than is realized by those who still think of another war in terms of the last. The present trend of conditions is by no means favorable to the formation of continuous fronts, at any rate in the early stages of a war. Mass armies do not lend themselves to mechanization, and since the mechanized fractions will be available earlier than the rest, there is a likelihood that the crucial first phase of a war will be fought out between these opposing fractions; thus we should see relatively small forces on large fronts. Furthermore, the assembly of the masses on the frontiers will be hindered by the danger of air attack on the marching columns and by the jeopardy of supply when their communications are exposed to interruption over so large an area in rear.

A factor common to all these alternative courses is the time factor. If the advantage is to be gained there must be an acceleration of action. The scales of war are inclining not to the side which has the "big battalions" but to the side which "gets there" first. I would suggest that it is an axiom of modern war that "a hundred men with machine guns who arrive at a spot first are stronger, at least in daylight, than five hundred and sometimes a thousand who arrive second."

This, in turn, suggests the value of using any fragment of one's force that is mechanized, or can be motor-moved, to jump ahead and secure key points. Nothing has been more disappointing in recent years' exercises than the way that mechanization has been wasted by moving units and formations at the pace of their slowest portion, owing to the desire to move complete. It shows a too-complete disregard of another modern axiom, arising from the advantage of defense over attack, which we may express in the phrase that "possession is nine tenths of the war."

Soldiers today are predominantly concerned with the problem of attack, so dubious of solution. They might wisely spare a little time to study the possibilities of a form of action which would throw the burden of that problem on the enemy. I refer to what I would term the "baited offensive," the combination of offensive strategy with defensive tactics. Throughout history it has proved one of the most effective of moves, and its advantages have increased as modern weapons have handicapped other types of move. By rapidity of advance and mobility of maneuver you may be able to seize points which the enemy, sensitive to the threat, will be constrained to attack. Thus you will invite him to a repulse which, in turn, may be exploited by a riposte. Such a counterstroke against an exhausted attacker is much less difficult than the attack on a defended position. The opportunity for it may also be created by a calculated withdrawal—what one may call the "luring defensive." Here is another gambit of future warfare.

Whatever form of action be adopted, its effectiveness will depend on concealment of intention. The mystification of the opponent acts upon him like a paralyzing drug. The surest method of producing it, as centuries of experience have shown, is that of *wide extension*. It is a method unsuited for use by military mediocrity. But in skilled hands its risks are far outweighed by its advantages. By operating on a wide front, one thickens the fog of war for one's opponent, yet minimizes it for oneself. It is a psychological smoke screen which disturbs the mind and may shake the nerve of the stoutest adversary. Under cover of it, one has the best chance of seizing points of leverage. The introduction of mechanized mobility has added to its potency while increasing its safety. But of itself it aids rapidity—by reducing the congestion inherent in the practice of operating on narrow fronts.

There have been some instances in recent exercises of a tendency toward movement on wider fronts, but it has not gone nearly far enough for its promise to mature. The greatest hindrance is the dogma of "concentration," imperfectly understood. It is not easy for the simple mind to grasp that concentration is in essence a matter of effect and not of form. The adaptation of methods to changing conditions is retarded by the soldier's customary reluctance to change his traditional terminology. By putting new ideas in old potted terms we cramp the growth of this understanding. I learned this lesson when compiling the postwar infantry manual. To eradicate the practice of a rigid linear advance and of direct reinforcement—a "building up of the firing line" which merely piled up the casualties—it was necessary to replace the terms "firing line" and "supports" which many, from habit or sentiment, desired to retain. The benefit of their disappearance was unmistakable. But today, in a higher sphere, we still suffer such needless handicaps. We still call the preliminary distribution of forces, however widely disposed, the "strategic concentration." We ought to drop this terminological absurdity. Again the idea of advancing on a wide front is cramped by the term "advanced guard," which is associated with the practice of moving on a narrow front —with the whole division on a single road. We are likely to be fettered to this obsolete method until we strike out the term.

The greatest need today is to recognize the evolution that is in progress. Until the end of the eighteenth century a physically concentrated approach, both strategic (*to* the battlefield) and tactical (*on* the battlefield), was the rule. Then Napoleon, exploiting Bourcet's ideas and the new divisional system, introduced a *distributed* strategic approach—the army moving in independent fractions. But the tactical approach was still, in general, a concentrated one. Toward the end of the nineteenth century, with the development of fire weapons, the tactical approach became *dispersed,* i.e., in particles, to diminish the effect of fire. But the strategic approach had again become concentrated; this was due partly to the growth of masses and partly to the misunderstanding of the Napoleonic method. Today we must recognize the need of reviving the distributed strategic approach, if there is to be any chance of reviving the art and effect of strategy. But two new conditions—air power and motor power—seem to point to its further development into a *dispersed strategic approach.* The danger of air attack, the aim of mystification, and the need of drawing full value from mechanized mobility suggest that advancing forces should not only be distributed as widely as is compatible with combined action, but be dispersed as much as is compatible with cohesion. And the development of radio is a timely aid toward reconciling dispersion with control.

If there is to be any hope of reviving any army's effectiveness, except in mere protectiveness, it lies in the development of such new methods: methods which aim at permeating and dominating areas rather than capturing lines; at the practicable object of paralyzing the enemy's action rather than the theoretical object of crushing his forces. Fluidity of force may succeed where concentration of force merely entails a helpless rigidity. The sea is stronger than a steam roller and should replace it as our military ideal. The main difficulty is the doubtful ability of soldiers trained on present lines to rise to the level of this new technique. Unless they can do so, it would be wiser to abandon any dreams of attack and resign ourselves to the present fact that the defensive is the only role an army can effectively play in a modern war where both sides are fairly equal in equipment.

TWENTY MILLION REDS

By Lieutenant Colonel (now Brigadier General) Charles A. Willoughby

American military men were early aware of the great growth of the Red Army. In 1939 General Willoughby summarized this growth. General Willoughby is a broad student of warfare and while on duty as an instructor at the Command and General Staff School was editor of the *Military Review,* the quarterly issued by the school (now a monthly), in which articles from all the world military magazines of every language were digested. General Willoughby has been a member of MacArthur's staff since well before the Japs first attacked Pearl Harbor and Manila.

WITH ITS ACTIVE FORCES of more than 1,500,000 men and a trained reserve estimated at 18,000,000, the army of Soviet Russia is probably the largest in the world in numbers, if not the strongest in any sense. Thus any tactical doctrine emanating from such a tremendous power and any information on the way its units are organized are worth the careful attention and study of those in every other army. In this article are presented, from many sources, late matters of Soviet military interest.

To consider, in beginning, the tactics and organization of the basic infantry units, we may turn briefly to the recent tentative infantry manual, of which a new edition became necessary through the introduction of the "combat unit," similar to the German reinforced-type infantry squad. In the new manual we find certain chapters of the old eliminated, viz., marches on skis, bayonet combat, hand-grenade manual, cyclist formations. These now appear in separate pamphlets. On the other hand, there is much more on anti-gas protection, particularly on measures for dealing with the degassing of large areas.

Of basic infantry units the new manual informs us that the standard combat team is the rifle squad grouped around the autorifle (light machine gun). It consists of one squad leader, eight riflemen, and one machine gun. In view of its small size it is not divided tactically into fire-support and maneuver units.

The platoon (there is no section unit) consists of three rifle squads and a rifle-grenade squad, which consists of one leader and six men. This high-angle fire within the platoon shows a tendency toward independence of ordinary support fire. The same thing is apparent in the organization of the company, which has its own heavy-machine-gun sections. These consist of eight men (gunner, assistant gunner, two observers, driver, and three ammunition carriers).

As in other armies of the world, we find that Soviet close-order formations have been simplified. In the platoon assembly formation the three rifle squads and one grenade squad are abreast, each in a single file of nine men. The heavy-machine-gun platoon takes post behind the center of the company. To form march column the flank platoon simply marches to the front, followed in column by the other platoons.

There are three open-order formations for the rifle squad: column of files, a skirmish line at intervals of four to five paces, and a wedge, or lozenge, formation—whichever is ordered or signaled. In battle the individual soldier advances by bounds and creeping. When he gets within fifty yards of the enemy line a concentrated salvo of hand grenades covers his final dash. The last hundred yards may, however, be made in bounds by the entire line. In open order the machine-gun crew conforms to the formation adopted by the nearest rifle units.

The organization of the infantry regiment is best shown in a table:

THE SOVIET INFANTRY REGIMENT

Regtl Staff:
  Commander of Engr Plat
  Commander of Gas Plat
  Commander of Accompanying FA
  Commander of Trains
  Commander of Med Dets and Vet Plat
  Political Officer
  Commander of Regtl School Det
Regtl Reconnaissance Det
Regtl Communications Co
3 Rifle Battalions
  Each Battalion:
  Bn Hqrs
  Bn Com Section
  1 heavy MG Co—3 MG Plats (12 guns)
  1 Sec Accompanying Arty (two 37-mm. guns and three light mortars)
  3 Rifle Cos
    3 Rifle Plats/1 Rifle Grenade Sec
    1 MG Sec
    Combat Train
Accompanying Arty:
  2 FA Btrys (76-mm.)
  1 Hqrs Btry
Regtl School Det (training cadre):
  3 Rifle Plats
  1 MG Plat
Regtl Reconnaissance Det:
  1 Mtd Plat (20 troopers, 3 light MGs)
  1 Bicycle Plat (heavy MGs)
1 Engr (Pioneer) Co
1 Gas Plat:
  4 Gas Squads
  1 Degassing truck (Mtz)
Supply and Service Elements:
  Combat Trains (Ammunition)
  Field Trains (Animal transport)

It is estimated that 285 such regiments have been organized as active units up to a recent date. There are also some 600 accompanying-gun batteries now active.

The next table shows the armament of infantry units:

Rifle: Model: 1891/1930; caliber: 7.62 mm. Rear sight (Vernier) modernized (meter readings); clip of 5 cartridges; rate of fire: 10–12 shots per minute. Weight: 9.9 lbs.; range: 2,500 yards.

Pistol: Model: Browning; caliber: 9 mm.; 7-round magazine; weight: 2.2 lbs.

Light Machine Gun: Model: Degtjarow; caliber: 7.62 mm. Gas-operated; air-cooled; range: 1,400–1,550 yards; rate: 500 rounds per minute; bipod support.

Heavy Machine Gun: Model: Maxim; caliber: 7.62 mm. Water-cooled; recoil actuated; belt 220 rounds; weight 43 lbs.; rate: 600 rounds per minute; range: 3,800 yards; transported in two-wheeled carts.

Hand Grenade: Model: Djakonow 1933 (PTD); defensive bursting radius: 100 yards (2,000 fragments) if covered by an auxiliary cylinder; without this cylinder radius of burst (offensive) is reduced to 25 yards.

Heavy weapons (Rifle Battalion):

Stokes mortar (and other types).

37-mm. Model: Rosenberg; range: 2,200 yards.

47-mm. cannon (AT guns); range: 1,600–3,300 yards.

The Soviet rifle (infantry) division, like our own, has been subject to experiment and change during the past few years. However, the main divisional sub-units are apparent from the outlines of tactical doctrine given below.

THE APPROACH MARCH

A Soviet division on the march has an unusual strength of advance guard—at least one third of the infantry and approximately one half of the divisional artillery. There is also an occasional attachment of corps artillery, even of long-range calibers. This strength is based on the desire to act offensively and fast and thus get the jump in early collisions with the enemy. The rest of the organic artillery moves at the head of the main body. Aviation and mechanized units furnish flank and frontal security.

The advance by bounds or phase lines is only favored in exceptional cases; it is regarded as time-consuming and as leading to loss of initiative. Soviet advance guards are expected to act independently and energetically. Their artillery is to act with equal aggressiveness from forward firing positions, even in advance of the support, seeking advantageous firing positions to establish fire superiority. The artillery conducts its reconnaissance with the leading infantry elements.

Thus, generally speaking, the Soviet advance-guard doctrine is to gain surprise and defeat the enemy by speed, aggressiveness, and the superior strength of leading elements. This means, of course, decentralization of command and independent action in many cases.

OFFENSIVE COMBAT

Normally the Soviet rifle division is grouped roughly into (1) an element of fixation (the advance guard) of about one third the available strength; (2) an element of maneuver, the main body, and (3) the reserve, of about one ninth of the available strength. Frontages for attack, where the enemy is in position, are as follows: 4,500–6,500 yards for a corps; 2,200 yards for a division; 1,100–2,200 yards for a regiment, and 600–1,100 yards for a battalion. Much larger frontages are used against an enemy in movement: corps, 9,000–13,000 yards; division, 4,500–6,500 yards; regiment, 2,200–3,300 yards, and battalion, 1,100–2,200 yards.

The heavy supporting weapons of the infantry regiments are employed by the regiment. They may, however, be released to battalions and companies for close-in support in close terrain, fog, and like conditions.

The divisional artillery furnishes direct support, with one battalion per infantry regiment. Corps artillery is often released to divisions but operates in groupments for unified firing. The corps ordinarily receives an artillery division from G.H.Q. reserve. Whenever it does it releases one regiment to each division and keeps the third for its own use.

Soviet doctrine conceives the offensive as one of relentless aggression like the advance-guard action. The mass of fires is placed far forward, notwithstanding the risks from lack of cover and vulnerable positions. Under cover of this fire, the maneuver element attempts flanking actions. Flank maneuver is sought always, whether the enemy is in position or in movement. Against an enemy in position a secondary attack is staged to gain a break-through. The line of departure is as close to the enemy as practicable, about 800 to 1,000 meters from his leading elements. Artillery command posts are from 600 to 1,700 yards from the enemy and the battery locations, from 2,000 to 3,500 yards. Notwithstanding the general aspect of aggressiveness which colors the Soviet tactical teachings, the artillery ordinarily undertakes an intensive preparation of three to five hours.

The battalions of the first attack wave, both preceded and accompanied by tanks, seek the enemy artillery and reserve locations. They are to advance resolutely and avoid centers of resistance that can be turned or outflanked, leaving their reduction to other attack echelons farther in rear. To quote,

. . . every unit advances as deeply as possible into the gaps of the enemy dispositions. Artillery must support as closely as possible, displacing forward, by echelons, in order to assure continuity of direct fire support.

This action, as it proceeds, leads to a complete decentralization and is maintained at "a rapid pace." In sum, the objective is to break the enemy's will, to destroy him, not to gain terrain.

DEFENSIVE COMBAT

The defensive, insist the Soviet regulations, is purely a provisional measure. Only part of the army will take up a defense, if it must, pending preparation for offensive action elsewhere, or during a regrouping of forces, or in any similar situation demanding economy of force.

The general zone of the defense is not strictly defined. There is an out-post and a main line of resistance, but here, too, considerable latitude is left to local commanders.

Normal defensive frontages are as follows: corps, 15–19 miles; division, 9,000–13,000 yards; regiment, 3,000–4,500 yards; battalion, 1,100–2,200 yards; company, 500–1,100 yards. The ratio of strength of the main de-fense elements runs about two thirds for the main defense and local counterattacks, about one third for major counterattacks, and about one ninth for reserves to take care of flanks.

In defensive battle the heavy infantry weapons operate against local targets and against tanks in particular. The organic divisional artillery furnishes direct support attached to specific infantry battalion and com-panies but has contingent missions in neighboring zones. Corps artillery fires counterbattery and is ordinarily kept in groupments for control.

Each light machine gun, in defensive combat, is to traverse across 75 yards and back at 250 yards' range, firing at a rate of two rounds per yard of traverse per minute. Thus the sector of fire of a section, based on its light machine guns, is 225–250 yards. To this density is added an addi-tional 200 rounds of rifle fire per minute, which enables a section to cover a front of approximately 300 yards. Additional weapons drawn from the rest of the company can be used to widen the section front to 500 yards. Interlocking fire is habitually used from front-line positions.

The above calculation is based on a rate of fire per gun of 300 rounds per minute. This, of course, is not the maximum rate but is considered reasonable in firing rapid sequences of bursts rather than continuous fire. The problem of frontages—always a controversial matter as solved by the Soviets—contains one striking element: density of fire per yard of front. This, after all, is probably the most important item in fire power.

During the enemy's preparation the divisional artillery fires concen-trate on his line of departure to break up his attack as it begins. After that its fire is concentrated on hostile tanks as they appear. All units of all sizes are to defend in place, even when surrounded. They deliver counter-attacks as soon as needed.

Soviet tactics also cover the possibility of larger unit frontages. Here a system of interlocking fires and loosely connected strong points is em-ployed or, where the situation requires it, a mobile defense of possible routes of enemy approach. In the latter case decentralization of units, especially of artillery, is considered logical. The infantry part of artillery-infantry teams may be as small as an infantry company.

TANK ATTACKS

The Soviet doctrine appears to favor mass tank attacks. In spite of the fact that there is a reasoned opinion that anti-tank weapons are only at the beginning of their ultimate development and that they are already capable of putting light and medium tanks out of action by single direct hits, the Soviet Army pins its hope upon mass attacks designed to overrun the anti-tank defense. It seems to be thought that an enemy will have only a limited number of anti-tank weapons in an average defensive sector.

In one recent article the author examines a typical tank attack. He assumes an attack by four companies of light tanks on a front of one thousand yards in four waves of twenty-five tanks each. The tanks are opposed by an infantry battalion on the defensive. The anti-tank guns, it is assumed, will probably be in depth, in three lines: first the three guns of the battalion anti-tank platoon, then three guns released by the regiment, and finally six guns from the divisional anti-tank company. Each gun commands a field of fire of about one thousand yards. The tanks advance at twelve miles per hour and consequently are under fire for about five minutes. In that period each gun can fire from fifty to sixty aimed rounds. This means 150 to 180 rounds from the first-line anti-tank guns. It is problematical, of course, how many hits the guns will obtain. It may be assumed, however, that they can score hits on tanks directly in their line of fire. And the tanks that get through will, many of them, run squarely into additional guns.

The author questions whether one hundred light (seven-ton) tanks can do the job. He thinks seven tanks of one hundred tons would be more to the point, thus favoring modern French thought rather than the Soviet mass light-tank attack.

Soviet authors also recommend the use of tanks by night. The attacker should, as a rule, they believe, employ at night only minor units attached to infantry. The tanks break through certain sectors of the hostile defensive position in order to facilitate the dawn attack. The tank attack should be timed so that infantry can occupy before dawn the ground the tanks capture. The tank units do not operate under orders of the attacking infantry because they cannot receive orders after their departure. Daylight should see only decisive tank attacks made to penetrate the entire depth of the hostile defenses. But the object of a tank attack by night is simply to penetrate as far as the hostile artillery positions in order to reduce daylight casualties. A second tank attack follows at dawn into the depth of the hostile position. During a night penetration of this kind tank fire is held to a minimum and is delivered only at frontal resistance. Because of the great difficulties attending night tank attacks, only well-trained and disciplined units should be employed. Radio communication is regarded as the solution for close control of maneuvering tanks. Tracer bullets are used to designate targets. One tank in each section reconnoiters for anti-tank targets. The commander of this tank should be a particularly accurate shot. This "scout tank" opens fire only against anti-tank weapons; the entire tank company is then expected to follow suit and clean them up.

TANKS IN DEFENSIVE OPERATIONS

The Soviet regulations provide, as we have already seen, for defense on a normal front, on an extended front, and on a mobile front. In the last two, tanks are attached to the reserve and from there are used to support counterattacks. If there are ample numbers of them they may be allotted to separate battalion sectors.

In normal defense operations one tank battalion is allotted to every infantry division. The commander places his tanks in areas from which he intends to assume the offensive. He may also use them within his defensive position wherever the enemy may penetrate.

Tanks are always attached to reconnaissance and outpost units. In a normal defense the Red Army sends weak outposts in front of the main line of resistance, from a platoon to a company per battalion, as the situation requires. Combat regulations advise attaching at least one platoon of tanks to these outpost troops to attack hostile reconnaissance and security units. They can also check the enemy's advance guards and compel his main body to deploy prematurely. From this position, too, they can also screen the outpost units when they pull back.

The most suitable moment for destroying hostile forces in the area in front of the main line of resistance is when the enemy is concentrating his forces in forward positions just before he jumps off. At this time his infantry and most of its organic supporting weapons, much of his artillery, not to say his observers, signal units, and command posts, are concentrated in a small area. At this time, also, he has no properly organized anti-tank defense. So all things considered, attacking tanks may gain a considerable success. This attack may be delivered by night or day, but preferably at dawn. The tanks may, of course, meet obstacles or mines, and the first tanks will encounter the fire of all the enemy's artillery and of the tanks supporting his attacks. This is particularly risky if the enemy happens to have better tanks. Whenever the enemy has fewer tanks or tanks with inferior armament, and his assembly positions have been accurately spotted, these should be attacked.

An infantry division on a normal front of defense, with a tank battalion at its disposal, should use the tanks in two waves. One tank company advances in the first wave against the hostile front line to a depth of some thousand yards. On the second wave two companies attack with the regimental and divisional reserves to a depth of thirteen hundred yards. Routes must be carefully reconnoitered, especially for mine fields. Preparation must also be made for friendly artillery barrages on routes of tank withdrawals to cover their return after executing their missions.

Soviet opinions differ with regard to employment of tanks within a defensive position. Some authors say that tanks should be allotted to the first line of defense, others that they should be left at the disposal of sector commanders for making counterattacks. Where tanks are allotted to the first line of defense, unit sectors may accordingly be widened. This, in turn, gives more room for counterattack maneuver, although it undoubtedly means also a dispersion of tank force and can be done only when there are plenty of tanks. When only limited numbers of tanks are available they are employed in platoons from behind the front line against hostile areas.

When tanks are under the control of sector commanders whole tank companies, alone or with infantry, are directed against the flank of the attacking hostile infantry before it reaches the main line of resistance. If a hostile attack peters out, all tanks support the units making the counterattack. Numerous routes of advance must be reconnoitered, however the tanks are to be used. Assembly positions before and after a fight should not be located near the line of departure because of hostile artillery concentrations.

If the attacking enemy has more and better tanks, the tanks of a Soviet counterattack are directed toward the enemy's infantry when it separates from its tanks. Where possible the tanks should attack from higher to lower ground to gain greater speed. The tanks should race to reach the hostile infantry as soon as possible, because this is the easiest way to get protection from anti-tank weapons. Tanks will also often be employed as stationary fire units, especially when fast tanks must halt in order to hold ground until friendly infantry comes up. The commander of tanks must be on the alert in case he encounters hostile tanks with superior armaments. In this event he can attack only when he is protected by mine fields and supported vigorously by previously prepared artillery fires.

A Soviet Map Problem

A map problem in the Soviet artillery journal designed for a rifle division throws an interesting light on Soviet views on the teamwork of artillery, infantry, and mechanized units. A division is making the main effort against an enemy established in a defensive position. The grouping of the artillery and the allotment of tank units here reveals definite tactical procedures.

The division had available one organic field-artillery regiment of three battalions; one heavy regiment (four battalions) attached from army reserve, and one medium regiment (three battalions) from corps reserve. The division commander directed groupments for direct support as follows: to the 1st Infantry, one battalion each of light and heavy; to the 2d Infantry, the same; to the 3d Infantry, one battalion of light and two of heavy. The corps medium regiment was placed in general support for distant fires.

A similar grouping in "direct" and "general" support is evident in the allotment of the four tank battalions attached to this division. The 1st Infantry received one tank company, the 2d Infantry two tank companies, the 3d Infantry one tank battalion. The other two tank battalions were held in a special group, for distant objectives.

This variable distribution of tank units was based on the terrain and on the strength to the main effort. The tanks were put under the orders of the infantry commanders as accompanying tanks to assist the advancing infantry in overcoming machine guns, infantry mortars, and like resistance. The tank group for distant objectives, however, operated under the division. Its mission was aimed generally at the hostile artillery areas and reserves. This group, however, attacked simultaneously with the infantry attack in order to explore the hostile disposition to its entire depth in a single battle action.

The problem also indicated considerable staff co-ordination and combat liaison. Preliminary staff conferences, attended by representatives from every major unit, were held to make clear and to co-ordinate the scheme of maneuver and the factors of time and space.

The tank-group commander indicated his zone of advance, itinerary, and probable duration of attack in the hostile areas, in order to co-ordinate with the fires of the artillery groupment in general support. The groupments in direct support arrived at similar understandings with the infantry commanders. Apparently the Soviet doctrine is well aware of liaison problems, already complicated when it was only a question of infantry-artillery liaison, and now far more so.

CONCLUSION

These Soviet tactical doctrines, gathered from official and other sources, contain little that is startling. But they do indicate an awareness of all modern tactical problems. Apparently Soviet thought on the uses of air infantry has not yet become settled and definite.

The views of Isserson, an instructor in tactics, will perhaps give us, in concluding, an indication of the trend of Soviet thought. This writer believes that the strategy of the World War, which failed, was "line strategy." "Depth strategy" must take its place, he thinks. He looks for a greater echelonment in depth than ever before. The modern attack he conceives as a series of waves which continue with increasing strength to batter against the obstacles in their front. Massed aviation operates as the first echelon; tanks and motorized units constitute the second echelon, and behind these follow the battering ram of large infantry units. The break-through was the major problem in 1914–18, but it was only a means to an end: to reach the enemy's rear areas. It failed because mobile units for exploitation were lacking. Now they are available in tanks. Isserson challenges the theories of Schlieffen, who stressed strength on the flanks for eventual maneuver, and believes in uniform echelonment in depth to gain penetration and decisive exploitation.

A TYPICAL FIGHT IN OPEN WARFARE

By CAPTAIN (now MAJOR GENERAL) ADOLF VON SCHELL,
German Army

General Adolf von Schell has been the Nazi high commander in charge of wartime transportation in Germany. He has been the co-ordinator of all kinds of transportation, not merely motor vehicles, but the railways and water and air transport, throughout the whole European area dominated by the Nazi army. Thirteen years ago he was sent to the United States as an observer and while here attended the Infantry School at Fort Benning, Georgia. Von Schell was an affable man with an able, tactical mind. He had seen a great deal of battle in the first World War. He discussed many military matters freely with friendly American officers while he was in this country, and he wrote several articles on the practical tactics of his World War experiences, some of which he gave as lectures at the Infantry School and some of which appeared in the *Infantry Journal*. The date of the one that follows is July 1931. It holds lessons for fighters as did everything he wrote. His articles written in this country appeared in a small book entitled *Battle Leadership*.

IT WAS ABOUT September 20, 1915. From a westerly direction a German battalion had been marching for some days, ever deeper into Russia. The roads were very bad. Sometimes there was a very hot sun, and then again it poured rain. About the middle of September the Germans had had heavy fighting for several days against the Russians in the vicinity of Vilna. Now they were marching eastward again. For several days they had seen no enemy.

The marches were very tiring. They had now come into a land of swamps. Forest, sand, swamp; between them a few villages. Whether they were marching as a part of the division or of the regiment, they did not know and did not care. That is, however, always true in wartime. In peace soldiers learn that even the last private should be acquainted with the situation, but in war no one knows anything about it and generally has no desire to. This last seems to be one of the main reasons for lack of knowledge of the situation. The soldier is satisfied if things go well with him. He has so much to do to look after himself; he must march, sleep, eat, and when he meets the enemy he fights. Whether the entire division is attacking, or only the battalion, is generally a matter of complete indifference to him. Such was the case here. The soldiers marched and marched, slept and ate. Where they were marching, or what they should do, was a matter of total indifference to them. Their higher commanders could make all the strategical plans they wanted; the soldiers marched. It is true that they discussed frequently among themselves what the mission could be. Then someone would say, "We are marching to Moscow." Then there was a laugh and the subject changed.

On one of those sunny autumn days this battalion turned suddenly toward the south at about ten o'clock in the morning. A couple of messengers galloped up and then left. Something must be wrong. The battalion was marching on narrow forest paths, often cross country. The battalion commander had ridden in advance. Suddenly he returned: "The Russians have attacked our cavalry with strong forces and pressed them back. We are to assist them. About two kilometers in front of us is a river which we are to defend."

Soon they reached the river. It was about forty yards wide but very deep. On the farther bank was a village. On this side the woods and fields lay in an irregular pattern. Not a shot could be heard; no Russians could be seen; nor was there any German cavalry visible. The battalion commander was the only one who had a map. He said to his company commanders: "Over there on the right, about five hundred meters away, is a farm; a battalion of the X Regiment will be there. We will defend from this edge of the wood to the left. The 9th, 10th, 11th companies in front, each with a sector three hundred meters wide; the 12th Company in reserve behind the middle of the battalion. To the left of our battalion is cavalry. We have no artillery for the time being. Send patrols across the river. I will get in touch with the cavalry."

Let us go with the 9th Company, which was on the right flank. The young company commander let his company bivouac about two hundred meters from the river in the wood and advanced with a few men to the river so as to look the situation over and see the real lay of the ground. Before he left his company he sent a patrol to the right to make contact with the battalion at the farm.

All was quiet at the river. The story about the Russians which the battalion commander had told did not seem to be as bad as he had painted it. The terrain was very unfavorable. All about were patches of woods, some small, some large, so that one could see only about one hundred meters in any direction.

This company was about eighty to ninety men strong. The company commander decided to use two platoons in the front line on the river and to hold back the third as a reserve. He therefore issued such an order. His platoon commanders were corporals but were men on whom he could rely. They returned to their platoons. He himself sought a boat along the river so as to reach the farther bank. He wanted to see what it looked like on the other side, but I must also admit that his principal reason was to see if he could find something to eat in the village across the river. Finally he found a boat. Then he looked back and saw his platoons coming forward from the wood. All was running smoothly. Suddenly a rifle-shot rang out over to the right. He thought that someone of the other battalion over at the farm was killing a pig for the field kitchen. Now another shot. He said to himself: "Aha! A bad shot. The man certainly ought to have been able to kill the pig with his first shot." More firing; two, four, seven shots. Can there be a fight over there? Heavier firing— and then, more quickly than it can be told, a flood of events, thoughts, and decisions.

The young officer's first thought was: "The neighboring battalion has located and driven back a Russian patrol. The firing, however, seems to be too strong for a mere patrol fight." He had in the meantime, however, climbed out of the boat. His patrol would certainly bring him information. Suddenly a few rifle bullets whistled over his head, coming from the right rear. By the sound he knew that the bullets came from Russian rifles. The situation suddenly became quite clear to him. The neighboring battalion could not be there, or the bullets could not have come from the right rear. The Russians had crossed the river and were at the farm.

What should he do? The battalion commander was not there; he must make his own decision and act. His train of thought was perhaps as follows: "Mission: defense of the river. The situation is changed. The Russians are across the river. Therefore, the decision is to attack quickly with as strong a force as possible."

He ran back with his runners to his reserve platoon. On the way he gave an order to a runner in whom he had entire confidence: "The left platoon will immediately retire into the wood and will then follow me in an attack on the farm. The right platoon will defend the entire company sector. Then report this decision to the battalion."

The company commander was soon with his reserve platoon. It had taken position with its front to the farm, which, however, was not visible. In that direction the firing was still going on. Without halting a moment he yelled: "The whole platoon will attack in double time in the direction of the farm." And then they all plunged into the wood as quickly as possible.

The Germans must attack the Russians quickly before they could get across the river in dense masses. Now a messenger came running up from the patrol, breathing hard. "The Russians are across the river near the farm. The patrol is lying down along a little road which leads north from the farm. The Russians are trying to get around us." A new situation had now arisen.

Since the first decision of the company commander scarcely ten minutes had passed. His thoughts were perhaps about as follows: "Has the situation changed? Do I now have to make a new decision? Is it possible to continue to attack? Are not the Russians already across the river in too-strong force?" He had only thirty men with him. He decided to attack. We do not want to try to decide whether this decision was right or not. We only want to state it.

He continued to advance through the wood with the platoon. Now it became lighter. There was the edge of the wood. Just beyond was another wood and the road leading to the north. Russians were on this road. "Lie down, fire, range four hundred meters." That was the only order given, and then the Germans' fire broke loose. For a moment it was quiet on the enemy's side, but then a storm of bullets came down on the men. There certainly must be a mass of Russians concealed over there. At this moment came a runner from the 2d Platoon. "The 2d Platoon is two hundred meters in rear of us." Again the young company commander had to make a decision. Should he continue the attack? No time was available for thinking long on this matter. He called out: "I am attacking with the 2d Platoon on the right. This platoon will keep up the fire and then join the attack." He ran back to the 2d Platoon and then led it forward through the wood toward the right. As they ran he gave the order: "There are Russians across the river near the farm. We are attacking." In a very brief time they reached the edge of the wood. As they came out of it they received very heavy fire from the right flank, which forced them to lie down. The Russians were already much farther across the river than they had believed possible. The situation had changed again. What should this company commander do? Would he have to make a new decision? At this moment a runner came from the battalion. "The Russians have broken through our cavalry"—his last words as he sank to the ground with a bullet through his head. Again the situation had changed. What should the poor officer do? Would he have to make a new decision?

Naturally the situation was not as clear to him as I tell it here. He did not have a map. He stood in the midst of combat. In every fight the impressions are tremendously strong, even when one has been at war for a long time. One thing seemed clear to him—to carry on the attack alone with fifty or sixty men would lead to failure. But what should he do? There were only two possibilities—to hold where he was, or to withdraw.

Defense could be advantageous only if fresh German troops were available which could drive the Russians back across the river. You will perhaps remember that of this battalion the 12th Company was still in reserve. But the 9th Company had neither seen nor heard anything of it. The company commander therefore believed that it had probably been used on the left flank of the battalion where the cavalry had retired. Still another body of troops which might be able to help was the battalion which should have been at the farm. It was not there. When would it arrive? Would it come at all? He did not know.

The situation was, therefore, that the 9th Company could hold its own if it received support immediately. If no support was coming it was high time to retire. To remain where it was fighting, without prospect for immediate support, was equivalent to destruction. The company commander decided to retire. We do not want to try to determine here whether his course was right or wrong. We want to make clear that this decision had rather to be felt than arrived at through logical thinking. We might recall again that the young officer had these thoughts in neither such clear form nor in so much time as it takes us to tell them here. He felt rather than thought.

They retired slowly. By afternoon they had gained touch again with their battalion. The cavalry was there too; then another battalion arrived, and a few batteries of light artillery. They had survived the crisis. They organized a defensive position on a little ridge in the middle of swamp and forest.

In the next few days they repulsed with heavy loss all attacks of the Russians but themselves suffered many casualties. I want to tell a little incident of this fighting because it shows how one often has to operate in war with the most unique methods.

The German line was very thin in this defensive position; the men were much dispersed. The battalion had a reserve of only thirty men which had to help in repulsing every Russian attack. The battalion lay in the swamp without trenches and without wire. In the terrain in front they could see only a short distance. Everywhere there were small bushes, small woods, so that they never could get a general view. Therefore, it was often very difficult to determine when the Russians were going to attack. They generally saw them for the first time when they were very close. They had also too few men to send out strong outguards. How could they help themselves in this situation? Then a corporal made a very simple but very good suggestion. About five hundred meters behind the lines there was a village in which there was a large number of cows. The corporal went to this village and drove all these cows in front of the position, where they could quietly graze. When the Russians approached the cows became uneasy and came toward the lines, and in this manner the Germans avoided surprise. These cows were the best and most valuable outpost ever seen in war.

Now, what can we learn from this little fight?

(1) We saw in this fight complete lack of intelligence of the enemy and knowledge about the situation. Although in this case the German cavalry had been in contact with the enemy and therefore was probably in a position to bring information, still this source failed. Suddenly the Russians were across the river; their strength was completely unknown.

Certainly the approach of the Russians in a future war would perhaps have been determined by aviators—I say perhaps. But it is my personal belief—I do not, of course, know whether this opinion will prove to be correct—that in the future we may not expect too much from our aviators.

In the first place, both sides will have aviators at their disposal who will fight each other. And before aviators can obtain good reconnaissance they must first beat the mass of the enemy's aviation. If the enemy is victorious in the air, we could naturally never hope for good information. Further, aviators in open warfare prior to combat will obtain principally intelligence of the large units of the enemy: marching columns, direction of march, and the like. This information will reach the higher staffs in the rear. What we at the front want to know about the enemy is where the machine guns and the centers of resistance are. Our fliers can rarely tell us, and then generally too late to do us any good.

Finally, we will constantly try to conceal ourselves from aviators by marching at night or by splitting our forces into small groups. If we expect these measures to be successful we must assume that the enemy's similar measures will be equally successful.

I believe, therefore, that in the war of the future we shall have to make decisions without satisfactory knowledge of the enemy. It is therefore important to practice this in peace and constantly remember that one can do in war only what one has learned in peace.

(2) This fight brought with it a very difficult situation which changed like lightning and demanded instantaneous decisions. How shall we solve difficult situations in war if we have not learned to do so in peace? If we read military history everything seems simple and clear because we can always see the entire situation, because generally we can obtain no glimpse of the minute details. We must get used to the fact in peace; we must teach ourselves and our men that in war we constantly come face to face with difficult situations. Good tennis or football players can be developed only by practice. What you are not able to do in practice you cannot do in a game, and what we soldiers do not learn in peace we cannot do in war.

(3) I believe that this example shows clearly that difficult situations can be solved only by simple decisions and simple orders. The more difficult the situation, the less time you have to issue a long order, and the less time your men have to understand a long order. If the situation is difficult all your men will be considerably excited. Only the simplest things can then be executed. We saw that this situation developed slowly and simply for a time. Then the difficulties came quick and fast. When I look back on the war this was the condition in almost all situations. I believe we can draw the following lessons about issuing orders. The first order for the fight can generally be given without hurry. It must there-

fore contain everything that is necessary—above all, the mission and the information at hand—but we should not expect that during the combat we can issue new, long orders, either written or verbal. They should be short but as clear as possible.

(4) And now the last point, which seems to me the most difficult of all. Our map problems generally close as follows: "It is now such and such an hour. Required, the decision." We know the situation; we have all the information, and we have to make a decision. I believe that the story of this fight has shown us very clearly that the most difficult thing is to know the *moment* when we have to make a decision. The information comes in by degrees. We never know whether the next minute will not give us further information. Shall we now make a decision, or should we wait still longer? In other words, to find the moment for making a decision is usually more difficult than the decision itself. Therefore, go out with your platoon commanders, your section and squad leaders, in the terrain. Tell them that they are marching with their platoons here on this road. When you then reach a selected point give to the leader a bit of information or an impression, then march quietly farther. Now give another bit of information. Never ask, however, for a decision, and you will see how terribly difficult it is to determine the time to make a decision.

We must learn all of these things in peace, and learn them in our first days in the service. But we must not know these things in only a general way; we must know them thoroughly. We can do in war only what we have learned to do in peace.

I want to close with a word of General von Seeckt's:

"Knowledge of a trade is essential, but gaining it is the work of an apprentice. The task of a journeyman is to utilize what he has learned. Only the master knows how to handle all things in every case."

SOME IMPRESSIONS OF THE UNITED STATES ARMY

By Colonel (now Major General) Hisao Watari,
Imperial Japanese Army

(*1930*)

When one reviews the great accomplishments and achievements of the belligerent nations in the World War one is particularly impressed by American overnight transition from a state of peaceful industry to a national mobilization of tremendous fighting forces on land and sea. I term this transition an overnight accomplishment, because when the United States of America entered the World War she was as wholly unprepared as it is possible for a nation of her potential resources to be. Yet in a remarkably short period of time her great expanse was dotted with temporary barracks and the streets of her cities were teeming with uniformed men. To be exact, within one month after the declaration of war the Selective Service Act was in operation, and within three months' time great military cities with a total housing capacity of 1,800,000 men had been erected to shelter the Republic's armies while they were training for future employment on the battlefield.

These myriads of men, recruited from all walks of American life, demonstrated during their training periods in the camps and the operations against the enemy that a quarter of a century of peace had not robbed American manhood of the finest qualities of the soldier. Not alone the literature of the Allies but the press and books of the enemy pay eloquent and sincere tribute to the abilities and qualities of the American as an offensive and defensive fighter.

It was my privilege in 1918 to cross the Atlantic on an army transport heavily laden with American troops, and it was my greater privilege to follow them into action and to observe their conduct at the front. This was my first close contact with United States troops, and I was particularly impressed by their youthful buoyancy and constant cheerfulness under all circumstances. I discovered, too, that although the Regular Army, the National Guard, the National Army troops considered themselves all part of one great army, nevertheless, each component had its own esprit de corps and pride of achievement. I found, too, that reported differences between the regular officer and the emergency officer did not exist, in fact, and that all personal differences, of whatever kind, were submerged in the common desire of all to achieve victory for American arms on the battlefield. I have always considered this unity of spirit, this comradeship, a remarkable tribute to American democracy, especially when it is recalled that so many hundreds of thousands of these officers and men had had no prior contact with the rigors of army life and discipline and no prior knowledge of the demands that modern warfare makes upon the individual.

I marveled, too, at the American soldier's aptitude in handling the complicated weapons of modern warfare. It would seem that this facility of his is particularly due to the fact that such a large percentage of American men are trained in the mechanical trades; but this in itself would not be sufficient, were it not accompanied by those remarkable American attributes of adaptability, ingenuity, and resourcefulness. It was the unusual American soldier who did not possess all three of these typical American characteristics. Just as these qualities set him apart, so was he distinguished above all others for his love of sports, an affection which he indulged at every possible opportunity. It is hard for that soldier to be disheartened and dispirited who, no matter how hard the day in the trenches, cannot resist the sight of a football or the trying out of a set of boxing gloves. This love of sport, innate in the American, I hold to be responsible not only for his physical superiority, but also for his mental alertness and youthful buoyancy.

Who will say that all these qualities of mind and heart were not most important factors in the nation's ability to create, in less than a year and a half, from a nucleus of two hundred thousand men, great armies numbering four millions, equipped with all the machineries of modern warfare?

In August 1919 I was recalled from the United States to Japan. But before leaving I had witnessed the amazing spectacle of these great armed forces absorbed back into civil life, until all that was left of their legions was a very small Regular Army and the troops occupying German territory.

In this rapid and smooth demobilization of their great armed forces the American people were again subscribing to their time-honored policy that the smallest possible standing army be maintained in time of peace and that men and money be raised without stint in time of war. They have adhered to this principle since the beginning of their national existence and should always find it a practicable and economical policy, provided that they do not make the mistake of reducing their standing army to the point of practical non-existence. Reduction beyond a rational minimum constitutes lack of defense.

In all my contacts with American troops through the years since 1917 I have noted their excellence in rifle marksmanship and musketry. In Tientsin, China, where detachments are stationed representing five foreign powers, and where frequent international competitions in rifle marksmanship are conducted, I observed that United States riflemen invariably won first place. This is undoubtedly due to the stress placed upon the marksmanship of the individual; and although they could not hope to do such superfine shooting under battle conditions, nevertheless, such supremacy with the rifle should make itself felt under any and all conditions.

I have made a study of the American system of bayonet instruction and consider it very practical and effective. It has undoubtedly been evolved and adopted after a careful study of the American soldier's physical characteristics.

Wherever I have observed American troops, in the United States, Europe, or China, I have had to admire their strict observance of sanitary precautions and principles. It is without question, too, that they are the best-fed troops in the world, both in time of peace and under campaign conditions in the field. In France in 1918 I was very careful to remain close to units of the AEF, for they were the only troops at the front who were enjoying the luxury of plenty of white bread and sugar. In October 1929, while attending the 1st Cavalry Division maneuvers in Texas, I made it a point to dine at a company mess of a colored infantry regiment. The company commander showed me through the kitchens, storerooms, and barracks, and I was greatly impressed by the spotless cleanliness of bedding, dishes, and cooking utensils. The weekly menu was varied and included all necessary kinds of food for soldier consumption.

The schools of military thought among most nations agree that victory cannot be won without good infantry. History tells us, too, that good infantry has won more than its share of the world's victories. While that holds true, the Infantry of the United States should continue its habit of victory, for I rate it the most efficient and capable of all infantry.

It is a happy thought for a Japanese Army officer to recollect historical incidents when the colors of Japanese and American troops advanced together, side by side, in common effort for a common cause. War has interrupted many international friendships since the days when Japanese and United States infantry advanced under scathing fire against the Boxers on the walls of Tientsin, and there have been many international misunderstandings and differences since the troops of these two great nations fought shoulder to shoulder against irresponsible foes in Siberia. But whatever problems may confront them, however distant may be their national opinions on political or commercial activities, I can conceive of no eventuality that could strain the traditional friendship that has existed between the peoples of Japan and the United States since Commodore Perry ended Japanese isolation from the outside world. This friendship, this spirit of good will and mutual sympathy which has characterized the relations of the armed forces of these two great nations whenever the soldiers and sailors of America have been the guests or hosts of the soldiers and sailors of Japan, is the surest guarantee of perpetual concord and amity between two peoples who are achieving great and worthy destinies.

MY AMERICAN IMPRESSIONS

By Captain Takashi Aoki, Imperial Japanese Army

(1934)

It has been a little over a year since I first landed in San Francisco. Consequently I do not feel fully qualified to give my impressions of the

United States and Americans except in a general way. I shall, however, endeavor to write down my observations to the best of my ability.

Having come into close contact with the younger men of this country, I very quickly learned that flattery and pretense are far removed from their lives. Outspoken words and sincerity are much preferred. With this in mind I shall attempt to make a frank disclosure of my thoughts, concerning the United States and Americans, my own country and countrymen, and of the relations between the two nations.

The very first thing which impressed me, almost immediately upon landing, was the extreme kindness of everyone. I discovered for myself a spirit of kindliness and helpfulness among all the Americans with whom I came into contact.

A United States Army officer, who had been at one time attached to the American Embassy in Tokyo, was the first American to greet me when I arrived. His warmhearted hospitality greatly impressed me, untutored as I was at that time in the ways of Americans. He was not only a generous and gracious host but a wonderful help in acquainting me with the customs of his country. One bit of advice which he gave to me and which I have ever since striven to follow was "to forget all about Japanese customs and try to do as Americans do." At times it has been difficult to carry out this advice to the letter, not because I am unwilling or not anxious to do so, but because of the inherent difficulties in always knowing what an American would do under a given circumstance.

After a brief stay in San Francisco I went straight to Baltimore, Maryland. My purpose in doing this was twofold. First, to learn English, and second, to acquaint myself with American customs. In either event, because of the fact that few of my countrymen live in Baltimore, I was assured of the almost certainty that for three months I would not be embarrassed with having to tell a white lie by saying that I had forgotten how to speak Japanese! Needless to say, it was very difficult for me at first, as I spoke precious little English, and that badly. But it is amazing how, under compulsion, one quickly learns a language. With the aid of a map of the city, it was not long before I could tell many Baltimoreans of points of interest which they had never seen! Often, while poring over my map, some kindly stranger would volunteer assistance, and once I was even accompanied to my destination, to be certain that I did not go astray. To me Baltimore was a city of friendly people. Everyone seemed only too anxious to help me with my language difficulties. I was invited to various churches and there asked to speak. Unfortunately I was unable to accept these invitations to be a speechmaker because I felt the language handicap to be too great, even though I secretly longed to tell my American friends of my sincere appreciation for their wholehearted reception. Thus it went: trips to schools, an involuntary inspection of a large hotel, trips through department stores. Wherever I went everyone seemed only too anxious to explain things to me and at the same time to seek from me information concerning similar things in Japan. In short, my three months' stay in Baltimore was a round of learning and of gathering first impressions.

It was not long before I grew accustomed to the typical American frankness. I enjoyed it. It was an entirely new experience to me. This is because of the inherent reserve which is so much a part of all Japanese. To be otherwise than reserved, for a Japanese, is to be considered ill bred. It is perhaps because of this reserve that we Japanese are so often misunderstood by people on this side of the globe. As a national characteristic, since my sojourn in America, I much prefer the buoyant frankness of the typical American to the cold, quiet reserve which forms so much a part of the Japanese character. Perhaps in the course of time, when we have had more opportunity to meet Americans, this desirable attribute will find its mark in Japan and leave its impress upon the Japanese, who, quite unsuspectedly, also loves his good times, picnics, and good cheer. The typical Japanese reticence, I might say in passing, is the fruit of careful teaching from earliest childhood not to display one's thoughts or emotions. Possibly, also, this reticence, if we can call it such, is an outward manifestation of the tenets of our national religion.

After my stay in Baltimore I came to Washington, where I found a repetition of my experience in Baltimore. Again I found the same spirit of kindliness, of friendliness, and, above all, the same frankness. Perhaps I have been particularly fortunate in my contacts, although I doubt that they have been unusual. Generally speaking, all my friends, be they Army officers, Navy officers, or civilians, seem to have the same characteristics.

Surrounded as I am by a spirit of friendliness, it is at times difficult for me to realize that below the surface, in both America and Japan, a spirit of ill feeling is smoldering. It always seems so absurd to me that such a condition should continue and that some positive means are not undertaken in both countries to clear away the veil of suspicion which has been allowed to becloud the friendly relations between our respective countries. I think such suspicions come from mutual ignorance.

It does not seem strange to the majority of my American friends that they have never been in Japan; to them it seems quite natural. This is home, and consequently, if the Japanese wish to learn to know the United States and Americans, the Japanese should come here. But likewise, to the Japanese in Japan, it does not seem strange that they, the Japanese, have never been to America; Japan is home to them, and if Americans wish to know Japan and the Japanese they should visit Japan! In my opinion this simple reasoning, or lack of it, is the root of most of the trouble. If and when the two nations again resume that familiar intercourse which was so general during the second half of the last century and during the first decade of the present century, then and only then will the spirit of good will and friendliness once more be the keynote of American-Japanese relations.

Relations between countries cannot be judged by the use or non-use by one country of the materials of the other. Were this not so, American-Japanese relations would be the hue of a rainbow! I say this because in Japan, on every hand, we find a steady process of Americanization taking place. Everywhere we see evidences of the United States: modern concrete buildings, asphalt boulevards, traffic lights, automobiles, filling stations, soda fountains, taxicabs, and a thousand and one other things. For this reason it is at times difficult for me to grasp the real cause of the great stone wall of misunderstanding which has so mysteriously arisen.

I am of the opinion that this atmosphere of suspicion and mistrust has been, in part, fostered by a portion of the press in both countries. I hold no brief for the press of my country, for I realize that a portion of it is just as sensational and unfair toward America as a powerful portion of the American press is toward Japan. In both cases it is not difficult to discover the motive. The masses in both countries easily understand sensationalism, and the American bugaboo increases circulation as well as the Japanese hobgoblin. We saw in the World War how very powerful the press can be in controlling the thoughts of a people. It follows that the press, in a like manner, could be a powerful medium for bringing our countries toward a closer understanding.

Japan has known what it means to have America as its friend. We have not forgotten the opening of Japan by Commodore Perry; the patience of the United States during the perilous and troublesome forty years of the Restoration; the friendly spirit of encouragement during the Russo-Japanese War, or the generous sympathy shown by your good people during the Great Earthquake.

A Japanese proverb says that after a rain the ground becomes firmer. Since the present misunderstanding is shared by only a portion of the people of both America and Japan, the near future will prove it to have been a rain which has served to make the bonds of our friendship closer and stronger.

VII

Today's War

As the war approached and began, the *Infantry Journal* made no attempt to report upon the war in the same sense in which the great news magazines and the newspapers and radio do so. The editors felt that it was beyond the scope of the magazine to attempt a news coverage and that its main value to the Army and to the growing number of non-Army readers lay in concentrating upon editorial matters which might help Americans become better fighters but which naturally contained nothing of aid and comfort—only discouragement—for the enemy—discouragement at the measure of alertness and will to victory indicated.

At the same time, the magazine has been found worthy of wide quotation by other magazines and newspapers. This is not because it has been able to obtain any exclusive battle stories through the fact that it is under direct military supervision. It is simply because the editors, being military men, seek for sides of war in their articles which may be overlooked or considered of too technical an interest by other editors.

Naturally, also, the editors have tried to emphasize not only the reasons for the great fight—the War for the World—but the practical common-sense battle habits that enable ground soldiers and ground leaders to fight as efficient fighting men—the measures and methods that enable a soldier to kill a Jap or a Nazi soldier with the least reasonable battle hazard to himself.

The magazine has also presented what its editors call "tactical news," the detailed accounts of military operations. These follow the news as it appears through the regular channels anywhere from three to eight or nine months. These accounts, though they contain many technical military details, are presented in as clear and simple a style as possible. In this section of the Reader there are several such articles, and they do not require for their understanding any particular breadth of technical knowledge beyond what the average alert newspaper reader has gained from following the war news.

Above all, there has been no attempt in the *Infantry Journal* to prognosticate. There are too many military experts busy sticking their necks out at that job. Besides, the only ones who have a chance at coming near the mark are the few members of the high command who know all the details about our widespread forces and those of our Allies and the latest reports on the German, Jap, and other enemy forces.

THE WAR FOR THE WORLD

Editorial

(*1942*)

THE NEWS COMES IN from the fronts. Our American effort, and that of our Allies, grows greater and broader in its spread. The official news recounts to the nation in proper time the expanding operations of our forces at arms.

The commanding general of the United States Air Forces in India . . .

The American commanding general of Chinese forces in Burma . . .

The supreme commander of the forces of the United Nations in the Southwest Pacific . . .

The commanding general of the United States Army forces in the Far East . . .

These distant designations of battle authority, and others of land and air and ocean that might be added, we accept already with little amazement. Even a year ago most American minds would not have been able to span to such foreign fields. But there was no reason last year, or in any year of peace since the last war ended, for a military man not to think in such possible terms.

Siberia, Italy, Russia, the Far East, France—these are all places our armies campaigned in before this War for the World began. Hence there is no astonishment now in the minds of reflective Army men that our forces are spread so far. It had happened before. It might happen again. No military man worth his pay and allowances could basically think in other terms. Widespread thought of peace and hope for peace, and a wish in the hearts of men, Army men among them, that war might go from the world—these were not enough to make a soldier say, "It cannot happen again." His place of trust, his duty, his thought for his country compelled him to remember that it could. He might not hold this thought close in his mind in years when his duties were often narrow and his Army not encouraged to think or speak. But it seldom took more than a moment's reflection to bring back the thought—the hard and terrible thought—that armies might one day surge again across the face of the world.

By now we have seen on both faces of the world what fighting nations can do when they plan, in secret, to conquer, when they gather their forces for years and loose them furiously across and adown the continents as the hour and day arrive. By now we have seen again what soldiers always know can be done if nations with strength endeavor to do it.

The fury and speed of the blows this time have astonished even the soldier. But it is no new thought to his mind that forces at arms might advance and seize what they sought and charge over thousands of miles of water and land, driving ill-prepared foemen before them. He is not amazed to see it again.

For it has been done again and again. And soldiers remember that fact if others forget it. It's been done by armies with swords and spears or bows for their weapons, as well as by armies with guns. It has been done without gasoline or wings, and even without powder.

And now it has almost happened again. The Nazi armies have sped and struck till they gained the heart of Europe. They have to halt them and force them to rest and gather their means of war. The Pacific foe has charged down the Asian seas and struck from mainland to island, and island to island, till he seized the Indies and threatened still other islands and continents. But not with a full success. For the troops of China have held them—had held them for years on lines that lay to the east of Chungking. And the head of one of those Nipponese arrows stopped for long in its onward course when it struck the hard mountain lines on Bataan.

The thought that always sticks in the minds of Army men, the thought that has stayed in their heads through every restricted year of peacetime activity—that thought has come to be true. Again have conquerors tried to encircle the sides of the earth. Again have they planned and built and trained their troops for doing what armed forces under conqueror captains have done before.

And now American forces grow. And the news comes in of their spread to the farthest waters, skies, and fields. They go to attack and block, and attack and attack again. They go to find the Enemies of the World and strike at their hearts.

They go wherever they need to go to find the Enemies of the World. This is the War for the World.

HOW THE GERMANS TOOK FORT EBEN EMAEL

By LIEUTENANT COLONEL (now COLONEL)
PAUL W. THOMPSON

(1942)

THE GREAT FORTRESS of Eben Emael, keystone of the Belgian defense line, was considered by many military men to be impregnable to direct assault. It might be besieged and at long last starved out, but taken by storm quickly?—never. Yet *less than forty-eight hours after the German Army had crossed the Belgian border* the fourteen hundred officers and men of Eben Emael filed out of their subterranean fastnesses and surrendered.

Immediately an incredulous world clamored for an explanation. Fanciful accounts of a new gas which had paralyzed the garrison appeared in print. Mysterious super fifth columnists, who had tunneled up to the fortress from below, got a play in the press. The air was full of conjecture, and the list of Hitler's "secret weapons" received some choice additions. But popular theorizing finally gave out, and the Eben Emael disaster was left as the one great unsolved mystery of the war.

Military men, however, whose business it is to leave no mystery of war unsolved, continued to study the case. And at length they got at the truth.

Their starting point was the history of the *Sturmbataillonen Boehm,* the heavily armed assault groups with which Germany had experimented in attempting to break the stalemate on the Western Front in World War I. Before the present war military reports had indicated that the experiments were being continued and extended. At a dozen points along the invasion fronts of 1940 there was corroborative evidence of the use of specially trained and equipped troops. And so at last the truth became known—Fortress Eben Emael had been reduced by a revolutionary new use of that familiar military high explosive, TNT.

Now, more than two years after the fact, it is possible to reconstruct accurately the whirlwind assault which succeeded in obliterating Belgium's Gibraltar in a matter of hours.

Let us first draw a picture of the fortress itself. It occupied a commanding strategic position on a plateau near the Meuse River and the Albert Canal, controlling the approaches to both. Ultramodern in design, it consisted of a score of lesser forts scattered over an area about one mile square. These individual works were of steel, armor plate, and reinforced concrete, deeply embedded in the native rock and connected by a system of deep tunnels. Each work had large-caliber guns for blasting the distant approaches and machine guns for close-in defense. Each one, and the fortress as a whole, was protected by dense barbed-wire entanglements and belts of mines. Judged in the light of the time, Belgium was justified in feeling secure behind the fortifications anchored on "impregnable" Eben Emael.

But the Germans had been working ceaselessly on that idea born in World War I. Certainly they were familiar with many of the details of Eben Emael, and very likely their advanced experiments were made on full-scale replicas of the fortress. We can surmise that sometime prior to May 10, 1940, a final report was made that all was ready for the supreme effort.

On that dawn of May 10 the German juggernaut pushed across the defenseless borders, and the campaign that was to shake the world was under way. Columns of tanks moved slowly but ominously through the winding roads of Luxemburg toward Sedan. Parachutists dropped on Rotterdam. Infantry choked the highways. Overhead, airplanes filled the skies. Everywhere there was action; everywhere, power.

Into this vast scene, on that memorable morning, there moved a certain motorized battalion, a pin point lost in the great mass, but with the right of way on all roads leading toward the crossings of the Meuse and the Albert Canal at Maastricht—the back door to Eben Emael. It was a battalion of engineers—or, more precisely, of *demolition engineers*. And it was peculiarly reinforced, for there were also a company of infantry, a battery of anti-tank guns, a battery of small-caliber (20-mm.) antiaircraft guns, and a detachment of chemical troops.

This strange new outfit was, in effect, a small combat team. First, the demolition engineer—his outstanding characteristic is his ability to handle the deadly pale yellow trinitrotoluene, TNT. Second, the infantry component—ready to move in, to occupy, and to hold. Third, the anti-tank and antiaircraft guns—tremendous accuracy and penetrating power. Lastly, the chemical troops—expert in making smoke and flame. The significance of these different attributes will soon be apparent.

By nightfall of May 10 the demolition battalion had crossed the river and canal at Maastricht and reached the base of the plateau, atop which lay Fortress Eben Emael. Meanwhile, war had come to the fortress in no uncertain way. Dive bombers had attacked from dawn until noon. Precisely at noon a flight of transport planes had appeared low overhead and disgorged perhaps fifty parachutists, who took refuge in shell holes and established radio communication with the battalion.

That evening the Belgians no doubt felt shaken but by no means hopeless. The works had been designed to withstand just such punishment and were essentially undamaged. The net result of the bombardment had been to blast some of the obstacles, to explode many of the mines, and to pock the terrain with shell holes. Fortunately for their night's rest, the Belgians did not grasp the significance of that last item.

But at dawn on May 11 the German engineers began working their way up the slopes toward the plateau. The operation was difficult and hazardous. The Belgian guns were in full action. But for one vital item the attackers must have been swept from the plateau as rapidly as they reached it. That one item was the bombardment of the morning before—which, while not damaging the works, had left the fields a mass of shell holes. Into these ready-made shelters the attackers dived.

Now began the climactic phase of the entire operation: the *assault*. The immediate objective was to get the engineers up to certain selected works. To protect their advance the flat-firing anti-tank and antiaircraft guns delivered point-blank fire against the embrasures, trying to put out Eben Emael's "eyes." The chemical troops blinded adjacent supporting works by smoke. The infantry covered the embrasures with rifle and machine-gun fire and stood ready to move up and consolidate any success the engineers might gain.

There is no minimizing the hazards involved, and the losses among the engineers, as they bounded and crawled from one hole to the next, were heavy. These men resembled walking arsenals. Hand grenades—the familiar potato-masher type of the Germans—were sticking out of the tops of boots and from between the buttons of blouses. Around almost every neck was slung a canvas container bulging with seven-pound blocks of TNT. Each soldier carried a carbine or a sub-machine gun. Many pushed or pulled fifteen-foot lengths of narrow board to which were tied, end to end, other blocks of TNT. Others carried twenty-foot "charge-placing poles" which looked like elongated bricklayers' hods. Still others lugged flame throwers. All in all, it was a strange and grotesque assembly—but one in which every last detail was the result of innumerable trials.

The boards loaded with TNT were used, as they were in the first World War, to blast a way through the barbed wire. Each one blew a path perhaps twenty feet wide and also destroyed near-by mines.

All the while the guns on both sides were being fired as fast as the men could load them. The action must have been terrific. Occasionally there must have been a crash louder than normal—indicating that one of the engineers and his bagful of TNT had gone up. But the advance continued. And finally the surviving engineers reached the works. Here, oddly enough, right up against the fortifications themselves, they were comparatively safe. For a fortification is like a tank: it can deliver deadly fire on areas far to the front, sides, and rear, but there is a small area *immediately adjacent* to it which the guns cannot reach because they cannot be sufficiently depressed to reach targets just below them.

The works, however, were still intact, still strong, and still angry. And now began the action to which all that had gone before was simple preparation. Those throwbacks to medieval war, the flame throwers, opened up against the embrasures. The engineers unslung their sacks and fused up the blocks of TNT. From their points of vantage they began systematically to demolish the works by detonating the blocks of TNT against sensitive parts: embrasures, ports, turrets, joints, and doors. Obviously the task was not easy. The Germans used a variety of methods to accomplish it. Where possible they placed the charge by hand, set off a delay fuse, and took cover around a corner. In other cases the charges were given a shorter delay fuse and tossed into embrasures like hand grenades. In still other cases the TNT was placed in the hod end of a "charge-placing pole" and pushed into place.

If the action during the advance of the engineers was terrific, that which now was taking place defies description. The flame throwers were active; the German anti-tank and antiaircraft guns continued to fire; the Belgian guns continued to answer. Smoke and flame and crashing detonations—it is doubtful if the history of warfare has ever seen the like. In a few minutes the work of the TNT began to make itself felt. Here an embrasure went out of action; there a turret was jammed. As the Belgian ability to fire decreased, the German engineers redoubled their efforts and multiplied their effectiveness. The Belgian sands were running out.

The action was too violent, the effects too decisive, to continue for long. After several works had been put completely out of action the Belgian commander saw the hopelessness of the situation. His great fortress, able to command the approaches to a country, had fallen prey to a band of men armed, not with great howitzers and cannon, but with seven-pound blocks of TNT. Early on the afternoon of May 11 the fortress surrendered.

Perhaps the newspapers were not so wrong after all in speaking of a "secret weapon"; new use of an old weapon, a strange new *method*, can be as effective as something completely original. If there is something new under the military sun, this revolutionary *offensive* use of TNT is it.

The conventional defensive uses of TNT, however, are still of great importance—and no article dealing with high-explosive combat would be complete without a word about them. TNT is handy stuff for the demolition of structures which would be of help to the enemy. It can be placed on the structure—most often a bridge—days or weeks in advance and fired at any given moment. Thus a bridge may be "prepared for demolition" at the first sign of danger; may be used by friendly troops up until the last moment, and the switch pulled as the vanguard of the enemy heaves into view.

The decision as to exactly when to "let 'er go," however, can be one of the most onerous a commander has to face. He wants to hold the bridge as long as possible, on the chance that it may be of further use, yet he must think of the consequences if the bridge falls intact into enemy hands.

The Dutch took a long step toward dooming all Holland when they hesitated too long over the demolition of the great Moerdyk Bridge over the lower Maas. German parachutists (aided by fifth columnists) beat the Dutch engineers to the draw and seized the bridge. A day or two later the panzer units crossed it and sealed the fate of Rotterdam.

Of course there are also horrible examples of demolitions set off too early. Hell hath no fury like that of a general who comes up to a river to find that the bridge leading to safety has been blown five minutes before by his own engineers. Napoleon lost an important part of his last great army when his engineers prematurely blew the bridges over the Saale at the Battle of Leipzig.

A remarkable incident took place during the British retreat down the Grecian peninsula in the spring of 1941. The issue in Greece had been decided and the only course left to the British Imperials was retreat into the Peloponnesos peninsula over the single highway bridge across the Corinth Canal. As the British soldiers streamed across the bridge engineers prepared the vital structure for demolition. The detonation caps—each about the size of a cigarette—were carefully adjusted. Meanwhile, the Nazi dive bombers gave the bridge a wide berth. The Germans hoped to use it themselves.

On May 26 the Germans decided to seize the Corinth bridge intact. That morning hundreds of parachutists were dropped near by. The engineer lieutenant commanding the bridge guard and charged with demolishing the bridge "when necessary" thus was thrown on the horns of as cruel a dilemma as ever faced an officer on the field of battle. If he blew the bridge and the parachutists were mopped up, irreparable harm would be done. If he failed to blow it and lost it to the Germans, the resulting harm might be even greater.

The lieutenant's dilemma was resolved by the parachutists, who were in greater force than he knew and advanced more rapidly than he had believed possible. They actually succeeded in seizing the bridge intact. The lieutenant, however, managed to escape. He took refuge in a briar-covered recess along the steep banks of the canal, perhaps 150 feet away.

The Germans crowded onto the captured bridge and began methodically to look for the charges of TNT which they knew must be around somewhere.

The British lieutenant watched the search with great anguish. But suddenly he spotted one of the small detonating caps (remember, about the size of a cigarette). And so as the Germans continued their systematic search he raised his rifle to his shoulder, drew a careful bead on that tiny target, and let go. There followed a terrific explosion, a deafening crash. The lieutenant's aim had been true; the detonating cap had exploded and so induced the explosion of all the charges of TNT. Bridge and Germans lay in a tangled mass far below in the canal.

From Eben Emael to the Corinth Canal—between the two there stands the gap which separates the offense from the defense, the new from the old. But TNT is one implement of war that now is found in both camps and is used in both ways. The trusted friend of the defender has become, in addition, the lusty ally of the attacker. And, incidentally, it has made of the engineer an elite combat soldier.

WE KNOW OUR FOES

Editorial

(1942)

THE GREAT OBJECTIVE of ending the threat from the armed forces of international gangsters has been stated in the plainest and most forceful terms by our Commander in Chief. Rule by Nazi and Nipponese terror must be banished from this earth without chance of return. That is our aim and our job. And it's not a job we can finish offhand with a battle or two in a few months of fighting.

It is no news at all to the leaders of our Army that the Jap and the German are hard-fighting soldiers. They have had that name for a long time, even to the point of exaggeration. We knew the Boche for a fighter in our first war against him. And we know what the Nazi has done since he first began war in earnest. Of the Jap we know how he fought against Russia early in the century. We know of his wide experience of war in China since his first "so-sorry" act ten years ago. Indeed, we know from the beginning that the treacherous Pacific enemy, like the treacherous European enemy, is a fighting soldier. But we know, at the same time, he's not good enough to end what he's trying to do.

The fact that we're facing, to east and west, a foe in no way second-rate, who knows how today's warfare is fought because he has been long in the field, can mean no short, sharp series of victories and then the finish. It means our smashing of the Jap and his Nazi masters, a scrap that may last for years before we and our Allies have ended the job.

We remember, for one thing, that we're still building our Army, though it has great strength in men and machines already. We think, too, of the flow, only now running faster and faster, of guns, planes, tanks, and ships—a torrent of the tools of war in the end, but not for a while. And we think of this war in terms of thousands of miles of air and ocean—

but of air and ocean that shall be the paths to our victories even before our strength is full.

The war's history in Europe, and its beginning for us in the Pacific, has told us one other thing that must be burned into the brain of every American fighter. We're fighting enemies who play the dirtiest kind of pool. There is no treachery and trickery we cannot look for as we begin our assault to set the Rising Sun and bend the Swastika into a pretzel.

We know from the methods of the Nazis that the Axis powers have killed whatever honorable rules of conduct men once may have had for battle. And we've seen from what our Jap foes have done in China and from what they have striven with an insane frenzy to do against our own possessions and people that they have as little thought as the Nazis of fighting with what soldiers once thought of as honor. A fanatic fights with distortion and destruction in his mind, but he can plan efficiently at the same time to deliver his mad fanatic assaults against the world that holds the freedom he's been taught to hate.

Jujitsu is a prime example of the Jap's idea of fighting. As an experienced wrestling instructor once said, jujitsu is mainly dirty wrestling. It has in it every foul trick that is barred from the sports of wrestling and fighting in the ring.

Well, this war is a fight against Nazi and Nipponese fighters who know no rules. And so long as we remember it, and stay on guard, and use whatever it takes to knock such fighting out for the count, we'll win our battles, and with our Allies we'll clean up the face of the world.

We should not get the idea, either, that simply because the Jap is a little man, or the German traditionally a follower, or because our men and teams have consistently beaten them both in athletic events, they have any weakness in campaign or combat. The hardened Japanese soldier is tough, and so is the Nazi. But it's simply a toughness that comes through training—it's nothing they are born with. The German or Jap recruit, unless he happened first to be a worker or an athlete, is as soft and flabby as any. Indeed, his physical condition will not meet the average of the American soldier.

The Jap has the extra disadvantage of being a runt. But a runt who is strong can fight, as we know from experience in every sport. He can march and he can fight, and his smallness is no particular disadvantage in the air or on the sea. His runtiness also makes him cocky and makes him hate the taller races of the earth, even though there are tall Japs in some regions.

It's well to remember, too, that the Jap, for all his imitativeness and his failure to improve on the inventions he has taken from our civilization, believes with an unshakable faith that he's the best man on earth. Though we know that the Nazi thinks this way because he's been told it so often, it is something we in America seldom stop to think of concerning the Jap. We've been sure in our hearts that ours is the best way of life and the best land with the best people in it, despite our faults. We're sure of it now beyond doubt. But never does the average Jap—and certainly not the Japanese soldier—see an American, or an Englishman, or a Russian, or, for that matter, even a German, without looking down upon him in his mind as he looks up at him with his eyes. The little brown Jap is taught from his childhood that his is the superior race of the earth—that white men are bragging scum, unfit to step upon the ground of the islands where the sun also rises.

Not until such ideas die in their world, die in Europe and die in Asia, can our world take any time for breath. And we, with Britain and China and the other Allies who have joined and will join in the fight, are chosen to make those ideas die. No people ever had a work that meant more than ours, either to themselves or to this earth. No army and navy of a people ever had a prouder, more glorious aim in hand and mind and heart than ours now has.

From where we look to the west the sun doesn't rise—it sets. And one day, when the might of our arms and the strength of our purpose have reached six thousand miles to do what it must and should, the sun that rises on the desperate, fanatic power that calls itself Nippon shall sink behind islands that know at last their place in a modern world. The force of our arms, now beginning its fight, shall smash alike the little Jap and his master, the Nazi, till their toughness is tired out and softened again and their people have learned that the world is a place to be shared and built up, not grabbed and exploited.

But to smash the ideas and smack down the strength of the Nazi conquerors and the Nipponese would-be conquerors is probably a job of years. And whether of months or years or decades, we take it up, knowing it for the great task it is, and knowing our enemies for just what they are. We know them across the Atlantic and across the Pacific as treacherous, tough, fanatical foes. We know them as foes whose ideas cannot live in the end and whose ways and weapons of fighting can never in the end stand up to our own. The *heils* and *banzais* may be loud for a while. But before it's over they'll be drowned out forever by good American razzberries.

DEFENSE BEHIND THE SEINE

By Lieutenant Robert M. Gerard

Lieutenant Gerard, a French reserve officer, called to active duty in time to face the blitzkrieg and now an American citizen in the employ of the War Department, wrote of his battle experiences in a book called

Tank-Fighter-Team, from which this is a chapter, since the book appeared serially in the *Infantry Journal*. There were a number of French units which held together and fought desperately to the end of the Battle of France. Lieutenant Gerard's was one of these. His stirring story held particular value to military men because of the detail with which he described the fighting he saw.

AFTER ALL THE MOVEMENTS our Groupe Franc had made, which I have told about in the earlier parts of this account, its gasoline was running dangerously low. My captain, accordingly, decided to send me with two gasoline trucks to get some more, wherever I could find it. We could no longer count on supplies coming up from the rear. We could only count on ourselves.

I left on June 10 at three in the morning with two drivers and two other men to help. At one gas station after another we found the pumps empty. We tried all the gas stations from Bourtheroulde to Pont Audemer and all those in Pont Audemer itself—but no gas. I then gave up as far as that particular area was concerned and decided to drive straight south for thirty miles, without stopping, to reach Lisieux, a good-sized town with a big Standard Oil tank depot near it.

There was nobody at the depot except two or three workers and an old French janitor. I told him I wanted a thousand gallons of gasoline for our Groupe Franc, whereupon he asked me to give him a blue requisition slip, Form No. 3. I had none, of course, and told him so, but "No slip, no gas," was all I could get out of him. I tried argument and even pleaded with him, telling him that if I didn't get the gas he alone would be responsible for the death and capture of the men of our Groupe Franc, who were, after all, defending him. But he could not rise from his long life of routine and Forms No. 3 to conceive a different world.

I finally cut things short, pulled my revolver out, and said I would shoot him if he didn't give us the gas. He just about collapsed but had strength enough left to call me a gangster. But we got the gas. And not just a thousand gallons but fifteen hundred gallons more in big barrels, more even than my two trucks could quite carry. I had also learned one fast way to cut red tape.

We then headed back toward the north and the front. On the running board of each truck I kept a man standing and constantly watching the sky for planes. It seemed a good idea not to be caught without warning while we were still in the gasoline trucks.

In a short time we were driving against the flow of refugees, and as we passed through Brionne there were houses still burning from a bombardment a short while before. As we came to Bourtheroulde, however, the refugees and fleeing troops grew fewer and fewer. "The Germans are already in Bourtheroulde," some of them cried. But they all seemed in a state of semihysteria, and in such a state false rumors spread at terrific speed. We did advance very slowly toward Bourtheroulde but found no enemy. Our Groupe Franc was still there. And the men acclaimed the arrival of more gas as if it had been gold. In short order it was distributed to the vehicles.

The captain then decided to move his headquarters platoon to a small hamlet off the main road, two miles to the southwest of Bourtheroulde, where the vehicles would be more secure. That morning he had sent two patrols, each consisting of an armored car and a few motorcycles, to La Bouille and to Elbeuf. But not a single German had they seen. The enemy was still not attempting to cross the Seine.

In the afternoon of that day (June 10) my captain received information from division headquarters that supposedly sixty German parachutists had just landed to the south of the Seine, in the loop below Rouen, and had sought cover in the woods of the Forêt de Rouvray. The captain decided to send me there to find out what the situation actually was. There were only a few sidecar motorcycles left. So I got only one for the job. But my driver and I were equipped. Each of us had a light machine gun and two revolvers, and several hand grenades besides. And as my captain put it before we left, if I didn't get back within three hours he would know that there were parachutists in the Forêt de Rouvray.

We followed a small dirt road winding through the woods. Our motorcycle noisily advertised our approach, and if there were any parachutists posted along the road it was not going to be hard for them to kill us. I rode with both feet hanging outside the "bathtub," ready to hit the ditch along the road. As we approached every curve we stopped to observe and listen intently. But not a sound. And not a German. We kept on toward Rouen and reached the suburbs. And then we took a small street leading to the Seine. The whole city was deserted. At the river we dismounted and watched the far bank where the two bridges, now demolished, had led. As we did this we held our light machine guns in our arms like two movie gangsters. But still we saw no German soldier. After a little we jumped in our sidecar and headed back full speed on the straight main road. What headquarters had told us was just another false rumor.

Not far out of Saint-Ouen and Bourtheroulde we were suddenly stopped by a group of French infantrymen hidden along the road. They sprang out at us with light machine guns and rifles at the ready. The sergeant in charge announced that I was under arrest, and they all surrounded us, looking as if they meant serious business. I told them that I was a French officer from the Groupe Franc coming back from a reconnaissance, but they did not believe me. I showed my officer's card with my fingerprints and photograph, but they were still suspicious. They took us to the young infantry lieutenant in command of their platoon. He, too, was fully as suspicious. In the end we were dragged to the lieutenant colonel commanding the infantry battalion, who recognized me, as I had met him the day before. Apparently these troops, misled by our special equipment and particularly by the new armored-force helmets we were wearing, padded in front with leather, had mistaken us for German parachutists. Back in Bourtheroulde I reported the negative results of my patrol.

To my great astonishment I found there the commander of the tank platoon whom I had thought killed in Rouen. He was the one who had gone out with his tank to hit the rear of the German column north of Rouen. His attack had been a successful surprise. He had destroyed three German tanks, then retreated full speed. A little later he had attacked the flank of the tank column that was in the city itself and got two more enemy tanks, about the time we had been fighting those same tanks hardest with our anti-tank guns. His tank was hit once, in the left of the cupola, but this did not disable it. He could still fire the gun, however, and managed to get hits on two more German tanks.

Then he had heard the two explosions of the bridges and decided he might be able to get back across the Seine with his tank on one of the ferries. The ferry at La Bouille had been destroyed, so he went as far as Caudebec and was amazed not to encounter a single enemy column all the way. At Caudebec he found the ferry still operating but had a hard time putting his tank on it, though he finally got it aboard. In the middle of the Seine the ferry was machine-gunned by a lone bomber, but three RAF pursuit planes which suddenly appeared opened on the German plane and drove it away.

Landed safely on the south side of the Seine, the tank-platoon commander had to spend all the next day (June 9) hunting for some gasoline. He kept asking all fleeing troops and refugees whether they had seen a French motorized unit with our Groupe Franc numeral painted in white on the sides of the vehicles and was finally directed to Bourtheroulde. He had some trouble, he reported, dodging colonels who wanted to commandeer his tank to ride in as they retreated to the south.

I had just about time to hear this story when some German bombers came in sight. Not far away from where I was there was an old 75-mm. gun in position, guarding one of the roads to the town. The officer in charge of it had lost his unit in the general retreat and had offered his services to my captain, who had gladly accepted. The German planes had first dropped a few bombs on the central square of the town near the church. Suddenly, as they came directly overhead, a man left a small group of refugees not far away and ran toward the 75-mm. gun, waving a white cloth. One of the planes saw it, diving straight on the gun, which was well camouflaged and had apparently not been seen from the air before. The plane released three bombs, one after the other, and got the small crew of the 75 and the officer. But it also killed the fifth columnist, too, in the middle of his dirty work. The gun was no longer usable.

That same night we heard a sudden shot in the street of the village. On investigation we found one of our men lying dead, with his papers gone and the identification plate on his wrist likewise stolen. By now this continual fifth-column activity had gotten thoroughly on our nerves. We began to hate such activities more than anything else, except attacks from the air.

The next morning, June 11, came one of the best surprises of the whole campaign. On a stolen bicycle, dirty, unshaved, and exhausted, the first lieutenant who commanded our 25-mm. anti-tank-gun platoon, and whom we had also thought had been killed in the Battle of Rouen two days before, came riding into Bourtheroulde. He told us, moreover, that ten miles from Bourtheroulde there were thirty infantrymen whom he had brought back from the north side of Rouen, and also the remnants of our anti-tank-gun crews—a few, like himself, who had survived the blowing of the bridges and the German artillery fire. At once we gave him two trucks to bring these men back to us.

When he returned two hours later, the lieutenant explained that the blowing of the bridge had put his anti-tank guns out of commission and killed nearly everyone in their crews. Those still alive had luckily found the men of the infantry platoon. Together they all marched toward the west along the banks of the Seine. A few miles out from Rouen they found a barge that would float. On this they got across to the south side, fifteen miles from Rouen, between Duclair and Caudebec. They marched from there toward Pont Audemer, inquiring as they went about our Groupe Franc. But soon they were so exhausted that the lieutenant ordered them to rest and continued the search himself with a commandeered bicycle, in the end finding us in Bourtheroulde.

Almost unbelievably our Groupe Franc was now regaining some of its past strength. We were now five officers and about 120 men. The infantrymen had brought back four of their six heavy machine guns, and this boosted our fire power a little. On the other hand, we had a new and serious problem because these thirty additional men had lost all their trucks—all transportation of every kind—and we could only cram them in the few vehicles we had left. But this, compared to the joy of getting them back, was a small thing.

What we were concerned about more deeply was our ammunition. It was low, after our battles at Boos and Rouen. But I got word from some retreating British that there was an abandoned munitions train on one of the railroad tracks near La Bouille in the middle of the forest. Immediately I took one of our trucks and four men to the spot, where we found the train. Near its front part and its rear part were enormous bomb craters, but by some miracle the attacking Nazi planes had missed the part that carried the ammunition. I posted a man in front of the train and another in its rear to give the rest of us warning with their whistles if any plane approached.

The bomb craters, the half-demolished train, the dead silence of the place, the lack of human activity gave us the feeling that we were far from substantial military protection and exposed to any sudden attack. Nervously we opened door after door of the freight cars. This took time, for the doors were all sealed. We looked rapidly inside each car to see whether it had the boxes of ammunition in it. All the first cars we opened contained artillery shells for 155-mm. and 75-mm. guns.

Suddenly one of the men whistled three times. We dashed across the tracks and under the train into the woods on the other side as three planes came over. They let go a few bombs in level flight but missed the ammunition train. We let our breaths out, crawled back again to the train, and in a few minutes more found what we wanted. We jammed one truck full as fast as we could, took the load back to the Groupe Franc, and then made a second trip to load the second ammunition truck. During the time we had three alerts and had to hit cover three times, but no bombs were dropped on us.

When we came back from the wrecked ammunition train the second time the Groupe Franc was about ready to leave Bourtheroulde for a small village, some fifteen miles to the west, called Bourneville. During the movement I performed the job of *serre-file*, that of the officer who is last in the column and sees to it that no vehicle is lost and that those with motor troubles get repaired and catch up. But no vehicle had such trouble this time. The mechanics had spent all night overhauling their motors and checking all possible weaknesses. Several Nazi planes machine-gunned us on the way to Bourneville, but their aim was bad and we had no casualties.

According to the reports of our patrols, there were still no signs that the enemy had tried a crossing anywhere in our sector. We had sent patrol after patrol along the Seine all day, in rotation, of course, to enable our men to get some rest. We now had to rely on continuous reconnaissance of this type because we had lost our radio truck in the bombardment of Bourtheroulde, which had been a major blow for the Groupe Franc. Without a radio truck we were continually losing contact with our armored cars and tanks during their march, and we were cut off from information from higher headquarters except for the news brought by the few motorcycle scouts that we could keep stationed at corps headquarters to bring us orders and new information on the latest developments.

Late in the evening of June 11 we arrived at Bourneville, a charming little village still full of refugees. It had not been bombed. We immediately felt better because of this peaceful atmosphere, even though the degree of danger here was exactly the same as it had been at Bourthe-roulde. We were lucky to find there also a few lambs and sheep, which we killed and ate with much delight. No food, of course, was reaching us from the rear, and we were getting sick of eating our *pain de guerre,* a very dry hardtack, and the cans of *singe* ("monkey meat" or canned beef) which we had in our supply truck. We were even luckier to find four hundred pounds of flour in the town bakery, and we immediately detailed two men to make some bread. For the next two days these men made bread without taking a single minute of rest. It tasted better than any bread I ever ate in my life.

We camouflaged our trucks in two orchards as soon as we arrived in the village. Beginning at once, also, and all during the night, the men constructed road blocks on all roads at the outskirts of the village. We took over the central switchboard at the post office simply by telling the girl in charge that the Germans were approaching full speed—another way of cutting red tape. She left at once, scared to death. Once an hour during the night we sent a patrol, on foot, around the village, mainly to listen. In the village the patrol saw to it that there were no lights, not even a match or a cigarette.

The next morning, June 12, my captain and I went around the village to determine the best emplacements for the heavy machine guns of the motorized-infantry platoon. We were walking along a little dirt road just outside of the village when suddenly, not fifty yards away, a man appeared and aimed a sub-machine gun directly at us. We threw ourselves into the ditch along the road as bullets whistled past our ears, automatically pulling our revolvers as we did so. My captain killed the German with his second shot. When we examined the fifth columnist and his little gun we found that he had fired some sixty bullets at us. This Mauser sub-machine gun of the Germans is a very inaccurate weapon, though its use had a marked psychological effect on the population. We found no identification papers on the German, only a map of the region. It was more detailed than the official French military maps we were using.

Since German fifth columnists were apparently mingled in with French refugees, my captain decided to take stern measures. We prepared a lot of small notices and pasted these on the walls of the village. The notice declared that to avoid any possibility of fifth-columnist activity and enable us to prepare our defense without being hampered by refugees, the commander of the Groupe felt compelled to order every civilian to leave the village within an hour. After two hours had passed any civilian found in the village without good reason would be locked up and, if there seemed grounds for it, shot. During the rest of the campaign we executed several. We may have made a mistake or two, but most of them were, in all probability, fifth columnists, and all others had been warned. Until we took this stern action, no matter how well our vehicles had been camouflaged, German bomber pilots always seemed to know where they were hidden. But from then on we suffered very few bombings in any village we defended. I feel, therefore, that the drastic measures taken by my captain were justified.

Bourneville was to be the headquarters of our Groupe Franc. We were not only assigned to defend this village, but also were assigned to protect a line behind the Seine that had a front of about twenty-five miles— from La Bouille near Rouen to the sea. To hold any such front with 120 men was practically an impossible task. If the enemy tried to cross by force it was evident we could not prevent them from doing so. We could, however, hinder their preparations on the far bank and could probably repulse any crossing attempted by a weak reconnaissance force. Our main mission, however, was that of warning the division headquarters of any crossing attempt. Thus we were, in effect, the rear guard of the French division. What puzzled me during that time was the fact that none of us had ever seen this division. Was it a myth, a ghost, or just a bunch of men too afraid to fight in the front lines? Or was it just retreating slowly on foot to new positions? I found out on June 18, a few days later, when I actually saw the men in the division surrounded.

A company of customs officers on bicycles, retreating from the coast, came into our area. They wore vivid blue uniforms with a red stripe down their pants. Their commander had very little push, and my captain persuaded him to stay with us, telling him he would have nothing to do, that my captain would take care of everything. We naturally welcomed any reinforcements as long as they would stay with us.

We set up our defense in the following manner. All along the banks of the river we posted these 300 customs officers with their rifles. (They had no machine guns.) Thus they were used as a line of sentries or scouts about 150 yards apart. Every two or three miles a sidecar or a solo motorcycle from the Groupe Franc was posted. If one of the customs officers saw the enemy trying to cross the Seine or preparing to make such a crossing, he was to fire several shots with his rifle to attract the attention of the motorcyclist, who would at once go to the place where the shots came from and then report to the headquarters of the Groupe Franc on the situation. At certain places the motorcyclist could use a telephone near by instead of racing to headquarters.

We installed the headquarters of our Groupe Franc in the post office of Bourneville. The town lay several miles south of the Seine behind a deep forest, and we made it the strong point of our defense, preparing its immediate defenses with mechanized attack mainly in mind. For the fixed defenses of the village the captain used the motorized-infantry platoon, the several road blocks, and a 47-mm. anti-tank-gun platoon under the energetic young artillery officer who had lost his unit and offered his services and those of his platoon to my captain instead of fleeing to the south, like most of the rest of the army. His two anti-tank guns, with their prime movers and the one cargo truck with them, were a great help to us and made up for our losses in the fight at Rouen.

The most essential part of our defense was the mobile reserve formed of two armored cars, the motorcycle platoon, and our three remaining tanks. The armored cars and motorcyclists were used also to effect numerous reconnaissances to the east, in order to cover our right flank if the Germans crossed the Seine east of Rouen. Our three tanks were ordered to go back and forth along the south bank of the Seine. Once an hour one of the tanks left La Bouille in the direction of Quillebeuf, moving along the Seine, stopping often to observe the other bank, and firing at any Germans who were sighted. The tank would come back to La Bouille again after a few hours. Thus our three tanks were constantly scouting along the Seine at different points, toward different directions. We hoped by using them that way to give the enemy the impression that there was a sizable mechanized force on the south side of the Seine and thus make them hesitate to attempt a crossing. I doubt very much whether we actually fooled the Germans, but at least if they attempted a crossing our fire would certainly harass them and slow them up. If the enemy tried to cross anywhere our three tanks were to assemble full speed and concentrate their fire on the point the customs-officer sentries indicated.

I did a good deal of that back-and-forth business in a tank myself because the tank-platoon commander was worn out and needed a rest. On the first day I saw nothing of the enemy, driving all the time with my turret open. Nor did our patrols to the east report any Germans either. When night came we drove our three tanks back to Bourneville, and that first night I stayed near the telephone with my captain.

About two o'clock in the morning (June 13) the telephone rang, and one of the motorcyclists told us that between Duclair and Caudebec a German motorized-infantry column was moving along the north bank of the Seine on the road that followed the river. Some of the customs officers had fired across at them to give the alarm, and at once the enemy had returned the fire, using tracer bullets of all possible colors—red, white, blue, yellow. The effect on the customs officers of seeing that kind of show was terrific; they had never seen such a thing. Half an hour later another motorcyclist phoned. The German column, he said, was still advancing to the west along the riverbank and was now keeping up a terrific noise for the purpose, he thought, of scaring our defending troops. The enemy would send a red rocket into the sky, and the whole column would stop dead. Then a green rocket would go up, and the column would resume its march. They also used white and yellow rockets for some purpose, and the whole performance was more than puzzling. From our own side of the Seine our motorcyclists and customs officers could hear officers shouting orders in German and even the enemy troops singing Nazi songs. The few customs officers who took up fire with their rifles didn't seem to bother the column, which was returning their fire with tracer bullets, now from machine guns. But daylight approached without any attempt by the enemy to cross the river.

At five o'clock that morning I again left Bourneville with my tank and resumed scouting along the Seine, but with much more care than before, because we knew for sure now that enemy troops were on the other side. Beyond Duclair I saw a few Germans but no vehicles. I systematically shelled their general area with the high-explosive shells of my 47-mm. gun and must have killed a few. I opened fire from a defiladed position with good protection against anti-tank-gun fire. But apparently the German force had no anti-tank guns with it and only returned the fire with small automatic arms. That kind of fighting continued at intermittent periods all during the day.

I learned later why the Germans had not appeared on the north side of the Seine right after our battle in Rouen. Contrary to our belief, the panzer division whose reconnaissance units we had met in Boos and Rouen did not stay along the Seine but headed northwest toward the sea and reached the sea at Saint-Valery-en-Caux, a little southwest of Dieppe, thus completely encircling the French and British troops retreating from the Somme River. Only when they had partly cleared up this pocket did the German motorized infantry turn south to take position along the lower part of the Seine between Rouen and the sea.

During the afternoon of June 13, as I arrived opposite Caudebec, I saw that the whole town was in flames. The Germans had just bombed the place. And all along the road leading to the ferry were hundreds of abandoned automobiles, all on fire with flames leaping into the sky. On my way back to Bourneville early that evening, I met a few British who had built a beautiful road block on the road my tank was following in the middle of the forest. They had two anti-tank rifles to defend it but were preparing to leave, which they soon did. They left a lot of equipment behind, which we salvaged eagerly the next day—excellent motorcyclists' goggles, some good light raincoats, and especially the two anti-tank rifles which they had evidently decided were too heavy for them to carry in their hasty retreat. We liked that particular anti-tank weapon, of which our army had none. It was called the Boys rifle from its inventor and was of caliber .55, weighing around thirty-six pounds with its bipod rest. It was effective against lightly armored vehicles at short distances.

I spent the night again at the telephone with my captain. One rumor after another to the effect that the Germans had crossed the Seine east of Rouen came to us over the phone. Louviers, a bridgehead on our side of the Seine, south of Pont de l'Arche, was reported in German hands. The German column was advancing at night toward the east, toward us, we were also told. To determine the part of reality and the part of fantasy in those rumors was impossible except by sending out our own patrols. At two in the morning a colonel telephoned us from division headquarters. He said a German column was already a few miles from Bourneville, in Bourtheroulde, our last previous position. If this was true our position with our right flank exposed was now untenable. The colonel wanted a patrol sent at once to confirm this information. My captain told him that to send out a tank at night on such a mission was hardly desirable. The tank couldn't see anything anyway and could be taken in ambush. It was finally decided to send a tank and a few motor-cycles with machine guns at dawn. My captain told me that I had been inside a tank enough during the past two days and that I should there-fore wake up the tank-platoon commander and direct him to take charge of the patrol. In view of the importance of this patrol my captain decided to send an entire motorcycle platoon with its commander.

This patrol left Bourneville at four-thirty on the morning of June 14. We waited and waited, until an hour later one of the men of the motor-cycle platoon reported by telephone. The patrol had been mistaken for a German column by the French artillery still in Bourtheroulde, which had opened fire. Several men were wounded, and the tank-platoon commander was dying. The motorcycle-platoon commander asked us to send a truck at once to transport the wounded to the nearest hospital or ambulance. My captain sent me with a truck and telephoned division headquarters to send two ambulances at once to Bourneville. Arriving in front of Bourtheroulde, I saw the disabled tank near the road. In Bourtheroulde itself I found the motorcycle-platoon commander, who told me the story very briefly.

The tank commander with his tank was out in front of the motor-cycle platoon. He was fired at without warning from the outskirts of Bourtheroulde. Thinking it was enemy fire, he quickly returned it. The motorcycle platoon dismounted and sought cover in the ditches along the road, opening on the supposed enemy with their machine guns. The "Germans" were firing a 77-mm. or 75-mm. gun, well camouflaged. Its high-explosive shells burst near the motorcycle platoon. The tank kept on firing shells at the gun, using fire and movement, stopping only to fire. After a couple of minutes the tank received a direct hit on its front, and the shell penetrated the tank as if through butter. Fragments of armor cut the left arm off the driver and tore the gunner's right shoulder apart. Another piece went through the tank-platoon commander's helmet into his head.

The motorcycle platoon advanced along the road in the ditches, ap-proaching the village, to determine the strength of the enemy forces, but they finally discovered that the enemy was French. Our tank had killed two men of the artillery gun crew. The tank commander was in bad shape when I arrived with the truck and was plainly dying. I carried the wounded back to Bourneville as fast as I could, and from there they were taken to the rear in two ambulances.

The mistake had occurred partly because of the morning fog. The artillerymen couldn't determine whether the tank was French or German. Our tanks had the blue-white-and-red circle of the Republic, and German tanks had the Iron Cross painted on the front of the tank. But the Germans had used French colors so many times that this means of identification was of little practical value. Since the French had so little mechanized equipment left in the area, the artillerymen could hardly be wrong in assuming that any mechanized equipment they would see would be German. The real reason for the mistake was because the crews of the artillery anti-tank guns had never had any thorough training in identifying the silhouettes of the different types of French, British, and German vehicles. And of course the lack of liaison between division headquarters and this particular artillery unit gave rise to the rumors that the Germans were there in Bourtheroulde and prevented the artillery unit from being warned in time that a French mechanized patrol was approaching.

The tank commander was also somewhat at fault. He would probably not have been killed if he had stayed with his tank along the edge of the woods west of Bourtheroulde and sent a few motorcycles to reconnoiter the village before he exposed his tank in the perfectly flat, open area between the woods and the village. With hindsight, however, it is always easy to criticize an action that has proved disastrous. Anyway, the result was a serious blow to the Groupe Franc. We now had only two armored cars and two tanks left as armored equipment. We had also lost a few sidecar motorcycles, destroyed by the 75-mm. fire in the same fight.

Shortly after I had come back to Bourneville we received an order from headquarters to retreat again. Other rumors that the Germans had crossed the River Seine east of Rouen had been confirmed by other units. Our movement had to be effected quickly, otherwise a German column advancing generally toward the southwest would cut our retreat. Our Groupe Franc was ordered to go to Campigny and establish its headquarters in this little village a few miles southeast from Pont Audemer and prepare a defense behind the Risle River. The French Army as a whole was abandoning the Seine as a defensive position.

What made us smile a bit at this news was that, as far as we had been able to see, the Seine had never been defended by French forces at all, except for a few rear-guard units like our own. All during the time we had been making reconnaissance after reconnaissance from one position after another behind the Seine, our division had been stationed back there behind the Risle, building a few road blocks. And now that the Seine line had been dented, our division was leaving the Risle and we were to take their place there. Things went this way, in fact, up to June 18, when the division was surrounded. During the whole time it did not fire a single shot to the best of our knowledge. For its own retreat, the division was lucky enough to have great numbers of Paris busses which the army had requisitioned. Without those busses it would probably have been captured a few days sooner.

My captain used our two tanks to protect the rear of our column as we dropped back from Bourneville to Campigny. The two armored cars, with what was left of the motorcycle platoon, protected our flanks by making small reconnaissances out on side roads, coming back to the main road after the column had passed. Thus the column had a mobile anti-tank defense on its flanks and rear. No hasty road blocks were built on the side roads because this would take too much time and work. Instead, my captain relied on the armored cars to repulse any small German mechanized column during the time it would take to re-establish the Groupe Franc quickly in a new defensive position. Preceding the column within sight were the solo motorcyclists, acting as scouts.

My captain decided to give me one of the two tanks to command. I was ordered to stay till the last in Bourneville—until ten o'clock in the morning, with the Groupe Franc leaving at nine-thirty. I waited near the east entrance of the village—the Germans were expected to come from the east near the crossroad of the main east–west and north–south roads—so that I could move my tank quickly in any direction.

On the road leading to the east we had built a stout road block by digging holes in the asphalt road and then sticking thick logs vertically in the holes. We had found this work half completed by some previous unit, with logs all cut and ready to be placed, and we had had time to finish it. The road block was of the staggered barricade type, to permit the traffic to flow through it. But at night, or if the enemy came in sight, the barricade could be closed by movable obstacles, such as abandoned vehicles and sliding beams. Just beyond this barricade the road turned to the right in a curve. An anti-tank gun had been defending this barricade but was now retreating with the main column. There were similar barricades on the roads leading south and north. We left them all open so that I could pass through them with my tank and attack the enemy if he came in sight.

At ten o'clock sharp, just as I was preparing to leave Bourneville with the tank, a German armored car drove suddenly into sight on the road from the east, stopped dead in front of the barricade, apparently saw my tank, and began to move back in reverse. It was not more than 150 yards away, and I fired and got a hit on it before it could get back around the curve in the road. This was probably the point, I thought,

of a whole armored-car platoon. And so I also said to myself, "Let's go!"
I then took my tank slowly out through the barricade, firing once more
at the armored car without stopping, but hitting it again. It hadn't fired
a single shot at my tank. It didn't have time to.

We now went out on the road beyond the disabled armored car and
moved on around the curve of the road. And there a second car was
heading toward the village to help the other. This was too good. I had
nothing to fear, anyway, as I knew the 20-mm. anti-tank gun on the
enemy armored car could not pierce my armor. It was much like a
battleship fighting a light cruiser. The moment this new German saw me
he headed toward a side road to escape my fire. He opened fire himself,
and a direct hit clanked on our armor but didn't come through. I had
been right in feeling safe. After firing twice myself this second armored
car was out of business. Several enemy motorcyclists following it had
pulled off to the left of the road and were firing at me with their
machine guns—probably with armor-piercing bullets. Several of them
hit the tank but didn't penetrate either. I continued on toward these
motorcyclists, leaving the road to do so, and now firing high-explosive
shells. I know I got several of them.

I headed back onto the road but couldn't see any other enemy cars
or troops. The rest of the armored-car platoon had probably decided
to pull back—the proper tactics for lightly armored vehicles in the face
of a medium tank. I decided not to follow for fear of an ambush. It
was well past ten o'clock now, and I had orders to stay only till ten.
And so I headed back to the village, passing the two disabled armored
cars and firing one good shot at each of them. It was probably pure waste
and child's play, but it made me feel good. All things considered, I had
nothing to brag about. Anyone in a medium tank could have destroyed
those two armored cars. But I don't think I would have been able to
destroy them at all if the enemy platoon commander had sent his motorcyclists out ahead to reconnoiter the village. I would probably have got
one or two of his motorcycle scouts but nobody else. His armored cars
would have had time to take cover.

Before leaving Bourneville I had my gunner and my driver close the
barricades. I stayed in the tank, covering them, ready to shoot, for by
now the Germans were probably preparing an attack on the village.
I had had a chance to fulfill my mission of slowing down the German
reconnaissance elements and thus give the Groupe Franc more time to
prepare its defense behind the Risle River. This made me feel a little
better than I had for several days. I had made up a little for my poor
marksmanship in our Battle of Rouen.

When I arrived in Campigny I found our two anti-tank guns already
in position in the village and road blocks half completed. My captain
decided to return the tank to its noncommissioned officer, who was in good

shape again. But I must have been bad luck for any tank I touched. The tank commander had been killed in my tank the very morning he took charge of it again. This time the noncommissioned officer of the tank was killed the next day by a bomb from a Stuka which penetrated his turret.

In Campigny my captain had installed the headquarters of the Groupe Franc in a small castle situated in the middle of a big park in which all the vehicles had been well concealed and camouflaged under the trees. For the first time in several days I now found the time to shave and wash my hands and face. In the afternoon I went around the village, supervising the work done on road blocks and on the anti-tank-gun and machine-gun emplacements. We had ordered all refugees out of the village.

At three o'clock I was sent in my sidecar to division headquarters, which had not given any orders since we had arrived in Campigny. I found the headquarters at Carsix, thirty miles to the south in a castle! The staff was standing around big maps, planning the withdrawal of the division to a new position. The Groupe Franc was again to be the last to move.

Shortly after I got back to Campigny several enemy bombers came over. I was in the middle of the town, and there was no time to seek cover in the woods that lay around the village. So I decided to go into the cellar of the nearest house. I found there one of my noncommissioned officers, a placid fellow who never seemed to be bothered by anything. He hadn't shaved for a week, and now, having some time to think about it, he went upstairs in the house, hunted around, and came back down in a few minutes with an old square mirror, an old blade and razor, and some soap. He hung the mirror on a nail and began shaving. By then the bombs were coming down, with attack apparently centered on the park and our vehicles. Some more good fifth-columnist information, I thought. But now the bombs were coming much nearer. It was funny to watch my noncom trying to shave. He had kept his helmet on as a precautionary measure. Every time a bomb fell a little nearer his mirror swung on its nail, and plaster fell from the ceiling. But he kept on shaving, unperturbed, until a terrific crash came and I thought for one moment it was the end of things for us both. Plaster came pouring down, covering us. A part of the ceiling above us broke. But the hit was not quite direct, and we were still safe even though the house above had been partly destroyed. My noncom, with razor still in his right hand, was now white with plaster. He slowly turned toward me and said very calmly, "The only trouble with this damn war is you can't even shave in peace!"

The planes dropped a few more bombs and left. They had destroyed many houses in the village. I now headed toward the park and saw that two of our trucks were demolished. One was a gasoline truck, and the men were busy keeping the flames from spreading. On the outskirts of the village one of our anti-tank guns had also been destroyed and some of its crew killed. Decidedly our Groupe Franc was getting smaller and smaller with each day.

Next morning, June 15, we got the order to withdraw once more, this time about sixty miles to the south, to Argentan. But before our Groupe Franc left it must blow up the two bridges on the Risle: one at Saint-Paul-sur-Risle, the other at Pont Audemer. Our tanks, armored cars, and sidecar motorcycles had been patrolling along the south bank of the river all the preceding afternoon but had seen no Germans. The enemy was, however, expected any minute. Our movement to the south had been ordered because the French Army was expected to make its next big stand along the Loire River.

The order to blow the two bridges was a perfect example of an impossible task. If even one staff officer from headquarters had visited the Groupe Franc since it left Rouen, the division commander would have known that we had no explosives. And so my captain sent a motorcycle scout back to tell them that we would have to be given some explosives if we were to do the job. We did have several tank mines and a few *pétards de cavalerie,* but it would take a good deal more to blow two bridges. The messenger came back an hour later to report that headquarters had already gone.

We had to do something. For the protection of our Groupe Franc itself we couldn't leave the bridges merely with a barricade on each side, especially since our tanks and armored cars would have to leave with our column in order to protect it on the march.

The captain decided to leave me behind with a sergeant and four men and three sidecar motorcycles to blow one bridge, and gave the lieutenant commanding the anti-tank guns the job of blowing the other; he had one truck and a few men. But first we had to find something to do it with. Together we hunted all along the Risle for some TNT left behind by some French unit in its hasty retreat. And we finally did find a few blocks in an abandoned British depot, but not as many as we needed. To our surprise, the supply depot seemed mainly full of British cigarettes in big wooden boxes, hundreds of them. We decided that a few thousand cigarettes were practically as important as TNT, in view of the boost they would give to the morale of our whole Groupe Franc. And so we left our truck there with two men to pack it full.

I then went on to Pont Audemer with my three sidecars and half of the explosives, and the other lieutenant took his half to the bridge at Saint-Paul-sur-Risle, only a few hundred yards from the British depot. I found Pont Audemer completely deserted. It had been bombed and many buildings destroyed. All stores had been looted, all shopwindows broken. Arriving at the river where it passes through the northern part of the town, I found that "the bridge" of Pont Audemer was, for practical purposes, three bridges!

True, one of them was nothing more than a small wooden lock to regulate the flow of the river, too small for vehicles, though troops could easily walk across it. And the middle bridge was no real bridge either, but simply a big building built across the river, which was very narrow at this point. The building served as the market place for the town. At both ends of this "bridge" French troops had piled sandbags and anchored them with cement. The floor of the building wasn't strong enough, it seemed to me, to bear the weight of a tank. A light armored car might cross without going through the flooring into the river, but I had my doubts. But enemy motorcycles and passenger cars could use it easily enough, provided the sandbags were cleared away first, which would be quite a job to do by hand but could easily be done with one or two blocks of TNT.

I simply didn't have enough explosives to blow this so-called bridge and the regular stone bridge where the main road crossed the river. I therefore decided to concentrate on the main bridge. At both ends of this bridge the French had also built sandbag barricades. My men began to dig a big hole in the middle of the bridge into the heavy pavements, working as fast as they could.

Meanwhile, with my driver, I reconnoitered what to do if we were surprised by a German column. I decided to put the three sidecars in the first side street to the right from the bridge, where they were protected by the buildings from machine-gun fire. We could get in them and then take another street to the left out of town and be out of German fire because of the cover given by a big building on the other side of the river. In this way we could hit the main road again a few hundred yards to the south. There a stretch of some fifty yards would be dangerous because it would be under direct machine-gun fire from the bridge, but this was a distance so short I thought we could cover it without casualties. I went back to the bridge. The hole was getting bigger and deeper.

Just at that moment we could hear an explosion off a few miles to the east. The anti-tank lieutenant had blown the other bridge. I then told my men they had dug deep enough and had them put the dynamite in the hole and cover it. It seemed to me time to act fast, and everybody helped. We put some big paving blocks on top and covered the hole with tightly compressed soil. Then I had my men leave the bridge and wait behind the sandbags. I started off the bridge myself, unrolling the wire that connected the detonator to the TNT. Just as I was climbing over the sandbags at the French end of the bridge I heard the noise of a motor. A German armored car was coming around the curve of the road just north of the bridge, and it at once began firing at us. I had just time to jump over the sandbags and throw myself flat. We had no machine guns or any weapon to do much good. The men behind the sandbags opened fire at the armored car with their rifles, using armor-piercing ammunition. We had to blow the bridge fast, now if at all. As I connected the cord with the detonator the sandbags gave excellent protection from the fire of the German car. Finally I was able to light the wick leading to the detonator. We then had exactly ninety seconds to get out before the bridge would go up. I lined the men behind the sandbags, and at a signal from my hand we leaped toward the little side street to the right all together at highest speed. We made the side street fifty yards away in about five seconds—I'm sure it was a record. The German gunner, surprised by this unexpected action, didn't hit any of us, we were so fast. In the side street we kept close to the walls of the houses on the north side of the street. A few seconds later up went the bridge, but none of its pieces hit us as they fell because we were protected by the houses. Arriving at the dangerous spot on our route, I lined the three sidecars up, and we dashed over it all together, instead of one after the other. The German fire missed us again. We heard some bullets whistle, though.

When we finally reached Campigny, our rallying point, I found the other lieutenant there waiting for me. He told me he had just blown his own bridge and was heading back to the British depot across the fields, when German motorcyclists appeared on the north bank and fired at him and his men, but by leaps and bounds they reached the depot. His men had kept their truck on the safe side of the building and were still loading cigarettes, even though the door was on the north side and they had to carry the boxes around under fire. The truck left the depot under long-range German fire, but nobody was hit. I looked in the truck. The lieutenant told me there were approximately 350,000 cigarettes. That made at least 3,000 cigarettes per man for our Groupe Franc. What a capture!

THE FIGHT AT PEARL HARBOR

By Blake Clark

The following passages from the author's *Remember Pearl Harbor* (part of which has also been published in a book limited in distribution to the armed services only under the same title as that given to this article) is as powerful writing on battle as this war has yet produced. It ran in the *Infantry Journal* during 1942.

Wheeler

Lieutenants welch and Taylor, sitting at the officers' club at Wheeler Field, saw the Japanese dive bombers swoop low over the ammunition hangar and drop their load. Sinewy steel and thick bastions of concrete were twisted and shattered from the high-power explosion. The lieutenants rushed outside, leaped into their car, and hit a hundred miles an hour on the way to a near-by airfield where they had their planes on special duty. They did not stop to hear the size, number, or type of the attacking planes but grabbed their airplane orders from the interceptor control and dashed for their pursuit planes on the field.

They rose to battle and headed straight for a squadron of a dozen or more Japanese planes over Barber's Point. Their planes were armed with only .30-caliber machine guns. The enemy planes were near now, and the two lieutenants bent to the attack. Lieutenant Welch made for one. It was a two-man dive bomber. The rear gunner was spraying lead at the attacking American, but Welch sat on the Japanese plane's tail and shot it down with one well-aimed burst from his three machine guns.

One gun jammed. An incendiary bullet hit his plane, passing through the baggage compartment behind the driver's seat. He climbed above the clouds and checked. The plane was not on fire. He dived through the clouds and returned to the attack. A Japanese plane was flying out to sea. He caught it, shot it down, and saw it fall into the broad Pacific below. His plane needed refueling, so he headed back for Wheeler Field.

Lieutenant Taylor's plane overtook his first victim so fast that he had to throttle back to keep from overshooting. He found his mark and the plane went down. During his second attack the enemy rear gunner nicked Taylor's arm. The bullet spattered when it hit the seat, and a fragment pierced the American's leg. He felt it but paid no attention. He joined Welch in the return for refueling, and the two landed together.

Before Welch's gun could be unlocked or Taylor's wounds receive first aid a second wave of fifteen Japanese planes swept in, flying low and heading for the two planes on the runway. Taylor had been advised not to return to the air because of his wounds. He leaped to his plane, took off, rising at high speed, and turned in a perfectly executed chandelle. The Japanese were on his tail. Welch, in the air behind them, swept fast upon Taylor's pursuers and dived on the one most dangerous to his partner. The Japanese rear gunner poured lead into Welch's plane. Bullets struck the motor, the propeller, the cowling. Still Welch pursued like an avenging fury, letting fly with all his guns. The enemy plane burst into flames and crashed. Taylor escaped. Welch followed another enemy plane seaward, caught it about five miles offshore, and gave its two-man team an ocean grave.

These fighters were not alone. Other squadrons were in the air. In another part of the sky Lieutenant Harry Brown saw his friend Lieutenant Robert Rogers in a dogfight with two Japanese planes. Brown singled out the one on Rogers' tail and began shooting. He got nearer and nearer to the Japanese plane, so close that he saw his bullets plowing into it from the belly to the tail. One of his guns jammed. He pounded it with his fist until the skin burst. The plane in front started wobbling, then shot into flames and crashed into the sea. Brown's throat was sore and his voice hoarse from yelling during the excitement.

An old-timer, Lieutenant Sanders, led a unit of four planes up through an overcast of six thousand feet. He saw a group of six Japanese bombing an airfield. He signaled his men to the attack, taking the enemy leader for himself. Although the sun was behind Sanders' unit, the Japanese saw them and fled north. The unit came in fast, dived on the Japanese, and started firing. Sanders opened up on the leader. The Japanese plane smoked up, faltered, and fell into the sea.

Lieutenant James Sterling was hot after one of the enemy.

A Japanese plane was on his tail. Lieutenant Sanders closed in, but the attacker was already pouring bullets into Sterling's plane, and it burst into flames. The American continued to fight the Japanese plane ahead, and the four went into a dive—the Japanese in front, Sterling still firing at him, the second Japanese after Sterling, and Sanders following through. They plunged down into the overcast at an altitude of six thousand feet, all motors roaring at full speed. Only Sanders pulled out.

Lieutenant Rasmussen was in a dogfight with a Japanese over the pineapple fields of Wahiawa. Each was desperately maneuvering to get on the other's tail. Bullets flew into Rasmussen's plane. His radio equipment fell to pieces before his eyes. The Japanese plane was fast, well armed. Below, thousands of people who had evacuated their homes at Hickam and Ford Island and thousands who had run outdoors at Schofield Barracks and Wahiawa stood anxiously watching the dogfight, the most exciting form of modern warfare.

Rasmussen pulled up out of a fast maneuver. He caught the Japanese plane in his sights. He pulled the trigger of his .50-caliber machine gun. Tracer bullets ripped into the enemy plane. He held the deadly stream straight on the Japanese. When he quit firing the plane was going down. All the anxious thousands broke into a great cheer of relief and pride when it fell to the ground in a burning, broken mass of wreckage.

When Rasmussen landed he looked at his plane. The rudder was shot away, and the fuselage was as full of holes as a sieve.

The Japanese got full satisfaction from their visit to "the eagles of Wheeler."

On the ground at Wheeler men were running through dust clouds arising from the Japanese strafers' incendiary bullets that were ripping up the ground. Dive bombers were planting demolition bombs on the hangars. Just before this blitz started Sergeant Bayham tore down to the supply house for a machine gun. He was breaking down a door when the supply sergeant, who was still thinking "practice," refused the gun and ammunition unless Bayham signed for it. By this time the door was down, and Bayham was dragging out a .50-caliber machine gun.

"I don't have time to sign for it!" he yelled.

When he finally mounted the gun somebody cried out, "Hey, you can't fire that water-cooled gun without water!"

"To hell with the water—I haven't got any water!"

Staff Sergeant Benton joined him and fed the ammunition as Bayham pumped it at the approaching Japanese two-motored bomber. The gunner in the rear cockpit was shooting at them. Dust popped up around them. Their own tracer bullets told them that they were hitting the attacker. Holes were going into the plane. When it had passed and was a couple of hundred yards away the plane shook like a dog shaking off water, circled jerkily to the right, and fell.

Oahu's defenders fought. They fought on the sea, in the air, and wherever men found guns to fight with. Two Japanese planes came strafing the streets of Wahiawa, a few miles from Pearl Harbor. At the sound of firing a lieutenant and a sergeant in charge of a communications section grabbed automatic rifles and rushed out to the sidewalk. The two planes flew low, slowly and deliberately. They raked everything in their path with machine-gun fire. Puffs of dirt exploded as the bullets whipped into the earth. One plane, blazing away, swooped down toward the unprotected communications station. Our men knelt, took a lead on the plane as if aiming at a duck, waited until it was within 150 feet, and emptied their magazines. The machine guns stopped firing. The plane went out of control. It slipped sideways and crashed in flames a hundred yards behind the communications post.

HICKAM

At Hickam Field, the airfield so near Pearl Harbor that it is virtually the same target, a long row of hangars and bombers invited the Japanese. The attack combined bombing and strafing. The enemy planes bombed the hangars and strafed the quarter-mile-long row of planes drawn up in front of the hangars in orderly parade formation.

A bomb hit on a hangar announced the news to the thousands on the post. Men came pouring out from all nine wings of the barracks—men in slacks, men in shorts, some in their underwear only, some without anything on at all. What was going on? Another mock war? No, bombs! Everyone ran for clothes and then for his battle station.

Colonel Ferguson was in a building up the street from the hangar line. He ran out into the open, saw the damaged planes, and jumped into the gutter. While strafers bounced bullets off the road by his side the colonel crawled down the gutter to the line. There he directed the tactical squadrons who were arriving a hundred to a hundred and fifty at a time on the double-quick.

"Disperse those planes!" was the order.

Up and back, up and back, the Japanese squadron was flying, strafing the airplanes on the wings. The men ran on, heedless of the rain of bullets. Some of the men faltered and fell.

A general's aide was already on the line. He was trying to taxi one of the big bombers. Strafers had put one motor out of commission. It was no easy job to taxi such a heavy plane with only one motor going. He did it by racing the one engine until it pulled its side of the plane brake, which forced the other wing up. Wading and crawling along under enemy fire, he brought the plane across the landing mat to comparative safety.

While the fire department fought flames at the tail end of some of the planes, daring crew men jumped upon the wings, disconnected the engines, and pulled their eight or nine hundred pounds' weight to the edge of the apron. Fine engines were saved by their quick thinking.

Inside one hangar twenty-one Hawaiians were fighting fire. Planes roared hoarsely; machine guns stuttered overhead. In the middle of the smoke-filled hangar Solomon Naauao, 245-pound athlete, trained the water from his fire hose on the fuselage of a four-motor Flying Fortress, pushing back the gasoline fire that leaped out from the fuselage onto the wings. Solomon is a giant Hawaiian, a true son of a warrior. Short, thick black hair fits his massive head like a fur cap. He was hoping the chief would come soon with the foamite. Water was not much good against gasoline.

One end of the burning hangar fell through to the floor, revealing a sky dotted with three approaching Japanese bombers. They were flying just a few feet above the hangar. The first one passed directly above Solomon and his fellow fighters. Solomon heard an explosion and felt hot pain.

"Lord help me!" he prayed, falling to the concrete floor. The inner side of his right leg was blown away.

With his arms and sound leg he crawled through the smoke, away from the flames. When two soldiers picked him up he learned that five others with him had been wounded, three more blown to pieces. They left him in the doorway to wait for the ambulance just coming in. As he lay there Japanese planes flew slowly above, just clearing the hangar, and strafed the men running to carry him to the ambulance. Others quickly picked him up and sped him to the hospital.

Sergeant Dwyer got a machine gun out of ordnance, put a corporal in charge of it, and dashed back for another. A bomb fell, and its deadly fragments flew. He got his second gun and set it up on the parade ground. He felt wet and looked at his shirt. It was soaked with blood.

The sergeant remembered that something he had thought was a stone had hit him when the bomb exploded. He was taken to the hospital with a shattered shoulder.

A lieutenant ran toward a plane. A Japanese flew over, strafing. The lieutenant fell to the ground, mortally wounded. A young corporal by his side lifted him to an ambulance, sped back across the apron, leaped in the plane, and taxied it out.

The raid lasted fifteen or twenty minutes. As soon as it ceased activity burst upon the streets and flooded them. Ambulances and all the cars that could be pressed into service as ambulances were whizzing up and back from the bombed area. School busses, Army station wagons, American Factors delivery trucks, and private cars helped to deliver the wounded and to rush surgical supplies from Honolulu to the hospitals.

Before half their work was completed they were caught in the second most destructive raid. Two rows of high-flying bombers dropped over twenty heavy and light demolition bombs from a height of ten to twelve thousand feet. They landed in the most populous section of Hickam Field. For what seemed a full minute after the bombs had landed there was a dead silence in which nothing happened. Then the new mess hall, large enough for six complete basketball courts inside, the photograph laboratory, the guardhouse, the fire station, the barracks built to house thousands, an immense hangar—everything in the entire area—seemed to rise intact from the earth, poise in mid-air, and fall apart, dropping back to the earth in millions of fragments and clouds of dust.

The third wave came strafing. Ground defenses were going full blast and accounted for several of the raiders. Guns were set up on the parade ground, on the hangar line, and even around the flagpole at post headquarters. One man—no one knows how—had lugged a machine gun up on top of one of the unbombed hangars and was perched up there, popping away at the strafing planes.

Green men under fire acted like veterans. All moved swiftly to their places without any confusion or disorder. The cooks ran back into the kitchen to remove all the stored food to a safer place. The kitchen was hit. The staff sergeant in charge was struck on the head by a piece of shrapnel. He ripped off his shirt, tied up his head to stop the blood, and went on directing the work.

Outside, a corporal was speeding across the parade ground to help man a machine gun. It was entirely in the open, without any protection whatever. Halfway there he was strafed by a low-flying Japanese pilot. Mortally wounded, he kept on, trying to get to the machine gun. He fell dead on the way.

His place was quickly taken. Eager privates ran out and took over the gun. They did this time and again, dashing out under fire and taking over free machine guns, even though the men who were operating them had just been strafed and killed.

On the apron opposite the hangars a lone man was firing a .30-caliber machine gun which he had carried out and set up on the mount of a B-18 bomber. It was unstable because the mount was made for an aerial gun. He braced it against his shoulder and kept up a steady stream of fire. An enemy plane flew low, strafed the plane he was in with incendiary bullets, and set it on fire. There was no way for the lone machine gunner to get out of his position in the nose of the bomber. All behind him was a flaming deathtrap. Spectators not far away said that he did not even try to get out but kept on firing. Long after the leaping flames had enveloped the nose of the plane they saw the red tracer bullets from his machine gun mounting skyward.

There was humor with the tragedy. When the Japanese came over Hickam the third time they placed a bomb squarely on the "Snake Ranch," the boys' name for their recently opened beer garden. A first sergeant of a truck company had endured the first two waves bravely enough, but this was too much. He dashed out of his barricade, shook his fist at the sky, and shouted, "You dirty S.O.B.s! You've bombed the most important building on the post!"

A group of United States bombers, all unarmed, were just flying in from the mainland when the bewildered pilots found themselves pounced upon by a fleet of armed and shooting bombers. Many of the Americans did not see the Rising Sun on the planes and simply could not imagine what had broken loose above their heads. What kind of Hawaiian welcome was this? The planes were to be delivered to one particular field, but they dispersed in every direction and landed wherever they could.

LESSONS OF BATAAN

By COLONEL MILTON A. HILL

(1942)

THERE WERE MANY THINGS among the battle and campaign experiences of our own troops and those of the Philippine Army during the whole of the fighting against our Japanese foes in the Philippine Islands which bring out lessons of marked value to all our troops in training. Some details we can't go into for military reasons. But there are many other things which to my mind should be known and discussed by our military forces in general, and especially by our infantry and other ground forces since the Philippine fighting was mainly warfare on the ground.

The Japs had planes, of course, and ours were gone in short order, a large part of them lost through the concentrated Japanese attacks on the airfields where most of our planes were standing. (There should be no need, any longer, of pointing to the folly of failing to disperse as widely as possible the planes used in any theater of war, but it ought to be repeated every so often just in case somebody forgets, even momentarily.) The small number of planes that did continue in service lasted for a time, but as the papers in the United States told you, they became casualties one by one till all were gone. Thus we never had any number of them with which to strike at the enemy, and what we had were more valuable, as long as they lasted, for the information they could quickly obtain of Japanese dispositions. And so the fighting was mainly ground warfare.

It would have been largely ground warfare, anyway, unless we assume that we had started the fighting with enough air forces to possibly prevent a landing. And if we had had that many planes it is doubtful whether the attempt would have been made at all. Under a reasonable assumption of greater air strength on our side, the added planes would have been a powerful addition to our total fighting power. But too much of the Philippines are made up of terrain over which air forces are at too heavy a disadvantage for them to contribute decisively to the result unless the comparative air power had been very one-sided.

This is shown by the way in which the fighting continued week after week on Bataan. The Japs had planes, a good many of them, and they did much scouting and bombing with them. But neither affected the hard ground fighting much, for as long as our troops were careful to make full use of camouflage and cover—they did very well on this; they soon learned they had to—the reconnoitering planes couldn't find many targets to report upon to their own artillery and aviation.

After our planes were gone we had observers on many high points, both for artillery observation and air-warning purposes. Often these observers had stations up in trees high up in the hills. Japanese planes would come circling over low to the ground, trying to detect our dispositions or find some installation to bomb or shell. They seldom, if ever, appeared to see these observers even when they came within a few hundred yards of them.

Where we had anything concentrated—supplies or troops—and the Japs spied them out from the air, they soon came bombing, as we could only expect in modern warfare. This meant, of course, as our tactical manuals have told us for years (this is a thing we used to neglect so badly in peacetime training that we had to learn it sharply in war), that a practically continuous deployment of troops was necessary and, also, as much dispersion as possible of supplies. For big dumps and storehouses cause too much traffic and concentrated activity. The Japs destroyed without much difficulty a big cold-storage warehouse. But such supplies as the gasoline hauled to Bataan during the withdrawal from the other Luzon sectors and hastily unloaded at a great many different spots were spread out too widely, either to be found by Jap fliers or to be worth bombing if they were found.

No, if we don't go into the big aspects of the Philippine campaign—the lack of preparedness not in any way due to President Quezon or General MacArthur, or anyone else in the islands themselves, and things like that —the big lessons we find are fighting lessons for ground troops. And those are the things I will especially stress in this article.

I find, when I think things over and go through my notebook to help the details come back to mind, that one thing above all else about the Philippine fighting needs emphasis—the proper training and hardening of the soldier for combat. The Filipino and American troops in the islands had all been training hard when war struck the islands. Some of the newly formed units were not far along in their training, but most of the older outfits had had a good deal of it. But superbly as they fought when the time came to fight, none of them had gone far enough in their training before then. They could shoot, some units better than others, but all of them probably better than the Japs. They were hard enough from the work they had had to cover the distances they had to on foot and keep fighting with good endurance. But they had not had what seems to me now to be utterly requisite in the training of all combat units in this war —a thorough toughening process through extended and realistic maneuvers.

When troops go into campaign and battle they often have to operate for days on little food and less sleep. They have to spend hours daily in close, hard contact with the ground. They have to drop automatically to the ground and the nearest cover when planes surprise them overhead. They have to use, in battle itself, every bump and pocket of ground for the life-preserving cover it gives when fire is heaviest. They have to dig themselves in habitually or find equivalent cover whenever they rest.

Our troops in the Philippines knew of these simple fighter's truths. They had not in general been omitted from tactical instruction except where shortness of service had not brought the training thus far. But these plain, vital matters of battle had not been pounded in and emphasized over and over until they were part of the very reactions of the troops.

Our prewar training in marching and endurance, I think, lacked reality most of all. The way to train troops for the rigors they are bound to meet sooner or later in war is to give them some actual practice, not only in making thirty or forty miles on foot, but in doing it hungry. This shows the troops what one of the tough sides of war may be like later on. But above all else it shows them—or most of them, anyway—that they have got the guts to do it. The American soldier—and the Filipino soldier too —has a splendid tenacity and toughness, as the whole story of Luzon and Bataan did show. But he's a far better soldier in his first battle if you give him beforehand every possible experience he is going to run into later, and this with all possible realism and emphasis on the things that count in actual campaign.

It shouldn't be necessary to say that our Jap and Nazi enemies do this. It's only good, common soldier sense to train in this way. And it's my positive belief that the American soldier thrives on such training and appreciates it to the full as what he must go through to be a soldier in the real meaning of the word.

I think every man in our Army of a few years' service will remember how it was always the toughest, longest hikes of peacetime training the troops remembered longest and talked about (and bragged about) most. And it's sure to be the same in all our newer units. The hard jobs, the hard maneuvers, when there was a sound reason for the hardness, make officers and their men alike proud of getting the hard jobs done, proud of going through the hard maneuvers.

But there's a better reason than pride. The soldier who knows what's coming is not surprised. He knows what to do and how to do it. He kills more men of the enemy's troops and preserves his own life for further fighting far more readily.

Take the simple business of hitting cover when the warning comes of planes, or no warning comes, as it sometimes doesn't, and the planes come over fast and low. There's no excuse whatever for a leader who neglects to train his men to get the advantage of the ground, not only as protection against bombs, but against bullets or shells. Readers of the *Infantry Journal* know how often this point has been pounded home in its pages. And every soldier with a few months of training knows what the training manuals say about it. It's all in the *Soldier's Handbook,* which every recruit receives to study. But just the same, there were a lot of men killed and wounded in the Philippines standing up when bombs came down. Somebody—a lot of somebodies, in fact—hadn't pounded it into them that a soldier flat on his stomach in even a small depression has ten or twenty times the chance of not getting hit by a piece of bomb or shell that a man does standing up.

It's all in the same general lesson of efficient soldiering that a fighting infantryman must make the most of the ground at any time he's fighting an enemy in strength or has reason to think he is. We lost men in the Philippines when they used the half-squat, semi-crouching method, common in peacetime maneuvers and training, as they approached the enemy. If the enemy is there, opposite, in strength, or if you have any reason to think he is there, your advance must either be a long-distance crawl from cover to cover, or a combination of crawling and rushes so short that the Japs or the Nazis can't take aim and fire or shift a machine gun upon you before you are down again.

It's all in the books we learn war from. We can't learn the experience of battle itself from tactical manuals and training instruction. But we can come so close to it, if we insist on realities and actually read for gospel and put into full effect in our training what the manuals say, that we can save the lives of hundreds in every battalion in the first few days of actual combat.

Naturally, troops learn these things for themselves very rapidly during heavy fighting—at least those who live or stay out of the hospital long enough to learn them do. At best this war is going to cost more American lives than we as a nation have been willing to think about. We who are American Army leaders have the knowledge, the authority, and the absolute responsibility to see to it that battle training is never slighted in any unit.

Make our troops tough and hard. Make our troops wise in the ways of battle. Do this by putting into their training as close to battle experience as it's possible to get without bullets and bombs and shells. Make sure not a man has to learn for himself in combat or waste his life or his service in the learning. Even give punishments to the soldier who is slow or careless. It may easily save his life.

To put all this another way—the platoon or company commander who brings his outfit in from tactical drill with no dust and dirt on their uniforms, the result of plenty of hard contact with the ground, is the leader who will lose 10 per cent or more of his men in their first fighting day.

I know I'm repeating. I intend to repeat, and I'm going to come back to it later. This, I am certain, was one of the biggest lessons of Luzon. There were reasons why at least some troops had to learn it the hard way there; they hadn't had time to train. There is no reason on earth why any of our other troops should have to do so. It's up to every American leader of fighting Army men to see that they don't.

Once our American and Filipino troops learned the simple, practical basic lessons of warfare, they excelled the Japs opposing them in several ways. Our men were better shots than the Japanese with every weapon, up to and including the artillery.

They were also wiser and more efficient in close-combat methods. Our troops didn't go in for letting the Japanese close in if they could kill them before they could do so. Our troops had plenty of will to close with the enemy. But they knew it was only common sense to use rifles and machine guns and then hand grenades, if they had to.

Most of the American and Filipino troops carried hand grenades on their belts as sidearms—they liked them better for close-in fighting than any other weapon.

Even when the Japs did manage to get close they weren't so good as bayonet fighters, so I was informed. I was also told, however, that they are very good with swords.

Our troops improvised grenades from bamboo, including the fuses. The joints of bamboo are closed by partitions and thus form a natural closed tube. The engineer troops would fill these tubes with nails or any other scrap iron or steel, tamp in some powder, close them, and attach a fuse, usually a match head. The troops saved cellophane from cigarette packages to keep the moisture out of the fuses.

There isn't a great deal to say about the use of tanks because we didn't have very many and I do not have any full reports on what they did. During the Luzon campaign the tank units were switched from one front to another, wherever they were needed worst. Unquestionably if we had had large numbers of good tanks they would have been of much value in the early fighting, but since much of the Philippines is not good tank ground it is hard to say what the final effect of an adequate number would have been. We could have used a lot more of them, just as we needed more planes, more artillery, and more troops of all kinds.

On Bataan the tanks that were left after the withdrawal were used to patrol narrow trails over which they could travel. They did some good work at such patrolling.

I have already made some references to planes in the Philippine fighting. Despite the lack of planes on our own side, our troops brought some down with their own fire. The big AA guns on Corregidor knocked down a number; the mobile AA-gun units on the mainland did, too, and so did the infantry and other troops fighting as infantry, when the planes came low. The Jap air units took their losses when they really meant business— when they had a mission they wanted to carry out. The losses to them from ground fire were not great, perhaps, considering the planes available to the Japs. But these losses from our own ground fire counted, as they always do.

When planes come over at low enough ranges for infantry to open up, it depends upon the situation whether they should open fire. Sometimes to do so betrays their positions to the enemy in the air, but this usually won't happen when fire is opened from under good overhead cover, as in firing upward between the branches of trees. Often the enemy fliers will already know that troops are in a given area, as when they come over to bomb repeatedly. Troops can open fire briefly at such planes but should dive for cover a second or so before the bombs hit the ground. What the manuals say about such fire is sensible, and I wouldn't suggest any changes in it.

You have to be fast when the bombs are about to fall. Once I wasn't anywhere near fast enough. I was riding in a command car, with a driver and two noncoms, on the way up to the 1st Division. On one side of the road which ran near the sea was a perpendicular bank about seven feet high. The road and the side out to the sea was flat and without a particle of cover in the ground. All of a sudden the car stopped running and I was sitting in it all by myself. I never saw anybody disappear faster than the driver and the two sergeants. We were near an area occupied by an AA-gun battery. They had heard Jap planes coming either to attack the guns or us or both. They assumed I heard them, too, but I didn't. But with the first bomb I was up over that seven-foot bank into a hollow in the ground in just as fast time as they made it. There were nine bombs altogether, but they didn't hit us or our car. One of the fliers saw the car, and the beaten zone of his machine-gun bullets passed close by it but didn't hit it.

Our troops made some use of reconnaissance patrols into the Jap lines to gather information. In the Filipino units some individual soldiers would steal out on their own into the Jap lines just to get a Jap or two and bring back some souvenirs. One soldier of the 41st Infantry was captured, and for some reason the Jap officer who took him got angry and drew his sword to cut off his head. The Filipino soldier took the sword away from him, killed the Jap, and escaped, bringing the sword back with him. There may have been individual scouts who went from our forces behind the Jap lines and stayed there for some time. If so, I did not hear of these, except for some men who crossed the bay to Cavite and sent back radio reports on the Japanese gun positions to Corregidor.

Since Bataan is largely covered with jungle or heavy growth there was much cutting to be done. Here the troops found the bolo absolutely essential. There is so much tough bamboo and cane in the Philippine jungle growth that a heavy blade, like the bolo, is needed. The lighter machete, which is probably better for a softer type of jungle growth, is too light for use in the Philippine jungles.

During the whole campaign on Luzon, and later on Bataan, I never once heard of any friction of any kind between the different branches of the fighting teams. Nor did I detect any signs of lack of co-ordination. Splendid teamwork was particularly noticeable between the infantry and the artillery. They worked together perfectly. The whole fighting force pitched in, and there weren't any hitches at all due to different collar ornaments. I should say that this extended also to the naval units and marines and the air units, which operated as ground troops after their planes were gone. An army is supposed to work as a combat team, according to all the tactical doctrines taught in our military manuals. Well, the teamwork was there, in our force, from the beginning to the end.

The work of the artillery can hardly be praised too highly. The artillery served the infantry time after time by breaking up Jap concentrations or convoys of trucks coming forward to attack. They used both direct and indirect fire, whichever served the purpose, and they gave quick, accurate support.

One day up on the front an outpost located a sizable number of Japs in an assembly position under some trees. The outpost commander picked up the telephone, called the artillery CP and told them about the Japs and where they were. In a fraction of a minute the shells of our artillery came down on the right spot.

The larger artillery fired at ranges up to ten thousand yards. There was excellent observation on Bataan at first since the northern part of that area is fairly open and flat, right up to the foothills and the mountains. It was possible even after that, when we dropped back to the south to new lines, to obtain very fair observation, and the artillery broke up Jap concentrations time and again. At first, of course, the few planes we had helped the effectiveness of our artillery also.

There was nothing special about the artillery methods to fit the situation. They just did their stuff as good artillery always does. After we had settled down on Bataan the artillery probably had accurate ranges worked out to every conceivable area to the front, which of course is the normal way of doing in such a situation.

Our artillery made good use of nets and foliage for camouflage. It isn't hard to do this on Bataan, where most of the area is heavily wooded. One artillery battery was especially good at this.

In fact, the Japs generally had a considerable amount of difficulty in locating our artillery. They did knock some guns out by bombs and some by shelling.

The firing of the Jap artillery was not as good as our own, probably owing to the lack of observation because of our good camouflage. Their artillery fire was pretty accurate when they could see the target. When they had captured Bataan and there was nothing to oppose them their heavy artillery fire was most accurate and effective against Corregidor.

I do not know of any use of chemicals of any kind by our forces during the whole campaign. We didn't even use smoke or tear gas, since there were strict orders out against it.

The Japs did try to use white phosphorus shells to set fire to the trees and undergrowth. But white phosphorus doesn't burn long enough to set fire to Philippine jungle growth. There were not many casualties from these white-phosphorus shells.

Most of the troops of the Philippine Army had no gas masks, and our own troops didn't carry theirs regularly.

Our troops wore their helmets only when it was necessary. Most of the men of the Philippine Army didn't have any. Those of us who went back and forth from the front to headquarters would take a helmet along but often would forget it. Most of the helmets our American troops and the Philippine Scout regiments had were of the old World War type.

Command and staff functioned generally according to our prescribed methods throughout the campaign. What we were taught about these methods is generally sound. The commander should be out with his fighting troops as much as he can, but his staff should stick at the command post unless there is some important reason for a staff member to leave it. The commander, however, by just being up with his troops, gives them confidence.

Our commanders followed this principle right up to and including General MacArthur and the different corps and army commanders. General Wainright liked to get into a pair of jumpers and take a rifle right up into the front defense areas. The troops were very fond of him, and the fact that he was there sometimes, bossing them around and fighting with them, meant a lot.

But the staff should stick to its work in the relative safety of the command post because it has all the work it can do. Besides, the command simply falls on the shoulders of the next ranking man if the commander becomes a casualty, but a hard-plugging, smooth-functioning staff can be badly disrupted by losses, thus in turn disrupting for some time the essential details of an operation.

This applies especially to the G-2 of large units. He should stay at headquarters and not go out trying to rustle up information on his own. He should send his assistants for any information that he needs which doesn't come in from other sources. But his own mind, with its grasp of the known information of the enemy, may be of vital value to the commander at any time. He must evaluate for his commander all information of importance as fast as it comes in. He must be able to give him a quick picture of the situation at any time. He is needed at headquarters constantly.

The same thing generally applies to the other main members of the General Staff. They, together, have the whole picture in mind for the commander to refer to for any particular details he needs. He, too, has the general picture. But when he is away he often loses it, even when he can keep frequent contact with his staff, and he has to be brought up to the moment by his staff as soon as he comes back.

As for an inspector general, which I was, he ceases to be an inspector in the customary sense of reporting on details of administrative operation and general housekeeping, and becomes a tactical investigator for his commander. The experience of Luzon points to duties of inspecting the tactical operation, combat efficiency, and fighting condition of specific units. That is what the Jap IG does, and every commander of a division or bigger unit does need a special assistant to help him in this respect. G-3 is too busy with the great number of details regarding our own operations to handle this duty. Either some G-2 agency or the inspector general should carry out this job.

Naturally we were short of officers on the Philippines, and I worked mainly by myself on such specific tasks of investigation as were needed. I'm not using the word "investigation" here particularly in its ordinary peacetime sense, which refers to the duty of looking into alleged offenses. I mean a general agent of the commander when he wants an especially detailed and firsthand report on any matter that arises under campaign conditions.

A good many of the staff customarily carried rifles when they went up to where the fighting was. I usually carried a Garand and almost always found somebody who needed it when I went forward. Then I would get another one when I went back to take along on my next trip up.

At the lower headquarters the usual necessary administrative duties continued right on through combat. The first sergeant kept the morning report and the sick report and made out the ration report. His main job was to keep track of the men of his company and help take care of them. Regimental headquarters kept the records required. Their load was not particularly heavy since there were no replacements, which greatly increases regimental paper work in most war situations.

There weren't any orderly rooms as such, of course. But you would find a first sergeant usually with a dugout of some kind, or other suitable protection, with his field desk in it and all he needed to keep up his customary and necessary administrative duties.

All other administrative offices appeared to function reasonably well under battle conditions. True, there were bound to be complete breakdowns of some activities. I never did get a bill from the commissary in Manila for my December purchases. I suppose they burned all records up when the city was evacuated and the QM left Manila. So this is one bill that will hang over me for a long, long time. Property records, too, eventually became meaningless. As accountable officer I had signed for all United States property the Philippine Army troops had received— millions of dollars in Ordnance and other equipment. The regulations were that the different American supply agencies—the Quartermaster, Ordnance, and so on—didn't deal directly with the Philippine Army. So an officer was appointed to sign for all such government property, and I happened to be the one. Then I, in turn, would get memorandum receipts from the Philippine Army. When General MacArthur's Far Eastern Forces Headquarters moved from Manila to Corregidor, the papers about this property were packed up and taken along. I had the papers all stored away carefully when we got over there. But a bomb hit it and destroyed it all, clearing me very simply of a good many million dollars of accountability.

There were, as the newspapers and radio said, a good many promotions made during the Philippine fighting. Promotion was recommended within each regiment and usually went through higher up, though I do recall one case of an enlisted man of marked ability who didn't get the full promotion recommended. I have not intended to take up space in this account by telling of individual exploits. There were many fine deeds, but others have done a better job than I possibly could in telling about them. However, I don't think the story of Frenchy Saulnier has been told, and it should be told. Frenchy Saulnier was an American private who somehow took command of a battalion of the Philippine Army in battle. This unit had had losses and was, for the time, without direction, and Frenchy took it in hand and straightened it out. Since his army commander had earlier received a report on Frenchy telling how he had assisted the artillery by taking over liaison duties and ordering the fire moved up until it was almost upon his own position but right on the enemy's, the army commander recommended that Frenchy Saulnier be commissioned as a major. He had proved in battle that he could handle the job, but it finally worked out that Frenchy was made a lieutenant. He was one of those natural leaders of men in combat every war brings out. He was later decorated, I believe. Everybody said that Frenchy Saulnier was a natural.

There was naturally a shortage of insignia on Bataan for those who gained promotions. Some had to go without. The soldiers of the Philippine Scout units, some of them long expert in such work, made beautiful insignia out of aluminum—better than you buy in some shops. They also made colonels' eagles out of 20-centavo pieces. The Ordnance came through with aluminum stars for the new generals.

The problem of supply, as everybody knew in the United States from the reports that were in the paper, was just about the worst trouble we had. When the troops moved out to the different defense sectors upon the opening of war they naturally took out with them a considerable amount of supplies. There was the usual system of railheads, dumps, and even "boatheads." If anything, we erred on the side of having too many supplies in the advanced sectors. For when we pulled back eventually to occupy Bataan, a lot of supplies were lost to the enemy, although great quantities were carried to Bataan by truck. How much more food we would have had on Bataan if those supplies had not been lost it is hard to tell, but I imagine it would have made a considerable difference in the length of time we could have held out.

On Bataan there were some main supply dumps established according to plan, but there were also a whole lot of small ones scattered well around where trucks unloaded hurriedly when they came out from Manila after we knew the withdrawal to Bataan would have to be made. The issuance of the rations on Bataan was kept under very good control both as to the supplies brought into the sector and as to those that existed in the area, such as rice. It was the harvesttime for rice and it was possible to gather all the crops on Bataan itself, but this wasn't a great deal since so much of Bataan is uncultivated. There wasn't much time to get anything from the areas farther north where there was a great deal more rice and other supplies. Our reports were that the Japs made the people continue their harvesting as fast as they occupied a new area.

The story of the food during the last few weeks has probably been thoroughly reported. One of the worst blows, of course, was the destruction of the big cold-storage plant on Corregidor. This had a large quantity of carabao and other meat in it—frozen meat. There was much of this not destroyed by the bombing, though the bombing put the refrigerator plant out of business. The only thing to do then was to get this meat out for the troops and refugees to eat as fast as possible before it spoiled. But a lot of it did spoil.

Toward the end, since there was no forage—no grain or hay—for the pack mules and other military animals, they were all slaughtered except a few pack mules which were still needed to carry supplies and weapons up into the different parts of the mountainous area of Bataan. I think some animals were still in use at the time of the surrender.

It might seem that it should have been possible to obtain sizable supplies of fish. Fishing fleets did go out, but the Japs bombed them. The bombs themselves killed a lot of fish, and it was possible to collect some of these in small boats. Some fishing was attempted at night, but it was almost impossible to co-ordinate the activities of the fishing boats with those of the defending troops both on Corregidor and on Bataan. For the Japs did make attempts to land by boat in the area we occupied, and it was only natural that our own troops would open up on any boats they saw.

All rice and carabao obtained from Filipino farmers, was, of course, purchased by the government. One thing it was possible for us to manufacture was salt. This was made from sea water.

There were some other special sources of food. The Filipino troops pieced out their meager rations with the leaves from certain trees which seemed to go all right as spinach. A small amount of Japanese rations was captured. The Jap ration was in a small compact package containing some little cakes of food and a few cigarettes. These rations were taken mainly during the attempted raid from the sea by several hundred Japanese troops on our west-coast flank. Jap planes brought the food over and dropped it. The aim of the Jap fliers was poor, and our troops got most of the food instead of the isolated Jap ground troops. A good deal of it also hung in trees.

One of our veterinary officers shot some crows and cooked them. He insisted that they were not bad at all. Practically anything fresh was very tasty when the rations got low.

There was never at any time any shortage of water on Bataan, although there was on Corregidor. On Bataan there was some artesian water and plenty of good, clear creek water coming down off the mountains.

There was some smuggling of liquor and cigarettes from Manila to the troops on Bataan after Manila was occupied. Very high prices were charged by the smugglers—for example, as high as two hundred dollars a carton for cigarettes. There was not a great deal of such smuggling, however, because of the high risk. The Japs killed a good many of the smugglers.

At first there was an issue of cigarettes to the troops. The smoking ration grew smaller as time went on, and finally tobacco ran out entirely, except on Corregidor. I think there was a little left there at the end, mainly for distribution in the hospitals. Coffee also got very low toward the end.

There was money to pay our American troops each payday but, of course, money didn't mean much on Bataan. There wasn't much of anything to spend it for. Stakes got pretty high in some of the card games, and a good many of the troops just didn't take their money on payday but permitted it to accumulate. Some took it and immediately deposited it with the finance officer. A good many got checks and mailed them home. Personally I found practically no use for money during almost all of the Philippine campaign until I reached Australia.

For the most part the normal methods of supply proved sound in the many emergency situations during the Philippine campaign. There were bound to be many improvised methods set up, but I observed no particular weaknesses in our prescribed supply methods for the field. The quartermaster and ordnance troops were eternally busy, and I often wondered how they got as much done as they did under the conditions.

There was so much for them to do in the line of their regular duties that it wasn't possible to consider using any of the service units as combat troops. The only special fighting units formed were those composed of air troops. They made very good ground soldiers after they got the hang of it. These "air-ground" units had to learn practically everything from the beginning. They held the western sector of the lines on Bataan—the strongest ground, which it was logical to assign to such inexperienced ground troops.

The engineers handled the demolition work most efficiently. They blew up many bridges, destroyed oil tanks, and demolished other installations. Among the things they destroyed were the big oil and gas tanks in Manila.

The work of demolishing bridges had to be done on close schedule during the withdrawal because, of course, the engineers couldn't blow up the bridges until the last of our units had cleared them. This required a timetable in close co-operation with the other ground-unit commanders. Only once that I know of did this co-ordination fall down. This happened in the Lingayen area a good many miles north of Manila when we lost a few tanks because the bridge was blown before the tanks got over, and there wasn't any way for them to go around and get across the stream somewhere else. Somebody must have blown the charge too soon.

The Philippine Army and our own troops both had a considerable number of motor vehicles. The motorization of our American units began a good many years ago and has continued steadily. But there were nowhere near enough vehicles in the military forces when it came to making the big-scale withdrawal into Bataan. The result was that hundreds of civilian busses and cars were requisitioned through the Quartermaster, and hundreds of others were simply commandeered. This is a possibility of warfare in any region where there are enough non-military motor vehicles to be of help to the armed forces. It is also a matter on which I recall little, if any, practical instruction in our military manuals. From what happened in the Philippines it seems to me highly desirable to work out some general method of commandeering and requisitioning non-military motor vehicles which could be applied in any region where there were vehicles to take over.

It is true that there were no great difficulties about this except for a good deal of confusion. Cars were taken out of dealers' display rooms; they were taken out of secondhand yards, and they were commandeered right on the roads and in the towns. Some of the bus lines, I believe, were taken over in accordance with long-standing plans. But for the most part the requisitioning and commandeering were emergency measures. Another thing that simplified matters was that there was no unwillingness on the part of car owners. Many were, in fact, glad to turn them over to the government and receive a receipt for them when things began to look bad, which was only natural.

The busses and cars thus taken over were used for every imaginable purpose. They were used for hauling supplies and troops, for evacuating wounded, for liaison and messenger purposes, and every other kind of military errand.

On Bataan itself it was possible to use trucks and cars to some extent. There was enough gasoline on Bataan so that I believe some was still left at the end. This was despite the fact that the rationing of gas and oil was not under good control for some time after the withdrawal. I have mentioned elsewhere how gasoline was brought into Bataan and dumped all over the area. Often a truck bringing food and other supplies from Manila would bring one or two drums of gasoline also. During the last few weeks the gasoline was rationed and there was very little allowed for administrative purposes but still enough for most tactical purposes. It was necessary, also, to mix the aviation gas with low-octane gas to get a product that would work well in motor vehicles.

It was my observation that the different means of signal communication we used held up very well throughout the whole campaign. Of course there is a considerable amount of long-distance commercial wire in the Philippines, and this was a good thing because one of the many things we were short of was military wire. Between the combined commercial and military wire nets and the radio net, we kept up fairly good communications at all times. There was also a system of scheduled messengers between the advanced command post of General MacArthur and the I and II Corps, and each corps had its own courier system down to the different divisions making up the corps. All three methods of communication—wire, radio, and courier—were used between Bataan and Corregidor.

There was also a system of observers up on the mountains of Bataan. These were, for the most part, trained spotters and were in wire communication with their units. Ladders were built up to the tops of tall trees, and then the observation nest was camouflaged. I never heard of a Jap flier being able to find one of these.

Colonel de Jesus, G-2 of the Philippine Army, kept up a messenger service through the Japanese lines back and forth to Manila. These messengers usually went by banca (a small native boat) across Manila Bay. Word was sometimes sent into Manila this way to friends held prisoners, and the messengers brought back reports of numbers, movements, and other military news.

We even had a newspaper on Bataan, a single sheet published both in English and Tagalog, as long as there was any paper which could be used for it. This little war newspaper contained brief items of news from the States, news about possible relief and anything that would help morale.

News also came in from outside from over the regular radio waves. I think all the American troops had radios in their companies. The Philippine Army units had a few of them, but since they were newly organized units most of them had not been able to build up any company funds with which to buy radios for their men. Some of the reports we heard from the United States didn't make much sense to us there on Bataan, especially because of the groundless and sugar-coated optimism on the part of a good many radio commentators. But all in all, radios were helpful to morale.

Our troops had some of the walkie-talkie type of radio. These proved most useful. One of the cleverest jobs of reconnaissance done during the whole campaign was the result of making use of these radios. The Japs had some big-gun emplacements near Cavite, which was several miles across Manila Bay from Corregidor. By then we didn't have any planes to observe the position of these big-gun batteries. A patrol of our men slipped over to the mainland from Corregidor with walkie-talkies—I believe they went over by night—succeeded in getting close enough to the Jap gun emplacements to report on their positions, and stayed there for the better part of a day, sending back information to the gun crews on Corregidor while keeping under cover. Our own guns silenced these big batteries that day, and the men who used the walkie-talkies got back to Corregidor O.K.

A good many men found comfort in religion as the situation grew tougher on Bataan. You would hear prayers pretty regularly from some men, and there was evidence that most of them felt comfort in religion during the hard days especially on the battle front. The chaplains were constantly busy holding services and conducting burials, and there were even three weddings that I know of.

When there was time to rest—and you have to take some time for rest in any long-drawn campaign; you can't keep going all the time—officers and men alike read anything they could lay hands on that was in print. I remember reading some thoroughly asinine novels and dipping into old, torn magazines and reading stuff I probably wouldn't ever have thought of reading in other circumstances. It was just tripe. It was much the same with everybody else. Old magazines were passed around until they were worn to tatters. It was the same way with such books as there were. Reading matter is practically a necessity wherever troops stay put for any length of time.

Music was also a help. The regimental bands apparently didn't have their instruments on Bataan, for I heard no bands playing. However, a number of men, both in the Philippine Army units and our own, had instruments of one kind or another, and there was a good deal of singing.

There was a chorus not far from the main headquarters which made some good music. I'm not musical, but it sounded good. The troops sang all the old songs that troops always sing—some newer ones too. A war will never interfere with the singing of American soldiers.

I haven't said much, so far, about the enemy, and there's a good deal to say. Others have described him in various ways, so a part, at least, of my own observations and information may be repetition, but some of it may be helpful.

The Jap can fight, and fight hard, and no question about it. And he has endurance and the spirit and will to keep on attacking.

When Japanese infantry attacks, you have to kill them to stop them. They use mass formations much more than we would, and they often assault in such formations. It is also generally true that a Jap will fight to the death rather than be taken prisoner.

The Japs will, however, retreat, and they often did. Once when the Japs attacked in an infantry sector they attacked in three waves. Our infantry simply mowed down these three waves, mainly by aimed rifle fire. A great number of other Jap casualties were due to our machine-gun fire, however. Once in another infantry regimental sector an American machine gunner whose gun was in a good position commanding a road got left at the gun position when his outfit pulled back. Somehow, it was nearly two days before a patrol went forward again and found him. They found him pretty well out of his head, yelling, "They're coming by thousands!" But there were hundreds of Japs piled up dead and dying in front of his position, and none of them had been able to get to the gun.

The Japs like to attack at night. They usually make a feint at one place and the real attack in another. They sometimes keep alignment at night by using a drummer who regulates the advance by different beats of the drum.

It shouldn't be thought that the Japs always attack in the open. They are good at infiltration, too, as good as Indians ever were. They will work forward and stay frozen in one position for hours at a time, until they get their chance. They like to work in behind the enemy and shoot him up and worry him. Our troops had to keep skirmish lines out to stop such infiltration.

We had nowhere near enough barbed wire or other similar defensive aids. It often seemed to me that if we had had something like sharp-pointed "jacks" of the type children play with, but a good deal larger— thousands of them scattered well out to the front of our defensive sectors —it would never have been possible for Jap troops to infiltrate either by day or by night. The sharp points would have injured their feet severely. But we had no particular amount of defensive obstacles of any kind.

The Japs left their dead on the field. When we made a counterattack the smell of the rotting bodies made it tough on our troops. When we gained an area they had been occupying we took their dead back by truckloads and burned the bodies. Grave-registration units took care of our own dead with the assistance of the troops.

Infiltrating small groups of Japanese were more than once successful in getting through our lines and then setting off firecrackers in the rear of our troops. Once one of our Filipino divisions was pretty badly panicked by this because the troops thought they were surrounded. If troops do keep their heads, as thoroughly trained troops will, such fire-cracker efforts are a waste of energy.

The Japs tried a number of other tricks besides firecrackers. The slang habit of calling everybody "Joe," which was common some time ago in the States, prevailed strongly among our American soldiers during the fighting in the Philippines. The Japs tried the trick of calling out, "Hey, Joe, come here and help me," or words to that effect. This worked a few times, but our men soon found ways to detect this trick. There are plenty of American words you can fire at a Jap who knows some English, which he can't understand or can't pronounce without an easily detectable accent. Our troops learned every trick of combat fast. They lost men unnecessarily in the beginning, as I have said earlier in this account. But they learned fast, and any initial unsteadiness soon disappeared as they settled down to the business of war.

When the Japs captured Filipino prisoners they stripped them naked and sent them to the rear without any guard. They did not take individual American prisoners, though they did apparently send some groups of captured Americans to the rear. Where a single American fought until surrounded he wasn't given any chance to give up. But at close quarters the fighting was usually to the death on both sides. We didn't take many prisoners ourselves, largely for the reason that the Jap soldier preferred to die.

It's true, also, that the Jap fliers didn't carry parachutes. All our own fliers said they never saw a Jap with one. When a Jap plane falls the flier falls.

The fact that the Japanese simply quit fighting and waited through a number of weeks for us to get weak and sick does not reflect on the battle courage of the individual Japanese soldier. For that must have been done on the orders of the high command, who decided that their forces could not stand the heavy losses we were inflicting. We did get reports from Manila to the effect that some enemy soldiers had been executed there for refusing to go to Bataan when the fighting was heavy in January and February. But there was little sign of fighting weakness in the troops immediately opposed to us. They apparently would attack anything they were ordered to attack, and do it in any formation, however vulnerable to our defensive fires. It is possible that the heavy losses broke the spirit of some Jap units, but in general there was no sign of it at any time.

Colonel Donald Hilton informed me of one operation which shows clearly the Jap military character. Some of his men found a diary of a dead Japanese officer. The entries in the diary were in a script that indicated a man of high education. In the diary this Jap officer told how he had come from Manchukuo and landed at Legaspi in southern Luzon, and from then on, there was a day-to-day account of his duties during the invasion.

Upon reaching the forces opposite our own lines in Bataan, his commander ordered him to take his unit in boats down the west coast of Bataan to land behind our lines. He carried out his orders by having a few of his men get ashore the first night and another fraction of his forces on succeeding nights. The first men who landed would not begin a fight but would simply lie quiet during the day until the force had been built up.

Our outguards discovered this attempt, and Colonel Hilton's battalion was ordered to drive the Jap forces out. The battle lasted about three days, and I understand much was said about it here at home in the papers.

The Japanese infantrymen carried an efficient rifle of small caliber—a bolt-action weapon which he loads from clips. This rifle has no windage regulator on it. The Jap soldier fires more from the standing or kneeling position than from the prone position, which we use for most of our firing.

A general exception to this was the Japanese sniper. These were good shots, especially selected. They learned to fire from almost any position, even tying themselves up in trees to shoot. They also used shell holes for sniper posts. The snipers used all kinds of camouflage. Their instructions apparently were to kill all officers possible, because they would let enlisted men go by in order to kill an officer. It was accordingly necessary for all officers not to wear their insignia of rank on their shoulders when they were up near the front.

One day an American officer of one of our Philippine Scout regiments was going through the jungle and noticed a dead Jap in the crotch of a tree. This enemy soldier had no shoes on, and one of the Philippine Scouts with the officer made a practice jab at the Jap's foot with his bayonet as he went by him. Another Scout a little to the rear happened to see the Jap's face wince and, realizing at once that he was alive, killed him.

Once it was decided by the Jap high command not to keep on taking losses but to wait for us to weaken—they knew what supplies we had, and their blockade was almost airtight—they just sat in front of us and harassed us by bombing whatever they could see to bomb. There was enough bombing to keep troops well on the alert in the daytime but very little at night; hence our troops could usually get rest at night. This continued until the Japs knew we were hungry and sick, and then they made their biggest push with everything they had.

I was sick myself and in the hospital for some time with a combination of malaria and diet-deficiency diseases, the illnesses that weakened most of us. From firsthand experience and from all of my direct observations and what was told to me by others during the whole campaign, I want to say that the work of the Medical Corps deserves much praise. It was untiring and efficient throughout. They were everywhere they were needed—first-aid men right with the troops, well-functioning first-aid stations just to the rear of the front-line fighting units, and larger installations farther to the rear. But the story of the hard-working nurses, doctors, and enlisted men on Bataan and Corregidor has been well told by others, and I will not go into it further except to say one other thing. It appeared to me that the medical methods of aid to the troops now established need no particular alteration; they worked out well under the most difficult conditions.

During the period when illness and hunger steadily weakened our forces they nevertheless begged more than once to go on the offensive. I don't know when the point came when we began to feel we knew the Japs had us. I do know we thought for a long time we could whip them and then toward the end began to realize we weren't going to make it.

That is what we must do—are doing now—to the Japs. They have never been licked in past wars or in the first months of this one. Until they know, through one defeat after another, that they can be whipped and whipped badly, they are going to stay cocky and keep on thinking they can whip the world. We have got to make them feel, time after time, what we Americans finally felt in the Philippines—that we *were* going to lose that particular fight.

I don't think the Jap propaganda had anything to do with our final defeat. They dropped a lot of leaflets advising the Filipino troops to surrender. The leaflets directed the soldier to take one along—that it would insure his safe passage into the Japanese lines. These were dropped on Corregidor as well as Bataan. They weren't at all convincing. I doubt whether a single one of them was ever used for the purpose it was intended for, though I know they were used for other purposes.

In these informal recollections of one of the hardest campaigns that troops have ever fought under the American flag, the thing I have so far tried to emphasize most is the absolute need for hard and complete battle training. A fighting soldier is still an amateur until his leaders have taught him every trick and made him practice over and over every hardship of war that can be practiced. Even then it will take at least one fight to make him anything of a professional. But if he receives the fullest training—in which nothing whatever he is going to need to know in battle is skimped or slid over—he'll round out into a real soldier fast, once he gets fighting. But if he goes into battle with any part of his training neglected or in the slightest ignorance of the demands battle is going to make upon him, we'll have the same old story of the early battles in our other war—great lists of casualties, most of them needless, and lost battles too.

I know that we're having more time to train, and train properly, for this war than for any other we've ever fought. The story of the half-trained troops, or replacements hardly trained at all, entering battle, as happened in France in 1918, is not going to have to be repeated in this present fight. With the time we have in this war for proper training there is no reason for putting even troops three-quarters trained into battle. We have the chance to make all our forces into hardened fighting men.

We are opposed by such fighters and not by amateurs. And to get any-where we shall have to be certain the troops we send in against them know all there is for them to know of modern fighting methods. It isn't a matter of highly complicated individual or small-unit tactics. It's just a matter of *complete* training and toughening in the trade of a fighting soldier. And it's every commander's first duty of all to see that his troops get such training.

There is, however, one other side of war today that is probably still more important, if you can make such a comparison. I think of it as "spiritual" training, though I don't care what name you give it. What I mean here is something to give American fighters the desire to *kill* their enemies.

Most American soldiers don't have much honest hate for the German or Jap until some of his comrades have been killed by the enemy, or until he himself has been made to suffer at the enemy's hands. This was true right on Bataan, and I say this without taking away one particle from the splendid fighting spirit I saw there or from the innumerable deeds of fighting craft and courageousness that were done there.

But the Jap hates the American with a downright hate that carries him through in battle to success or death. And we could do with more of a similar individual fighting spirit. On Bataan our troops soon learned the usual lesson of battle—that it is a case of kill or be killed. And as I have said, a lot of them were killed or wounded because they had not had complete training in this basic idea of combat. They learned this lesson, but by no means all of them gained the spirit that goes beyond it—the belief in the heart of every man that he must kill the enemy, and the feeling that he *wants* to kill him to the extreme of his own fighting ability.

I don't mean here a spirit of wild rashness that will make a man forget to fight as a thoroughly trained fighter ought to fight—forget to apply every skill and craft of battle whether it meets ideas of fair play or not. I don't mean a spirit of useless sacrifice among commanders that will lead them to waste their troops, as sometimes happened in France. I don't even mean a blind, unthinking hatred based on lies and psychologi-cal deceit from the high command, which is what the Jap soldier has in his heart. But I do mean a spirit just as strong and stronger, because it can be based on the truths of this war.

I consider this too big a thing for me to preach about. It needs more expert thought than I could give it. I simply know from what I saw that it's needed. I think about it more than anything else in this war because its building seems most important of all.

It can't be a separate thing, given to troops through lectures, movies, and reading matter. These all help, but it's got to be mixed right in with the battle training. Every time a soldier handles his weapon in training he needs to remember its purpose. An infantryman's rifle, for example, has only one purpose. It's made for him to kill Japs or Nazis with, not to keep clean, to practice with, or carry to parades. The same with every other weapon up to planes and tanks.

So the spirit that makes a soldier want to kill the enemies of his country has to be instilled in him from the very beginning. It has to be put before him, with reasons, from the first day of his training right on through all of his combat training to his time of battle.

It makes little difference, as I said, what name you call it by. I don't think it ought to take the form of constant preaching or any other form that gets tiresome. I think it ought to be treated always as an utterly serious matter, and not as a matter for joking.

But I'm not an expert. There are plenty of practical students of the human mind who ought to know how to make a man understand the thing I'm trying to express. I think an appeal to American pride has a place in what I am suggesting. We have pride in many things now, but we as a nation have lost out on pride in our fighting abilities. We just haven't thought much about it. No American soldier would even think of admitting that a fanatic Jap, with his mind plugged full of what his leaders have told him about his being the best fighter in the world, *is* the best fighter in the world. But he *is* a good fighter, bent on killing every American he possibly can. So there's only one answer, to be better at killing than he is. If we are not, then what the Japs think about being better fighters than we are is true.

I think the toughening processes of training have something to do with it too. We're accustomed to think of plenty of good food and a lot of passes to town as important things in building morale. Yet with all the good food and chances to relax, I've seen marches not long before this war when men would begin to fall out of the column with sore feet after six or seven miles of marching. Now that we're training for war the troops undoubtedly do far better. But do we use heavy marches for the kind of practice we need to? And do we make them hard enough to get men's minds out of the idea that steak every day and ice cream on Sundays are important matters?

Unless the morale we build is based on pride in overcoming hardships, such as a day or two of hard marching with no food, it is a morale that won't hold up in battle. When demands like this are made on troops in training, every man must understand why he is being tested—why American troops, if they really are better than the troops we are fighting—must equal and surpass them in hardness and endurance and ability to kill.

I don't expect anybody to make the American character over again into some imitation of our enemies' that wouldn't be American at all. I only think that we need to take more steps to toughen up the character we have. It is always news in our wars to great numbers of new soldiers that killing the enemy is the principal work of an army and that expert killing is the only thing that will save us from defeat and, this time, slavery. We've got to make this sink in deeper, whether you call what you use to do it propaganda, indoctrination, or, as more experienced soldiers would say, military common sense plus love of our country and what it is. I think that there are enough fine things to fight for to make men eager to kill the enemies who want to destroy them. That's why I think of it as "spiritual" training, though some may object to the word.

I know that others have thought even more about this, perhaps, than I have, and that a good deal is being done about it. From what I saw on Bataan, there is nothing else so important in winning this war.

NO TIME FOR A DRY RUN

By Major (now Lieutenant Colonel) Leonard H. Nason

(1942)

This is my third emergency, or war, whichever you care to call it. Three times in a man's short life I have had to leave my peaceful pursuits and train for combat. Each time my regiment was organized, reorganized, and disorganized, changed from one branch to the other, and finally cast into battle, where it always did well for itself. And we discovered there how war boils men down, how a few minutes of battle show whether a man is made of oak or only covered with a thin veneer quickly warped and cracked in the heat of conflict.

Maybe a lot of the warping and cracking is due to the sudden shock of contact with an alert and active enemy. Every nation, once a war is started, at once begins to vilify the enemy in press and pulpit and call him hard names. This, of course, has its place, but the soldier who reads and hears these things, too, is misled. I know, because when I was younger, in the last great peril, I believed what I read and heard, and when I first met up with what we then called a Hun I was surprised. I was surprised to find out that though he might be abased and brutal and the ravager of Belgium, he was a better shot than I was with a machine gun. And so I was carried out feet first.

The last time, the last two times, I was much younger. I had no responsibilities, at home or in the Army, and war was pretty much of a romp, with periods of repose mixed in during which I acquired a working knowledge of local beverages. But in this one I have a grown-up family and some three hundred earnest youths in my battalion who look to me to get them through this thing.

These last are my main worry. They have been brought up proud of the fact that they were Americans and could do as they pleased. Many of my young officers have graduated from places where it was smart to be "collegiate," that is, to be dirty. I knew a man once who died because he wouldn't clean his pistol and wouldn't wash his shirt. And when his pistol jammed a low Hun shot him and the bullet carried a bit of dirty shirt into the wound.

We will, of course, eventually lick the Japs and the Germans and all their rabble following. But when the two great forces, Democracy and Tyranny, come head-on into collision, there are going to be a few basketfuls of human fragments after the party is over. I don't want to be in one of the baskets and I don't want any of my boys in one either. I can't reproduce a battle for them; it's like trying to describe a sunset to a blind man. But I can train them to the utmost before they actually fight. I can explain the purpose of a lot of things that seem useless and stupid. I can point out, for instance, that a man who leaves the lid of the coal box up will probably forget to clean his pistol after a dusty march, and so becomes a poppy in Flanders Field. I can tell them that the man who does not salute because he "did not see the officer, sir," will not see the lurking Jap scout.

The day when you and I and our buddy from the next bunk come face to face with the enemy, nothing will stand between us and death but what we learned before the battle. There is no time, then, to learn how to clear a jammed machine gun. No time to fill the gas tank that should have been filled that morning. No time, with the enemy at the bend of the road, for a dry run. If you've got it you can put it out. If you haven't you had better say your prayers.

The responsibility of a commander in wartime is heavy. He has to order men to possible death. Not to certain death, as the unthinking sometimes say, because if death is certain a commander who is any good won't order his men into it. But if men are killed as a result of his orders, the commander's conscience will be clear if he knows he has done his utmost to train them, to teach them skill in their weapons, alertness, and self-confidence in all their actions.

So before combat the commander who has the welfare and safety of his men at heart insists that they be smart in appearance, that they march well, that they go to formations promptly, that they have the benefit of his constant attention to see that they know how to use their weapons.

FROM AN OLD SOLDIER TO THE NEW[1]

By Gerald W. Johnson

(1942)

This . . . is a word from an old member of the AEF to the men who now go to war more than two decades later.

Gentlemen, I am sorry for you—but not too sorry. You are going to catch hell for a while. Even though you may not stop a bullet you will have what we used to call *beaucoup* trouble, hard work, hard living, hard beds, and hard rations, not to mention hard men over you. This is not pleasant, and nobody likes it. For all that it implies, I am sorry. Any man who has to do active service in time of war is entitled to sympathy, as everyone knows who has done it.

But I am not too sorry, for you are going to win a victory that is worth winning. I do not speak of glory. Never mind glory. Too much of it is rather tin-pot stuff, won by doing things that really are pretty idiotic. Every old soldier knows that the man with the most hardware on his chest is not necessarily the best man. Sometimes fakers get away with the medals and good men go without.

But apart from glory, you are called on to do a job that needs doing. This country of ours is not perfect, God knows, but it is a pretty good old country, at that, and it is by way of getting better. It has been getting better for 150 years in spite of occasional setbacks, and it is because of you that it is going to stand and continue to get better in the future.

You know, gentlemen, you have had it pretty soft for the last twenty years. Times have been hard, and all that, but by comparison with the young man in any other country in the world, the young American has been doing right well. At least he could call his soul his own. He hasn't had to get off the sidewalk and hold up his hand in a silly attitude every time some swine in a Sam Browne belt passed by. He has been able to read the news in his papers. He has been able to go to a school where they taught the facts. He has been able to cast his vote as he pleased, without a thug with a blackjack in his hand standing looking over his shoulder as he marked his ballot. He has been able to collect his pay and spend it as he pleased, without having to cough up for the party funds, in order that a lot of plug-uglies called party chiefs might live at ease.

And why? Well, if I may say so, because in 1917 and 1918 a lot of us old fellows also caught hell—worked hard, lived hard, slept on hard

[1]Reprinted from the Baltimore *Evening Sun*.

beds, and jumped when hard men told us to jump. And because, long before us, other men did the same—in 1861, and in 1846, and in 1812, and in 1776. Say what you will, this country has survived because, whenever it was threatened, it was able to produce a tough man with a gun; a man a little tougher than the toughest any enemy could bring against it.

In between, whole generations of Americans have had it easy. Most of us who were caught in the jam a quarter of a century ago hoped that you were going to be one of those generations. We have done our best to make it so, but our best efforts have failed. You are in for it now.

All right, you will stand up and take it. I am sorry, but there is nothing else for it; and, after all, when this business is over you will have something in the consciousness that you belong to one of the generations that didn't take everything and give nothing.

Maybe that doesn't seem much to you now, but it will in time to come. The man who has gone under fire for his country is forever after a man apart. He has paid for his keep. He has paid his part of the debt we all owe to the long line of brave men who won our freedom and have maintained it. He can look George Washington in the eye, with respect, yes, but without servility. He is, in the fullest sense, a free man, for he has met the final test of a freeman and has passed it.

It's a great thing, gentlemen, worth a lot of hard work, worth a lot of risk.

Unfortunately some of you will not experience it. Some of you have already died, and more will die. But if you die in this service you will go out cleanly and, since you have to die sometime, anyhow, that is something. In other words, while you may not win the greatest prize, you who serve honorably in this war cannot lose altogether. At worst you will go in a way that becomes a man, and your family and friends will never think of you without a glow of happy pride.

For there isn't going to be any disillusionment about this war. We didn't want it. We know there isn't any profit in it, and we don't want the sort of glory that may be won in it. We did everything we honorably could to keep out of it. But it was thrust upon us.

But we did not try to get out of it because we were afraid, although the enemy apparently thought so. Now that we are in it we are going to fight it in a way that will make those who thrust it upon us wish that they had never been born. When we get through this world is going to be pretty safe for decent nations, who want no more than a chance to attend to their own business, letting other people alone.

It is you, gentlemen, who are destined to establish that state of affairs, by your efforts and by your risks. It is an honorable task which will win you the right to the gratitude of many generations. Therefore, it is not altogether a hard duty. It is also an enviable opportunity. Yours is the chance to establish yourselves as one of the great generations of American history, to take a place alongside the men of 1776, and of 1812, and of 1846, and of 1861. It is an enviable place, but you will fill it worthily.

Therefore, I am not too sorry for you. Only in the shortsighted view are you to be listed among the unfortunate, for if you are called upon to endure hardness it is without fault on your part, and therefore it opens the door to greatness. It is not to every generation that such an opportunity comes. Take your fortune, then, realizing that it is not altogether ill, and as you do valiantly, so shall all the future admire and envy you.

GROUND TROOPS' AA METHODS

By Major (now Lieutenant Colonel) Carl T. Schmidt

(*1942*)

IN A GREAT MANY of the general accounts of battle since the war began there has been much emphasis on the effect of dive bombers and hedgehoppers on ground troops. There has been so much, in fact, that we have been apt to discount the possible action of ground troops in the face of such attacks. But by now there has been enough detailed information to furnish a clear answer to the old question of whether ground troops would fire back or duck when attacked from the air.

The answer is easy. It is the only one you could expect to a question of such breadth. The only answer, indeed, that can be given to any broad tactical question. It depends upon the specific situation.

But before we get into the details we should first try to clear up two or three general aspects of the matter. For example, is the fire of ground troops effective enough against fast planes at short ranges to warrant its use at all? And if so, why was it apparently so ineffective in the battles of Poland, Flanders, and France? In other words, how could it be disregarded by the enemy's planes as freely as it apparently was?

Here we can undoubtedly find the answer in two facts. The Polish and French armies, besides having no adequate amount of special AA weapons, were not thoroughly trained to pour lead into the skies at attacking planes with every possible weapon, as we have been taught for many years to do. Moreover, the French method of getting a machine gun ready for AA fire was particularly slow, and their infantry in general used passive measures rather than active ones. And, to be sure, the French morale was not conducive to sustained AA firing by the troops in general.

As for the general effectiveness of ground fire at low-flying planes, both British and German tactical doctrines, like our own, emphasize the use of small-arms fire in addition to that of heavier infantry AA weapons. But we should note a continual tendency toward giving ground troops more special weapons for AA uses. For example, the British infantry division of 1939–40 contained no AA guns of its own. But after the Flanders campaign a regiment of forty-eight Bofors 40-mm. automatic AA guns was incorporated in the division. One twelve-gun battery of this regiment is permanently allotted to each of the three rifle brigades (equivalent to American regiments), and the fourth battery protects the divisional artillery. Each brigade headquarters has a "defense-and-employment" platoon that has, among its duties, to protect the headquarters against air attacks. Furthermore, each infantry battalion now contains a platoon with four dual Bren guns on AA mounts.

Again, the German infantry division of early 1940 apparently relied mainly on rifles and machine guns (approximately caliber .30) as its organic weapons for firing at aircraft. It is now probable that the AT company of every regiment has a platoon with four 20-mm. AA machine guns.

The Nazi motorized division is said to include an AA battalion with sixteen 15-mm., twelve 20-mm., and eight 37-mm. AA machine guns. Armored divisions appear to have a still heavier AA armament.

If we could watch a squadron or two of planes attacking a Nazi armored division we would probably see the division keep on rolling with its tanks deployed if the country were open enough and all AA machine guns opening fire. This would not include any fire from the tanks themselves unless they have recently been equipped with high-angle weapons for this purpose. It probably would include, however, the fire of some fifty 20-mm. AT-AA heavy machine guns on as many light scout cars, and that of fifty more 7.9-mm. machine guns on these same vehicles. There might also be an additional blast of AA fire from three different AA battalions with the division. From a "motorized AA battalion" would probably come the fire of some thirty to forty weapons—single 20-mm. AT-AA superheavy machine guns, four-barreled 20-mm. superheavy machine guns, and 37-mm. dual-purpose AT-AA guns. An "air-force mixed battalion" would probably have five batteries containing altogether twelve 88-mm. guns (too big to fire at low-flying planes), thirty 20-mm. machine guns, and eight searchlights. And the five batteries of an "air-force light AA battalion" might have an additional thirty-six 20-mm. guns and nine 37-mm. guns (also sixteen searchlights). This would make a possible total of some 160 weapons of 0.8-inch or 1-inch caliber, and many more machine guns of over .30 caliber. This is a powerful lot of special AA fire and indicates clearly the tendency to increase such armament and the belief in its effectiveness.

As for the effectiveness of ordinary AA rifle and machine-gun fire, there have been reports in this present war of planes brought down by such fire, just as there were in the first World War. At the same time, it is true that the armor now built into low-bombing planes to protect the pilots and other vital spots (at least against ball ammunition) narrows down the probability of seriously damaging hits from such fire.

But even when planes lacked armor it took on the average (simply through the operation of the law of chance) the firing of thousands of rifle and machine-gun bullets, with perhaps several score hits on the plane itself among them, to give any certainty that one or two bullets would strike a spot vital enough to bring the plane down. But an intense concentration of small-arms fire would often bag a hostile plane. And it was therefore worth it if *every* man with a rifle or larger weapon opened fire, applying the methods of such fire in which he had been trained.

For two reasons this habitual blasting away at low-flying planes is probably still worth while, provided there are no tactical reasons to the contrary in a given situation. In the first place, the armor covers only a few square yards, for low-bombing planes simply cannot sacrifice much of their pay load to armor and have enough left for bombs, weapons, ammunition, and gasoline. Hence most hits on a plane do *some* damage, the total of which will inevitably add to the hours the plane must stay on the ground for repairs. And some hits, especially with armor-piercing ammunition, can still do serious damage, since the armor cannot cover every partially vulnerable spot and may even destroy the plane. Again, if the man who habitually pots at a plane with rifle or machine gun knows there is even a small chance of doing real damage, his morale is helped by the fact that he is accomplishing *something* against his enemy in the air.

There is, however, no question at all regarding the effectiveness of *concentrated* AA fire from the next-heavier weapons beyond small arms. The armor a plane of suitable size for ground-target bombing can carry can hardly be enough to ward off, say, the fire of a 37-mm. AA weapon. And when bombers happen to dive or strafe an area containing a number of such weapons the air losses may be heavy indeed.

Right here it may be well to consider the effect upon troops of the difficulty of determining the direct effect of their fire. It is, for example, a plainly observable fact of battle when a dive bomber comes shrieking down several times in succession to turn loose its bombs at a definite target in a definite locality. Most men on the ground within hundreds of yards can see the plane, the bombs, and the destruction they cause. But the results of any fire they direct back at such a plane are extremely vague. The speed of the plane is such that a man firing any kind of infantry weapon at it almost never knows whether he hit it or, if he did, whether his fire caused any substantial damage. Even if his fire actually caused the plane to crash he will seldom, if ever, know it, for many others will have been firing at the same target at the same time. And the speed of a plane is so great that even if it is struck in a vital spot it will hit the ground many hundreds of yards away.

These things being true, it is evident that troops may gain the feeling, after some experience of air attack, that their fire against planes is wholly ineffective. But so long as there continues to be evidence that heavy ground fire has effect on low-flying planes, there are at least two ways of offsetting any particular effect upon the morale of troops which such lack of specific knowledge of results might bring about. One is a frequent emphasis in orders of large units, giving probable credit for crashed enemy planes to all troops within a mile or so of its point of crash. The other, of course, is the use in training of actual damaged parts of planes to show the effect of small-arms fire, and a full explanation of how hard it is to tell just what man or what small unit brought a plane down.

Another general point we may clear up here is that of the so-called "paralyzing" effect of dive bombing on troops that have to take it. The fact is that any heavy bombardment, whether of air or artillery, may have such an effect. And of the two, it is entirely probable that a modern artillery concentration is the more intense, for more shells may fall within a given area in a given time. But the general moral effect here, it is plain, will depend upon the degree of training and battle experience of the troops bombarded, and therefore very largely on their habitual measures for protection against such attacks.

The number of ground troops killed by machine-gunning from the air in this war has certainly been small. Even in Poland, where this form of attack was frequent, the casualties are reported to have been light, though the confusion caused among horse-drawn transport was considerable. As with bombing, however, the moral effect is considerable and often disproportionate. Here again the soldier's instinctive reactions need breaking down—he assumes too readily, when he hears a rattle in the sky, that the plane is shooting at him. It is a frequent practice of German bombers, even when flying at three thousand feet or more, to fire large quantities of ammunition in what appears to be a more or less indiscriminate manner. The tendency is for inexperienced troops to take far too much notice of this sort of thing and also to indulge in a good deal of loose talk about it afterward. No casualties may occur and probably no more than one soldier in a hundred even sees a bullet strike the ground. But the enemy will achieve his object of intimidation, if only by virtue of the fact that every man believes himself to have "been machine-gunned" and says so. Inevitably this delusion spreads and has its effect on morale.

There may indeed be a marked moral effect in the air instead of on the ground, as Axis forces have demonstrated in at least one battle instance in Africa. German columns attacked by British planes proved to have flank guards with so many AA weapons (probably 15-mm., 20-mm., or 37-mm. automatic guns on special mounts) that the planes had to fly through a regular barrage to attack. The air losses were so heavy that the morale of pilots making such attacks was plainly lowered.

It is clear enough from the methods given in our training manuals that small-arms AA fire from troops that have not been thoroughly trained in it may only result in wasting much good ammunition. The methods of AA fire taught on the range must be kept fresh in mind, for example, through frequent practice in estimating altitudes and aiming at planes.

It is also of great importance for troops to learn to distinguish between hostile and friendly aircraft, and this again is simply a matter of training. Given plenty of practice, men can come to recognize types of planes as readily as they can tell the makes of cars on the road. But under combat conditions it may often be necessary to distinguish hostile planes by their actions rather than their appearance.

Troops with some knowledge of bombing tactics and technique derived from watching not one or two demonstrations, but a series of demonstrations and exercises, will settle down much more quickly in the field than troops to whom every aircraft in sight is an immediate potential menace. In combat troops soon learn things they should have known before they went into action—for example, that a large formation of aircraft flying in the usual V-shaped formation down a narrow road is not going to bomb that road so long as the planes keep that formation. Troops who do not learn this lesson until they are in action learn it at some expense to their nerves and morale. The expense is unnecessary.

There are, of course, many situations in which purely passive measures are better than active AA firing. If concealment of a unit or an installation from either ground or air observation is desired, the position must obviously not be given away by small-arms firing, and this requires a strict AA discipline, since troops have normally the impulse to let fly at repeatedly attacking planes with the weapons in their hands. However, the fact that planes are attacking an area is certainly a sign the enemy has a good idea it is worth attacking.

It is also rarely advisable to open fire at night, not only because of the inaccuracy of such fire, but even more because the flashes may give away the position. Again, when troops are engaged in an intense fire fight with a ground enemy, as our field manuals plainly say, it seldom will be desirable to divert front-line or close-support weapons against hostile planes. At times, also, the ammunition supply is bound to be an important consideration.

In situations where AA fire is desirable, there can never be the maximum of fire placed on attacking planes unless constant readiness is an ingrained habit. And no military unit can be considered a trained unit today without this habit. During the past fifteen years the *Infantry Journal* has published many articles explaining in detail how fleeting a low air target is but also how, in a few seconds' fire, an alert infantry unit can direct a storm of bullets toward attacking planes.

Indeed, it is worth repeating here that a deployed infantry regiment in open country—for example, a desert—has the organic weapons to fire over twenty-five thousand rounds in five seconds' time, *provided every man who carries a weapon is ready to fire it when an air attack comes.*

The bulk of this is armor-piercing caliber .30, but there is a sizable fraction of heavier stuff. And all of it that hits a plane may do serious damage. With trained troops at least 1 per cent of it will strike a plane fired at from the side and perhaps 5 per cent a head-on target. In other words, there are sure to be several hundred hits from the organic AA fire of a regiment in five seconds. Not all units will be firing at the same planes during the same five seconds, but this does not change the total quantity of fire.

The duties of air guards are emphasized plainly in infantry tactical manuals. They work in pairs for frequent relief, scanning the sky in every direction and listening for planes and sounding their warning when they come.

Though night restricts air operations, attacks by bombing and machine-gunning may nevertheless be delivered through the use of flares or by moonlight. But troops are not usually visible from the air at night unless they give themselves away through lights, such as vehicle lamps, flash-lights, fires, matches, cigarettes, and lights of buildings. Obviously windows and doors of buildings or shelters must be screened and outdoor lights covered. This may, however, be carried to excess in at least one respect. The British found it better in Greece for motor convoys to risk air observation than to suffer heavy losses from blind driving.

Except when hostile planes use flares, marching troops should usually push on at night even when planes come over. But if they are on a road its center should be kept open, since a pilot can readily see an unlighted road but not troops moving in single file along its sides. If flares are dropped every movement must cease, for then movement more than anything else will betray the presence of troops. And it is generally best to withhold the fire of infantry weapons at night since the flashes establish the troop locations.

The fact that concentrated infantry fire is often desirable against planes that attack by day does not mean at all that troops should not use passive measures as well as active. Every unit must ordinarily employ AA camouflage habitually, not only for protection against attack but chiefly for concealment against the planes that may serve as the far-seeing eyes of the enemy's artillery. Naturally this is more applicable to resting or defending troops than to troops in an attack. Camouflage is practically impossible during an attack, and in no circumstances do troops let air reconnaissance deter them from carrying out their mission. Besides, active

AA measures are not generally the concern of troops leading an attack—these are carried out by units farther back. It is also worth noting that fully deployed infantry is, on the whole, a poor target for air attack, and that often in the course of the present war German planes have paid no attention to deployed troops, seeking out more remunerative column targets.

This, of course, may well indicate that deployed troops are hard to see from fast-flying planes. And it most certainly shows that deployment, even of rear echelons, is highly desirable whenever it can be done—not only to avoid detection but to reduce casualties if an air attack is actually delivered.

The number of casualties from air attacks in the present war has proved to be surprisingly small. So long as troops lie down, even where they have no trenches or other depressions, they suffer little from bombs. And this can likewise be said of machine-gun fire—except when planes attack along roads. There the fire appears to be more accurate. It will be remembered that in the Russo-Finnish fighting in 1939 the Finns got so used to low-bombing attacks that they considered it simply as harassment. They fired, if they had warning of approaching planes, then ducked, and then went ahead with their business at hand on the ground. Here, of course, the terrain was largely wooded and the work of the Soviet airmen therefore often inaccurate. It appears, however, from accounts in later theaters, that steady, disciplined troops, though they may receive casualties from the air, can rarely be defeated by aviation alone.

At every halt and rest troops must take advantage of cover if air attack is at all possible. The slit trench has proved one of the best protective means, especially against dive bombers. It protects its occupant from bomb fragments and bullets and also from the blasts of heavy bombs. Whenever a unit halts for any time men should dig these trenches at once. The trench is simply large enough for a man to lie down in—about two feet wide, six feet long, and three or four feet deep.

The British have learned the lessons of aerial security from bitter experience. British troops who made habitual use of slit trenches in Greece suffered almost no casualties from air attacks. Once men realized the protection these trenches gave they dug them enthusiastically and became nonchalant about hostile planes. At one place in North Africa during a single day dive bombers attacked a division headquarters seventeen times and machine-gunned it from the air eighteen times. But slit trenches had already been dug, and there were no casualties. In the campaign in East Africa a South African brigade was bombed steadily for nine days. Eight men taking cover in a single trench were killed by one direct hit, and the only other casualties were two men wounded. Other examples of the almost complete protection given by suitable trenches have been numerous.

Troops certainly should not be trained to scramble at all cost into whatever cover is available and there remain prostrate with their faces to the ground. This practice has a negligible effect, if any at all, on their chances of surviving an attack, and it has an extremely bad effect on morale. Indeed, frantic running may enable the hostile aviator to spot a target that he would otherwise not have seen.

At most halts in bivouac British troops now dig slit trenches immediately; orders are no longer necessary. Vehicles and installations are separated by at least one hundred to two hundred yards—sometimes much more. Bivouacs are usually established by battalions or other small units. At least one third of the light machine guns are mounted for anti-aircraft defense. When available, a section of two 40-mm. AA guns may be assigned to cover such an area. Every uniform formation of troops, vehicles, armament, and shelter is avoided. Sentries sound warning signals when enemy planes appear. Hostile planes are seldom able to approach without detection, for in a threatened area every man of any experience is thoroughly aware of what a surprise air attack may do, and whenever a plane comes within hearing someone invariably tries at once to identify it. Nevertheless, this excellent habit does not warrant dispensing with sentries, no matter how small the group. For example, one detachment of six men did not post an air sentry; four men were killed and the other two wounded, although slit trenches were available for them. They simply had no warning.

On the march troops and vehicles must be widely scattered. Air attacks on columns are focused on the most conspicuous and valuable targets. Consequently anything that might become a target should not be closer than two hundred to five hundred yards to its neighbor if this is possible. That the maximum number of vehicles on a single road should certainly be no more than ten per mile is the opinion expressed by troop leaders experienced in such attacks. The British disperse Bren machine guns on antiaircraft mounts throughout their marching columns and place an antiaircraft sentry on each vehicle. But when a column is attacked every effort is made to keep the formation moving. (On the desert vehicles may disperse off the roads and still keep rolling.)

Before one action a British column of thirty thousand men advanced to concentration spread out over an area of fifteen by forty miles. Hostile scouting aircraft were active as low as three thousand feet, but apparently the troops were so scattered that they were not observed or at least not as being a force of any size. For when the fighting began this large force obtained surprise. On the other hand, a battery of two-pounder AT guns (sixteen guns) was attacked by aircraft while going into position. Here, because the unit disregarded dispersion and permitted a temporary laxness in its air sentinels and AA personnel, it was practically annihilated.

Men must be trained not to take shelter under motor vehicles, for these are always a mark for airplanes. The best protection is obtained by the side of a truck, not under it. For example, the commanding general of the British forces in Greece habitually stood on the running board of his car when in movement, and when an air attack came along he took cover in the ditch or any other defiladed spot along the road. Two of his cars were destroyed practically at his side. His aide-de-camp, however, took cover under a truck and was killed by a well-aimed bomb.

A few general methods we can arrive at in addition are as follows: When it is deemed best by a unit commander to deliver fire at attacking planes, machine guns must be sited so that there is as little dead space as possible for each gun. All weapons should be already alerted and ready to fire the moment hostile planes appear. But fire should never be opened by riflemen or machine gunners without command or without a reasonable certainty that the situation is such that their leader, if present, would authorize it. The use of infantry small arms against planes is a decision of the unit commander, not of the individual soldier. It may, however, be covered by standing operating procedures or exceptions to SOP for a given situation. Very evidently, no single hard-and-fast rule can be given on small-arms AA fire except the old and none-too-satisfactory dictum: "It depends upon the situation." One broad conclusion, however, is plain to see: Air support and adequate special AA weapons—properly mounted and sited—are essential to the active protection of ground troops against air attack. Better yet is such an aerial superiority that hostile aircraft can operate over our troops only at excessive cost.

CONQUEST BY AIR

By Major (now Colonel) Paul W. Thompson

During 1941 and 1942 there was seldom an issue of the *Infantry Journal* which did not contain an article by Colonel Thompson. The same was true of the *Military Engineer,* the service journal of the Corps of Engineers of which Colonel Thompson is a member. Colonel Thompson's *Modern Battle,* a collection of his *Infantry Journal* articles, including "Conquest by Air," has reached the distribution of over 200,000 copies. He is also the author of *Engineers in Battle* and *What the Citizen Should Know about the Army Engineers,* and of articles which have appeared in general magazines. Colonel Thompson has the ability to explain for military readers what went on during a battle in terms so clear that the general reader doesn't have to concentrate very hard to find out how much more there is to a battle than what he read in his newspaper. Colonel Thompson is now on duty in a war theater.

THIS IS THE STORY, necessarily incomplete and probably somewhat inaccurate, of the conquest of Crete. It is a story of conquest by air, a conquest in which a small mixed ground force, without heavy supporting weapons, without transportation, and without important land or sea communications, was literally blasted into victory by overpowering support from the air.

This war of tremendous events has produced no more significant or lesson-rich campaign. Indeed, the danger is that the spectacle of a defended *island* being reduced without control of the sea tends, by its very uniqueness, to suggest unjustified conclusions. Therefore, let us attempt to recast the events as they occurred and then attempt to divine what they mean.

PHYSICAL CONSIDERATIONS

Of all the unfavorable theaters to which this current war has one time or another spread (Ardennes, Albania, Greece, North Africa), perhaps the most unfavorable is the island of Crete. Unfavorable, that is, in the sense of imposing grave limitations on movement, observation, supply. Nature must have intended Crete to be anything other than a theater for modern war.

Nevertheless, Nature did endow Crete with the inherent characteristic of *strategic position* and thereby made of the island a military prize of importance. Geography tells the story: Crete is a barrier dominating the entrance to the Aegean Sea. It is a steppingstone between Sicily and the Dodecanese Islands. Held by Great Britain, it is a base for air operations against objectives on the Grecian mainland and even against objectives farther to the north and west. Held by the Axis, it is a base for air operations against Cyprus, Syria, Suez, and the North African coast. The strategic situation being what it is, it is not surprising that, following the occupation of Greece, Germany decided that the further occupation of Crete was worth a major effort.

Our estimate of Crete as a theater of operations may be facilitated by reference to a large-scale map. Crete is long (160 miles) and narrow (average, eighteen miles in width). Crete consists essentially of the upper levels of a range of mountains which rises out of the very deep eastern Mediterranean waters. Along the axis of the island the mountains rise to elevations above 7,000 feet. The various mountain masses are connected by high, rough saddles. The mountains are composed largely of limestone and igneous rock. They are not wooded but in general are covered by wild bushes and thickets.

There are very few plains or flat areas on the island. Generally speaking, the mountains fall precipitously into the very deep surrounding waters. As a result the island has a regular coast line with very few acceptable harbors. Indeed, along the entire south coast there is nothing deserving the name of a harbor, and along the north coast the only harbor which is at all suitable for deep-draft vessels is the one at Suda Bay. Even Suda Bay is far from ideal—it offers little protection against the north wind; its anchoring grounds are too deep, and its docking waters are too shallow. Suda Bay formed the base for such British naval units as operated from Crete after the British occupation in October of 1940.

An indication as to the climate of Crete is the fact that the island lies in the latitudes not of Europe, but of North Africa. Thus the spring and summer days may be very hot (say to 120 degrees), while the nights may be quite cold. Water supply for troops in the field is a problem almost as difficult as in Libya.

Crete has a population of about 400,000. A few of the people eke out a living in the mountains, chiefly by sheep raising, and a few cling to the fishing villages of the south coast. Most of them, however, live along the narrow northern coastal plains where the chief means of livelihood is the raising of olives. Thus the few flat places on the island are usually covered by olive trees—trees which have a low, thick foliage, such as to make observation for military purposes very difficult.

The road net of Crete is exceedingly simple and sparse. There is one road running generally along the north coast, connecting all the principal centers of population. This road, poor as it is, is the backbone of the island's communications system. A few subsidiary roads (trails is a better word) extend south from the main coastal road to specific points in the interior or on the south coast. These subsidiary roads run through the saddles which connect the mountain masses. An example of such a road is the one from Kalami (just east of Suda) to a point just short of Sphakia on the south coast. (The fact that this particular road stops short of its logical terminus—to which it is connected by a footpath— is illustrative of the general status of Cretan communications.) All Cretan roads, including the main coastal one, pass through many defiles. Meanwhile, the country between and off the roads is exceedingly rough, being practically impassable for any sort of self-propelled vehicle.

The Cretan terrain being what it is, it is clear that good airfields on the island are few and far between. As a matter of fact, in their six months of occupation, the British appear to have attempted to develop only three sites: the chief one at Maleme, ten miles west of the island capital of Canea; one at Rethymnon, and one at Candia. Little is known concerning the characteristics of these fields, but certainly none of them offered any exceptional natural advantages.

THE FORCES INVOLVED

To arrive at an estimate of the forces with which Crete was being held at the time of the attack, we must resort to deduction. At the time of the British occupation, during the closing months of 1940, it was generally understood that the occupying force was a single division. During the Grecian campaign certain Australian and New Zealand units were evacuated to Crete. One unofficial source puts the number of Australians so evacuated at about 6,500. Since the entire British force in Greece did not itself amount to more than about two divisions, it is logical to conclude that no more than, say, the equivalent of a division could have been landed at Crete, and the figure for Australian strength quoted above leads to the conclusion that the *évacués* were about equally divided between Australians and New Zealanders. In addition to the British military forces, there were, according to the Prime Minister, about 2,000 marines in action. Finally, along with the British, of course, were some Greek troops.

All in all, this evidence leads us to estimate the British forces in Crete at about 32,000 (15,000 English soldiers, 15,000 Australians and New Zealanders, and the 2,000 marines), and to this we may add a guess of, say, 10,000 Greeks. (Pursuing the same process of deduction, German commentators arrive at a total British-Greek force of about 50,000—a reasonable check under the circumstances.)

The defenses of Crete were commanded during the critical days by Major General Freyberg, a distinguished New Zealander whose "exploits in war and peace rival those of the heroes of antiquity" and who had commanded the New Zealand division during the Grecian campaign. One of General Freyberg's peacetime exploits had been an almost-successful attempt to swim the English Channel in 1925.

An estimate of the German forces employed in the attack on Crete involves further uncertainties. Prime Minister Churchill is authority for the statement that 3,000 parachutists were dropped near Suda Bay during the first day of the attack, and if we double that figure we have a reasonable estimate as to the total number dropped on the various objectives over the island. Meanwhile, as the battles progressed German reinforcements poured in constantly. Regardless of the total number of Germans thus involved, however, we shall see that the critical actions were fought and won by two regiments of mountain troops and a special "pursuit detachment," acting in conjunction with what was left of the parachutists.

The German action against Crete was in general charge of Reichsmarschall Göring. The "tactical operations" were under the direct command of Generaloberst Löhr, commanding the 4th Air Fleet. The chief figures in the Löhr task force were the following: General-of-Aviation Student, "with strong parachute, air-borne, and mountain units," and General-of-Aviation Richthofen, "with his strong VIII Air Corps." The commander of the mountain division which, as we shall see, played so important a part in the battle was one General Ringl, an Austrian.

It is likely that the British division (?) which originally occupied Crete was deficient in equipment and especially in supporting AA artillery. There is evidence of a few light tanks having been on hand, but it is certain that the units evacuated from Greece were lacking in almost all types of equipment and armament—so much so, in fact, as to suggest the thought that these évacués may have been more of a liability than an asset in the fight. Finally, it is clear that the British had never reached the point where they were basing considerable numbers of aircraft on the Cretan airdromes.

During the critical phases of the battle the German troops also were operating with only light equipment and armament, but between the German and the British cases there was one far-reaching difference. The German attackers were supported by the practically unlimited resources of Richthofen's air corps. It was a case, as we shall see, of poorly armed ground forces advancing behind a terrific artillery preparation.

The fundamental relationship which delivered into German hands absolute air supremacy over Crete was set up at the moment the Germans moved into southern Greece and occupied the airfields there. Six of the occupied fields—two near Athens, one each at Argos, Sparta, the island of Melos, the island of Scarpanto (one of the Dodecanese Islands)— were within effective fighter-plane range of Crete. On the other hand, the distance from Crete to the British bases in North Africa was about 400 miles—beyond effective fighter-plane range. The net result of this situation was to make the Cretan airfields untenable for British aircraft. This condition had been reached even before the invasion proper took place, with the result that the defenders of the island were almost completely without air support from beginning to end.

THE PARACHUTIST OPERATIONS

The actual invasion of the island came as no surprise to the defenders. As early as May 12 large assemblies of Ju-52 troop-carrying airplanes had been reported on the various Grecian fields listed above. Meanwhile, German activity in the air over Crete had been becoming progressively more intense. The British installations were bombed constantly, and it is safe to assume that every critical part of the terrain was carefully reconnoitered and photographed from the air. All of these signs pointed to an attempt at invasion. Finally, on May 18, two German aviators fished out of the sea confided to their Greek rescuers (whom they naïvely believed to be friendly to the Germans) that the zero hour was set for the morning of the twentieth.

The invasion did come on the morning of the twentieth. The sequence of events at each of the points of attack appears to have been about as follows: first a terrific bombardment by high-level and dive bombers, followed by and mixed in with machine-gun strafing by fighter planes;

then the attack by "several thousands" of parachutists, still with the support of the dive bombers.

It is possible to build up a fair picture of the parachute-dropping phase of the action by analyzing several eyewitness accounts. The violent preparatory bombardment had the effect of pinning the defenders to the ground and of shaking them up. Everything was perfectly co-ordinated by the Germans, the troop-carrying transports appearing on the scene immediately following the preparatory bombardment and before the defenders could regain their cohesion. The transports came in from the sea in formations of about fifteen planes each. They were flying very low—some accounts say as low as 200 feet—and before the parachutists from one formation had much more than touched ground another would be overhead discharging its load. Apparently the parachutists came in waves of about 600 each—the inference being that there was a lapse of time between successive waves. Perhaps one third of the parachutes carried equipment. There are authentic accounts of the dropping of infantry howitzers and anti-tank guns—by means of double and triple chutes.

The parachutists were dropped, as usual, from three-motored "Junkers 52" planes. The Ju-52 is a large (wing span 100 feet), cumbersome plane with a maximum speed of less than 200 miles per hour and a range, fully loaded, of about 500 miles. Each Ju-52 accommodates about thirty parachutists.

Interspersed with the parachutists were a few glider-borne troops. The normal German glider is only slightly smaller than the Ju-52 (wing span of glider seventy feet), and accommodates about twelve men. Reports indicate that the gliders came in low trains of four to six, towed by a loaded Ju-52 (giving the tow unit a strength of as much as 100 men). They were released as they approached the landing fields. They "looked more ominous than the parachutists," but frequently they were carried away from their landing objectives by contrary air currents. Since the gliders were used so sparingly, it is likely that, so far as they are concerned, the operation was nothing more than an experiment.

The parachutist himself carried a tommy gun with bands of ammunition slung around his neck. He carried also a knife and at least one hand grenade. There are reports of parachutists firing with their tommy guns as they descended.

On the point of picking the parachutists off while in the air there is some conflicting evidence, this possibly being illustrative of the confusion into which a large-scale bombing-parachute attack may throw a defending force. One account states that out of ten typical parachutists one was killed through failure of the chute to open in the short descent (this witness says the jumps were from 300 feet) ; one was picked off by the defending riflemen on his descent; one was put out of action by breaking a wrist or ankle on alighting, and the others "spouted about helplessly with tommy guns," only to be "picked off with rifles at 600 or 700 yards' distance." Another account states that it is impossible to hit a descending parachutist with a pistol and it is almost impossible with a rifle but that it is "easy enough with a (captured) German tommy gun if you can get close enough."

The very first action on the part of the parachutist after cutting himself loose from his chute was to seek local cover. Here again the *Luftwaffe* entered the picture: the most readily available covers often were the craters resulting from the bombing attacks. After gaining local cover the parachutists attempted to orient themselves, to form into small combat groups, and to reach their equipment chutes.

As has been indicated, the German parachute attack was directed against four vital points and four only. These four points were:

(1) The airfield at Maleme;
(2) The city at Canea;
(3) The airfield and town of Rethymnon, and
(4) The airfield and town of Candia.

In general the parachutists were dropped outside their objectives and hence outside the lines of the defenders. The descents on Maleme and Canea came early in the morning, but those on Rethymnon and Candia began during the afternoon. As to numbers, we have already noted the estimate of 3,000 men dropped in the Suda Bay area (Maleme and Canea) and have already ventured the estimate that a like total applies to Rethymnon and Candia (1,500 on each objective).

Obviously, as of May 20, there was nothing to indicate to the defenders which of the attacks constituted the main effort. As a matter of fact, there is some evidence that the Germans themselves were in doubt on the point and were awaiting developments. Significantly the German communiqués were silent on the entire operation until May 24, by which time the crisis had passed and success was all but assured. This indicates more than a German doubt as to the point of main effort. It also indicates a doubt as to the success of the operation as a whole. Perhaps the Germans undertook the operation as an experiment and were agreeably surprised at the quick results.

German accounts emphasize that the critical hours of the entire operation were the ones immediately following the initial descents. Those accounts throw some light on the matter of the German conception of the psychology of the parachutist in such an operation. During the critical first hours the parachutist must operate with no knowledge of the general situation. He must be prepared to undergo the most severe physical hardships and to carry on against any enemy elements which may be encountered. The parachutist must have complete faith in the high command and must operate in the belief that he will be supported and relieved in due course.

It is clear that the British and Greek defenders must have exacted a considerable toll from the parachutists dropped on May 20, but any estimates as to percentages or numbers lost at present are nothing better than guesses. Whatever the losses may have been, the fact remains that the parachutists, with their ever-present dive-bomber support, were not wiped out but after passing a hot and thirsty day and a cold night were situated about as follows on the morning of May 21: holding areas around the edges of the airfields at Rethymnon and Candia (the fields and towns being in British hands), holding areas close to the city of Canea (the city itself being in British hands), and *holding the airfield at Maleme.*

The italics are mine, and they are completely justified. The seizing of an airfield was the key to the German plan. As of the morning of the twenty-first the German hold on the field at Maleme was precarious. The British were still *controlling* the field by artillery emplaced in positions among the hills to the east. Thus the Germans had the field, but they could not use it—at least not effectively. The situation appears analogous to a river over which there is a shallow bridgehead but on which there is still falling observed artillery fire and across which, accordingly, a pontoon bridge may not yet be constructed.

Details of the manner in which the German parachutists seized the field at Maleme are not available. One eyewitness British account lays it all at the feet of the bombers and the strafing fighter planes which "did what the parachutists failed to do" and "forced us off Maleme." This is a reasonable—almost an obvious—explanation. During those first hours the artillery of the air did the leading, and the parachutists did the following.

From the German standpoint everything now depended upon gaining full use of the Maleme field. However, the parachutists were barely holding their gains, and the dive bombers were proving ineffective against the well-emplaced artillery. The inadequacy of the parachutist-bomber team to complete occupation of the airfield is tacitly acknowledged by the German decision to land infantry on the field, come what may.

OPERATIONS AROUND SUDA BAY

Therefore, as of the afternoon of May 21, the Germans began to land Ju-52s on the fire-swept field at Maleme. It must have been an expensive proposition although, considering the results obtained, it was cheap at half the price. There are several eyewitness accounts to help us build up the picture. One German aviator describes how his first attempts to land were completely frustrated, how he returned his first load to the Grecian base, and how he was able to return and land with great difficulty later. A British officer describes how the first twelve Ju-52s **to** attempt the landing were "smashed to pieces," but how "that did not stop them . . . they went on landing, one plane regularly every three minutes, losing one, then getting another down, then losing another."

By nightfall of this second day one battalion of mountain infantry had been landed on the field at Maleme. No details are available, but it appears that this battalion had with it no armament heavier than its machine guns. The packs of the men were stripped to the minimum (the soldiers suffered severely during the cold nights for lack of blankets and overcoats), and there was no transportation.

This first mountain battalion—the 1st Battalion of the 85th Regiment—had the definite mission of eliminating the artillery fire on the Maleme field. It seems likely that attempts to land additional air-borne elements on the field were suspended pending the actions of the 1st Battalion. Few details concerning those actions are available. Authentic German accounts place the main British positions on the heights of Hag Marina, four miles east of the field, and tell of an envelopment effected over difficult terrain to the south. In any event it is certain that the advance of the 1st Battalion was supported by the usual—or perhaps in this instance by the more than usual—number of dive bombers. British and German accounts agree that the Maleme airfield was free of artillery fire and was completely in German hands by the morning of May 23. Everyone agrees that this was the decisive development of the Cretan campaign.

We may be sure that the Ju-52s poured into Maleme during the twenty-third and the days following. Full details again are not available, but as of the evening of the twenty-third we find the 1st Battalion of the 85th Mountain Infantry swinging off to the southeast along the road Maleme–Episcope, "protecting the right flank of a mountain regiment attacking along the coastal road toward Canea." By this time contact had been established with the parachutists dropped on the first morning of the attack near Canea.

During the next two days (May 24 and 25) the remaining elements of the 85th Mountain Infantry—the regimental headquarters, the 2d and 3d Battalions, and the light-howitzer company—were landed at Maleme. By evening of the twenty-fifth the regiment was assembled in the area southeast of Modion.

Now we may reconstitute the situation as it stood on the evening of May 25. Certain combat elements of the Mountain Division, consisting chiefly of two regiments, had been landed and were in action. One of the regiments was attacking due east from the vicinity of Hag Marina against the main British positions at the head of Suda Bay. This was in the nature of a holding attack. The other regiment—the 85th—was assembled as already described, ready to move due east from the vicinity of Episcope toward Stylos. This advance, which would take the regiment straight across the pathless mountain wastes, was directed against the flank and rear of the main British positions. The British, on their part, were holding to the west and south of Canea, and in the sector of the 85th Regiment they were holding lightly the heights southwest of Alikianou and south of Episcope.

We are able to follow the advance of the 85th Regiment in some detail, and since that is something we have not often been able to do in this campaign, let us do it here. The advance was an exercise in pure mountain warfare, conducted under conditions which called for the greatest physical exertion on the parts of the troops. The terrain was exceedingly rough and rocky; it was roadless and almost pathless. By day the sun was broiling-hot and there was no shade and very little water. There was no transportation of any kind—weapons, ammunition, water, rations, all had to be carried by the soldiers. In the course of the fighting units were often separated from their ration dumps and often went a day or more without food. No attempt at all was made to warm the food. By night it was cold and there were no overcoats. There was also little sleep since it was invariably necessary to post a large part of each company on security missions.

The technique of the advance of the 85th Regiment seems to have involved assigning definite terrain features as objectives to certain battalions. Often one battalion would be held back until another battalion had reached its objective, whereupon the first battalion would be pushed ahead, and so on. The regiment had no artillery of its own, the guns of the light-howitzer company having been left behind with orders to be brought up later along the coastal road. Dive-bomber support is not mentioned in the German accounts, but perhaps it had become too commonplace to receive special mention.

The advance across country began on the morning of May 26. The 3d Battalion led out and forthwith discovered that the British had abandoned the positions southwest of Alikianou and south of Episcope. As the 3d Battalion reached the heights south of Barypetras the regimental commander ordered the 1st Battalion to smash ahead. It encountered some resistance but by nightfall had reached the line of Pyrgos–Hill 542. Early on the morning of May 27 the advance was resumed, this time with two battalions abreast: the 1st Battalion on the left and the 2d Battalion on the right. The objective for the day was the road running southeast through Stylos down which the British would necessarily withdraw. On this day the assault battalions covered about eight miles (they had covered five miles the day before), but they fell short of their objective by a mile or so. On the twenty-eighth the regiment reached the road at many points, and one company of the 1st Battalion is reported to have pushed ahead on its own initiative and seized a bridge on the main road one mile south of Kalami. From a point of vantage the regimental commander watched columns of British soldiers moving south toward Neon Chorion. His reaction was to regret his lack of artillery for use against the "highly observable targets."

While the 85th Regiment was advancing from Pyrgos to Stylos it was by-passing the fight which all the time was raging to the west and south of Canea. As the 85th Regiment approached the main coastal roads in the vicinity of Stylos and Kalami the British positions near Canea became untenable. The positions were abandoned on the afternoon of the twenty-seventh. As we shall see, many of the defenders managed to slip away to the southeast that night, using the roads which the 85th Regiment had fallen just short of reaching.

Having reached and cut the vital roads on the twenty-eighth, the 85th Regiment, following a division order, sent its reserve battalion (the 3d) down the road to a point south of Neon Chorion. There the battalion was to take up a position covering the assembly of a "pursuit detachment" then being formed back at Maleme.

OPERATIONS OF THE PURSUIT DETACHMENT

This pursuit detachment deserves a few paragraphs. The first noteworthy point is the one just made: the detachment was being formed at Maleme while the attack on the Canea position was still in progress. Therefore, the detachment was ready to move out the moment the roads were clear. Obviously the detachment was composed of all-fresh units which had not yet seen action. In fact, the clear indication is that most of the units had just been landed, and there is the good possibility that they were components not of the Mountain Division but of an air-infantry division.

The chief elements of the pursuit detachment were:

(1) One motorcycle battalion;

(2) One mountain-reconnaissance battalion;

(3) Several mountain-artillery batteries;

(4) One platoon of tanks, and

(5) One section of engineers.

No further details concerning any of these units are available. It is probable that all except the tank platoon were air-borne. The tanks may have been small ones brought in by air, or they may have been boated over to Suda Bay by night.

In any event the detachment moved out of its assembly area near Platanias at 3:30 A.M. on May 28. There had been a little delay in departure, due to failure of the tanks and the motorcycles to arrive, and, in fact, these elements were missing when the movement started. Just east of Suda the column was delayed for three or four hours, due to demolitions on the road, and during this enforced wait tanks and motorcycles caught up. The detachment continued the march in a formation concerning which we have only one detail: the leading unit was a bicycle company (apparently from the reconnaissance battalion). Just west of the road junction north of Stylos the bicyclists were brought up short by fire from the cliffs which lined the road. The rest of the reconnaissance battalion (the "heavy" company) came up and took over the frontal advance, and the bicycle company turned south for the inevitable envelopment. After bringing mortars, anti-tank guns, and artillery into action the enemy was finally dislodged; a crater in the road at the junction was by-passed, and the advance continued. The time was about noon. It will be noted that the pursuit detachment had reached the Stylos road practically simultaneously with the 85th Mountain Regiment. It is likely that the enemy dislodged by the detachment were cut off, or barely escaped being cut off, by the mountain troops.

Following the action north of Stylos, the pursuit detachment took up an advance-guard formation. The advance guard consisted of one motorcycle company, the section of engineers, one platoon of artillery, one platoon of anti-tank guns, and the "heavy" company of the reconnaissance battalion. Meanwhile, the bicycle company with one platoon of anti-tank guns attached was sent down the alternate route, Kalami–Vamos.

As the advance guard passed through Stylos it made contact with the 85th Regiment and no doubt was brought up to date on the current situation. The object of the detachment now was to push ahead as rapidly as possible in the hope of disrupting the British withdrawal. At a point about a mile south of Neon Chorion—apparently just beyond the position held by the 3d Battalion—the point of the advance guard was taken under heavy rifle fire. This evidently was from the rear guard of the withdrawing enemy column. It was still early in the afternoon.

An attempt by the advance party to steam-roller its way through the pass was repulsed, apparently with considerable losses ("The party got itself into a difficult situation," says the German account). During the afternoon the remainder of the advance guard and finally the main body came up and joined the action. Finally the 3d Battalion of the 85th was called in to serve as the enveloping force. Obviously the British were fighting a determined action. The German commander got the impression that "the enemy was employing all means at hand in order to hold out until dark with the intention of withdrawing during the night . . . [the British] made occasional small counterattacks, so that much of the action was at close quarters." He found his own artillery was ineffective, owing to poor observation, and so he decided to await the withdrawal.

The British did withdraw shortly after midnight—withdrew to the south, and away from further contact with this pursuit detachment. The detachment resumed the advance early on the morning of the twenty-ninth. There were occasional delays due to road blocks, mines, and weak or demolished bridges, but there was no enemy resistance worthy of the name. At 1:00 P.M. the advance guard reached Rethymnon and a few minutes later made contact with the "Rethymnon west" group of parachutists. This group of parachutists were defending themselves near where they had fallen about two miles east of Rethymnon. The town had remained in Australian-Greek hands. Here as elsewhere along the coastal road the defenders appear to have abandoned their positions after the fall of Canea and to have moved to the south coast in the hopes of being evacuated.

Up to this point—the road junction east of Rethymnon—there continued to be little or no enemy resistance (although a few hundred Greeks had given themselves up as prisoners). However, the road farther east of Rethymnon is cut out of the sides of the hills which rise from the sea. The parachutists reported that the hills were strongly held and that the road was covered by enemy fire. Under the circumstances the detachment commander decided to bivouac for the night where he was—near Rethymnon.

At 5:00 A.M. on May 30 the detachment again moved out. This time the advance was led by two tanks, closely followed by two infantry howitzers (on self-propelled mounts?). Apparently the tanks and infantry howitzers went on down the road a distance of about three miles while the mass of the detachment awaited the results of an artillery bombardment of the sides of the hills. When the artillery fire at the near end of the pass was supplemented by fire from the tanks and infantry howitzers at the far end, the defending Greeks and Australians (1,100 of them, the Germans say) came down and surrendered.

The action east of Rethymnon was over by 7:30 A.M. At 8:30 A.M. the advance guard of the detachment made contact with the "Rethymnon east" group of parachutists. This group, like the "Rethymnon west" one, had been unable to better its position and so had simply held on through the ten tough days.

At 1:30 P.M. the detachment was resting on the airfield at Candia, having made contact a half an hour before with the Candia group of parachutists which had been held west of the town. Leaving Candia at 4:00 P.M., the detachment marched to Neapolis. There one platoon of motorcyclists was detached and sent on ahead to the day's march objective, Herapetra. As the platoon passed through Spakia it made contact with a motorized *Italian* reconnaissance party. With the battle already won, the Italians had landed (by boat) the day before. Their current mission was to hold the insignificant village of Spakia. The German motorcycle platoon reached Herapetra at 10:00 P.M. An hour later the remainder of the motorcycle battalion came up. The distance covered during the day figured up at about 120 miles.

Throughout the operations of the pursuit detachment there is no mention of support by dive bombers. The conclusion seems to follow that although the Germans provide dive bombers liberally when needed, they do not provide them at all when not needed.

PURSUIT TO THE SOUTH COAST

By now there will have arisen the question of what happened to the defenders who succeeded in getting away. Light on this matter is thrown by the further activities of the 85th Regiment of mountain infantry. It will be recalled that we left that regiment along the Stylos road on the afternoon of May 28. The regiment's 3d Battalion had just assisted the pursuit detachment in an attack on a British delaying position near Neon Chorion. By the afternoon of May 29 the 85th Regiment (less the 2d Battalion) had occupied a pass two miles south of Alikampos, where we again pick up its story. The British troops who had evacuated the Suda Bay region were heading south toward Sphakia on the southern coast (not to be confused with Spakia, where we left the Italians). The mission of the 85th Mountain Regiment was to turn that retreat into a rout.

About 9:30 A.M. on May 30 the 1st Battalion, leading the advance, came into contact with scouts of the British rear guard near Imvros. There was an exchange of rifle fire, following which the weak British screen withdrew to what developed to be another main delaying position in the vicinity of Hill 798 and the end of the road. (It will be recalled that the road ends at Komedates and that from there on there is nothing but a footpath.) The British had thrown up field fortifications. Their position was so strong as to induce automatically the adoption by the 85th Regiment of the *Umfassung* (envelopment) tactics which characterize German operations, even minor ones. There was no frontal attack but, as indicated on the map, the 1st and 2d companies of the leading battalion moved out across country for a double envelopment of the enemy flanks. Apparently the 3d Company was in battalion reserve.

This envelopment operation of the 1st Battalion progressed during the night (May 29–30), but when morning came it was found that the British had extended their flanks. The German reaction to this new development was again to decline a frontal attack and again to resort to a double envelopment. This time the 7th and 8th companies of the 3d Battalion were sent wide around the flanks. This was a double envelopment of a double envelopment.

Meanwhile, during the course of May 31 a regimental OP had been established on the commanding heights of Hill 892. From this point of vantage a long stretch of coast could be observed. The British were seen to be crowding into the area between Kometades and Sphakia. They were continuing to hold the line of Hill 798 and were erecting field

fortifications facing east between Kometades and Wraskos. The attack
on Hill 798 (by the enveloping forces) had been set for dawn of June 1,
but after observing the strength of the British position the regimental
commander decided to hold up the attack until he could get dive-bomber
and artillery support.

The dive bombers (four of them) appeared early on the morning of
June 1. Meanwhile, a light infantry howitzer had been installed on Hill
892 (being pulled up by man power) and, beginning at 8:30 A.M., it
added its fire to that of the bombers. The observation being excellent, the
fire of the infantry howitzer was highly effective—by inference, more
effective than the bombs of the Stukas. The combined fires of howitzer
and bombers is alleged to have "forced the enemy to leave his positions
and to seek safety by dispersion in the fields."

At 9:00 A.M., under cover of the bombardment, the 7th and 8th companies launched their converging attack on Kometades and Sphakia. By
10:00 A.M. the 8th Company was in Kometades, and by 1:30 P.M. the
7th Company had broken through to Sphakia. By 8:00 P.M. the 85th
Regiment was in possession of the coast from Wraskos to Loutrou, and
the final action on Crete soil was finished.

NAVAL OPERATIONS

The operations around Crete constituted one of the most heroic but
altogether one of the saddest experiences in the history of the Royal Navy.
When the parachutists began to drop on May 20 the Navy waded into
the thick of the action. At the time it was generally believed that the
parachute-and-air attack was preliminary to a large-scale water-borne invasion, and the Royal Navy undertook to prevent it.

All during the twentieth strong units of the Mediterranean fleet,
operating out of the base at Alexandria, patrolled the northern Cretan
beaches, particularly those at Canea and Candia along which landings
were likely to be attempted. Nothing happened that day, and at night
the units of the fleet withdrew from the Aegean waters. During the night
there was a brush with Italian E-boats, as a result of which several of
those fast motor-driven craft were sunk. A short time later, as the fleet
was passing through the straits between Crete and the Dodecanese
Islands, it was attacked from the air and one destroyer, the *Juno,* was
sunk. Even with that loss by nighttime of May 20 it looked as though
things were going well enough at sea.

The day of May 21 appears to have passed quietly, with the main
British fleet units keeping out of the Aegean. During that night (May
21-22), however, there came reports that the water-borne invasion was
under way. The fleet which had been standing by in readiness moved
immediately to the danger points. During the very early hours of May 22

the ships encountered the convoy—a convoy of about thirty small Greek ships, escorted, apparently, by a single destroyer. The action was short and decisive, the convoy and its destroyer being quickly and completely annihilated. The Germans later put their losses at 200 men—a figure probably as far under the true mark as British estimates of 5,000 lost were over the mark. There is good evidence to show that the convoy was made up of mountain troops. This suggests the thought that the unit involved may have been the missing third regiment of that mountain division which figured so prominently in the land operations.

Apparently the British fleet had disposed of the convoy before the *Luftwaffe* could get into action, but a little later in the morning the bombers arrived. There followed a plane-versus-ship fight which likely will go down in history as a military epic.

Details of the historic battle are lacking. Apparently as it began only "light" units of the fleet were in the Aegean while the "heavy" units were patrolling the nearby Ionian Sea. The light squadron, or a part of it consisting of four cruisers and three destroyers, was attacked by dive bombers at 8:30 A.M. between Candia and the island of Melos. Apparently the technique of the dive bombers was to concentrate on any ship which happened to get separated from the others and, conversely, the technique of the squadron was to keep all ships within mutual supporting distances. The ships themselves kept moving at high speeds, "repeatedly changing course, dodging the falling bombs, while speeding at over thirty knots."

Meanwhile, as the battle in the Aegean raged the heavy squadron was speeding through the straits northwest of Crete to the rescue of the lighter units. During the afternoon all units, heavy and light, were violently engaged. Heavy losses were suffered and inflicted. At 1:30 P.M. the destroyer *Greyhound* fell back, was heavily attacked, and was sunk. Two destroyers and two cruisers went back, the destroyers to pick up survivors, and the cruisers to provide antiair protection. Both cruisers (the *Gloucester* and the *Fiji*) were sunk.

The terrible day in the Aegean finally ended, and the British ships withdrew to their base. The two cruisers and perhaps four destroyers had been lost, and practically every ship had been subjected to a terrific pounding from the air.

The elements of the Battle of the Aegean were clear. It had been a case of land-based aircraft against ships with no protection other than their own antiair guns.

It appears that the British fleet never again entered the Aegean in strength after the battle of the twenty-second. At the same time it appears that the Germans never resorted to large-scale water-borne troop transport during the operations on the island. Possible answers to this seeming inconsistency are the following: Having effected the air-borne landing of the battalion of mountain infantry of May 22, the Germans had no burning need of water-borne transport and, with the British fleet still strong and still in position to move into the Aegean quickly, the Germans feared to risk the loss of another convoy.

The Royal Navy did indeed continue to perform invaluable services during the remainder of the Cretan campaign. Perhaps the most important of these services was in aiding the evacuation of troops from the southern coasts. It appears that light units of the fleet—such as destroyers —would lay well off the southern coast of the island. By night these vessels would come in close and would send boats ashore to pick up any troops who happened to have reached the points in question. Thus while the British were fighting that delaying action north of Sphakia, it is probable that each night saw the evacuation of hundreds of troops via the destroyers lying offshore.

The clearest evidence of the work of the Royal Navy during those later days of the operations on Crete lies in the official British figures of number of troops evacuated: approximately 15,000. About half of that number were English. The remainder was divided between Australians and New Zealanders. Incidentally, it will be noted that the British succeeded in evacuating about one half of the force which garrisoned Crete at the start of the invasion. Of course most of the force's equipment was lost.

The figures for British losses, according to British sources, have been indicated above: approximately 15,000 killed, wounded, or missing. On the other side of the picture, German figures for German losses, officially announced, give a total of about 6,000 killed, wounded, or missing. The British say this German figure is about one third of the true one, and they add that the Germans lost on the order of 250 troop-carrying planes and 180 fighters and bombers. One thing is clear: On a percentage basis, the losses on both sides were extremely high. In view of the nature of the operations that fact comes as no surprise.

THE LESSONS

The campaign in Crete gives us a remarkable and clear-cut example of unity of command. Absolute co-ordination of land and air forces was a prerequisite to German success. That co-ordination was attained by placing all the forces concerned—the VIII Air Corps, the mountain division, the parachute units, the air-borne units—under the direct command of General Löhr. The action in so constituting the "Task Force Crete" was typical of German doctrine. Under that doctrine the question as to the merits or demerits of a "separate" or a "non-separate" air force becomes merely a play on words. When it comes to the fighting no one element is separate—everything is blended, by deliberate directive, into a co-ordinated whole.

The command of the Task Force Crete was not only unified; it was also especially fitted for the task at hand. General Löhr is a general of aviation. The selection of such an officer to command an operation in which air power played so important a role is another item typical of German doctrine.

Also typical was the composition of the task force itself. It might have been expected that the first air-borne troops to land would be the air-infantry units which had operated the year before in Holland. However, Crete is a mass of mountains, and so it was logical (and typical) for the mountain troops to be landed first. We have seen that these mountain troops had, in fact, broken the back of the defense before other units arrived.

The campaign in Crete was another powerful illustration of the Dunkirk-proven fact that an air force is only effective when it has bases within range of the action. Much of the explanation of the events in Crete lies in the following picture: hundreds of German fighters and bombers operating out of bases between ninety (Melos) and two hundred (Athens) miles away; against an insignificant number of British bombers operating out of African bases beyond effective fighter range (400 miles).

The sad situation cited just above has one cheerful angle: It reassures us as to the chances of success of an invasion of England. Just as the invasion of Crete turned on acquiring complete control of the air, so does a successful invasion of England presuppose complete control of the air. But the island of England is dotted with airdromes, and the invader will meet not bombers that have flown four hundred miles, but fighters that left the ground five minutes ago. Owing to the unfavorably located African bases, Germany seized the air over Crete practically by default. The price of seizing the air over England would be an all-out encounter with the RAF pursuit fleet. Judging by past events, the price will be beyond the invader's means.

The events of May 22 in the Aegean Sea will long be cited as prime evidence in discussions of air and sea power. These events seem to have established definitely a fact which already had been widely accepted, namely, that naval vessels can operate in narrow waters covered by hostile land-based aircraft only at the cost of heavy losses.

As it happened, the tragic losses of the British Mediterranean fleet were largely in vain since the Germans were able to make the invasion stick without benefit of sea-borne convoys. However, the fact remains that the fleet was able to destroy the convoy, and the strong indication is that it could have destroyed subsequent convoys had any appeared and had the fleet been willing to take the losses. Thus the fact that land-based aircraft can inflict heavy losses on naval vessels in narrow waters does not mean that shipping friendly to the aircraft may sail such waters with impunity. And under some conditions that fact may be very important indeed.

The tactical developments of the campaign were a demonstration of the possibilities of the bomber used as artillery in conjunction with ground troops armed with automatic weapons (tommy guns). While "the destructive power [of the bomber] is less than its paralyzing power, it does paralyze . . . and it is able to ferret out anything." It is only belaboring the obvious to note once again that the parachutists were sustained by the bombers and that the mountain troops were literally blasted into victory by them.

The direct strategical consequences of the fall of Crete are not yet discernible. There was a prevalent expectation that the successful invasion would be followed rapidly by an attack on the long-established British naval base at Cyprus. But such an attack has not materialized, and if it did it would find Cyprus a harder nut to crack. However, there seems no doubt but that the occupation of Crete has materially restricted the British use of the eastern Mediterranean and has given Germany an advanced bastion of great value both from the offensive and defensive standpoints. Among other possibilities there is the one that Crete-based bombers may play an important role in any forthcoming action around Suez or in North Africa.

THEY SAY . . .

By Colonel R. Ernest Dupuy

Colonel Dupuy is the author of several books on military subjects and a contributor for many years to the service journals. "They Say . . ." appeared in 1942.

". . . A convoy will sail tomorrow for . . ." "The new mortar has a range of . . ." "General MacArthur will hit first at . . ." "Our latest bomber carries . . ." "We're going to seize . . ." "The Navy lost . . ." "Our troops are griping because . . ."

So runs the gabble full tilt in cocktail bar and at soda fountain; in home, restaurant, bus, and smoking car; in gossip columns and under the by-lines of "military experts"; in letters home to Mother and the best girl and the guy who worked across the desk before the war.

Who are *They?* Who told you? More to the point—why in hell should you be wagging your jaw? Do you work for Hitler, or are you just a big goodhearted guy who doesn't care who dies so long as you get the credit for knowing something?

Snap out of it, soldier. The limber-lipped boys have always played the enemy's game for him. That's why we—and our enemies—have that patient puzzle-picture solver we call "military intelligence."

Maybe you've never bothered much about military intelligence. Maybe you think it some newfangled thing. Have you ever read your Bible? Take a peek at Joshua 2: 1 to 24:

> And Joshua the son of Nun sent out of Shittim two men to spy secretly, saying, Go view the land, even Jericho. And they went, and came into an harlot's house, named Rahab, and lodged there.

That's the way the first story of military intelligence opens. Look it up. It's all there, down to the final successful assault of the city, based on the information gained. There was no counterintelligence in those days, no protective censorship. Censorship, be it of our own lips, or of the written word, or the picture, in so far as the military are concerned, consists of barring from the enemy knowledge of the things he wants to know in order to defeat us.

These are matters which we call "military information." They are the same things we want to know about the enemy so that we can defeat him the more easily. They are facts which, when collected, evaluated, and fitted into a mosaic, become military intelligence. Unless we recognize these facts, recognize the inherent danger in publishing them, inadvertent publication of such things in effect penalizes our side. In war this means death and disaster.

What are these elements of military information of value to the enemy? Let us look them over. They are: factual information of the strength, armament, equipment, morale, state of training or tactical doctrines of our armed forces; information which may affect the morale of our own people or that of allied, neutral, or enemy peoples and which may be used by the enemy for propaganda; strategic information which would lead the enemy to an interpretation of our own war plans or intelligence.

Basically the enemy, in order to crush us, must know what we are doing, how we propose to do it, and what resources we can command. From all the information which he can gather he makes an estimate of the situation which is nothing more or less than a trial balance. This estimate is continuous, and it must be projected into the future. If the enemy can obtain accurate knowledge of our plans, strength, and resources as of a given date, either global or in a given theater of operations, that is so much grist in his mill.

Let me repeat. These enemy estimates are continuous. They consist in piecing together a mass of fragmentary information, bits of news themselves seemingly unimportant but which, put together, make an important picture.

Whether we talk loosely or write loosely, the results are grist in the enemy's mill. Perhaps, however, by looking at historical examples of the printed word we can get a better idea of the evils of loose talk. History is full of instances of battles lost, campaigns wrecked, nations shattered, because of the disclosure of information by the press.

Who would believe that there would be harm in publishing the fact that in a certain camp a measles epidemic had broken out and that there were so many cases hospitalized? Measles? Nothing serious about an outbreak of measles. Such things happen all the time. Yet for that very reason actuarial expectancy tables based on past experience exist; one can predict the number of cases per one thousand persons in any given group. How easy, then, to reverse the process, given the number of cases, and arrive at the group total. This has actually happened in this war.

Who would think that there would be harm in the publication of a picture showing British soldiers handling an unexploded delayed-action bomb in London? It was the enemy's own bomb; surely he knew all about it. Quite so. But, having found out the British method of handling these bombs, the enemy made such changes in his detonators as to ensure that future unexploded delayed-action bombs would and did explode on handling!

Let's go back to World War I. On April 16, 1917, just ten days after the United States declared war on Germany, the French so-called Nivelle offensive was launched and failed. As a result, six weeks later, had Germany but known, a large part of the French Army was practically in mutiny. But the Germans did not know—and neither did we, by the way. Before General Pershing had ever arrived in France a confidential report to the French Minister of War, on April 24, stated, "By the end of the summer we will have guns, planes, to say nothing of the Americans—but there will be no French soldiers!" A determined German drive would have won the war. But Germany didn't know, or wasn't convinced—and no less a personage that Ludendorff admits it—until June 5. By then it was too late. The mutiny had been checked. French military intelligence had choked the news, delayed it until too stale to be of any use to the enemy. That was plain suppression of news. Was it justified? I leave the answer to you.

The identification of units—the order of battle—is something to be sought, particularly if there be prior knowledge of the time of organization of the unit or the state of its training. It is the starting line-up, important in sports, doubly so in war. Thus in war we must discourage much of the regional or home-town news coverage which in peacetime is one of our great means of letting Mr. and Mrs. John Q. Public know how their son is getting along. The mention of a group of men hailing from a specific locality leads to the conclusion that they belong to some specific division—everyone knows our normal territorial organization in divisions. On the other hand, the cessation of news from a particular division which has been widely publicized in a certain area may lead to the assumption that that division has left for some battle front.

The publication of society notes, harmless enough in themselves, may give information to the enemy. It was only a comparatively short time ago that a Washington newspaper mentioned the name of a young naval officer present at a social gathering, adding the chirpy gossip that he "was waiting until repairs to his ship, the U.S.S. *Blank,* had been completed." The U.S.S. *Blank,* one of our battle fleet, had been at Pearl Harbor, but until that time it was not known she had received even a scratch. Here was confirmation of damage well calculated to cheer an enemy's heart, to set him right on casualties he had inflicted.

One of our former military attachés, through careful and continued study of social notes in the press of one of our present enemies, succeeded in making a very accurate analysis of the divisional organization and strength of that country's army—carefully guarded facts which he could have obtained by no other means. Just one man, sitting in an office poring over the newspapers.

It was only a few weeks ago that an irresponsible reporter published a fanciful story relating to a "mighty armada" of American ships traversing the South Pacific. He related the story as an eyewitness, although he had actually never been in the South Pacific. That was plenty to set our blood running cold, for by coincidence there was, in fact, a convoy of United State troops on the Pacific seas at that time. Had a single ship been sunk as a result of that yarn whose would have been the responsibility?

Let's look at the Civil War. In September 1863 General Rosecrans put into operation a plan for crushing the Confederacy by whipping first Bragg and then Johnston in detail in the Chattanooga area. The Chicago *Times* published the plan in full, the correspondent ending his story with the statement: "Twenty days from this time, if I mistake not, the signs will see Georgia redeemed and thoroughly regenerated."

Bragg read and digested the story, sent it on to Richmond and the Confederate War Department. As a result came the Federal disaster at Chickamauga, September 19, 1863. Instead of seeing Georgia redeemed in twenty days, the Union Army was almost destroyed. Instead came a long succession of bloody battles up to September 2, 1864, when Atlanta fell, and April 9, 1865, when Lee surrendered at Appomattox. What price in blood, tears, and sweat that newspaper story?

In the Spanish-American War the entire plan for, and destination of, the expeditionary force to invade Puerto Rico was published in the American press. The result was that General Miles had to reroute his defenseless transports, thus disclosed to the enemy, to an entirely different destination on the opposite side of the island from that originally chosen.

Going back to the Crimean War, we find Lord Raglan complaining, with reason, that the London *Times* was publishing full information of the British losses from disease, location of British strong points, effect of hostile fire—all items of great value to the enemy both directly and indirectly.

In the Franco-Prussian War, as before it in the Austro-Prussian War of 1866, the German military authorities received from the British press priceless information on enemy plans and dispositions, including news of French concentrations which enabled them to attain the victory of Sedan.

In World War I the British, prior to the great German offensive of March 1918, which resulted in the destruction of Gough's Fifth Army, received a tip-off—that they did not act on it is another story—on the enemy's intentions. The fact that General von Hutier, heretofore a leader in violent and successful offensives on other fronts, was on the Fifth Army front was disclosed by reading an item in an obscure Baden newspaper. The British had downed a German aviator in the Fifth Army area. They knew his name. A few days later this Baden newspaper published a letter of sympathy to his parents from General von Hutier, and a Briton read it in Berne, Switzerland. Just a question of adding two and two, *provided* one were furnished with both facts.

So much for the disclosure of military information. Let's look at the aggressive side of the tongue-wagging picture—the spreading of rumor campaigns by whispers or by reprinting what the enemy sends out to attract our attention. These are the artillery fire of psychological war—the war of nerves.

A skillful enemy, well versed in the art, today sets trap after trap to catch our press and our newscasters. The traps are baited with news interest; they are timed to deadlines; they carry the punch that in peacetime news gathering would ring a flash bell on every news ticker in the nation. And they are just as deadly as the spray of high-explosive shell fragments.

There is more to wartime radio broadcasting than just that, however, because of the instantaneous action of radio, its immediate impact. The enemy speaks and his voice is heard by thousands of our own people. If, topping that, the American radio rebroadcasts his utterances, millions of Americans hear. Therein lies danger. Why? Cannot Americans be trusted to draw their own conclusions, to evaluate his words? Of course they can, given a complete presentation. But unless this accurate documentation is made, they are as wide open to the hostile emotional attack as unprotected soldiers to the physical bomb blast.

These things we are combating by the protective shield of censorship, by tight-lipped reticence. And we will aggressively combat them successfully, too, despite the continuous enemy effort. Already we have started.

What must be scored as the most brilliant psychological blow on our part in the present war is the cloud of secrecy which hung over the details of the bombing of Tokyo. From the viewpoint of the Japanese General Staff it is a "must" that they know whence came the bombers that hit their country, where they were bound. Where are these mysterious bases? Where Shangri-la? They don't know yet. Not only the Japanese propagandists but, in fact, the entire Axis propagandist machinery developed in this case a severe hotbox, as evidenced in the halting, conflicting stories they sent out, childish attempts to goad us into telling them these all-important facts.

The story includes also a very neat bit of shoe fitting on the other foot. The bombers who performed that task under Jimmy Doolittle winged their way into battle, in broad daylight, riding the radio beam of a Japanese station which at the time was broadcasting a little rhapsody on the scenic beauties of Japan, nestling peacefully in the assurance that it could never be bombed. That's exactly what the Nip was saying, in English. Suddenly he went off the air. On came an excited voice, talking Japanese. The monitor, who of course understood Japanese, listened while the Jap announcer screamed, "Enemy bombers coming! Coming fast! They are flying low; they go too fast to be caught!"

As the bomb sticks whirled down this Nip announcer kept on the job. Screaming in high-pitched panic, he called our shots in a play-by-play description, noted the fires caused, shouted casualty bulletins. Our bomber monitor kept him on as our ships winged their way on. And from the Nip station they received the fullest information that anyone would want on their accomplishments. It was not until twenty-four hours later that the tone began to change, that casualties and damage were played down. But in the meantime *we knew—we had received from the enemy*—precious confirmation of our successes. Why? Because it was a complete surprise, because there apparently existed at that time in Japan no internal defense against psychological warfare, no linking of national effort to combat panic.

Someday we in the United States are going to get a token air raid. Its objective will be the production of fear, panic, and uncertainty in the minds of our people. Are we going to play it like soldiers or are we going to cackle and squawk on the air like barnyard hens when a hawk flies over?

Let's play it safe. Let's play it all safe, by tongue, by pen, by photograph. To transpose the adage—what the enemy don't know can't hurt us.

GAS ON A HOSTILE SHORE

By Colonel (now Brigadier General) Alden H. Waitt

(1942)

After two weeks of preparation the Greek fleet and army assembled at Aulis in Boeotia to avenge the seduction of Helen, wife of Menelaus, by Paris, son of Priam, king of Troy.

"The wind thereupon proving fair, the fleet made sail and brought the forces to the coast of Troy. The Trojans opposed the landing valiantly. At the first onset many were slain and one of the noblest of the Greeks, Protesilaus, fell by the hand of Hector."

Several thousand years later another fleet stood off Gallipoli within cannon shot of Troy. The Turks opposed the landing valiantly. At this first onset and at the other bloody subsequent assaults, thousands of British troops were slain.

The passage of years has not lessened the problem which confronted Greek and British in other wars. The landing of troops on a hostile shore is still one of the most difficult of operations. And if the defender adds chemical weapons to his inherent defensive advantage the task of the attacking force becomes still more difficult.

One of the important obstacles that must be foreseen by any commander planning such an operation is the *chemical obstacle*. Every plan for a landing on the enemy's shore must take into account the chance of running into chemical agents, and it must provide a means of overcoming them. These things must be covered by the plan whenever there is any probability that the enemy may use gas.

As defensive means of warfare, chemicals are highly valuable and flexible. They serve many purposes, and not the least of them is to provide an effective defense over a period of several days without the necessity of holding a large number of troops at the area to be defended.

The commander must first foresee the obstacles. He must estimate all ways in which a defender might make use of chemicals. After this is done, then he must find the means to overcome these possible chemical defenses.

On any stretch of shore the practicable landing places are generally few, owing to the irregularities of the shore line, the depth of the water, the surf, or the prevailing winds. Thus a defending enemy will often be able to make a fairly accurate estimate of where a landing is likely to be made and to plan his defense ahead of time. Some of the things that make a particular section of shore a good landing beach also make it a good place for chemical defense. For example, quiet water is desirable, and quiet water is usually found along the parts of shore where the wind comes from the land more than from the sea. Such spots lend themselves to the release of gas in cylinders from the headlands or even from beaches.

While landing troops are still aboard their transports, and even until they come close to land, they run no great risk from chemicals. There can be little effective chemical fire against a ship. Certainly the use of non-persistent gases against ships need not be considered, and except for tear gas in combination with shell or shrapnel there will be no likelihood of chemicals fired by mobile artillery. Armor-piercing shell from shore batteries may carry a proportion of irritant gases mixed with high explosive.

Bombers may use phosphorus or mustard-gas bombs, but it is doubtful if either of these would be substituted for high explosive. The defending enemy commander seeks destruction, and there is no substitute for HE as a destructive agent. But some bombs of mustard gas may be mixed in with explosive bombs to increase confusion and make the landing troops put on their masks.

At the same time an attack by bombardment aviation against a landing operation seems unlikely, since the landing would not be attempted without local air superiority or at least a definite air advantage. Supporting aviation would fail in its mission if enemy planes were able to deliver a bombing attack against the transports or their protecting naval vessels. Nevertheless, large ships which have stopped in the open ocean are excellent air targets, and their vulnerability to air attack should not be lost sight of since the enemy may be able to hold back some of his air strength for the critical moment when troops are disembarking in small boats for the landing.

Thus if gas is used by the defending enemy his first important chemical attack on the landing force will perhaps occur as the troops are disembarking into landing boats and the tows are being formed, for then the attacker is most vulnerable. A few planes carrying mustard spray can cover a wide area and cause tremendous damage and confusion. Here the conditions favor the use of the chemical spray, and the results may be so important that the enemy will use a number of planes for this purpose at this critical moment.

If the wind is right the enemy may easily release a heavy cloud if irritant gas from the headlands in such a way that it will cover the waters the small boats must pass through coming to shore. Wearing the gas mask would then be an absolute requirement, and landing in a mask is, to say the least, a difficult job.

As soon as the first boats come within range of enemy machine guns, the run-in may be covered by smoke laid by friendly airplanes, either sprayed as a screen or laid by dropping floating smoke pots. This presupposes, of course, that surprise has been lost and the landing is being attempted against resistance. The smoke stops the enemy from delivering aimed fire. Hence where resistance is expected smoke is essential, and the wise landing commander will use plenty of it in gaining his toe hold on the beach and in securing and holding it. And he will improvise ways of making smoke, if he has to, as well as to use every standard smoke device.

As the attack reaches the beach and the troops rush to gain a foothold, the enemy again has an excellent opportunity to use mustard sprayed from planes. It takes a few planes a matter of seconds to lay a band of chemical a mile long and several hundred yards wide.

But it is after the troops have gained their beach head that their chemical difficulties may really begin. Up to this point the use of chemicals has been largely a question of opportunity, but now they offer a sure advantage to the defender.

The next job of the landing troops, after securing the beach head, is to push ahead to their final objective. They must organize and go forward at once. The forward impulse must not be lost. After passing any obstacle, whether a bridge, defile, or beach, there must be a fanning out in order to gain shoulder room. Troops hemmed in by natural or created obstacles on their flanks will have tough going when the ground to their front is held by determined men.

This lack of shoulder room because of natural obstacles was one of the reasons for the failure of the British on Gallipoli. The actual landings were accomplished successfully. The British gained a foothold, but that was all.

Persistent chemicals are most effective for increasing the difficulties of natural obstacles. And where these do not exist a liberal sprinkling of mustard is often a first-class substitute. If the ground does give the attacking troops ample room to deploy, wide bands of mustard, perpendicular to the shore line, will delay their lateral movement. The mustard can be put down in this manner by means of land mines or by artillery, airplanes, or chemical mortars.

It is true that passage is not physically barred by any chemical agent. But maneuver over contaminated ground is hazardous; it cannot be accomplished without wearing the gas mask, and it is certain to result in a large number of casualties. Thus by making full use of chemical obstacles the enemy on the shore can hold a given area of ground with a smaller number of men than would otherwise be possible. He will also sweep the contaminated areas by fire from machine guns and artillery, thus further slowing the attacking troops and keeping them down close to the ground surface where the contamination is greatest.

Where winds are dependable, as they are in many cases, and narrow corridors exist along which landing troops must pass, the enemy may use gas clouds of non-persistent chemicals released from cylinders or projectors. Indeed, a landing force may meet with chemical attack in all of its many forms if the enemy has been able to anticipate the landing.

Now what can be done to offset and overcome the chemical defense an enemy may try to use along his shores? In the first place, a landing on a hostile shore begins back on friendly soil, weeks or months before embarkation. Perfect gas training and the best possible anti-gas equipment are essentials for every landing force that may run into gas.

The organization for chemical defense should be even more complete than what is ordinarily required for operations on land. Each company will need its regular quota of two gas noncommissioned officers. Each battalion, in addition to its gas officer and noncommissioned officer, must have a squad of selected men carefully trained in chemical reconnaissance methods and equipped to conduct degassing operations on a small scale. Each regiment should have a similar squad under the direction of the regimental gas officer.

Before embarkation the commander should make certain that all anti-gas equipment is available, serviceable, and ready to go over with each landing wave. Every man must know how to use his protective equipment and understand how to behave if he becomes exposed to chemicals. First-aid training for gas casualties should be included. There must be repeated exercises aboard ship to accustom all men to wearing the mask for long periods. Working while masked develops the ability to fight while masked.

During the landing itself protection is largely an individual problem, for there is little chance for measures of group protection. As soon as the first sub-wave has reached the beach its mission is to push forward and secure the landing for the succeeding sub-waves. As soon as it is possible to gain the beach head the first wave must push forward at once to the principal objective. Therefore, all steps possible will have to be taken to overcome any slowing of the attack from enemy gas.

Regimental gas officers with their assistants should accompany the shore-party commanders or at all events land with an early sub-wave. They reconnoiter as soon as they land to find whether the enemy is using gas, and particularly whether or not he has laid down barriers of mustard.

Chemical-defense squads under battalion gas officers accompany their units in each sub-wave as a part of the combat team. These squads must all be equipped with protective clothing so they can go through gassed areas. They carry cutting tools, small entrenching shovels, and material with which to clear lanes through heavily contaminated brush and undergrowth. They cannot eliminate entirely the danger of bodily contact with mustard-type gases on grass, undergrowth, or overhanging branches, but they can reduce it greatly.

It is an open question whether or not it will be possible for the members of chemical-defense squads to carry some small amount of degassing material. If it is found practicable each man should carry about twenty-five pounds of chloride of lime in a knapsack. Obviously this will be enough only for degassing on the smallest scale, but that is essential.

For example, the degassing of the small area for portable radio apparatus is most important since communication between the landing party and the commander of the operation must be maintained. Degassing material is extremely useful at the entrances and exits of contaminated trails. Foot burns may be reduced by requiring troops to scuff their feet in chloride of lime at these places.

As soon as the anti-gas squads land they help the gas officers reconnoiter to find gassed areas. They determine the extent of the chemical obstacles and find ways around them if possible. If not they make the best way through them. Some will act as guides for the advancing troops.

Active countermeasures are, of course, taken against enemy gas as soon as possible. When artillery becomes available it directs counterbattery fire against guns that may be laying down persistent gas. Degassing may be necessary at battery positions.

Medical units have special duties to carry out if gas is encountered. It should be possible to set up field stations near the beach where men can be bathed who have run into mustard or similar gas. There will be plenty of salt water at hand, and a bath with issue soap or any other will reduce casualties materially.

When the beach head is secured the anti-gas units take measures for degassing areas that must be occupied or along which troops and supplies must pass. They take extra precautions to protect food and water being carried from the shore inland. Dangerous areas are posted with signs and sentries placed where necessary to prevent passage through them. If wind and weather conditions favor continued use of chemicals by the enemy, all precautions must be taken against non-persistent clouds. Constant inspection of the protective equipment is also necessary.

A definite plan of protection is essential, for without such a plan a landing force is liable to find it impossible to accomplish its mission against a well-trained enemy.

The other side of this problem, that of protecting a beach defense of our own against enemy gas, is equally important and demands as careful consideration as the protection of landing parties. Again it is necessary to foresee the obstacles before attempting to set up a system of defense.

In a landing operation there is a point when advantage in the use of chemicals passes from the attacker to the defender. Up to the time the attack reaches the beach and the landing party leaves its boats, the chemical advantage, such as it is, is with the attack. But as soon as the attack does reach the beach it changes hands and rests with the defense.

There are several rather remote possibilities of chemical attack that a beach defense might be prepared to resist. It is possible that swift-moving destroyers may run in to within a few thousand yards of a beach and discharge clouds of irritant gas under cover of darkness. This, of course, presupposes that the weather will favor the drift of the cloud. But if it is practicable it should prove an effective form of attack. Only an alert gas sentry and alarm system and a high degree of training in mask adjustment could cope with it. Surface or underwater craft might also discharge high concentrations of non-persistent gases such as phosgene. Irritant gases may be fired from naval guns in combination with high explosive.

Frequent attacks by either of these methods, if they can be accomplished, would do much to wear down the beach defenders and reduce their effectiveness. Unless men have been trained to work and fight in their masks, the efficiency of the defense will be badly cut down.

There is also a possibility that persistent gas may be used in spray or bombs from naval aircraft. Persistent gas would not be used directly on beaches where landing is contemplated but could be used on places outside the intended landing area or against reserves to prevent their reaching critical points. This would make it necessary for the defense to have protective clothing, protected shelters, and degassing materials, and also to be prepared to move to alternate positions chosen in advance.

The defender must expect a landing to be made under cover of smoke either from planes, destroyers, or naval gunfire, or from smoke mortars and guns on landing craft. Aiming points close to the guns defending the beach should be provided (a normal requirement) in order to permit some accuracy of fire while more distant reference points are obscured by smoke.

A protective scheme for a beach defense must take account of all methods that are not unreasonable to expect since every enemy must be credited with the ability to accomplish all that is reasonably possible.

In the protective scheme against a landing attack all means of individual protection are necessary.

The training requirement of wearing the gas mask for long periods so that efficiency will not be too greatly reduced when men are compelled to wear it in action is also most important. Training is necessary in the operation of beach guns while wearing the mask and training in firing while in smoke. Men must be able to make repairs and correct stoppages in the dark or in heavy smoke. Beach groups are often isolated, hence a high state of gas discipline and training is particularly desirable. All troops must be trained to meet gas situations alone and to have confidence in their ability to protect themselves without the help or advice of an officer or a noncommissioned officer. A knowledge of first aid, if gassed, is an essential.

Since the defense of a beach is conducted by very small groups, there is little opportunity for collective protection of the forward elements. Gasproofing of the beach guns may not be practicable. There should be, however, gasproof shelters near the guns and command posts, and communication centers should be gasproofed. Communications must function effectively if the defense is to be successful.

Reserve positions require gasproof shelters. Gasproofing is entirely practicable back in these positions under all conditions.

Somewhere within the sector, probably in the neighborhood of the reserves, there should be stores of degassing materials with trained men ready for any needed degassing operations. The need for an efficient gas alarm and sentry system is obvious. This is tied in with the security measures normally taken. Frequent weather reports will also help the defender in forecasting the probability of enemy gas and smoke operations.

All men, especially those of anti-gas units, should be trained to watch the weather carefully and take note of prevailing wind currents in their own small sectors.

Whether we are concerned with the protecting of a landing party or a beach defense, the use of chemicals as a weapon introduces three principal requirements aside from proper equipment. These are careful training, perfect gas discipline, and a complete and well-integrated organization.

THE INVISIBLE WEAPON

By CAPTAIN (now LIEUTENANT COLONEL)
JOHN V. GROMBACH

(1940)

WORLD WAR II and the year 1940 have wrought fundamental and unforeseen changes in warfare. Neutral non-belligerent and warring powers have found themselves faced with a hundred new problems—air power, motorized and mechanized units, new tactics, parachutists, and, by no means least, the fifth column. In all this change communication remains vital to the participant in war. And propaganda and the protection of military secrets are vital both to participants and to nations near the brink of involvement. Thus a mighty power in the struggle for world dominion by nations, forms of government, and ideals is radio.

International radio is just now beginning to be evaluated adequately as the powerful though invisible weapon it is. Just as dominance in the air by plane may be the key to victory on land and sea, so the use of the ether waves may be the most potent means for mastery of the minds and hearts of men, without which no nation or ideal can survive.

Let us imagine, if we can, the invisible and increasing world-wide host of lightning messengers impressed on carrier waves. A magic which in effect has banished time and space throughout the entire globe. In a minute fraction of a second a mere whisper is audible from the Antipodes to the Arctic and from Cathay to the Caribbean, to one hundred million radio receivers, each capable of listening in to hundreds of messages. There is one radio receiver for every twenty inhabitants, almost sixty million, in the Western Hemisphere alone. The air around our world seethes with long and short waves radiating to those hundred million receivers from more than fifty thousand transmitters of commercial, government, military, and naval stations, and from those of over one hundred thousand efficient and indefatigable amateurs. From any point in the world hundreds of powerful short-wave transmitters are easily contacted, relaying messages from the most remote points of all continents and from seventy-eight different countries. Such, briefly, is the most potentially powerful agency for many purposes that the world has ever known.

While the present airplane, tank, and automatic weapon have changed conditions of combat, radio and broadcasting have completely revolutionized the problems of the intelligence sections of the services. For example, before and during the present war Englishmen and Frenchmen have cleverly sold over the air, in impeccable English and French, Nazi and Fascist ideals and beliefs. The strongest effort has been made to discourage the English and French civilian public on war. In France radio propaganda was used to create suspicion and break down confidence in the English alliance. Moreover, before the war and since, a steady stream of information has been sent secretly, quickly, and effectively by the German espionage system by way of the radio. The perfect co-ordination of troops with aviation, fifth columnists, and parachutists, particularly in Poland, Norway, and Holland, was accomplished largely through radio broadcasting. Also, the German submarine that threaded its way through the safeguards, mines, patrols, nets, and booms of Scapa Flow on October 14, 1939, and sank the British battleship *Royal Oak* was undoubtedly guided by some seemingly innocent radio broadcast in England or Holland, perhaps even a band concert or a dramatic presentation.

Just as the ancient counterpart of the tank, the elephant, was employed by the Persians centuries ago, codes and ciphers have been used as long as there has been war. In fact, recorded history tells us that a cryptogram to Lysander of Sparta saved a general, an army, and the empire later to be enlarged by Alexander the Great. At the same time all authorities from Julius Caesar, one of the first cryptographers, to the Black Chamber of the last World War agree that there is really no secret writing code or cipher created by man that cannot be broken by man. But as Francis Bacon, Lord Verulam, himself one of the world's greatest cryptologists, said in his *Advancement of Learning:* "The only truly secret system of writing conceals the existence of a secret." Little did Bacon know of the day when the secret would be even better concealed by not even being written. Seconds may now send a crucial cryptogram hurtling thousands of miles through space, whose secret meaning and presence is known only to sender and receiver. And an instant after it is delivered there is not one shred of evidence, nor even a record of any kind by which the message can be deciphered into the "clear." Such is the blitzkrieg in the cryptographic battle of radio in World War II.

A practical illustration will be far more effective, perhaps, than dissertations in history and literature. Not long ago a former world's heavyweight boxing champion, in an interview on a major network of thirty-nine United States stations, capable of being picked up over thousands of miles, broadcast a message in the most simple jargon code, so simple that any amateur cryptographer or alert listener should have made it out. The broadcast had a potential audience of twenty-eight million radio homes in the United States alone. Evidently not a single listener was expecting it. The message was: "*S 112–SS. Queen Elizabeth* sails tonight with hundreds of airplanes for Halifax, N.B." Neither the sponsor, the network, the world's champion, nor the sports commentator interviewing the champion knew anything about the message. This particular message, of course, was sent out only as an experiment to see whether anyone would pick it up from the air waves. But if such a message can be sent with millions listening in, is it safe to assume that there have not been far more important uses made of this agency here in America?

If radio could be used with such devastating effect in Europe, it can be used here with even more telling effect. In America, because of our commercial radio system, our programs are the best in the world. Single radio performances of many of our network programs would be events of outstanding importance in other countries. As a result we have by far the greatest radio-listening audience in the world, and in no country can more people be reached by radio than here. Also, in no country is there any greater freedom and tolerance. All these facts, it seems most evident, constitute a new and serious military problem.

There are some 813 commercial (long-wave) broadcasting stations in the United States, over six hundred more than in all Europe combined, and, in addition, all of ours are privately owned. Then there are thirteen short-wave stations, twenty-one television stations, and sixteen facsimile stations. There are over fifty-three million radio receiving sets, including eight million automobile sets, in the United States, and a potential audience of over one hundred million. The problem of planning the control of radio by the War Department to cover both prewar and wartime necessities is staggering. All stations should be carefully guarded or controlled:

(1) Against cryptic broadcasting, which either relays military information by enemy espionage agents or co-ordinates fifth-column activities, this in addition to providing ordinary censorship of news that might be of value to the enemy.

(2) For the broadcasting of propaganda and information to combat the enemy's short-wave propaganda which would be intensified in case of war (there are many foreign short-wave broadcasting stations easily picked up here); also, propaganda to serve as a deterrent against fifth-column activity.

(3) For the proper kind of recreation and morale-building entertainment, which would require minimum attention from the War Department, since this is a radio station's ordinary service in peacetime.

(4) In order to minimize or neutralize the effects of possible physical seizure by enemy armed forces or the fifth column.

According to reports from excellent authority, though so far unconfirmed, the break-through at Sedan on May 14, 1940, which caused the separation of the Belgian and English forces and the French Army of the North from the main French Army and resulted in the encirclement and destruction of the northern units and the final crushing of France, was a German victory in the radio war of cryptography. Over one of the government-owned and -operated stations spies or traitors concealed messages in code appraising the Germans of the thinly held line at the elbow between the Maginot and Little Maginot lines, and of the temporary gap between the armies moving rapidly into Belgium and the few divisions under General Corap holding the northern end of the Maginot Line. If this report is true it shows that government-owned stations are as liable to subversive use as stations privately owned. It also proves that the Battle of France was lost in large part by radio.

This is doubly strange when one considers the fatalistic parallel this war has with World War I. In World War I the turning point was the Battle of the Marne. It was won by radio. In 1914, however, there was little radiotelephony but much radio telegraphy. The air was filled by radio traffic with many jammed wave lengths. French, British, Belgian, and German communications transformed the German offensive into a mess of faulty co-operation. On September 2, 1914, Von Kluck was ordered to close up on Von Bulow to his left and push the French away from Paris. He never received this message, but the French did. He radioed that he was following his original orders to swing southwest to Paris. This message was also intercepted by the French but never received by the German G.H.Q. The French cryptographers laid the deciphered messages side by side before Joffre, and from them developed the Battle of the Marne, won by radio and cryptography.

However, ordinary military radio telephonic or telegraphic messages, their interception and the cryptography relating to them, do not constitute, strictly speaking, a new problem. Although perhaps more complex now than it was before, and more exacting, particularly with respect to time, this is a fairly established military problem handled by the Signal Corps. According to the latest booklet on our armed forces, *The Army of the United States*, the Signal Corps is charged with intercepting enemy radio messages and locating enemy (military) radio stations by radio goniometry.

The new military problem which is the subject of this article is more in the province of the Military Intelligence Division (G-2) which has duties "that relate to collecting, studying, analyzing, and furnishing all kinds of military information," which "supervises any army activities dealing with military surveys, maps and photographs, codes and ciphers, and translations," and which "also directs a press-relations branch which prepares and issues War Department press releases and handles other matters concerning relations with the press and with the public at large." To these extensive duties must be added the new military problem of radio propaganda and counterpropaganda, fifth-column and counter-fifth-column radio activities, and the audio aspects as against the trans-mitter aspects of radio from the creation and production of radio enter-tainment to preventing fifth-column or espionage secret communications by way of radio.

The problem does not always stop at any given line, nor is it any too well defined. Here, for instance, is an actual case: One of the most powerful short-wave stations in Europe, heard all over the world, often emitted either before or after a scheduled evening broadcast a buzzing signal resembling static, so fast in vibration it would not be recognized as consisting of separate noises. However, that was not the answer. The noise was actually a message concealed not only in code or cipher, but by speed of transmission, and intended for their nationals in a country six thousand miles away. First the message had been recorded, and then the record was broadcast as played at perhaps ten times the normal velocity. The key to its reception and solution lay, of course, in reversing the operation.

Returning again to the four points of control which together represent the new military problem of radio, we can label them:

(1) Espionage and fifth-column cryptography and censorship;
(2) Propaganda and counterpropaganda;
(3) Recreation, entertainment, and morale building;
(4) Neutralization of physical seizure of stations by enemy or fifth column.

These form a staggering new assignment for the Intelligence Division of our service. And on the basis of European experience, they offer as vital and as difficult a problem as any encountered in the warfare of 1940.

With regard to espionage and fifth-column cryptography and censor-ship, it will be well to explain and describe in detail how a message can be inserted in a commercial radio-program broadcast. It should be clear that if by the adaptation of a well-known system a cryptogram can easily and secretly be transmitted through audio means and doubly concealed in the music, sound effects, and dramatic dialogue of the program, superior cryptographers would have no trouble doing a far better and more original job for espionage purposes or for the organization and control of a fifth column.

While many different methods can be used to conceal a cipher or code message in a radio program, including simple jargon, the most obvious cipher is the radio equivalent of the grille or "cardan" method, in which the sender writes his "clear" through the holes of the grille, the letters following the order of the numbered grilles, and then fills up the vacant spaces with innocent letters to make a message. In radio actual words in most cases could be used as letters and the grille replaced by key numbers, all based on the order of words in the program from its beginning or from some key word. Here the difficulty of even suspecting, much less deciphering without both a recording and stenographic transcript of the broadcast, is to be noted. This is what makes sending and receiving cryptographic messages by radio easier than their discovery or prevention.

A reverse of the Gronsfeld cipher especially adapted for radio can also be effectively used. In the Gronsfeld there is a set of key numbers in a series that can be easily memorized. These numbers are written down over the "clear" and repeated as often as necessary. Each letter of the "clear" is then represented in the written message by a letter which is the number of letters farther in the alphabet called for by the key number over it. In the radio adaptation a key word would be written down over the "clear" and repeated as often as necessary. Each letter of the "clear" can then be represented by a number equivalent to the number of letters in the alphabet separating the letter of the "clear" from the corresponding letter of the key word. In the radio program words with the number of letters equivalent to those numbers could be designated at indicated spots or key breaks.

However, the most effective and practical cipher which would lend itself to radio is what might be called a radio adaptation of the Nihilist Bacon biliteral.

In this system the key is a square, as follows:

	2	3	4	5	6
2	A	B	C	D	E
3	F	G	H	IJ	K
4	L	M	N	O	P
5	Q	R	S	T	U
6	V	W	X	Y	Z

In writing the cipher the numbers describing the position of a letter (its co-ordinates) are substituted for it. In the original the numbers start with 1, but due to the fact that here also numbers of the message will be given by the number of letters in a word in the radio program, there are too few one-letter words to make the original key practicable. In writ-

mass reaction to radio, one has but to remember the famous *War of the Worlds* broadcast which completely disrupted a quiet and peaceful New Jersey countryside. Perhaps H. G. Wells did not discover a secret weapon, but Orson Welles discovered that radio was certainly a weapon through which man's mind and imagination could be successfully attacked.

With regard to propaganda, it is a fact that there are definite propaganda short-wave programs already reaching America. In addition, there are definite programs and a considerable number of domestic broadcasts in foreign languages aimed at the large colonies of foreign-born.

In Europe before and during the war German propaganda by radio was as far ahead of the French and English as German superiority in military equipment of ground and air. Many times a week, at regularly scheduled times, outstanding symphonic concerts featuring French music or radio adaptations of French musical comedies and L'Opéra Comique were broadcast all over France by German stations. These programs built up a tremendous audience because of the superiority of their entertainment and production. They could be compared with certain commercial advertisers' programs in the United States which, through superior entertainment such as Charlie McCarthy and Jack Benny, attain such tremendous audiences that the networks have hard work selling any time competing directly against them. In other words, in radio propaganda, as in radio advertising, "the show's the thing." The size of the audience is directly in ratio to the entertainment and showmanship of the program.

After obtaining a large audience by superior entertainment an advertiser in America takes care to see that his commercials sell his product and are as sugar-coated and innocuous as possible. In the more serious game of selling ideals and ideas, races, countries, and men, radio propaganda and counterpropaganda have become correspondingly adept.

In the German broadcast featuring French music and drama occasionally a French speaker spoke to the French people, explaining that Germany definitely did not want to go to war with France. That the social advantages in France were only a beginning, but that France was still in the grip of capitalists, and that the French people were forced to fight for England and her economic control of the world. This was all done in excellent taste, with superior production and accurate statistics, and featured native Frenchmen or Germans speaking perfect French. In England the propaganda took a different tack, and from September to May millions of English and French soldiers listened to Lord Haw Haw and Paul Ferdonnet prove that they were fighting for nothing.

How efficient this invisible weapon can be is evidenced by "The Link," an English fifth column of English Fascists meeting regularly in London. It can be positively stated that this organization owes more to radio than to any other single factor. When Fascist Sir Oswald Mosley visited Paris as a member of the British fencing team at the world's championship a number of years ago he was wined and dined by the radio executives of the government radio agencies of France, Italy, Belgium, Holland, Germany, and, strangely enough, Denmark, and also by the owners of several of the few commercial stations on the Continent.

The importance of the radio weapon is still paramount in the most militarily efficient country in the world. On June 27, the German advance guard arrived at the Spanish-French border. The first German unit to reach the border consisted of twenty specialists of the radio-propaganda section traveling in radio-equipped trucks. They stated to correspondents that they broadcast many times a day both from their trucks and from radio stations taken over in their advance.

Yes, mastery of the sea may be vital to England; mastery of the air may win the present war for Germany, but mastery of the minds and hearts of men must be gained today to wage war successfully, and that mastery can be attained in full only by radio.

The actual recreation, entertainment, and morale-building qualities of radio are almost as important as the propaganda and counterpropaganda which are in most cases carried within the talks and shows broadcast. If radio is a "weapon," then we can carry the comparison farther and call the entertainment the "propellant" by which it reaches the ears of millions, and propaganda the "disruptive" that either explodes theories and ideals and leaves a horrible debris of apprehension and confusion, or crystallizes the understanding and gives men the urge to fight on.

The actual physical seizure of radio stations is our least important topic because it can come only at a stage in war at which radio will already have done its worst. Only upon invasion or revolution will the armed forces or the civil agencies of law and order be so helpless as to permit the seizure of radio stations by the enemy or by the fifth column. Yet plans should nevertheless be formulated to neutralize the effect of such a seizure in part of a nation just as plans are made for every other military eventuality.

In a visit to England just before the war it was my very good fortune to discuss World War II with my friend, the late Sir Basil Thomson, who was head of Scotland Yard for eleven years and head of the British secret service in World War I. His last remark to me was, "Remember that in the next war radio will be the secret as well as the invisible weapon one always wonders about when a new war comes along." I know now he was right, and I hope that this article may at least serve to prevent its readers from underrating the problems created by this new weapon.

HOW MANY DOES IT TAKE?

Editorial

(1942)

OUR PEACETIME PLANS for a big war, if it came, envisaged an army of as many as four million men, and more if they proved to be needed. Here in this War for the World we're passing that figure now, and it may be doubled or even trebled in the years of bloody fighting that probably lie ahead.

Once in a while some misled voice still speaks in terms of "small mechanical armies" and forces exclusively made up of air power as adequate to defeat our millions upon millions of foes, regain the millions of square miles already lost, and gain the other vast areas the United Nations may have to seize before the job of their armies is done. But most men have no longer a question in their minds on the numbers it is going to take to win. It can't, in fact, be stated now, even in round figures. The best way to say it is simply, "We shall have to have enough to finish the biggest, most desperate, meaningful task the world has known."

This is the only way, right now, we can think in terms of the total. And this means, in practical effect, only one thing—plans for the possible use in uniform of every man and woman who is not more needed on other work.

When it comes to breaking down the armed forces into echelons and allotments for different kinds of troops and different grades and ranks of men and officers—organization planning—the same general answer must guide those who determine the strengths of particular units and categories. There must be *enough* men in every unit for it to be able to do its fighting work to best advantage, with due allowance for the wieldliness of the fighting team as a whole. There must also be adequate means of replacement—replacement not merely in numbers but in specific trained classes of men. For in overseas campaigning, as the first World War so plainly showed, losses from accident, illness, detachment, wounds, death, and capture may even require a one-for-one replacement in a combat unit in six months' time. Indeed, in all our wars of the past, replacement is the one great problem of war we have never adequately solved.

One special problem of allotment that always comes up is the strength needed for the groups of command, the headquarters groups all the way up to and including the highest headquarters in the field and at home. Here again the guiding word can be only "enough." And no one can determine how many is enough but the high commanders themselves.

For units in the field the needs of headquarters can be generally arrived at through careful advance planning of tables of organization. The tendency in all such planning is to give the commander, as far as it can be determined in advance, the staff he will need but no more. A commander may find when he reaches a theater that one section of his staff is undermanned whereas another has more personnel than it needs, and he can adjust this as the situation demands. But if he finds, as sometimes happens, that his staff as a whole can't keep up with its tasks, he must bring up the men he needs from the lower units of his total force, thus weakening these all the way down, until his needs for additional staff, if permanent, can be adjusted from above. Our own experience and that of our Allies, however, helps avoid this by determining well in advance what the needs will be.

But in the end, whether it's a company headquarters or the highest command, the one basis of judgment is "enough"—enough personnel to keep the plans for fighting, moving, reconnoitering, communicating, feeding, and supplying abreast of the hour, even in battle—and enough officers and men to see that all these plans and orders of the commander are promptly and efficiently put into effect, this without demanding that they work so continuously and hard that minds cannot stay quickened and fresh for each new task.

The numbers as such have nothing to do with it. It is simply a matter of what it takes to keep things moving, to keep things from getting behind, to obviate all possible delays, to win battles and campaigns—and in the end the War for the World.

This applies equally to the highest headquarters, the agencies that govern the different theaters in the field, and the whole war effort at home. Such matters as whether there are "too many officers" in a given locality cannot be determined merely by counting noses or by noting the apparent numbers of uniforms that meet the eye. They can be determined only by finding the answer to one question: "Are there more than enough?" Are there more than enough for every activity, every agency, every office to do today what it should accomplish today to win this war? Or is vital work, needing careful study and decision, piling so high that it takes days and weeks to get things done? Things that should get done today? Is it piling so high that key personnel must keep on going for seventy and eighty hours a week in a desperate endeavor to keep things moving onward to victory—a state of affairs that inevitably slows things down from sheer cumulative exhaustion of nerves and power to think?

In actual campaign it is to be expected that commanders and their assistants may sometimes have to keep going in battle for several days on end with snatches of rest. But this can continue only for a matter of days till rest or relief must come. A fresh division or wing goes in to bear the brunt while another takes rest and reorganizes. This is common to war, and we've seen it become necessary again and again in this present war we are fighting. We've seen battles and campaigns lost because it couldn't be done.

At a higher headquarters there is usually less physical strain and more comfort of existence than for lower ones. There may even be little chance of undergoing attack, and conditions of life may be well-nigh normal. But there is a continuous mental pressure, particularly in the face of accumulating tasks on the completion of which a final success depends, which at bottom puts much the same type of strain on the mind as the pressure found in headquarters in the field. The better, more regular conditions make it possible for men to keep going long hours, with too little rest, for weeks and months on end. But nervous exhaustion eventually slows down the toughest, most enduring mental powers if heavy overwork continues.

This is the only basis for judgment of personnel needs in war. Are there enough to do the work as it should be done? Does work back up so that accomplishment seems often at a standstill? And if so could a greater number of assistants get more done? For in building an enormous army from what we had in peace there are some things that cannot be sped, things like construction and production for which there is needed an irreducible minimum of time. If there are more than enough for the daily tasks or the soon-expected tasks, then there's room for reducing. But if there's a single agency of war where the work is jammed up and more workers can speed it along, then there's room only for an increase of workers. This cannot be viewed as a whole in arbitrary fashion. It has to be determined separately for each agency and each subagency. Inspection may show that shifting is possible without increasing the total numbers. But the total itself means nothing if shifting brings no rapid solution. The work this war must see done is what measures the number of workers, whether they are fighting soldiers in the field or fighting soldiers and their clerical assistants at desks.

Every man and woman in uniform and every non-uniformed helper of the armed forces is directly engaged in the work of this war. Numbers, of themselves, mean nothing anywhere until we are certain the numbers are enough. But insufficient numbers both of men and machines mean a loss of time and a prolongation of the war until there are enough. The whole risk lies in underestimation, not in making certain there are *enough* for the job to be done.

VIII

The Soldier Looks Ahead—2

THERE IS NOTHING in this final section about a third World War and how its battles might be fought, though professional Army men will believe there will be none only if this war is completely won and the world so controlled that new wars cannot come. They will also believe that those who will form the instrument of armed strength that might ensure a world without great wars must assume that fighting may be needed to keep such wars from arising.

But now the soldier giving his utmost to the cause of immediate success can think but briefly of the future. He can, however, find time to think of the extensive problems of military government that will follow the capture of enemy soil. And time to hope that his nation will see how improbable it is that its armed services will ever have the chance again to catch up with warfare if a new conqueror did arise.

There are, accordingly, reminders from the past in this final section as well as the beginnings of thought for the future. For the Army men who remember the 1900s and the 1920s hope that their country will remember them, too, when this war is over.

THREE HUNDRED YEARS OF WAR

From an article by PROFESSOR (later MAJOR) ROBERT M. JOHNSTON

(*1914*)

WHATEVER the immediate results of the present war may be, it is clear that in western Europe it is bound to stimulate the opposition to conscript armies. Partial disarmament, if it should come, would, therefore, mean a return to professional armies. Navies swallow up fewer men than armies, and that of England is a professional force. The sentiment against them is now, and presumably will be in the future, less marked. But, on the other hand, if government in western Europe becomes more democratic as a result of the war, as seems probable, then the vast expense of navies is likely to prove an incentive toward naval disarmament. If England should embark on such a course the change would be momentous and not without its effects on this country.

But disarmament, even on land, is not so certain to follow as many believe. It is clear that east of the Bohemian mountains the present war is far more likely to accentuate than to settle the complicated conflicts of nationality and of creed from the borders of Poland to those of Greece. If Germany should suffer a democratic reaction it is doubtful whether she could even partially disarm before a still-warlike Russia. And if Germany, under any conditions, remains armed the outlook is gloomy. Belgium has already found out what it costs to practice pacifism with such a neighbor. What blood, and treasure, and agony she would have saved had she had the common prudence to maintain an efficient army of two to three hundred thousand men!

The question of the size of the European states is bound to emerge from the war in some shape or other. If a congress is the conclusion, as is likely, then this country is at once confronted by the problem. For it is one of the interesting features of Japan's participation in the conflict that, if it is concluded by a congress, she will be entitled to meet the other powers there on equal terms. Perhaps the United States alone of world powers would not participate. This might be a good thing or it might not, but it is at all events worth while inquiring whether the stock argument against our wishing to participate in such an international deliberation has any validity at the present day, and that brings us at once to the question of the size of the world of international politics.

The stock argument is nearly one hundred years old. It carries us back to the epoch of President Monroe, when it took as many weeks to communicate between America and Europe as it now takes seconds. The policy then enunciated, and it was wise at the time, was that we had no more concern in the affairs of Europe because of its remoteness than Europe had in American affairs. Since then we have consistently maintained this attitude, save in matters relating to international law and arbitration. Can we maintain that attitude any longer? Is Europe still remote? Have not the digging of Panama and the participation of Japan in the war really placed us in the very center of world politics instead of on the remote edge? Our interest in the humanizing of international politics, the fact that we are acting diplomatically for most of the belligerents—that we have participated in congresses for the regulation of international intercourse—all these are reasons why we should enter such a congress and, by entering it, why we should broaden its scope and its general utility.

Turning back to the nations of Europe, and still following out the question of size, it seems probable that among the readjustments following the war will be extensions of customs, if not of political boundaries. The pooling of military interests almost inevitably follows the pooling of economic interests, and a customs federation of any two or three European states would probably establish peace firmly as between such states and enable them to take higher rank in the economic world. Such changes as these involve great hopes of the pacification of large areas but entail at the same time grave dangers of military shocks on an even larger scale than that which the year 1914 is witnessing. Europe is already battling to form two or three new groups capable of holding their own with the really great powers of the world: Russia, China, the United States. In that sense we are directly interested in the conflict. Let us, therefore, prepare to play a part not in the conflict but in the pacification.

IT WILL TAKE SOMETHING MORE

Editorial

(1943)

THE ARMED SERVICES and the nation behind them are centering their energies on winning the war. There is so much of battle yet ahead, so much planning, sweating, and fighting to be done, that the men who are doing most of it, the men already in battle and those on the way, haven't time to think very far beyond the vast immediate job.

But there are many others who do have time to. Books, articles, speeches, round-table discussions, a big part of every means of widespread discussion, are now given to the future of the country and the world. From serious students of world affairs, from men with no other equipment for such discussion than loud voices and the chance to make them heard, from practical men, from dreamers, from unselfish men seeking a way for the future, from selfish or fearful men afraid of all new conceptions—from all these flow the words about the future world. From all these come the ideas, the final resultant of which may determine the kind of existence that Americans, soldiers and civilians, will lead for a lifetime to come, to say nothing of how they may affect the rest of the world.

Hardness and Integrity of Mind

It is not at all sure, however, that the thoughts for the future now commonly under discussion will, in the end, be applicable to the world as it develops. An obvious historical lesson—the rise of the conqueror—was generally ignored, not only before this war but before the first World War. Yet the growth of the spirit of conquest and the development of means for conquest are things no nation can hide. And they are therefore plain to the observant citizen and soldier of any land who doesn't let his wish for world peace and prosperity keep him from seeing with open eyes. Peace and prosperity in the world can be planned with hope of attainment only by men who have the hardness and integrity of mind to weigh all things that might prevent it.

Such planning is of deepest interest to the millions of Americans in the armed services. The men in uniform may have less time to think of the future, but the future will belong to the millions who return from the war as to all other citizens.

The men in the armed services, however, are those who are experiencing the most direct consequences of this new war, of the rise of conquest which a few fully observant men and women did see and warn against. Thus in one way the troops in uniform have the deepest interest of all men in the kind of world that comes out of this war. And it is they, and especially those among them who are fighting in their second World War, who can give the clearest warning to those who have more time than they do to think and talk about the future.

War Is a Habit of Man

The one warning of utmost importance they can give is this—that war is a habit of mankind and that fighting one more war to a finish will not, of itself, change that habit. It will take something more to achieve this change than a full defeat of our enemies.

The threat of other wars will stay in the world until men and nations can be helped to form a new habit in place of the old one—the habit of not fighting wars to settle things. For the habit of fighting wars is millenniums old. This doesn't mean it would necessarily take thousands of years to change it, but it does most certainly mean that the habit of going to war cannot merely be talked away by men who now speak freely of "the postwar world." It is the post-second-World-War world they are actually concerning themselves with and that is all. It is not the "postwarfare" world. To think of it this soon as a postwarfare world is to begin again the nineteen-twenty and -thirty kind of talking that made this present war such a surprise to those who listened to that talk and believed it. The postwarfare world can come only when men everywhere have put a new habit in place of the old one.

How long it may take for this time to come can hardly be guessed. It will depend upon the efficiency with which the strong nations at the end of this war can help their own people and those of all other nations to replace the habit of war. Fifty years, a century, two centuries—even less or even more? We can only say it would take time, and probably much time.

"Postwar" and "Postwarfare" Worlds

It is the period during which the habit of war will continue in the minds of men that many now speaking of the future shrink from facing. They appear to confuse the "postwar" and "postwarfare" worlds. They are inclined to skip the first to reach the second. Similar men were so inclined in the nineteen-twenties and -thirties.

The soldier is facing the hardest of war's realities. When he has time to think of anything else and consider the future himself and what men are saying about it, he can find no sense except in ideas that face the things he faces. He knows that if there is ever to be a world in which his sons and grandsons will not be following him into battle, the spirit of the ruthless conqueror of humans must first be gone from the hearts of men. He knows—from the hatred his Jap and Nazi enemies show him—that the thought of changing this hatred to permanent good will seems far off indeed, seems a dream of the distant future. It's a good dream to him, as it is to most men of the democracies. But it can never be anything but a dream unless the dream is remembered, considered, and worked toward by wide-awake men who never forget the continuing possibility of war in the postwar period.

He's too busy with this present war to think much about the postwar period. But he has arms in his hands now. He is busy preparing to use them or actually using them daily to kill enemies bent on conquest. When he does think of a postwar time he thinks first of all in terms of practical armed means to keep down wars of the future. He can see no other insurance, no other firm guarantee of peace, no other safeguard for the freedoms Americans and similar peoples treasure than efficient armed strength.

The Thought of "No More Wars"

For the sake of the world and the nation there is every reason to hope that there will be no more wars. But this can never be achieved without continuous expert thought upon new wars that might arise. Thought of "no more wars" with the iron of armed enforcement as its basis may give the world a chance to learn in the end some other habit than fighting wars. Thought of "no more wars" which excludes practical thought of possible war is the kind of thought most likely to bring our country to the end of its course. Twenty years of it almost brought us there this time. Twenty years more of it in the postwar period, and it will not be Pearl Harbor but New York Harbor or San Francisco Bay.

OUR GREATEST NEED

From an editorial by Captain (now Colonel) H. C. Clark

(*1907*)

We need an army—not artillery or cavalry or staff; not even infantry, helpless as we are in that arm, overworked as what we have of it is, bitter as will be the lesson that may come without it. None of these is sufficient of itself for an army, so none is sufficient of itself for our need. We need an army—not large, let us repeat, lest we frighten the peaceful citizen with the bogey of militarism—but large enough for the first time. It is a need that may at any time become suddenly pressing. Such needs always press suddenly. If this presses suddenly now, we shall see our old history rewritten, with perhaps a darker page at the close—our old history of confusion and unnecessary sickness and unnecessary death. These have been with us always in war—God forgive us!—but always success of some sort has rested with us at the end and we have fain been content. Rather, we have been proud. We have forgotten the confusion, pensioned the unnecessary sick, decorated the unnecessary graves, and boasted brazenly to the world of our civilization.

AFTER THE WAR

Editorial by Major (later Colonel) John R. M. Taylor

(*1918*)

It may be that after the war there will be no more armies. If Germany should win decisively there would be no more—outside of Germany. Fortunately that will not happen, but after it is all over will there be no more armies; will the big guns go into the melting pot, and will all the airplanes be set to work on rural mail routes? Perhaps, but the decision will not be left to the men who now form the governments of the belligerent states. It will be in the hands of the men who are now in uniform. It is they who will dictate the future policies of the world.

It well may be that all, or at least most, of them will be utterly sick of war. They will not want to think of war. They will want to go home and sleep in a bed, eat three meals a day from china plates, have a bath when they want it, and take up their work where they laid it down to take up a rifle.

THE AMERICAN "MILLION ARMY"

By Dr. Leo Brenner

(1917)

UNDER THE CONDITIONS one will understand why the resolution of Congress struck me as being funny. Resolutions can be made for all things, but it is a question whether or not they can be carried out. From where are the one million to come, when it is not even possible to drum up enough to maintain the miserable strength of eighty thousand? If it is believed the militia and volunteers will furnish the million, it is very questionable whether there are as many willing to play soldier, in spite of the American's fondness for dressing himself in grotesque uniforms. But even if the million really comes, there are neither officers (who cannot simply be appointed) nor arms, and least of all artillery or other war materials. Therefore, I maintain, throwing a scare amounts to nothing.

COMMUNAL DISPERSION

By Robert Strausz-Hupé

(1942)

SO SPECTACULAR have been the exploits of air power, so eloquent the voices of its exponents from Douhet to Seversky, that supremacy in the air is now being widely accepted as axiomatic in planning for victory. The writer is not an aviation expert, hence unqualified to discuss the tactics of air battle, the virtue of individual plane types, and the rate of their production. He perceives, however, albeit dimly, the shape of human society and economy in the age of aviation, and feels sufficiently concerned as regards the emerging pattern to ask the question: Air supremacy precisely over what?

What planes can do to ships in straight duels has been amply demonstrated from the coasts of Norway to the shores of the Pacific; a host of eyewitnesses testified to what they did to the tightly packed roads of northern France and to the narrow streets of London; and aerial photography renders accurately the effects of intense bombing upon compact industrial targets. The impress of air warfare upon areas thinly settled or spacious enough to allow for a wide geographic distribution of industry is less clearly marked. The role of the air arm over the plains of Russia and the Libyan desert appears circumscribed not only by the relative strength of the contending air forces but also by the topography of the respective theaters of war favoring the rapid movement and the prompt dispersal of the ground forces. Similarly, the Chinese, once they had been pushed by their Japanese foes from the densely settled and highly industrialized coastal sectors into their roomier hinterland, showed themselves perversely indifferent to the doctrines of General Douhet.

If, in the search for facts by which to judge the role of air power in modern war, one fact towers above all others, it is the fact that the effectiveness of air power depends largely on the nature of the ground over which it operates. The doctrine of the most extreme and most popular exponents of air-power-and-nothing-but-air-power can be fairly and simply stated as follows: an air fleet powerful enough to seek out the enemy's air fleet, to defeat it in battle or destroy it on the ground, then to pound the enemy's territory into submission by massive bombing. Thus victory will be won.

It may be beside the point in a discussion of theory to insist upon the fact that thus far no victory of this kind has been won and that the Chinese and Russians, for example, refused to comply in just that way with the claims of the air-power enthusiasts. But it is not beside the point to emphasize those by no means so recent trends in industrial and communal planning which are modifying the geography of the world's aviation targets—if they have not profoundly modified that geography already. Air power will, in this war and in wars to come, remain the sharp edge of a nation's total fighting power. Preponderance in the air has been tactically decisive on many a battlefield and will be so on many more. But the case history of Warsaw, Rotterdam, London, and Cologne can no more be taken as the final and conclusive evidence as to what planes can do to civilian targets than the triumph of the Stuka over massed Polish cavalry can be accepted as the final verdict in the case of plane versus mobile ground forces.

Early fliers gave big cities a wide berth, and city councils enacted ordinances to keep early fliers at a safe distance. To this day peculiar air currents and impediments to emergency landings require—over large urban centers—special precautions in the operation of more weakly powered craft. Experiments have shown that it is possible, but by no

means yet safe and practical, to operate special types like gyroplanes and
helicopters from city roofs and city streets. The comparative remoteness
of airports from municipal centers leaves the average big-city dweller
with the inescapable impression that the layout of his metropolis is awkward for air traffic. This not-so-remarkable discovery antedates the second
World War and the rise of air power by a good many years. Shortly after
the first World War, town planning, its literature and applied designs,
reflected a growing interest in the problems posed by developments in
aviation.

M. le Corbusier, the Swiss architect, published in 1922 a scheme for a
city of three million which—besides providing for decentralized communal services, spacious parks and fresh air for all inhabitants—included
airports as integral parts of the town plan. The American school of city
planners, represented by Frank Lloyd Wright and Henry Wright, practicing architects, and Lewis Mumford, theoretician and publicist, early recognized the increasing importance of aviation in the life of modern communities. German town planning—before the advent of Hitler—sought
to harmonize the requirements of a rapidly expanding commercial aviation with communal demands for easily accessible and safe airdromes.

The partnership of town planner, whether architect, social worker, or
sanitary engineer, and air-traffic expert, whether builder or operator of
airdromes, is a logical one. Their common enemy is congestion—the awful
congestion of the big cities and industrial centers which planlessly spill
across and devour their rustic environs.

The demand of decent communal living and safe flying mutually is for
spaciousness. Before the outbreak of the second World War it had become
apparent that the adjustment of the modern community to the requirements of air communication would bring about as far-reaching changes
of the maps of towns and cities as the motorcar had imposed during the
preceding two decades. Henceforth, in town plans the characteristics of
flight would have to be given consideration similar to that heretofore
bestowed on vehicular traffic. The location of airdromes—true public
utilities—would have to be purposefully planned instead of being made
dependent on the fluctuations of the real-estate market and the vagaries
of sectional interest.

The menace of the bombing plane imparted to the business of planning
more spacious communities a slant wholly different from that contemplated by the Le Corbusiers, Wrights, Mumfords, and their pre-Nazi
German colleagues. On first glance, to plan for a more spacious way of
human living and to plan for safety from explosive and incendiary bombs
appear not at all as related activities. Yet to the communal planner the
fundamental problems inherent in both tasks bear a close resemblance.
The threat from the air forcibly imposes on countless communities the
very same structural reforms for which the advocates of better communal

living have vainly sought the public's approval in peacetime. Such ideas as, for example, the decentralization of communal services and industries, the garden city and the conversion of slum districts into parks are kindred to the military conception of dispersion. While ultimate purposes appear to differ, the task at hand is the same: to break down congestion.

In Germany economic recovery and social changes after the first World War had imparted a powerful impetus to communal building and rehousing activities. It would have been only by a strange oversight that the Nazis and their generals could have overlooked the accumulated capital in German and international thought on communal and regional planning. True, in the Nazi cannon-instead-of-butter economy the schemes for improving the dwellings of German workers were only scantily provided for. Such notable successes as the conversion of Vienna's worst slum districts into handsome and airy workers' quarters and the magnificent garden suburbs created by the municipality of Frankfurt were accomplished under democratic government. The Nazis can boast of no similar achievements. But the progressive ideas of the municipal and regional planners on decentralization and functional architecture met halfway with the purely military cerebrations of the Nazis. The latter, indeed, seized upon the obvious analogy between decentralization for spacious living and dispersion as passive defense in air warfare. They applied the technical experience which German architects had gained in modern housing projects to the design of air-raid shelters, underground factories, and camouflage.

Perhaps one of the most important official organizations in Germany concerned with the strategy of passive air protection is the Institute for Space Research and Space Organization (*Reichsstelle für Raumforschung und Raumordnung*). Ostensibly organized for the study of internal migration and resettlement problems, the publications of the institute reflect an intense preoccupation with the planned transfer of industries from Germany's borderlands to centrally located shelter areas. The scope of this article does not permit me to review the literature of this institute. Many of its publications are available in this country. They represent a systematic approach to the problem of dispersion on a national scale— "space strategy," as the institute calls it. It is reported that the institute planned the removal of certain key industries with their respective labor complements from the Rhineland and southwestern Germany to the east-central provinces and, later, to Czechoslovakia and western Poland. It stands to reason that Germany does not care to advertise her accomplishments in industrial dispersion. But the official German statistics for persons employed in industry, published May 17, 1939, reflect the trend toward a wider diffusion of war industries over the Reich. Aircraft and allied industries whose spectacular growth dates from the inception of the Nazi regime appear well distributed over the central regions of the Reich.

No amount of ingenuity on the part of the Institute for Space Research and Space Organization—which, incidentally, is closely affiliated with Dr. Haushofer's Institute for Geopolitics—could have solved the problems of removing all of Germany's war industries beyond hostile bombing range. That task would have required more years than the Nazi timetable conceded to the planners. Moreover, the geography of central Europe allows for a wide dispersion of war industries but never for that immunity from air attack which mere distance bestows on Soviet factories located beyond the Urals. It is, however, precisely the geographic limitations of the German planners which make their methods of vital interest to us. Their handling of the problem of dispersing strategic industries within an area densely populated and highly industrialized as a whole should furnish food for thought not only to the advocates of victory through bombing at the exclusion of all else, but also to the planners of our own passive defenses.

It is known that German architects, on the personal behest of Hitler, have thoroughly explored the technical aspects of underground living. Hitler's own chancellery in Berlin has been equipped with spacious duplicate installations underground, complete with hospital, operating room, air-conditioning apparatus, and sundry comforts. It is a fair guess that the average German citizen must sit out air raids in far less luxurious quarters. But it is reliably reported that important factories, especially those catering to the *Luftwaffe,* possess underground facilities, both for work and recreation, fortified by heavy concrete construction. As regards reports concerning the extent and accessories of these subterranean plants, it is difficult to determine where fact becomes fiction. Yet we need not doubt that such plants were built and are being built far beyond the experimental stage.

No plausible arguments can be advanced why underground factories, equipped with modern devices of air conditioning and lighting should not operate as efficiently as surface plants. Under optimum conditions the maintenance of constant temperatures and illumination present less of a problem in workshops underground than in those on surface level. There remains the psychological element: protracted confinement underground, it is argued, will lower the workers' spirits. It should be remembered, however, that such confinement is accepted as a matter of course in several peacetime trades. Moreover, ingenuity in the choice of decorative effects, such as painted walls and partitions, sensibly furnished rooms for rest and recreation, and a solid feeling of security from being blown to bits, may compensate the worker for the psychological strains imposed by subterranean living.

Underground working and living is only one answer, and by no means the uniformly best one, to the question of passive defense against air attack. Neither is the air-raid shelter of various shapes, more or less hastily built beneath or near existing building types. The best long-range answer is the planned decentralization of communal services, industries, and residential quarters propounded by the modern town and regional planners. This does not mean that we can now or in the future, by foolhardy neglect, discontinue the construction of bombproof shelters and the enforcement of other safety measures for our overcrowded cities. But it is precisely the crowded community which is the most inviting target of the bomber. What happened to the tenement districts of London under the blitz can logically happen to the tenement districts of any metropolis. Even under peacetime conditions the danger of conflagration is mainly curbed by the efficiency of fire departments rather than by the intrinsic merit of structural design or the wisdom of zoning laws. It takes little imagination to foresee what an air raid—even a light one by London standards—could do to our own little publicized but large slums.

If some of our cities seem to have been built for congestion rather than for circulation, and hence present their inhabitants with exorbitant hazards in air warfare, some of our most important industrial plants likewise testify to a blissful unawareness of hostile air potentials. Two important aircraft factories are cases in point. Their prominent locations, the one in pistol range of the eastern seaboard's main highway and the other within slingshot distance from the East's most traveled railroad track, appear as proof against effective camouflage. Yet it should be emphasized that blame—if anyone is to be blamed at all—cannot be placed at the door of individuals. No one, the German least of all, was able to predict accurately the nature of today's air warfare, and our builders of aircraft plants can no more be stigmatized for a lack of foresight than our best international experts for their low score in global prophecy.

But the tardy recognition accorded by the authorities and the public in this country as well as in Great Britain to the evils of overcrowding and its remedies can be blamed on these authorities and that public. For the evils were sorely evident to anyone with eyes to see, and the remedies could have been easily applied. Had these remedies been undertaken in the days of peace and plenty the benefits from a healthier communal life would have largely justified the outlay; the task of providing adequate passive defense for the big city and the overgrown coke town would be a great deal simpler than it is now.

There has sprung up in Great Britain a new school of architects. These British builders propose to build for today's blitz and a better future. They maintain that there need not be a conflict between building for protection against the more common bombing hazards and building for use and comfort. The British engineer Ove N. Arup designed multi-family buildings subdivided into two-story houses accommodating one to two families. Floors and interior walls are of reinforced concrete, while exterior walls are of brick with horizontal slit windows. These small windows are to minimize the effects from bomb fragmentation and provide an outlet for possible bomb explosions within the building. The brick construction permits the windows to be enlarged easily for peace-time use. Reinforced cross walls tend to localize the effects of direct hits and near misses. The living room is set back from a roofed balcony from which the family may enjoy fresh air. The building's overall appear-ance is pleasing to the eye; simplicity of design and execution make for low cost and cheap rentals. Notwithstanding its emphasis on principles applied to the design of splinterproof shelters, this project appears as an ingenious approach to the problem of rehousing tenement dwellers.

Reviewing the current literature of the British building trades, we find considerable space devoted to manifold uses of reinforced concrete in the construction of private and public buildings. Le Corbusier, as early as 1922, advocated the flat roof garden, its thick concrete flags laid on sand, with grass-sown joints, insulating the house beneath. This idea happily meets the requirements of hygiene and comfort, splinterproof shelter and camouflage. The principle laid down by the great Swiss archi-tect is flexible enough to lend itself to various adaptions. A rich field lies before forward-looking architects and engineers.

In this country we have at our disposal the unrivaled know-how of American engineers and building trades. On the scale of town planning there are Henry Wright's execution of the town plan of Radburn, New Jersey, and the United States Resettlement Administration's layout for Greenbelt, Maryland. Both must be ranked as classical examples of the new order of design. For both projects stressed not only openness, and hence a high degree of dispersion, but also took advantage in harmony with natural contours, of wooded areas and existing trees, and hence an effective kind of camouflage.

Evidence is accumulating fast, from published material in this country and abroad, that the logical partnership of city planner and air-protection designer is being increasingly recognized. This fact demands the close attention of the air strategist. It is doubtful that the conditions which so singularly favored the bomber up to the third year of the second World War will prevail in the future. More likely the effectiveness of the same weight of explosives delivered at the target will never be as great as in the heyday of Herr Göring's blitz. The ratio of bomb weight to destruction of that period can be restored by improvements in aviation design and chemistry only if creative imagination in architecture is lag-ging behind. At present all indications point in the opposite direction.

The study of the complex problems of air-protective design vitally concerns the soldier and the citizen. It is sound military policy and good statesmanship to plan for all emergencies yet wrest from the exigency of total war the opportunities for more spacious and healthy living.

A SOLDIER LOOKS AT MILITARY GOVERNMENT

By Colonel Elbridge Colby

(1943)

OF ALL INTRODUCTIONS to this subject there is none better for a military audience than that used by Colonel H. A. Smith at Fort Leavenworth in 1920, where he denied that military government was anything mysterious and said that it reminded him of the way certain artillerists in former years had attempted to make mysterious their own profession, hoping thereby to exalt it. Although lawyers, and military lawyers too, have been deeply concerned in military government, it is primarily a military and administrative subject rather than a legal one. In the "Old Army" there was many an officer who had acted as *alcalde* of a Filipino town during the Insurrection and what we call the days of the Empire, or as town major in Germany in 1919. Our army is experienced in this matter. Without being lawyers our officers have handled it "in addition to their other duties," and well.

It is true that military government has gotten into the courts of law, even into the Supreme Court of the United States, which has handed down decisions regarding the British occupation of Castine, Maine, in 1814, the American occupation of Tampico, Mexico, and the Insurgent occupation of the island of Cebu in 1899. But this article will not be filled with legal citations and legal phrases. These decisions were handed down after the conflicts were over. They were made to settle certain rights and to answer questions about payments of money. They were legal. They were remote from events on which they were based. Whatever their implications, they could have no effect upon events on the spot.

On this subject there is already a great deal of what the scholars call literature. Most of it has been written by lawyers and for lawyers, even most of that actually written by military men. This is unfortunate. What the soldier wants to know is what he should do, not what some judge will say about it afterward. In fact, about the latter he should not concern himself. His situation is like that of which Viscount Wolseley wrote to his wife: "If every general feels that his proceedings may form the subject of an official inquiry, no general will risk anything." His problem is immediate. He must do the intelligent thing. He may take comfort from the story of Andrew Jackson in New Orleans, who defied a court which interfered with his military necessity, who afterward was fined by that court for his defiance, and who later was reimbursed by a grateful government.

Military government is a part of war, indeed even an act of war. It has received its greatest notoriety in the last century from the control exercised by Germany in a disturbed and revolutionary France in 1870–71 and in a prostrate and bitter Belgium in 1914–18. Too much of the viciousness of Prussianism has been attached to its reputation as a whole. Yet it is not necessarily un-American. It can be conducted in a thoroughly American fashion as it was by our forces in Mexico in 1846–48 and again in 1914, in Puerto Rico and the Philippines in 1898, and by the Third Army on the Rhine in 1919. Its principal characteristic is that it is military—both in purpose and in personnel. It is, as the Duke of Wellington once said, nothing more or less than the will of the military commander. His will in this respect must be based upon a good judgment of circumstances, just as much as his will in combat must be based upon a sound estimate of tactical facts and not upon mere theory, regulation, or whim.

What is military government? A clear understanding of the general term is necessary, lest applications in detail go awry from its general concept and purpose. We need not approach the matter by insisting that each paper must open with a formal definition of its topic. But in matters that depend so much upon policy it is necessary to be understood. "When I use a word," said Humpty Dumpty to Alice, "it means just what I want it to mean." We must understand meanings, or we may be talking about different things. The British have another term for military government; they call it "martial law." Publicists and professors have spoken of it as "belligerent occupation" and as "hostile occupation." William H. Taft—and he was there himself as governor—said that our military government in Cuba was military in name only. The differences in name and in meaning have caused confusions. So we had better be clear. The classic statement as to what military government is was made, as an aside, in the famous Milligan case by Chief Justice Chase, who distinguished it from martial law and from military law and said that it is a form of military jurisdiction exercised by the military commander and superseding the local law as far as may be deemed expedient.

Let us see, then, what happens when an army enters a foreign country and has to set up more or less a military government. The army is generally acknowledged to be subject only to the military law of its own country, which accompanies it wherever it goes. The reason is that military law is personal and not territorial. Most law is territorial. The difference between divorce laws in the various states of the Union are ample evidence of this. Even if an army enters a friendly country with permission, its members are not subject to the laws of that country. When it enters an allied country the exception still holds, as we have recently seen acknowledged in an act of Parliament exempting American soldiers from British law and relying upon courts-martial of the United States for trial for offenses, even for such serious crimes as murder and rape. How much more necessary, therefore, the established rule that members of an army in an enemy country are not subject to local, territorial law. The learned professors will talk of sovereignty and of agents or representatives of a sovereign power who cannot be disturbed in their duties at the behest of the courts of another country. But—practically speaking—it is of course natural that soldiers of an invading force cannot be hampered individually by the requirements of local laws, except for such restrictions as their commander himself applies to them.

But there must be law in this territory which has been occupied. Government of an occupied area, therefore, must be something quite apart from "military law" as such, which goes on just the same in the military establishment wherever the army may be. Although in some circumstances at home, and especially in time of peace, an army at home must recognize the supremacy of civil government over army personnel, this necessity does not hold in time of war in a foreign country, especially not in an enemy country.

There are thus two laws in effect, the military law of the army and the law of the military government over the area.

Let us suppose an offense which both soldiers and civilians may commit—and it is hardly necessary to suppose, for the thing frequently happens. It may be breach of the peace or public misbehavior. If it is committed by the soldier on the same street and in the same town and at the same time as by a civilian resident his act is an offense against the Articles of War—say it is a "disorder . . . to the prejudice of good order" or simply "conduct of a nature to bring discredit upon the military service." He is tried by court-martial. If it is committed by a civilian he is tried by the local law, as maintained and enforced by the military government, and probably tried in the local courts for disorderly conduct, breach of the peace, or something of the sort. But if the trouble is one which involves both a soldier and a civilian inhabitant of the occupied territory that civilian will be tried by a special "provost court" of the military government—not under military law, not under local law, but under the law set up by the military government to protect its armies against civilians and to prevent them from interfering with its work. The power of the military commander is supreme, but he may exercise it in three different ways, according to the circumstances of the case.

As we go, then, with an army into enemy country we must recognize three basic factors: (1) the army must control that country; (2) the army must be free for the purpose which brings it there; (3) the country has ordinary civilian activities which must continue and must therefore be regulated. This third and final factor is the principal reason for having a military government at all. The occupying army could isolate itself; it could protect itself against local attacks, but it could not live in the midst of the confusions and disturbances which would result from sudden abolition of all regulation among the people around it. It has seized control of the country by force of arms, and that seizure imposes upon it an obligation to make that control effective in all the life of the country.

The tone and temper with which it does this will be the character of the military government established under that branch of international law called the "laws of war."

There are two conflicting theories in international law regarding the legal effect of a state of war. One is old and Anglo-Saxon and logical today. It holds that every citizen or subject of an enemy state is an enemy of our state and of each of our citizens. It says that even neutrals and neutrally owned property in an enemy country are tainted with the "enemy" brush. It is what the courts still apply in cases at law, in spite of national declarations that "we do not make war upon the German people." The other theory arose in the eighteenth century under the influence of French humanitarians like Rousseau and is perhaps best expressed in the words of the classic Vattel, who has had such a tremendous influence on international law: "War is made by regular troops; the people, peasants, and middle-class folk are not concerned in it and, ordinarily, have nothing to fear from the enemy."

This theory, created in a day when dynastic kings were fighting with professional armies almost solely, entered all the books for a century and a half. It influenced the increasing efforts for the amelioration of the effects of war at Geneva and at The Hague. It must, however, be admitted to have broken down very largely today, in the face of such wars of man power and resources as we are waging.

These may be theories to plain soldiers like ourselves. But even as theories they are facts and have an impact upon action. They determine policy. It makes a world of difference, when you have occupied a hostile country, which theory you follow. Are all of those inhabitants enemies or potential enemies? Or are they just spectators? Can you just go on about your own military business and feel sure that they will not interrupt or irritate you at all, or needle you or fifth-column you?

Any army entering an enemy country does not come there as a tourist or temporary vacationist. It comes there for a purpose. One purpose might be to break the will of the people and to force an end to the war. Another purpose might be to use the people who live there. In fact, the exploitation of conquered countries by modern Germany is evidence of a complete reversion to the old Anglo-Saxon theory. Action rests more upon the old doctrine of universal enmity than upon modern sentimentality. These are harsh words. But they do not mean that any military occupation must include oppression of civilian populations. They do, nevertheless, mean that any action deemed necessary for the security of that army, or reasonably aimed to accomplish the military purpose of that army, is perfectly justifiable, so long as it is humane and just and not unduly harsh and cruel.

If all inhabitants withdrew under a scorched-earth policy or all took up arms and became fighters the problems of military government would be simplified. Perhaps they would be entirely eliminated. But these things do not happen. Conquest is not achieved by the onrush of a long line of metal; it results from penetrations and infiltrations which cut off parts of the enemy army, and in the same regions with them large parts of the enemy population, wedded to their soil or perhaps simply unable to flee. These people, so long as they are not guilty of what is technically called "war treason" and do not commit acts against the occupying army, are—in spite of basic law and the old theory— treated so far as possible as separate from the war and as peaceable noncombatants, so that they shall in the words of Vattel "have nothing to fear from the enemy."

With that established, follow me now in this line of reasoning. All areas of the earth are under some sovereignty or political control. Occupation of an area by an enemy severs the bonds which tie the people to their former national government. Even if military government is temporary only, until confirmed in a treaty of peace, it is apparent that temporary sovereignty must be assumed by an occupying army. It is not merely a privilege but a duty. The situation was exactly described in Admiral Fletcher's announcement to the people of Vera Cruz on April 26, 1914, in which he said: "In accordance with the law of nations, I am vested with the power and responsibility of government in all its branches throughout the territory."

There must be some control, even over people engaged only in the ordinary processes of living. These people are parts of a human society, which is, after all, a very complicated thing. Men die and there is property to be inherited and cared for. Men want to sell, and deeds must be recorded. Marriages must be legalized and births registered. Food and clothing must be produced and sold in stores. Repairs to buildings must be made. Contracts must be enforced and bills of sale acknowledged as final. Indebtednesses must be met or adjusted. Burglars must be apprehended and punished. Wrongs of man against man must be righted in courts of equity. Streets must be cleaned, garbage collected; electrical, water, and sewage utilities must be operated; schools and hospitals must continue to function. All of these things must be done or the communities will sink to barbarism. Responsibility for control of these activities rests in the hands of the commander of the occupying army. His exercise of this control is military government. The question of military law and jurisdiction over members of his own forces is a separate question. The problem of special regulations to prevent espionage and fraternization, to secure necessary facilities for his army, and to settle frictions between enemy civilians and individuals of his own force is allied to this government but not the sole root of it. Beyond these new matters the old must have attention.

When an occupying general takes over a region he inherits control over both public and private business. To exercise this control he does not have to sit up all night writing out new codes of law. There were laws governing the businesses and the homes of men before he arrived. These probably differ in many respects from those in his own home country. They are unfamiliar to him. Yet they are as well known to the local inhabitants as his own laws are unfamiliar to them. Why try to administer unfamiliar laws? Why try to upset laws already valid and permanent in effect? It has generally been understood, therefore, as proper in law as well as practicable in execution to permit local municipal and provincial laws to remain in force—excepting, of course, those that might be of present benefit to the enemy state. Let us say, then, that if the commander is going to inherit the normal human business of the country he might as well inherit the laws of the country which govern that business.

Yet—note it well—he inherits them and makes them his own. He does not merely let them run. He adopts them. He can change them if he wishes. The change will be temporary only, unless confirmed in a treaty of peace. Yet such changes are customarily held to a minimum, because changes too many or too deep are likely to be confusing. This fact was acknowledged when in California in 1847 much of the Spanish, or Mexican, law was allowed to remain unaltered and still remains unaltered after nearly a century. The change is not so unusual; sometimes it appears desirable, and in such instances it is made. When the governing general thinks it necessary to express his will on local affairs he does it unhesitatingly, and his action is legal and final. In California, General Kearny even promoted the holding of free elections of local officials. On the Rhine in 1919 the Third Army permitted voting for representation in the Reichstag, although forbidding elections for local officials. Whether the commander makes changes or not, what he does is recorded as done and a legal basis for the future. Those whom he appoints, or permits to be elected, or retains in office are legal officials with full powers of their offices.

If the commander sets aside the customs laws and collects customs dues of his own, the goods which come in and pay duty under his government cannot later be charged duties by the government whose control he has abrogated. His law is the law of the land. He generally strives, however, for reasons of simplicity and policy, to retain the old laws and to supersede them with new ones, as Chief Justice Chase has said, only "so far as may be deemed expedient."

Most of the new laws and regulations which he makes will have to do with relations between his military men and local inhabitants. The old courts will judge civilian matters, but new ones will be created— provost courts we now call them—to try civilians for violation of his regulations and for crimes or torts against his soldiers. He may abolish the use of the old national currency and substitute currency of his own for it, and should in any event take strict control over all fiscal operations, public and private. He may create new customs taxes. He may require payment of taxes for work on the roads, for necessary sanitation, and for police.

Who, then, is going to administer these laws, especially the laws governing the ordinary business of the country?

Municipal administration is very complicated. Equally as bad as changing it unnecessarily would be changing the persons who know how to handle it, except in so far as military necessity dictates. It is customary to use to the utmost local officials. The American Army on the Rhine did this with signal success. The Germans did it in France in 1870–71, although they ran into the difficulty that some resident officials held office from the national government and would not serve under an enemy power, although many municipal officials were willing to and did serve. General Scott was able to utilize local Mexican officials in 1847, although in 1914 most withdrew and would not serve under General Funston. During the American Civil War, Sherman wrote to Grant: "We have a right to use any sort of machinery to produce military results, and it is the commonest thing for military commanders to use civil governments in actual existence as means to an end."

Even if the commanding general leaves the mayors or the alcaldes in place, the military commander still sits above them and controls them. In peace the local officials receive their authority from the local people and government; in a war-occupied area they receive it from the occupying commander. That commander of course does not spend his time running about the country sitting at the elbow of each mayor or superintendent of sanitation. He has other things to do. Who, then, shall do it for him?

In 1914, during the joint Army-Navy occupation of Vera Cruz, the staff which headed up the various departments of the government was composed of specially selected American civilians. In 1919, during the occupation of the Rhineland, the staff was military in character, although composed of specialists with expert knowledge of the various functions of civil government. The latter procedure is deemed to be the better.

Japanese tried to use civilians in China in 1894 and found that the plan did not work. French mixed in both military men and civilians in Belgium in 1793 and got into an awful mess. The commanding general has better control over military personnel than over separately appointed civilians; also—and more importantly—he has greater confidence that the military will act always in the interest of the military occupation and its military purposes and not be swayed by sentimental theories of government and social order. The main purpose of the occupation of enemy territory, he knows, is not to remake the world but to keep control over an area from or through which he must operate for the purposes of war. For such a purpose he prefers soldiers under him doing his work.

His every act must be bent toward those purposes of the war. If the country is rich in produce he must use some of it to feed his army and thus reduce the logistic burden of distant supply. If it has fuel deposits which he can use to run his railways, to warm his troops in winter quarters, or to cook their food, he must use some of these too. Whatever aid he may secure for the support of his operation is his to take, to make "war support war" in the Napoleonic phrase, provided always that he does not absolutely impoverish the local population, or starve them, or freeze them, to such an extent as to result in inhumanity and in such world-wide abhorrence and condemnation as the Germans of the twentieth century have called down upon themselves. It has always been the American practice to buy and pay for materials needed, and this practice will probably be continued, unless we occupy an enemy area where inhabitants refuse to sell. His needs may be great, but his demands should not be greater than the people he rules can actually bear. Our best reminder on this point is the classic American statement in the famous General Order No. 100 of Civil War days that "men who take up arms against one another in public war do not cease on this account to be moral beings responsible to one another and to God." If this still be true as against an armed enemy, except one who forfeits consideration by his atrocious behavior, it must be at least equally true as to a noncombatant even in days when entire populations are pressed into the war effort.

Before we leave off we must consider another situation which may arise. What, it may well be asked, will a commander do if he finds no well-established government in the region which he occupies? Suppose the officials have all fled the country, or suppose the country is so undeveloped that there are no officials in the modern sense of the word. It is composed merely of native tribes, perhaps. These have been under foreign control, either as imperial colonies or as mandated lands. With the advent of battle, whatever control had existed has been dropped. Or perhaps the area is one which has been completely fought over, conquered, stripped of its people of responsible power, if not also of most of its inhabitants, and is reconquered with that turn of the tide which brings it into our hands.

In any case, so long as there is any civil population, the responsibility for government rests with the commander into whose military control the land has come. If there is an existing government he controls it, as we have already seen. If there is no existing government or none that can be trusted the commander must create one. If there are laws he may adopt them or change them; if there are none he must make them, even if only simple ones to keep the peace. He creates a new government in more or less of a complex form in accordance with the complex or the simple nature of the society which he finds on the ground. Perhaps there are no inhabitants capable of assuming minor administrative posts under his direction. If so, he must furnish them from his Civil Affairs staff and get more men for that staff if those he has are not enough.

It is always possible that on an isolated island or in a wild or devastated country there may be nothing upon which to build, in accordance with the general principles set down in the paragraphs above. Here, of course, if there are only a few inhabitants, he can put them on the pay roll in some way or other and control them by court-martial under military law as "retainers" of the Army under the Articles of War. But this course is not recommended. It is best, even for a few, to set up a civilian control separate from the military control. In fact, there will, except on some rare atolls, always be more than a few. Of these there may still be a smaller few whom he can enroll, instruct, and organize to help him. If he does this he must avoid a serious possible pitfall. He must avoid playing into the hands of any single faction or clique, however small. If a local leader who does not hold public office offers his "gang"—be it native banditti or private army—as a unit for police service, the offer should be refused.

The commanding officer should do his own building, even though it be from the ground up—as it may very well be in recaptured colonies or mandated areas from which shot and shell and bomb have only just driven the previous overlord. This situation may require the construction of an entire frame of government, from police to postage stamps, in accordance with the blueprint laid down in the War Department manual. We did this in Cuba for the Cubans after 1898. We can do it again, even if again someone may call it a government "military in name only." If the situation requires such action the task must be accepted and accomplished. It is the commander's responsibility—one which he cannot escape any more than he can escape any other responsibility.

This, then, is military government. In authority it replaces, even though in some particulars it uses, the old government of an area. Its purpose is military. If it is not completely administered by military men and utilizes local officials in some particulars, or its own imported civilian experts in others, its top control is military and its key posts should be filled by military men and operated in a military manner, although always still in accordance with what the British manual calls "the dictates of religion, morality, civilization, and chivalry."

THE DAY OF THE WALRUS

Editorial by MAJOR (later BRIGADIER GENERAL) GEORGE H. SHELTON

General Shelton was the most fluent writer ever to be editor of the *Infantry Journal* (1909–12). His brilliance of intellect is often recalled by senior officers of the Army today. He wrote this editorial in 1910.

IT IS RECORDED, the careful student will recall, in Lewis Carroll's classic history of the golden age, that the walrus, at a certain eventful period of his career, decided that the time had come to talk of many things, after which with profound wisdom he announced the topics for discussion to remove any possibility of misapprehension on the part of those interested. But it will also be recalled that the walrus and his companion had then the more important matter in hand of devouring the oysters that had accompanied them on their stroll, and this having been efficiently attended to, there was no audience left, except the carpenter, who seems to have been an unintelligent sort of person, to hear the opinions of the walrus or to record them if uttered. Wherefore the world has ever since been left in darkness. Doubtless it was in this that the walrus showed the real profundity of his wisdom. Nevertheless, it has always appeared to us that there was much of importance to be said on the subjects so carefully selected and that in the failure to secure permanent record of the walrus' views the world is a distinct loser. It seems worth while, therefore, to attempt, in the light of modern research into the general character of the distinguished philosopher, to reconstruct, so to speak, what was probably on his mind in reference to these matters at a period of which record of his movements and other observations is so clear. To our notion there is little room to doubt that, could record now be obtained, it would be very close in meaning to what follows.

I OF SHOES AND SHIPS

His name is legion—the man who knows it can't be done. He is a constant reader of *Cold Water,* which at once inspires him with the darkest of forebodings and reflects his most dismal views. He belongs to the Amalgamated Brotherhood of Gloom of which Major Growler is Present Grand Master. You probably know him.

He is most prominent and numerous in holding the world back, in sticking to traditions, however evil. But he is not the only undesirable citizen. The cold-water thrower is perhaps worse. The cold-water thrower not only makes his own existence miserable but dampens the ardor of all he touches. He is worse than the thrower of vitriol because he is more common, and the law permits you to put the vitriol thrower in jail. Yet the vitriol fiend has never done a hundredth part of the evil of the cold-water thrower. Frequently, but not always, the man who knows it can't be done and the cold-water thrower are one and the same. Combined, they make the pessimist at his best, and the pessimist at his best is the biggest force for evil and for reversion there is in all the world.

Optimism is a virtue, albeit negative. The optimist is a desirable citizen. In the first place, you don't have to build jails for him and, in the second place, if you did he would make jails a pleasanter place of residence. The optimist pure and simple has never done much directly for the world. His sense of proportion, which, as Buster Brown says, is all there is to a sense of humor, is not sufficient. But indirectly he has paid his board and deserved his place by the cheer cheerfully given to the real humorist, the man who is doing the work. For men of this kind, too, thank God, still exist. Out of his wisdom, we may believe, the Creator never labored unnecessarily. The pessimist as well as the optimist must have his purpose. For the man who is doing the work, perhaps one is a goad, the other an inspiration.

But the men who are doing the work (altogether a different classification, be it noted, from men who are simply working) are the world builders. They have their hours of gloom—depths unknown to the pessimist—and their hours of enthusiasm—finer than the optimist wots of —but through all they retain their sense of proportion and their faith. They do not believe the world is hollow and they know that the moon is not made of green cheese. But they intend before the summit is reached that it shall be known just what is inside of the world and of what the moon is made. They intend to do their part in this and to add their mite to the sum total of human happiness and world development. For above all these are men of faith, of faith in themselves, in their fellows, and, beyond everything, in their work.

Of these, then, are all the inhabitants of the earth. Classify yourself, friend, before going farther, and turn, if doubtful, to pleasanter things, for the walrus (having devoured the oysters, and the carpenter being an unintelligent sort of person) kept his thought on these momentous subjects for intelligent vertebrates.

II Of Sealing Wax

Recently a member of Congress made a speech on the general subject of national defense. It was a very good speech. It contained much of interest to the military services and of importance for their future. It has not been the habit of Congress, except in time of national emergency, to manifest much interest in the military service. Never before in peace, probably, had there been a display of such intelligent interest as this. It would seem, therefore, under the circumstances, that it might well have been regarded as a favorable sign. "But," observed Major Growler, "it doesn't mean anything. It is just for home consumption. Congress won't notice it." As it happened, this speech does not appear to have been made purely for home consumption, and Congress did notice it. On the same subject a service newspaper, after characterizing it as one of the most important speeches delivered during the session, said: "It is to be feared, however, that it will not receive the attention it deserves either in or out of the halls of the national legislature."

While it is not likely that any reference to this subject would receive the attention that military minds regard as desirable, it happened, nevertheless, that this particular reference received considerable attention both in and out of the halls of Congress—to the extent, at least, of achievement of the purpose for which it was made. Again, on the same subject another service newspaper said: "There is a justifiable suspicion that Congress will resist the efforts to obtain provision for adequate defense until we have a demonstration which shall show, at much public cost and national humiliation, the deficiency . . . It is still necessary to obtain legislation in a haphazard way with increase of partial effect and by the piecemeal process."

Congress, like every other human institution, is open to suspicion. But there is also justifiable reason for belief that Congress, out of the many difficulties that surround legislation, seeks honestly, in the main, to find the road that will lead to the best goal attainable by this nation.

III Of Cabbages and Kings

The day has gone when pessimism is to control. Pure pessimism, let it be repeated, has never done a stroke of constructive work in the whole building of the world. Pure pessimism can do nothing to help us now. We need not be optimists; nothing so radical is thought of. But if we cannot be reasonably enthusiastic in our own behalf and exercise reasonable faith in our own work we can certainly expect neither enthusiasm nor faith on the part of others in securing development. The newspapers that say it is still necessary to seek service legislation by the haphazard process of the past may speak, perhaps, out of the fullness of their knowledge of legislative affairs and with due reverence to tradition, but they are in ignorance certainly of the spirit of the Army that is now in control of its own desires and prefers to see no legislation for the services at all rather than the piecemeal variety from which it has suffered in the past and which has resulted in our present costly and inefficient military system.

It is not to be thought that this spirit is yet universal in the Army, even in the Infantry. But it is growing and it is already a power, since it is strong enough to control its own desires and curb its own selfishness. This spirit believes that haphazard legislation can be made to give way to a general plan—to a military policy, if you will. It believes that today we have no army, only an aggregation of troops that costs the government far beyond any possible return in efficiency. The time has come when we should face this fact, when we should put it into words and, all unashamed, tell it to ourselves and our world.

Out of the improvements that have come since the war with Spain, out of the greater study we have given to the problems of organization, out of greater knowledge, greater interest, and greater work has come realization of these things. The Army today is not an army except in name. This country either needs an army or it does not need an army. There is no middle ground. If it can get along in a military way without an army, with a mere aggregation of troops, it may as well disband most of the troops it has and save most of the expense to which it is now put. If this country needs an army it is our business to help create an army, and no army can ever be created by the haphazard system of military legislation that has provided the present aggregation to which we apply the name.

IV Of Why the Sea Is Boiling Hot

If we, possessing this knowledge, however carefully hidden, can be content with this state of affairs we must be satisfied to be mere time servers. However much we may love our profession, however honorable that profession may be, if we do not seek in every proper way to develop our present military establishment into an army capable of meeting the necessities that this nation is bound, like all others, to encounter, we are simply holding our places—we are simply satisfied with our jobs.

V Of Whether Pigs Have Wings

We may go on hoping, on and on, but if we are ever to expect better things out of the system of which we are a part today we must do more than hope. The responsibility is ours and we cannot rid ourselves of it. We have blamed Congress and the people in the past for a fault that is almost entirely ours. Congress would go on, doubtless, as it has always gone on, increasing or decreasing the Army; go on with its haphazard military legislation through years innumerable and never, until brought to sudden realization by national disaster, create an army or create anything more than an aggregation of troops. The people would go on as they have gone on, ignorant of the Army and of its purpose; go on in the belief that armies for this country are unnecessary and that in time of stress heaven, as always, will be kind to the United States. If we believe in ourselves, if we believe in our profession, if we believe in the necessity of an army for this country, our highest and most patriotic duty is not to rest content with a system we know to be wrong, but to strive in every proper way to develop a system we believe to be right. With all our knowledge we are committing a wrong against ourselves, against our country, and against its government if we do not spread that knowledge before the world.

The plain business of the Army today seems to be, while clinging faithfully to its traditions and principles of subordination and loyalty, to strive to put before the people whose Army it is its own just conception of what for their best service it should be. This done wisely and well will result in the end in the creation of such a military establishment as is thus devised and as the country needs. Ever to attain this end, however, ever even to interest the people largely, the Army itself must have a just conception of what such a military establishment should be, not merely in strength but in organization. It must not only have this just conception but must be in full agreement within itself. It must strive wholly for the whole; it must put selfish interests aside; it must put the well-being of any part aside for the well-being of the whole. And it can do this in the full knowledge of reward to come—moral reward in the consciousness of duty well performed and material reward in the assurance that by the benefit of the whole every part will in the end attain far more than can possibly be attained by its own selfish and individual pursuit of numbers or power. United, the Army can do its greatest service to the country by creating an army. Divided, neither is it an army nor can it create an army worth the name.

And we all know these things; yet it is necessary, we are told, to go on with our past piecemeal method of army building; that Congress will never grant at one time legislation that will of itself at once create an army. This last is no doubt true. It is neither to be expected nor desired that Congress should attempt to create an army at one stroke. Successful army building is a matter of time, and to attempt to absorb at one time the numbers and changes necessary to create an army out of the present establishment could be expected to end only in disaster. Nothing of the kind is suggested, but when the service, even as it is today, can be brought to the point where it will agree upon what should constitute the military system of this country and will outline a system that will do reasonable justice to all concerned and will agree within itself to avoid every effort to secure legislation not applicable to the general plan, Congress will not only have occasion to rejoice but will, beyond all doubt, sooner or later accept that plan and apply thereon whatever in its wisdom it sees fit to grant. And the knowledge of this is not only in the hearts of all of us but spread at length upon the records of military legislation for whosoever so desired to read. And the proof thereof lies in this: There has never yet, certainly in time of peace, been a line of legislation for the Army that was not urged on Congress by some part of the Army. There never was a line of piecemeal legislation that some piece of the Army was not behind. When, therefore, the Army ceases to urge piecemeal legislation, piecemeal legislation will cease. When piecemeal legislation ceases there will be hope for a general plan.

The Army has before it a plain duty, and it is for the Army to say just how it shall acquit itself of that duty. The past is gone, but the future is ours to use as we will. Let us profit by the past and use the future wisely.

Whereupon the walrus, observing the bewilderment of the carpenter, but sustained by a sense of humor, smiled sadly and, putting away his pocket handkerchief, flopped back into the sea; while the carpenter, being an unintelligent sort of person, murmured, "Interesting but incomprehensible. Besides, I know it can't be done," and, reaching for a bucket of cold water with either hand, went back to his steady job.

EQUIPMENT ON ITS LAST LEGS

Editorial by MAJOR (now MAJOR GENERAL) PAUL J. MUELLER

(*1927*)

WHEN Congress provided for 125 new passenger automobiles for the Army it inaugurated what is hoped will be an annual partial replacement of motor transport. Practically every motorcycle and passenger car of the Army is today on its "last legs," all being veterans of the World War and past the stage where repairs are economical. No commercial concern would consider it a business proposition to keep on repairing the old machines that the Army has been obliged to keep going in order to have transportation for the most urgent needs. And despite what demagogues may say concerning the use of Army transportation for the social benefits of officers, there is not a post in the Army where the personnel does not use its private cars for transacting "the people's business." It has to be done if business is to be transacted with dispatch. And incidentally, this expense on personal funds was not contemplated when the pay act was written.

Notwithstanding all the efforts of the efficient motor-repair shops to maintain as many cars as possible in running condition, 1,702 cars were junked in 1926. Losses in 1927 will be greater, even though many cars are kept running, after a fashion, when they really should be retired.

The days of living on the leftovers from the World War are rapidly approaching an end. Many items of issue are already depleted; others are deteriorating. All of which makes the upkeep of the Army cost more now, and this cost will increase in the future.

Replacement of horses and mules was begun last year, and funds are provided for more next year. Ammunition has likewise been taken care of in a small way. But there is one item whose passing will not be regretted. That is the wartime shabby, multicolored uniform of which there seems no end. When that is gone and provision is made for neat and fitting uniforms—not out of the pockets of the soldier—Army morale will get a boost that it needs.

GO TO IT

From an editorial by LIEUTENANT COLONEL (now COLONEL) WILLIAM H. WALDRON

(1920)

THE ARMY is no stranger to seasons of discontent. In common with the rest of the world, it has its ups and downs, ascending the heights on some occasions and plumbing the depths on others. With these fluctuations in the tide of its material fortunes, the Army suffers corresponding spiritual variation—which is to admit that the Army, individually and collectively, is inclined to be temperamental.

Nor is there anything strange in such a premise. The Army, in its being as well as its purpose, is like no other institution on earth. Physically and functionally it stands apart from the main current of life, drifting from its appointed place only at long intervals to enter the flow of common purpose and effort. Its mission is one of service. Its rewards are largely intangible as measured by the ordinary standards of modern success, and it is this fact alone that gives the Army an excuse for the temperamental eccentricities that it exhibits from time to time.

As a matter of fact, the Army as a rule has little of a material sort to show for its work. Satisfaction derived from the consciousness of duty well done is, after all, its chief reward. Deprived of that satisfaction, the military man has but little with which to content himself. In other lines of endeavor a man may achieve success through the employment of bungling methods, and the material rewards will recompense him for any chagrin he may feel over his lack of polish and technique. There is no such compensating balm in the Army. All of which leads to the conclusion that if circumstance puts it beyond the power of the Army to do good work, there is little incentive for doing any kind of work.

The past year has been a trying one for the Army, a period of little promise and great uncertainty. Scattered, depleted, seemingly neglected, the Army has had little, actual or in prospect, to inspire it with confidence in the future.

A year ago summer came upon us in the midst of the confusion and disorganization incident to demobilization, when officers were witnesses to the depressing spectacle of a magnificent military machine dissolving before their eyes. Scattered over the country with the pitiful wreckage of this machine, faced with the uncertainty, and harassed by the acuteness of personal problems, it is small wonder that the Army lost heart.

Winter brought with it little promise of relief. The task of providing for reorganization proceeded with discouraging deliberateness. The eccentricities of demotion added their share to the burden of depressing circumstance. Relieving legislation hovered discouragingly in the background, toying with the Army's hopes. Professionally there seemed to be little to stimulate the Army's interest or to divert it from its personal but disconcerting problems. What little was left of the Army occupied itself halfheartedly in the prosaic details of daily routine. In a word the Army appeared to be facing a blank wall. This condition, following upon the heels of the Army's finest achievement, served only to paint the future as a drab and uninteresting anticlimax.

Old-timers in the service had foreseen all of this. Drawing lessons from their past experience, they knew in advance what was sure to come. Following the Armistice, they knew that the war army must be speedily demobilized. They knew that the processes of demobilization would leave disorganization and demoralization in their trail. They knew that a wearisome period of waiting for reorganization must inevitably ensue. More to the point, they knew to a certainty that the tide of public interest in military affairs would ebb, leaving the remnants of the little Regular Army stranded amid the wreckage and salvage of the war. They realized fully that a feeling of depression must follow as a reaction from the war period. All of this they foresaw, and they sought about them for means and ways with which to fortify themselves against it.

PREPAREDNESS IN THE UNITED STATES

From an editorial by MAJOR (later COLONEL)
JOHN R. M. TAYLOR

(*1918*)

THE UNITED STATES has never been a military nation, but it has always been a warlike nation. The number of our wars belies our constant claim to be the most pacific of states. From these wars grew the idea that we could form an army of a million men overnight. We are trying it at present, not overnight, and finding difficulties in doing it. Still it does not follow that the idea was as fallacious as it seems and that there was no foundation for it.

. . .

The time has passed when it is safe to rely upon the progressively diminishing military efficiency of the men who will be discharged when this war is over. We have accumulated a great armament. We are teaching the Army the art of war. It would seem expedient that the soldiers under arms today should not remain the sole depositories of the knowledge they have acquired. Some form of military training, of military preparation, must be adopted which will permit them to transmit what they know to their younger brothers, so that if we again have to confront an enemy we shall be able to mobilize an army in place of being under the necessity of creating one. Next time we may have to fight alone.

PREPAREDNESS

From an article by CAPTAIN (now LIEUTENANT GENERAL)
WALTER KRUEGER

(*1917*)

. . . THE TROUBLE IS that our people still believe, in spite of the handwriting on the wall, that military amateurs are practically as good as professionals. They may be argued out of this belief apparently, but way down in their hearts they cling to it with a persistence that defies everything. This is at the root of all our military problems. This belief must be eradicated before we can hope to have anything in the way of real preparedness. Our people can easily see that it would be the height of folly to make out of the most efficient officer of our Regular Army a business manager of a department store, but they do not deem it unwise at all to make an intelligent businessman a general. Of course the officer-manager of a department store would so quickly make a failure of his job that money would be lost, and this fact is so apparent even to the unintelligent that the experiment would never be tried. But that a businessman could possibly fail, or rather is sure to fail, if he attempts to hold down the office of general, or any military office for which he is not trained, is not so apparent. To make that failure patent to the public eye would require the crucial test of war, and of course war is but a remote possibility in the mind of the people. That any man, unless he devotes his whole time to the work, can possibly master the military profession is out of the question.

* * *

This is the literal and unvarnished truth. We cannot hope to put up a real fight against a real enemy unless we have made all our resources in men and material available in times of peace and unless we have molded them into an army, a *real army,* commanded by men as thoroughy trained and as capable in every respect as those of any army that may be launched against us.

To accomplish this will necessitate the adoption of universal liability to service; that is to say, not military service at odd moments in any military body whatsoever, but real, businesslike, intensive military training and discipline, extending over a certain period in the Army of the United States.

THE GROWTH OF WAR

From an article by PROFESSOR (later MAJOR) ROBERT M. JOHNSTON

(*1915*)

. . . ON THE OTHER HAND, the present status of industrial democracy is on a scale so vast, so international, and so intense, that historical analogies are of very doubtful value for guiding our judgments. On the whole, though, it would seem that the strife for money and for external happiness, which makes up the substance of human effort at the present day, does not tend to reduce the probability of war to any great extent. Without discussing this large topic the fact remains that modern war demands greater study and skill than at any previous epoch, that it involves more deeply than ever before the prosperity of nations, and that unless a community has studied the organization and equipment of armies in as technical and scientific spirit as it studies the organization and equipment of its great industrial enterprises, it can stand no chance when it comes to the final arbitrament.

IN THE MIDDLE OF THE FIGHT

Editorial

(*1943*)

EVERY NEW OPERATION of the war seems to show more clearly how much the infantry means to the whole fighting team. We think of infantry as Queen of Battles as we have always thought of it. We take such pride in the hard jobs the infantry has to do that we think of them as the hardest jobs. And in a lot of battles they are.

The fighting man who comes to closest grips with the fighting men of the enemy, who gets closest to them in the hottest part of the scrap, and who must, with his dozen weapons, tackle and meet whatever fighting means the enemy has, can never be criticized for believing his job is the toughest.

He gets closer, too, to the swamp and the sand, to the ice and the hot desert rock. He does most of his fighting right in them and on them. It's not only the man and his weapon but the man, his weapon, and the ground. It takes these three to get at and capture or kill the other side's fighters in the end.

To think these things takes nothing away from the fighting man of the air and the sea. Or the other men on the ground upon whose tanks and guns an army heavily depends. It takes nothing away from those whose services—and often whose fighting, for all may fight in war as it is today —enable the combat units to shoot, eat, move, and keep warm. They can all have pride. For they can all know the fighting force can't fight without them.

But think back through the battles of the war and pick out the hard fights, the hard campaigns. And think of the hard parts of the easy campaigns. Think of Dunkirk, the Dyle Line, the mountain passes of Greece, the capture of Crete and Tobruk, Bataan, Burma. But think still more of Russia which, in fury and vastness of battle, has been greater than all the other campaigns combined.

Think of the Nazi charge to the east on a thousand-mile front with its spearheads driving in fast at first, then ever more slowly. Think of the

Don and the Volga, the Caucasus—of Sevastopol, Stalingrad, and Leningrad.

And think of El Alamein.

Think of these all and the story of the fighting is a story of infantry fighting always as infantry must fight. It's a dozen epics of the doughboy gaining his ground, holding his ground, or relinquishing his ground to other men on the ground who have fought with a better will or better weapons and numbers. It's ever a battle tale of the infantry, fighting with the utmost help of every other kind of fighter.

And look, too, at the slashing seizure of Morocco, Algeria, and Tunis— and the slower, tougher going on Guadalcanal. The hard work in these sectors, as in every other campaign, found the infantry there where the work was heaviest, where other means of war could make no progress, where the whole great combat team with the doughboy in the center, moving by land or sea or air, was needed to do the job.

It must seem to some who knew little of war as this war began and who saw in machines the end of the separately fighting soldier still an inexplicable thing why the machine is not enough. This is only because they were too ready to believe in the easier way of war. Or too lazy to consider what machines cannot do as well as applaud their tremendous combat power.

The machines of war were invented to do more than the fighting soldier by himself. They can. For he has no armor and he has no wings. With machines, therefore, he can do what he cannot do without them. He must have machines.

But there is the other side of it to see. There are many things the combat soldier cannot do with machines that he can do without them. He cannot find large numbers of widely deployed and fighting men and attack them effectively with any of his machines. And such as he finds he often cannot shoot at accurately. But without his machines he can do both these things.

If ever man can invent a fighting machine that can clamber and crawl as well as fly, and preserve full vision or improve it, and has armor reasonably proof from penetrating or heat-creating weapons that can readily and accurately be directed against it, then perhaps will the infantry disappear as a separate class of fighting men. For the ground fighter would merge with the fighting man of the tank and the plane. And then the old doughboys would say that armies were now made up of "mechanical infantry." Old tankers would say that the tank had "absorbed" the doughboy and the plane. And the old flier would still insist that now that all fighters had wings we could forget all obsolete kinds of warfare.

But there is no promise of science for a war machine like that, for an all-purpose, keen-eyed, armored, creeping-flying machine that combines the fighting features of each known means of today's warfare. Wings are too broad to fold for creeping; armor is too heavy for creeping or flying and cannot keep out heat or heavy shells, and the speed of wings and the closeness of armor prevent clear vision.

That is at least the way things stand here in the middle of this great war. No new superweapon on a new scientific principle seems at hand, though the powerful machines we have are utterly necessary tools of the fighting team.

And so the unarmored, unwinged infantry is in the heart of the fight, tackling what its men believe are the hardest jobs of war. It is there in the center of battle, attempting the feats of combat no other kind of fighter can hope to succeed in, but constantly needing and relying upon the winged and armored fighting strength of the other men of battle and upon the services of all other men who aid it to reach and keep in the middle of the fight.

IX

Appendix

The Editors, the *Infantry Journal*
1904–40

Date	Name and Rank while on *Journal* Staff	Highest Rank and Assignment during Career; American Decorations
May 31, 1904, to July 7, 1904	Lieutenant Colonel James Sumner Pettit	Lieutenant Colonel; member of War Department General Staff; died June 30, 1906.
	Captain Harry Clay Hale	Major General; Division Commander; Distinguished Service Medal.
	Captain Frank McIntyre	Major General; Executive Assistant to Chief of Staff; Distinguished Service Medal.
July 7, 1904, to February 7, 1905	Captain Harry Clay Hale	See above.
	Captain Charles Henry Muir	Major General; Corps Commander; Distinguished Service Cross; Distinguished Service Medal; died December 8, 1933.
	Captain Dennis Edward Nolan	Major General; Army Commander; Distinguished Service Cross; Distinguished Service Medal; Silver Star (Oak Leaf Cluster).
February 7, 1905, to September 21, 1905	Major William Pierce Evans	Colonel; Regimental Commander; died September 28, 1916.
	Captain Harry Clay Hale	See above.
	Captain Charles Henry Muir	See above.
	Captain Dennis Edward Nolan	See above.

September 21, 1904, to June 30, 1906	Lieutenant Colonel James Sumner Pettit	See above.
June 30, 1906, to December 31, 1906	Captain Charles Henry Muir	See above.
December 31, 1906, to May 15, 1909	Captain Hollis Chenery Clark	Colonel; member of Adjutant General's Department; Silver Star.
May 15, 1909, to December 31, 1912	Major George Henry Shelton	Brigadier General; Brigade Commander; Distinguished Service Medal; died November 2, 1920.
July 1, 1909, to December 31, 1909	*Captain Samuel Tilden Ansell	Brigadier General; Acting Judge Advocate General; Distinguished Service Medal.
July 1, 1909, to June 30, 1910	*Lieutenant George Catlett Marshall	General; Chief of Staff, Army of the United States; Distinguished Service Medal.
January 1, 1910, to October 31, 1911	*Lieutenant Harry Surgisson Grier	Colonel; Regimental Commander; died October 27, 1935.
July 1, 1910, to October 31, 1911	*Captain George Franklin Baltzell	Colonel; Regimental Commander; died August 6, 1937.
September 1, 1910, to February 28, 1912	*Captain Alpha Templeton Easton	Lieutenant Colonel; Silver Star.
January 1, 1911, to August 31, 1912	*Captain Palmer Eddy Pierce	Brigadier General; Brigade Commander; Distinguished Service Medal; died January 17, 1940.
November 1, 1911, to April 30, 1912	*Lieutenant Jay Leland Benedict	Major General; Corps Commander; Distinguished Service Medal.
May 1, 1912, to February 1, 1913	*Captain Rufus Estes Longan	Brigadier General; Chief of Staff, Port of Embarkation; Distinguished Service Medal; died September 3, 1936.

*Associate editors.

Date	Name and Rank while on *Journal* Staff	Highest Rank and Assignment during Career; American Decorations
September 1, 1912, to August 31, 1914	*Major George Davis Moore	Brigadier General; Brigade Commander.
January 1, 1913, to June 15, 1914	Major Evan Malbone Johnson	Brigadier General; Brigade Commander; died October 13, 1923.
January 1, 1913, to June 30, 1914	*Lieutenant George Arthur Lynch	Major General; Chief of Infantry; Distinguished Service Medal.
March 1, 1913, to August 20, 1914	*Major Peter Murray	Brigadier General; Brigade Commander; Distinguished Service Medal; died December 26, 1940.
June 15, 1914, to June 8, 1915	Colonel William Pierce Evans	See p. 676.
June 8, 1915, to September 10, 1915	Major Irvin Leland Hunt	Colonel; Assistant to Judge Advocate General; Distinguished Service Medal; died August 21, 1933.
September 10, 1915, to September 7, 1916	Lieutenant George Arthur Lynch	See above.
September 7, 1916, to December 20, 1917	Major Merch Bradt Stewart	Major General; Superintendent, United States Military Academy; Distinguished Service Medal; died July 3, 1934.
November 1, 1916, to January 31, 1917	*Lieutenant Parker Cromwell Kalloch	Colonel; on staff of Provost Marshal General's School; Distinguished Service Cross.
June 1, 1917, to September 30, 1917	Major Fred Radford Brown	Colonel; Regimental Commander; Distinguished Service Medal; died August 30, 1941.
December 20, 1917, to March 8, 1919	Major John Rodgers Meigs Taylor	Colonel; Military Attaché to Turkey; three Silver Star citations.

March 8, 1919, to September 15, 1919	Major Robert Christie Cotton	Colonel; Executive, Historical Section, War Plans Division, War Department General Staff.
September 15, 1919, to August 10, 1924	Colonel William Henry Waldron	Colonel; Regimental Commander; Distinguished Service Cross; Distinguished Service Medal.
March 1, 1924, to June 30, 1924	*Captain Joseph Hamilton Grant	Colonel; Regimental Commander.
August 11, 1924, to June 15, 1927	Major Paul John Mueller	Major General; Division Commander; Silver Star.
June 15, 1927, to June 30, 1931	Major Thomas Benton Catron	Colonel; Executive, Women's Army Corps; Distinguished Service Medal.
September 1, 1927, to August 31, 1928	*Captain James Edward Wharton	Brigadier General; Assistant Division Commander.
March 1, 1931, to June 1, 1931	*Major John Walton Lang	Colonel; Military Attaché to Argentina.
July 1, 1931, to June 26, 1934	Major Thomas James Camp	Brigadier General; Assistant Commander of Armored Division.
March 15, 1932, to December 15, 1932	*Captain Harris Marcy Melasky	Major General; Division Commander.
June 14, 1933, to June 15, 1936	*Staff Sergeant Robert William Gordon	Captain, United States Marine Corps.
June 26, 1934, to July 11, 1938	Lieutenant Colonel Edwin Forrest Harding	Major General; Division Commander; Silver Star.
February 5, 1935, to July 11, 1938	*Captain Charles Trueman Lanham	Colonel; Regimental Commander.
July 12, 1938, to June 25, 1940	Major John Halpin Burns	Major; Chief of Publications Section, the Infantry School; died June 25, 1940.

*Associate editors.